Deviations

A John Hope Franklin Center Book

DEVIATIONS

A Gayle Rubin Reader

GAYLE S. RUBIN

Duke University Press   *Durham & London*   2011

© 2011 Gayle S. Rubin

All rights reserved

Printed in the United States of America on acid-free paper ∞

Designed by Amy Ruth Buchanan

Typeset in Minion by Tseng Information Systems, Inc.

Library of Congress Cataloging-in-Publication Data appear
on the last printed page of this book.

FOR JAY

CONTENTS

Acknowledgments

This book has been a long time coming. The essays collected here span almost four decades. Since each of the essays included acknowledgments when they were published, the comments here address those who helped in the preparation of this collection, and the individuals and institutions that have had an enduring impact on my life and work.

As a reviewer recently noted, I have had an atypical career. For much of my working life I was part of the itinerant academic labor force, or what Richard Walker (Geography Department, University of California, Berkeley), calls the "lumpen professoriat." While marginality is commonly romanticized, I am acutely aware of its challenges. I have been sustained by a network of exceptional friends and colleagues, a series of informal study groups, and some of the more anomalous institutions of academia. This book is a joyous occasion to express my gratitude and appreciation.

I have been immensely privileged to have been educated and inspired by many brilliant thinkers and scrupulous scholars. Richard Bailey, Alton (Pete) Becker, Kent Flannery, Raymond Kelly, Marshall Sahlins, Charles Tilly, and Henry Wright were among my most influential teachers when I was a student at Michigan. Each had a unique and formative impact on my intellectual habits and sensibilities. Since my return to Michigan as a faculty member, Tomoko Masuzawa and Tom Trautmann have been similarly influential as colleagues: their work has profoundly reshaped my own. I can never thank Gillian Feeley-Harnik, David Halperin, Erik Mueggler, Abigail Stewart, and Valerie Traub enough for their generosity, wise counsel, and intense engagement with my work. I am deeply grateful for the support of a small writers group into which I was warmly welcomed: Rebecca Hardin, Nadine Naber, Julia Paley, Damani Partridge, Elizabeth (Liz) Roberts, and Miriam Ticktin, all struggling with manuscripts of their own.

There are a handful of rarified academic programs and places that operate on the periphery of departmental structures and the demands of regular teaching. By providing a respite from the routines of academic life, they nurture new scholarly and artistic endeavors. Several such institutions have aided my unconventional career. The first of these was the Michigan Society of Fellows, in which I was a Junior Fellow from 1975 to 1978. Junior Fellows were appointed for three years, during which they were prohibited from teaching and encouraged to focus entirely on whatever research and creative tasks they chose. The freedom of that Junior Fellowship and its generous stipend enabled me to inaugurate a dissertation on gay leathermen when other possibilities for funding such an unusual project were remote.

During the recession of the early 1970s the society's funds shrank with the swooning Dow Jones. The program was reconstituted, such that the Junior Fellows were required to do some teaching in departments that partially subsidized their cost. Despite this increase in Fellows' obligations and some dents in the original vision, the society survived and has thrived. However, the changes were a cautionary lesson on the impact of hard economic times on academic institutions whose value may not be immediately obvious or easily measurable.

I was extremely fortunate to be invited as a Visiting Fellow at the Humanities Research Centre of the Australian National University (ANU) in 1993. We visitors had few responsibilities aside from attending daily tea and having conversations with one another and a fantastic group of ANU faculty. This visit was intellectually and professionally rejuvenating. I am intensely grateful to John Ballard, Graeme Clarke, and Jill Julius Matthews for having hosted the events and including me among the participants.

The Social Science Research Council launched the Sexuality Research Fellowship Program (SRFP) in 1995, with funds provided by the Ford Foundation. For ten years the SRFP facilitated an unprecedented avalanche of social and behavioral research on sexuality at the doctoral and post-doctoral levels. I suspect that only the Rockefeller Foundation grants for the original Kinsey studies have had as significant a cumulative impact on the academic study of sexuality in the United States. I applaud the Ford Foundation for having supported such an innovative program, and was exceedingly fortunate to have participated as a pre-doctoral Research Fellow (1999–2001) and as a Research Consultant (2005–6). I am grateful to Diane di Mauro for running the program so brilliantly, and for the opportunity it gave me to meet so many other social scientists actively working on sexual topics. The SRFP facilitated several pilgrimages to the Kinsey Institute and Library and enabled me to spend precious time with John Gagnon, one of the most inspirational figures in the study of sexuality in the second half of the twentieth century.

In 2001 I was invited to be the Norman Freehling Visiting Professor at the Institute for the Humanities at the University of Michigan. This was an exhilarating experience, the most thrilling aspect of which was the opportunity to read through classical texts of European and American race theory with Tom Trautmann. Mary Price and Eliza Woodford helped make that visit memorable and productive.

In 2006–7 I was a Fellow at the Center for the Advanced Study in the Behavioral Sciences (CASBS), a bucolic site overlooking the campus of Stanford University. For over fifty years CASBS has provided a chance for scholars in the social sciences to do their own work, wander intellectually, and discover new interests. The vibrant cross-disciplinary interchanges made my sojourn on the hill one of the most intense learning experiences I have had since graduate school, and the presence of Paula Fass, Dolores Hayden, Alison Isenberg, Peter Marris, and Stephen Mintz was markedly serendipitous for my work. The CASBS staff was superb, and I was especially appreciative of the efforts of its director, Claude Steele, director of services, Linda Jack, housing and meetings coordinator, Christy Duignan, and chef, Susan Beach. The library services were outstanding, and I am indebted to Tricia Soto and assistant librarian Jason Gonzales. Ravi Shivana provided exceptional technical support. Like the Michigan Fellows during the recession of the 1970s, CASBS faces financial perils and an uncertain future. I fervently hope that it will survive, and that its uniquely revitalizing intellectual culture will emerge intact from the Great Recession in which the country is currently mired.

I have a passion for libraries and archives, several of which have been critically important at various stages of my work. The first was the Labadie Collection at Michigan, where Ed Weber amassed an unparalleled collection of homophile and gay liberation documents and Julie Herrada continues to cultivate and shepherd the collection. When I first visited the incomparable Kinsey Library, Paul Gebhard was my tour guide through its wonders; Katherine Johnson-Roehr, Jennifer Yamashiro, and Liana Zhou have performed that function on subsequent visits. The GLBT Historical Society in San Francisco is a treasure trove whose navigation has been made possible by a succession of dedicated archivists: Paula Jablons, Willie Walker, Kim Klausner, and Rebekah Kim. Susan Goldstein has steered me to crucial resources held by the San Francisco History Room of the San Francisco Public Library. Rick Storer keeps the Leather Archives and Museum running smoothly, and also serves as a pilot through its as yet largely uncharted holdings. I am also grateful to the superb staff of the Bentley Historical Library at the University of Michigan.

Advances in certain kinds of knowledge, especially stigmatized subjects, depend not only on scholars, libraries, and archives but also on collectors and dealers who occupy the front lines of resource acquisition. Rare-book dealers and collectors are often the unsung heroes of the "primitive accumulation" phase of new areas of exploration. They are frequently the first to assemble primary sources before institutional libraries become aware of new topics of inquiry, or when such subjects are still considered disreputable. With the exception of a handful of places such as Labadie and Kinsey, this has certainly been the case for LGBTQ sources specifically and for sexual materials more generally.

Dealers and collectors are often exceptionally erudite as well. Several have provided me not only with sources but also with a good bit of my education, much of it unavailable elsewhere. My earliest purchases of rare lesbian books were from Ed Drucker, who ran a gay out-of-print book service called Elysian Fields Booksellers. He was succeeded by Bob Manners of Books Bohemian. C. J. Scheiner was one of the earliest dealers from whom I was able to acquire erotica and sexological texts. His catalogues were like a graduate seminar in the field of sexuality, and I was privileged to visit his mammoth collection all too briefly in the early 1980s. I have also benefited from Joseph Vasta's deep knowledge of erotic publication. The bulk of my sexology collection was provided by Ivan Stormgart, who has been incredibly generous in sharing his own encyclopedic command of sexual bibliography.

Todd Pratum helped build my collections on right-wing occultism and nineteenth-century racial taxonomy. For decades David Sachs has provided me with all sorts of literature I did not know I needed until he explained its relevance. Among many other things, he introduced me to the early right-wing pamphlet literature on sex education. Sachs and P. Scott Brown supplied me with the core of what has become a substantial library of government reports on urban planning and land use. Bolerium in San Francisco keeps me well provisioned with gay books, left and anarchist texts, and right-wing literature on homosexuality. Gerard Koskovich wears many hats: collector and dealer extraordinaire, but also scholar, curator, editor, and educator. Many of these people have helped build not only my library but also the special collections of many universities.

This book has benefited from many skilled editors, including Dianna Downing, Linnea Due, Lynn Eden, Liz Highleyman, and David Lobenstine.

Jill Matthews devoted several days of her vacation to some of the chapters. Carole Vance was positively heroic in her detailed comments on many parts of the book as it neared completion. It was a joy to work with Tim Elfenbein, my excellent editor at Duke University Press. I deeply appreciated the meticulousness of the Duke copy editors. I am deeply appreciative of Fred Kameny's Herculean efforts to shepherd this project to completion. Ken Wissoker's persistence and willingness to go the extra mile made this book possible. I have a deep sense of books as physical objects, and am delighted by Amy Ruth Buchanan's elegant design.

Melinda Chateauvert, Susan Freeman, Sally Miller Gearhart, Rebecca Jordan-Young, Gerard Koskovich, Rostom Mesli, and Carole Vance supplied last-minute citations and factual details. Sora Counts has helped tame my papers and manage my files for over two decades: she is the finder of lost folders, clippings, and obscure leaflets. Moonyean has systematized my library and kept it usable when its growth threatened to make it unmanageable. Andrew McBride was a matchless research assistant throughout the preparation of this manuscript: he edited and formatted the text and bibliography, and tracked down innumerable citations. Linda Alperstein, Neal Powers, Lana Sandahl, and Erda Sanders have kept my body and soul together and functioning.

I have been exceptionally blessed with many long-term friends and interlocutors. Some go back to my undergraduate days, and many date from graduate school. I have encountered others during my subsequent peregrinations. I would not think as I do, or know what I know, were it not for conversations over the years with Henry Abelove, Allan Bérubé, Sally Binford, Wendy Brown, Judith Butler, Lawrence Cohen, Lynn Eden, John D'Emilio, Ellen Dubois, Lisa Duggan, Jeffrey Escoffier, Estelle Freedman, Eric Garber, Barbara Grier, David Halperin, Susan Harding, Amber Hollibaugh, Isabel Hull, Nan Hunter, Jonathan Ned Katz, Liz Kennedy, Gerard Koskovich, Ellen Lewin, Donald Lopez, Jay Marston, Jill Matthews, Joan Nestle, Esther Newton, Rayna Rapp, Lisa Rofel, Eric Rofes, Mary Ryan, Erda Sanders, Ruth Schoenbach, Tobin Seibers, Larry Shields, Victoria Sork, Judith Stacey, Susan Stryker, Daniel Tsang, Carole Vance, and Martha Vicinus. Several of these have been so much a part of my life and in so many capacities that it is difficult to even articulate all the ways they have contributed to my work and well-being. Carole Vance has been friend, colleague, and comrade in arms: we have talked through countless issues and walked through many hells together. I have known Lynn Eden, Isabel Hull, and Victoria Sork since we were all students. They are more than close friends and treasured colleagues: they are family.

One of my regrets is that my parents are no longer alive to see this book come to fruition. My father read constantly and was rarely without a book in his hand. He had an extensive home library in which I spent countless happy hours. His love of reference books was contagious. We used to play a game that might have been called "Look It Up." We would argue heatedly about some factual matter, then eagerly rush to consult an encyclopedia or dictionary to determine who was more correct. His boundless curiosity and his fierce joy in learning are no doubt primarily responsible for my having ended up as an academic.

My mother applied her own considerable intelligence to practical matters, but she was no less thorough. She was an information hound, with a knack for asking the right questions and an instinct for detecting flawed answers. She could recognize patterns with lightning speed, based on minimal data. She was a logistical whiz, fanatically attentive to small details, and a perfectionist in all things. If my father made me an intellectual, my mother made me a careful and probing one. Their training, example, unconditional love, and enduring support made my work possible even when its content left them uneasy or bemused.

Above all, Jay Marston has been my best friend and beloved partner for over two and a half decades. She has given me support, motivation, contentment, and purpose. She has put up with long absences, the stresses of my writing, and the anxieties of my career with fortitude, love, and humor. Going through life with her makes every day a joy. This book is for her.

Introduction

Sex, Gender, Politics

Men make their own history, but they do not make it as they please; they do not make it under self-selected circumstances, but under circumstances existing already, given and transmitted from the past.
—**Karl Marx**, *The Eighteenth Brumaire of Louis Bonaparte*, 1852

Text, Time, and Space

Texts are produced in particular historical moments and with specific horizons of possibility. They are part of a repertoire of conversations, questions, assumptions, political environments, available data, and theoretical resources. These discursive conglomerates shift over time—sometimes by slow increments, and sometimes with dramatic jolts. When new formations become the familiar terrain, it becomes difficult to recall the previous landscape with its distinctive assemblage of what could be thought and what seemed significant. Durable texts find new meanings in new historical contexts and evolving preoccupations. But as texts are read in new circumstances, the issues that formed them are often forgotten, as the edges of the old landscape are eroded by time.

When we go to the library to find out about something, we encounter a huge heap of literature all at once. This creates a tendency to treat a large body of texts as if they all exist on the same temporal plane.[1] But the various layers of accretion were produced at specific moments and under specific conditions. It is important to understand texts in their times. This allows us to think about the temporal aspects of their relationships to one another, and to distinguish the dialogues which produced them from those with which we are now engaged.

Geology is one of my recreational obsessions, and one from which I tend to draw metaphors. Take fossils. We look at fossils, extracted from their matrices, to understand the qualities of the once living entity of which they are remnants, and to think about their genealogical relationships with other life forms. We learn other things, such as the environment in which the organism once lived, from examining a fossil's matrix. Similarly, texts can be approached from both angles of vision. We can see the qualities of a text and its genealogical relationship to other texts that came before or come later, but we can also learn something about a text from the qualities of the matrix in which it was formed.

All of the essays collected here deal in some way with a set of concerns I have been engaged with during the last four decades: gender, sexuality, power, politics, institutions, and what Charles Tilly has called "durable inequalities."[2] I have been concerned with how these things are located in specific times, places, and cultural contexts, and in how knowledge of them is assembled, preserved, and transmitted (or not). While these essays manifest a consistent lineage of theoretically interconnected interests, they are also artifacts of very particular circumstances. They have different matrices. Preparing this collection has forced me to think about why they were written, the conditions that molded them, and the persistent themes with which they have wrestled.

Nerd Out of Carolina

In 1968, I was riding a wave, but had no idea that there was a wave or that my own trajectories were being shaped by its motion.[3] I was pursuing various intellectual, political, and personal passions. In retrospect it has become blindingly obvious that things I perceived as personally compelling were part of large social paroxysms and tectonic shifts. We are all so much inside our times and places that it is difficult to see them. Nineteen sixty-eight was when I joined the nascent women's liberation movement in Ann Arbor, Michigan. This of course changed my life in countless ways.

In addition to being oblivious to the fact that I was participating in some large-scale social upheavals, I was equally unaware of the impact of accident, coincidence, and chance. Had I been a few years older, I would have graduated from college before encountering the early second-wave feminist movement. Had I been a few years younger, I would have missed that first crest and no doubt have ended up in some other eddy. Had I been at some other institution, there would have been a different constellation of people, ideas, and re-

sources. This book would have turned out differently. Life is path dependent, and chance affects what roads are, or are not, there to be taken.

I have spent most of my life in three places. I grew up in the still apartheid South Carolina of the 1950s and early 1960s. I got my college education at the University of Michigan in the late 1960s and my graduate training at the same institution in the 1970s. I have lived in San Francisco since the late 1970s. Now I split my time between San Francisco and Ann Arbor, where I have been teaching back at my alma mater since 2003. My preoccupations and the ways I have approached them have been profoundly shaped by these three places: South Carolina, Ann Arbor, and San Francisco.

Growing up in the South gave me an intimate familiarity with many of the racist assumptions and constituencies that still have such a grip on our political process. The black–white color line cut through institutions and daily life like a rift valley, dividing occupations, housing, religious worship, medical care, political access, recreation, consumption, and death. The binary racial system overrode or displaced many other social differences, including groups whose "racial" character or ethnicity did not quite fit into the hegemonic bifurcation.[4]

Like the rest of Southern society, the public schools I attended were segregated. The conflict over desegregating the school system in my hometown erupted when I was in junior high, and a handful of African American students were finally admitted to the "white" high school the year I was a senior. As soon as the public schools were integrated, local elites set up a private school for white students; this was typical of the "segregation academies" that popped up all over the South in the wake of desegregation.

The struggles to end segregation ripped the covers off a tacit set of assumptions that had been largely unstated among whites during the Jim Crow era. As the racial regime came under siege, those who rose to its defense began to explicitly articulate their beliefs about why it was necessary. I vividly recall sitting in the school cafeteria listening to my friends spew abhorrent, paranoid, and wild statements to justify racial separation. These were not bad people; they were teenagers who for the most part repeated in school what they heard over their dinner tables at home. But their outbursts revealed a belief system I found as factually challenged as it was morally reprehensible. I too was mostly parroting what I heard from the adults in my life, so claim no moral high ground. However, I did learn from these experiences. They were a sharp lesson in the ways that institutions, beliefs, passion, and power work to maintain systemic inequalities. They left me with an abiding hatred for racism in all its forms and a healthy respect for its tenacity. Growing up during that time as a white student who supported integration also taught me to stand my ground when I held an opinion that almost no one else shared and which offended a vociferous majority. This would later prove to have been a good preparation for the feminist sex wars.

My Southern childhood also means that the assorted elements that make up the political and religious Right in the United States early in the twenty-first century are familiar characters, worldviews, and agendas. Strom Thurmond was my senator for most of my life. Carl McIntire spun reactionary and conspiratorial tales daily on the local A.M. radio. Respected members of the community participated in the White Citizens Council, a relatively moderate alternative to the Klan, but still deeply committed to white supremacy.[5] I watched in stunned horror in the late 1970s and early 1980s, when their successors began to acquire the kind of influence and presence in national politics and media they had previously wielded in the South.[6] I take the Right, from its mainstream to its extremist manifestations, extremely seriously.

The South of my youth was a white Protestant theocracy. My hometown had dozens of Protestant churches, one small Catholic church, and a smaller Jewish congregation to which my family belonged. There were of course plenty of black Protestant congregations, but I never quite knew if there were any African American Catholics or Jews, and if so, where they worshiped. Like the churches, the cemeteries were segregated by religion and race. There was a small Jewish cemetery, a slightly larger Catholic one, and a vast sprawling necropolis for white Protestants. The black cemeteries were located elsewhere in town.

Protestantism was the default setting for all public venues, including the public schools. We began each day with a compulsory recitation of the Protestant version of the Lord's Prayer. This insured that both Catholic and Jewish kids would be alienated. The handful of Catholic kids stopped reciting when we got to the doxology; I would endure the entire exercise in resentful silence. I did not know it at the time, but the imposition of Protestant observance on Catholic school children had historically been a source of bitter conflict, and the passive resistance of the Catholic pupils was a well-developed tactic.

The Elliot School Rebellion in Boston in 1859 resulted when a Catholic student, Thomas Whall, refused to recite the King James version of the Ten Commandments. "Typically, the Catholic students would mutter a different version of the commandments—avoiding the Protestant second commandment, which cautioned against the worship of any 'graven image'—and the substitution would be lost in the general din."[7] When Whall refused to participate at all, McLaurin Cooke, the school principal, promised to "'whip him till he yields if it takes the whole forenoon.' And so Cooke did, beating Whall's hands with a rattan stick for half an hour until they were cut and bleeding."[8] Our punishments, thankfully, were far less harsh.[9]

We were lucky to have good hot lunches, prepared and served by a staff consisting mostly of African American women. However, we could not eat until the food had been duly sanctified in the name of Jesus. So there were at least two obligatory Christian observances every day, and sometimes three: special events such as school assemblies and football games always began with yet another invocation in Christ's name.

The acme of this routine religious indoctrination came when I was in high school. On two separate occasions, we were herded into a week of compulsory daily assemblies in which an Evangelical preacher spent an hour exhorting us to take Jesus as our personal savior. These roughly fourteen obligatory hours of attempted conversion occurred well after the Supreme Court ruled against religious instruction (*McCollum v. Board of Education*, in 1948) and even nondenominational prayers (*Engel v. Vitale*, in 1962) in the public schools. But there were few Catholics and fewer Jews to protest. I was the only Jewish kid in my elementary school. There were two of us in junior high. When I got to (the white) high school, there were about a half dozen Jews in a student body of 1,400.[10] As a result of these experiences, I retain a deeply felt antagonism toward both the overt imposition and the creeping infiltration of sectarian dogma into what should be nondenominational and secular public venues.

Despite some heretical opinions, however, I was hardly a political activist. I was just a bookish kid who read as much as possible. When I was punished in elementary school for refusing to recite the Lord's Prayer, the sentence was light and it failed utterly in its disciplinary intent: I was forced to stay inside during recess. This suited me just fine since it was much easier to read in an empty classroom than in the schoolyard, which was dirty, noisy, and had no good place to sit. Mostly I read fiction, but I was also interested in fossils, natural history, and of course, dinosaurs. I read all the books on mythology and medieval romance in the local Carnegie Public Library. Kids were generally not allowed in the adult area, but once I had exhausted everything of interest in the children's section, my father and a couple of friendly librarians quietly arranged for me to have the run of the building.

My reading material, clothing preferences, and interests violated most of the local norms for a proper girlhood. This was after all the 1950s. Middle-class girls were not supposed to be smart, wear glasses, or have career ambitions. The glass ceiling was much lower then. Women had few economic alternatives to marriage, and the elite jobs for working women were nursing, dental assistance, secretarial services, and elementary school education. Most of the schoolteachers were female, but even there women's advancement was limited. All of our school principals and superintendents were men. The highest ranking woman in the local school administration was a vice-principal, who was respected but treated as anomalous.[11]

When people asked me what I wanted to be when I grew up, I usually told them I was going to be a scientist. Once the space program was under way I decided instead to become an astronaut, although in the United States these were then all male.[12] Almost every adult (apart from my very supportive father) found my answer so startling that they would ask, incredulously, didn't I want to be a wife and mother? I was quite clear that while I had not decided between physics and astronomy, wife and mother were not among my career goals. In many respects, my childhood in the post–Second World War South preprogrammed me for feminism. I chafed at the suffocating conventions of respectability, claustrophobic gender roles, limited career opportunities, restrictive dress codes, and vicious double standard of sexual morality. When I finally encountered second-wave feminism, it was like finding a bubbling spring in the Kalahari.

There were also many things I loved about the South. My small town was the county seat of an agrarian region; this taught me a good deal about the relationships between even very small urban centers and their rural hinterlands. I worked one summer for the city-planning department, where I learned some of the basic features of real property: taxation, zoning, mapping, and the way private ownership is a function of state systems of registration, record keeping, and contract enforcement. I spent time in fields and forests. My father loved the woods and took me hiking in the forests. He made sure I knew how timber was managed and harvested. Although he was not an enthusiastic hunter, he gave me basic lessons in handling rifles and shotguns.

The rural economy was heavily dependent on cotton and tobacco. Even city kids were expected to be familiar with these products at every stage of cultivation. My kindergarten class was taken to the cotton fields after the harvest to pick the leavings, which taught us how cotton grew, what it felt like, and how hard it was to pick. We saw the cotton gins at work converting the big piles of fluffy seed cotton into tight bales stacked up for shipping. I walked through rows of tobacco in the fields and still remember the intoxicating smell of the leaves as they cured in special barns. I attended tobacco auctions, where buyers for the cigarette factories evaluated bundled leaves in baskets and the bidding was too fast and furious for me to follow.

We were close to our food. There were supermarkets, but they had not supplanted direct contact between consumers and producers. Some neighbors still bought live chickens from the nearby farms and killed them in their backyards. In the summer farmers would drive through town selling produce off the backs of their flatbed trucks. We would get peaches directly from the orchards, and fresh peanuts to boil were a plentiful delicacy. The pecan harvest was a beloved ritual of autumn: we would fill big buckets from some trees my mother owned, and she would spend much of the winter shelling, picking, packaging, and freezing the nuts.

Hunting and fishing brought deer, quail, and fresh fish to local tables. My mother disliked most wild game, but seafood was another matter: she would often drive to the coast just to buy fresh shrimp right off the boats when they docked. During the summers, we usually spent time at the beach where we could catch our own crabs for dinner. I have fond memories of going crabbing on a small rowboat with my father and bringing buckets of wriggling crustaceans home to my mother, who already had a pot of water boiling, ready, and waiting.

The Carolina beaches are glorious, and I especially loved those that were still old, funky, and not yet modernized. "The beach" was not just a strip of coastal sand where people swam and sunned: it was also a space in the cultural imaginary, a place redolent with illicit pleasures. The beaches were real places of unruly behavior, liminal spaces where the usual rules of propriety were somewhat suspended. "The beach" meant drinking and petting, and rumors of sex in the dunes. The coast was an odd combination of quiet backwaters and a thoroughly raunchy night life.

No visit was complete without at least one trip to the honky-tonk amusement park of Myrtle Beach, and the Carolina shoreline was dotted with clubs and pavilions where young people dated, mated, and danced to both records (seven-inch 45 RPM singles) and live bands.[13] The beaches in particular and the South in general moved to a unique blend of rhythm and blues, Motown, soul, and rock-and-roll. I loved that dance music, the erotic soundtrack of my teens.[14] I started to collect records in junior high and became an occasional DJ. I still DJ whenever there is an opportunity to do so, and there is little I enjoy more than giving a crowd the musical motivation to get up and shake their booties.

Life in the South was also embedded within a dense web of gift exchange, consisting primarily of food, small services, and personal care. The stereotypes of Southern hospitality are (or at least were) largely accurate. People were genuinely nice, friendly, and amazingly helpful, as long as you were part of whatever was defined as their extended community. An illness, accident, or death triggered an immediate escalation in this system of circulating favors and labor: the women, and a few men, would immediately get to work making casseroles, preparing aspics, baking cakes, and organizing shifts of onsite assistance.

My mother did this for years for just about everyone to whom we were socially connected, and it did indeed all come back around. When my father and later my mother died, flotillas of food quickly materialized. So did a managerial army of efficient hands who answered the door and the phone, ushered the callers in and out, made sure that everyone was fed, took care of cleaning up, kept lists of the gifts that poured in, and freed me and the other dazed members of my family to stagger through the details of death. There was, in short, a very vital communalism that I did not fully appreciate when I was young, and only began to understand when I ran into anthropology and Marcel Mauss.[15] That happened at Michigan. The University of Michigan gave me my education and provided me with a set of analytic tools with which to think, learn, and investigate. If the South shaped my political and social reflexes, Michigan formed my intellectual interests and scholarly habits.

Go Blue

Michigan was a lucky accident. Since this was the period of the space race, the federal government spent money to train young scientists. Among the results were summer science programs for high-school students sponsored by the National Science Foundation (NSF). Michigan held an NSF program in microbiology at the music camp at Interlochen. I played the oboe, so the Michigan program seemed ideal: I could study microbiology in the morning and take oboe lessons in the afternoon. My parents drove me to Interlochen, and we stopped to check out the Ann Arbor campus en route. I applied to Michigan almost as an afterthought. Had I actually understood the severity of the climate, I probably would have ended up at some nice southern school such as Duke or the University of North Carolina. But we had visited in the early summer, when Ann Arbor is at its verdant finest. Despite a fervent hatred for Michigan winters, I have endured many of them. The university is an exceptionally well-administered and functional institution.

The bureaucracy is large but efficient, and the faculty is treated well. At least in the units with which I have been associated, people are extremely nice and generally reasonable. Intellectually, the institution fosters interdisciplinarity and interaction on a scale I have rarely encountered elsewhere. Michigan is a very nutrient rich environment, in which one can prosper by mimicking a large filter feeder, swimming around and sucking up the abundant intellectual plankton.

These features are, in part, a consequence of geography. Because Ann Arbor is a small town, it is easy to get around but there are fewer places to go than in a large city. By contrast, the university is huge and there is always something of interest happening. So people connected to the university tend to hang around campus and talk to each other.

The architecture and layout of the central campus also facilitate frequent contact. A large diagonal walkway (a.k.a. "the Diag") connects the two far corners of the main quadrangle, passes in front of the graduate library, and links most of the buildings on central campus. At each end it terminates at a commercial strip where there are coffee shops, bars, and restaurants. This traffic pattern results in unplanned encounters, and the close proximity of small-scale retail provides quick access to places to get a drink or a meal and continue a conversation. Michigan is also unusual in the strength of the social sciences (an observation for which I am indebted to Claude Steele). Some universities favor the humanities, the hard sciences, or their professional schools. Michigan has all of these, but social science is a substantial institutional and intellectual presence. All of this makes the winters almost bearable.

I enrolled as a freshman at Michigan in the fall of 1966 and quickly went into extreme culture shock. The school had a larger population than my hometown. I was unprepared for much college-level work. South Carolina had one of the worst public-school systems in the United States, but I had been lucky to have some superb teachers. They had provided me with reasonable competence in reading, writing, and languages. My background in math and science, however, was woeful. After a disastrous freshman year it was clear that I was not going to be a physicist.

I was equally unprepared for the political environment. Fights over school desegregation were familiar territory, but I had never heard of Vietnam, much less the movement against the Vietnam War. Ann Arbor was one of the epicenters of a spirited antiwar movement, the New Left, and the counterculture. Students for a Democratic Society (SDS) had its origins there. One of its founders, Tom Hayden, edited the student newspaper, the *Michigan Daily*, in the early 1960s. The first anti-Vietnam war teach-in was held at Michigan, in 1965. By the time I arrived, demonstrations were as common as pep rallies.

Like chance encounters, such large gatherings were facilitated by the spatial layout of the central campus. In front of the graduate library, the Diag opens up into an expansive plaza that is well suited for public events. A crowd could gather in front of the library, and speakers could address the assembly from the elevated platform provided by the capacious library steps. This format was used for everything from football rallies to antiwar demonstrations. When there was no large event, the plaza became an open-air public market of ideas. People would gather on the Diag to discuss and debate politics, or set up tables from which they could disseminate literature promoting various groups, causes, or products. In inclement weather these activities were moved inside to the Fishbowl, an enclosed but also spacious area that linked three (and now four) major classroom buildings.

After the initial shock wore off, I got involved in various aspects of campus politics. In the fall of 1967, some friends and I led a successful movement in our dorm house to end the curfews and dress codes for female students. We thought we were acting on our own, unaware that another dorm across campus was engaged in the same struggle, and that similar rules were collapsing on campuses across the country. And there was more: none of us knew that a court case in 1961, *Dixon v. Alabama*, had previously established the conditions for ending administrative supervision of students' time, sexual conduct, dating patterns, and private lives. This decision probably made our spontaneous assault on the women's curfew possible.[16]

Eventually, I gravitated to the periphery of the antiwar movement and acquired a boyfriend, Tom Anderson, who was active in draft resistance. This led me into the feminist movement. The sociologist Barrie Thorne has written about the relationship between the draft-resistance movement and the formation of early second-wave feminist groups in the late 1960s.[17] Since women were not subject to the draft, the female partners of resisters were invariably involved in support roles for the men who were. This structural marginality may have helped propel large numbers of such women into the early versions of what later came to be called consciousness-raising groups.

Sometime in 1968, Tom mentioned that I might be interested in a discussion group being organized by some of the wives and girlfriends of other local antidraft activists. I eagerly joined what became Ann Arbor's first ongoing second-wave feminist organization, the Thursday Night Group. At first, we mostly came together to talk about our frustrations with the gender relations encountered in what was then the New Left. The New Left was probably no more sexist than the rest of society, and possibly a good bit less. Because its explicit values were egalitarian, however, we expected more of our male colleagues and were often bitterly disappointed when they failed to live up to those principles or to apply them to women. The story of how much of women's liberation emerged from such inconsistencies and dashed expectations has been written about elsewhere.[18]

As our Thursday night conversations continued, we expanded our focus beyond the antiwar and New Left movements to think about the situation of women in society at large. We later staged the first teach-in on women in Ann Arbor, wrote articles on feminism for the local underground newspaper (the *Ann Arbor Argus*), and protested the Miss Ann Arbor contest.[19] We also joined the political conversations on the Diag and in the Fishbowl by setting up a literature table from which we distributed the early texts of women's liberation. At first these were mimeographed, but soon they were published as pamphlets by the Radical Education Project and the New England Free Press, the same printers who produced much of the antiwar literature.[20]

After physics, I had briefly declared a major in philosophy. But feminism engaged all of my passions. There was not yet a program in women's studies at Michigan, and the field itself was embryonic. I took advantage of an option available to students in the honors program to declare an independent major in women's studies, with which I ultimately graduated.

In the fall of 1970, I stumbled into anthropology. I needed to find one elective course to get a few credits toward graduation. My roommate, Arlene Gorelick, was an anthropology major. She thought I would enjoy a class she was taking on "primitive" economics from some professor named Marshall Sahlins. So I went to check it out. Sahlins is a mesmerizing speaker and a brilliant thinker. By the time he finished the first lecture, I was hooked: I knew almost immediately that anthropology had the theoretical and empirical tools to explore the issues that mattered to me. By the end of the semester, despite having taken only one anthropology class, I decided to pursue graduate training in the field. I started graduate school at Michigan in the fall of 1971. I loved grad school, and was very lucky to have landed in the Michigan department in the early 1970s.

Sahlins soon decamped for Chicago, but I was in good hands. The intellectual culture of the department was both theoretically vibrant and empirically rich. It was then, as now, a four-field department, something increasingly rare but exceedingly precious. Although I was preparing for a career in sociocultural anthropology, I eagerly took advantage of the opportunity to learn from the other subfields. The linguists deepened my interest in classification and taxonomy and the ways language shapes perception. The archaeologists introduced me to urban geography and gave me ways to think about space and place. They were also intensely engaged in the formation of archaic states and closely related topics: the emergence of bureaucratic systems, the intensification of social stratification, and the increase in social and economic specialization.[21]

I learned about both evolution and plate tectonics from the biological anthropologists. Plate tectonics and continental drift had only recently been widely accepted as explanatory frameworks for geologic processes and these theories were reshaping large bodies of information across the earth sciences and natural history. One set of implications was of particular interest to scholars of evolution: continental drift resolved issues of the geographic distribution of species that had puzzled Darwin.[22] I took a course on human evolution from Frank Livingstone and can still remember his excited lecture about how plate tectonics explained why Madagascar had lemurs, why marsupials were dominant Australian fauna, and most importantly for human evolution, the differences between new and old world primates.[23] Such observations, so commonplace now, were startlingly fresh then.

Frank also introduced me to the critique of race as a useful way of describing human biological variation. The biological anthropologists at Michigan were centrally involved in deconstructing racial taxonomy and the category of race itself.[24] A department in which race was a suspect and unstable category was certainly one in which the concept of gender could be similarly dissected.

While the departmental power structures and accepted bodies of knowledge were still heavily male dominated, the intellectual resources for the development of feminist anthropology were readily available. Although there were only two tenured women on the faculty (Norma Diamond and Niara Sudarkasa), this compared favorably with most other departments, only a few of which had any female senior faculty.[25] The department did not punish students for political activism, and some of the most respected senior faculty, such as Marshall Sahlins, Eric Wolf, and Joseph Jorgensen, were prominently involved in the antiwar movement.

The generally supportive atmosphere allowed new ideas to flourish. The graduate students were encouraged to be collaborative. We talked incessantly and passionately. The first essay in this present collection is very much a product of the Michigan department in the early 1970s. It began as a term paper for Sahlins's course and was completed when I was in graduate school. For me, "The Traffic in Women" is something like a piece of amber that preserves those heady conversations and that moment in time.

"The Traffic in Women" was published in *Toward an Anthropology of Women*, edited by Rayna Reiter (later Rayna Rapp). Rayna and I had both been in the Thursday Night Group, and she was also a graduate student in anthropology.[26] In 1971, Rayna and a fellow grad student, Lembi Congas, under the faculty sponsorship of Norma Diamond, cotaught the first course at Michigan on the anthropology of women. Rayna had left Michigan to teach at the New School for Social Research by the time the anthology was published, but the book was very much a product of the Michigan department: of the seventeen essays, nine were authored by Michigan graduate students, PhDs, or faculty.

While my paper was thus a profoundly local product, it also resulted from both happy coincidence and deeper structural shifts affecting many feminist intellectuals. The accidental quality is best illustrated by an anecdote about timing. The English translation of Lévi-Strauss's *Elementary Structures of Kinship* was published in the United States in 1969. Similarly, Althusser's article on Freud and Lacan (and Lévi-Strauss) appeared in the summer 1969 issue of *New Left Review*. Both texts were essentially hot off the presses when I read them in the fall of 1970. Had I taken the same class a year or two earlier, neither would have been available. Had I read them later, the possibilities they presented for feminist thought would have already been extracted, digested, and articulated by others. If the connections they suggested were glaringly obvious to me, they were equally accessible to others. French feminists of various factional persuasions were already familiar with these texts and had been working out their own understandings of the implications of Lacanian psychoanalysis, Lévi-Strauss's models of kinship, and structural linguistics. In England, Juliet Mitchell published her synthesis of Marxism, Freud, and Lévi-Strauss in *Psychoanalysis and Feminism* (1974).

One important factor that shaped my paper was the availability of a historically specific concept of gender. I coined the phrase "sex/gender system" while groping for an alternative to "patriarchy," which I considered a hopelessly imprecise and conceptually muddled term. Sandra Harding has posed an interesting question in the title of her essay "Why Has the Sex/Gender System Become Visible Only Now?" Harding is more interested in the epistemological questions than the linguistic ones; she interrogates the historical developments that made such a concept possible and necessary, while taking no note of the introduction of the terminology.[27]

Jennifer Germon's book *Gender* is a fascinating exploration of why the conceptual language of gender was itself available as a theoretical resource. Germon argues that:

> Gender did not exist 60 years ago—at least not in the way we understand it today. . . . A lack of attention to gender's origins has led to the common assumption that it has always been available, an assumption due in

no small part to gender's formidable conceptual, analytical, and explanatory power. Yet gender does indeed have a history, and a controversial one at that. Until the 1950s, gender served to mark relations between words rather than people. While there is evidence that it was used sporadically during the nineteenth and twentieth centuries, the mid-1950s stand as the historical moment in which gender was codified into the English language as a personal and social category and so began its ascent as a potent new conceptual realm of sex.[28]

Germon attributes the introduction of gender in its current analytic form primarily to John Money, although she also credits Robert Stoller with helping to establish this usage. In her chapter on the feminist appropriation of the term, starting in the very early 1970s, she credits me with having introduced "gender" into feminist anthropology.[29] She comments that "Rubin's analysis demonstrated that she was—on some level—drawing on Money's concept of gender, yet nowhere in 'The Traffic in Women' is there an indication of whence she took the term."[30] Germon observes that in 1972 Money's and Ehrhardt's book *Man & Woman, Boy & Girl* appeared in the collective bibliography of *Toward an Anthropology of Women*, but was not explicitly cited by me.

While I did not cite Money and Ehrhardt, I was indeed influenced by their book and had clearly absorbed aspects of their analytic framework, without grasping its novelty. Their disaggregation of the presumed unity of chromosomal sex, hormonal exposure, internal reproductive organs, external genitalia, and psychological identifications was extremely important, as was their insistence that gender identities could be both disconnected from and more resistant to change than physical bodies.[31]

As Germon and others have discussed, Money's impact is complex, but its relevance for early feminist theory has often been unremarked and underestimated. Germon observes, "That gender is indispensable to feminist theorizing . . . seems so self-evident that it surely goes without saying. Yet it is precisely because gender has achieved that status that its historical legacy is worth examining. . . . Over the past 25 years or so, gender has often been attributed to feminism as though the term had no history outside of that tradition."[32] She further argues that Money's research was useful to feminism precisely because it argued for the strength of gender socialization: "That idea was seized upon to demonstrate that women's subordinated sociocultural, political, and economic status was neither natural nor inevitable. Instead it was quite literally produced by culture—itself a production."[33]

I used gender in exactly this sense. Such ideas were in the air, the water, the conversations, and the feminist pamphlet literature I so eagerly consumed. "Gender" was one of the resources at hand with which to build feminist frameworks. Money's concept of gender was an element that I crunched with Marx's discussions of reproduction, Lévi-Strauss's analysis of kinship, Freud's theories of femininity, and Lacan's linguistic reading of Freud. It must have contributed to my choice of terminology.

I almost did not bother to revise "Traffic" for publication. I told Rayna that Mitchell's book had made my version superfluous. Rayna insisted that I had my own perspective and pressured me to finish the article. I am grateful that she did, and she was correct: my take on Lévi-Strauss, Freud, Lacan, and Marx was different from that of Juliet Mitchell, Monique Wittig, or the French group Psychanalyse et Politique.[34] Many different feminists were working with common bodies of literature to address a similar set of problems. But local conditions, accidents of timing, and individual idiosyncrasies produced distinctive responses to big seismic changes. We do not make our histories as we please, but we do make them.

Lesbian and Gay Histories

By the spring of 1971, gay liberation had come to Ann Arbor. The local Gay Liberation Front had several men and a single visible lesbian. I came out shortly after that lone lesbian activist visited the Thursday Night Group to explain the new gay politics. Prior to that visit, I had no real concept of homosexuality. Naming is a powerful tool, and the sudden availability of situated and meaningful words such as *lesbian, homosexual,* and *gay* was revelatory. The language enabled me to reinterpret my own experience and emotional history. I realized I was in love with one of my feminist comrades and had two immediate goals: to seduce the object of my desire, and to read all about this exciting discovery. Since the girl was unavailable, I headed to the library.

After a disappointing traipse through the card catalogue at the graduate library, I decided to compile a bibliography on lesbianism. This turned out to be superfluous, as there already was a considerable bibliographic literature. These lesbian bibliographies were difficult to find, but once located they provided a ready roadmap into the available source material circa 1970. Rather than having to reinvent the wheel, I was able to use Jeannette Foster's *Sex Variant Women in Literature* (1956) and Gene Damon's (Barbara Grier) and Lee Stuart's *The Lesbian in Literature* (1967), as well as some early compilations by Marion Zimmer Bradley.[35]

Luck, timing, and location were all involved. The Damon and Stuart bibliography was the most complete, and it was then of relatively recent vintage. What was more remarkable was that these bibliographies were actually in the Michigan library, in a special collection called the Labadie Collection. The Labadie had originally been dedicated to anarchist materials, but over the years its scope had expanded to include radical politics and social-protest movements, from Left to Right. That it also boasted a focus on "alternative sexuality" and "sexual freedom" was mainly due to Ed Weber, who became the curator of the collection in the early 1960s. By the time I stumbled into the Labadie in 1971, Weber had amassed one of the most significant collections of homosexual publications in any major research library. The pre–gay-liberation homophile movement had generated several important magazines as well as a bibliographic corpus, and the Labadie had them all. This was at a time when university libraries did not generally consider such material worthwhile. As far as I know, the Labadie was unique.[36] And it was on my campus.

I spent much of the ensuing year in the special-collections reading room, working my way through the lesbian publications (I had as yet little or no interest in gay male materials). I became especially fascinated by Djuna Barnes, Natalie Barney, Romaine Brooks, and Renée Vivien, all of whom crossed paths in Paris in the early decades of the twentieth century. I spent the summers of 1972 and 1973 in Paris (courtesy of the Center for Western European Studies at University of Michigan) researching this crowd. I had a wonderful time reading lesbian novels and poetry in the Salle de la Réserve at the Bibliothèque Nationale, visiting the buildings where some of these women had lived, searching for their publications in dingy used bookstores, and putting flowers on the graves of Barney and Vivien in the cemetery at Passy.

However, this topic was not a viable long-term project. It did not lend itself to an ethnographic approach, and I was trained in neither literature nor history. I was ill-equipped to undertake research in French, as my language skills could be charitably described as rudimentary. On this occasion, time was not on my side. The archival materials were extremely limited and most were not yet available during my window of opportunity. Barney had only recently died when I arrived in Paris. Her papers were at the Bibliothèque Doucet, but they had not yet been processed.[37] The curator, François Chapon, allowed me to gaze hungrily at shoeboxes full of letters, but I was not able to read any of them. For these and other reasons, my research focus shifted away from the lesbians in Paris circa 1900.

I had by then become acquainted with Barbara Grier (a.k.a. Gene Damon). Grier succeeded Marion Zimmer Bradley in writing "Lesbiana," a bibliographic column for *The Ladder* (the major lesbian publication of the homophile period). She subsequently edited *The Ladder*, and her work on "Lesbiana" morphed into *The Lesbian in Literature*, the bibliography she coauthored with Lee Stuart. In 1973, Grier and her partner started Naiad Press to publish lesbian books. Grier, who seemed to know everyone, was in touch with Jeannette Foster, who had translated Renée Vivien's novel, *A Woman Appeared to Me*. When Naiad undertook the publication of Foster's translation of the novel, Grier asked me to write the biographical introduction. I hesitate to include it in this collection, as I have not kept up with what is now a considerable literature on the Paris lesbian crowd.[38] There are probably errors I am in no position to know, much less to correct. But it is an artifact of a time when this cast of characters was coming into clearer focus for a generation of lesbian and other scholars, as well as a time when they enthralled me.[39]

Among my essays, this one is relatively obscure and rarely cited. So I was both amused and honored to discover that Elaine Marks had taken the piece seriously enough to subject it to some fairly withering critical attention.[40] Marks takes me to task for creating an "imaginary Renée Vivien," for reading Vivien "in terms of post-1968 Lesbian feminist consciousness," and above all, for failing to recognize the pervasive racism and anti-Semitism of the world Vivien and Natalie Barney inhabited.[41] She compares and contrasts my essay with one on Vivien by Charles Maurras, who was a major figure of the French Right, a "nationalist, monarchist, and anti-Semite."[42] And she warns that "it is incumbent upon readers of Gayle Rubin's text to question the unqualified praise she lavishes on Renée Vivien and Natalie Clifford Barney."[43] I can only plead guilty as charged and heartily concur with the substance of her critique.

When I wrote that essay I had no idea who Charles Maurras was, apart from his association with Vivien. I had minimal knowledge of the history of European racism, a subject which now, decades later, has become a major preoccupation, commanding much of my time and a substantial amount of my library shelf space. With two colleagues, I have now cotaught a seminar that specifically excavates some of the tangled history of the racial taxonomies to which Marks refers.[44]

Forty years ago, when I was prowling the streets and cemeteries of Paris, hunting for traces of vanished lesbians, I certainly shared the narrow and myopic focus that characterized so much of that era of lesbian feminist scholarship. I have since been quite critical of that particular form of tunnel vision, and the kind of lesbian history it tended to produce.[45] Ironically, the research on which this essay was based was largely responsible for a turning point in how I, and as it turned out, many other gay-liberation-era scholars, were reconceptualizing homosexuality and its histories.

Jeannette Foster had titled her book with the term *sex variant women*, rather than with *lesbian. Sex variance* is a term with many uses. Sometimes it seems to have been deployed to minimize stigma, and at other times because it was broad enough to include a range of gender as well as sexual transgressions. Whatever Foster's reasons, *sex variant* worked better for the material she amassed than did *lesbian*. Spanning several centuries and multiple countries, the lives and literatures she compiled did not readily conform to the modern taxonomies of lesbianism. On the other hand, the artifacts produced by the Paris crowd as early as the 1890s resonated easily with lesbian feminists (like me) of the 1970s. These women seemed as familiar as some of Foster's other examples seemed remote.

This project convinced me that lesbianism itself had a history. The time I spent trying to digest all the available (nonmedical) literature on lesbianism, as well my obsessive effort to learn the details of this crowd in Paris, turned me into a "social constructionist" with respect to homosexuality. It became clear that "lesbianism" was a historically specific concatenation of same-sex desires, gender variability, forms of identity, and institutional repertoires. It did not easily translate indefinitely backward in time or across cultural boundaries. A number of individuals working on gay materials independently came to similar conclusions at about the same time. Another wave was breaking.

Between 1973 and 1976, the Gay Academic Union (GAU) held annual conferences in New York. When I presented my work on the Paris lesbians on a panel on lesbian aesthetics, in 1974, it was within the framework of looking for the "great lesbians" of the past. In 1976 I spoke on a panel on gay and lesbian history held in concert with a subsequent GAU conference a year or two later.[46] Reflecting on the Paris material in relation to the broader trajectory of what might be considered a lesbian past, I argued that what might be called "modern" lesbianism was a distinctive development. In the two years between those panels, my paradigm had shifted.[47]

I was not alone. Responding to my comments, one of the men from *The Body Politic*, Toronto's gay liberation newspaper, mentioned that I might be interested in the work of Jeffrey Weeks, who, he said, was making a similar argument. The outlines of Weeks's argument were already clear in an article published in 1976.[48] The following year, his landmark book, *Coming Out: Homosexual Politics in Britain, from the Nineteenth Century to the Present*, offered a fully developed argument about "the making of the modern homosexual," as Ken Plummer titled a 1981 collection on the topic. Weeks's book was a powerful and coherent articulation of the "social construction of sex" paradigm that came to dominate gay history, the anthropology of homosexuality, and much subsequent LGBTQ studies. It continued to shape my own work, which was about to change direction in terms of topics, content, and location.

Fieldwork as a Vocation

In 1978 I moved to California, taught temporarily at Berkeley, started my dissertation fieldwork, and ran headlong into the early feminist antipornography movement. I have now lived in San Francisco for over half of my life, except for sporadic visiting positions and seasonal migrations to teach in the frigid Midwest. San Francisco has left indelible imprints on my research projects, political involvements, and personal maturation. Most of the work collected in this volume resulted from research undertaken and experiences encountered in San Francisco. Many forces propelled me to the West Coast. Intellectually, I was shifting from thinking about gender to thinking more about sexuality, from a focus on feminism to lesbian and gay studies, from research on lesbians to research on gay men, and from working in libraries to working in the field. I had begun to wrestle with the politics of pornography, the re-emergence of the socially conservative Right, and the political economies of sexual space. All of these changes started in Ann Arbor, but the move west was a definitive pivot: a permanent turn in direction, focus, and methodologies. I was also unknowingly joining the Great Gay Migration of the late 1970s. I arrived in Berkeley a few months after Harvey Milk was elected to the San Francisco Board of Supervisors, and moved to San Francisco a few months after his murder. Life and work became enmeshed in the trajectories of gay urban politics.

I had never quite understood the imperative to do fieldwork. My interests in anthropology were forged in theory and I would have been happy to satisfy them in the library. One did not, however, become an anthropologist (at least not in my department) without doing fieldwork. It was the unavoidable initiatory rite of passage. Since fieldwork was inevitable, I was determined to do some kind of research on homosexuality, preferably lesbianism, but I was having difficulties in formulating a project and choosing a field site. The topic of homosexuality was still intensely stigmatized and academically disreputable. I was especially interested in the formation of gay communities and territories, but finding one that had coalesced recently enough so that it could be studied in both the present and a recent past was challenging.

A series of serendipitous events led me to a rather unexpected project: studying the gay male leather community in San Francisco. By then I had concluded that it would be a really bad idea for me to study lesbians. Given the politics and culture of the lesbian community at that time, I decided that some separation between my research and my personal life would be salutary. With gay men, I could study a homosexual population and yet have a social life elsewhere. I was not a lesbian separatist, but since most of my gay career had been spent firmly ensconced in Lesbian Nation, gay men seemed strange and quite fascinating. The gay male leather community was of recent vintage, having only coalesced after the Second World War. There were men involved in its initial formation who were very much alive and available to interview. In San Francisco, the leather population was highly visible, institutionally complex, and had acquired a territory by establishing a presence in the South of Market neighborhood.

There was some general literature on gay communities that had noted the existence of this group in passing. Esther Newton had recorded observations of "the leather queens" in *Mother Camp* (1972), her pathbreaking study of female impersonators. *Mother Camp* was at that point the only full-length ethnographic monograph on any modern gay population, and it was also the only study of any of the stylistically distinct gay subcultures. She had done the drag queens, but no one had studied the "leather queens."[49]

As I was starting the field research in 1978, Michel Foucault's *History of Sexuality, Volume I* was translated and published in English. I have argued elsewhere that Foucault is often incorrectly credited as solely responsible for the paradigm shift that was under way across a number of thinkers and several fields.[50] Nonetheless, his book had an enormous impact.

The History of Sexuality is a brilliant literature review of early sexology, the medicine of sexuality that was coalescing in the late-nineteenth and early-twentieth centuries. Foucault's previous work on French medicine and the history of psychiatry contributed to his wide angle of vision, since much of the development of the science of the "perversions" took place in French psychiatry.[51] His book focuses on the production of authoritative knowledges of sexuality, rather than on the populations of inverts and perverts who were increasingly visible in the streets, cafes, and newspapers of Paris, Vienna, Berlin, and London. But the expanding involvement of physicians and urban police in managing such persons produced records of their encounters. These points of contact became a nexus from which new theories were elaborated.[52] Foucault's interests in medicine and criminology were ideally suited for exposing a developing set of relationships between governance, health, and sexual practice.

Foucault sketched out relationships between the emerging structures of variant sexuality and the creation of modern childhood, especially the wars on masturbation; changes in the social roles of women, especially as these were expressed in their medical complaints and diagnoses; and the increasing involvement of nation-states in managing the physical bodies and procreative activities of their citizens.[53] He furthermore made suggestive links between the forces reshaping sexual emotion and practice to the construction of theories of race and the eruptions of state racism.

Among the most salient passages for my own thinking was his discussion of "alliance" and "sexuality." I took the former to refer to kinship systems generally, and in particular to the work of Lévi-Strauss, who seemed to be the referent for much of this section.[54] Foucault notes:

> It will be granted no doubt that the relations of sex gave rise, in every society, to a *deployment of alliance*: a system of marriage, of fixation and development of kinship ties, of transmission of names and possessions. This deployment of alliance, with the mechanisms of constraint that ensured its existence and the complex knowledge it often required, lost some of its importance as economic processes and political structures could no longer rely on it as an adequate instrument or sufficient support. Particularly from the eighteenth century onward, Western societies created and deployed a new apparatus which was superimposed on the previous one, and which, without completely supplanting the latter, helped reduce its importance. I am speaking of the *deployment of sexuality*: like the *deployment of alliance*, it connects up with the circuit of sexual partners, but in a completely different way. The two systems can be contrasted term by term. . . . For the first, what is pertinent is the link between partners and definite statutes; the second is concerned with the sensations of the body, the quality of pleasures, and the nature of impressions, however tenuous or imperceptible these may be. . . . It is not exact to say that the deployment of sexuality supplanted the deployment of alliance. One can imagine that one day it will have replaced it. But as things stand at present, while it does tend to cover up the deployment of alliance, it has neither obliterated the latter nor rendered it useless. Moreover, historically it was around and on the basis of the deployment of alliance that the deployment of sexuality was constructed."[55]

Foucault's comments on "alliance" and "sexuality" were a kind of "*gemeinschaft* and *gesellschaft*" moment: they situated his project squarely in the long sociological interrogation of what distinguishes traditional from modern societies, and how those differences can be adequately articulated without distortion and gross oversimplification. Understanding the "great transformation" has been at the heart of social theory, sociology, and social history.[56] Since

Tönnies, Durkheim, Marx, and Weber, the social sciences have continually tackled these issues, but the questions had to be posed for sexuality as much as for political economies, state polities, and civil societies.

I have often wished that Foucault had written the planned volumes on children, women, perverts, and populations; I would love to have read them. Nonetheless, in *The History of Sexuality* Foucault provided a kind of unified field theory for the contemporary study of sex. My colleague Tom Trautmann is fond of observing that we never read the same book twice. I reread *The History of Sexuality* about once a year, when I teach it at the culmination of a seminar on sexology. In each reading I find some important insight I was not previously equipped to notice. The more I know, the more I see in it. In 1978, I also joined the fledgling San Francisco Lesbian and Gay History Project.[57] The history project was a small discussion group for individuals conducting investigations into lesbian and gay history. It soon became clear that one of the problems in doing such work was the lack of institutional repositories of primary source material. The Labadie was an exceptional resource: few research libraries or archives collected gay-related documentation. The university libraries in the Bay Area did not even have copies of the major local gay newspapers. Some of Allan Bérubé's early work on gay San Francisco was made possible by a collection of clippings by Bois Burk, a Bay Area resident who contacted Allan and "presented him with folders full of gay-related news articles that Burk had systematically clipped from the San Francisco press for decades."[58]

There were collections in Los Angeles that had emerged out of the homophile movement of the 1950s and 1960s. What is now the One National Gay and Lesbian Archives at the University of Southern California grew out of a tangled organizational history and the Herculean efforts of Jim Kepner. Kepner had amassed a vast collection under various organizational names, including the Western Gay Archives, the National Gay Archives, the International Gay and Lesbian Archives, and at one time, the Natalie Barney/Edward Carpenter Library.[59] But until these collections were finally safely installed in a building at USC, they were only sporadically accessible and inadequately stored. I visited the Kepner collection around 1979, during a brief period when it was opened to the public in a rented storefront. The walls were lined with file cabinets, the floors were covered with stacks of newspapers, and the catalogue was in Jim's head. He was living on a cot in the basement among the stacks and bookshelves.

In the 1970s, the gay liberation and radical lesbian movements generated a new push for community-based lesbian and gay archives. The Lesbian Herstory Archives in New York, founded in 1974, was one of these new institutions. The Gay, Lesbian, Bisexual, Transgender Historical Society (GLBTHS) was founded in San Francisco in 1985, as an offshoot of the History Project.[60] The Leather Archives and Museum (LAM) in Chicago was incorporated in 1991.

In their early days, these community-based archives mostly consisted of the determination of a few souls to collect documents, artifacts, and ephemera with the goal of preserving them and eventually making them accessible. The conditions in these archives were a far remove from the world of well-funded, carefully housed, meticulously tended and temperature controlled collections of the more prosperous universities and private foundations. The Lesbian Herstory Archives were initially housed in the apartment of its founders. What is now the GLBTHS began as boxes of gay and lesbian periodicals in the living room of Willie Walker, a founder and later one of its archivists. Although many have become far better funded and more institutionally stable, most of the early community-based queer archives were closer to Jim Kepner's cot in the basement of his rented storefront than to the Beinecke Rare Book and Manuscript Library at Yale University.

Archives, museums, and libraries need space. Space must be rented or bought. Preservation is labor intensive and ideally requires specialized, and expensive, media such as acid free folders and boxes. Collections need to be catalogued, and access to them requires a secure facility as well as staff to retrieve and reshelve the document boxes. This will seem terribly obvious to anyone who has used a library, but what is not obvious is how much money and labor is involved in setting up new collections and maintaining them. Public and university libraries generally have budgets, even if they are often inadequate and now shrinking to previously unimaginable levels. By contrast, however, the early community-based queer archives had no budgets, no paid staff, and no buildings. All of this had to be accumulated.

When I began my ethnographic research on gay leathermen in San Francisco in 1978, there were few archival, documentary, or artifactual resources with which to work. The GLBTHS and LAM did not yet exist. Much of the primary documentation was still in private hands, housed in basements, attics, and storage lockers. It was unprocessed, inaccessible, and often deteriorating. I traveled to any place that seemed likely to have source material. In addition to visiting Kepner's collection, I made a pilgrimage to the Kinsey Institute Library at Indiana University in Bloomington. The Kinsey Library did have some very helpful material, but little relating to San Francisco gay male leather. Most researchers have the luxury of consulting archival collections that have been assembled and maintained by others. But like other queer scholars at the time, I did not. Because of the paucity of such material, I began to assemble, store, and maintain my own research collection. In addition, I later became involved with both the GLBTHS in San Francisco and the LAM in Chicago.

As a consequence, I have struggled for over three decades with the problems of collection, storage, preservation, and access, both with my own materials and those of the community institutions with which I have been affiliated. I have learned that if information is to endure, it requires infrastructure: staff, storage, and the cash flow to pay for them. The final essay in this collection emerges from these experiences.

Such challenges were part of what made fieldwork as exciting as library research and as interesting as theory. The process has given me a profound sense of the importance of empirical research, an appreciation for the craft involved in doing it well, and an understanding of how assumptions must respond to observation. There is no substitute for direct engagement in the details of a specific group of people in a particular place. The canonical literatures of social science become stale without infusions of freshly gathered data from primary sources. I am deeply grateful that my teachers enforced the imperative to conduct a field study. I am happy to have learned so much about one small corner of the social universe, and through a learning process that could not have occurred in a library.

I had initially planned to focus on the issues of gay-community formation, the emergence of new sexual identities and subcultures, and urban sexual location. I had come to study the "rise" of gay and leather South of Market, but it was immediately clear that gay and leather South of Market had a very limited future. The neighborhood was about to undergo dramatic change as the city, the Redevelopment Agency, and private developers were starting to build a new convention center and museum complex on the site of what had once been a thriving light industrial and working-class residential neighborhood.

I arrived in Berkeley in April of 1978. Ground for the convention center was broken that August. This massive construction project initiated a cascade of changes in land use that altered the ecology of the neighborhood. Rising rents, changes in zoning, increased policing, and even the reduced availability of parking were symptoms of a broader process of displacement. It was clear that any study of South of Market, gay or otherwise, had to grapple with redevelopment and real estate. I probably spent as much time in meetings of the planning commission and learning about zoning as I did sitting in leather bars. Sex was, after all, enmeshed in the political economy of the city.

In November of 1978, Supervisor Dan White assassinated Supervisor

Harvey Milk and Mayor George Moscone. The convention center, whose construction had begun that summer, opened, in 1981, as the Moscone Center, in honor of the slain mayor. That same year, reports of strange new diseases affecting urban gay men began to appear in the medical and gay press.[61] HIV and AIDS tore through my research population, killing many people I knew and affecting the social institutions I had come to study. The epidemic necessitated another change in focus as I tried to document the impact of AIDS as well as the reactions to it.

The bulk of that material has been or will be published elsewhere. Most of the results of my fieldwork are collected in another book, a monograph on gay male leather in San Francisco.[62] There is only one essay from that project in this volume, a piece on a sex club called the Catacombs. However, the engagement with the city, urban space, neighborhood succession, and the scholarly literatures that address these topics became an integral part of all my subsequent work and is especially reflected in this collection in both "Thinking Sex" and "Studying Sexual Subcultures."

Moreover, the impact of HIV/AIDS was mediated by social structures, political agendas, and sexual stigma. Like all natural disasters, AIDS was also unnatural: a human catastrophe in which cultural frameworks, institutional structures, and individual actors shaped its effects. Many of the responses to it—both inside and outside the gay community—were driven more by fear and sexual squeamishness than by detached science, thoughtful policies, or sound principles of public health.[63] In short, one way to think about the impact of AIDS is through the analytic lens of moral or sex panics. The sex-panic paradigm has shaped much of the work represented in this book.

Panics, Pornography, and Perversion

Social and political change was under way in the late 1970s. The sixties (the cultural period, not the decade) were ending with the resurgent "New Right." There is no single year to mark the shift, but there were harbingers well before the election of Reagan, in 1980. Anita Bryant's successful campaign to repeal the Dade County ordinance prohibiting discrimination against gay people took place in 1977. The Moral Majority was founded in 1979. The New Right had been mobilizing funding, think tanks, and political organizations throughout the 1970s; their impact became obvious by the end of the decade. Sex and gender were salient aspects of the social and political agenda of the revived Right: to roll back feminism, restore the Right's notion of traditional family and gender roles, eliminate comprehensive sex education, promote sexual purity (abstinence) among the young, recriminalize medical abortion, raise the costs for sexually active youth, combat obscenity and pornography, and insure that homosexuals remained less than full citizens.[64]

Moral and sex panics have been a singularly effective mechanism for enacting these agendas. The concept of "moral panic" was introduced by Stanley Cohen in *Folk Devils and Moral Panics* (1972). Cohen's book was a study on the Mods and the Rockers, youth subcultures in midcentury Britain. Cohen described the public hysteria over these youth subcultures in the 1950s and 1960s as a "moral panic." Following Cohen, the concept became widely used in sociology, particularly in Britain.

In *Sex, Politics and Society: The Regulation of Sexuality since 1800*, Jeffrey Weeks introduced the sociological language of moral panic into the emergent field of sexual history. Weeks is a brilliant scholar who was trained in both sociology and history. One of his characteristic intellectual habits has been the creative injection of sociological analytic frameworks into historical narratives. He quickly grasped the applicability of Cohen's concept of "moral panic" for thinking about the mechanisms of structural changes in sexual regulation. My own work has been profoundly affected by Weeks, and I expanded on his discussion in "Thinking Sex." But I was still using the phrase *moral panic*. Carole Vance started to use the phrase "sex panic" to reference moral panics about sexuality in particular in her book *Pleasure and Danger: Exploring Female Sexuality*.[65] Whether called moral panics or sex panics, they are potent engines of social change. The United States, since the late 1970s, has been in an almost perpetual state of panic over sex: over pornography, prostitution, trafficking, homosexuality, sex offenders, and, especially, children.

During this same period, starting in the last 1970s and continuing into the present, the feminist movement has been rent by a series of poisonous disputes over many of these same issues, particularly pornography, prostitution, and "perversion," but also including transsexuality and some aspects of homosexuality. While most feminists are supportive of homosexuals and gay rights, there have also been vituperative denunciations of gay male behavior and even some lesbian practices, notably butch and femme roles. On many issues, the agendas of some feminists have at times converged with those of social conservatives.

As a combatant in the feminist sex wars, I have watched with considerable dismay as sex panics within feminism have been used repeatedly to push what I consider to be a fundamentally reactionary sexual agenda. Many of the essays in this collection are marked by those concerns, and some have addressed them directly. "The Leather Menace" was written in response to the controversies over lesbian sadomasochism in the late 1970s. "Misguided, Dangerous, and Wrong" was directed at the feminist antipornography movement and analysis.

The battle lines of the sex wars have shifted, with much of the focus now on issues of "trafficking." Many of the former antipornography activists have moved into the antiprostitution wing of the antitrafficking movement, which they see as a means toward the abolition of all commercial sex, including pornography and prostitution. Opposition to trafficking began as a form of antiprostitution mobilization in the late nineteenth century, and the current discourse on trafficking has a tendency to revert into attacks on sex work, sex workers, and their customers. Contemporary antiprostitution organizations tenaciously promote this amalgamation of trafficking with the sex industry. The essay "The Trouble with Trafficking" addresses the historical background of the powerful undertow that continually drags popular understandings and legal definitions of trafficking toward prostitution rather than toward coercion, labor abuse, and the challenges facing migrant workers in many occupations.

The essay "Of Catamites and Kings" addresses issues of lesbian gender, butches, and female-to-male transsexuals. It has a more tangential relationship to the sex wars. However, long before the fights over pornography, transsexuality had exposed many of the fault lines in feminism that would fracture in the sex wars. Disputes over transsexuality in the early 1970s were harbingers of the outbreak of hostilities that tore through the feminist movement in the early 1980s.[66] "Thinking Sex" has a complicated relationship to the sex wars.[67] It had multiple agendas that expressed many of the changes of direction taking place in my life, politics, and work. The essay and several comments on it occupy considerable space in this collection. For further reflections on the context and career of "Thinking Sex," see Chapter 8, "Blood Under the Bridge."[68]

Then and Now

A cartoon titled "In the Nostalgia District" appeared in the New Yorker while I was editing this introduction.[69] The image depicted a row of shops, all obsolete: Joe's Fix-it Shop, Photo Developing, Stationery Supplies, Acme Travel Agency, and the Kwik-Konnect Internet Café, this last showing several CRT monitors available for customers to use in the days, not all that long ago, before flat screens, laptops, smart phones, iPads, and WiFi. Rereading these essays has made me feel like a permanent resident of the nostalgia district. I have had to confront how young I was then, and how old now; how much I did not know then, and how much I wish I did not know now.

Small details have been continual reminders of how much time has passed. When I wrote "The Traffic in Women," anthropologists were still using the term *primitive*. Transistor radios were a recent invention, when semiconductors were replacing vacuum tubes in consumer audio equipment. Psychiatry was still dominated by psychoanalysis. Freud was the canonical authority, for any discussion addressing sexual "deviation," including homosexuality. Today, psychoanalysis is widely considered passé, and hardly anyone feels a need to genuflect in Freud's direction. There is still a lively academic and queer theoretical literature that engages with Freudian psychoanalysis and finds it useful.[70] But among practitioners, the primary consumers of psychoanalytic literature on homosexuality are the ex-gay ministries and conversion specialists who promote the idea that gay people can and should become heterosexual. This is a very different landscape.

All of the older essays are evidence of how much technological, intellectual, and political change has taken place. The music at the Catacombs was recorded from vinyl records onto reel to reel tapes. There were no CDs, much less digital downloads. When the porn wars erupted in feminism, most pornography consisted of printed material purchased in porn shops or movies seen in porn theaters. By the early 1980s, the latest innovation in pornographic media was home video: the VCR was a dramatic change that allowed people to easily consume porn films in the privacy of their homes. No one was "sexting," or downloading porn from the Internet. The Internet itself was still text based, and mainly used by the tiny cadre of programmers who were creating it. Much of the software that made the Internet accessible to ordinary users was developed in the 1990s and a tipping point toward mass access and use was only reached with consumer friendly browsers such as Netscape (1994) and Explorer (1995).

For the Internet to expand beyond universities, government, and the defense industries, computers had to shrink from the size of rooms to fit on desktops, and their cost had to plummet. Personal computers began to penetrate the consumer market only in the early 1980s. The early essays here were written on a typewriter, when my idea of technological paradise was to own an IBM Selectric. I bought my first computer in 1984. Early versions of "Misguided, Dangerous, and Wrong," and "The Catacombs" were the first of the essays in this collection to be composed with word processing.

The scholarly literature on sexuality has exploded since the early 1980s, and we know a lot more now than we did about many things. One of the examples that jumped out while I was going over these essays is the expansion in knowledge of the "lavender scare," the post–Second World War crusades against homosexuals that included a total ban on federal employment of "sex deviates."[71] The emergence of the early gay-rights movement in the United States after the Second World War was in part a response to these witch hunts, policies, and legal persecution. Much has changed politically. Gay activists finally succeeded in getting the ban on federal employment lifted in 1975.[72] The removal of homosexuality from the list of sexual pathologies in the *Diagnostic and Statistical Manual* in 1973 was a huge step.[73] So was the Supreme Court decision that declared sodomy laws unconstitutional in 2003.[74] I did not expect to see the end of sodomy laws in my lifetime, and I am ecstatic to have lived to see this come about.

On the other hand, I am troubled that there is still such a huge and dangerous apparatus of sexual regulation, and concerned that some of it is expanding rather than contracting. The front line of the battle for gay rights has moved from decriminalization and depathologization to areas of impaired citizenship: mainly marriage and military service. Gay activists have been fighting the restrictions on military service for decades, since they were first instituted during the Second World War. Prior to "Don't Ask, Don't Tell," all homosexuals were simply barred from the military.[75] "Don't Ask, Don't Tell" was implemented in the early 1990s when attempts to lift the previous ban failed. As this book goes to press, the restrictions barring openly gay personnel from serving in the military are due to be removed, but are still in force.

The first of the articles in this collection was published over three decades ago, whereas others were written for this book. There is, therefore, a problem of tense. Each of these pieces inhabits a different present. Often when I speak of "now," the text is addressing something that was "then." And "then" can be quite a long time ago.

Nothing dates scholarly literature more than references to current events, so most academics leave such commentary to journalists, or, these days, post them on their blogs. Yet I feel strongly that we should use all the intellectual tools we possess to think about the present, so I live with the consequences. One is that my essays are full of comments on current events which are no longer current. Nevertheless, while there are ways these essays are obviously dated, in other respects they seem contemporary, and occasionally eerily prescient. We are still enmeshed in conflicts that have roots in the late 1970s and early 1980s. Much of the political conversation and social concern with issues such as pornography, sex work, civil equality for gay and lesbian citizens, transsexuality, AIDS prevention, sexual variation, women's roles, and children's sexuality occurs within frameworks that were constructed then and have been cultivated ever since.

In March of 2009, Frank Rich, in his *New York Times* column, announced that "Americans have less and less patience for the intrusive and divisive moral scolds who thrived in the bubbles of the Clinton and Bush Years. Culture wars are a luxury the country—the G.O.P. included—can no longer afford." He also predicted that "When the administration tardily ends 'don't ask, don't tell,' you can be sure that this action . . . will be greeted by more yawns than howls." Furthermore, "In our own hard times, the former moral 'majority' has been downsized to more of a minority than ever. . . . Even the old indecency wars have subsided."[76]

Unfortunately, the announcement of the death of the culture wars was all too premature. In the two years since Rich's column, the culture wars have come roaring back, if indeed they ever went away. Social conservatives have been pressuring the Obama Justice Department to be more aggressive in their prosecution of pornography. Abortion rights have been under their most sustained assault since *Roe v. Wade.* The war over same-sex marriage has intensified. To Rich's credit, in an earlier column, he did note that gay civil rights were an exception to his otherwise rosy forecast, commenting that Karl Rove's and George W. Bush's "one secure legacy will be their demagogic exploitation of homophobia. . . . [But], that lagging indicator aside, nearly every other result . . . suggests that while the right wants to keep fighting the old boomer culture wars, no one else does."[77] And Rich was especially optimistic about abortion rights.

That was before anti-abortion forces in the House of Representatives used the Affordable Health Care Act as a toehold to re-launch campaigns for increased federal restrictions on abortion, mainly through newly inventive restrictions on insurance coverage for the medical procedure. Since the 2010 midterm elections put Republicans in complete control of twenty-one states, several of those states have proposed or passed unprecedented anti-abortion regulations.[78] These include forcing women to take medically unnecessary sonograms, imposing mandatory "counseling" that requires doctors to read government written anti-abortion scripts to their patients, shortening the number of weeks in which abortion can be legally performed, and instituting onerous new architectural regulations on abortion clinics that are intended to make code compliance difficult or impossible. Requirements that both parents of girls under seventeen provide notarized signatures raise the bar of parental notification for minors seeking abortion. Other tactics include novel bans or restrictions on even private insurance coverage for abortion, laws ostensibly protecting embryos from "fetal pain," and proposals to define an egg as a legal person as soon as it is fertilized.

Attacks on funding for Planned Parenthood have become common at both federal and state levels. Defunding Planned Parenthood will go well beyond abortion services, and eliminate much of the routine health care the organization provides.[79] And these are only the legislative maneuvers. In addition to the episodic murders of physicians providing abortion services, abortion providers have been subjected to sustained harassment and threats of violence to them and to their families. Many anti-abortion activists are also opposed to legal contraception. They do not just want to roll back *Roe v. Wade*. They want an end to *Griswold v. Connecticut*.

Then there is that pesky "lagging indicator" of the alleged truce in the culture wars: gay rights. Marriage is a conduit for an extraordinary range of redistributive benefits, citizenship rights, and social privileges.[80] Much of the language around same-sex marriage emphasizes sentiment, but much of the impact of bans on marriage (and even domestic partnerships and "marriage-like arrangements") is practical: confiscatory taxation and costs for medical insurance and care, bureaucratic unintelligibility, Kafkaesque dramas when conducting routine business such as filing tax returns, and impenetrable barriers to rights and privileges available to other citizens, such as immigration for partners.[81]

While much of the rhetoric about same-sex marriage is religious, the bans on gay marriage do not prevent clergy from performing religious ceremonies in denominations that permit them, nor does legal gay marriage require ceremonies from denominations that prohibit them.[82] There are battles within specific religions over the conduct of their own clergy, but these are internal matters to those organizations. The dispute over the legality of gay marriage is entirely over civil marriage: bans on same-sex marriage simply prevent states (or the federal government) from giving the same civil status to all marriages. While they differ in scale, the bans on same-sex marriage are similar in some respects to the apartheid racial rules of my Southern childhood. The racial regime was more systematic and reached further into the social capillaries, but both carve gashes through the social landscape and the activities, events, and institutions of everyday life. While public opinion in the United States appears to be slowly drifting toward favoring equality for gay citizens, there are well-funded and dedicated constituencies who would like to reduce it. Many of the individuals and organizations that are battling same-sex civil marriage also promote the restoration of criminal penalties for homosexuality.

Sex is often imagined to be marginal to the really important political issues: power and war, the relations of production, and social stratification in the old sense of wealth and status. Yet I am continually stunned by the persistent salience of sex, gender, stigma, and panic. Some of this is simple opportunism: While the Bush administration was promoting its orgy of homophobia, it was presiding over a massive transfer of assets from the bulk of the population—low-income, middle-class, and even lower-rich—to a tiny sliver of the extremely, extraordinarily, and incomprehensibly wealthy. Indeed, one of the most significant political and social developments of the last thirty years is what has probably been one of the greatest transfers of wealth in human history.[83]

Human history is full of pillaging, but it is usually accomplished by overt means and the threat or exercise of lethal force. Armies of conquest simply seized the wealth of their defeated enemies. Imperial, royal, and feudal states were mechanisms to enable ruling elites to exact tribute and treasure from their subordinate populations. But for a democratic state to legalize the looting of the many for the benefit of the few, large numbers of people must be persuaded to vote against their interests. For the last several decades, race and sex have been especially reliable means to do so. The "threat" of gay civil marriage has been a repetitively effective tactic to motivate people to vote for politicians whose policies have brought many of those voters increased misery, greater poverty, and insufficient medical care. The manipulation of sexual anxieties continues to be a potent instrument for making the process of systemic wealth extraction both culturally palatable and politically viable.[84]

I do not think, however, that the politics of sexuality are only matters of expediency, however effective they have proven to be. There are real material, cultural, and emotional stakes to these intense social conflicts over morals and values. Much of my work has been dedicated to exposing them, and to understanding how much they matter.

Sodomy has been (mostly) decriminalized. Some gay partners can get benefits, although unlike heterosexual spousal benefits these are taxed as income, which makes them considerably less beneficial. Gay studies are (somewhat) institutionalized in major universities, and doing gay research is no longer automatic career suicide. Yet, the Defense of Marriage Act requires legalized discrimination against same-sex couples and families. Gay civil marriage is illegal in most states, and its illegality is more systematically codified now than it was even a decade ago. We have spent a billion or two dollars teaching kids that sex is dangerous and that promises will protect them from pregnancy and STDs more efficiently than condoms. Uganda has been in the news because of a proposed law that would, among other things, mandate the death penalty for some homosexuals. There are calls for making homosexuality a capital crime in the United States as well, although no one has seriously (yet) introduced legislation to that effect.

I hope someday sex really is marginal.

The Traffic in Women

Notes on the "Political Economy" of Sex

1

The literature on women—both feminist and antifeminist—is a long rumination on the question of the nature and genesis of women's oppression and social subordination. The question is not a trivial one, since the answers given it determine our visions for the future, and our evaluation of whether or not it is realistic to hope for a sexually egalitarian society. More important, the analysis of the causes of women's oppression forms the basis for any assessment of just what would have to be changed in order to achieve a society without gender hierarchy. Thus, if innate male aggression and dominance are at the root of female oppression, then the feminist program would logically require either the extermination of the offending sex, or else a eugenics project to modify its character. If sexism is a byproduct of capitalism's relentless appetite for profit, then sexism would wither away in the advent of a successful socialist revolution. If the world-historical defeat of women occurred at the hands of an armed patriarchal revolt, then it is time for Amazon guerrillas to start training in the Adirondacks.

It lies outside the scope of this paper to conduct a sustained critique of some of the currently popular explanations of the genesis of sexual inequality—theories such as the popular evolution exemplified by *The Imperial*

Chapter 1 was originally published in Rayna Reiter, ed., *Toward an Anthropology of Women* (New York: Monthly View Press, 1975), 157–210. The version included here is from Karen Hansen and Ilene Philipson, eds., *Women, Class, and the Feminist Imagination* (Philadelphia: Temple, 1990), 74–113.

Animal, the alleged overthrow of prehistoric matriarchies, or the attempt to extract all of the phenomena of social subordination from the first volume of *Capital*.[1] Instead, I want to sketch some elements of an alternate explanation of the problem.

Marx once asked: "What is a Negro slave? A man of the black race. The one explanation is as good as the other. A Negro is a Negro. He only becomes a slave in certain relations. A cotton spinning jenny is a machine for spinning cotton. It becomes *capital* only in certain relations. Torn from these relationships it is no more capital than gold in itself is money or sugar is the price of sugar."[2] One might paraphrase: what is a domesticated woman? A female of the species. The one explanation is as good as the other. A woman is a woman. She only becomes a domestic, a wife, a chattel, a playboy bunny, a prostitute, or a human Dictaphone in certain relations. Torn from these relationships, she is no more the helpmate of man than gold in itself is money . . . and so on. What, then, are these relationships by which a female becomes an oppressed woman?

The place to begin to unravel the system of relationships by which women become the prey of men is in the overlapping works of Claude Lévi-Strauss and Sigmund Freud. The domestication of women, under other names, is discussed at length in both of their oeuvres. In reading through these works, one begins to have a sense of a systematic social apparatus which takes up females as raw materials and fashions domesticated women as products. Neither Freud nor Lévi-Strauss sees his work in this light, and certainly neither turns a critical glance upon the processes he describes. Their analyses and descriptions must be read, therefore, in something like the way Marx read the classical political economists who preceded him.[3] Freud and Lévi-Strauss are in some sense analogous to Ricardo and Smith: they see neither the implications of what they are saying, nor the implicit critique that their work can generate when subjected to a feminist eye. Nevertheless, they provide conceptual tools with which one can build descriptions of the part of social life that is the locus of the oppression of women, of sexual minorities, and of certain aspects of human personality within individuals. I call that part of social life the "sex/gender system," for lack of a more elegant term. As a preliminary definition, a "sex/gender system" is the set of arrangements by which a society transforms biological sexuality into products of human activity, and in which these transformed sexual needs are satisfied.

The purpose of this essay is to arrive at a more fully developed definition of the sex/gender system, by way of a somewhat idiosyncratic and exegetical reading of Lévi-Strauss and Freud. I use the word *exegetical* deliberately. The dictionary defines *exegesis* as a "critical explanation or analysis; especially, interpretation of the Scriptures." At times, my reading of Lévi-Strauss and Freud is freely interpretive, moving from the explicit content of a text to its presuppositions and implications. My reading of certain psychoanalytic texts is filtered through a lens provided by Jacques Lacan, whose own interpretation of the Freudian scripture has been heavily influenced by Lévi-Strauss.[4]

I will return later to refine the definition of a sex/gender system. First, however, I will try to demonstrate the need for such a concept by discussing the failure of classical Marxism to fully express or conceptualize sex oppression. This failure results from the fact that Marxism, as a theory of social life, is relatively unconcerned with sex. In Marx's map of the social world, human beings are workers, peasants, or capitalists; that they are also men and women is not seen as very significant. By contrast, in the maps of social reality drawn by Freud and Lévi-Strauss, there is a deep recognition of the place of sexuality in society, and of the profound differences between the social experiences of men and women.

Marx

No theory accounts for the oppression of women—in its endless variety and monotonous similarity, cross-culturally and throughout history—with anything like the explanatory power of the Marxist theory of class oppression. Therefore, it is not surprising that there have been numerous attempts to apply Marxist analysis to the question of women. There are many ways of doing this. It has been argued that women are a reserve labor force for capitalism, that women's generally lower wages provide extra surplus to a capitalist employer, that women serve the ends of capitalist consumerism in their roles as administrators of family consumption, and so forth. However, a number of articles have tried to do something much more ambitious—to locate the oppression of women in the heart of the capitalist dynamic by pointing to the relationship between housework and the reproduction of labor.[5] To do this is to place women squarely in the definition of capitalism, the process in which capital is produced by the extraction of surplus value from labor by capital.

Briefly, Marx argued that capitalism is distinguished from all other modes of production by its unique aim: the creation and expansion of capital. Whereas other modes of production might find their purpose in making useful things to satisfy human needs, or in producing a surplus for a ruling nobility, or in producing to insure sufficient sacrifice for the edification of the gods, capitalism produces capital. Capitalism is a set of social relations—forms of property, and so forth—in which production takes the form of turning money, things, and people into capital. And capital is a quantity of goods or money which, when exchanged for labor, reproduces and augments itself by extracting unpaid labor, or surplus value, from labor and into itself. "The result of the capitalist production process is neither a mere product (use-value) nor a *commodity*, that is, a use-value which has exchange value. Its result, its product, is the creation of *surplus-value* for capital, and consequently the actual *transformation* of money or commodity into capital."[6]

The exchange between capital and labor which produces surplus value, and hence capital, is highly specific. The worker gets a wage; the capitalist gets the things the worker has made during his or her time of employment. If the total value of the things the worker has made exceeds the value of his or her wage, the aim of capitalism has been achieved. The capitalist gets back the cost of the wage, plus an increment—surplus value. This can occur because the wage is determined not by the value of what the laborer makes, but by the value of what it takes to keep him or her going—to reproduce him or her from day to day, and to reproduce the entire workforce from one generation to the next. Thus, surplus value is the difference between what the laboring class produced as a whole, and the amount of that total which is recycled into maintaining the laboring class.

> The capital given in exchange for labour power is converted into necessaries, by the consumption of which the muscles, nerves, bones, and brains of existing labourers are reproduced, and new labourers are begotten. . . . [T]he individual consumption of the labourer, whether it proceed within the workshop or outside it, whether it be part of the process of production or not, forms therefore a factor of the production and reproduction of capital; just as cleaning machinery does.[7]

> Given the individual, the production of labour-power consists in his reproduction of himself or his maintenance. For his maintenance he requires a given quantity of the means of subsistence. . . . Labour-power sets itself in action only by working. But thereby a definite quantity of human muscle, brain, nerve, etc., is wasted, and these require to be restored.[8]

The amount of difference between the reproduction of labor power and its products depends, therefore, on the determination of what it takes to reproduce that labor power. Marx tends to make that determination on the basis of the quantity of commodities—food, clothing, housing, fuel—that would be necessary to maintain the health, life, and strength of a worker. But these commodities must be consumed before they can be sustenance, and they are not immediately in consumable form when they are purchased by the wage. Additional labor must be performed upon these things before they can be turned into people. Food must be cooked, clothes cleaned, beds made, wood chopped. Housework is therefore a key element in the process of the reproduction of the laborer from whom surplus value is taken. Since it is usually women who do housework, it has been observed that it is through the reproduction of labor power that women are articulated into the surplus-value nexus which is the sine qua non of capitalism.[9] It can be further argued that since no wage is paid for housework, the labor of women in the home contributes to the ultimate quantity of surplus value realized by the capitalist. But to explain women's usefulness to capitalism is one thing. To argue that this usefulness explains the genesis of the oppression of women is quite another. It is precisely at this point that the analysis of capitalism ceases to explain very much about women and the oppression of women.

Women are oppressed in societies which can by no stretch of the imagination be described as capitalist. In the Amazon Valley and the New Guinea Highlands, women are frequently kept in their place by gang rape when the ordinary mechanisms of masculine intimidation prove insufficient. "We tame our women with the banana," said one Mundurucu man.[10] The ethnographic record is littered with practices whose effect is to keep women "in their place" — men's cults, secret initiations, arcane male knowledge, and so on. And precapitalist, feudal Europe was hardly a society in which there was no sexism. Capitalism has taken over and rewired notions of male and female which predate it by centuries. No analysis of the reproduction of labor power under capitalism can explain foot-binding, chastity belts, or any of the incredible array of Byzantine, fetishized indignities — let alone the more ordinary ones — that have been inflicted upon women in various times and places. The analysis of the reproduction of labor power does not even explain why it is usually women rather than men who do domestic work in the home.

In this light it is interesting to return to Marx's discussion of the reproduction of labor. What is necessary to reproduce the worker is determined in part by the biological needs of the human organism, in part by the physical conditions of the place in which it lives, and in part by cultural tradition. Marx observed that beer is necessary for the reproduction of the English working class, and wine necessary for the French.

The number and extent of his [the worker's] so-called necessary wants, as also the modes of satisfying them, are themselves the product of historical devel-opment, and depend therefore to a great extent on the degree of civilization of a country, more particularly on the conditions under which, and consequently on the habits and degree of comfort in which, the class of free labourers has been formed. *In contradistinction therefore to the case of other commodities, there enters into the determination of the value of labour-power a historical and moral element.*[11]

It is precisely this "historical and moral element" which determines that a "wife" is among the necessities of a worker, that women rather than men do housework, and that capitalism is heir to a long tradition in which women do not inherit, in which women do not lead, and in which women do not talk to God. It is this "historical and moral element" that presented capitalism with a cultural heritage of forms of masculinity and femininity. It is within this "historical and moral element" that the entire domain of sex, sexuality, and sex oppression is subsumed. And the briefness of Marx's comment only serves to emphasize the vast area of social life that it covers and leaves unexamined. Only by subjecting this "historical and moral element" to analysis can the structures of sex oppression be delineated.

Engels

In *The Origin of the Family, Private Property, and the State*, Engels sees sex oppression as part of capitalism's heritage from prior social forms. Moreover, Engels integrates sex and sexuality into his theory of society. *Origin* is a frustrating book. Like the nineteenth-century tomes on the history of marriage and the family which it echoes, the state of the evidence in *Origin* renders it quaint to a reader familiar with more recent developments in anthropology. Nevertheless, it is a book whose considerable insight should not be overshadowed by its limitations. The idea that the "relations of sexuality" can and should be distinguished from the "relations of production" is not the least of Engels's intuitions.

> According to the materialistic conception, the determining factor in history is, in the final instance, the production and reproduction of immediate life. *This, again, is of a twofold character: on the one hand, the production of the means of existence, of food, clothing, and shelter and the tools necessary for that production; on the other side, the production of human beings themselves,* the propagation of the species. The social organization under which the people of a particular historical epoch and a particular country live is determined by both kinds of production: by the stage of development of labor, on the one hand, and of the family on the other.[12]

This passage indicates an important recognition—that a human group must do more than apply its activity to reshaping the natural world in order to clothe, feed, and warm itself. We usually call the system by which elements of the natural world are transformed into objects of human consumption the "economy." But the needs that are satisfied by economic activity even in the richest, Marxian sense do not exhaust fundamental human requirements. A human group must also reproduce itself from generation to generation. The needs of sexuality and procreation must be satisfied as much as the need to eat, and one of the most obvious deductions to be made from the data of anthropology is that these needs are hardly ever satisfied in any "natural" form, any more than are the needs for food. Hunger is hunger, but what counts as food is culturally determined and obtained. Every society has some form of organized economic activity. Sex is sex, but what counts as sex is equally culturally determined and obtained. Every society also has a sex/gender system—a set of arrangements by which the biological raw material of human sex and procreation is shaped by human, social intervention and satisfied in a conventional manner, no matter how bizarre some of the conventions may be.[13]

The realm of human sex, gender, and procreation has been subjected to, and changed by, relentless social activity for millennia. Sex as we know it— gender identity, sexual desire and fantasy, concepts of childhood—is itself a social product. We need to understand the relations of its production, and forget, for awhile, about food, clothing, automobiles, and transistor radios. In most Marxist tradition, and even in Engels's book, the concept of the "second aspect of material life" has tended to fade into the background or to be incorporated into the usual notions of "material life." Engels's suggestion has never been followed up and subjected to the refinement it needs. But he does indicate the existence and importance of the domain of social life that I want to call the sex/gender system.

Other names have been proposed for the sex/gender system. The most common alternatives are "mode of reproduction" and "patriarchy." It may be foolish to quibble about terms, but both of these can lead to confusion. All three proposals have been made in order to introduce a distinction between "economic" systems and "sexual" systems, and to indicate that sexual systems have a certain autonomy and cannot always be explained in terms of economic forces. "Mode of reproduction," for instance, has been proposed in opposition to the more familiar "mode of production." But this terminology links the "economy" to the production, and the sexual system to the "reproduction." It reduces the richness of either system, since "productions" and "reproductions" take place in both. Every mode of production involves reproduction—of tools, labor, and social relations. We cannot relegate all of the multifaceted aspects of social reproduction to the sex system. Replacement of machinery is an example of reproduction in the economy. On the other hand, we cannot limit the sex system to "reproduction" in either the social or biological sense of the term. A sex/gender system is not simply the reproductive moment of a "mode of production." The formation of gender identity is an example of production in the realm of the sexual system. And a sex/gender system involves more than the "relations of procreation," reproduction in a biological sense.

The term *patriarchy* was introduced to distinguish the forces maintaining sexism from other social forces, such as capitalism. But the use of *patriarchy* obscures other distinctions. Its use is analogous to using *capitalism* to refer to all modes of production, whereas the usefulness of the term *capitalism* lies precisely in that it distinguishes between the different systems by which societies are provisioned and organized. Any society will have some system of "political economy." Such a system may be egalitarian or socialist. It may be class stratified, in which case the oppressed class may consist of serfs, peasants, or slaves. The oppressed class may consist of wage laborers, in which case the system is properly labeled "capitalist." The power of the term lies in its implication that, in fact, there are alternatives to capitalism.

Similarly, any society will have some systematic ways to deal with sex, gender, and babies. Such a system may be sexually egalitarian, at least in theory, or it may be "gender stratified," as seems to be the case for most or all of the known examples. But it is important—even in the face of a depressing history—to maintain a distinction between the human capacity and necessity to create a sexual world, and the empirically oppressive ways in which sexual worlds have been organized. *Patriarchy* subsumes both meanings into the same term. *Sex/gender system*, on the other hand, is a neutral term that refers to the domain and indicates that oppression is not inevitable in that domain, but is the product of the specific social relations which organize it.

Finally, there are gender-stratified systems that are not adequately described as patriarchal. Many New Guinea societies are viciously oppressive to women.[14] But the power of males in these groups is founded not on their roles as fathers or patriarchs, but on their collective adult maleness, embodied in secret cults, men's houses, warfare, exchange networks, ritual knowledge, and various initiation procedures. Patriarchy is a specific form of male dominance, and the use of the term ought to be confined to the ecclesiastical offices and authorities to which the term initially referred, or to the Old Testament-type pastoral nomads and similar groups whose political structures the word usefully describes. Abraham was a Patriarch—one old man whose absolute power over wives, children, herds, and dependents was an aspect of the institution of fatherhood, as defined in the social group in which he lived.

Whichever term we use, what is important is to develop concepts to adequately describe the social organization of sexuality and the reproduction of the conventions of sex and gender. We need to pursue the project Engels abandoned when he located the subordination of women in a development within the mode of production.[15] To do this, we can imitate Engels in his method rather than in his results. Engels approached the task of analyzing the "second aspect of material life" by way of an examination of a theory of kinship systems. Kinship systems are and do many things. But they are made up of, and reproduce concrete forms of socially organized sexuality. Kinship systems are observable and empirical forms of sex/gender systems.

Kinship: On the Part Played by Sexuality in the Transition from Ape to "Man"

To an anthropologist, a kinship system is not a list of biological relatives. It is a system of categories and statuses which often contradict actual genetic relationships. There are dozens of examples in which socially defined kinship statuses take precedence over biology. The Nuer custom of "woman marriage" is a case in point. The Nuer define the status of fatherhood as belonging to the person in whose name cattle bridewealth is given for the mother. Thus, a woman can be married to another woman, and be husband to the wife and father of her children, despite the fact that she is not the inseminator.

In pre-state societies, kinship is often the idiom of social interaction, organizing economic, political, and ceremonial, as well as sexual activity. One's duties, responsibilities, and privileges vis-à-vis others are defined in terms of mutual kinship or lack thereof. The exchange of goods and services, production and distribution, hostility and solidarity, ritual and ceremony, all take place within the organizational structure of kinship. The ubiquity and adaptive effectiveness of kinship has led many anthropologists to consider its invention, along with the invention of language, to have been the developments that decisively marked the discontinuity between semihuman hominids and human beings.[16]

While the idea of kinship's importance enjoys the status of a first principle in anthropology, the internal workings of kinship systems have long been a focus of intense controversy. Kinship systems vary wildly from one culture to the next. They contain all sorts of bewildering rules which govern whom one may or may not marry. Their internal complexity is dazzling. Kinship systems have for decades provoked the anthropological imagination into trying to explain incest taboos, cross-cousin marriage, terms of descent, relationships of avoidance or forced intimacy, clans and sections, taboos on names—the diverse array of items found in descriptions of actual kinship systems. In the nineteenth century, several thinkers attempted to write comprehensive accounts of the nature and history of human sexual systems.[17] One of these was *Ancient Society*, by Lewis Henry Morgan. It was this book which inspired Engels to write *The Origin of the Family, Private Property, and the State*. Engels's theory is based upon Morgan's account of kinship and marriage.

In taking up Engels's project of extracting a theory of sex oppression from the study of kinship, we have the advantage of the maturation of ethnology since the nineteenth century. We also have the advantage of a peculiar and particularly appropriate book, Lévi-Strauss's *The Elementary Structures of Kinship* (1969). This is the boldest twentieth-century version of the nineteenth-century attempt to understand human marriage. It is a book in which kinship is explicitly conceived of as an imposition of cultural organization upon the facts of biological procreation. It is permeated with an awareness of the importance of sexuality in human society. It is a description of society that does not assume an abstract, genderless human subject. On the contrary, the human subject in Lévi-Strauss's work is always either male or female, and the divergent social destinies of the two sexes can therefore be traced. Since Lévi-Strauss sees the essence of kinship systems to lie in an exchange of women between men, he constructs an implicit theory of sex oppression. Aptly, the book is dedicated to the memory of Lewis Henry Morgan.

"Vile and precious merchandise."—Monique Wittig, *Les Guérillères*

The Elementary Structures of Kinship is a grand statement on the origin and nature of human society. It is a treatise on the kinship systems of approximately one-third of the ethnographic globe. Most fundamentally, it is an attempt to discern the structural principles of kinship. Lévi-Strauss argues that the application of these principles (summarized in the last chapter of *Elementary Structures*) to kinship data reveals an intelligible logic in the taboos and marriage rules that have perplexed and mystified Western anthropologists. He constructs a chess game of such complexity that it cannot be recapitulated here. But two of his chess pieces are particularly relevant to women—the "gift" and the incest taboo, whose dual articulation adds up to his concept of the exchange of women.

The Elementary Structures is in part a radical gloss on another famous theory of primitive social organization, Marcel Mauss's *Essay on the Gift* (1967).[18] It was Mauss who first theorized the significance of one of the most striking features of primitive societies: the extent to which giving, receiving, and reciprocating gifts dominate social intercourse. In such societies, all sorts of things circulate in exchange—food, spells, rituals, words, names, ornaments, tools, and powers: "Your own mother, your own sister, your own pigs, your own yams that you have piled up, you may not eat. Other people's mothers, other people's sisters, other people's pigs, other people's yams that they have piled up, you may eat."[19]

In a typical gift transaction, neither party gains anything. In the Trobriand Islands, each household maintains a garden of yams and each household eats yams. But the yams a household grows and the yams it eats are not the same. At harvest time, a man sends the yams he has cultivated to the household of his sister; the household in which he lives is provisioned by his wife's brother.[20] Since such a procedure appears to be a useless one from the point of view of accumulation or trade, its logic has been sought elsewhere. Mauss proposed that the significance of gift-giving is that it expresses, affirms, or creates a social link between the partners of an exchange. Gift-giving confers upon its participants a special relationship of trust, solidarity, and mutual aid. One can solicit a friendly relationship in the offer of a gift; acceptance implies a willingness to return a gift and a confirmation of the relationship. Gift exchange may also be the idiom of competition and rivalry. There are many examples in which one person humiliates another by giving more than can be reciprocated. Some political systems, such as the Big Man systems of highland New Guinea, are based on exchange that is unequal on the material plane. An aspiring Big Man wants to give away more goods than can be reciprocated. He gets his return in political prestige.

Although both Mauss and Lévi-Strauss emphasize the solidary aspects of gift exchange, the other purposes served by gift-giving only strengthen the point that it is a ubiquitous means of social commerce. Mauss proposed that gifts were the threads of social discourse, the means by which such societies were held together in the absence of specialized governmental institutions. "The gift is the primitive way of achieving the peace that in civil society is secured by the state. . . . Composing society, the gift was the liberation of culture."[21]

Lévi-Strauss adds to the theory of primitive reciprocity the idea that marriages are a most basic form of gift exchange, in which it is women who are the most precious gifts. He argues that the incest taboo should best be understood as a mechanism to insure that such exchanges take place between families and between groups. Since the existence of incest taboos is universal, but the content of their prohibitions variable, they cannot be explained as having the aim of preventing the occurrence of genetically close matings. Rather, the incest taboo imposes the social aim of exogamy and alliance upon the biological events of sex and procreation. The incest taboo divides the universe of sexual choice into categories of permitted and prohibited sexual partners. Specifically, by forbidding unions within a group it enjoins marital exchange between groups. "The prohibition on the sexual use of a daughter or a sister compels them to be given in marriage to another man, and at the same time it establishes a right to the daughter or sister of this other man. . . . The woman whom one does not take is, for that very reason, offered up. . . . The prohibition of incest is less a rule prohibiting marriage with the mother, sister, or daughter, than a rule obliging the mother, sister, or daughter to be given to others. It is the supreme rule of the gift."[22]

The result of a gift of women is more profound than the result of other gift transactions, because the relationship thus established is not just one of reciprocity, but one of kinship. The exchange partners have become affines, and their descendants will be related by blood: "Two people may meet in friendship and exchange gifts and yet quarrel and fight in later times, but intermarriage connects them in a permanent manner."[23] As is the case with other gift-giving, marriages are not always simply activities to make peace. Marriages may be highly competitive, and there are plenty of affines who fight each other. Nevertheless, in a general sense the argument is that the taboo on incest results in a wide network of relations, a set of people whose connections with one another compose a kinship structure. All other levels, amounts, and directions of exchange—including hostile ones—are ordered by this structure. The marriage ceremonies recorded in the ethnographic literature are moments in a ceaseless and ordered procession in which women, children, shells, words, cattle, names, fish, ancestors, whale's teeth, pigs, yams, spells, dances, mats, and so on, pass from hand to hand, leaving as their tracks the ties that bind. Kinship is organization, and organization gives power.

But who is organized? If it is women who are being transacted, then it is the men who give and take them who are linked, the woman being a conduit of a relationship rather than a partner of it.[24] The exchange of women does not necessarily imply that women are objectified, in the modern sense, since objects in the primitive world are imbued with highly personal qualities. But it does imply a distinction between gift and giver. If women are the gifts, then it is men who are the exchange partners. And it is the partners, not the presents, upon whom reciprocal exchange confers its quasi-mystical powers of social linkage. The relations of such a system are such that women are in no position to realize the benefits of their own circulation. As long as the relations specify that men exchange women, it is men who are the beneficiaries of the product of such exchanges—social organization. "The total relationship of exchange which constitutes marriage is not established between a man and a woman, but between two groups of men, and the woman figures only as one of the objects in the exchange, not as one of the partners. . . . This remains true even when the girl's feelings are taken into consideration, as, moreover, is usually the case. In acquiescing to the proposed union, she precipitates or allows the exchange to take place; she cannot alter its nature."[25]

To enter into a gift exchange as a partner, one must have something to give. If women are for men to dispose of, they are in no position to give themselves away.

> "What woman," mused a young Northern Melpa man, "is ever strong enough to get up and say, 'Let us make *moka*, let us find wives and pigs, let us give our daughters to men, let us wage war. Let us kill our enemies!' No, indeed not! . . . they are little rubbish things who stay at home simply, don't you see?"[26]

What women indeed! The Melpa women of whom the young man spoke cannot get wives; they *are* wives, and what they get are husbands, an entirely different matter. The Melpa women can't give their daughters to men, because they do not have the same rights in their daughters that their male kin have, rights of bestowal (although *not* of ownership).

The "exchange of women" is a seductive and powerful concept. It is attractive in that it places the oppression of women within social systems, rather than in biology. Moreover, it suggests that we look for the ultimate locus of women's oppression within the traffic in women, rather than within the traffic of merchandise. It is certainly not difficult to find ethnographic and historical examples of trafficking in women. Women are given in marriage, taken in battle, exchanged for favors, sent as tribute, traded, bought, and sold. Far from being confined to the "primitive" world, these practices seem only to become more pronounced and commercialized in more "civilized" societies. Men are of course also trafficked—but as slaves, hustlers, athletic stars, serfs, or as some other catastrophic social status, rather than as men. Women are transacted as slaves, serfs, and prostitutes, but also simply as women. And if men have been sexual subjects—exchangers—and women sexual semi-objects—gifts—for much of human history, then many customs, clichés, and personality traits seem to make a great deal of sense (among others, the curious custom by which a father gives away the bride).

The "exchange of women" is also a problematic concept. Since Lévi-Strauss argues that the incest taboo and the results of its application constitute the origin of culture, his analysis implies that the world-historical defeat of women occurred with the origin of culture, and is a prerequisite of culture. If his analysis is adopted in its pure form, the feminist program must include a task even more onerous than the extermination of men; it must attempt to get rid of culture and substitute some entirely new phenomena on the face of the earth. However, it would be a dubious proposition at best to argue that if there were no exchange of women there would be no culture, if for no other reason than that culture is, by definition, inventive. It is even debatable that "exchange of women" adequately describes all of the empirical evidence of kinship systems. Some cultures, such as the Lele and the Kuma, exchange women explicitly and overtly. In other cultures, the exchange of women can be inferred. In some—particularly those hunters and gatherers excluded from Lévi-Strauss's sample—the efficacy of the concept becomes altogether questionable. What are we to make of a concept which seems so useful and yet so difficult?

The "exchange of women" is neither a definition of culture nor a system in and of itself. The concept is an acute, but condensed, apprehension of certain aspects of the social relations of sex and gender. A kinship system is an imposition of social ends upon a part of the natural world. It is therefore "production" in the most general sense of the term: a molding, a transformation of objects (in this case, people) to and by a subjective purpose.[27] It has its own relations of production, distribution, and exchange, which include certain "property" forms in people. These forms are not exclusive, private property rights, but rather different sorts of rights that various people have in other people. Marriage transactions—the gifts and material which circulate in the ceremonies marking a marriage—are a rich source of data for determining exactly who has which rights in whom. It is not difficult to deduce from such transactions that in most cases women's rights are considerably more residual than those of men.

Kinship systems do not merely exchange women. They exchange sexual access, genealogical statuses, lineage names and ancestors, rights, and *people*—men, women, and children—in concrete systems of social relationships. These relationships always include certain rights for men, others for women. "Exchange of women" is a shorthand expression for the social relations of kinship systems specifying that men have certain rights in their female kin, and that women do not have the same rights either to themselves or to their male kin. In this sense, the exchange of women is a profound perception of a system in which women do not have full rights to themselves. The exchange of women becomes an obfuscation if it is seen as a cultural necessity and when it is used as the single tool with which an analysis of a particular kinship system is approached.

If Lévi-Strauss is correct in seeing the exchange of women as a fundamental principle of kinship, the subordination of women can be seen as a product of the relationships by which sex and gender are organized and produced. The economic oppression of women is derivative and secondary. But there is an "economics" of sex and gender, and what we need is a political economy of sexual systems. We need to study each society to determine the exact mechanisms by which particular conventions of sexuality are produced and maintained. The "exchange of women" is an initial step toward building an arsenal of concepts with which sexual systems can be described.

Psychoanalysis and Its Discontents

The battle between psychoanalysis and the women's and gay movements has become legendary. In part, this confrontation between sexual revolutionaries and the clinical establishment has been due to the evolution of psychoanalysis in the United States, where clinical tradition has fetishized anatomy. The child is thought to travel through its organismic stages until it reaches its anatomical destiny and the missionary position. Clinical practice has often seen its mission as the repair of individuals who somehow have become derailed en route to their "biological" aim. Transforming moral law into scientific law, clinical practice has acted to enforce sexual convention upon unruly participants. In this sense, psychoanalysis has often become more than a theory of the mechanisms of the reproduction of sexual arrangements; it has been one of those mechanisms. Since the aim of the feminist and gay revolts is to dismantle the apparatus of sexual enforcement, a critique of psychoanalysis has been in order.

But the rejection of Freud by the women's and gay movement has deeper roots in the rejection by psychoanalysis of its own insights. Nowhere are the effects on women of male-dominated social systems better documented than within the clinical literature. According to the Freudian orthodoxy, the attainment of "normal" femininity extracts severe costs from women. The theory of gender acquisition could have been the basis of a critique of sex roles. Instead, the radical implications of Freud's theory have been radically repressed. This tendency is evident even in the original formulations of the theory, but it has been exacerbated over time until the potential for a critical psychoanalytic theory of gender is visible only in the symptomatology of its denial—an intricate rationalization of sex roles as they are. It is not the purpose of this paper to conduct a psychoanalysis of the psychoanalytic unconscious; but I do hope to demonstrate that it exists. Moreover, the salvage of psychoanalysis from its own motivated repression is not for the sake of Freud's good name. Psychoanalysis contains a unique set of concepts for understanding men, women, and sexuality. It is a theory of sexuality in human society. Most important, psychoanalysis provides a description of the mechanisms by which the sexes are divided and deformed, of how bisexual, androgynous infants are transformed into boys and girls.[28] Psychoanalysis is a feminist theory *manqué*.

un fullfilled

The Oedipus Hex

Until the late 1920s, the psychoanalytic movement did not have a distinctive theory of feminine development. Instead, variants of an "Electra" complex in women had been proposed, in which female experience was thought to be a mirror image of the Oedipal complex described for males. The boy loved his mother, but gave her up out of fear of the father's threat of castration. The girl, it was thought, loved her father, and gave him up out of fear of maternal vengeance. This formulation assumed that both children were subject to a biological imperative toward heterosexuality. It also assumed that the children were already, before the Oedipal phase, "little" men and women.

Freud had voiced reservations about jumping to conclusions about women on the basis of data gathered from men. But his objections remained general until the discovery of the pre-Oedipal phase in women. The concept of the pre-Oedipal phase enabled both Freud and Jeanne Lampl de Groot to articulate the classic psychoanalytic theory of femininity.[29] The idea of the pre-Oedipal phase in women produced a dislocation of the biologically derived presuppositions which underlay notions of an "Electra" complex. In the pre-Oedipal phase, children of both sexes were psychically indistinguishable, which meant that their differentiation into masculine and feminine children had to be explained, rather than assumed. Pre-Oedipal children were described as bisexual. Both sexes exhibited the full range of libidinal attitudes, active and passive. And for children of both sexes, the mother was the object of desire.

The characteristics of the pre-Oedipal female challenged the ideas of a primordial heterosexuality and gender identity. Since the girl's libidinal activity was directed toward the mother, her adult heterosexuality had to be explained:

"It would be a solution of ideal simplicity if we could suppose that from a particular age onwards the elementary influence of the mutual attraction between the sexes makes itself felt and impels the small woman towards men. . . . But we are not going to find things so easy; we scarcely know whether we are to believe seriously in the power of which poets talk so much and with such enthusiasm but which cannot be further dissected analytically."[30] Moreover, the girl did not manifest a "feminine" libidinal attitude. Since her desire for the mother was active and aggressive, her ultimate accession to "femininity" had also to be explained: "In conformity with its peculiar nature, psychoanalysis does not try to describe what a woman is . . . but sets about enquiring how she comes into being, how a woman develops out of a child with a bisexual disposition."[31]

In short, feminine development could no longer be taken for granted as a reflex of biology. Rather, it had become immensely problematic. It is in explaining the acquisition of "femininity" that Freud employs the concepts of penis envy and castration, which have infuriated feminists since he first introduced them. According to Freud, the girl turns from the mother and represses the "masculine" elements of her libido as a result of her recognition that she is castrated. She compares her tiny clitoris to the larger penis, and in the face of its evident superior ability to satisfy the mother, falls prey to penis envy and a sense of inferiority. She gives up her struggle for the mother and assumes a passive feminine position vis-à-vis the father. Freud's account can be read as claiming that femininity is a consequence of the anatomical differences between the sexes. He has therefore been accused of biological determinism. Nevertheless, even in his most anatomically stated versions of the female castration complex, the "inferiority" of the woman's genitals is a product of the situational context: the girl feels less "equipped" to possess and satisfy the mother. If the pre-Oedipal lesbian were not confronted by the heterosexuality of the mother, she might draw different conclusions about the relative status of her genitals.

Freud was never as much of a biological determinist as some would have him. He repeatedly stressed that all adult sexuality resulted from psychic, not biologic, development. But his writing is often ambiguous, and his wording leaves plenty of room for the biological interpretations which have been so popular in American psychoanalysis. In France, on the other hand, the trend in psychoanalytic theory has been to de-biologize Freud, and to conceive of psychoanalysis as a theory of information rather than organs. Jacques Lacan, the instigator of this line of thinking, insists that Freud never meant to say anything about anatomy, and that Freud's theory was instead about language and the cultural meanings imposed upon anatomy. The debate over the "real" Freud is extremely interesting, but it is not my purpose here to contribute to it. Rather, I want to rephrase the classic theory of femininity in Lacan's terminology, after introducing some of the pieces on Lacan's conceptual chessboard.

Kinship, Lacan, and the Phallus

Lacan suggests that psychoanalysis is the study of the traces left in the psyches of individuals as a result of their conscription into systems of kinship.

> Isn't it striking that Lévi-Strauss, in suggesting that implication of the structures of language with that part of the social laws which regulate marriage ties and kinship, is already conquering the very terrain in which Freud situates the unconscious?[32]

> For where on earth would one situate the determinations of the unconscious if it is not in those nominal cadres in which marriage ties and kinship are always grounded. . . . And how would one apprehend the analytical conflicts and their Oedipean prototype outside the engagements which have fixed, long before the subject came into the world, not only his destiny, but his identity itself?[33]

> This is precisely where the Oedipus complex . . . may be said, in this connection, to mark the limits which our discipline assigns to subjectivity: that is to say, what the subject can know of his unconscious participation in the movement of the complex structures of marriage ties, by verifying the symbolic effects in his individual existence of the tangential movement towards incest.[34]

Kinship is the culturalization of biological sexuality on the societal level; psychoanalysis describes the transformation of the biological sexuality of individuals as they are enculturated.

Kinship terminology contains information about the system. Kin terms demarcate statuses and indicate some of the attributes of those statuses. For instance, in the Trobriand Islands a man calls the women of his clan by the term for "sister." He calls women of clans into which he can marry by a term indicating their marriageability. When the young Trobriand male learns these terms, he learns which women he can safely desire. In Lacan's scheme, the Oedipal crisis occurs when a child learns of the sexual rules embedded in the terms for family and relatives. The crisis begins when the child comprehends the system and his or her place in it; the crisis is resolved when the child accepts that place and accedes to it. Even if the child refuses that place, he or she cannot escape the knowledge of it. Before the Oedipal phase, the sexuality of the child is labile and relatively unstructured. Each child contains all the sexual possibilities available to human expression. But in any given society, only some of these possibilities will be expressed, while others will be constrained. Upon leaving the Oedipal phase, the child's libido and gender identity have been organized in conformity with the rules of the culture which is domesticating it.[35]

The Oedipal complex is an apparatus for the production of sexual personality. It is a truism to say that societies will inculcate in their young the character traits appropriate to carrying on the business of society. For instance, E. P. Thompson speaks of the transformation of the personality structure of the English working class as artisans were changed into good industrial workers.[36] Just as the social forms of labor demand certain kinds of personality, the social forms of sex and gender demand certain kinds of people. In the most general terms, the Oedipal complex is a machine which fashions the appropriate forms of sexual individuals.[37]

In the Lacanian theory of psychoanalysis, it is the kin terms that indicate a structure of relationships that will determine the role of any individual or object within the Oedipal drama. For instance, Lacan makes a distinction between the "function of the father" and a particular father who embodies this function. In the same way, he makes a radical distinction between the penis and the "phallus," between organ and information. The phallus is a set of meanings conferred upon the penis. The differentiation between phallus and penis in contemporary French psychoanalytic terminology emphasizes the idea that the penis could not and does not play the role attributed to it in the classical terminology of the castration complex.[38]

In Freud's terminology, the Oedipal complex presents two alternatives to a child: to have a penis or to be castrated. In contrast, the Lacanian theory of the castration complex leaves behind all reference to anatomical reality.

> The theory of the castration complex amounts to having the male organ play a dominant role—this time as a symbol—*to the extent that its absence or presence transforms an anatomical difference into a major classification of humans, and to the extent that, for each subject, this presence or absence is not taken for granted, is not reduced purely and simply to a given, but is the problematical result of an intra- and intersubjective process* (the subject's assumption of his own sex).[39]

The alternative presented to the child may be rephrased as an alternative between having, or not having, the phallus. Castration is not having the (symbolic) phallus. Castration is not a real "lack," but a meaning conferred on the genitals of a woman: "Castration may derive support from . . . the apprehension in the Real of the absence of the penis in women—but even this supposes a symbolization of the object, since the Real is full, and 'lacks' nothing. Insofar as one finds castration in the genesis of neurosis, it is never real but symbolic."[40]

The phallus is, as it were, a distinctive feature differentiating "castrated" and "noncastrated." The presence or absence of the phallus carries the differences between two sexual statuses, "man" and "woman."[41] Since these are not equal, the phallus also carries a meaning of the dominance of men over women, and it may be inferred that "penis envy" is a recognition thereof. Moreover, as long as men have rights in women which women do not have in themselves, the phallus also carries the meaning of the difference between "exchanger" and "exchanged," gift and giver. Ultimately, neither the classical Freudian nor the rephrased Lacanian theories of the Oedipal process make sense unless at least this much of the Paleolithic relations of sexuality are still with us. We still live in a "phallic" culture.

Lacan also speaks of the phallus as a symbolic object which is exchanged within and between families.[42] It is interesting to think about this observation in terms of primitive marriage transactions and exchange networks. In those transactions, the exchange of women is usually one of many cycles of exchange. Usually, there are other objects circulating as well as women. Women move in one direction, cattle, shells, or mats in the other. In one sense, the Oedipal complex is an expression of the circulation of the phallus in intrafamily exchange, an inversion of the circulation of women in interfamily exchange. In the cycle of exchange manifested by the Oedipal complex, the phallus passes through the medium of women from one man to another—from father to son, from mother's brother to sister's son, and so forth. In this family *Kula* ring, women go one way, the phallus the other. It is where we aren't. In this sense, the phallus is more than a feature which distinguishes the sexes: it is the embodiment of the male status, to which men accede, and in which certain rights inhere—among them, the right to a woman. It is an expression of the transmission of male dominance. It passes through women and settles upon men.[43] The tracks which it leaves include gender identity, the division of the sexes. But it leaves more than this. It leaves "penis envy," which acquires a rich meaning of the disquietude of women in a phallic culture.

Oedipus Revisited

We return now to the two pre-Oedipal androgynes, sitting on the border between biology and culture. Lévi-Strauss places the incest taboo on that border, arguing that its initiation of the exchange of women constitutes the origin of society. In this sense, the incest taboo and the exchange of women are the content of the original social contract.[44] For individuals, the Oedipal crisis occurs at the same divide, when the incest taboo initiates the exchange of the phallus.

The Oedipal crisis is precipitated by certain items of information. The children discover the differences between the sexes, and that each child must become one or the other gender. They also discover the incest taboo, and that some sexuality is prohibited—in this case, the mother is unavailable to either child because she "belongs" to the father. Lastly, they discover that the two genders do not have the same sexual "rights" or futures.

In the normal course of events, the boy renounces his mother for fear that otherwise his father would castrate him (refuse to give him the phallus, and make him a girl). But by this act of renunciation, the boy affirms the relationships which have given mother to father and which will give him, if he becomes a man, a woman of his own. In exchange for the boy's affirmation of his father's right to his mother, the father affirms the phallus of his son (does not castrate him). The boy exchanges his mother for the phallus, the symbolic token which can later be exchanged for a woman. The only thing required of him is a little patience. He retains his initial libidinal organization and the sex of his original love object. The social contract to which he has agreed will eventually recognize his own rights and provide him with a woman of his own.

What happens to the girl is more complex. She, like the boy, discovers the taboo against incest and the division of the sexes. She also discovers some unpleasant information about the gender to which she is being assigned. For the boy, the taboo on incest is a taboo on certain women. For the girl, it is a taboo on all women. Since she is in a homosexual position vis-à-vis the mother, the rule of heterosexuality which dominates the scenario makes her position excruciatingly untenable. The mother, and all women by extension, can be properly beloved only by someone "with a penis" (phallus). Since the girl has no "phallus," she has no "right" to love her mother or another woman since she is herself destined to some man. She does not have the symbolic token which can be exchanged for a woman.

If Freud's wording of this moment of the female Oedipal crisis is ambiguous, Lampl de Groot's formulation makes the context which confers meaning upon the genitals explicit: *"If the little girl comes to the conclusion that such an organ is really indispensable to the possession of the mother, she experiences* in addition to the narcissistic insults common to both sexes still another blow, namely *a feeling of inferiority about her genitals.*"[45] The girl concludes that the "penis" is indispensable for the possession of the mother because only those who possess the phallus have a "right" to a woman, and the token of exchange. She does not come to her conclusion because of the natural superiority of the penis either in and of itself, or as an instrument for making love. The hierarchical arrangement of the male and female genitals is a result of the definitions of the situation—the rule of obligatory heterosexuality and the relegation of women (those without the phallus, castrated) to men (those with the phallus).

The girl then begins to turn away from the mother, and to the father. "To the girl, it [castration] is an accomplished fact, which is irrevocable, but the recognition of which compels her finally to renounce her first love object and to taste to the full the bitterness of its loss. . . . [T]he father is chosen as a love-object, the enemy becomes the beloved."[46] This recognition of "castration" forces the girl to redefine her relationship to herself, her mother, and her father.

She turns from the mother because she does not have the phallus to give her. She turns from the mother also in anger and disappointment, because the mother did not give her a "penis" (phallus). But the mother, a woman in a phallic culture, does not have the phallus to give away (having gone through the Oedipal crisis herself a generation earlier). The girl then turns to the father because only he can "give her the phallus," and it is only through him that she can enter into the symbolic exchange system in which the phallus circulates. But the father does not give her the phallus in the same way that he gives it to the boy. The phallus is affirmed in the boy, who then has it to give away. The girl never gets the phallus. It passes through her, and in its passage is transformed into a child. When she "recognizes her castration," she accedes to the place of a woman in a phallic exchange network. She can "get" the phallus—in intercourse, or as a child—but only as a gift from a man. She never gets to give it away.

When she turns to the father, she also represses the "active" portions of her libido.

> The turning away from her mother is an extremely important step in the
> course of a little girl's development. It is more than a mere change of object
> . . . hand in hand with it there is to be observed a marked lowering of the
> active sexual impulses and a rise of the passive ones. . . . The transition to
> the father object is accomplished with the help of the passive trends in so

far as they have escaped the catastrophe. The path to the development of femininity now lies open to the girl.[47]

The ascendance of passivity in the girl is due to her recognition of the futility of realizing her active desire, and of the unequal terms of the struggle. Freud locates active desire in the clitoris and passive desire in the vagina, and thus describes the repression of active desire as the repression of clitoral eroticism in favor of passive vaginal eroticism. In this scheme, cultural stereotypes have been mapped onto the genitals. Since the work of Masters and Johnson, it is evident that this genital division is a false one. Any organ—penis, clitoris, vagina—can be the locus of either active or passive eroticism. What is important in Freud's scheme, however, is not the geography of desire but its self-confidence. It is not an organ which is repressed but a segment of erotic possibility. Freud notes that "more constraint has been applied to the libido when it is pressed into the service of the feminine function."[48] The girl has been robbed.

If the Oedipal phase proceeds normally and the girl "accepts her castration," her libidinal structure and object choice are now congruent with the female gender role. She has become a little woman—feminine, passive, heterosexual. Actually, Freud suggests that there are three alternate routes out of the Oedipal catastrophe. The girl may simply freak out, repress sexuality altogether, and become asexual. She may protest, cling to her narcissism and desire, and become either "masculine" or homosexual. Or she may accept the situation, sign the social contract, and attain "normality."

Karen Horney is critical of the entire Freud/Lampl de Groot scheme. But in the course of her critique she articulates its implications.

> When she [the girl] first turns to a man (the father), it is in the main only by way of the narrow bridge of resentment. . . . We should feel it a contradiction if the relation of woman to man did not retain throughout life some tinge of this enforced substitute for that which was really desired. . . . The same character of something remote from instinct, secondary and substitutive, would, even in normal women, adhere to the wish for motherhood. . . . The special point about Freud's viewpoint is rather that it sees the wish for motherhood not as an innate formation, but as something that can be reduced psychologically to its ontogenetic elements and draws its energy originally from homosexual or phallic instinctual elements. . . . It would follow, finally, that women's whole reaction to life would be based on a strong subterranean resentment.[49]

Horney considers these implications to be so far-fetched that they challenge the validity of Freud's entire scheme. But it is certainly plausible to argue instead that the creation of "femininity" in women in the course of socialization is an act of psychic brutality, and that it leaves in women an immense resentment of the suppression to which they were subjected. It is also possible to argue that women have few means for realizing and expressing their residual anger. One can read Freud's essays on femininity as descriptions of how a group is prepared psychologically, at a tender age, to live with its oppression.

There is an additional element in the classic discussions of the attainment of womanhood. The girl first turns to the father, because she must, because she is "castrated" (a helpless woman). She then discovers that "castration" is a prerequisite to the father's love, that she must be a woman for him to love her. She therefore begins to desire "castration," and what had previously been a disaster becomes a wish. "Analytic experience leaves no room for doubt that the little girl's first libidinal relation to her father is masochistic, and the masochistic wish in its earliest distinctively feminine phase is: 'I want to be castrated by my father.'"[50] Deutsch argues that such masochism may conflict with the ego, causing some women to flee the entire situation in defense of their self-regard. Those women to whom the choice is "between finding bliss in suffering or peace in renunciation" will have difficulty in attaining a healthy attitude to intercourse and motherhood.[51] Why Deutsch appears to consider such women to be special cases, rather than the norm, is not clear from her discussion.

The psychoanalytic theory of femininity is one that sees female development based largely on pain and humiliation, and it takes some fancy footwork to explain why anyone ought to enjoy being a woman. At this point in the classic discussions biology makes a triumphant return. The fancy footwork consists in arguing that finding joy in pain is adaptive to the role of women in reproduction, since defloration and childbirth are "painful." Would it not make more sense to question the entire procedure? If women, in finding their place in a sexual system, are robbed of libido and forced into a masochistic eroticism, why did the analysts not argue for novel arrangements, instead of rationalizing the old ones?

Freud's theory of femininity has been subjected to feminist critique since it was first published. To the extent that the theory is a rationalization of female subordination, this critique has been justified. To the extent that it is a description of a process that subordinates women, this critique is a mistake. As a description of how phallic culture domesticates women, and the effects in women of their domestication, psychoanalytic theory has no parallel.[52] And since psychoanalysis is a theory of gender, dismissing it would be ill advised for a political movement dedicated to eradicating gender hierarchy (or gender itself). We cannot dismantle something that we underestimate or do not understand. The oppression of women is deep; equal pay, equal work, and all the female politicians in the world will not extirpate the roots of sexism. Lévi-Strauss and Freud elucidate what would otherwise be poorly perceived parts of the deep structures of sex oppression. They serve as reminders of the intractability and magnitude of what we fight, and their analyses provide preliminary charts of the social machinery we must rearrange.

Women Unite to Off the Oedipal Residue of Culture

The precision of the fit between Freud and Lévi-Strauss is striking. Kinship systems require a division of the sexes. The Oedipal phase divides the sexes. Kinship systems include sets of rules governing sexuality. The Oedipal crisis is the assimilation of these rules and taboos. Compulsory heterosexuality is the product of kinship. The Oedipal phase constitutes heterosexual desire. Kinship rests on a radical difference between the rights of men and women. The Oedipal complex confers male rights upon the boy and forces the girl to accommodate herself to her lesser rights.

This fit between Lévi-Strauss and Freud is by implication an argument that our sex/gender system is still organized by the principles outlined by Lévi-Strauss, despite the entirely nonmodern character of his data. The more recent data on which Freud bases his theories testifies to the endurance of these sexual structures. If my reading of Freud and Lévi-Strauss is accurate, it suggests that the feminist movement must attempt to resolve the Oedipal crisis of culture by reorganizing the domain of sex and gender in such a way that each individual's Oedipal experience would be less destructive. The dimensions of such a task are difficult to imagine, but at least certain conditions would have to be met.

Several elements of the Oedipal situation would have to be altered in order that the phase not have such disastrous effects on the young female ego. The Oedipal phase institutes a contradiction in the girl by placing irreconcilable demands upon her. On the one hand, the girl's love for the mother is induced by the mother's job of child care. The girl is then forced to abandon this love because of the female sex role—to belong to a man. If the sexual division of labor were such that adults of both sexes cared for children equally, primary object choice would be bisexual. If heterosexuality were not obligatory, this early love would not have to be suppressed, and the penis would not be overvalued. If the sexual property system were reorganized in such a way that men did not have overriding rights in women (if there was no exchange of women) and if there were no gender, the entire Oedipal drama would be a relic. In short, feminism must call for a revolution in kinship.

The organization of sex and gender once had functions other than itself—it organized society. Now, it mainly organizes and reproduces itself. The kinds of relationships sexuality established in the dim human past still dominate our sexual lives, our ideas about men and women, and the ways we raise our children. But they lack the functional load they once carried. One of the most conspicuous features of kinship is that it has been systematically stripped of its functions—political, economic, educational, and organizational. It has been reduced to its barest bones—*sex and gender.*

Human sexual life will always be subject to convention and human intervention. It will never be completely "natural," if only because our species is social, cultural, and articulate. The wild profusion of infantile sexuality will always be tamed. The confrontation between immature and helpless infants and the developed social life of their elders will probably always leave some residue of disturbance. But the mechanisms and aims of this process need not be largely independent of conscious choice. Cultural evolution provides us with the opportunity to seize control of the means of sexuality, reproduction, and socialization, and to make conscious decisions to liberate human sexual life from the archaic relationships which deform it. Ultimately, a thoroughgoing feminist revolution would liberate more than women. It would liberate forms of sexual expression, and it would liberate human personality from the straightjacket of gender.

"Daddy, daddy, you bastard, I'm through."—Sylvia Plath

In the course of this essay I have tried to construct a theory of women's oppression by borrowing concepts from anthropology and psychoanalysis. But Lévi-Strauss and Freud write within intellectual traditions produced by a culture in which women are oppressed. The danger in my enterprise is that the sexism in the traditions of which they are a part tends to be dragged in with each borrowing. "We cannot utter a single destructive proposition which has not already slipped into the form, the logic, and the implicit postulations of precisely what it seeks to contest."[53] And what slips in is formidable. Both psychoanalysis and structural anthropology are, in one sense, the most sophisticated ideologies of sexism around.[54]

For instance, Lévi-Strauss sees women as being like words, which are misused when they are not "communicated" and exchanged. On the last page of a very long book, he observes that this creates something of a contradiction in women, since women are at the same time "speakers" and "spoken." His only comment on this contradiction is this.

> But woman could never become just a sign and nothing more, since even in a man's world she is still a person, and since insofar as she is defined as a sign she must be recognized as a generator of signs. In the matrimonial dialogue of men, woman is never purely what is spoken about; for if women in general represent a certain category of signs, destined to a certain kind of communication, each woman preserves a particular value arising from her talent, before and after marriage, for taking her part in a duet. In contrast to words, which have wholly become signs, woman has remained at once a sign and a value. *This explains why the relations between the sexes have preserved that affective richness, ardour and mystery which doubtless originally permeated the entire universe of human communications.*[55]

This is an extraordinary statement. Why is he not, at this point, denouncing what kinship systems do to women, instead of presenting one of the greatest rip-offs of all time as the root of romance?

A similar insensitivity is revealed within psychoanalysis by the inconsistency with which it assimilates the critical implications of its own theory. For instance, Freud did not hesitate to recognize that his findings posed a challenge to conventional morality: "We cannot avoid observing with critical eyes, and we have found that it is impossible to give our support to conventional sexual morality or to approve highly of the means by which society attempts to arrange the practical problems of sexuality in life. *We can demonstrate with ease that what the world calls its code of morals demands more sacrifices than it is worth,* and that its behavior is neither dictated by honesty nor instituted with wisdom."[56]

Nevertheless, when psychoanalysis demonstrates with equal facility that the ordinary components of feminine personality are masochism, self-hatred, and passivity, a similar judgment is *not* made.[57] Instead, a double standard of interpretation is employed. Masochism is bad for men, essential to women. Adequate narcissism is necessary for men, impossible for women. Passivity is tragic in man, while lack of passivity is tragic in a woman.

It is this double standard which enables clinicians to try to accommodate women to a role whose destructiveness is so lucidly detailed in their own theories. It is the same inconsistent attitude which permits therapists to consider lesbianism as a problem to be cured, rather than as the resistance to the bad situation that their own theory suggests.[58] There are points within the analytic discussions of femininity where one might say, "This is oppression of women," or "We can demonstrate with ease that what the world calls femininity demands more sacrifices than it is worth." It is precisely at such points that the implications of the theory are ignored and are replaced with formulations whose purpose is to keep those implications firmly lodged in the theoretical unconscious. It is at these points that all sorts of mysterious chemical substances, joys in pain, and biological aims are substituted for a critical assessment of the costs of femininity. These substitutions are the symptoms of theoretical repression, in that they are not consistent with the usual canons of psychoanalytic argument. The extent to which these rationalizations of femininity go against the grain of psychoanalytic logic is strong evidence for the extent of the need to suppress the radical and feminist implications of the theory of femininity (Deutsch's discussions are excellent examples of this process of substitution and repression).

The argument which must be woven in order to assimilate Lévi-Strauss and Freud into feminist theory is somewhat tortuous. I have engaged it for several reasons. First, while neither Lévi-Strauss nor Freud questions the undoubted sexism endemic to the systems they describe, the questions which ought to be posed are blindingly obvious. Second, their work enables us to isolate sex and gender from "mode of production," and to counter a certain tendency to explain sex oppression as a reflex of economic forces. Their work provides a framework in which the full weight of sexuality and marriage can be incorporated into an analysis of sex oppression. It suggests a conception of the women's movement as analogous to, rather than isomorphic with, the working-class movement, each addressing a different source of human discontent. In Marx's vision, the working-class movement would do more than throw off the burden of its own exploitation. It also had the potential to change society, to liberate humanity, to create a classless society. Perhaps the women's movement has the task of effecting the same kind of social change for a system of which Marx had only an imperfect apperception. Something of this sort is implicit in Wittig—the dictatorship of the Amazon *guérillères* is a temporary means for achieving a genderless society.

The sex/gender system is not immutably oppressive and has lost much of its traditional function. Nevertheless, it will not wither away in the absence of opposition. It still carries the social burden of sex and gender, of socializing the young, and of providing ultimate propositions about the nature of human beings themselves. And it serves economic and political ends other than those it was originally designed to further.[59] The sex/gender system must be reorganized through political action.

Finally, the exegesis of Lévi-Strauss and Freud suggests a certain vision of feminist politics and the feminist utopia. It suggests that we should not aim for the elimination of men, but for the elimination of the social system which creates sexism and gender. I personally find a vision of an Amazon matriarchate, in which men are reduced to servitude or oblivion (depending on the possibilities for parthenogenetic reproduction), distasteful and inadequate. Such a vision maintains gender and the division of the sexes. It is a vision which simply inverts the arguments of those who base their case for inevitable male dominance on ineradicable and *significant* biological differences between the sexes. But we are not only oppressed *as* women; we are oppressed by having to *be* women—or men as the case may be. I personally feel that the feminist movement must dream of even more than the elimination of the oppression of women. It must dream of the elimination of obligatory sexualities and sex roles. The dream I find most compelling is one of an androgynous and genderless (though not sexless) society, in which one's sexual anatomy is irrelevant to who one is, what one does, and with whom one makes love.

The Political Economy of Sex

It would be nice to be able to conclude here with the implications for feminism and gay liberation of the overlap between Freud and Lévi-Strauss. But I must suggest, tentatively, a next step on the agenda: a Marxian analysis of sex/gender systems. Sex/gender systems are not ahistorical emanations of the human mind; they are products of historical human activity.

We need, for instance, an analysis of the evolution of sexual exchange along the lines of Marx's discussion in *Capital* of the evolution of money and commodities. There are an economics and a politics to sex/gender systems that are obscured by the concept of "exchange of women." For instance, a system in which women are exchangeable only for one another has different effects on women than one in which there is a commodity equivalent for women.

> That marriage in simple societies involves an "exchange" is a somewhat vague notion that has often confused the analysis of social systems. The extreme case is the exchange of "sisters," formerly practiced in parts of Australia and Africa. Here the term has the precise dictionary meaning of "to be received as an equivalent for," "to give and receive reciprocally." From quite a different standpoint the virtually universal incest prohibition means

that marriage systems necessarily involve "exchanging" siblings for spouses, giving rise to a reciprocity that is purely notational. But in most societies marriage is mediated by a set of intermediary transactions. If we see these transactions as simply implying immediate or long-term reciprocity, then the analysis is likely to be blurred. . . . The analysis is further limited if one regards the passage of property simply as a symbol of the transfer of rights, for then the nature of the objects handed over . . . is of little importance. . . . Neither of these approaches is wrong; both are inadequate.[60]

There are systems in which there is no equivalent for a woman. To get a wife, a man must have a daughter, a sister, or other female kinswoman in whom he has a right of bestowal. He must have control over some female flesh. The Lele and Kuma are cases in point. Lele men scheme constantly in order to stake claims in some as yet unborn girl, and scheme further to make good their claims.[61] A Kuma girl's marriage is determined by an intricate web of debts, and she has little say in choosing her husband. A girl is usually married against her will, and her groom shoots an arrow into her thigh to symbolically prevent her from running away. The young wives almost always do run away, only to be returned to their new husbands by an elaborate conspiracy enacted by their kin and affines.[62]

In other societies, there is an equivalent for women. A woman can be converted into bridewealth, and bridewealth can be in turn converted into a woman. The dynamics of such systems vary accordingly, as does the specific kind of pressure exerted upon women. The marriage of a Melpa woman is not a return for a previous debt. Each transaction is self-contained, in that the payment of a bridewealth in pigs and shells will cancel the debt. The Melpa woman therefore has more latitude in choosing her husband than does her Kuma counterpart; still, her destiny is linked to bridewealth. If her husband's kin are slow to pay, her kin may encourage her to leave him; on the other hand, if her consanguineal kin are satisfied with the balance of payments, they may refuse to back her in the event that she wants to leave her husband. More-over, her male kinsmen use the bridewealth for their own purposes, in *moka* exchange and for their own marriages. If a woman leaves her husband, some or all of the bridewealth will have to be returned. If, as is usually the case, the pigs and shells have been distributed or promised, her kin will be reluctant to back her in the event of marital discord. And each time a woman divorces and remarries her value in bridewealth tends to depreciate. On the whole, her male consanguines will lose in the event of a divorce, unless the groom has been delinquent in his payments. While the Melpa woman is freer as a new bride than a Kuma woman, the bridewealth system makes divorce difficult or impossible.[63]

In some societies, like the Nuer, bridewealth can only be converted into brides. In others, bridewealth can be converted into something else, such as political prestige. In this case, a woman's marriage is implicated in a political system. In the Big Man systems of Highland New Guinea, the material which circulates for women also circulates in the exchanges on which political power is based. Within the political system men are in constant need of valuables to disburse, and they are dependent upon input. They depend not only upon their immediate partners, but upon the partners of their partners, to several degrees of remove. If a man has to return some bridewealth, he may not be able to give it to someone who planned to give it to someone else who intended to use it to give a feast upon which his status depends. Big Men are therefore concerned with the domestic affairs of others whose relationship with them may be extremely indirect. There are cases in which headmen intervene in marital disputes involving indirect trading partners in order that *moka* exchanges not be disrupted.[64] The weight of this entire system may come to rest upon one woman kept in a miserable marriage.

In short, there are other questions to ask of a marriage system than whether or not it exchanges women. Is the woman traded for a woman, or is there an equivalent? Is this equivalent only for women, or can it be turned into something else? If it can be turned into something else, is it turned into political power or wealth? On the other hand, can bridewealth be obtained only in marital exchange, or can it be obtained from elsewhere? Can women be accumulated through amassing wealth? Can wealth be accumulated by disposing of women? Is a marriage system part of a system of stratification?[65]

These last questions point to another task for a political economy of sex. Kinship and marriage are always parts of total social systems and are tied into economic and political arrangements.

> Lévi-Strauss . . . rightly argues that the structural implications of a marriage can only be understood if we think of it as one item in a whole series of transactions between kin groups. So far, so good. But in none of the examples which he provides in his book does he carry this principle far enough. The reciprocities of kinship obligation are not merely symbols of alliance, they are also economic transactions, political transactions, charters to rights of domicile and land use. No useful picture of "how a kinship system works" can be provided unless these several aspects or implications of the kinship organization are considered simultaneously.[66]

Among the Kachin, the relationship of a tenant to a landlord is also a relationship between a son-in-law and a father-in-law. "The procedure for acquiring land rights of any kind is in almost all cases tantamount to marrying a woman from the lineage of the lord."[67] In the Kachin system, bridewealth moves from commoners to aristocrats, women moving in the opposite direction.

> From an economic aspect the effect of the matrilateral cross-cousin marriage is that, on balance, the headman's lineage constantly pays wealth to the chief's lineage in the form of bridewealth. The payment can also, from an analytical point of view, be regarded as a rent paid to the senior landlord by the tenant. The most important part of this payment is in the form of consumer goods—namely cattle. The chief converts this perishable wealth into imperishable prestige through the medium of spectacular feasting. The ultimate consumers of the goods are in this way the original producers, namely, the commoners who attend the feast.[68]

In another example, it is traditional in the Trobriands for a man to send a harvest gift—*urigubu*—of yams to his sister's household. For the commoners, this amounts to a simple circulation of yams. But the chief is polygamous, and marries a woman from each subdistrict within his domain. Each of these subdistricts therefore sends *urigubu* to the chief, providing him with a bulging storehouse out of which he finances feasts, craft production, and *kula* expeditions. This "fund of power" underwrites the political system and forms the basis for chiefly power.[69]

In some systems, position in a political hierarchy and position in a marriage system are intimately linked. In traditional Tonga, women married up in rank. Thus, low-ranking lineages would send women to higher-ranking lineages. Women of the highest lineage were married into the "house of Fiji," a lineage defined as outside the political system. If the highest-ranking chief gave his sister to a lineage other than one which had no part in the ranking system, he would no longer be the highest-ranking chief. Rather, the lineage of his sister's son would outrank his own. In times of political rearrangement, the demotion of the previous high-ranking lineage was formalized when it gave a wife to a lineage which it had formerly outranked. In traditional Hawaii, the situation was the reverse. Women married down, and the dominant lineage gave wives to junior lines. A paramount would either marry a sister or obtain a wife from a distant land. When a junior lineage usurped rank, it formalized its position by giving a wife to its former senior line.

There is even some tantalizing data suggesting that marriage systems may be implicated in the evolution of social strata and perhaps in the development of early states. The first round of the political consolidation which resulted in the formation of a state in Madagascar occurred when one chief obtained title to several autonomous districts through the vagaries of marriage and inheritance.[70] In Samoa, legends place the origin of the paramount title—the *Tafa'ifa*—as a result of intermarriage between ranking members of four major lineages. My thoughts are too speculative, my data too sketchy, to say much on this subject. But a search ought to be undertaken for data which might demonstrate how marriage systems intersect with large-scale political processes like state-making. Marriage systems might be implicated in a number of ways: in the accumulation of wealth and the maintenance of differential access to political and economic resources; in the building of alliances; in the consolidation of high-ranking persons into a single closed stratum of endogamous kin.

These examples—like the Kachin and Trobriand ones—indicate that sexual systems cannot, in the final analysis, be understood in isolation. A full-bodied analysis of women in a single society, or throughout history, must take *everything* into account: the evolution of commodity forms in women, systems of land tenure, political arrangements, subsistence technology, and so on. Equally important, economic and political analyses are incomplete if they do not consider women, marriage, and sexuality. The traditional concerns of anthropology and social science—such as the evolution of social stratification and the origin of the state—must be reworked to include the implications of matrilateral cross-cousin marriage, surplus extracted in the form of daughters, the conversion of female labor into male wealth, the conversion of female lives into marriage alliances, the contribution of marriage to political power, and the transformations that all of these varied aspects of society have undergone in the course of time.

This sort of endeavor is, in the final analysis, exactly what Engels tried to do in his effort to make coherent so many of the diverse aspects of social life. He tried to relate men and women, town and country, kinship and state, forms of property, systems of land tenure, convertibility of wealth, forms of exchange, the technology of food production, and forms of trade—to name a few—into a systematic historical account. Eventually, someone will have to write a new version of *The Origin of the Family, Private Property, and the State*, recognizing the mutual interdependence of sexuality, economics, and politics without underestimating the full significance of each in human society.

The Trouble with Trafficking

Afterthoughts on "The Traffic in Women"

2

When I was preparing the essay that became "The Traffic in Women" for publication, I needed a title. And I found one in Emma Goldman's essay "The Traffic in Women" (1910).[1] Her title was a great and catchy phrase that seemed to convey the sense of my argument. Our topics were distinct, but her sensibilities were similar to my own. However, I did not realize at the time that the phrase smuggled in a whole collection of associations of which I was blissfully unaware. Nor could I have known that a revived movement against "trafficking" in the closing decades of the twentieth century would resuscitate many of the very problems which Goldman addressed.

When my essay "The Traffic in Women" was published in France, in 1998, the translators contacted me about changing the title. They did not want to use the phrase "traffic in women" because it was too readily associated with a discourse on trafficking that is assumed to be and often is a call for the suppression of prostitution. So the title to the French translation became "Transactions sur les Femmes."[2] Periodically a student will ask me about some article they think I have written about "sex trafficking." However, I had not written about sex trafficking, and certainly not in the sense in which that term is now often used. Specifically, I do not embrace the pervasive contemporary confusions between trafficking and prostitution, and in fact oppose them.

As Carole Vance notes, trafficking as currently defined in international law is not elided with prostitution. "In both the new international law . . . and U.S. law . . . trafficking no longer focuses exclusively on prostitution, but instead on all extreme forms of labor exploitation."[3] Article 3, Section A of the UN Protocol defines trafficking as follows:

"Trafficking in persons" shall mean the recruitment, transportation, transfer, harbouring or receipt of persons, by means of the threat or use of force or other forms of coercion, of abduction, of fraud, of deception, of the abuse of power or of a position of vulnerability or of the giving or receiving of payments or benefits to achieve the consent of a person having control over another person, for the purpose of exploitation. Exploitation shall include, at a minimum, the exploitation of the prostitution of others or other forms of sexual exploitation, forced labour or services, slavery or practices similar to slavery, servitude or the removal of organs.[4]

Moreover, in popular rhetoric and media coverage, trafficking is often treated as indistinguishable from prostitution. "Trafficking" often slides imperceptibly into "trafficked into sex slavery," which in turn is equated with all commercial sex. Antiprostitution activists tend to cultivate these elisions and treat trafficking as simply an alternative language for commercial sex. Such rhetoric is an effective way to target prostitution by mobilizing anger about exploitation, coercion, and abuse. As Vance notes, "the trafficked person" is assumed to be "a woman or a female minor; the danger and injury are sexual; and the nature of the crime is an offense against society and morality (for evangelical activists) or against women's equality (for antiprostitution feminists)."[5]

The constant conflation of trafficking and prostitution is neither accidental nor new. In fact, these contemporary confusions derive from the discourse about trafficking that emerged in the late-nineteenth and early-twentieth centuries, about which Goldman was speaking and whose assumptions she largely rejected. The contemporary deployments of the term *trafficking*, and especially the notion of "trafficking in women" are deeply inflected by the meanings these terms gathered at the turn of the last century. The trafficking rhetoric emerged in battles over prostitution that generated voluminous public attention and extensive social activism in the United States, Great Britain, and Europe. More than a distant relative of contemporary campaigns and concerns, these earlier mobilizations shaped law, policy, and interventionist paradigms that remain potent today.

Current debates about what trafficking is, the nature of the problem to which it refers, and what solutions should be adopted to address it, are rooted in the social movements that made these terms significant a century ago. Hence, it is worthwhile to revisit the origins of the political language of trafficking in women. That language continually tugs at "trafficking," pulling the term into the semantic orbit of prostitution, "sex trafficking," or "sex slavery." The ghosts of trafficking past haunt the politics of trafficking present, and in all likelihood will hound the policies of trafficking in the future.

The Construction of the Problem

Around 1900, "trafficking" was used more or less interchangeably with the terms *white slavery*, *white slave trade*, or *white slave traffic*. These terms were, along with *the social evil* and *immoral purposes*, codes for prostitution as well as rhetorical vehicles for denouncing prostitution. The language of the white slave traffic first emerged in the context of British activism around prostitution in the late nineteenth century. Edward Bristow writes,

> In the environment of regulated and migratory prostitution, the issue of "white slavery" swept the West like wildfire late in the nineteenth century. Just what was white slavery all about? Outside the Orient, were women really abducted into prostitution on a regular basis? As for the phrase itself, white slavery was first used in the context of prostitution in the 1930s by Dr. Michael Ryan, a London reformer. Referring to the local campaign against vice, Ryan noted that: "it has been proved in several cases that have come before our public magistrates, especially at the eastern end of town, that the infernal traffic in question is still carried on to a great extent, principally by Jews. These white-slave dealers trepan young girls into the dens of iniquity, sell them to vile debaucheries."[6]

"White slavery" had become broadly associated with prostitution by the 1870s, with or without allegations of entrapment. By the end of the decade, "the term changed connotation. . . . In [activist] rhetoric and in public opinion white slavery decisively took on the suggestion of recruitment to prostitution by force or fraud."[7] It was also broadly assumed, however, that prostitution invariably involved force or fraud. Bristow notes that the campaigns around white slavery were shaped by the "prevalent Victorian assumptions of the day, that prostitution could never be a rational vocational choice" and that it was "inherently cruel." Reformers also seized upon "migratory prostitution" as what they considered "the worst form of an inherently exploitative business."[8] Bristow and others have noted how effective this language was in propelling antiprostitution agitation and legal regulation. It culminated in the sensational journalism of W. T. Stead's series "The Maiden Tribute of Modern Babylon" and the subsequent passage of the Criminal Law Amendment Act of 1885.[9]

The issue first gained popular traction when reports surfaced of British girls allegedly being held captive in brothels in Brussels.[10] The language of the white slave traffic thus fused several elements: opposition to prostitution, the assumption that prostitution invariably involved coercion, and some kind of movement across a national border or internal boundary. Quite apart from the elements of "whiteness" or "slavery," the term *traffic* itself connoted commercial activity and geographical mobility. Racism and anti-Semitism were also frequently part of the brew.[11]

Despite the efficacy of the rhetoric about the white slave trade in changing law and policy, the claims made about the trade's size, characteristics, and prevalence have been challenged by many historians who suggest that the scale of the traffic was grossly exaggerated. In her study of prostitution reform in England from 1890 to 1914, Paula Bartley states that while the London police supported antiprostitution groups in their crusades against white slavery, they were privately skeptical about the existence of the trade.

> In a confidential memorandum, the Criminal Investigation Department (CID) reported that the White Slave Traffic Branch, which had been in existence for a year, had found little evidence of actual trafficking. It complained that Britain had "been aroused by a number of alarming statements made by religious, social and other workers, who spread the belief that there was a highly organized gang of 'White Slave Traffickers' with agents in every part of the civilized world, kidnapping and otherwise carrying off women and girls from their homes to lead them to their ruin in foreign lands."[12]

According to Bartley, "The White Slave Branch believed that there was an utter absence of evidence to justify the alarming statements put forward by social purists since every case it investigated proved to be false. As far as they were concerned, white slavery was of such a small proportion and so sporadic that it did not justify police attention."[13]

Judith Walkowitz made a similar point in her magisterial study of Victorian prostitution: "The evidence for widespread involuntary prostitution of British girls at home or abroad is slim. During the 1870s and 1880s officials and reformers were able to uncover a small traffic in women between Britain and the Continent, although the women enticed into licensed brothels in Antwerp and Brussels were by no means the young innocents depicted in the sensational stories."[14] And Bristow reports that by 1901, "Scotland Yard reported that it was five years since they had received a complaint 'as to any English girl having been procured for immoral purposes on the Continent.'"[15] Nonetheless, beliefs about a vast network of shady men snatching huge numbers of innocent girls and condemning them to lives of sexual horror were widely accepted. Furthermore, they propelled changes in British law as well as the adoption of the International Agreement for the Suppression of the "White Slave Traffic" (1904) and the International Convention for the Suppression of the White Slave Traffic (1910).[16]

The wildfire of concern over white slavery in the United States in the early twentieth century was also part of a multifaceted movement against prostitution. As David Langum has observed, during the first two decades of the twentieth century, "America worried about prostitution with an intensity never before or after equaled. During those years, the 'social evil,' as it was often called, became the focus of at least six feature motion pictures, about the same number of plays and novels, and at least twelve 'white slavery narratives,' a special genre hovering uncomfortably between fact and fiction. Over thirty-five local, state, and national commissions probed the causes, practice, and possible escalation of prostitution."[17]

In his book on these mobilizations against prostitution in the early twentieth century, Mark Thomas Connelly noted that "antiprostitution in the progressive era was exceedingly protean."[18] Antiprostitution agitation took many forms, but among the most popular and prominent was the crusade against "white slavery." As in England, the "white slave traffic" in America was a composite category in which prostitution, coercion, and movement across borders were melded together and treated as intrinsically related phenomena. The language of white slavery involved an easy slippage among the terms *slavery*, *trade*, and *traffic*, and the category incorporated the prevailing assumptions that force and violence were inherent qualities of prostitution. As in England, the white slave discourse in the United States tended to assume that prostitution was distinctively exploitative, uniformly coercive, and almost invariably fatal.

According to Langum, the white slave hysteria erupted in the United States after a muckraking journalist and a crusading prosecutor began to publicize claims that young women were being held as slaves in the brothels of Chicago.

> It began with an article published in *McClure's Magazine* by the muckraker George Kibbe Turner. . . . In it he charged that a "loosely organized association . . . largely composed of Russian Jews" was furnishing most of the women for the Chicago brothels, with the connivance of city officials. Then Clifford G. Roe, a crusading Chicago prosecutor, claimed to have recovered a note thrown from a brothel in which a young prostitute claimed she was held as a "white slave." Roe began a sensational series of prosecutions, charging that brothels were holding young girls in actual confinement. Soon there were allegations of sales and auctions of women held as slaves.

On October 17, 1909, the *Chicago Tribune* published a vivid cartoon depicting a young seminaked girl, sobbing into her handkerchief with shame, while buyers bid for her auction as a new acquisition for their brothels.[19]

Roe claimed that: "Chicago has at last waked up to a realization of the fact that actual slavery that deals in human flesh and blood as a marketable commodity exists in terrible magnitude in the city today. It is slavery, real slavery, that we are fighting. . . . The white slave of Chicago is a slave as much as the negro [*sic*] was before the civil war [*sic*] . . . that is the condition of hundreds, yes thousands of girls in Chicago at present."[20] As Langum details, "Panic quickly spread to the rest of the nation. Soon a substantial segment of the population believed that young girls in America's cities were being lured to brothels by false pretenses, or pierced by poisoned darts or hypodermic needles and then dragged off to dens of iniquity. They were held there as slaves, bought and sold as chattels."[21]

Such beliefs were articulated and disseminated by what Connelly calls "an exotic literary genre" that "flourished in the United States during the early decades of the twentieth century."[22] In *The Response to Prostitution in the Progressive Era*, Connelly notes that numerous

> books and pamphlets appeared announcing a startling claim: a pervasive and depraved conspiracy was at large in the land, brutally trapping and seducing American girls into lives of enforced prostitution, or "white slavery." These white slave narratives, or white slave tracts, began to circulate around 1909. . . . The plot lines were strikingly uniform. Typically, a chaste and comely native American country girl would forsake her idyllic country home and family for the promise of the city. On the way, or shortly after arrival, she would fall victim to one of the swarm of panders lying in wait for just such an innocent and unprotected sojourner. Using one of his vast variety of tricks—a promise of marriage, an offer to assist in securing lodging, or if these were to no avail, the chloroformed cloth, the hypodermic needle, or the drugged drink—the insidious white slaver would brutally seduce the girl and install her in a brothel, where she became an enslaved prostitute. Within five years she would end up in the potters field, unless she had the good fortune to be rescued by a member of one of the dedicated groups fighting white slavery.[23]

"White slavery" thus became a vehicle for the more general set of sentiments about prostitution, albeit one drenched in considerable narrative hyperbole.

"White slavery" fused prostitution with several other social concerns, many of them involving people in motion. The language and legal apparatus of anti-trafficking have always involved issues of migration and movement. One facet of such anxieties in early-twentieth-century America addressed internal flows of people, especially the large numbers of young women who were leaving the farms and small towns of rural America for the cities, where they found jobs as factory laborers, retail clerks, and secretaries. Connelly observes that the anxiety over white slavery was concerned "in the broadest sense, with two obvious facts of early-twentieth-century American life: the migration of rural and small town young women to the cities in search of jobs and social opportunities, and the existence of open and teeming red-light districts in these same cities. The cutting edge of the white slave tracts was a question concerning the relationship between these two circumstances: What was happening to the American girl who struck out for the city?"[24]

Concern about migration across national borders and into the United States also became entangled in the narrative of white slavery. The increased immigration from southern and eastern Europe, especially Jews and Catholics, was met with a nativistic defense of northern European (generally thought of as "Anglo-Saxon" or "Nordic") Protestant supremacy against groups seen as socially and "racially" inferior. Books such as Madison Grant's *The Passing of the Great Race* and Lothrop Stoddard's *The Rising Tide of Color* articulated the beliefs that animated a determined movement to restrict immigration from countries other than northern and western Europe.[25]

At the federal level, anti-immigration agitation resulted in the establishment of a commission to study the "problem." The United States Immigration Commission—popularly known as the Dillingham Commission, after the senator who was its chair—produced a forty-one volume report in 1911. The anti-immigration movement resulted in a series of legislative reforms, culminating in the 1924 Johnson-Reed Act, which virtually stopped the flow of immigrants from southern and eastern Europe by establishing quotas based on national origin.[26] These restrictions based on national origin were only relaxed in 1965.

Volume 37 of the Dillingham Report includes a section on "Importing and Harboring of Women for Immoral Purposes," tucked in between sections on steerage conditions, immigrant homes and aid societies, and immigrant banks. The mobilizations against prostitution and white slavery were thoroughly enmeshed with the debates about race and immigration. While the Dillingham Report focused on prostitution among immigrant women, much of the white-slave literature warned of the ostensible dangers of immigrant men. The alleged procurers were assumed to be disproportionately drawn from the racially suspect populations whose immigration threatened to undermine the ostensibly virtuous native-born population.

In the typical melodramatic formula, the enslaved girls were generally depicted as white and native born, while the slavers tended to be, by contrast, alien, dark, and swarthy men.[27]

> The innocent country girls were debauched into the captivity of prostitution by urban denizens invariably identified as Jewish, Italian, or Eastern European. The white-slave traffic, warned the author of *America's Black Traffic in White Girls*, is "carried on and exploited by a foaming pack of foreign hellhounds, . . . the moral and civic degenerates of the French, Italian, Syrian, Russian, Jewish or Chinese races. . . . an American or Englishman conducting such a business is almost entirely unknown."[28]

The association of prostitution and pimping with all things foreign was not the only reason that movement across territorial boundaries became so embedded in the definitions of trafficking. State and national boundaries were also a source of regulatory and legal jurisdiction. The "white slave" panic had many consequences in law and policy, both domestically and internationally. In the United States, the most critical legal consequence was the passage, in 1910, of the White Slave Traffic Act, popularly known as the Mann Act.[29]

The Mann Act made it a federal crime "to transport or cause to be transported or aid or assist in obtaining transportation for, or in transporting, in interstate or foreign commerce, or in any Territory or in the District of Columbia, any woman or girl for the purpose of prostitution or debauchery, or for any other immoral purpose, or with the intent and purpose to induce, entice, or compel such woman or girl to become a prostitute or to give herself up to debauchery, or engage in any other immoral practice."[30] The Act specified a number of prohibited activities, including helping a woman or girl obtain a ticket for any such travel. It instituted new immigration regulations to prevent the entry into the United States of alien women or girls who might be inclined toward prostitution or debauchery or any immoral purpose, and to make it easier to deport them (or their equally alien pimps) if they were later discovered. Anyone who harbored or sheltered such a woman or girl was also guilty of a felony. Provisions of the law applied to movement within the Territories or the District of Columbia, as these were also under federal jurisdiction. While the Mann Act was explicitly aimed at prostitution, the residual classification of "immoral purposes" was extremely broad and vague. It would later allow expansive interpretations of the Act to permit federal prosecution of almost any nonmarital sexuality that involved interstate travel, immigration, or even mobility within the federally administered Territories and the District of Columbia.

The consequences of the Mann Act were numerous. For example, it was through the enforcement of the Mann Act that the FBI was transformed from "a modest agency concerned with odds and ends of Federal law enforcement to a nationally recognized institution." According to Langum, before 1908, federal investigations were handled by "a makeshift system of borrowing detectives from other agencies or hiring private detectives." In 1908 a small subagency was created within the Department of Justice. Initially, "it had only a director and twenty-three agents, and because there was substantial fear of a national police force it was given only a limited jurisdiction. . . . This changed with the acquisition of Mann Act jurisdiction. The Mann Act resulted in the Bureau's first major field office, in Baltimore, and a dramatic increase in manpower . . . The Mann Act provided the real takeoff for the FBI." Langum observes that by 1912 "the white slave investigations overshadowed the entire balance of the Bureau's work."[31] To enforce the Act, the FBI used its own expanding force of agents, and also began to recruit others, such as railroad agents and postal workers, as spies. Train companies advised their agents not to deliver prepaid tickets to women or girls thought to reside in brothel districts. The postal service, also a federal agency, was recruited to help compile information about prostitutes.[32]

Federal agents had no authority over prostitution within local jurisdictions, in many of which prostitution was legal or tolerated. Since the Mann Act applied to transportation, primarily across state lines, the Bureau needed to monitor the movement of prostitutes. Information on where they lived and worked was needed in order to detect, and prosecute, movement that triggered federal jurisdiction. So the emergent FBI began to compile a census of prostitutes. "Forms were filled out at the brothel by the regular Bureau agent with information on each prostitute, including the names by which she had been known, age, identifying statistics, country where her parents were born, and detailed information on addresses and owners of all houses in which she had practiced prostitution. For each new prostitute who arrived at the brothel the madam was asked to fill out such a form and send it to the local white slave agent."[33] This was sexual surveillance of women on a grand scale and must have involved a considerable infrastructure of personnel and information storage. It may have been an early template for the elaborate systems used in later decades by the FBI to spy on politicians and homosexuals.

After the elimination of most of America's old red-light districts during the

First World War, Mann Act prosecutions shifted toward nonmarital sex. The language of "immoral purposes" was successfully construed more broadly to mean noncommercial sexual activity outside of marriage. From approximately 1917 through the 1920s, both the Department of Justice and local police collected thousands of reports on "sexual irregularities" from gossips, neighbors, and busybodies. Hundreds of individuals were prosecuted under the Mann Act, mostly for consensual adultery, even when such acts were unconsummated.

> Once the Mann Act was extended to noncommercial, boyfriend–girlfriend travel . . . it meant that any man who has taken his girlfriend from New York City to New Jersey on a date, hoping for sexual romance that evening, has violated the Mann Act. . . . Likewise, the man who invites his girlfriend to fly by herself from Detroit to Birmingham for a visit, with the same hope, has committed a federal felony if he held that hope while she crossed the state line, notwithstanding that he is subsequently disappointed and no sexual conduct occurs. This Orwellian "badthought," plus transportation, defined the essence of the crime.[34]

Women as well as men were liable under the Act for transporting other women; they also could be, and often were, prosecuted for conspiracy to aid males (such as their boyfriends and lovers) with *their own transportation*. David Langum provides many examples of women who were subjected to federal charges for traveling voluntarily with men to whom they were not married. Between 1927 and 1937, some 23 percent of the female prisoners in the federal prison in Alderson, West Virginia, were incarcerated for violations of the Mann Act, almost none of them prostitutes.[35] Presumably, they had violated the provision prohibiting travel for other "immoral purposes."

The Mann Act proved useful in racially and politically motivated prosecutions, such as those of the black heavyweight-champion boxer Jack Johnson, rock-and-roll's Chuck Berry, and Charlie Chaplin. The pioneering sociologist W. I. Thomas lost his job at the University of Chicago in 1918 after being charged for a Mann Act violation when he was found in a Chicago hotel with a woman to whom he was not married.[36] The provisions of the Mann Act are still in force, though now made "gender-neutral." The threat of a Mann Act prosecution for transporting a woman across state lines for purposes of prostitution is likely what forced Eliot Spitzer to resign the governorship of New York in 2008.

Prior to the passage of the Mann Act, laws regulating prostitution had been matters of state or local governments. The Mann Act federalized the crime. It did so by invoking the commerce clause of the Constitution. Article 1, section 8 gives Congress the authority "to regulate Commerce with foreign Nations, and among the several States, and with the Indian Tribes." Similarly, as international treaties addressed the issue of "trafficking," they too, were grounded in the jurisdictions of nation-states over movement across their borders. Thus, for a variety of ideological, practical, and jurisdictional parameters, movement and transportation have been incorporated into the taxonomies and crimes of "trafficking."

The Mann Act's official title—the White Slave Traffic Act—embodies an enduring legacy of these early crusades, a rhetoric in which distinctions between the issues of coercion, immorality, prostitution, and mobility across borders are blurred. The same elision often resurfaces in the current international movement against "trafficking," although the language has been purged of the term *white*.[37]

The Mann Act and other legal codes and conventions dating from the crusades against the white slave traffic singled out prostitution and other forms of "immorality." They were not applicable to abuses that were nonsexual, and incorporated a great deal of sex that was not abusive. By contrast, the current UN Protocol has detached trafficking from an exclusive focus on all forms of prostitution. There is a residual rhetorical and institutional undertow, however, that tends to reforge the link to prostitution and other forms of sexual commerce, and to divert attention from abuses in domestic labor, factory work, marriage, or other ostensibly "non-immoral" purposes.

David Feingold observes that "it has been both politically more expedient and emotionally more rewarding to focus on trafficking for sexual exploitation, rather than for labor exploitation. Under the influence of a politically well connected 'abolitionist' lobby, *prostitution* has been conflated with *trafficking*; a crusade against the former is seen as synonymous with a victory against the latter."[38] To the general public, "trafficking" probably evokes far more images of brothels than of factories, farms, or private homes. Crusading journalists and documentary filmmakers reinforce these associations. Some politically mobilized antiprostitution constituencies, both feminist and conservative, still find trafficking to be an effective rhetorical and institutional vehicle for their agendas and still treat trafficking and prostitution as largely interchangeable.

Contemporary antitrafficking organizations differ in how they define their concerns and targets. Some address abuse and coercion in all types of work; others aim to abolish prostitution or further criminalized it. For example, the Global Alliance Against Trafficking in Women (GAATW) defines trafficking as "all acts involved in the recruitment and/or transportation of women within and across national borders for work or services by means of violence or threat of violence, abuse of authority or dominant position, debt bondage, deception or other forms of coercion."[39] For GAATW, the focus is on the social relations of exploitation and abuse, rather than on any particular kind of labor or activity, and the problem of trafficking is not framed in terms privileging prostitution and commercial sex. By contrast, prostitution is the primary focus of many other organizations. In this context, "trafficking" is largely reduced to commercial sex, whether forced or not. One such organization is the Coalition Against Trafficking in Women (CATW), which describes itself as an NGO that promotes women's human rights, and states that its purpose is to

> work internationally to combat sexual exploitation in all its forms, especially prostitution and trafficking in women and children, in particular girls. . . . CATW brings international attention to all forms of sexual exploitation, including prostitution, pornography, sex tourism, and mail order bride selling. . . . CATW researches and documents the situation of women who have been trafficked and are in prostitution; educates the public about the extent of harm sustained by women and girls in prostitution. . . . All prostitution harms women, regardless of women's consent. Prostitution includes casual, brothel, escort agency or military prostitution, sex tourism, mail order bride selling and trafficking in women.[40]

Despite some modernization in rhetoric, the CATW platform reproduces many of the presumptions about prostitution and coercion that characterized the old white-slavery crusades. The cumulative burden of that rhetorical baggage is difficult to escape, despite the fact that the new international protocol on trafficking adopted an inclusive definition, and does not equate all prostitution with trafficking.[41]

The Scope of the Problem

> Old numbers—like old habits—die hard.
> —**David Feingold,** "Trafficking in Numbers"

The trafficking panic of the early twentieth century also provides a cautionary lesson about numbers, size, significance, and definition. For any social problem, the definitions should be carefully formulated and explicitly stated, and the sources of numerical estimates should be made extremely clear. Unfortunately, when individuals, constituencies, and assorted claims makers are trying to establish a social problem or mobilize action to address it, definitions tend to be slippery and numbers are presented with little or no provenance.

The sociologist Joel Best comments that it is often "the combination of big numbers, broad definitions, and horrible examples make . . . claims compelling."[42] Large numbers make a social problem seem important, and dangerous to ignore. As Best puts it, "Big numbers are better than little numbers," "official numbers are better than unofficial numbers," and "big official numbers are best of all."[43] The putative size of a particular problem or phenomenon is frequently deployed as an argument to buttress claims of its malevolent status. When sexual stigma is mixed with large numerical estimates, the resulting cocktail can be particularly heady.

Best also notes that "claims makers' figures often cannot bear close inspection. Some estimates are little more than guesses plucked from thin air, others are extrapolations from minimal data."[44] There are many examples—such as pornography, homosexuals, missing children, and trafficking—in which estimates of vast size and scope have dubious sources. Once introduced, however, such figures can endlessly circulate, gaining credibility through repetition. Their frequent reiteration is taken as some kind of factual assessment of the dimensions of a problem, which under more careful scrutiny may turn out to be difficult to substantiate, conceptually flawed, of uncertain origin, or completely preposterous.[45]

In the early-twentieth-century United States, "white slavery" was constructed as a social problem with the aid of narratives depicting a huge problem involving vast numbers of prostitutes. It is interesting to look back at some of the contemporary attempts to quantify prostitution. Exactly how many prostitutes, or "white slaves," were there in the United States during this period? What was the scale of the trade? And why were the figures so unreliable?

One problem with counting prostitutes was figuring out what and whom to count. Best warns that broad definitions produce large numbers. In the early twentieth century, the definitions of prostitution were often exceptionally broad, resulting in inflated statistics of the scope of the ostensible problem. This was a problem not only in white slave fiction, which tended toward hyperbole as a matter of course, but even in the more sober antiprostitution documents, such as the report of the Chicago Vice Commission, published in 1911, as *The Social Evil in Chicago*. The Chicago Commission attempted to produce a rigorous study of prostitution. Prostitution, however, could mean almost any nonmarital sex, or even conjugal relations that were unduly enthusiastic (at least for women). Connelly notes, in *The Response to Prostitution in the Progressive Era*, that the commission

> regularly turned its attention to aspects of urban social life that only the most ecumenical definition of prostitution would include, such as dance halls where young working women met men, assignation houses where married individuals conducted extramarital affairs, lake boats where adolescents congregated, unsupervised picnics, summer amusement resorts, saloons, and vaudeville halls. In the Chicago report and elsewhere, the sexual activity that purportedly occurred in these situations often was categorized as "clandestine" prostitution.... Clandestine prostitution was taken to include almost any premarital or nonmonogamous female sexual activity, whether or not financial exchange was involved. Thus, in the moral world of *The Social Evil in Chicago*, potentially all sexual activity unsanctioned by marriage could be characterized as prostitution.[46]

Connelly notes that many other definitions of prostitution were "equally imprecise and similarly all-inclusive. For instance, in 1912 the *Outlook* defined prostitution as 'the attempt to isolate the sensuous element in love from the social affectations and family responsibilities it was meant to support.'"[47] The president of the New York Medico-Legal Society described prostitution as "an insane impulse for the unrestrained gratification of the sexual functions of the body" and "an obsession that dominates every consideration of duty and obligation and purpose in life, in which procreation is not considered." Another physician defined a prostitute as "a woman who satisfies the physical side of the sexual desire of man without regard as to whether the passion is associated with admiration and respect . . . or any woman who will cohabit with any man for the pleasure that it gives her."[48] Such definitional flexibility was one of the ways in which the estimates of the population of prostitutes were grossly inflated, since much of the female population could be included.

Another factor in the inflated statistics was what Connelly calls "the five year theory." One pervasive assumption in the early-twentieth-century literature on prostitution was that the life of a prostitute was not only nasty and brutish, but exceedingly short, with the ostensibly high rate of mortality requiring thousands of new replacements every year.

> It was a dominant belief that a prostitute's fate was a slow physical and mental degeneration to death within five years of beginning "the life." . . . The "five year" theory was never proven, but its general acceptance made it necessary to assume that large numbers of women were needed each year to

fill the death ravaged ranks.... [T]he vision of tens of thousands of women debauched into immorality each year fanned the fires of the more extreme reactions to prostitution, particularly the white slave panic.[49]

Indeed, in 1912, the American Federation for Sex Hygiene estimated that 50,000 prostitutes died each year. John S. Fulton, a contemporary critic cited by Connelly, noted that if this estimate were accurate "there would be 20,000 more prostitutes than 'decent' women in the death roll for those between the ages of fifteen and thirty-five, the years in which prostitutes allegedly expired."[50]

Connelly describes an acerbic controversy over the claimed numbers of prostitutes in an exhibit by the American Federation of Sex Hygiene at the Fifteenth International Congress on Hygiene and Demography, held in Washington, D.C. in 1912.

> The newly formed American Federation for Sex Hygiene sponsored an exhibit stressing the need for sex hygiene education, complete with charts and photographs illustrating the tragedy and horror of venereal disease. The exhibit, prepared by Robert N. Wilson, a Philadelphia physician who was secretary of the federation, also presented figures on the extent of prostitution in the United States. Wilson's "ultraconservative estimate of the number of public female prostitutes and earnings" was 544,350 prostitutes at a yearly cost to the public of over $272 million. Wilson also estimated there to be three "clandestine" prostitutes for each public prostitute, which brought the total to 1,633,050 at a cost of $408,262,500. "There is every reason to believe," he concluded, that, conservative estimates aside, "we are spending on immorality and the social diseases ... not less than $3,000,000,000."[51]

John S. Fulton savaged these numbers in the *American Journal of Public Health*.

> Fulton flatly stated that the federation's "statistical misadventures," "numerical confections," and "guesstimates" could not be substantiated; and although he did not himself offer ironclad figures to contradict those of the federation, he did point out some interesting contradictions. "In the light of a few concrete facts," he observed, with reference to the claim that prostitution was a $3 billion a year business, "the Federation might have delayed for a few years at least the announcement that the molly-coddled males in this country can deliver into the hands of the mollies every year, one-fourth of all the money in the world, all the money there is in the United States, enough to pay a fourth of the world's total debt, a billion dollars more than enough to discharge the public debt of the United States."[52]

According to Connelly, "Wilson countered Fulton's accusations with an equally polemical repartee, asserted the validity of the federation's estimates, and then launched an ad hominem attack on Fulton's character and motives."[53]

Similarly, when trafficking is in the headlines now, vast numbers of trafficked individuals are frequently alleged, but the sources of such estimates of size and scope are often both unquestioned and unclear. David Feingold writes, "It is crystal clear . . . that in the case of human trafficking, no one knows the true value of the trade. The trafficking field is best characterized as one of numerical certainty and statistical doubt. . . . When it comes to statistics, trafficking of girls and women is one of several highly emotive issues which seem to overwhelm critical faculties. Numbers take on a life of their own, gaining acceptance through repetition, often with little inquiry into their derivations."[54]

When trafficking is conflated with prostitution, the numbers are especially unreliable. The means for obtaining estimates of sexual commerce are often particularly speculative and seldom checked for credibility, source, or definitional consistency. Expressing concerns similar to those of John S. Fulton a century ago, Feingold notes

> In 1997, the organization to End Child Prostitution, Child Pornography, and Trafficking of Children for Sexual Purposes (ECPAT) claimed that there were 800,000 child prostitutes in Thailand (a figure that, to their credit, they now disown). Other NGOs and journalists were claiming that there were 4 million sex workers in Thailand. However, had this number been correct, it would have meant that 24 percent of the female population of Thailand between the ages of ten and thirty-nine was engaged in commercial sex work—an unlikely proposition at best.[55]

Feingold also analyzes statistics presented by what he calls "an otherwise reliable NGO" that claimed that approximately one million girls are forced into commercial sex each year, and that the "sex trafficking industry exploits children to the tune of $10 billion a year." Feingold asks: "Where did these figures come from? How were they derived? If 1 million girls are forced into the sex industry each year, how many leave? For how long have 1 million girls each year been forced into the sex industry?"[56] These claims are reminiscent of the 50,000 white slaves who were supposed to have died each year in the brothels of the early twentieth century, and the legions of young women supposedly abducted to replace them.

Of course, sex sells social problems as efficiently as it sells cars, beer, and televisions. "Sex slaves" sell far more newspapers than do workers coerced into making athletic shoes or cleaning toilets. Feingold comments wryly:

> Rarely is there as much excitement about exploited migrant farm workers. The *frisson* of sex slaves down the street in suburbia is too good to pass up. . . . The mere mention of "trafficking" and "sex slavery" seems to dull critical sensibility—even for the fact-checked *New York Times*. As with other moral panics, people are so appalled by the enormity of the crime that they do not question whether it is occurring—and if so, whether it is occurring on the scale that is alleged.[57]

Joel Best notes a frequent discrepancy between the large numbers alleged for a social problem, and the atypical stories that are used to characterize it. "Opening with an emotionally riveting 'grabber' is a standard journalistic technique. . . . Horrific examples give a sense of the problem's frightening, harmful dimensions. . . . Atrocity tales perform another, less visible function. The atrocity—usually selected for its extreme nature—typifies the issue; it becomes the referent for discussions of the problem in general."[58] But such atrocities are rare. The big numbers refer to much more prevalent, but less dramatic, situations. The currently popular narratives of trafficking are classic examples of this genre. Broad and vague definitions generate spurious statistics. These are linked to examples of extreme, but infrequent abuse, and spiked with an infusion of sexual prurience. This makes for a persuasive package, but one that can obscure as much as it illuminates. Some oppression is dramatic, spectacular, and grotesque. Most exploitation and oppression, however, takes place in the realm of the everyday, the routine, and the quotidian.

Emma Goldman's "The Traffic in Women"

Emma Goldman's essay, "The Traffic in Women," was her own rather critical assessment of claims of the white-slave tracts then in such vogue.

> Our reformers have suddenly made a great discovery—the white slave traffic. The papers are full of these unheard of conditions, and lawmakers are already planning a new set of laws to check the horror. It is significant that whenever the public mind is to be diverted from a great social wrong, a crusade is inaugurated against indecency, gambling, saloons, etc. . . . The "righteous" cry against the white slave traffic is such a toy. It serves to amuse the people for a little while, and it will help to create a few more fat politi-

cal jobs—parasites who stalk about the world as inspectors, investigators, detectives, and so forth.[59]

Throughout her tract, Goldman sympathized with prostitutes and defended their dignity, called for gender equality in wages, demanded equal access for women to sex education and sexual freedom, explained prostitution as an economic decision, condemned sexual moralists, and treated all exchanges of sex for money as similar, whether or not sanctified by church or state.

She proposed a causal theory of prostitution that linked it to economic exploitation, gender inequality, the sexual double standard, and lack of sex education for women. She asked, "What is really the cause of the trade in women? Not merely white women, but yellow and black women as well. Exploitation of course; the merciless Moloch of capitalism that fattens on underpaid labor, thus driving thousands of women and girls into prostitution. . . . Naturally, our reformers say nothing about this cause." Goldman added that "Nowhere is woman treated according to the merit of her work, but rather as a sex. It is therefore almost inevitable that she should pay for her right to exist . . . with sex favors. Thus it is merely a question of degree whether she sells herself to one man, in or out of marriage, or to many men. Whether our reformers admit it or not, the economic and social inferiority of woman is responsible for prostitution . . . which is the direct result, in many cases, of insufficient compensation for honest labor."[60]

Goldman put prostitution on a continuum with marriage, rather than on a separate moral plane. "To the moralist," she states, "prostitution does not consist so much in the fact that the woman sells her body but rather that she sells it out of wedlock. That this is no mere statement is proved by the fact that marriage for monetary considerations is perfectly legitimate, sanctified by law and public opinion, while any other union is condemned and repudiated."[61] In her tract, Goldman also managed to vociferously condemn women's lack of access to sex information: "Woman is being reared as a sex commodity, and yet she is kept in absolute ignorance of the meaning and importance of sex. Everything dealing with that subject is suppressed, and persons who attempt to bring light into this terrible darkness are persecuted and thrown into prison." Goldman includes a fervent denunciation of the double standard: "It is due to this ignorance that the life and nature of the girl is thwarted and crippled. We have long ago taken it as self-evident that the boy may want to follow the call of the wild, that is to say, that the boy may, as his sex nature asserts itself, satisfy that nature; but our moralists are scandalized at the very thought that the nature of a girl should assert itself."[62]

When I wrote "The Traffic in Women," I agreed with Goldman's condemnation of the double standard, her call for more and better sex education, her denunciation of women's low wages and unequal economic resources, and her antagonism toward morality crusades. Most important, though, was her level comparison of marriage and prostitution as relationships that both involved women's exchange of sex for sustenance. Goldman did not accept that the blessings of the church or registration by the state were a valid justification for the distribution of honor or vilification, or that marriage should be spared critical scrutiny. The inequalities of gender and class structured respectable institutions such as marriage as much as they did disreputable occupations such as prostitution. Putting marriage on an even plane with prostitution highlighted how their shared elements, such as the exchange of sex, love, intimacy, or domestic service for room and board, revealed much about women's limited choices, poor pay, and marginal power.

Goldman's general refusal to grant marriage special status was compatible with a key element of my argument in "The Traffic in Women." Marriage and prostitution are, of course, both complicated institutions. While marriage and kinship (and prostitution) involve sentiment, intimacy, and many other emotions, feminist analysis called for an unsentimental approach in which affect could be disentangled from systemic effects: marriage could be at the same time an emotionally fulfilling relationship and a mechanism for the unequal distribution of power and resources. Such an approach to intimate relationships was, in fact, one of the key projects of second wave feminism, expressed in the slogan "the personal is political." Lévi-Strauss's analysis, which located the exchange of women at the heart of kinship and marriage, provided tools to think about marriage and kinship systems as a material apparatus of women's oppression. "The traffic in women" seemed an apt phrase to convey a feminist reading of Lévi-Strauss's analysis of the exchange of women in kinship and marriage.

When I wrote "The Traffic in Women," however, I was unfamiliar with the early-twentieth-century crusades against which Goldman was speaking. I was attracted by the progressive, egalitarian, and antimoralistic tenor of her remarks. Like her, I certainly did not intend (or make) a critique that singled out prostitution as a particularly insidious institution of gender inequality. Unfortunately, there is now a strain within feminism that does just that, following similar paths trod by many feminists a century ago.[63]

In the last two decades, a resurgent movement against prostitution, often using the language of antitrafficking, has resuscitated many of the problematic assumptions that circulated in the early 1900s. Now, as then, "trafficking" is too often equated with prostitution and other forms of commercial sex. Because of the stigma and marginal legality of prostitution, it is still far too easy to think that sex work is always coercive, or to believe that it is uniquely exploitative in a way that marriage, domestic labor, or factory work are not. Now, as then, the media circulate unverified and sometimes demonstrably false statistics that make the problem seem Gargantuan and hence exceptionally menacing. Now, as then, atrocity stories typify the issue. Now, as then, the common problems of poverty, migration, racism, and sexual moralism are often submerged behind melodramatic horror stories of abused and imperiled women and children.[64] Now, as then, there are feminists involved in antiprostitution activism, and now, as then, the major actors are social conservatives, Evangelicals, and other religious denominations whose agendas are by and large antagonistic to feminist ones.[65]

Such political dynamics are not entirely new. In her work on Victorian prostitution, Judith Walkowitz delineated how British feminist activists addressing prostitution and "white slavery" were ultimately bypassed by moral conservatives who were hostile to women's advancement: "It was these more repressive forces that eventually won the day."[66] In a prescient essay summarizing her work on Victorian prostitution and the social movements that addressed it, Walkowitz warned that "commercial sex as a locus of sexual violence against women is a hot and dangerous issue for feminists," largely because the issues were so readily coopted.[67] She commented that feminist mobilizations around these issues were

> easily subverted into repressive campaigns against male vice and sexual variation, controlled by men and conservative interests whose goals were antithetical to the values and ideals of feminism. . . . We have to be aware of the painful contradictions of our sexual strategy, not only for the sex workers who still regard commercial sex as the "best paid industry" available to them, but also for ourselves as feminists. We must take care not to play into the hands of the New Right or the Moral Majority, who are only too delighted to cast women as victims requiring male protection and control, and who desire to turn feminist protest into a politics of repression.[68]

Walkowitz's book was published in 1980, and her essay cautioning feminists to be wary of moral crusades in 1982.[69] The New Right to which she referred is no longer new. Over the intervening decades it has gained enormous traction over the institutions of local, state, and federal government. It has halted or rolled back many gains for which feminists have fought, and these struggles are ongoing. The Moral Majority is long gone, but its agendas live on and are arguably more influential now than they were in the heyday of the organization. Walkowitz's admonitions about the perils of the politics of commercial sex for feminists are as pertinent now as they were when she made them thirty years ago.

I could not have imagined in 1975 that the language of trafficking with its pernicious baggage would return with such a vengeance in the late twentieth century. Nor would I have imagined in my wildest nightmares that late-nineteenth-century rhetoric would be revived to mobilize another international crusade against prostitution. I would not have anticipated that a portion of the feminist movement would join with antifeminist social conservatives and Evangelicals under the banner of antitrafficking to further criminalize or abolish prostitution, rather than to address the conditions that constrain women's economic choices and social power. I could not have dreamed that anyone would think my title signaled an antiprostitution tract. If I had been aware of these possibilities, I would have searched very diligently for another title.

It is important to keep Goldman's warning in mind: when the public is to be diverted from great social wrongs, crusades are inaugurated against indecency and vice. I am sure she would advise us to resist the hypnotic pull of the endless media-fed sex scandals du jour, and to pay closer attention to whose pockets are being picked and what mechanisms are being employed to pick them.

3

History is lies agreed upon by the victors.

—**Anonymous**

The first novel, Adam's and Eve's, has been overprinted.

—**Natalie Barney,** *Pensées d'une Amazone*

I know that these are the women our fathers stole us from. Know thy women; know thyself.

—**Bertha Harris,** "The More Profound Nationality of Their Lesbianism"

I

It is notoriously difficult to maintain the memory of the past. But groups which are socially marginal are particularly relegated to the fringes of historical discussion. Lesbians, suffering from the dual disqualification of being gay and female, have been repeatedly dispossessed of their history. The generation of lesbians who emerged out of the women's movement in the late 1960s had to discover their immediate predecessors of the 1950s, who had already undertaken the task of retrieving earlier ancestors from scanty archives. The same

---

The "Introduction" in Chapter 3 was originally published in Renée Vivien, *A Woman Appeared to Me* (Weatherby Lake, Miss.: Naiad, 1976), iii–xxxi. The "Afterword" was originally published in the reprinted edition of *A Woman Appears to Me* (Weatherby Lake, Miss.: Naiad, 1979), xxi–xxii.

silence which makes the practice of lesbian history so arduous also obscures the work of those who have succeeded in illuminating a lesbian past.

Such considerations make the publication of this translation of *Une Femme m'apparut* an event to be relished. The translator is Jeannette Foster, whose *Sex Variant Women in Literature* (1956) is the principal reference book on lesbian history. It had been out of print for two decades, until this year, when a women's press rescued it from the underground. I doubt that Foster was very surprised by the general neglect of her work, which painstakingly documents the extent to which lesbian lives and literature are routinely forgotten. The author of *A Woman Appeared to Me* is Renée Vivien, whose own career is an object lesson in historical amnesia. Vivien's poetry was lavishly praised by critics in the early part of this century, but it has since been consigned to obscurity.[1]

Renée Vivien's twenty-odd volumes of poetry and prose comprise one of the most remarkable lesbian oeuvres extant. While her celebration of lesbian passion has contributed to her lack of literary recognition, it has conversely guaranteed her a modest cult reputation as a homosexual poet. Her collected poems were reprinted (in the original French) in the recent Arno Press collection on homosexuality and several poems were translated into English in *The Ladder*.[2] Vivien's prose poems, short stories, and her one novel (*A Woman Appeared to Me*), have remained even less known than her verse, and her prose work never reached second printings even in her lifetime when her poetry was widely read and something of a scandalous sensation. Much of her prose writing is both beautiful and fascinating; it should be more accessible. Hopefully, this translation of *A Woman Appeared to Me* will encourage a revival of interest in all of Renée Vivien's work.

If *A Woman Appeared to Me* were merely a lost work by an obscure lesbian writer, its publication would be welcome. But the novel is also a historical document, part of the archival remains of one of the most critical periods in lesbian history. *A Woman Appeared to Me* is Renée Vivien's feverish, dreamlike account of her tormented relationship with her muse and mistress, Natalie Clifford Barney. "Between Sappho and Gertrude Stein . . . these women represent practically the only available expressions of lesbian culture we have in the modern western world."[3] Since the novel evokes both the relationship and the milieu in which it took place, it can be better understood with some knowledge of both its historical and biographical contexts. I will first describe some aspects of the complex world in which the two main protagonists of the novel lived.

Part of the unwritten history of the nineteenth century is that of the profound historical changes in sexuality. The nineteenth century saw the culmination of trends which began as Europe changed into modern society.

The massive social transformations — such as industrialization, urbanization, etc. — have long engaged the historical imagination. Historians have recently become interested in the changes that took place in the family and in sexual life, but few have noticed that these changes included a revolution in homosexuality. It was in the nineteenth century that homosexuality assumed its modern form.

In the Middle Ages homosexuality was defined as a form of behavior, a sinful activity. The idea of a type of person who is homosexual is a product of the nineteenth century. It was the nineteenth century sexologists who recognized a category of homosexual individuals and who evolved a terminology to describe such persons. Writers of the period also record evidence of the urban subcultures which still characterize so much of homosexual experience.[4] The nineteenth-century cities contained specialized homosexual communities centered around bars, restaurants, informal networks, and semi-secret clubs.

Colette charmingly described the variety of lesbian society in Paris before 1910. Between 1906 and 1911, Colette left her first husband, made her living by performing in music halls, and had a woman lover — Missy, the Marquise de Belboeuf. Through the music halls, Colette was familiar with the popular homosexual culture. She frequented a lower-class bar called the Palmyre. The clientele was mostly poor, the food was cheap, and the proprietor a rough, maternal Amazon who fed the most indigent for nothing.

> I go to the bar kept by Sémiramis, appropriately named — Sémiramis, warrior queen, helmeted in bronze, armed with the meat cleaver, who speaks a colorful language to her crowd of long-haired young lads and short-haired young girls. . . .
>
> . . . [Y]ou find there a majority of young men who are not at all interested in women. At dinnertime there they are, comfortably at home, enjoying a rest. They are recovering their strength for suppertime. They have no need to waggle their hips or cry out shrilly or flutter a handkerchief soaked in ether, or dance together. . . . They are gentle, weary, with their painted eyelids heavy with sleep.
>
> . . . While dining at Sémiramis's bar I enjoy watching the girls dancing together, they waltz so well. They're not paid for this, but dance for pleasure between the cabbage soup and the beef stew. They are young models, scapegraces of the neighborhood, girls who take bit parts at the music hall but who are out of work. . . . I see only two graceful bodies united, sculptured beneath thin dresses by the wind of the waltz. . . . They waltz like habitués of cheap dance halls, lewdly, sensuously, with that delicious inclination of

a tall sail of a yacht. . . . I can't help it! I really find that prettier than any ballet.[5]

Through her lover Missy, Colette met the disgruntled aristocrats. Remembering them thirty years later, she wrote: "The adherents of this clique of women exacted secrecy for their parties, where they appeared dressed in long trousers and dinner jackets and behaved with unsurpassed propriety. . . . Where could I find, nowadays, messmates like those . . . Baronesses of the Empire, lady cousins of Czars, illegitimate daughters of grandukes, exquisites of the Parisian bourgeoisie, and also some aged horsewomen of the Austrian aristocracy, hand and eye of steel."[6]

It was to this Paris, vibrant capital of homosexual society, that Renée Vivien and Natalie Barney came shortly before 1900, when they were both in their early twenties. It was here that the two young women instigated a lesbian renaissance. They distinguished themselves from their contemporaries in Paris lesbian society by what we would now call their "gay consciousness." Beneath the florid, belle epoque, upper-class texture of their lives, one can discern two forerunners of the contemporary gay women's movement.

II

> . . . sick with anguish,
> Stood the crowned nine Muses
> about Apollo,
> Fear was upon them,
>
> While the tenth sang
> wonderful things they
> knew not,
> Ah, the tenth, the Lesbian!
> —**Swinburne,** "Sapphics"

> Is it sapphism which
> nourishes her intelligence,
> or is it intelligence which
> makes her a lesbian?
> —**Jean Royére,** speaking of Natalie Barney in "Sapho et Circé"

Renée Vivien was born Pauline Mary Tarn in England on 11 June 1877.[7] Her mother was American and her father British. The Tarn family apparently amassed their fortune in the London dry-goods business. Renée was sent to study in Paris, where she met Violet Shilleto, a young American who was to become one of the most important figures in her life.[8] The two girls became close friends. They shared an intense concern with religion and related questions. As children, they refused Anglican communion together, and both were to die as Catholics. With adolescence, Renée developed an intense, but unconsummated, passion for Violet. Renée had probably not yet understood the implications of her feelings when her parents brought her back to England to prepare her for her debut. She did know that she was miserable, missed her friend, and was in a constant state of rage at having to go through the motions of a conventional upper-class girl preparing for marriage. Renée was finally presented in 1897, when she was twenty. She escaped back to Paris the next year, and had her first sexual relationship in 1899 with Natalie Barney, whom she met through Violet Shilleto.

Natalie Barney was born in Dayton, Ohio, on Halloween 1876.[9] The Barney family then lived in Cincinnati where they made a fortune manufacturing railroad equipment. The Barney family subsequently moved to Washington, D.C. Natalie spent much of her youth in France, where she attended Les Ruches, the school immortalized in *Olivia*.[10] She lived for a while in Paris, where her mother, Alice Pike Barney, studied painting.[11] Natalie's memoirs convey the impression of an extraordinary precocity. She says that she became a feminist during one of the family excursions to Europe, where she saw a woman and a dog pulling a cart while the man walked alongside.[12] She was ten years old. That same year, her mother arranged for Carolus Duran to paint Natalie's portrait. Displaying the fine sense of camp which never deserted her, Natalie posed as a young prince wearing a green velvet doublet.[13] Natalie knew that she was a lesbian from an early age, and later commented that if her studies had come to nothing, it was because "my only books were women's looks."[14] She had her first lesbian affair at the age of sixteen, with a red-haired beauty named Eva Palmer. The two girls had met at Bar Harbor, Maine, where their families had summer homes.

Natalie settled in Paris in 1899. She immediately seduced Liane de Pougy, one of the most celebrated courtesans in Paris. Pougy wrote *Idylle Saphique*, a roman à clef of the relationship.[15] The novel portrays young Natalie orating against the injustice of male laws and referring to lesbianism as "a religion of the body, whose kisses are prayers."[16] The character based on Barney refuses to call lesbianism a perversion. Instead, she refers to it as a "conversion."[17]

Natalie was still involved with Liane when she met Renée. The affair between Natalie and Renée commenced on a winter night in 1899 in a room full of lilies. It lasted until a bitter rupture in 1901 and resumed again briefly in 1904. It would be difficult to understand how such a short liaison could have had the impact that it did upon both women, were it not for the intensity generated by their shared vision of a society in which women would be free, and homosexuality honored.

When Renée Vivien and Natalie Barney began their relationship, they each found a comrade in their literary war on behalf of women and lesbianism. Searching for their own roots, they discovered Sappho and Hellenism. They dreamed of establishing a group of women poets dedicated to Sappho, preferably on the island of Mytilene (Lesbos). Vivien learned Greek in order to read Sappho in the original, and she eventually translated Sappho's poetry into French. The two women declared themselves pagans, spiritual descendants of the Greeks.

Vivien and Barney were part of the emergence of the early homosexual movement in the late nineteenth century. In Britain this movement mainly consisted of Victorian gentlemen who wrote homoerotic poetry. In Germany, the movement was explicitly political and fought for the legalization of homosexuality.[18] Renée Vivien and Natalie Barney were unique in that they achieved and articulated a distinctively lesbian self-awareness. Their writings show that they understood who they were and what they were up against. There were few homosexuals of either sex who comprehended the dimensions of the homosexual situation.

Both women understood that prejudice against homosexuals had to be fought, and they realized the importance of living openly. Before Radclyffe Hall argued for tolerance, they argued for pride. Hall's consciousness was largely that of sexologists, such as Havelock Ellis and Magnus Hirschfeld, who believed that homosexuality was an inborn anomaly for which no one should be held legally culpable. By contrast, Vivien and Barney adopted an attitude for which they found support in nineteenth-century French literature, in which the lesbian was often a romantic figure.[19] Radclyffe Hall believed that pride was possible in spite of homosexuality; Vivien and Barney were proud *of* homosexuality.

At a time when Krafft-Ebing classified homosexuality as a degenerative disease, Vivien and Barney considered it a thrilling distinction. They responded to anti-homosexual disdain with insolent extremism, as illustrated by this interchange between two of the characters in *A Woman Appeared to Me*.

> "In fact, San Giovanni, has a woman ever loved a man?"
> "I can hardly conceive of such a deviation of the senses. Sadism and the rape of children seem more normal to me."[20]

Vivien read widely in myth, legend, and ancient literature. She rewrote many of Western culture's most cherished myths, replacing their male and heterosexual biases with female and lesbian ones. In these excerpts from "The Profane Genesis," Vivien changes the biblical story into the creation myth of lesbian poetry.

I. Before the birth of the Universe, there existed two eternal principles, Jehovah and Satan.

II. Jehovah was the incarnation of Force, Satan the incarnation of Cunning.

VII. Jehovah breathed upon the Infinite, and the sky was born of his breath.

VIII. Satan covered the implacable azure with the fleeting grace of clouds.

XIII. Jehovah kneaded clay, and from this clay, fashioned man.

XIV. From the very essence of this flesh flowered, idealized, the flesh of woman, the work of Satan.

XV. Jehovah bent the man and the woman with the violence of the embrace.

XVI. Satan taught them the piercing subtlety of the caress.

XVIII. He [Jehovah] inspired the Bar of Ionia, the mighty Homer.

XIX. Homer celebrated the magnificence of carnage and the glory of spilt blood, the ruin of cities, the sobs of widows. . . .

XX. Satan leaned toward the west, over the sleep of Sappho, the Lesbian.

XXI. And she sang the fugitive forms of love . . . the ardent perfume of roses . . . the sacred dances of Cretan women . . . the immortal arrogance that scorns suffering and smiles in death and the charm of women's kisses.[21]

Renée Vivien and Natalie Barney were as outspoken in their feminism as in their lesbianism. Vivien scoured her sources for themes of female independence. Amazons, androgynes, and archaic female deities abound in her writing. Many of her prose pieces are tales of women as magnificent rebels. There are noble virgins, independent prostitutes, queens who choose poverty and freedom to the slavery of an unloved royal bed. "The Veil of Vashti" is a story based on the Old Testament Book of Esther.[22] The Jewish festival of Purim celebrates Esther's rescue of the Jews from the machinations of a Persian court functionary. Vivien was inspired by the part of the story which is generally ignored in Hebrew school. She wrote about Queen Vashti, whom Esther replaced. The biblical account says that Vashti refused to obey an order of King Ahasuerus. The king's advisors warn that she must be punished or the Persians and the Medes will be faced with a feminist revolt:

> For this deed of the queen shall come abroad unto all women, so that they shall despise their husbands in their eyes, when it shall be reported, The king Ahasuerus commanded Vashti the queen to be brought in before him, but she came not.
>
> Likewise shall the ladies of Persia and Media say this day unto all the king's princes, which have heard of the deed of the queen. Thus shall there arise too much contempt and wrath.[23]

In Vivien's story, Vashti's provocation is deliberate.

> For my action will come to the attention of all women and they will say, "The King Ahasuerus had ordered that Queen Vashti be brought into his presence and she did not go." And, from that day, the princesses of Persia and Media will know that they are no longer the servants of their husbands, and that the man is no longer the master in his house; but that the woman is free and mistress equally to the master in his house.[24]

When Queen Vashti is informed of her banishment from the court, she declares,

> I am going into the desert where human beings are free like lions. . . . I shall perish there perhaps of hunger. I shall perish there perhaps in the teeth of savage beasts. I shall perish there perhaps of solitude. But, since the rebellion of Lilith, I am the first free woman. My action will come to the attention of all women, and all those who are slaves in the houses of their husbands or of their fathers will envy me in secret. Thinking of my glorious rebellion, they will say: Vashti disdained being a queen that she might be free.
>
> And Vashti went into the desert where dead serpents lived again under the light of the moon.[25]

Renée Vivien also wrote stories of women as victims of male injustice. One of the most striking is "The Eternal Slave." It is worth quoting in full.

> I saw the Woman encumbered with chains of gold and chains of bronze. Her bonds were at once tenuous like a spider's web, and heavy like the mass of mountains, and the Man, sometimes tyrant and sometimes parasite, dominated her and lived off of her.

Docile, she submitted to his tyranny. And what was most dismaying was to hear the hypocritical words of love which were mingled with the orders of the master.

I cried out to the Woman (and my cry passed despairingly through the bars which separated us):

"O You, the eternally Afflicted, Tenderness deceived, Martyr of love, why do you resign yourself in degrading patience to the ignominy and baseness of this false companion? Do you submit out of love or out of fear?"

She replied to me: "I submit neither from love nor from fear, but through ignorance and habit."

And with these words, an immense sadness and an immense hope came to me.[26]

Because of her sensitivity to the male sexual monopoly on women, Renée Vivien was fascinated by stories of women who refused men. She often wrote about women who preferred to mate with monsters or to die rather than to accept the desire of a human male. Many of her stories are told from the viewpoint of some bemused man who has unwittingly encountered such a woman and been humiliated by her refusal. "Brown Like a Hazel-Nut" is narrated by a young man named Jerry, and consists of his bitter recollection of Nell.[27] Jerry wants Nell to be his mistress, but she refuses. She tells him that she would rather swallow a toad than be embraced by him. He catches a toad and tells her that he will take her by force unless she swallows it. She does.

Renée Vivien is chiefly remembered for her poetry, the vast bulk of which is devoted to the passion of women. There is no poet who wrote as openly, as single-mindedly, and as prolifically of lesbian love. Colette said of the Poet of Lesbos, "Renée Vivien has left a great many poems of unequal strength, force, merit, unequal as the human breath, as the pulsations of human suffering."[28] It would be impossible to begin to present the range of Vivien's poetry here, so these verses from "Words to my Friend" will have to suffice.

See: I am at the age when a maiden gives her hand
To the Man whom her weakness seeks and dreads,
And I have not chosen my traveling companion,
Because you appeared at the turn of the road.

The hyacinth bleeds on the red hills,
You dreamt and Eros walked by your side . . .
I am a woman, I have no right to beauty,
They have condemned me to the ugliness of men.

And I had the inexcusable audacity to want
The sisterly love made up of light purities,
The furtive step that does not bruise the ferns
And the soft voice which blends with the evening.

They had forbidden me your hair, your eyes
Because your hair is long and fragrant
And because your eyes hold strange ardors
And become muddy like rebellious waves.

They pointed their fingers at me in an angry gesture,
Because my eyes were seeking your tender glance . . .
On seeing us pass by, no one has wished to understand
That I have chosen you with simplicity.

Consider the vile law that I transgress
And judge my love, which knows nothing of evil,
As candid, as necessary, and fatal
As the desire which joins the lover to his mistress.[29]

If Renée Vivien was the poet of Lesbos, Natalie Barney was its muse. Barney was also a writer and a poet, but her impact came less from her writing than from her powerful personality, her arrogant disregard for convention, the lucidity of her ideas, and her astounding capacity for seduction. She lived among writers, many of whom used her colorful personality as a model for barely disguised fictional characters. Besides Vally in *A Woman Appeared to Me*, Barney's most memorable appearances include Laurette in Delarue-Mardrus's *L'Ange et les pervers* (1930); Dame Evangeline Musset in Barnes's *The Ladies Almanack* (1928); Florence Temple Bradford (Flossie) in *Idylle Saphique* (Pougy 1901); and Valerie Seymour in Hall's *The Well of Loneliness* (1959). These characters depict Natalie in her favorite roles—muse of poets, high priestesses of lesbianism, missionary and seductress of the unconvinced. Natalie was a living advertisement for the healthful benefits of the gay life.

Natalie did not restrict the exercise of her charm to women. She has a considerable reputation as a patron of literature and her salon at 20, rue Jacob, is legendary. In contrast to Gertrude Stein's, Natalie's salon was a center for French literature. Her guest list reads like a Who's Who in twentieth-century French and American arts and letters.

During the 1920s, Natalie's home was also a gathering place for the international homosexual underground. Radclyffe Hall and Una Troubridge visited her frequently during this time, and in *The Well of Loneliness* Hall wrote about the ambiance Natalie created.

> And such people frequented Valerie Seymour's, men and women who must carry God's mark on their foreheads. For Valerie, placid and self-assured, created an atmosphere of courage; everyone felt very normal and brave when they gathered together at Valerie Seymour's. There she was, this charming and cultured woman, a kind of lighthouse in a storm-swept ocean. The waves lashed round her feet in vain. . . . The storms, gathering force, broke and drifted away, leaving behind them the shipwrecked, the drowning. But when they looked up, the poor spluttering victims, why what should they see but Valerie Seymour! Then a few would strike boldly for the shore, at the sight of this indestructible creature.[30]

An impressive number of talented and articulate women continued to gather around Natalie Barney well into the twentieth century. Some were, at one time or another, her lovers—including Lucie Delarue-Mardrus, Elizabeth de Gramont (Duchesse de Clermont-Tonnerre), Dolly Wilde (Oscar Wilde's niece), and Romaine Brooks. They wrote about each other, painted portraits of each other, wrote poetry to each other, and engaged in Byzantine sexual intrigue. They left an extraordinary collection of artifacts scattered about in museums and libraries. Many of them are famous, and this period of Paris history, in the 1920s, is relatively well known. It should be remembered, however, that these women were carrying on a tradition already established by 1900 by Renée Vivien and Natalie Barney.

III

> "Some women," said Dame Musset, "are Sea-Cattle, and some are Land-Hogs, and yet others are Worms crawling about our Almanacks, but some," she said, "are Sisters of Heaven, and these we must follow and not be sidetracked."
> —Djuna Barnes, *Ladies Almanack*

In spite of their shared ideology, Renée Vivien and Natalie Barney were emotionally mismatched. Although *A Woman Appeared to Me* reflects their common lesbian consciousness, it is primarily a record of their incompatibility. Renée wrote *A Woman Appeared to Me* sometime before their reconciliation in 1904.[31] The novel is based on the events and people in her life between 1899 and

1903, and its aesthetic is *fin de siècle*. The novel is biographical, but it records less the events themselves than her emotional response to them. Moreover, Renée experienced her emotions very symbolically. Perhaps as part of her poetic craft, particular people became associated with any number of levels of imagery and significance. Her inner cosmology associated colors, flowers, and legendary figures with personal archetypes.

There are two primary emotional sources for *A Woman Appeared to Me*. The first was the failure of Renée's relationships with Natalie. During the same period in her life, Renée faced another crisis. Her friend Violet Shiletto died in 1901. Violet's death haunted Renée for the rest of her own short life, and it complicated the relationship with Natalie.

A Woman Appeared to Me is the story of a doomed love affair between the narrator (Renée Vivien) and Vally (Natalie Barney). The first part of the novel covers the years from 1899 to 1901. Vally is portrayed as incapable of love and utterly faithless. The narrator is distressed at Vally's dalliances with other women, but she is most outraged by the "Prostitute," a man who wants to marry Vally. Natalie did in fact have male suitors at that time, and she led them on. But men were never of any sexual or romantic significance to her.

The narrator realizes that her obsessed relationship with Vally is undermining her friendship with Ione (Violet Shiletto), who had been her most dear and intimate friend. Completing the initial cast of characters, there is the orientalist Petrus (J. C. Mardrus, a friend of Natalie's and the translator of *Arabian Nights*), the wife of Petrus (Lucie Delarue-Mardrus), and San Giovanni.

The character of San Giovanni is a composite alter ego of the narrator. She is Renée's better half, her common sense, the courageous poet of Lesbos: in short, the core of Renée's identity, which remained intact from the devastation of her unhappy passion. Sometimes San Giovanni is the wise Renée of 1903, while the narrator is the innocent Renée of 1900. San Giovanni is also one of the archetypes of Renée's personal mythology: the androgyne.

Vally, the narrator, and San Giovanni travel together to America, where they visit a women's college (Bryn Mawr); Ione gets sick and dies shortly after they return. The narrator is desolate with grief for Ione and jealous of Vally's affairs. San Giovanni—her common sense—warns her: "If you don't alter your jealous melancholy and your savage moods, *you will lose Vally*. She will simply stay out of the dark mists in which you wrap yourself and which smother her. She needs fresh air, space, and sunlight."[32] And, indeed, Vally soon expels the narrator from her divine presence.

The rest of the novel covers the years 1901 to 1903. The narrator attempts to console herself with Dagmar (Olive Custance), until Dagmar finds her

"Prince" (Lord Alfred Douglas, whom Olive married in 1902 and who had been the lover of Oscar Wilde). Then the narrator finds Eva, and the two women embark on a year of happy love. Like San Giovanni, Eva defies precise classification. Eva is based in part on Eva Palmer. Renée seems to have fallen in love with Palmer, who gently refused her.[33] Renée plays up on the connotations of Eva's name to evoke the archetypal primal woman. Just as San Giovanni is Renée's ideal self, Eva is the ideal lover of her dreams. Finally, Eva also seems to represent Hélène, Baronne Van Zuylen de Nyevelt, who also became Renée's lover after the break with Natalie in 1901.

While the narrator is living happily with Eva, Vally returns to claim her. The last part of the novel records the struggle to decide between these two arch-angels of her destiny.

A Woman Appeared to Me was written out of Renée Vivien's need to come to terms with her relationship with Natalie Barney. Renée wanted to understand what went wrong and whom to blame. Although the novel occasionally presents Natalie's analysis of the affair, it is fundamentally an expression of Renée's confusion, pain, anger, and guilt. Natalie wrote about her side of the relationship in her memoirs (*Souvenirs indiscrets* [1960] and *Aventures de l'esprit* [1929]) and in a group of prose poems (*Je me souviens* [1910]). All of these accounts are partisan and must be measured against what actually happened.

When Renée met Natalie, in 1899, Violet Shilleto was still the center of her emotional life. As Renée became increasingly involved with Natalie, she began to lose touch with Violet. Early in 1901, Violet asked Renée to go with her to the south of France. Renée elected to stay in Paris with Natalie, promising Violet she would come later. When she received word that Violet was ill, Renée hastened to the Riviera. While Renée was gone, Natalie dabbled in an unsuccessful liaison with Olive Custance. Renée meanwhile had arrived in Nice to find that Violet was dying and had converted to Catholicism. Renée's grief for Violet was compounded by her guilt for having become estranged from her friend. She felt that she had been led to betray the friendship by her absorption in the carnal delights of her first affair.

Renée's grief did not abate. Hoping that a change of scenery would help Renée out of her depression, Natalie persuaded Renée to go with her to the United States. They spent the summer of 1901 in Bar Harbor, where Renée met Eva Palmer, who had been Natalie's first lover. Eva was much more understanding of Renée's grief than Natalie. While Natalie went to a round of social events, Eva studied Greek with Renée. In the fall, all three traveled to Bryn Mawr, where Eva was a student.[34] While Natalie again went to balls and parties, Renée wrote poetry in an abandoned cemetery. Renée finally departed to visit her family in London, and Natalie left for her family's home in Washington. They were to meet back in Paris.

In her memoirs, Natalie says she did not hear from Renée during that winter, and was filled with disquiet. She says she was surprised to find that Renée would not see her when she returned to Paris. Natalie ascertained that Renée had become involved with Hélène, Baronne Van Zuylen de Nyevelt (née Rothschild). Renée avoided all of Natalie's attempts to communicate with her, which included moonlight serenades and messages tossed over garden walls. Natalie speculates in her memoirs that the Baroness had paid Renée's governess to intercept her letters, leading Renée to believe that Natalie had abandoned her. The Baroness was jealous and did try to sequester Renée from her former lover, but Natalie's account is somewhat disingenuous. The relationship had been in trouble for some time, and Natalie already knew that Renée was trying to avoid her quite apart from any possible intrigue by the Baroness.

From the beginning of the affair, Renée was both exhilarated and terrorized by its carnality and its power. Natalie was the incarnation of her dreams, a lover who could inspire an incinerating passion. But Renée was ambivalent about such passion. She had a curious kind of chastity, both emotional and physical. Her chaste love for Violet seemed to embody a passion untouched by impurity. If anything, her experiences with Natalie were sufficiently confusing to exacerbate the conflict. On the other hand, much of Natalie's ability to seduce was the result of her religious devotion to the pleasures of the flesh. One of Natalie's early complaints was that she wanted a more ardent reality and fewer ardent words. She evidently felt that Renée's love was largely lived in the imagination. She accused Renée of being more willing to speak of love than to love, and she wrote these words to her: "And would you have put all of your courage and all your poetry into your verses if there is so little left for your life? Is it you who will write these audacious and beautiful words, and will I alone dare to live that of which you sing?"[35]

Renée and Violet had shared a fascination with death and religion when they were children. When Natalie met Renée, she thought her own lusty paganism would give Renée more of an interest in life. While Renée was coping with Natalie's vitality, which both attracted and hurt her, the drama of Violet's death heightened the polarity she already felt. Renée thought that Natalie — and sex — were responsible for the unforgivable lapse in her friendship with Violet. Renée's endless mourning was in part an effort to expiate the guilt she felt toward Violet's memory. Natalie, on the other hand, hated to think about death and even avoided funerals. Renée's grief seemed to Natalie to exceed the limits of decency. Renée argued for her right to mourn, and wrote a poem called "Let the Dead Bury Their Dead." Natalie commented in the margin, "But not the Living."[36]

The most acute issue in the relationship, and the one around which all other conflicts crystallized, was monogamy. I cannot do justice here to Natalie's complex theories about sex roles and erotic relationships. Suffice it to say that Natalie evolved a critique of the sex roles which included a critique of the structure of erotic emotion. She felt that sex roles hurt each person by dictating the suppression of the personality traits assigned to the other sex. She also thought that erotic relationships drew their structure from this artificial division of the sexes, such that each individual sought its missing wholeness in the other. Natalie felt that the emotions of jealousy, possessiveness, and exclusivity derived from this sexual system, which she also held responsible for women's secondary status. Natalie maintained that a relationship should be based on mutual independence, rather than on dependence, and that love should never be constrained by fidelity. Fidelity, she thought, meant that love and desire were dead.

Natalie lived by such ideals as much as possible. When Natalie gave her love, she gave it forever; but this did not preclude her from giving it to others in the meantime. Such loyalty was not always appreciated by lovers whose idea of love was more conventional or whose emotional constitutions were less rugged. Natalie maintained that she did not suffer from jealousy, but from the jealousy of others. Of all her lovers, only Romaine Brooks shared Natalie's perspective on relationships. Although Romaine and Natalie were lovers for half a century, they lived apart. When they built a villa in the south of France, it consisted of two residences joined by a set of common rooms. Natalie's other lovers were generally less than pleased by her promiscuity.[37] Quite apart from her ideals, Natalie had all the instincts of a hamadryas baboon. Chalon describes her pattern best, noting that her harem usually contained a ruling "Sultana," a "Favorite" or two, and a bevy of lesser delights.

Unlike Natalie, Renée Vivien did not attempt to express her own needs in terms of a systematic philosophy. She was simply romantic. To Renée, love was forever, and forever meant fidelity. When Natalie dallied about and yet assured Renée that she loved her, Renée could not believe in her sincerity. Natalie responded by saying that if Renée loved her, she would try to understand her; and that such understanding would lead Renée to cease the suspicious possessiveness that threatened to destroy the very liveliness that made Natalie so attractive. Renée tried to understand, but was unable to stop the anguish caused by Natalie's constant infidelities. Renée began to identify Natalie's vitality as the source of her pain. The circumstances of Violet's death led her to link Natalie's sensuality with betrayal. It was Violet's death that finally gave Renée enough desperate strength to remove herself from this emotionally unbearable relationship. She wrote the following letter late in 1901, from London, to Natalie, who was still in Washington.

> I am sad that you have thus broken the promise which you made me before leaving. You had promised not to call me to serve as a distraction for an hour of boredom, only to call me when you had need of me to console you, to help you in a bad moment. Now, there is no necessity for me to come. Nothing serious has taken place in your life. . . . [Y]ou are calling me for the simple pleasure of trying out, once again, your power over me, or of having once again, next to you, one who is in pain, an easy dupe whom you will use again for all your little amorous and whimsical projects.
>
> I am sad to the bottom of my heart for having to tell you this, to you whom I love still and in spite of everything. But you forget to what point you martyred me, you forget the anguish, the humiliations, the wounds that you inflicted on me; you forget that I am still bleeding and bruised with all that you made me suffer, unconsciously, perhaps, but fatally. Far from you, I do not suffer with the same intensity the pains, the jealousies, the anxieties which I endure when I see you giving out smiles and provocative glances like a merchant of kisses to everyone, female or male. . . .
>
> . . . I will always love you, but no longer with that blind love of the first days. I love you now with a love more bitter, more sad, more skeptical. . . . I no longer have an irrational faith; I doubt and I seek to know what there is that is true at the base of the lies—what there is that is false at the base of the truths—for you are a being so complex that you are not entirely true or false.
>
> . . . But I beg you leave me a little peace of mind, let me bathe in solitude and silence and recover a bit of strength.
>
> . . . To return to you for a while in order to leave again afterwards, what madness! I could not do it, I would not have the courage to absent myself a second time. There are sacrifices that one cannot remake.
>
> . . . [B]elieve me when I tell you again that I love you "unalterably." . . . I love you as I will love you always.[38]

Natalie therefore must have known when she returned to Paris that Renée considered the relationship over, although she was genuinely surprised by the

Baroness Van Zuylen. Renée had already tried to console herself with Olive Custance in late 1901, before succeeding in the new relationship with the Baroness. Natalie was still quite in love with Renée and determined to win her back. Natalie's larger project did not however prevent her from having an affair with Lucie Delarue-Mardrus in 1902.[39]

Eva Palmer was also in Paris, and she became Natalie's emissary to Renée. It was only through Eva and music that Natalie had any success in her quest.[40] When Renée invited Eva to share her box at the opera, Natalie took Eva's seat and Renée seemed happy to see her. Renée promised to meet Natalie again, but failed to make the rendezvous. Natalie was then called away to attend her father, who was dying in Monte Carlo. She took his ashes back to Washington and apparently stayed away for some time.[41]

Finally, in the summer of 1904, Natalie heard that Renée was planning to attend the Wagner festival in Bayreuth, and that she would be going without the Baroness, whose constant jealous surveillance had hampered Natalie's efforts. Natalie left with Eva for Bayreuth. Seats were exchanged so that Natalie and Renée could be together. Natalie had brought some prose poems which protested the sincerity and depth of her love for Renée, and Renée was finally convinced.[42] She decided to resume the relationship, but only at Mytilene.

Renée and Natalie traveled to Mytilene where they rented two villas in an orchard and revived their old dreams of establishing a cult of Sappho. Their happy idyll was interrupted by a cable from the Baroness Van Zuylen, who was on her way to the island. Natalie left for Paris, having been assured that Renée was going to break with the Baroness and return to her. Renée was torn between the two women, but finally decided to drop Natalie and stay with the Baroness instead.

It becomes increasingly difficult to trace Vivien's personal history after the second break with Natalie, in 1904. Renée seems at last to have come to terms with her feeling for Natalie. The two women developed a friendship, which Renée had earlier declared impossible; after 1904 Renée had more understanding for her difficult lover but also understood that she could not stay with her. Renée was satisfied with her choice and kept to it, although she always thought of her earlier love with wistfulness. Colette recounts a conversation in which Renée expressed some regret about a lover from her past: "Then it was a question of the satisfactions of another epoch, another woman, and regrets and comparisons."[43]

Renée traveled extensively during the last years of her life, in the Mediterranean, the Middle East, and the Orient. She filled her apartment at 23, Ave.

du Bois with art treasures acquired on her journeys.[44] Romaine Brooks knew Renée before 1909, and she described the apartment in her memoirs.[45]

> There comes before me the dark, heavily curtained room, overreaching itself in lugubrious effects: grim life-sized Oriental figures sitting propped up on chairs, phosphorescent Buddhas glowing dimly in the folds of black draperies. The air is heavy with perfumed incense. A curtain draws aside and Renée Vivien stands before us attired in Louis XVI male costume. Her straight blond hair falls to her shoulders, her flower-like face is bent down. . . . We lunch seated on the floor Oriental fashion and scant food is served on ancient Damascus ware, cracked and stained. During the meal Renée Vivien leaves us to bring in from the garden her pet frogs and a serpent which she twines round her wrist.[46]

Colette lived across the courtyard, and became one of Renée's friends. She also described the apartment: "I became almost wickedly intolerant there, yet never wore out the patience of the gossamer angel who dedicated offerings of lady apples to the Buddhas. One day, when the spring wind was stripping the leaves from the Judas trees in the avenue, I was nauseated by the funereal perfumes and tried to open the window: it was nailed shut."[47]

The data on Renée's romantic attachments after 1905 are not very definitive. Some of the confusion arises from the fact that although the Baroness Van Zuylen was not popular, her identity was well protected in a literature that usually specialized in indiscretion. She is referred to as the Valkyrie, *La Brioche*, or as Madame de Z. Colette did describe the Baroness, but did not directly link her to Renée: "We heard from J. de Bellune that at that gala evening in Nice the Baroness Van Zuylen lorded it in a box, wearing a white tie and tails—and a mustache! The Baroness Ricoy accompanied her, likewise in tails and looking quite emaciated beside that elephantine monster. They were recognized and were pestered by visitors to their box, although the Baroness Van Zuylen responded to the intruders with broadsides of very masculine oaths."[48]

The actual dimensions of the affair between Vivien and the Baroness remain unclear. It seems that at least until 1905, the relationship was a healing one for Renée. She did much of her best work during this period and seemed to be happy. The Baroness encouraged Renée's work, and the two of them collaborated on a few volumes of poetry published under the collective pseudonym of Paule Riversdale.[49] But after 1905, something happened—either the relationship ended, or it changed.

In *Souvenirs indiscrets*, Natalie Barney says that Renée became outraged by the discovery that the Baroness had been unfaithful to her. Natalie implies that the relationship ended, and that Renée's decline subsequently became cataclysmic. In his notes on Renée Vivien, Salomon Reinach is definite that the liaison with the Baroness lasted between 1901 and 1905, and he gives no indication that it continued after 1905. The Riversdale collaboration only lasted until 1904. We also know that Renée had several affairs in the last years of her life, between 1906 and 1909, but we do not know to what extent the Baroness was still her primary concern.[50] It is clear that by 1908 Renée was both depressed and unhealthy, and that her poetry was increasingly obsessed with themes of death. She wrote the epitaph which is engraved on her tomb, and many of her late poems evoke the shadow of the dead Violet Shilleto. According to Colette, Renée was at that time engaged in a very disturbing relationship with a mysterious "master." It is usually assumed that the "master" was still the Baroness Van Zuylen. "This 'master' was never referred to by the name of woman. We seemed to be waiting for some catastrophe to project her into our midst, but she merely kept sending invisible messengers laden with jades, enamels, lacquers, fabrics."[51] The "master" would summon Renée erratically, and Renée often had to leave in the midst of a dinner party. As Colette arrived for one soirée, she found Renée on her way out the door. Renée explained: "Hush, I am requisitioned. *She* the terrible is present."[52] At another time, Renée explained to Colette that she was leaving Paris to get away before her lover killed her: "In four words she explained how she might perish. Four words of a frankness to make you blink. This would not be worth telling, except for what Renée said then. 'With her I dare not pretend or lie, because at that moment she lays her ear over my heart.'"[53] Even Colette did not know whether this imperious lover was real, or a creation of Vivien's imagination. Perhaps the "master" was the Baroness, perhaps she was someone else, or perhaps Renée created her last lover in the image of her fantasies.

By this time, Renée was acutely unhappy. She drank a lot and ate very little. Her regime of melancholy, alcohol, and starvation finally killed her, on 18 November 1909, after a deathbed conversion to Catholicism. The poet had written these words only a few years earlier.

If the Lord should bend His head toward my passage,
I would say to Him: "O Christ, I do not know you.

"Lord, your strict law was never mine,
And I lived thus a simple pagan.

"See the simplicity of my poor and naked heart.

I do not know you, I never knew you at all."[54]

But by 1909, Renée had followed her friend Violet into Christianity and an early death. Renée Vivien's tomb, at Passy, is a small, ornate, gothic chapel, full of crosses, plastic flowers, and a portrait of the poet.

Natalie Barney died a pagan on 2 February 1972. Her grave, also at Passy, is simple, unornamented, and bears no religious emblems. At the time Barney died, the legacy of these women was being rediscovered by a new generation of lesbian feminists in search of their ancestry.

Afterword from the New Edition of *A Woman Appeared to Me*

This new edition of *A Woman Appeared to Me* has given me a welcome opportunity to correct errors and make some stylistic revisions in my introduction. I have resisted the impulse to make substantive changes since to do so would entail either major surgery or a new article. However, I cannot resist a few comments on what has changed since I wrote this one.

The scholarship on Vivien and Barney has expanded. *The Amazon of Letters* by George Wickes was published in 1976 and is available in paperback. The rumored biography of Vivien materialized in 1977, when *Sapho 1900: Renée Vivien* by Paul Lorenz was published in Paris by Julliard. Also in 1977, Naiad Press published *The Muse of the Violets*, the first book of Vivien's poetry in English translation. The National Collection of Fine Arts exhibited part of its collection of Barney family artifacts in 1978. Donald McClelland's catalogue of the exhibit, *Where Shadows Live: Alice Pike Barney and Her Friends*, is a delightful account of Natalie's milieu from the perspective of her mother's life.

In spite of all the excellent research, our image of this network of lesbians is largely based on what some of its members thought of themselves. Natalie Barney was particularly talented at generating her own legend. Now that her letters and papers can be studied, I expect that future research will not only correct the details, but that it will also result in changes in the larger picture of what occurred among these women.

I had a foretaste of such a shift in perspective when I ran across Mabel Dodge Luhan's memoir of Violet Shilleto in Jonathan Ned Katz's *Gay American History*. Because she died so young and made no direct contribution to the literary record of this group, Violet is a very shadowy historical presence.

Her wraithlike existence in the written sources led me to underestimate her substantial personal impact. Luhan writes,

> I have never known any man or woman with such wisdom and such love as she had. She knew everything intuitively and at the same time she had a very unusual intelligence — teaching herself Italian for her pleasure in order to read Dante in the original when she was sixteen. . . .
>
> Violet was, of all the people I have ever known . . . the highest evolved, the one who had reached the farthest. . . .
>
> . . . [S]he belonged to all ages, she was like a synthesis of the past. . . . Once in a great while Nature creates a marvelous human being, but very rarely. . . . After all these years, Violet's great significance lives in me yet.[55]

Luhan's memoir is evidence of Violet's charisma and of her religious mysticism. It corroborates the picture of Violet in *A Woman Appeared to Me* and renders the relationship between her and Renée more intelligible. It alters my earlier understanding that *A Woman Appeared to Me* is primarily about Renée's relationship with Natalie. Renée was dealing with some very strong personalities.

The level of detail with which one can chronicle the bedroom wars of this group of women would be enough to make them historically fascinating. But the significance of Barney and Vivien has been brought into increasingly clear focus by recent developments within lesbian and gay history. It has become apparent that gay/lesbian history is undergoing a revolution in its paradigms, projects, and practices. Jeffrey Weeks's *Coming Out* (1977) perhaps best exemplifies the trend away from compiling a history of homosexuals and toward constructing a social history of homosexuality. The "new" gay history is characterized by the insight that "however people have behaved sexually throughout European history, they did not live in a world of heterosexual and homosexuals until quite recently."[56] The object of the new gay history is to describe, date, and explain the emergence of this world of sexually specialized persons and its concomitant sociology and politics. While the periodization is by no means settled, there is a growing consensus among gay historians that this modern sexual system was consolidated in or by the last two decades of the nineteenth century in western Europe.

The transformation of gay history has been largely brought about by the study of several key figures of the late nineteenth century. The new gay history is primarily grounded in research on Edward Carpenter, John Addington Symonds, Magnus Hirschfeld, Karl Heinrich Ulrichs, Natalie Barney, Renée Vivien, and Havelock Ellis. It became necessary to develop a new conceptual framework in order to understand the implications of the activities, ideas, writings, and sexual careers of these emblematic individuals. The significance of Vivien and Barney lies not as much in their emotional and sexual pyrotechnics as in their status as two of the most important lesbians among these late-nineteenth-century heroes of sexual freedom.

The Leather Menace

Comments on Politics and s/m

4

I

Since Christianity upped the ante and concentrated on sexual behavior as the root of virtue, everything pertaining to sex has been a "special case" in our culture, evoking peculiarly inconsistent attitudes.
—**Susan Sontag,** *Styles of Radical Will*

It is difficult to simply discuss the politics of sadomasochism when the politics of sex in general are so depressingly muddled. In part, this is due to the residue of at least a century of social conflict over sex during which conservative positions have dominated the terms of discussion as well as the outcome of many discrete struggles. It is important to know and to remember that in the United States and Britain, there were extensive and successful morality campaigns in the late-nineteenth and early-twentieth centuries. Social movements against prostitution, obscenity, contraception, abortion, and masturbation were able to establish state policies, social practices, and deeply entrenched ideologies which still affect the shape of our sexual experience and our ability to think about it. In the United States, the long-term agenda of the conservative right has helped to maintain deep reservoirs of ignorance and sexual bigotry by its

Chapter 4 was originally published in Samois, ed., *Coming to Power: Writing and Graphics on Lesbian* s/m (San Francisco, Samois, 1981). The version included here is from the second edition of *Coming to Power: Writing and Graphics on Lesbian* s/m (Boston: Alyson, 1982), 192–225.

unrelenting opposition to sex research and sex education. More recently, the Right has been spectacularly successful in tapping these pools of erotophobia in its accession to state power. The Right will now use its hegemony over the state apparatus to renew and deepen its hold over erotic behavior.

Even the elementary bourgeois freedoms have never been secured in the realm of sexuality. There is, for instance, no freedom of sexual speech. Explicit talk about sex has been a glaring exception to first amendment protection since the Comstock Act was passed, in 1873. Although there have been many skirmishes to establish exactly where the line will be drawn or how strongly it will be enforced, it remains true that it is still illegal in this country to produce (or show or sell) images, objects, or writing which have no other purpose than sexual arousal. One may embroider for relaxation, play baseball for the thrill, or collect stamps merely for their beauty. But sex itself is not a legitimate activity or goal. It must have some "higher" purpose. If possible, this purpose should be reproductive. Failing that, an artistic, scientific, or literary aim will do. Minimally, sex should at least be the expression of a close personal relationship.

In contrast to the politics of class, race, ethnicity, and gender, the politics of sex are relatively underdeveloped. Sexual liberals are defensive, and sexual radicals almost nonexistent. Sex politics are kept far to the right by many forces, among them a frequent recourse to terror. Our sexual system contains a vast vague pool of nameless horror. Like Lovecraft's pits, where unmentionable creatures perform unspeakable acts, this place of fear is rarely specified but always avoided. This reservoir of terror has several effects on our ability to deal with sex politically, making the whole subject touchy and volatile. It makes sex-baiting painfully easy. It provides a constant supply of demons and boogiemen with which otherwise rational people can be stampeded.

In the United States throughout the twentieth century, there have been periodic sex scares. In the late 1940s and early 1950s the Cold War was inaugurated with a wave of domestic repression. Along with anticommunism, loyalty oaths, and the postwar reconstruction of gender roles and the family, there was a paroxysm of sex terrorism whose most overt symptom was a savage repression against homosexuals. Gay people were purged from government positions, expelled from schools, and fired from jobs (including academic jobs with tenure). Newspapers carried screaming headlines as police rounded up suspected perverts and gay bars were raided. Government agencies, legislative bodies, and grand juries held hearings and investigated the "sex deviate problem." The FBI conducted surveillance of gay people. All of these activities were both justified by, and contributed to, the construct of the homosexual as a social menace.

The repression of gay people during the Cold War has been absent from histories of the period, and the abuses suffered by homosexuals during the 1950s have never been questioned.[1] The antigay repression was seen as a hygienic measure since gay life was depicted as seedy, dangerous, degraded, and scary. The impact of the repression was in fact to degrade the quality of gay life and raise the costs of being sexually different. During the 1950s, the Communist Party was just as apt to purge homosexuals as the state department. The ACLU refused to defend homosexuals who were being persecuted by federal, state, and local governments. The entire political spectrum, from Protestant Republicans to godless communists, accepted more or less the same analysis of homosexuals as scum. This period is an object lesson in the mechanics of sexual witch-hunting and needs to be better known.[2]

It should be fairly obvious that the late 1970s and early 1980s are similar in many ways to the period in which the Cold War began. For whatever reason, military build-up, family reconstruction, anticommunism, and enforced sexual conformity all merge in the right-wing program. But we are not simply repeating history. Among other important differences, the positions of target sexual populations have changed dramatically. The gay community is under attack and is vulnerable, but it is simply too large and too well organized to be attacked with the impunity of the 1950s. Instead of a few tiny organizations whose names, like the Mattachine Society, gave no indications of their focus, there are now hundreds of explicitly gay political organizations. More important, there is an effective and extensive gay press which can document and publicize the war against homosexuals. Gay people enjoy some political legitimacy and support in the nongay population. This does not imply complacency. The Jewish community in pre–Second World War Poland was large, literate, and possessed a thriving press and was nevertheless wiped out by the Nazis. But it does mean that people know what is going on and can mount some resistance. It means that it is more difficult and politically expensive to conduct antigay persecution.

It is the erotic communities which are smaller, more stigmatized, and less organized which are subject to virtually unrestrained attack. Just as the political mobilization of black people has been emulated by other racial and ethnic groups, the mobilization of homosexuals has provided a repertoire of ideology and organizational technologies to other erotic populations. It is these smaller, more underground groups who enjoy even fewer legal rights and less social acceptance who are bearing the brunt of current sexual repression. Moreover, these communities, particularly boy-lovers and sadomasochists, are being used as wedges against the larger gay community.

It lies well outside the scope of this essay to fully analyze the issues of cross-generational sex. But thus far, it has been the most strategically located, so a few comments are in order. In the United States, gay lovers of youth have been *the* front line of the Right's battle against the gay community, which has been picking up steam since the spring of 1977.³ Lovers of youth enjoy virtually no legal protection, because any sexual contact between an adult and a minor is illegal. This means that a fully consensual love affair is, in the eyes of the law, indistinguishable from a rape. Moreover, sentences for consensual sex with a minor are usually longer and harsher than sentences for violent rape of adult women, assault and battery, or even murder. Second, lovers of youth are the cheapest targets for inflammatory rhetoric. Very little public education has occurred to dislodge the stereotypes which depict adult-youth relationships in the ugliest possible terms. These images of drooling old sickies corrupting or harming sweet innocent children can be relied upon to drum up public hysteria. Such stereotypes have also been used to quash any discussion of the complex ways that statutory-rape laws function, not only to protect young people from abuse, but also to prevent them from acquiring sexual knowledge and to interfere with their own sexual explorations. Sex between people of different ages is not an exclusively gay phenomenon. On the contrary, all statistics on cross-generational sex indicate that the majority of instances, and the vast majority of nonconsensual incidents, are heterosexual (older male, younger female). Nevertheless, most of the media coverage and legal attention has been directed at gay men. Each time another gay person is arrested for an age offense, the ensuing headlines serve to reinforce the stereotype that it is primarily a gay practice.

This claustrophobic and demonic discourse, the illegality of the sexual practices, and the ease with which the issue can be used to smear other gay people have made boy-lovers the favored target of state repression. The community of men engaged in cross-generational sex has been under siege for over four years and has been subjected to the kinds of police activity and media propaganda that were directed at homosexuals in the 1950s. Recently NAMBLA, the North American Man/Boy Love Association, has had the dubious honor of becoming the first gay-civil-rights organization directly attacked by the government in the current wave of repression against dissenting sexuality. Sadly, this community has been treated by the Left and the women's movement in much the same way that homosexuals were treated by so-called progressives in the 1950s. The gay movement has been repeatedly baited on this issue. When homosexuals are all accused of being "child molesters," it is legitimate to deny that all, or even a large percentage of, gay people engage in cross-generational sex. But it is crucial to add that not all adults who do have sex with minors are harming them. All too often, homosexuals have defended themselves against the accusation of child stealing by joining with the general condemnation of all adult-youth sex and by perpetuating the myths about it. Many lesbians have been doubly baited, disassociating themselves from the practice but accepting stereotypes not only that all lovers of youth are rapists, but also that gay men tend to be lovers of youth.

Sadomasochism is the other sexual practice which to date has been used with great success to attack the gay community, and at greatest cost to those who actually practice it. Unlike sex between adults and minors, s/m is not, per se, illegal. Nevertheless there are a variety of laws which have been interpreted to apply to s/m sexual encounters and social events. It is easy to bend the applicability of existing laws because s/m is so stereotyped and stigmatized, and thus shocking and frightening. The shock value of s/m has been mercilessly exploited by both media and police.

In 1976, Los Angeles police used an obscure nineteenth-century antislavery statute to raid a "slave auction" held in a gay bathhouse. The next morning, four-inch headlines screamed, "POLICE FREE GAY SLAVES." The slaves were, of course, volunteers, and proceeds from the auction were to benefit gay charities. The event was about as sinister as a Lions Club rummage sale. But sixty-five uniformed officers, two helicopters, a dozen vehicles, at least two phone taps, several weeks of surveillance of the staff of a local gay magazine, and over $100,000 were expended to bust the party and arrest some forty people. Once arrested, they were detained for many hours in handcuffs, not allowed to go to the bathroom, and subjected to full strip searches. It is only the moral stupidity induced by anti-s/m attitudes that could make anyone think that the volunteer slaves had been rescued, or that the tender mercies of the L.A.P.D. were preferable to those of their intended Masters. The statute used was actually an antiprostitution law aimed at forcible prostitution. All charges under that statute were dropped, but four of the principals were charged with felony pandering and eventually pleaded guilty to misdemeanors.

s/m sex has occasionally been prosecuted under assault laws. Since assault is a felony, the state can press charges without a complaint from or even over the objections of the "victim." Once a sexual activity is construed as assault, the involvement of the partner is irrelevant, since one cannot legally consent to an assault. Since few judges or jurors can imagine why anyone would do s/m, it is easy to obtain convictions and brutal sentences. In a recent case in Massachusetts, Kenneth Appleby was sentenced to ten years in prison for hitting his lover lightly with a riding crop in the context of a consensual s/m relationship.[4] The Appleby case has some murky elements, but it sets a frightening precedent. It could happen that an s/m couple is making love. Police, perhaps called by neighbors alarmed by the noise, or perhaps looking for an excuse to arrest one of the parties, break in on the scene. They arrest the top and charge her (or him) with assault. The bottom could protest that they were only making love as her or his lover is hauled off to jail. If the couple is gay or otherwise unmarried, the submissive could even be subpoenaed and forced to testify against her or his partner in court. While the protests of the bottom might not save the top from prison, they might be used as evidence to declare the bottom mentally incompetent. Again, only the distortions of anti-s/m bigotry could locate the abuse of power in this scenario within the s/m relationship rather than with outsiders who interfere with it.[5]

The legal vulnerability of s/m is also demonstrated by a string of police actions in Canada. In December 1978, Toronto police raided a local leather-oriented gay bath, the Barracks. They charged several men under the bawdy-house laws and confiscated lots of sex toys, including dildos, butt plugs, leather harnesses, and whips. The bawdy-house laws were originally passed as anti-prostitution measures. No prostitution was alleged to have occurred at the Barracks. But the law contains a vague phrase referring to a "place where indecent acts take place." The police were arguing that gay s/m sex is indecent and that any place where it occurs is a bawdy house. While this interpretation has not been clearly upheld in court, the arrests and trials have continued and generated much havoc in the interim.

Press coverage of the Barracks raid was sensationalistic. The news media jumped at the opportunity to show, in loving detail, the confiscated equipment. The Toronto gay community protested the nature of the charges, the raid, and the press coverage. A defense committee was formed.

In June of 1979, one of the members of the defense committee was arrested for "keeping a common bawdy house" in his own home. Again, no prostitution was alleged. The redefinition of a bawdy house as a place where indecent acts took place, and of s/m sex as indecent, enabled police to bring the charges based on the man's s/m playroom. His toys, equipment, even his leather jacket and hat were confiscated as evidence, along with membership lists of the Barracks defense committee and the gay caucus of a political party.

In February 1981, the four major gay baths in Toronto were hit with a massive raid. Over three hundred men were charged under the same bawdy-house laws and hauled out into the winter snow in their towels. The Barracks was raided a second time, but the other three baths catered to a mainstream gay clientele. Having first redefined the bawdy-house laws with regard to gay s/m, the police were now expanding their application to cover ordinary gay sex. This neatly circumvented Canada's consenting-adults law and provoked a gay riot.

On April 14 of this year (1982), the scope of the crackdown expanded again. Robert Montgomery, who runs a small business making custom leather gear and sex toys, was charged with fifteen separate offenses. In addition to the now obligatory bawdy-house laws relating to his apartment, several charges were brought having to do with making, selling, distributing, and possessing to distribute obscene material. The obscene material in question included the leather items and sex toys. In effect, the Canadian police have now reclassified sex toys and leather gear as pornography, therefore prosecutable under the obscenity laws.

The reason behind Montgomery's arrest became clear a week later. Six men who own or have interests in gay baths in Toronto were charged with an array of offenses including keeping a common bawdy house, distribution and sale of obscene matter, and conspiracy to live off the proceeds of crime. The men charged were prominent gay businessmen, lawyers, and gay political activists, including George Hislop, a gay political official. The charges against them relied upon the whole carefully constructed edifice of redefined sex laws which the police had been building for three years. Any gay bath can be prosecuted as a bawdy house. Sex toys, leather items, enema bags, dildos, and even lubricants can be treated as contraband. In this case, the obscenity charges were related to the sale of sex equipment (including some items made by Montgomery) in shops at the baths. If these charges stick, anyone who owns or has an interest in a gay bath or sex-related business can be prosecuted for conspiracy to live off the proceeds of crime.

On 30 May, the gay baths were raided in Edmonton. On 12 June two men were convicted in the original Barracks case, and on 16 June the last two gay baths in Toronto were raided. What has happened very clearly in Canada is that s/m has been used to set several legal precedents which are now being used to decimate mainstream gay institutions and the bastions of mainstream gay political and economic power. Police have used the media and manipulated sexual prejudice and ignorance to criminalize whole categories of erotic behavior without a single new law being passed.

Nothing quite so blatant has happened yet in the United States, but we already have similar laws on the books. In California, for instance, a bawdy house is defined as a place resorted to for "purposes of prostitution *or lewdness*" (my emphasis). There is also a clause which prohibits keeping a house "for purposes of assignation." Given the current sexual climate in the United States, where Congress has just allocated some twenty million dollars to promote teenage chastity, it does not seem farfetched to imagine people here getting arrested for having assignations in their own living rooms. It takes even less foresight to predict that the next few years will see a rash of morality campaigns to exterminate vulnerable sexual populations. There are many signs that s/m is on the verge of becoming a direct target of such a campaign.

Police already harass the institutions of the leather community with a great deal of impunity. Within the last five years, the vice squad and the Alcoholic Beverage Commission (ABC) have either warned, raided, brought suspension proceedings against, or revoked the licenses of virtually every leather bar in San Francisco. Since 1970 no other group of gay bars, let alone heterosexual drinking establishments, has faced anything like this kind of concerted enforcement of the liquor laws. This unrelenting harassment of the leather bars has not raised a peep of protest from the rest of the city's gay community. In fact, from reading the local gay press, it would be difficult to even know that it was taking place. By contrast, when mainstream gay institutions like the Jaguar bookstore have been hassled, both press coverage and gay community support have been extensive.[6]

Meanwhile, the straight media have discovered that they can bait homosexuals, smear sadomasochists, and increase their circulation or ratings all at once. The infamous CBS "documentary" *Gay Power, Gay Politics* used s/m to question the credibility of gay political aspirations. The program implied that if gay people are allowed to acquire significant political power, s/m will be rampant, and people will be killed doing it. This analysis rested on three completely phony connections.

The program gave the false impression that s/m is especially prevalent in San Francisco, and that this high level of s/m activity results from gay political clout. The New York-based reporters failed to mention that almost every major city has an s/m population, that San Francisco's is not particularly large, and that s/m institutions are more numerous and developed in New York, a city that has failed to pass a gay-rights ordinance, than in San Francisco, which has.

Second, the program gave the false impression that s/m is a specifically gay (male) practice. The reporters failed to mention that most sadomasochists are heterosexual and that most gay men do not practice s/m. In fact, most of the s/m section of the program was filmed at the Chateau, a heterosexually oriented establishment.

Third, s/m was presented as a dangerous and often lethal activity. Most of the evidence for this assertion consisted of the reporter, George Crile, asking leading questions in order to get his interviewees to confirm his prejudices.[7] At one point, Crile told a story about a place "where they have a gynecological table . . . with a doctor and a nurse on hand to sew people up."[8] There is no such place in San Francisco, although there are certainly people who do have sex on surplus hospital equipment, and some establishments have physicians on call. This is a responsible attitude, since health problems can occur during sexual activities, just as they can during sports events, academic lectures, or at the opera. Yet it was presented in a completely sinister light.

Crile interviewed Dr. Boyd Stephens, the San Francisco coroner, who estimated that 10 percent of the homicides in San Francisco were gay related and that some were s/m related. Dr. Stephens later told the reporter Randy Alfred that the 10 percent figure included the killing of homosexuals by heterosexuals. Alfred points out that this percentage is about the same, or less than, the percentage of homosexuals in the population of San Francisco.[9] On another occasion, Dr. Stephens estimated that about 10 percent of the city's homicides were *sex* related (given the amount of sex which takes place, it would appear to have a remarkable safety record). Yet the coroner has been widely misquoted (in *Time* magazine, *Peoria Journal Star*, and several different times in the *San Francisco Chronicle*) as the source of a completely fabricated statistic that 10 percent of San Francisco's homicides are related to s/m.

After *Gay Power, Gay Politics* was aired, KPIX, the local CBS affiliate, presented a panel of local gay figures to respond. Most of them were successfully baited on the issue of s/m, hastening to disassociate themselves from it without challenging the distorted picture of s/m itself. Harry Britt, gay member of the board of supervisors, was the only panelist who criticized the coverage of s/m as well as the coverage of homosexuality. The CBS special has been widely censured for its reporting on homosexuality. But its coverage of s/m has escaped scrutiny and has set a new low standard for the treatment of s/m in the media.

In March 1981, KPIX ran a four-part series on s/m on the 11 o'clock news. Called *Love and Pain*, the series used sensational, unsubstantiated claims, and a half-digested version of the antiporn movement's analysis to present s/m as a public menace. The program repeatedly equated s/m with violence, called sex toys dangerous weapons, and made a wild claim that the city's emergency rooms were inundated with injuries caused by s/m activity.

Injuries and accidents do occur in the course of sexual activity, and s/m is not exempt. But by and large, s/m, particularly when practiced by people in touch with s/m communities, has a safety record most sports teams would envy. Among the people I know, there are more health problems caused by softball or long-distance running than by whipping, bondage, or fist-fucking. The s/m community is obsessed with safety and has an elaborate folk technology of methods to maximize sensation and minimize danger. These techniques are transmitted largely by older or more experienced members to neophytes. s/m oppression renders this transmission difficult. Scaring people away from the community puts people in some real danger of trying things they do not know how to do.

A point of competition among tops, sadists, dominants, Mistresses, and Masters is over who is the safest (as well as the hottest, the most imaginative, and the most proficient). People who do not play safely—tops who get too drunk, bottoms who are too reckless—are identified, and others are warned of them. Reputations in a small, gossip-ridden community are always fragile, so there is in fact a good deal of social control over patterns of play. People who are scared into viewing this community as dangerous are outside the protections it actually affords.

No community can completely protect its members from accidents or from people who are, for whatever reason, actually violent or dangerous. The s/m community has its fair share of sociopaths and criminals, just like any other. It is just as concerned that they be apprehended and put out of commission. But far more people end up in the hospital as a result of playing sports, driving cars, or being pregnant than from having s/m sex. One of the biggest sources of injury in San Francisco right now is queer-bashing, fed in part by anti-s/m hysteria. One of the worst things that I have heard of happening to an s/m person occurred when a gay man who was leaving a leather bar was assaulted by a gang of bashers. He suffered serious head injuries and the loss of an eye.

The idea that s/m is dangerous is self-perpetuating. A friend of mine died recently. He had a heart attack while he was having sex in his lovingly built playroom. When the police saw the s/m equipment they threatened to charge his lover with manslaughter. They notified the press, which aired lurid stories of "ritual sadomasochistic death." When the death was ruled accidental, the stories were quietly pulled, but no retraction or follow-up appeared to correct the lingering impression that s/m had caused the death. When men have coronaries while fornicating with their wives, the papers do not print stories implying that intercourse leads to death. Nor are their widows threatened with criminal charges. The only reason to link my friend's death to his sexual orientation was the preconception that s/m leads to death. That preconception generated the news stories. The news stories reinforced the preconception. Many people will have their prejudices about s/m corroborated by these ill-conceived "news" reports.

Besides promulgating the idea that s/m is dangerous to its practitioners, the KPIX program also alleged that s/m is harmful to those who do not do it. The program argued that s/m imagery in the media is a kind of miasma from which no one can escape. Therefore, s/m was "corroding the fabric of society," it was affecting everyone, and something ought to be done about it. Historically, crackdowns on activities which primarily affect those who are involved in them are rationalized on the basis of some similarly flimsy connection with social decay. Notions that marijuana, prostitution, or homosexuality by some vague mechanism lead to violent crime, disease, or creeping communism are used to rationalize punitive social or legal action against otherwise innocuous activities.

Love and Pain did not call for new laws to make s/m activity criminal. But the reporter, Gregg Risch, did propose that parents who do s/m be relieved of the custody of their children. The program did a whole segment on a woman who is living with her lover and her two-year-old child in a rural s/m community in Mendocino County. The reporter interviewed the child's grandmother, who was horrified and wanted to take the child. He also interviewed a therapist who pontificated that the child might be damaged by exposure to its mother's sexual orientation. He called for the Mendocino County authorities to come in and take the kid away from its mother.

Custody law is one of the places where sex dissenters of all sorts are viciously punished for being different. Lesbians and gay men are not the only groups whose rights to keep or raise offspring are drastically limited. The state may come in and snatch the children of prostitutes, swingers, or even "promiscuous" women. Society has a great deal of power to insure that sex dissenters are separated from young people, including their own children as well as the next generation of sex perverts. A rough rule of sexual sociology is that the more stigmatized the sexuality, the higher the barriers are to finding one's way into that community, and the older people are when they finally get over them.

Risch expressed great dismay that so many s/m people were of child-rearing age. All that this means is that the s/m community is full of adults—hardly cause for alarm. He did concede that s/m people might be allowed to keep their children if they were careful to hide their sexuality from them. But he felt that out-of-the-closet sadomasochists should relinquish their offspring. One of the functions of custody law and practice is to reproduce conventional values. When lesbian mothers are granted custody on the condition that they do not live with their lovers, when swingers are forbidden to swing, when s/m people are required to hide, it is clear that sex dissenters are being denied the right to raise their children according to their value systems. This insures that even if perverts have and keep their children, those kids will be inculcated with the dominant social mythology about sex.

In the wake of both *Gay Power, Gay Politics* and *Love and Pain*, local news coverage of s/m has gotten worse. Less than two weeks after the KPIX series, the *San Francisco Chronicle* reported that the coroner had been conducting workshops on s/m safety, and that there was an "alarming increase in injuries and deaths from sado-masochistic sex."[10] Again, the phony statistic was quoted that 10 percent of the city's homicides were s/m related. Dr. Stephens, the coroner, is currently suing the paper for libel. Aside from the inaccuracies of the article, it is true that the coroner has displayed a remarkable professionalism in dealing with the minority sexual populations of San Francisco. He has taken the trouble to learn about these communities, has displayed good judgment in dealing with them, and has earned their respect. For his trouble and his professionalism, he was given harsh treatment in the press and was chastised by Mayor Feinstein, who was quoted as saying, "It is my belief that s&m is dangerous to society and I'm not eager to have it attracted to San Francisco."[11]

In July of 1981, a major fire burned a large area south of Market Street, and press coverage was entirely sensational. The fire started on the site of a former gay and leather oriented bathhouse, the Folsom Street Barracks. The Barracks has been closed for years and the building was being remodeled as a hotel. But the press reported that the fire started in a "gay bathhouse." The burned area is in the midst of the leather bars, so many gay men and s/m people lived in the vicinity. But the neighborhood is mixed. There were old people, artists, Filipinos, and a good assortment of low-income families living there. The largest single group of fire victims consisted of over twenty displaced children. Yet the media portrayed the fire as a gay and s/m event, as if the sexual orientation of some of the victims had somehow caused it.

One of the buildings that burned belonged to a man who manufactures Rush, a brand of poppers. The fire department suspected that Rush had caused or fed the fire and was searching for large quantities of it. No Rush was ever found. The fire department also hypothesized that since s/m people were known to live on the alley, that there might be bodies of slaves chained to their beds in the rubble. No bodies were ever found.

Media coverage of the fire promulgated the image that masochists are completely helpless, that they spend their time chained in their quarters, and that in the event of an emergency, they are simply abandoned by their callous keepers. Buried far back in the news reports on the third day were comments by neighborhood residents, who pointed out that if anyone had been in bondage when the fire broke out, their lover or trick or friend would have done everything to save them. If a parent fails to save a child caught in a fire, no one assumes that the family caused the death. Had anyone been accidentally burned anywhere in proximity to s/m equipment or space, the tragedy would have been interpreted as sinister evidence that s/m people are inhuman monsters. Coverage of the fire was premised on the idea that s/m people do not care about one another. The straight media simply did not report on the human dimensions of a great community crisis.[12]

The papers did not mention, for instance, that the initial relief effort was run out of the Folsom Street Hotel, a fuck palace catering to the gay male leather community. They did not report that the Hothouse, a leather-oriented bathhouse, immediately held a benefit for the victims. No whisper hit the papers that every South of Market bar and bath contributed some kind of aid and that all the leather bars became drop-off points for donations of food, clothing, and equipment for the fire victims, gay and straight. The *Chronicle* ran a picture of a burned-out s/m playroom next to the story about how there might be dead slaves lying in the ruins. It did not report that an auction of used jockstraps was held at the Gold Coast, a leather bar, to raise money for the homeless.

All of this slanted media coverage is constructing a new demonization of s/m and probably heralds a campaign to clean it up. It is very similar to what happened to homosexuals in the 1950s. There were already plenty of antigay ideas, structures, and practices. But during a decade of headlines, arrests, investigations, and legislation, those preexisting elements of homophobia were reconstituted into a new and more virulent ideology that homosexuality was an active menace which needed to be actively combated. Currently, there are already plenty of anti-s/m ideas, structures, and practices, and they are being drawn into the creation of a new ideological construct that will call for a more active extermination campaign against s/m. It is likely that many sadomasochists will be arrested and incarcerated for such heinous thought crimes as wanting to be tied up when they come.

The form such campaigns often take is that police use old laws, as they have done in Canada, to make a few spectacular arrests. The media cover the arrests the way they covered the fire, or my friend's death, and turn tragedy into an excuse to further harass the victims and their community. At some point, there will be an outcry for new laws to give police more power to deal with and control the "menace." These new laws will give police more summary powers against the target population and will lead to more arrests, more headlines, and more laws, until either the s/m community finds a way to stop the onslaught or until the repression runs out of steam.

Already, in the wake of the fire, a San Francisco supervisor considered introducing legislation to ban the sale of s/M equipment in the city. Many "feminist" antiporn groups would support legislation against s/M material on other grounds. If our reading material and sexual technology were contraband, our community could be decimated by the police. And this kind of campaign, like those against homosexuals thirty years ago, will be seen as a hygienic measure, supported by conservatives and radicals alike. It will scapegoat a bunch of people whose only crime is exotic sexual tastes. And while all of this has been taking shape, what has the women's movement been doing? Why, it has been conducting a purge against its own rather tiny s/M population. The rhetoric of this purge is what most feminists think of as the "politics of s/M."

II

Homosexuality is a response—consciously or not—to a male supremacist society. Because it is a response to oppressive institutions and oppressive relationships it is not necessarily a progressive response or one that challenges the power of the monopoly capitalist. We see that the pressures that capitalist society puts on each individual are tremendous. . . . Today people are grasping at all kinds of straws, at exotic religious sects, mysticism, sex orgies, Trotskyism, etc.

—**Revolutionary Union,** *On Homosexuality*[13]

While gay people can be anti-imperialists we feel that they cannot be Communists. To be a Communist, we must accept and welcome struggle in all facets of our lives, personal as well as political. We cannot struggle with male supremacy in the factory and not struggle at home. We feel that the best way to struggle out such contradictions in our personal lives is in stable monogamous relations between men and women. . . . Because homosexuals do not carry the struggle between men and women into their most personal relationships, they are not prepared, in principle, for the arduous task of class transformation.

—**Revolutionary Union,** *On Homosexuality*

I see sadomasochism as resulting in part from the internalization of heterosexual dominant-submissive role playing. I see sadomasochism among lesbians as involving in addition an internalization of the homophobic heterosexual view of lesbians. Defending such behavior as healthy and compatible

with feminism, even proselytizing in favor of it is about the most contra-feminist antipolitical and bourgeois stance that I can imagine.
—**Diana Russell,** "Sadomasochism as a Contra-feminist Activity"

Sadomasochistic activity between/among lesbians is an outcome and perpetuation of patriarchal sadistic and masochistic culture.
—**ry,** "S/M Keeps Lesbians Bound to the Patriarchy"

The fact is, the whole culture is S/M, we're all sadomasochists. The people in SAMOIS, or gay people who wear leather, have a more severe form of the disease.
—**Susan Griffin**[14]

SAMOIS is entitled to exist as a group devoted to S/M, but why should we let them get away with calling themselves lesbian-feminist?
—**tacie dejanikus,** "Our Legacy"

The first time I came out was over a decade ago, when I realized, at the age of twenty, that I was a lesbian. I had to come out again, several years later, as a sadomasochist. The similarities and differences between these two experiences have been most instructive. On both occasions, I spent several months think-ing that I must be the only one on earth, and was pleasantly surprised to dis-cover there were large numbers of women who shared my predilections. Both debuts were fraught with tension and excitement. But the second coming out was considerably more difficult than the first.

I came out as a lesbian just when a bad discourse on homosexuality, the product of the antigay wars of the 1950s, was coming apart. I did not experi-ence the full force of homophobia. On the contrary, to be a baby dyke in 1970 was to feel great moral self-confidence. One could luxuriate in the knowledge that not only was one not a slimy pervert, but one's sexuality was especially blessed on political grounds. As a result, I never quite understood the experi-ence of being gay in the face of unrelenting contempt.

When I came out as an s/m person, I got an unexpected lesson in how my gay ancestors must have felt. My youth as a sadomasochist has been spent at a time when, as part of a more general reconsolidation of antisex and anti-gay ideology, a new demonization of s/m is taking shape. This is happening in the society at large and in the women's movement. Watching the images of your love turning uglier by the day, fearing arrest, and wondering how bad things will get seems a long way from 1970. It is especially depressing if a once-progressive movement in which you have spent your entire adult life is leading the assault. The experience of being a feminist sadomasochist in 1980 is similar to that of being a communist homosexual in 1950. When left ideology condemned homosexuality as bourgeois decadence, many homosexuals were forced out of progressive political organizations. A few of them founded the Mattachine Society. Now that large parts of the feminist movement have similarly defined s/m as an evil product of patriarchy, it has become increasingly difficult for those of us who are s/m-practicing feminists to maintain our membership in the women's community.

Some feminist bookstores have refused to carry Samois publications or books having a positive attitude toward s/m.[15] Some stores which do carry such material have it shelved obscurely, or have put up cards warning customers against the contents. One store has even prepared packets of anti-s/m readings which are included with any purchase of pro-s/m books. "Sadomasochistic" is routinely used as an epithet. A group is putting out a book called *Against Sadomasochism*, the advertising for which has promised a response to the "threat" posed by the existence of Samois. The flyer for the book expresses horror that some of us have actually been "invited speakers at university classes" and that there has been an effort to "normalize sadomasochism."

I used to read the feminist press with enthusiasm. Now I dread each new issue of my favorite periodicals, wondering what vile picture of my sexuality will appear this month. Papers and journals are reluctant to print pro-s/m articles, and usually only do so if accompanied by reams of disclaimer and at least one anti-s/m essay. However, essays that trash s/m are not held over until the magazine can solicit a positive viewpoint.

Recently the Board of the Women's Building in San Francisco decided that Samois cannot rent space there. Among the stated purposes of the building are a commitment to end oppression based on sexual orientation and a promise to respect the diversity of individual women. The Women's Building has a very open policy. Mixed groups, men's groups, community groups, nonfeminist groups, and private parties regularly rent space. The building has frequently rented space for weddings. It is a sad commentary on the state of feminism that heterosexual weddings, sanctioned by religion and enforced by the state, are less controversial than the activities of a bunch of lesbian sex perverts.[16]

In 1980, the National Organization of Women passed a misleadingly labeled resolution of "lesbian and gay rights." What this resolution actually did was condemn s/m, cross-generational sex, pornography, and public sex. The resolution denied that these were issues of sexual or affectional preference and declared now's intention to disassociate itself from any gay or lesbian group that did not accept these definitions of sexual preference. When there was an attempt ten years ago to purge NOW of lesbian members, NOW was not stampeded into denying the legitimacy of gay rights. The campaign against the leather menace has succeeded where the attack on the lavender menace failed. It has put NOW on record as opposing sexual freedom and the civil rights of erotic minorities.[17]

There are many reasons why s/m has become such a bête noire in the women's movement, and most originate outside of feminism. With the glaring exception of monogamous lesbianism, the women's movement usually reflects society's prevailing sexual prejudices. Feminists have no monopoly on anti-s/m attitudes. The medical and psychiatric establishments have moved somewhat on homosexuality, but on virtually every other sexual variation they hold barely modified nineteenth-century views. The psychiatric theories of sex in turn reflect the sexual hierarchies which exist in society. Another general rule of sexual sociology is that the more persecuted a sexuality, the worse its reputation.

A second force for which the women's movement is not responsible is the state of sex research and sex education. While the movement has a lamentable tendency to adopt some of the worst elements of sex research, the field as a whole is underdeveloped. Sex is so loaded and controversial in Western culture that research on it is loaded and controversial. Sex research is inscribed within the power relations that organize sexual behavior. Challenging those power relations with new data or original hypotheses brings one into conflict with deeply held folk theories of sex.

The sex field also reflects its marginality. Whereas almost every institution of higher learning has a department of psychology, there are virtually no departments of sexology. There are fewer than a dozen academic sites in the United States where sex research is conducted. There are few courses taught on sex at the college level, and pre-college sex education is still tenuous. Knowledge of sex is restricted. Getting into the Institute for Sex Research is like getting into Fort Knox.[18] Almost every library has its sexual materials in a locked case, or in a special collection, or oddly catalogued. The younger one is, the harder it is to access information about sex. The systematic restraints on curiosity about sex maintain sexual ignorance, and where people are ignorant, they are manipulable.

There are other reasons for the controversy over s/m which are more intrinsic to the women's movement and its history. One of these is the confusion between sexual orientation and political belief, which originated in the idea that feminism is the theory, lesbianism is the practice. There are elements of truth in the idea that being a lesbian brings one into conflict with some basic elements of gender hierarchy. But like many good ideas, this insight has been overused and overapplied. It has made it difficult to accept that there are heterosexuals who are feminists, and that there are lesbians who are not. It has actually inhibited the development of lesbian politics and consciousness. It has led to the belief that lesbianism is only justified politically insofar as it is feminist. This in turn has encouraged feminist lesbians to look down on non-movement dykes. It has led feminist lesbians to identify more with the feminist movement than with the lesbian community. It has encouraged many women who are not sexually attracted to women to consider themselves lesbians. It has prevented the lesbian movement from asserting that our lust for women is justified whether or not it derives from feminist political ideology. It has generated a lesbian politic that seems ashamed of lesbian desire and made feminism into a closet in which lesbian sexuality is unacknowledged.[19]

If feminist politics entail or require particular sexual positions or forms of erotic behavior, then it follows that other kinds of sexual activity are specifically antifeminist. Given prevailing ideas of appropriate feminist sexual behavior, s/m appears to be the mirror opposite. It is dark and polarized, extreme and ritualized, and above all, it celebrates difference and power. If s/m is understood as the dark opposite of happy and healthy lesbianism, accepting that happy and healthy lesbians also do s/m would threaten the logic of the belief system from which this opposition was generated. But this analysis is not based on the realities of sexual behavior. It is predicated on a limited notion of the symbolic valences of both lesbianism and s/m. Torn from real social context, sexual differences can symbolize all kinds of other differences, including political ones. Thus, to some people, homosexuality is fascist, and to others it is communist. Lesbianism has been understood as narcissism and self-worship, or as an inevitably unfulfilled yearning. To many right-wingers, gayness in any form symbolizes the decline and fall of empires.

There is nothing inherently feminist or nonfeminist about s/m. Sadomasochists, like lesbians, gay men, heterosexuals, and so on, may be anarchists, fascists, Democrats, Republicans, communists, feminists, gay liberationists, or sexual reactionaries. The idea that there is an automatic correspondence between sexual preference and political belief is long overdue to be jettisoned.

This does not mean that sexual behavior should not be evaluated. How people treat each other in sexual contexts is important. But this is not the same issue as passing judgment on what are essentially cultural differences in sexual behavior. There are plenty of lesbian relationships which are long term and monogamous, in which both partners switch roles or do the same thing, in which all touching is gentle, but in which the partners are mean and nasty to each other in their daily lives. The idea that lesbianism, especially when practiced by feminists, is a superior form of sex often leads people to ignore actual interpersonal dynamics. Conversely, the idea that s/m is intrinsically warped leads to an inability to perceive love, friendship, and affection among s/m people. s/m partners may occupy polarized roles, the touching may be rough, and yet they may treat each other with respect and affection. In all sexualities, there is a range of how people act toward one another. Ranking different sexualities from best to worst simply substitutes for exercising judgment about specific situations.

The ease with which s/m has come to symbolize the feminist equivalent of the Anti-Christ has been exacerbated by some long-term changes in feminist ideology. Few women in the movement seem to realize that what currently passes for radical feminism has a tangential relationship with the initial premises of the women's movement. Assumptions which now pass as dogma would have horrified activists in 1970. In many respects the women's movement, like the society at large, has quietly shifted to the right.

Feminists in 1970 were angry because women, the things women did, and female personality traits were devalued. But we were also enraged at the restrictions placed on female behavior. Women were not supposed to engage in a range of activities considered masculine. A woman who wanted to fix cars, get laid, ride a motorcycle, play sports, or get a Ph.D. could expect criticism from the society and support from the women's movement. The term *male identified* meant that a woman lacked consciousness of female oppression.

By 1980, the term *male identified* had lost that meaning (lack of political consciousness) and became synonymous with "masculine." Now women who do masculine things are accused of imitating men not only by family, church, and the media, but by the feminist movement.[20] Much contemporary feminist ideology maintains that everything female—persons, activities, values, personality characteristics—is good, whereas anything pertaining to males is bad. By this analysis, the task of feminism is to replace male values with female ones, to substitute female culture for male culture. This line of thinking does not encourage women to try to gain access to male activities, privileges, and territories. Instead, it implies that a good feminist wants nothing to do with "male" activities. All of this celebration of femininity tends to reinforce traditional gender roles and values of appropriate female behavior. It is not all that different from the sex-role segregation against which early feminists revolted. I, for one, did not join the women's movement to be told how to be a good girl. There are many labels for this brand of feminism, but my preferred term is *femininism*.[21]

Femininism has become especially powerful with regard to issues of sexuality and issues of violence, which it not surprisingly links together. Sexuality is seen as a male value and activity. The femininist view of sex is that it is something that good/nice women do not especially like. In this view, sex is not a motivating force in female behavior. Women have sex as an expression of intimacy, but orgasm is seen as a male goal. The idea that sexuality is most often something men impose upon women leads to the equation of sex with violence, and the conflation of sex with rape. These were the sexual theories I was taught growing up. I never expected to have them rammed down my throat by the women's movement. Man the Id and Woman the Chaste are Victorian ideas, not feminist ones.[22]

The re-emphasis on feminine values, especially sexual chastity, has led to a shift in the mode of argument for feminist goals. Instead of arguing for justice or social equality, much feminist polemic now claims a female moral superiority. It is argued that we should have more, or total, power in society because we are more equipped for it, mainly by virtue of our role in reproduction, than men. I did not join the women's movement to have my status depend on my ability to bear children.

I fear that the women's movement is repeating the worst errors of a century ago. The nineteenth-century feminist movement began as a radical critique of women's role and status. But it became increasingly conservative and similarly shifted the burden of its argument onto a reconstituted femininity in the form of alleged female moral superiority. Much of the nineteenth-century movement degenerated into a variety of morality crusades, with conservative feminists pursuing what they took to be women's agenda in antiprostitution, anti-masturbation, anti-obscenity, and anti-vice campaigns. It will be a historical tragedy of almost unthinkable dimensions if the revived feminist movement dissipates into a series of campaigns against recreational sex, popular music, and sexually explicit materials. But this appears to be the direction in which feminism is moving.[23]

By a series of accidents, and through the mediating issue of pornography, s/m has become a challenge to this entire political tendency, which has ridden to power by manipulating women's fears around sex and violence. Therefore, when feminists argue about s/m, there is much more at stake than sexual practice. Some women are arguing for the logical coherence of their political beliefs. Others of us are arguing that political theory about sex is due for a major overhaul based on a more sophisticated sociology of sex. But what often seems most at stake is the shape of feminist ideology and the future direction of the movement. There are ways of understanding s/m which are compatible with "femininism" and its attendant political programs. When these become more articulated (and they will in the not too distant future), s/m will seem to be less of a threat to the hegemonic ideology of the women's movement. But for now, the fight over s/m has been the locus of a struggle over deep political differences in the women's movement.

Given the immense symbolic load that s/m has acquired, it is not surprising that it is difficult for participants in this debate to absorb information about s/m that would undermine the assumptions upon which certain genres of feminist theory, ideology, and politics are built. Nevertheless, the picture of s/m which is assumed in the current diatribes has almost no relationship to the actual experience of anyone involved in it.

III

> For "consent" to be a meaningful criteria all the parties involved must have some measure of real choices. Women, for instance, have been "consenting" to marriage for centuries. Women in China had "consented" to the footbinding of their own daughters. This is coerced-consent, and it hardly constitutes freedom. The most "heavy" masochist, who gives his hands and feet to be shackled to some rack, who offers his body to be gang-banged, fist-fucked, and pissed upon—he "consents," but if he has so internalized society's hatred of him as to offer his own body for a beating, then his "consent" is merely a conditioned reflex.
> —**Neil Glickman,** "Letter to the Editor," *Gay Community News*,
> 22 August 1981

Coming out has several meanings. Sometimes it refers to the point at which people realize that they are gay or have some other variant sexuality. Coming out in this sense is a form of self-recognition. Another meaning of coming out is that of public declaration, a willingness to let other people know about it. In yet another sense, coming out is a kind of journey people take from the straight world where they begin, into the gay or other variant world they want to occupy. Most of us are born into and raised by straight families, educated in straight schools, and socialized by straight peer groups. Our upbringing does not provide us with the social skills, information, or routes of access into nonconventional sexual lifestyles. We must find our way into those social spaces where we can meet partners, find friends, get validation, and participate in a community life which does not presuppose that we are straight. Sometimes this journey is fairly short, from the suburbs of large cities to the gay bars downtown. In small towns, it usually means finding an underground network or building a more public community. Often it means migrating from middle America to a bigger city such as New York, Los Angeles, Chicago, or San Francisco. A classic account of this kind of coming out is the fifties pulp novel *I Am a Woman*.[24] Laura, the heroine, suffers vague malaise in the Midwest, so she takes a bus to New York City. Eventually, she stumbles into a lesbian bar in Greenwich Village. She instantly realizes who she is, that there are others like her, and that this is home. She finds a lover, develops a gay identity, and becomes an adult, functioning lesbian.

This kind of migratory behavior is characteristic of sexual minorities. There are many barriers to the process. These include the marginality of dissenting sexual communities, the amount of legal apparatus built to control them, the social penalties to which their members are subject, and the unrelenting propaganda that portrays them as dangerous, sleazy, horrid places full of dreadful people and unspecified pitfalls. It is extraordinary that young perverts, like salmon swimming upstream, continually and in great numbers make this journey. Much of the politics of sex consists of battles to determine the costs of belonging to such communities and how difficult it will be to get into them.

I came out as a lesbian in a small college town that had no visible lesbian community. A group of us formed a radical lesbian feminist group which eventually grew into a fairly large, albeit young, public lesbian community. The nearest pre-movement lesbian community was thirty miles away, where there were actually a couple of lesbian bars. But locally, there was one mostly male gay bar, called the Flame. For years, I had heard that it was the kind of place you wanted to stay away from. There were vague implications that if you went there, something bad would happen. But it was the only gay bar in town, and I was drawn to it. I finally screwed up my courage and walked in. The minute I got past the front door I relaxed. It was full of very innocuous looking gay men and a couple of lesbians. I instantly realized that these were my people, and that I was one of the people I had been warned against.

Before I walked into the Flame, I still thought that gay people were rare and scarce. Going through that door was like going through the looking glass. The other side of that taboo entrance is not a place of terror, but a huge, populous, prosperous, bustling world of homosexuals. What is most incredible about the whole experience is that so large a part of reality could have been kept so invisible to so many for so long. It is as if one grew up under the impression that there were no Italians, or Jews, or Chinese in the United States.

Seven years later, I was again sweating in front of another tabooed threshold. This time it was the door to the Pleasure Chest in New York City. I must have walked up and down Seventh Avenue twenty times before I finally got a friend to go in with me. It took a little longer to get used to the s/m world than to the gay world. But now I feel as at home in leather bars and sex-toy shops as I do in lesbian bars and gay restaurants. Instead of the monsters and slimy perverts I had been led to expect, I found another hidden community. The s/m community is not as large as the gay community, but it is complex, populated, and quite civilized. Most parts of the s/m community take a responsible attitude to newcomers, teaching them how to do s/m safely, s/m etiquette, and acquired wisdom. Preconceived chimeras disappear in the face of actual social practice. I had been worried that my eroticism would require that I give up control over my life or become some kind of mindless nebbish. One of the first lessons I learned was that you can do s/m by agreement *and* it can still be a turn-on. There is a lot of separation between the straight, gay, and lesbian s/m communities. But there is also pan-s/m consciousness. As one wise woman who has been doing this for many years has said, "Leather is thicker than blood."

The largest subpopulation of sadomasochists is the heterosexuals. Of these, most appear to be male submissive/female dominant. Much of the straight s/m world revolves around professional female dominants and their submissive clients. There are also some straight or predominantly straight social clubs and political organizations through which heterosexual sadomasochists can meet one another. In the last few years, the straight s/m community in New York City began to have regular nights at a bar. And even more recently, an s/m sex club opened which has a predominantly heterosexual clientele.

I should point out that contrary to much of what is said about straight s/m in the feminist press, heterosexual s/m is *not* standard heterosexuality. Straight s/m is stigmatized and persecuted. Whatever the metaphoric similarities between standard sex and s/m, once someone starts to use whips, ropes, and all the associated theater, they are considered to be perverts, not normal. The relationship between heterosexual s/m and "normal" heterosexuality is at most like the relationship between high-school faggots and the high-school football team. There is some overlap of personnel, but for the most part, all that fanny-patting and even an occasional blow-job does not make the jocks into fags. And the former would often rather beat up the latter than accompany them to the nearest gay bar.

Gay male sadomasochists are less numerous than heterosexual ones, but they are much better organized. Gay men have developed an elaborate technology for building public institutions for sexual outlaws. When the gay male leather community emerged, it followed the organizational patterns of the larger homosexual community, in which bars and baths are central institutions. The first gay male leather bar opened in New York around 1955. The first one in San Francisco opened about five years later. There was a population explosion of leather bars along with gay bars in general (including lesbian bars) around 1970. In San Francisco today, there are five to ten leather bars and about five baths or sex clubs that cater to the gay male leather community. There are also several social or charitable organizations, motorcycle clubs, a performance space, assorted shops, and a couple of restaurants for the South of Market crowd. Although leather styles were faddish in the larger gay community for a couple of years, and leather/macho has replaced drag queen fluff as the dominant gay stereotype, the leather community is a distinct subgroup. The average gay man is not into leather or s/M. But the average gay man is probably more aware of sexual diversity and erotic possibilities than most heterosexuals or lesbians.

Lesbian social organization is smaller in scale but institutionally similar to gay male. Bars have been for many years the most important public lesbian community space. Since 1970, feminist political organizations and cultural institutions have provided another major context for lesbian social life. Unlike gay men, lesbians have not yet developed more specialized sexual subgroups. There are lesbians who do everything that gay men and heterosexuals do. There are girl-lovers, sadomasochists, and fetishists (probably for flannel shirts, hiking boots, cats, softball uniforms, alfalfa sprouts, and feminist tracts). There are many transvestites and transsexuals (especially female to male). But lesbian sexual diversity is relatively unnoticed, unconscious, and unorganized.

When I came out as a lesbian sadomasochist there was no place to go. A notice I put up in my local feminist bookstore was torn down. It took months of painstaking detective work to track down other women who were into s/M. There was no public lesbian s/M community to find, so I had to help build one. At least in San Francisco, there is now a visible, accessible avenue for lesbians to find their way into an s/M context. Samois is a motley collection. We have lots of refugees from Lesbian Nation, a good number of bar dykes, and many women who work in the sex industry. It is clear in retrospect that what has happened in the last three years or so is another mass coming out. There are probably now about as many sadomasochists in most lesbian communities as there were radical feminist lesbians in 1970. There would be groups like Samois in virtually every lesbian community in the United States if the costs of coming out were not so excruciating. It takes someone willing to put out the word and serve as a focus for other dyke perverts to start coming out of the woodwork.

But most women have watched Samois get trashed and are afraid to be treated the same way.

The s/m community is more underground and harder to find than the lesbian community and its routes of access are even more hidden. The aura of terror is more intense. The social penalties, the stigma, and the lack of legitimacy are greater. I have rarely worked so hard or displayed such independence of mind as when I came out as an s/m person. I had to reject virtually everything I had been told about it. Having struggled this hard to assume a stigmatized identity (one "they taught me to despise"), I find the idea that I have been brainwashed infuriating and ludicrous. A sadist is likely to be regarded as a dangerous character. A top is vulnerable to legal prosecution. In the current debate on s/m, a top risks having his or her testimony dismissed. A masochist has more credibility in defending s/m, but risks being held in contempt. I am in much less danger of being treated badly by tops or sadists than by the people who want to protect me from them.

It is an unfortunate habit of sexual thought that people so readily assume that something they would not like would be equally unpleasant to someone else. I hate to run. I might someday change my mind, but at this point it would take a lot of coercion to get me to run around the block, let alone for five miles. This does not mean that my friends who run in marathons are sick, brainwashed, or at gunpoint.

People who are not into anal sex find it incomprehensible that anyone else could enjoy it. People who gag at the thought of oral sex are baffled that anyone else would actually relish sucking cock or eating pussy. But the fact remains that there are uncountable hordes for whom oral sex or anal sex are exquisitely delightful. Sexual diversity exists, not everyone likes to do the same things, and people who have different sexual preferences are not sick, stupid, warped, brainwashed, under duress, dupes of the patriarchy, products of bourgeois decadence, or refugees from bad child-rearing practices. The habit of explaining away sexual variation by putting it down needs to be broken.

The idea that masochists are victims of sadists underlies much of the debate on s/m. But tops and bottoms are not two discrete populations. Some individuals have strong and consistent preferences for one role or the other. Most s/m people have done both, and many change with different partners, at different times, or according to situation or whim.

Nor are the social relations between tops and bottoms similar to the social relations between men and women, blacks and whites, straights and queers. Sadists do not systematically oppress masochists. Of course, class privilege, race, and gender do not disappear when people enter the s/m world. The social power individuals bring to the s/m community affects their ability to negotiate within it, whether as tops or bottoms. But class, race, and gender neither determine nor correspond to the roles adopted for s/m play. The most frequent oppressions connected to s/m come from a society bent on keeping people from engaging in nonconventional sex and which punishes them when they do.

The silliest arguments about s/m have been those which claim that it is impossible that people really consent to do it. The issue of consent has been clouded by an overly hasty application of Marxian critiques of bourgeois contract theory to sex law and practice. Marxists argue that just because someone voluntarily enters into an agreement to do something, does not mean that they have not been coerced by forces impinging on the decision. This is a useful distinction since social relations of class, gender, race, and so forth in fact do limit the scope of possible decisions which can be made. So do the social relations of sexuality, but not by forcing people to be perverts.

While the word is the same, the meanings of consent in sex law are distinct from those involved in critiques of contract theory. In sex law, consent is what distinguishes sex from rape. But consent is a privilege which is not enjoyed equally by all sexualities. Although it varies according to state, most sexual activity is illegal. The fewest restrictions apply to adult heterosexuality. But adult incest is illegal in most states, and adultery is still a felony in many. In some states, sodomy laws even apply to heterosexuals, who may be prosecuted for oral or anal sex. Homosexuality is much more restricted than heterosexuality. Except for the states which have passed consenting adult statutes decriminalizing homosexuality, it is still illegal to have gay sex. Before 1976, a gay person in California did not have the legal right to have oral sex with his or her lover, and could be prosecuted for doing it. Minors have no right at all to consent to sex, although it is usually adult partners who are prosecuted. But sexually active youth can be sent to juvenile homes and are subject to other penalties.

In addition to clearly defined legal restrictions, sex laws are unequally enforced. And in addition to the activities of police, forces like religion, medicine, media, education, family, and the state all function to pressure people to be married, heterosexual, monogamous, and conventional. One may more reasonably ask if anyone truly "consents" to be straight in any way. Coercion does occur among perverts, as it does in all sexual contexts. One still needs to distinguish rape and abuse from consensual situations. But the overwhelming coercion with regard to s/m is the way in which people are prevented from doing it. We are fighting for the freedom to consent to our sexuality without interference and without penalty.

IV

We are sworn that no boy or girl, approaching the maelstrom of deviation, need make that crossing alone, afraid, or in the dark ever again.
—The Mattachine Society, 1951[25]

Current radical (mostly feminist) writing on s/M is a hopeless muddle of bad assumptions, inaccurate information, and a thick-headed refusal to accept evidence which contravenes preconceptions. It needs to be taken apart point by point. But prejudice is like a hydra. As soon as one avenue of sexual bigotry is blocked, alternative channels are developed. Ultimately, acceptance is gained by political power as much as by rational argument. Bigotry against s/M will flourish until it is more expensive to maintain than to abandon. Like the social discourse on homosexuality, this discourse on s/M sets up phony issues and poses phony questions. At some point, we need to step out of this framework and develop an alternative way to think about sexuality and understand its politics.

Minority sexual communities are like religious heretics. We are persecuted by the state, the mental-health establishment, social-welfare agencies, and the media. When you are a sex pervert, the institutions of society do not work for you, and often work against you. Sexual dissenters face an endless stream of propaganda that rationalizes abuses against them, attempts to impair their self-esteem, and exhorts them to recant.

In addition to social hierarchies of class, race, gender, and ethnicity, there is a hierarchy based on sexual behavior. The most blessed form of sexual contact is heterosexual, married, monogamous, and reproductive. Unions that are unmarried, nonmonogamous, nonreproductive, involve more than two partners, are homosexual, or which involve kink or fetish are judged as inferior and punished accordingly. This hierarchy has rarely been challenged since its emergence, except by the gay movement. But it is a domain of social life in which great power is exercised. The "lower" sexual orders are human fodder for the prisons and the mental institutions.

It is time that radicals and progressives, feminists and leftists, recognize this hierarchy for the oppressive structure that it is instead of reproducing it within their own ideologies. Sex is one of the few areas in which cultural imperialism is taken as a radical stance. Neither the therapeutic professions, the women's movement, nor the Left have been able to digest the concept of benign sexual variation. The idea that there is one best way to do sex afflicts radical as well as conservative thought on the subject. Cultural relativism and the ability to respect diversity are not the same thing as liberalism.

One of the sad things about the current debates on sex in the women's movement is that they are so stupid and regressive. Once the impulse to purge all sex freaks from feminist organizations passes, we will still have to face more intelligent arguments. Among them will be a kind of neo-Reichian position which is pro-sex but which understands the more stigmatized sexualities and practices (pornography, s/m, fetishism) as symptoms of sexual repression. Unlike Reich, the neo-Reichian position may accept homosexuality as a healthy or natural eroticism.

What is exciting is that sex—not just gender, not just homosexuality—has finally been posed as a political question. Rethinking sexual politics has generated some of the most creative political discourse since 1970. The sexual outlaws—boy-lovers, sadomasochists, prostitutes, and transpeople, among others—have an especially rich knowledge of the prevailing system of sexual hierarchy and of how sexual controls are exercised. These populations of erotic dissidents have a great deal to contribute to the reviving radical debate on sexuality.

The real danger is not that s/m lesbians will be made uncomfortable in the women's movement. The real danger is that the Right, the religious fanatics, and the Right-controlled state will eat us all alive. It is sad to be having to fight to maintain one's membership in the women's movement when it is so imperative to create broad-based coalitions against fascism. The level of internal strife around s/m should be reserved for more genuine threats to feminist goals. If we survive long enough, feminists and other progressives will eventually stop fearing sexual diversity and begin to learn from it.

Thinking Sex / **5**

Notes for a Radical Theory of the Politics of Sexuality

The Sex Wars

Asked his advice, Dr. J. Guerin affirmed that, after all other treatments had failed, he had succeeded in curing young girls affected by the vice of onanism by burning the clitoris with a hot iron. . . ."I apply the hot point three times to each of the large labia and another on the clitoris. . . . After the first operation, from forty to fifty times a day, the number of voluptuous spasms was reduced to three or four. . . . We believe, then, that in cases similar to those submitted to your consideration, one should not hesitate to resort to the hot iron, and at an early hour, in order to combat clitoral and vaginal onanism in little girls."
—**Demetrius Zambaco,** "Onanism and Nervous Disorders in Two Little Girls"

The time has come to think about sex. To some, sexuality may seem to be an unimportant topic, a frivolous diversion from the more critical problems of poverty, war, disease, racism, famine, or nuclear annihilation. But it is precisely at times such as these, when we live with the possibility of unthinkable destruction, that people are likely to become dangerously crazy about sexuality. Contemporary conflicts over sexual values and erotic conduct have much in common with the religious disputes of earlier centuries. They acquire immense

---

Chapter 5 was originally presented at the Scholar and the Feminist 9 Conference, 24 April 1982, Barnard College, New York City; and first published in Carole S. Vance, *Pleasure and Danger: Exploring Female Sexuality* (Boston: Routledge and Kegan Paul, 1984), 267–319.

symbolic weight. Disputes over sexual behavior often become the vehicles for displacing social anxieties, and discharging their attendant emotional intensity. Consequently, sexuality should be treated with special respect in times of great social stress.

The realm of sexuality also has its own internal politics, inequities, and modes of oppression. As with other aspects of human behavior, the concrete institutional forms of sexuality at any given time and place are products of human activity. They are imbued with conflicts of interest and political maneuvering, both deliberate and incidental. In that sense, sex is always political. But there are also historical periods in which sexuality is more sharply contested and more overtly politicized. In such periods, the domain of erotic life is, in effect, renegotiated.

In England and the United States, the late nineteenth century was one such era. During that time, powerful social movements focused on "vices" of all sorts. There were educational and political campaigns to encourage chastity, to eliminate prostitution, and to discourage masturbation, especially among the young. Morality crusaders attacked obscene literature, nude paintings, music halls, abortion, birth-control information, and public dancing.[1] The consolidation of Victorian morality, and its apparatus of social, medical, and legal enforcement, was the outcome of a long period of struggle whose results have been bitterly contested ever since.

The consequences of these great nineteenth-century moral paroxysms are still with us. They have left a deep imprint on attitudes about sex, medical practice, child-rearing, parental anxieties, police conduct, and sex law.

The idea that masturbation is an unhealthy practice is part of that heritage. During the nineteenth century, it was commonly thought that "premature" interest in sex, sexual excitement, and above all sexual release would impair the health and maturation of a child. Theorists differed on the actual consequences of sexual precocity. Some thought it led to insanity, while others merely predicted stunted growth. To protect the young from premature arousal, parents tied children down at night so they would not touch themselves; doctors excised the clitorises of onanistic little girls.[2] Although the more gruesome techniques have been abandoned, the attitudes that produced them persist. The notion that sex per se is harmful to the young has been chiseled into extensive social and legal structures designed to insulate minors from sexual knowledge and experience.[3]

Much of the sex law currently on the books also dates from the nineteenth-century morality crusades. The first federal anti-obscenity law in the United States was passed in 1873. The Comstock Act—named for Anthony Comstock, an ancestral antiporn activist and the founder of the New York Society for the Suppression of Vice—made it a federal crime to make, advertise, sell, possess, send through the mails, or import books or pictures deemed obscene. The law also banned contraceptive or abortifacient drugs and devices and information about them.[4] In the wake of the federal statute, most states passed their own anti-obscenity laws.

The Supreme Court began to whittle down both federal and state Comstock laws during the 1950s. By 1975, the prohibition of materials used for, and information about, contraception and abortion had been ruled unconstitutional. However, although the obscenity provisions have been modified, their fundamental constitutionality has been upheld. Thus it remains a crime to make, sell, mail, or import material which has no purpose other than sexual arousal.[5]

Although sodomy statutes date from older strata of the law, when elements of canon law were adopted into civil codes, most of the laws used to arrest homosexuals and prostitutes come out of the Victorian campaigns against "white slavery."[6] These campaigns produced myriad prohibitions against solicitation, lewd behavior, loitering for immoral purposes, age offenses, and brothels and bawdy houses.

In her discussion of the British "white slave" scare, Judith Walkowitz observes, "Recent research delineates the vast discrepancy between lurid journalistic accounts and the reality of prostitution. Evidence of widespread entrapment of British girls in London and abroad is slim."[7] However, public furor over this ostensible problem,

> forced the passage of the Criminal Law Amendment Act of 1885, a particularly nasty and pernicious piece of omnibus legislation. The 1885 Act raised the age of consent for girls from 13 to 16, but it also gave police far greater summary jurisdiction over poor working-class women and children. . . . [I]t contained a clause making indecent acts between consenting male adults a crime, thus forming the basis of legal prosecution of male homosexuals in Britain until 1967. . . . [T]he clauses of the new bill were mainly enforced against working-class women, and regulated adult rather than youthful sexual behaviour.[8]

In the United States, the Mann Act, also known as the White Slave Traffic Act, was passed in 1910. Subsequently, every state in the union passed antiprostitution legislation.[9]

In the 1950s, in the United States, major shifts in the organization of sexuality took place. Instead of focusing on prostitution or masturbation, the anxieties of the 1950s condensed most specifically around the image of the "homosexual menace" and the dubious specter of the "sex offender." Just before and after the Second World War, the "sex offender" became an object of public fear and scrutiny. Many states and cities, including Massachusetts, New Hampshire, New Jersey, New York State, New York City, and Michigan, launched investigations to gather information about this menace to public safety.[10] The term *sex offender* sometimes applied to rapists, sometimes to "child molesters," and eventually functioned as a code for homosexuals. In its bureaucratic, medical, and popular versions, the sex offender discourse tended to blur distinctions between violent sexual assault and illegal but consensual acts such as sodomy. The criminal justice system incorporated these concepts when an epidemic of sexual psychopath laws swept through state legislatures.[11] These laws gave the psychological professions increased police powers over homosexuals and other sexual "deviants."

From the late 1940s until the early 1960s, erotic communities whose activities did not fit the postwar American dream drew intense persecution. Homosexuals were, along with communists, the objects of federal witch hunts and purges. Congressional investigations, executive orders, and sensational exposés in the media aimed to root out homosexuals employed by the government. Thousands lost their jobs.[12] The FBI began systematic surveillance and harassment of homosexuals which lasted at least into the 1970s.[13]

Many states and large cities conducted their own investigations, and the federal witch hunts were reflected in a variety of local crackdowns. In Boise, Idaho, in 1955, a schoolteacher sat down to breakfast with his morning paper and read that the vice president of the Idaho First National Bank had been arrested on felony sodomy charges; the local prosecutor said that he intended to eliminate all homosexuality from the community. The teacher never finished his breakfast. "He jumped up from his seat, pulled out his suitcases, packed as fast as he could, got into his car, and drove straight to San Francisco. . . . The cold eggs, coffee, and toast remained on his table for two days before someone from his school came by to see what had happened."[14]

In San Francisco, police and media waged war on homosexuals throughout the 1950s. Police raided bars, patrolled cruising areas, conducted street sweeps, and trumpeted their intention of driving the queers out of San Francisco.[15] Crackdowns against gay individuals, bars, and social areas occurred throughout the country. Although antihomosexual crusades are the best-documented examples of erotic repression in the 1950s, future research should reveal similar patterns of increased harassment against pornographic materials, prostitutes, and erotic deviants of all sorts. Research is needed to determine the full scope of both police persecution and regulatory reform.[16]

The current period bears some uncomfortable similarities to the 1880s and the 1950s. The 1977 campaign to repeal the Dade County, Florida, gay-rights ordinance inaugurated a new wave of violence, state persecution, and legal initiatives directed against minority sexual populations and the commercial sex industry. For the last six years, the United States and Canada have undergone an extensive sexual repression in the political, not the psychological, sense. In the spring of 1977, a few weeks before the Dade County vote, the news media were suddenly full of reports of raids on gay cruising areas, arrests for prostitution, and investigations into the manufacture and distribution of pornographic materials. Since then, police activity against the gay community has increased exponentially. The gay press has documented hundreds of arrests, from the libraries of Boston to the streets of Houston and the beaches of San Francisco. Even the large, organized, and relatively powerful urban gay communities have been unable to stop these depredations. Gay bars and bath houses have been busted with alarming frequency, and police have gotten bolder. In one especially dramatic incident, police in Toronto raided all four of the city's gay baths. They broke into cubicles with crowbars and hauled almost 300 men out into the winter streets, clad in their bath towels. Even "liberated" San Francisco has not been immune. There have been proceedings against several bars, countless arrests in the parks, and, in the fall of 1981, police arrested over 400 people in a series of sweeps of Polk Street, one of the thoroughfares of local gay nightlife. Queer-bashing has become a significant recreational activity for young urban males. They come into gay neighborhoods armed with baseball bats and looking for trouble, knowing that the adults in their lives either secretly approve or will look the other way.

The police crackdown has not been limited to homosexuals. Since 1977, enforcement of existing laws against prostitution and obscenity has been stepped up. Moreover, states and municipalities have been tightening regulations on commercial sex. New restrictive ordinances have been passed, zoning laws altered, licensing and safety codes amended, sentences increased, and evidentiary requirements relaxed. This subtle legal codification of more stringent controls over adult sexual behavior has gone largely unnoticed outside of the gay press.

For over a century, no tactic for stirring up erotic hysteria has been as reliable as the appeal to protect children. The current wave of erotic terror has reached deepest into those areas bordered in some way, if only symbolically, by the sexuality of the young. The motto of the Dade County repeal campaign was "Save Our Children" from alleged homosexual recruitment. In February 1977, shortly before the Dade County vote, a sudden concern with "child pornography" swept the national media. In May, the *Chicago Tribune* ran a lurid four-day series with three-inch headlines, which claimed to expose a national vice ring organized to lure young boys into prostitution and pornography.[17] Newspapers across the country ran similar stories, most of them worthy of the *National Enquirer*. By the end of May, a congressional investigation was under way. Within weeks, the federal government had enacted a sweeping bill against "child pornography," and many of the states followed with bills of their own. These laws have reestablished restrictions on sexual materials that had been relaxed by some of the important Supreme Court decisions. For instance, the court ruled that neither nudity nor sexual activity per se were obscene. But the child-pornography laws define as obscene any depiction of minors who are nude or engaged in sexual activity. This means that photographs of naked children in anthropology textbooks and many of the ethnographic movies shown in college classes are technically illegal in several states. In fact, the instructors are liable to an additional felony charge for showing such images to each student under the age of eighteen. Although the Supreme Court has also ruled that it is a constitutional right to possess obscene material for private use, some child-pornography laws prohibit even the private possession of any sexual material involving minors.[18]

The laws produced by the child-porn panic are ill-conceived and misdirected. They represent far-reaching alterations in the regulation of sexual behavior and abrogate important sexual civil liberties. But hardly anyone noticed as they swept through Congress and state legislatures. With the exception of the North American Man/Boy Love Association and the American Civil Liberties Union, no one raised a peep of protest.[19]

A new and even tougher federal child-pornography bill has just reached House-Senate conference. It removes any requirement that prosecutors must prove that alleged child pornography was distributed for commercial sale. Once this bill becomes law, a person merely possessing a nude snapshot of a seventeen-year-old lover or friend may go to jail for fifteen years, and be fined $100,000. This bill passed the House 400 to 1.[20]

The experiences of the art photographer Jacqueline Livingston exemplify the climate created by the child-porn panic. An assistant professor of photography at Cornell University, Livingston was fired, in 1978, after exhibiting pictures of male nudes which included photographs of her seven-year-old son masturbating. *Ms. Magazine, Chrysalis,* and *Art News* all refused to run ads for Livingston's posters of male nudes. At one point, Kodak confiscated some of her film, and for several months Livingston lived with the threat of prosecution under the child-pornography laws. The Tompkins County Department of Social Services investigated her fitness as a parent. Livingston's posters have been collected by the Museum of Modern Art, the Metropolitan, and other major museums. But she has paid a high cost in harassment and anxiety for her efforts to capture on film the uncensored male body at different ages.[21]

It is easy to see someone like Livingston as a victim of the child-porn wars. It is harder for most people to sympathize with actual boy-lovers. Like communists and homosexuals in the 1950s, boy-lovers are so stigmatized that it is difficult to find defenders for their civil liberties, let alone for their erotic orientation. Consequently, the police have feasted on them. Local police, the FBI, and watchdog postal inspectors have joined to build a huge apparatus whose sole aim is to wipe out the community of men who love underage youth. In twenty years or so, when some of the smoke has cleared, it will be much easier to show that these men have been the victims of a savage and undeserved witch hunt. A lot of people will be embarrassed by their collaboration with this persecution, but it will be too late to do much good for those men who have spent their lives in prison.[22]

While the misery of the boy-lovers affects very few, the other long-term legacy of the Dade County repeal affects almost everyone. The success of the antigay campaign ignited long-simmering passions of the American Right, and sparked an extensive movement to compress the boundaries of acceptable sexual behavior.

Right-wing ideology linking nonfamilial sex with communism and political weakness is nothing new. During the McCarthy period, Alfred Kinsey and his Institute for Sex Research were attacked for weakening the moral fiber of Americans and rendering them more vulnerable to communist influence. After congressional investigations and bad publicity, Kinsey's Rockefeller grant was terminated in 1954.[23]

Around 1969, the extreme Right discovered the Sex Information and Education Council of the United States (SIECUS). In books and pamphlets, such as *The Sex Education Racket: Pornography in the Schools* and *SIECUS: Corrupter of Youth*, the Right attacked SIECUS and sex education as communist plots to destroy the family and sap the national will.[24] Another pamphlet, *Pavlov's Children (They May Be Yours)* (1969), claims that the United Nations Educational, Scientific and Cultural Organization (UNESCO) is in cahoots with SIECUS to undermine religious taboos, to promote the acceptance of abnormal sexual relations, to downgrade absolute moral standards, and to "destroy racial cohesion," by exposing white people (especially white women) to the alleged "lower" sexual standards of black people.[25]

New Right and neoconservative ideology has updated these themes, and leans heavily on linking "immoral" sexual behavior to putative declines in American power. In 1977, Norman Podhoretz wrote an essay blaming homosexuals for the alleged inability of the United States to stand up to the Russians.[26] He thus neatly linked "the anti-gay fight in the domestic arena and the anti-communist battles in foreign policy."[27]

Right-wing opposition to sex education, homosexuality, pornography, abortion, and premarital sex moved from the fringes to the political center stage after 1977, when right-wing strategists and fundamentalist religious crusaders discovered that these issues had mass appeal. Sexual reaction played a significant role in the Right's electoral success in 1980.[28] Organizations like the Moral Majority and Citizens for Decency have acquired mass followings, immense financial resources, and unanticipated clout. The Equal Rights Amendment has been defeated, legislation has been passed that mandates new restrictions on abortion, and funding for programs like Planned Parenthood and sex education has been slashed. Laws and regulations making it more difficult for teenage girls to obtain contraceptives or abortions have been promulgated. Sexual backlash was exploited in successful attacks on the Women's Studies Program at California State University, Long Beach.

The most ambitious right-wing legislative initiative has been the Family Protection Act (FPA), introduced in Congress in 1979. The Family Protection Act is a broad assault on feminism, homosexuals, nontraditional families, and teenage sexual privacy.[29] The Family Protection Act has not and probably will not pass, but conservative members of Congress continue to pursue its agenda in a more piecemeal fashion. Perhaps the most glaring sign of the times is the Adolescent Family Life Program. Also known as the Teen Chastity Program, it gets some 15 million federal dollars to encourage teenagers to refrain from sexual intercourse, and to discourage them from using contraceptives if they do have sex, and from having abortions if they get pregnant. In the last few years, there have been countless local confrontations over gay rights, sex education, abortion rights, adult bookstores, and public-school curricula. It is unlikely that the antisex backlash is over, or that it has even peaked. Unless something changes dramatically, it is likely that the next few years will bring more of the same.[30]

Periods such as the 1880s in England, and the 1950s in the United States, recodify the relations of sexuality. The struggles that were fought leave a residue in the form of laws, social practices, and ideologies which then affect the way in which sexuality is experienced long after the immediate conflicts have faded. All the signs indicate that the present era is another of those watersheds in the politics of sex. The settlements that emerge from the 1980s will have an impact far into the future. It is therefore imperative to understand what is going on and what is at stake in order to make informed decisions about what policies to support and oppose.

It is difficult to make such decisions in the absence of a coherent and intelligent body of radical thought about sex. Unfortunately, progressive political analysis of sexuality is relatively underdeveloped. Much of what is available from the feminist movement has simply added to the mystification that shrouds the subject. There is an urgent need to develop radical perspectives on sexuality.

Paradoxically, an explosion of exciting scholarship and political writing about sex has been generated in these bleak years. In the 1950s, the early gay-rights movement began and prospered while the bars were being raided and antigay laws were being passed. In the last six years, new erotic communities, political alliances, and analyses have been developed in the midst of the repression. In this essay, I will propose elements of a descriptive and conceptual framework for thinking about sex and its politics. I hope to contribute to the pressing task of creating an accurate, humane, and genuinely liberatory body of thought about sexuality.

Sexual Thoughts

> "You see, Tim," Phillip said suddenly, "your argument isn't reasonable. Suppose I granted your first point that homosexuality is justifiable in certain instances and under certain controls. Then there is the catch: where does justification end and degeneracy begin? Society must condemn to protect. Permit even the intellectual homosexual a place of respect and the first bar is down. Then comes the next and the next until the sadist, the flagellist, the criminally insane demand their places, and society ceases to exist. So I ask again: where is the line drawn? Where does degeneracy begin if not at the beginning of individual freedom in such matters?"
> —Fragment from a 1950s fictional discussion between two gay men trying to decide if they may love each other, **James Barr,** *Quatrefoil*

A radical theory of sex must identify, describe, explain, and denounce erotic injustice and sexual oppression. Such a theory needs refined conceptual tools which can grasp the subject and hold it in view. It must build rich descriptions of sexuality as it exists in society and history. It requires a convincing critical language that can convey the barbarity of sexual persecution.

Several persistent features of thought about sex inhibit the development of such a theory. These assumptions are so pervasive in Western culture that they are rarely questioned. Thus, they tend to reappear in different political contexts, acquiring new rhetorical expressions but reproducing fundamental axioms.

One such axiom is sexual essentialism—the idea that sex is a natural force that exists prior to social life and shapes institutions. Sexual essentialism is embedded in the folk wisdoms of Western societies, which consider sex to be eternally unchanging, asocial, and transhistorical. Dominated for over a century by medicine, psychiatry, and psychology, the academic study of sex has reproduced essentialism. These fields classify sex as a property of individuals. It may reside in their hormones or their psyches. It may be construed as physiological or psychological. But within these ethnoscientific categories, sexuality has no history and no significant social determinants.

During the last five years, a sophisticated historical and theoretical scholarship has challenged sexual essentialism both explicitly and implicitly. Gay history, particularly the work of Jeffrey Weeks, has led this assault by showing that homosexuality as we know it is a relatively modern institutional complex.[31] Many historians have come to see the contemporary institutional forms of heterosexuality as an even more recent development.[32] An important contributor to the new scholarship is Judith Walkowitz, whose research has demonstrated the extent to which prostitution was transformed around the turn of the century. She provides meticulous descriptions of how the interplay of social forces such as ideology, fear, political agitation, legal reform, and medical practice can change the structure of sexual behavior and alter its consequences.[33]

Michel Foucault's *The History of Sexuality* has been the most influential and emblematic text of the new scholarship on sex. Foucault criticizes the traditional understanding of sexuality as a natural libido yearning to break free of social constraint. He argues that desires are not preexisting biological entities, but rather that they are constituted in the course of historically specific social practices. He emphasizes the generative aspects of the social organization of sex rather than its repressive elements by pointing out that new sexualities are constantly produced. And he points to a major discontinuity between kinship-based systems of sexuality and more modern forms.[34]

The new scholarship on sexual behavior has given sex a history and created a constructivist alternative to sexual essentialism. Underlying this body of work is an assumption that sexuality is constituted in society and history, not biologically ordained.[35] This does not mean the biological capacities are not prerequisites for human sexuality. It does mean that human sexuality is not comprehensible in purely biological terms. Human organisms with human brains are necessary for human cultures, but no examination of the body or its parts can explain the nature and variety of human social systems. The belly's hunger gives no clues as to the complexities of cuisine. The body, the brain, the genitalia, and the capacity for language are all necessary for human sexuality. But they do not determine its content, its experiences, or its institutional forms. Moreover, we never encounter the body unmediated by the meanings that cultures give to it. To paraphrase Lévi-Strauss, my position on the relationship between biology and sexuality is a "Kantianism without a transcendental libido."[36]

It is impossible to think with any clarity about the politics of race or gender as long as these are thought of as biological entities rather than as social constructs. Similarly, sexuality is impervious to political analysis as long as it is primarily conceived as a biological phenomenon or an aspect of individual psychology. Sexuality is as much a human product as are diets, methods of transportation, systems of etiquette, forms of labor, types of entertainment, processes of production, and modes of oppression. Once sex is understood in terms of social analysis and historical understanding, a more realistic politics of sex becomes possible. One may then think of sexual politics in terms of such phenomena as populations, neighborhoods, settlement patterns, migration, urban conflict, epidemiology, and police technology. These are more fruitful categories of thought than the more traditional ones of sin, disease, neurosis, pathology, decadence, pollution, or the decline and fall of empires.

By detailing the relationships between stigmatized erotic populations and the social forces which regulate them, work such as that of Allan Bérubé, John D'Emilio, Jeffrey Weeks, and Judith Walkowitz contains implicit categories of political analysis and criticism. Nevertheless, the constructivist perspective has displayed some political weaknesses. This has been most evident in misconstructions of Foucault's position.

Because of his emphasis on the ways that sexuality is produced, Foucault has been vulnerable to interpretations that deny or minimize the reality of sexual repression in the more political sense. Foucault makes it abundantly clear that he is not denying the existence of sexual repression so much as inscribing it within a larger dynamic.[37] Sexuality in Western societies has been structured within an extremely punitive social framework, and has been subjected to very real formal and informal controls. It is necessary to recognize repressive phenomena without resorting to the essentialist assumptions of the language of libido. It is important to hold repressive sexual practices in focus, even while situating them within a different totality and a more refined terminology.[38]

Most radical thought about sex has been embedded within a model of the instincts and their restraints. Concepts of sexual oppression have been lodged within that more biological understanding of sexuality. It is often easier to fall back on the notion of a natural libido subjected to inhumane repression than to reformulate concepts of sexual injustice within a more constructivist framework. But it is essential that we do so. We need a radical critique of sexual arrangements that has the conceptual elegance of Foucault and the evocative passion of Reich.

The new scholarship on sex has brought a welcome insistence that sexual terms be restricted to their proper historical and social contexts, and a cautionary skepticism toward sweeping generalizations. But it is important to be able to indicate groupings of erotic behavior and general trends within erotic discourse. In addition to sexual essentialism, there are at least five other ideological formations whose grip on sexual thought is so strong that to fail to discuss them is to remain enmeshed within them. These are sex negativity, the fallacy of misplaced scale, the hierarchical valuation of sex acts, the domino theory of sexual peril, and the lack of a concept of benign sexual variation.

Of these five, the most important is sex negativity. Western cultures generally consider sex to be a dangerous, destructive, negative force.[39] Most Christian tradition, following Paul, holds that sex is inherently sinful.[40] It may be redeemed if performed within marriage for procreative purposes and if the pleasurable aspects are not enjoyed too much. In turn, this idea rests on the assumption that the genitalia are an intrinsically inferior part of the body, much lower and less holy than the mind, the "soul," the "heart," or even the upper part of the digestive system (the status of the excretory organs is close to that of the genitalia).[41] Such notions have by now acquired a life of their own and no longer depend solely on religion for their perseverance.

This culture always treats sex with suspicion. It construes and judges almost any sexual practice in terms of its worst possible expression. Sex is presumed guilty until proven innocent. Virtually all erotic behavior is considered bad unless a specific reason to exempt it has been established. The most acceptable excuses are marriage, reproduction, and love. Sometimes scientific curiosity, aesthetic experience, or a long-term intimate relationship may serve. But the exercise of erotic capacity, intelligence, curiosity, or creativity all require pretexts that are unnecessary for other pleasures, such as the enjoyment of food, fiction, or astronomy.

What I call the fallacy of misplaced scale is a corollary of sex negativity. Susan Sontag once commented that since Christianity focused "on sexual behavior as the root of virtue, everything pertaining to sex has been a 'special case' in our culture."[42] Sex law has incorporated the religious attitude that heretical sex is an especially heinous sin that deserves the harshest punishments. Throughout much of European and American history, a single act of consensual anal penetration was grounds for execution. In some states, sodomy still carries twenty-year prison sentences.[43] Outside the law, sex is also a marked category. Small differences in value or behavior are often experienced as cosmic threats. Although people can be intolerant, silly, or pushy about what constitutes proper diet, differences in menu rarely provoke the kinds of rage, anxiety, and sheer terror that routinely accompany differences in erotic taste. Sexual acts are burdened with an excess of significance.

Modern Western societies appraise sex acts according to a hierarchical system of sexual value. Marital, reproductive heterosexuals are alone at the top of the erotic pyramid. Clamoring below are unmarried monogamous heterosexuals in couples, followed by most other heterosexuals. Solitary sex floats ambiguously. The powerful nineteenth-century stigma on masturbation lingers in less potent, modified forms, such as the idea that solitary pleasures are inferior substitutes for partnered encounters. Stable, long-term lesbian and gay male couples are verging on respectability, but bar dykes and promiscuous gay men are hovering just above the groups at the very bottom of the pyramid. The most despised sexual castes currently include transsexuals, transvestites, fetishists, sadomasochists, sex workers such as prostitutes and porn models, and the lowliest of all, those whose eroticism transgresses generational boundaries.

Individuals whose behavior stands high in this hierarchy are rewarded with certified mental health, respectability, legality, social and physical mobility, institutional support, and material benefits. As sexual behaviors or occupations fall lower on the scale, the individuals who practice them are subjected to a presumption of mental illness, disreputability, criminality, restricted social and physical mobility, loss of institutional support, economic sanctions, and criminal prosecution.

Extreme and punitive stigma maintains some sexual behaviors as low status and is an effective sanction against those who engage in them. The intensity of this stigma is rooted in Western religious traditions. But most of its contemporary content derives from medical and psychiatric opprobrium.

The old religious taboos were primarily based on kinship forms of social organization. They were meant to deter inappropriate unions and to provide proper kin. Sex laws derived from or justified on the basis of biblical pronouncements were aimed at preventing the acquisition of the wrong kinds of affinal partners: consanguineous kin (incest), the same gender (homosexuality), or the wrong species (bestiality). When medicine and psychiatry acquired extensive powers over sexuality, they were less concerned with unsuitable mates than with unfit forms of desire. If taboos against incest best characterized kinship systems of sexual organization, then the shift to an emphasis on taboos against masturbation was more apposite to the newer systems organized around qualities of erotic experience.[44]

Medicine and psychiatry multiplied the categories of sexual misconduct. The section on psychosexual disorders in the *Diagnostic and Statistical Manual of Mental Disorders* (DSM) of the American Psychiatric Association (APA) is a fairly reliable map of the current moral hierarchy of sexual activities. The APA list is much more elaborate than the traditional condemnations of whoring, sodomy, and adultery. The most recent edition, DSM-III, removed homosexuality from the roster of mental disorders after a long political struggle. But fetishism, sadism, masochism, transsexuality, transvestism, exhibitionism, voyeurism, and pedophilia are quite firmly entrenched as psychological malfunctions.[45] Books are still being written about the genesis, etiology, treatment, and cure of these assorted "pathologies."

Psychiatric condemnation of sexual behaviors invokes concepts of mental and emotional inferiority rather than categories of sexual sin. Low-status sex practices are vilified as mental diseases or symptoms of defective personality integration. In addition, psychological terms conflate difficulties of psychodynamic functioning with modes of erotic conduct. They equate sexual masochism with self-destructive personality patterns, sexual sadism with emotional aggression, and homoeroticism with immaturity. These terminological muddles have become powerful stereotypes that are indiscriminately applied to individuals on the basis of their sexual orientations.

Popular culture is permeated with ideas that erotic variety is dangerous, unhealthy, depraved, and a menace to everything from small children to national security. Popular sexual ideology is a noxious stew made up of ideas of sexual sin, concepts of psychological inferiority, anticommunism, mob hysteria, accusations of witchcraft, and xenophobia. The mass media nourish these attitudes with relentless propaganda. I would call this system of erotic stigma the last socially respectable form of prejudice if the old forms did not show such obstinate vitality and new ones did not continually become apparent.

All these hierarchies of sexual value—religious, psychiatric, and popular—function in much the same ways as do ideological systems of racism, ethnocentrism, and religious chauvinism. They rationalize the well-being of the sexually privileged and the adversity of the sexual rabble.

Figure 1 diagrams a general version of the sexual value system. According to this system, sexuality that is "good," "normal," and "natural" should ideally be heterosexual, marital, monogamous, reproductive, and noncommercial. It should be coupled, relational, within the same generation, and occur at home. It should not involve pornography, fetish objects, sex toys of any sort, or roles other than male and female. Any sex that violates these rules is "bad," "abnormal," or "unnatural." Bad sex may be homosexual, unmarried, promiscuous, nonprocreative, or commercial. It may be masturbatory or take place at orgies, may be casual, may cross generational lines, and may take place in "public," or at least in the bushes or the baths. It may involve the use of pornography, fetish objects, sex toys, or unusual roles.

Figure 2 diagrams another aspect of the sexual hierarchy: the need to draw and maintain an imaginary line between good and bad sex. Most of the discourses on sex, be they religious, psychiatric, popular, or political, delimit a very small portion of human sexual capacity as sanctifiable, safe, healthy, mature, legal, or politically correct. The "line" distinguishes these from all other erotic behaviors, which are understood to be the work of the devil, dangerous, psychopathological, infantile, or politically reprehensible. Arguments are then conducted over "where to draw the line," and to determine what other activities, if any, may be permitted to cross over into acceptability.[46]

All these models assume a domino theory of sexual peril. The line appears to stand between sexual order and chaos. It expresses the fear that if anything is permitted to cross this erotic demilitarized zone, the barrier against scary sex will crumble and something unspeakable will skitter across.

Most systems of sexual judgment—religious, psychological, feminist, or socialist—attempt to determine on which side of the line a particular act falls. Only sex acts on the good side of the line are accorded moral complexity. For instance, heterosexual encounters may be sublime or disgusting, free or forced, healing or destructive, romantic or mercenary. As long as it does not violate other rules, heterosexuality is acknowledged to exhibit the full range of human experience. In contrast, all sex acts on the bad side of the line are considered utterly repulsive and devoid of all emotional nuance. The further from the line a sex act is, the more it is depicted as a uniformly bad experience.

As a result of the sex conflicts of the last decade, some behavior near the border is inching across it. Unmarried couples living together, masturbation, and some forms of homosexuality are moving in the direction of respectability (see fig. 2). Most homosexuality is still on the bad side of the line. But

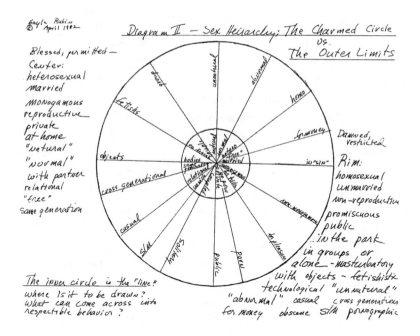

Figure I. **The Sex Hierarchy: The Charmed Circle vs. the Outer Limits**

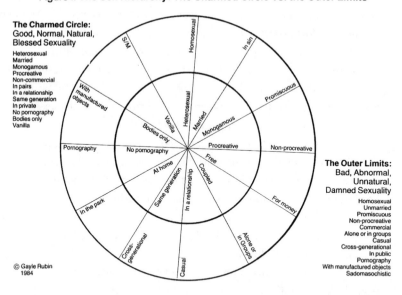

Figure 1. Sex Hierarchy: The Charmed Circle vs. the Outer Limits.

Top: Version distributed as handout at Rubin's workshop at the Barnard Conference, 1982.

Bottom: Version published in 1984. Courtesy of Gayle Rubin

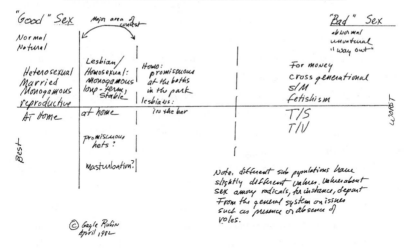

Diagram I - Sex Heirarchy: The Struggle over
Where to draw the line

"Good" Sex   Major area of contest   "Bad" Sex

Normal
Natural   abnormal
                                unnatural
                                "way out"

Heterosexual   Lesbian/   Homo: For money
Married   Homosexual: promiscuous   cross generational
Monogamous   Monogamous   at the baths   S/M
reproductive   long-term,   in the park   fetishism
          stable   lesbians:
At Home   at home   in the bar   T/S
                                T/V

Best   promiscuous   WORST
      hets?

     masturbation?

                      Note, different sub populations have
                      slightly different values. values about
                      sex among radicals, for instance, depart
                      From the general system on issues
                      such as presence or absence of
                      roles.

       © Gayle Rubin
         April 1982

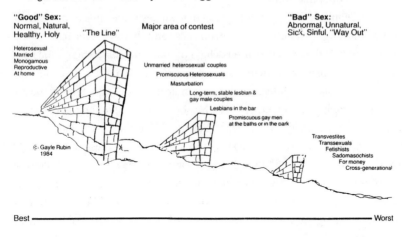

Figure II. **The Sex Hierarchy: The Struggle Over Where to Draw the Line**

"Good" Sex:
Normal, Natural,
Healthy, Holy   "The Line"   Major area of contest   "Bad" Sex:
                                           Abnormal, Unnatural,
                                           Sick, Sinful, "Way Out"

Heterosexual
Married
Monogamous
Reproductive
At home

                      Unmarried heterosexual couples

                       Promiscuous Heterosexuals

                         Masturbation

                           Long-term, stable lesbian &
                           gay male couples

                             Lesbians in the bar

                               Promiscuous gay men
                               at the baths or in the park

                                        Transvestites
                                         Transsexuals
© Gayle Rubin   Fetishists
1984   Sadomasochists
                                         For money
                                         Cross-generational

Best ——————————————————————————————— Worst

Figure 2. Sex Hierarchy: The Struggle over Where to Draw the Line.

Top: Version distributed as handout at Rubin's workshop at the Barnard Conference, 1982.

Bottom: Version published in 1984. Courtesy of Gayle Rubin

if it is coupled and monogamous, the society is beginning to recognize that it includes the full range of human interaction. Promiscuous homosexuality, sadomasochism, fetishism, transsexuality, and cross-generational encounters are still viewed as unmodulated horrors incapable of involving affection, love, free choice, kindness, or transcendence.

This kind of sexual morality has more in common with ideologies of racism than with true ethics. It grants virtue to the dominant groups, and relegates vice to the underprivileged. A democratic morality should judge sexual acts by the way partners treat one another, the level of mutual consideration, the presence or absence of coercion, and the quantity and quality of the pleasures they provide. Whether sex acts are gay or straight, coupled or in groups, naked or in underwear, commercial or free, with or without video should not be ethical concerns.

It is difficult to develop a pluralistic sexual ethics without a concept of benign sexual variation. Variation is a fundamental property of all life, from the simplest biological organisms to the most complex human social formations. Yet sexuality is supposed to conform to a single standard. One of the most tenacious ideas about sex is that there is one best way to do it, and that everyone should do it that way.

Most people find it difficult to grasp that whatever they like to do sexually will be thoroughly repulsive to someone else, and that whatever repels them sexually will be the most treasured delight of someone, somewhere. One need not like or perform a particular sex act in order to recognize that someone else will, and that this difference does not indicate a lack of good taste, mental health, or intelligence in either party. Most people mistake their sexual preferences for a universal system that will or should work for everyone.

This notion of a single ideal sexuality characterizes most systems of thought about sex. For religion, the ideal is procreative marriage. For psychology, it is mature heterosexuality. Although its content varies, the format of a single sexual standard is continually reconstituted within other rhetorical frameworks, including feminism and socialism. It is just as objectionable to insist that everyone should be lesbian, non-monogamous, or kinky, as to believe that everyone should be heterosexual, married, or vanilla—though the latter set of opinions are backed by considerably more coercive power than the former.

Progressives who would be ashamed to display cultural chauvinism in other areas routinely exhibit it toward sexual differences. We have learned to cherish different cultures as unique expressions of human inventiveness rather than as the inferior or disgusting habits of savages. We need a similarly anthropological understanding of different sexual cultures.

Empirical sex research is the one field that does incorporate a positive concept of sexual variation. Alfred Kinsey approached the study of sex with the same uninhibited curiosity he had previously applied to examining a type of wasp. His scientific detachment gave his work a refreshing neutrality that enraged moralists and caused immense controversy.[47] Among Kinsey's successors, John Gagnon and William Simon have pioneered the application of sociological understandings to erotic variety.[48] Even some of the older sexology is useful. Most early sexology was articulated within the scientific language of the period, which included social evolution, racism, and eugenics. Nonetheless, texts of Krafft-Ebing, Havelock Ellis, and Magnus Hirschfeld are resplendent with detail. Ellis was an especially astute and sympathetic observer of sexual behavior and emotion. In their work, Hirschfeld and Ellis argued eloquently for the decriminalization and destigmatization of homosexuality.[49]

Much political writing on sexuality reveals complete ignorance of both classical sexology and modern sex research. Perhaps this is because so few colleges and universities bother to teach human sexuality, and because so much stigma adheres even to scholarly investigation of sex. Neither sexology nor sex research has been immune to the prevailing sexual value system. Both contain assumptions and information which should not be accepted uncritically. But sexology and sex research provide abundant detail, a welcome posture of calm, and a well-developed ability to treat sexual variety as something that exists rather than as something to be exterminated. These fields can provide an empirical grounding for a radical theory of sexuality more useful than the combination of psychoanalysis and feminist first principles to which so many texts resort.

Sexual Transformation

> As defined by the ancient civil or canonical codes, sodomy was a category of forbidden acts; their perpetrator was nothing more than the juridical subject of them. The nineteenth-century homosexual became a personage, a past, a case history, and a childhood, in addition to being a type of life, a life form, and a morphology, with an indiscreet anatomy and possibly a mysterious physiology. . . . The sodomite had been a temporary aberration; the homosexual was now a species.
> —**Foucault,** *The History of Sexuality*

In spite of many continuities with ancestral forms, modern sexual arrangements have a distinctive character which sets them apart from preexisting systems. In Western Europe and the United States, industrialization and urbanization reshaped the traditional rural and peasant populations into a new urban industrial and service workforce. They generated new forms of state apparatus, reorganized family relations, altered gender roles, made possible new forms of identity, produced new varieties of social inequality, and created new formats for political and ideological conflict. They also gave rise to a new sexual system characterized by distinct types of sexual persons, populations, stratification, and political struggle.

The writings of nineteenth-century sexology suggest the appearance of a kind of erotic speciation. However outlandish their explanations, the early sexologists were witnessing the emergence of new kinds of erotic individuals and their aggregation into rudimentary communities. The modern sexual system contains sets of these sexual populations, stratified by the operation of an ideological and social hierarchy. Differences in social value create friction among these groups, who engage in political contests to alter or maintain their place in the ranking. Contemporary sexual politics should be reconceptualized in terms of the emergence and ongoing development of this system, its social relations, the ideologies that interpret it, and its characteristic modes of conflict.

Homosexuality is the best example of this process of erotic speciation. Homosexual behavior is always present among humans. But in different societies and epochs it may be rewarded or punished, required or forbidden, a temporary experience or a life-long vocation. In some New Guinea societies, for example, homosexual activities are obligatory for all males. Homosexual acts are considered utterly masculine, roles are based on age, and partners are determined by kinship status.[50] Although these men engage in extensive homosexual and pedophile behavior, they are neither homosexuals nor pederasts.

Nor was the sixteenth-century sodomite a homosexual. In 1631, Mervyn Touchet, Earl of Castlehaven, was tried and executed for sodomy. It is clear from the proceedings that the earl was not understood by himself or anyone else to be a particular kind of sexual individual. "While from the twentieth-century viewpoint Lord Castlehaven obviously suffered from psychosexual problems requiring the services of an analyst, from the seventeenth-century viewpoint he had deliberately broken the Law of God and the Laws of England, and required the simpler services of an executioner."[51] The earl did not slip into his tightest doublet and waltz down to the nearest gay tavern to mingle with his fellow sodomites. He stayed in his manor house and buggered his servants. Gay self-awareness, gay pubs, the sense of group commonality, and even the term *homosexual* were not part of the earl's universe.

The New Guinea bachelor and the sodomite nobleman are only tangentially related to a modern gay man, who may migrate from rural Colorado to San Francisco in order to live in a gay neighborhood, work in a gay business, and participate in an elaborate experience that includes a self-conscious identity, group solidarity, a literature, a press, and a high level of political activity. In modern, Western, industrial societies, homosexuality has acquired much of the institutional structure of an ethnic group.[52]

The relocation of homoeroticism into these quasi-ethnic, nucleated, sexually constituted communities is to some extent a consequence of the transfers of population brought about by industrialization. As laborers migrated to work in cities, there were increased opportunities for voluntary communities to form. Homosexually inclined women and men, who would have been vulnerable and isolated in most preindustrial villages, began to congregate in small corners of the big cities. Most large nineteenth-century cities in Western Europe and North America had areas where men could cruise for other men. Lesbian communities seem to have coalesced more slowly and on a smaller scale. Nevertheless, by the 1890s, there were several cafés in Paris near the Place Pigalle that catered to a lesbian clientele, and it is likely that there were similar places in the other major capitals of Western Europe.

Areas like these acquired bad reputations, which alerted other interested individuals to their existence and location. In the United States, lesbian and gay male territories were well established in New York, Chicago, San Francisco, and Los Angeles in the 1950s.[53] Sexually motivated migration to places such as Greenwich Village had become a sizable sociological phenomenon. By the late 1970s, sexual migration was occurring on a scale so significant that it began to have a recognizable impact on urban politics in the United States, with San Francisco being the most notable and notorious example.[54]

Prostitution has undergone a similar metamorphosis. Prostitution began to change from a temporary job to a more permanent occupation as a result of nineteenth-century agitation, legal reform, and police persecution. Prostitutes, who had been part of the general working-class population, became increasingly isolated as members of an outcast group.[55] Prostitutes and other sex workers differ from homosexuals and other sexual minorities. Sex work is an occupation, while sexual deviation is an erotic preference. Nevertheless, they share some common features of social organization. Like homosexuals, prostitutes are a criminal sexual population stigmatized on the basis of sexual activity. Prostitutes and male homosexuals are the primary prey of vice police everywhere.[56] Like gay men, prostitutes occupy well-demarcated urban territories and battle with police to defend and maintain those territories. The legal persecution of both populations is justified by an elaborate ideology that classifies them as dangerous and inferior undesirables who are not entitled to be left in peace.

Besides organizing homosexuals and prostitutes into localized populations, the "modernization of sex" has generated a system of continual sexual ethnogenesis. Other populations of erotic dissidents—commonly known as the "perversions" or the "paraphilias"—also began to coalesce. Sexualities keep marching out of the *Diagnostic and Statistical Manual* and on to the pages of social history.[57] At present, several other groups are trying to emulate the successes of homosexuals. Bisexuals, sadomasochists, individuals who prefer cross-generational encounters, transsexuals, and transvestites are all in various states of community formation and identity acquisition. The perversions are not proliferating as much as they are attempting to acquire social space, small businesses, political resources, and a measure of relief from the penalties for sexual heresy.

Sexual Stratification

> An entire sub-race was born, different—despite certain kinship ties— from the libertines of the past. From the end of the eighteenth century to our own, they circulated through the pores of society; they were always hounded, but not always by laws; were often locked up, but not always in prisons; were sick perhaps, but scandalous, dangerous victims, prey to a strange evil that also bore the name of vice and sometimes crime. They were children wise beyond their years, precocious little girls, ambiguous schoolboys, dubious servants and educators, cruel or maniacal husbands, solitary collectors, ramblers with bizarre impulses; they haunted the houses of correction, the penal colonies, the tribunals, and the asylums; they carried their infamy to the doctors and their sickness to the judges. This was the numberless family of perverts who were on friendly terms with delinquents and akin to madmen.
>
> —**Foucault**, *The History of Sexuality*

The industrial transformation of Western Europe and North America brought about new forms of social stratification. The resultant inequalities of class are well known and have been explored in detail by a century of scholarship. The construction of modern systems of racism and ethnic injustice has been well documented and critically assessed. Feminist thought has analyzed the prevailing organization of gender oppression. But although specific erotic groups, such as militant homosexuals and sex workers, have agitated against their own mistreatment, there has been no equivalent attempt to locate particular varieties of sexual persecution within a more general system of sexual stratification. Nevertheless, such a system exists, and in its contemporary form it is a consequence of Western industrialization.

Sex law is the most adamantine instrument of sexual stratification and erotic persecution. The state routinely intervenes in sexual behavior at a level that would not be tolerated in other areas of social life. Most people are unaware of the extent of sex law, the quantity and qualities of illegal sexual behavior, and the punitive character of legal sanctions. Although federal agencies may be involved in obscenity and prostitution cases, most sex laws are enacted at the state and municipal levels, and enforcement is largely in the hands of local police. Thus, there is a tremendous amount of variation in the laws applicable to any given locale. Moreover, enforcement of sex laws varies dramatically with the local political climate. In spite of this legal thicket, one can make some tentative and qualified generalizations. My discussion of sex law does not apply to laws against sexual coercion, sexual assault, or rape. It does pertain to the myriad prohibitions on consensual sex and the "status" offenses such as statutory rape.

Sex law is harsh. The penalties for violating sex statutes are universally out of proportion to any social or individual harm. A single act of consensual but illicit sex, such as placing one's lips upon the genitalia of an enthusiastic partner, is punished in many states with more severity than rape, battery, or murder. Each such genital kiss, each lewd caress, is a separate crime. It is therefore painfully easy to commit multiple felonies in the course of a single evening of illegal passion. Once someone is convicted of a sex violation, a second performance of the same act is grounds for prosecution as a repeat offender, in which case penalties will be even more severe. In some states, individuals have become repeat felons for having engaged in homosexual love-making on two separate occasions. Once an erotic activity has been proscribed by sex law, the full power of the state enforces conformity to the values embodied in those laws. Sex laws are notoriously easy to pass, as legislators are loath to be soft on vice. Once on the books, they are extremely difficult to dislodge.

Sex law is not a perfect reflection of the prevailing moral evaluations of sexual conduct. Sexual variation per se is more specifically policed by the mental-health professions, popular ideology, and extralegal social practice. Some of the most detested erotic behaviors, such as fetishism and sadomasochism, are not as closely or completely regulated by the criminal-justice system as somewhat less stigmatized practices, such as homosexuality. Areas of sexual behavior come under the purview of the law when they become objects of social concern and political uproar. Each sex scare or morality campaign deposits new regulations as a kind of fossil record of its passage. The legal sediment is thickest—and sex law has its greatest potency—in areas involving obscenity, money, minors, and homosexuality.

Obscenity laws enforce a powerful taboo against direct representation of erotic activities. Current emphasis on the ways in which sexuality has become a focus of social attention should not be misused to undermine a critique of this prohibition. It is one thing to create sexual discourse in the form of psychoanalysis, or in the course of a morality crusade. It is quite another to graphically depict sex acts or genitalia. The first is socially permissible in a way the second is not. Sexual speech is forced into reticence, euphemism, and indirection. Freedom of speech about sex is a glaring exception to the protections of the First Amendment, which is not even considered applicable to purely sexual statements.

The anti-obscenity laws also form part of a group of statutes that make almost all sexual commerce illegal. Sex law incorporates a very strong prohibition against mixing sex and money, except via marriage. In addition to the obscenity statutes, other laws impinging on sexual commerce include anti-prostitution laws, alcoholic-beverage regulations, and ordinances governing the location and operation of "adult" businesses. The sex industry and the gay economy have both managed to circumvent some of this legislation, but that process has not been easy or simple. The underlying criminality of sex-oriented business keeps it marginal, underdeveloped, and distorted. Sex businesses can only operate in legal loopholes. This tends to keep investment down and to divert commercial activity toward the goal of staying out of jail rather than the delivery of goods and services. It also renders sex workers more vulnerable to exploitation and bad working conditions. If sex commerce were legal, sex workers would be more able to organize and agitate for higher pay, better conditions, greater control, and less stigma.

Whatever one thinks of the limitations of capitalist commerce, such an extreme exclusion from the market process would hardly be socially acceptable in other areas of activity. Imagine, for example, that the exchange of money for medical care, pharmacological advice, or psychological counseling were illegal. Medical practice would take place in a much less satisfactory fashion if doctors, nurses, druggists, and therapists could be hauled off to jail at the whim of the local "health squad." But that is essentially the situation of prostitutes, sex workers, and sex entrepreneurs.

Progressives tend to discuss capitalist commerce as though socialism is the sole alternative. They often fail to compare capitalism with less salutary systems of economic extraction and political domination: for example, the many varieties of feudalism and premodern despotism. Marx himself considered the capitalist market a revolutionary, if limited, force. He argued that capitalism was progressive in its dissolution of precapitalist superstition, prejudice, and the bonds of traditional modes of life. "Hence the great civilizing influence of capital, its production of a state of society compared with which all earlier stages appear to be merely local progress and idolatry of nature."[58] Keeping sex from realizing the positive effects of the market economy hardly makes it socialist. Rather, legal marginality tends to push sexual commerce in the opposite direction: closer to the despotic and the feudal.

The law is especially ferocious in maintaining the boundary between childhood "innocence" and "adult" sexuality. Rather than recognizing the sexuality of the young and attempting to provide for it in a caring and responsible manner, our culture denies and punishes erotic interest and activity by anyone under the local age of consent. The amount of law devoted to protecting young people from premature exposure to sexuality is breathtaking.

The primary mechanism for insuring the separation of sexual generations is age-of-consent laws. These laws make no distinction between the most brutal rape and the most gentle romance. A twenty year old convicted of sexual contact with a seventeen year old will face a severe sentence in virtually every state, regardless of the nature of the relationship.[59] Nor are minors permitted access to "adult" sexuality in other forms. They are forbidden to see books, movies, or television in which sexuality is "too" graphically portrayed. It is legal for young people to see hideous depictions of violence, but not to see explicit pictures of genitalia. Sexually active young people are frequently incarcerated in juvenile homes, or otherwise punished for their "precocity."

Adults who deviate too much from conventional standards of sexual conduct are often denied contact with the young, even their own. Custody laws permit the state to steal the children of anyone whose erotic activities appear questionable to a judge presiding over family court matters. Countless lesbians, gay men, prostitutes, swingers, sex workers, and "promiscuous" women have been declared unfit parents under such provisions. Members of the teaching professions are closely monitored for signs of sexual misconduct. In most states, certification laws require that teachers arrested for sex offenses lose their jobs and credentials. In some cases, a teacher may be fired merely because an unconventional lifestyle becomes known to school officials. Moral turpitude is one of the few legal grounds for revoking academic tenure.[60] The more influence one has over the next generation, the less latitude one is permitted in behavior and opinion. The coercive power of the law ensures the transmission of conservative sexual values with these kinds of controls over parenting and teaching.

The only adult sexual behavior that is legal in every state is the placement of the penis in the vagina in wedlock. Consenting-adults statutes ameliorate this situation in fewer than half the states. Most states impose severe criminal penalties on consensual sodomy, homosexual contact short of sodomy, adultery, seduction, and adult incest. Sodomy laws vary a great deal. In some states, they apply equally to homosexual and heterosexual partners, and regardless of marital status. Some state courts have ruled that married couples have the right to commit sodomy in private. Only homosexual sodomy is illegal in some states. Some sodomy statutes prohibit both anal sex and oral-genital contact. In other states, sodomy applies only to anal penetration, and oral sex is covered under separate statutes.[61]

Laws like these criminalize sexual behavior that is freely chosen and avidly sought. The ideology embodied in them reflects the value hierarchies discussed above. That is, some sex acts are considered to be so intrinsically vile that no one should be allowed under any circumstance to perform them. The fact that individuals consent to or even prefer them is taken to be additional evidence of depravity. This system of sex law is similar to legalized racism. State prohibitions of same-sex contact, anal penetration, and oral sex make homosexuals a criminal group denied the privileges of full citizenship. With such laws, prosecution is persecution. Even when they are not strictly enforced, as is usually the case, the members of criminalized sexual communities remain vulnerable to the possibility of arbitrary arrest or to periods in which they become the subjects of social panic. When those occur, the laws are in place and police action is swift. Even sporadic enforcement serves to remind individuals that they are members of a subject population. The occasional arrest for sodomy, lewd behavior, solicitation, or oral sex keeps everyone else afraid, nervous, and circumspect.[62]

The state also upholds the sexual hierarchy through bureaucratic regulation. Immigration policy still prohibits the admission of homosexuals (and other sexual "deviates") into the United States. Military regulations bar homosexuals from serving in the armed forces.[63] The fact that gay people cannot legally marry means that they cannot enjoy the same legal rights as heterosexuals in many matters, including inheritance, taxation, protection from testimony in court, and the acquisition of citizenship for foreign partners.[64] These are but a few of the ways that the state reflects and maintains the social relations of sexuality. The law buttresses structures of power, codes of behavior, and forms of prejudice. At their worst, sex law and sex regulation are simply sexual apartheid.

Although the legal apparatus of sex is staggering, most everyday social control is extralegal. Less formal, but very effective social sanctions are imposed on members of "inferior" sexual populations.

In her marvelous ethnographic study of gay life in the 1960s, Esther Newton observed that the homosexual population was divided into what she called the "overts" and the "coverts." "The overts live their entire working lives within the context of the [gay] community; the coverts live their entire *nonworking lives* within it."[65] At the time of Newton's study, the gay community provided far fewer jobs than it does now, and the nongay work world was almost completely intolerant of homosexuality. There were some fortunate individuals who could be openly gay and earn decent salaries. But the vast majority of homosexuals had to choose between honest poverty and the drain of maintaining a false identity.

Though this situation has changed a great deal, discrimination against gay people is still rampant. For the bulk of the gay population, being out on the job is still impossible. Generally, the more important and higher paid the job, the less the society will tolerate overt erotic deviance. If it is difficult for gay people to find employment where they do not have to pretend, it is doubly and triply so for more exotically sexed individuals. Sadomasochists leave their fetish clothes at home and know that they must be especially careful to conceal their real identities. An exposed pedophile would probably be stoned out of the office.[66] Having to maintain such absolute secrecy is a considerable burden. Even those who are content to be secretive may be exposed by some accidental event. Individuals who are erotically unconventional risk being unemployable or unable to pursue their chosen careers.

Public officials and anyone who occupies a position of social consequence are especially vulnerable. A sex scandal is the surest method for hounding someone out of office or destroying a political career. The fact that important people are expected to conform to the strictest standards of erotic conduct discourages sex perverts of all kinds from seeking such positions. Instead, erotic dissidents are channeled into positions that have less impact on the mainstream of social activity and opinion.

The expansion of the gay economy in the last decade has provided some employment alternatives and some relief from job discrimination against homosexuals. But most of the jobs provided by the gay economy are low status and low paying. Bartenders, bathhouse attendants, and disc jockeys are not bank officers or corporate executives. Many of the sexual migrants who flock to places like San Francisco are downwardly mobile. They face intense competition for choice positions. The influx of sexual migrants provides a pool of cheap and exploitable labor for many of the city's businesses, both gay and straight.

Families play a crucial role in enforcing sexual conformity. Much social pressure is brought to bear to deny erotic dissidents the comforts and resources that families provide. Popular ideology holds that families are not supposed to produce or harbor erotic nonconformity. Many families respond by trying to reform, punish, or exile sexually offending members. Many sexual migrants have been thrown out by their families, and many others are fleeing from the threat of institutionalization. Any random collection of homosexuals, sex workers, or miscellaneous perverts can provide heart-stopping stories of rejection and mistreatment by horrified families.

In addition to economic penalties and strain on family relations, the stigma of erotic dissidence creates friction at all other levels of everyday life. The general public helps to penalize erotic nonconformity when, according to the values they have been taught, landlords refuse housing, neighbors call in the police, and hoodlums commit sanctioned battery. The ideologies of erotic inferiority and sexual danger decrease the power of sex perverts and sex workers in social encounters of all kinds. They have less protection from unscrupulous or criminal behavior, less access to police protection, and less recourse to the courts. Dealings with institutions and bureaucracies—hospitals, police, coroners, banks, public officials—are more difficult.

Sex is a vector of oppression. The system of sexual oppression cuts across other modes of social inequality, sorting out individuals and groups according to its own intrinsic dynamics. It is not reducible to, or understandable in terms of class, race, ethnicity, or gender. Wealth, white skin, male gender, and ethnic privileges can mitigate the effects of sexual stratification. A rich, white, male pervert will generally be less affected than a poor, black, female pervert. But even the most privileged are not immune to sexual oppression. Some of the consequences of the system of sexual hierarchy are mere nuisances. Others are quite grave. In its most serious manifestations, the sexual system is a Kafkaesque nightmare in which unlucky victims become herds of human cattle whose identification, surveillance, apprehension, treatment, incarceration, and punishment produce jobs and self-satisfaction for thousands of vice police, prison officials, psychiatrists, and social workers.[67]

Sexual Conflicts

> The moral panic crystallizes widespread fears and anxieties, and often deals
> with them not by seeking the real causes of the problems and conditions
> which they demonstrate but by displacing them on to "Folk Devils" in an
> identified social group (often the "immoral" or "degenerate"). Sexuality has
> had a peculiar centrality in such panics, and sexual "deviants" have been
> omnipresent scapegoats.
>
> —**Jeffrey Weeks**, *Sex, Politics, and Society*

The sexual system is not a monolithic, omnipotent structure. There are continuous battles over the definitions, evaluations, arrangements, privileges, and costs of sexual behavior. Political struggle over sex assumes characteristic forms.

Sexual ideology plays a crucial role in sexual experience. Consequently, definitions and evaluations of sexual conduct are objects of bitter contest. The confrontations between early gay-liberation and the psychiatric establishment are an excellent example of this kind of fight, but there are constant skirmishes. Recurrent battles take place between the primary producers of sexual ideology—the churches, the family, and the media—and the groups whose experience they name, distort, and endanger.

The legal regulation of sexual conduct is another battleground. Lysander Spooner dissected the system of state-sanctioned moral coercion over a century ago in a text inspired primarily by the temperance campaigns. In *Vices Are Not Crimes: A Vindication of Moral Liberty* (1977), Spooner argued that government should protect its citizens against crime, but that it is foolish, unjust, and tyrannical to legislate against vice. He discusses rationalizations still heard today in defense of legalized moralism—that "vices" (Spooner is referring to drink, but homosexuality, prostitution, or recreational drug use may be substituted) lead to crimes and should therefore be prevented; that those who practice "vice" are *non compos mentis* and should therefore be protected from their self-destruction by state-accomplished ruin; and that children must be protected from supposedly harmful knowledge. The discourse on victimless crimes has not changed much. Legal struggle over sex law will continue until basic freedoms of sexual action and expression are guaranteed. This requires the repeal of all sex laws except those few that deal with actual, not statutory, coercion; and it entails the abolition of vice squads, whose job it is to enforce legislated morality.[68]

In addition to the definitional and legal wars, there are less obvious forms of sexual political conflict, which I call the territorial and border wars. The processes by which erotic minorities form communities and the forces that seek to inhibit them lead to struggles over the nature and boundaries of sexual zones.

Dissident sexuality is rarer and more closely monitored in small towns and rural areas. Consequently, metropolitan life continually beckons to young perverts. Sexual migration creates concentrated pools of potential partners, friends, and associates. It enables individuals to create adult, kin-like networks in which to live. But there are many barriers which sexual migrants have to overcome.

According to the mainstream media and popular prejudice, the marginal sexual worlds are bleak and dangerous. They are portrayed as impoverished, ugly, and inhabited by psychopaths and criminals. New migrants must be sufficiently motivated to resist the impact of such discouraging images. Attempts to counter negative propaganda with more realistic information generally meet with censorship, and there are continuous ideological struggles over which representations of sexual communities make it into the popular media.

Information on how to find, occupy, and live in the marginal sexual worlds is also suppressed. Navigational guides are scarce and inaccurate. In the past, fragments of rumor, distorted gossip, and bad publicity were the most available clues to the location of underground erotic communities. During the late 1960s and early 1970s, better information became available.[69] Now groups like the Moral Majority want to rebuild the ideological walls around the sexual undergrounds and make transit in and out of them as difficult as possible.

Migration is expensive. Transportation costs, moving expenses, and the necessity of finding new jobs and housing are economic difficulties that sexual migrants must overcome. These are especially imposing barriers to the young, who are often the most desperate to move. There are, however, routes into the erotic communities which mark trails through the propaganda thicket and provide some economic shelter along the way. Higher education can be a route for young people from affluent backgrounds. In spite of serious limitations, the information on sexual behavior at most colleges and universities is better than elsewhere, and most colleges and universities shelter small erotic networks of all sorts.

For poorer kids, the military is often the easiest way to get the hell out of wherever they are. Military prohibitions against homosexuality make this a perilous route. Although young queers continually attempt to use the armed forces to get out of intolerable hometown situations and closer to functional gay communities, they face the hazards of exposure, court-martial, and dishonorable discharge.

Once in the cities, erotic populations tend to nucleate and to occupy some regular, visible territory. Churches and other anti-vice forces constantly put pressure on local authorities to contain such areas, reduce their visibility, or to drive their inhabitants out of town. There are periodic crackdowns in which local vice squads are unleashed on the populations they control. Gay men, prostitutes, and sometimes transvestites are sufficiently territorial and numerous to engage in intense battles with the cops over particular streets, parks, and alleys. Such border wars are usually inconclusive, but they result in many casualties.

For most of this century, the sexual underworlds have been marginal and impoverished, their residents subjected to stress and exploitation. The spectacular success of gay entrepreneurs in creating a variegated gay economy has altered the quality of life within the gay ghetto. The level of material comfort and social elaboration achieved by the gay community in the last fifteen years is unprecedented. But it is important to recall what happened to similar miracles. The growth of the black population in New York in the early part of the twentieth century led to the Harlem Renaissance, but that period of creativity withered with the Great Depression. The relative prosperity and cultural florescence of the gay "ghetto" may be equally fragile. Like blacks who fled the South for the metropolitan North, homosexuals may have merely traded rural problems for urban ones.

Gay pioneers occupied neighborhoods that were centrally located but rundown. Consequently, they border poor neighborhoods. Gays, especially low-income gays, end up competing with other low-income groups for the limited supply of cheap and moderate housing. In San Francisco, competition for low-cost housing has exacerbated both racism and homophobia, and is one source of the epidemic of street violence against homosexuals. Instead of being isolated and invisible in rural settings, city gays are now numerous and obvious targets for urban frustrations.

In San Francisco, unbridled construction of downtown skyscrapers and high-cost condominiums is causing affordable housing to evaporate. Megabuck construction is creating pressure on all city residents. Poor gay renters are visible in low-income neighborhoods; multimillionaire contractors are not. The specter of the "homosexual invasion" is a convenient scapegoat which deflects attention from the banks, the planning commission, the political establishment, and the big developers. In San Francisco, the well-being of the gay community has become embroiled in the high-stakes politics of urban real estate.

Downtown expansion affects all the territorial erotic underworlds. In both San Francisco and New York, high-investment construction and urban renewal have intruded on the main areas of prostitution, pornography, and leather bars. Developers are salivating over Times Square, the Tenderloin, what is left of North Beach, and South of Market. Antisex ideology, obscenity law, prostitution regulations, and the alcoholic beverage codes are all being used to dislodge seedy adult businesses, sex workers, and leathermen. Within ten years, most of these areas will have been bulldozed and made safe for convention centers, international hotels, corporate headquarters, and housing for the rich.[70]

The most important and consequential kind of sex conflict is what Jeffrey Weeks has termed the "moral panic." Moral panics are the "political moment" of sex, in which diffuse attitudes are channeled into political action and from there into social change.[71] The white-slavery hysteria of the 1880s, the anti-homosexual campaigns of the 1950s, and the child-pornography panic of the late 1970s were typical moral panics.

Because sexuality in Western societies is so mystified, the wars over it are often fought at oblique angles, aimed at phony targets, conducted with misplaced passions, and are highly, intensely symbolic. Sexual activities often function as signifiers for personal and social apprehensions to which they have no intrinsic connection. During a moral panic, such fears attach to some unfortunate sexual activity or population. The media become ablaze with indignation, the public behaves like a rabid mob, the police are activated, and the state enacts new laws and regulations. When the furor has passed, some innocent erotic group has been decimated, and the state has extended its power into new areas of erotic behavior.

The system of sexual stratification provides easy victims who lack the power to defend themselves, and a preexisting apparatus for controlling their movements and curtailing their freedoms. The stigma against sexual dissidents renders them morally defenseless. Every moral panic has consequences on two levels. The target population suffers most, but everyone is affected by the social and legal changes.

Moral panics rarely alleviate any real problem because they are aimed at chimeras and signifiers. They draw on the preexisting discursive structure which invents victims in order to justify treating "vices" as crimes. The criminalization of innocuous behaviors such as homosexuality, prostitution, obscenity, or recreational drug use is rationalized by portraying them as menaces to health and safety, women and children, national security, the family, or civilization itself. Even when activity is acknowledged to be harmless, it may be banned because it is alleged to "lead" to something ostensibly worse (another manifestation of the domino theory).[72] Great and mighty edifices have been built on the basis of such phantasms. Generally, the outbreak of a moral panic is preceded by an intensification of such scapegoating.

It is always risky to prophesy. But it does not take much prescience to detect potential moral panics in two current developments: the attacks on sadomasochists by a segment of the feminist movement, and the Right's increasing use of AIDS to incite virulent homophobia.

Feminist antipornography ideology has always contained an implied, and sometimes overt, indictment of sadomasochism. The pictures of sucking and fucking that comprise the bulk of pornography may be unnerving to those who are not familiar with them. But it is hard to make a convincing case that such images are violent. All of the early antiporn slide shows used a highly selective sample of s/M imagery to sell a very flimsy analysis. Taken out of context, such images are often shocking. This shock value was mercilessly exploited to scare audiences into accepting the antiporn perspective. The use of s/M imagery in antiporn discourse is inflammatory. It implies that the way to make the world safe for women is to get rid of sadomasochism.

A great deal of antiporn propaganda implies that sadomasochism is the underlying and essential "truth" toward which all pornography tends. Porn is thought to lead to s/M porn which in turn is alleged to lead to rape. This is a just-so story that revitalizes the notion that sex perverts commit sex crimes, not normal people. There is no evidence that the readers of s/M erotica or practicing sadomasochists commit a disproportionate number of sex crimes. Antiporn literature scapegoats an unpopular sexual minority and its reading material for social problems they do not create.

Feminist rhetoric has a distressing tendency to reappear in reactionary contexts. For example, in 1980 and 1981 Pope John Paul II delivered a series of pronouncements reaffirming his commitment to the most conservative and Pauline understandings of human sexuality. In condemning divorce, abortion, trial marriage, pornography, prostitution, birth control, unbridled hedonism, and lust, the pope employed a great deal of feminist rhetoric about sexual objectification. Sounding like the lesbian feminist polemicist Julia Penelope, His Holiness explained that "considering anyone in a lustful way makes that person a sexual object rather than a human being worthy of dignity."[73]

The right wing opposes pornography and has already adopted elements of feminist antiporn rhetoric. The anti-s/m discourse developed in the women's movement could easily become a vehicle for a moral witch hunt. It provides a ready-made defenseless target population. It provides a rationale for the re-criminalization of sexual materials that have escaped the reach of current obscenity laws. It would be especially easy to pass laws against s/m erotica based on rationales similar to those used for child-pornography laws. Such laws are justified as protecting individuals from actual or potential harm. The ostensible purpose of new laws against s/m imagery would be to reduce violence by banning so-called violent porn. A focused campaign against the leather menace might also result in the passage of laws to criminalize s/m behavior that is not currently illegal. The ultimate result of such a moral panic would be the legalized violation of a community of harmless perverts. It is dubious that such a sexual witch hunt would make any appreciable contribution toward reducing violence against women.

An AIDS panic is even more probable. When fears of incurable disease mingle with sexual terror, the resulting brew is extremely volatile. A century ago, attempts to control syphilis led to the passage of the Contagious Diseases Acts in England. The Acts were based on erroneous medical theories and did nothing to halt the spread of the disease. But they did make life miserable for the hundreds of women who were incarcerated, subjected to forcible vaginal examination, and stigmatized for life as prostitutes.[74]

Whatever happens, Acquired Immune Deficiency Syndrome (AIDS) will have far-reaching consequences on sex in general, and on homosexuality in particular. The disease will have a significant impact on the choices gay people make. Fewer will migrate to the gay meccas out of fear of the disease. Those who already reside in the gay villages will avoid situations they fear will expose them. The gay economy, and the political apparatus it supports, may prove to be evanescent. Fear of AIDS has already affected sexual ideology. Just when homosexuals have had some success in throwing off the taint of mental disease, gay people find themselves metaphorically welded to an image of lethal physical deterioration. The syndrome, its peculiar qualities, and its transmissibility are being used to reinforce old fears that sexual activity, homosexuality, and promiscuity lead to disease and death.

AIDS is both a personal tragedy for those who contract the syndrome and a calamity for the gay community. Homophobes have gleefully hastened to turn this tragedy against its victims. One columnist has suggested that AIDS has always existed, that the biblical prohibitions on sodomy were designed to protect people from AIDS, and that AIDS is therefore an appropriate punishment for violating the Levitical codes. Using fear of infection as a rationale, local right-wingers attempted to ban the gay rodeo from Reno, Nevada. A recent issue of the *Moral Majority Report* featured a picture of a "typical" white family of four wearing surgical masks. The headline read: "AIDS: Homosexual Diseases Threaten American Families."[75] Phyllis Schlafly has recently issued a pamphlet arguing that passage of the Equal Rights Amendment would make it impossible to "legally protect ourselves against AIDS and other diseases carried by homosexuals."[76] Current right-wing literature calls for shutting down the gay baths, for a legal ban on homosexual employment in food-handling occupations, and for state-mandated prohibitions on blood donations by gay people. Such policies would require the government to identify all homosexuals and impose easily recognizable legal and social markers on them.

It is bad enough that the gay community must deal with the medical misfortune of having been the population in which a deadly disease first became widespread and visible. It is worse to have to deal with the social consequences as well. Even before the AIDS scare, Greece passed a law that enabled police to arrest suspected homosexuals and force them to submit to an examination for venereal disease. It is likely that until AIDS and its methods of transmission are understood, there will be all sorts of proposals to control it by punishing the gay community and by attacking its institutions. When the cause of Legionnaires' Disease was unknown, there were no calls to quarantine members of the American Legion or to shut down their meeting halls. The Contagious Diseases Acts in England did little to control syphilis, but they caused a great deal of suffering for the women who came under their purview. The history of panic that has accompanied new epidemics, and the casualties incurred by their scapegoats, should make everyone pause and consider with extreme skepticism any attempts to justify antigay policy initiatives on the basis of AIDS.[77]

The Limits of Feminism

> We know that in an overwhelmingly large number of cases, sex crime is associated with pornography. We know that sex criminals read it, are clearly influenced by it. I believe that, if we can eliminate the distribution of such items among impressionable children, we shall greatly reduce our frightening sex-crime rate.
>
> —**J. Edgar Hoover**, cited in Hyde, *A History of Pornography*

In the absence of a more articulated radical theory of sex, most progressives have turned to feminism for guidance. But the relationship between feminism and sex is complex. Because sexuality is a nexus of the relationships between genders, much of the oppression of women is borne by, mediated through, and constituted within sexuality. Feminism has always been vitally interested in sex. But there have been two strains of feminist thought on the subject. One tendency has criticized the restrictions on women's sexual behavior and denounced the high costs imposed on women for being sexually active. This tradition of feminist sexual thought has called for a sexual liberation that would work for women as well as for men. The second tendency has considered sexual liberalization to be inherently a mere extension of male privilege. This tradition resonates with conservative, antisexual discourse. With the advent of the antipornography movement, it achieved temporary hegemony over feminist analysis.

The antipornography movement and its texts have been the most extensive expression of this discourse.[78] In addition, proponents of this viewpoint have condemned virtually every variant of sexual expression as antifeminist. Within this framework, monogamous lesbianism that occurs within long-term, intimate relationships and does not involve playing with polarized roles has replaced married, procreative heterosexuality at the top of the value hierarchy. Heterosexuality has been demoted to somewhere in the middle. Apart from this change, everything else looks more or less familiar. The lower depths are occupied by the usual groups and behaviors: prostitution, transsexuality, sadomasochism, and cross-generational activities.[79] Most gay male conduct, all casual sex, promiscuity, and lesbian behavior that involve roles or kink or nonmonogamy are also censured.[80] Even sexual fantasy during masturbation is denounced as a phallocentric holdover.[81]

This discourse on sexuality is less a sexology than a demonology. It presents most sexual behavior in the worst possible light. Its descriptions of erotic conduct always use the worst available example as if it were representative. It presents the most disgusting pornography, the most exploited forms of prostitution, and the least palatable or most shocking manifestations of sexual variation. This rhetorical tactic consistently misrepresents human sexuality in all its forms. The picture of human sexuality that emerges from this literature is unremittingly ugly.

In addition, this antiporn rhetoric is a massive exercise in scapegoating. It criticizes nonroutine acts of love rather than routine acts of oppression, exploitation, or violence. This demon sexology directs legitimate anger at women's lack of personal safety against innocent individuals, practices, and communities. Antiporn propaganda often implies that sexism originates within the commercial sex industry and subsequently infects the rest of society. This is sociologically nonsensical. The sex industry is part of a sexist society and reflects the sexism of its culture. The sex industry is hardly a feminist utopia. We need to analyze and oppose the manifestations of gender inequality specific to the sex industry. But this is not the same as attempting to wipe out commercial sex or blaming it for all the ills that afflict women.

Similarly, erotic minorities such as sadomasochists and transsexuals are as likely to exhibit sexist attitudes or behavior as any other politically random social grouping. But to claim that they are inherently antifeminist is sheer fantasy. A good deal of current feminist literature attributes the oppression of women to graphic representations of sex, prostitution, sex education, sadomasochism, male homosexuality, and transsexualism. Whatever happened to the family, religion, education, child-rearing practices, the media, the state, psychiatry, job discrimination, and unequal pay?

Finally, this so-called feminist discourse recreates a very conservative sexual morality. For over a century, battles have been waged over just how much shame, distress, and punishment should be incurred by sexual activity. The conservative tradition has promoted opposition to pornography, prostitution, homosexuality, all erotic variation, sex education, sex research, abortion, and contraception. The opposing, pro-sex tradition has included individuals like Havelock Ellis, Magnus Hirschfeld, Alfred Kinsey, and Victoria Woodhull, as well as the sex-education movement, organizations of militant prostitutes and homosexuals, the reproductive-rights movement, and organizations such as the Sexual Reform League of the 1960s. This motley collection of sex reformers, sex educators, and sexual militants has mixed records on both sexual and feminist issues. But surely they are closer to the spirit of modern feminism than are moral crusaders, the social-purity movement, and anti-vice organizations. Nevertheless, the current feminist sexual demonology generally elevates the anti-vice crusaders to positions of ancestral honor, while condemning the more liberatory tradition as antifeminist. In an essay that exemplifies some of these trends, Sheila Jeffreys blames Havelock Ellis, Edward Carpenter, Alexandra Kollantai, "believers in the joy of sex of every possible political persuasion," and the 1929 congress of the World League for Sex Reform for making "a great contribution to the defeat of militant feminism."[82]

The antipornography movement and its avatars have claimed to speak for all feminism. Fortunately, they do not. Sexual liberation has been and continues to be a feminist goal. The women's movement may have produced some of the most retrogressive sexual thinking this side of the Vatican, but it has also produced an exciting, innovative, and articulate defense of sexual pleasure and erotic justice. This "pro-sex" feminism has been spearheaded by lesbians whose sexuality does not conform to movement standards of purity (primarily lesbian sadomasochists and butch/femme dykes), by unapologetic heterosexuals, and by women who adhere to classic radical feminism rather than to the revisionist celebrations of femininity that have become so common.[83] Although the antiporn forces have attempted to weed out of the movement anyone who disagrees with them, the fact remains that feminist thought about sex is profoundly polarized.[84]

Whenever there is polarization, there is an unhappy tendency to think the truth lies somewhere in between. Ellen Willis has commented sarcastically that "the feminist bias is that women are equal to men and the male chauvinist bias is that women are inferior. The unbiased view is that the truth lies somewhere in between."[85] The most recent development in the feminist sex wars is the emergence of a "middle" that seeks to evade the dangers of antiporn fascism, on the one hand, and a supposed "anything goes" libertarianism, on the other.[86] Although it is hard to criticize a position that is not yet fully formed, I want to draw attention to some incipient problems.[87]

The emergent middle is based on a false characterization of the poles of the debate, construing both sides as equally extremist. According to B. Ruby Rich, "The desire for a language of sexuality has led feminists into locations (pornography, sadomasochism) too narrow or overdetermined for a fruitful discussion. Debate has collapsed into a rumble."[88] True, the fights between Women Against Pornography (WAP) and lesbian sadomasochists have resembled gang warfare. But the responsibility for this lies primarily with the antiporn movement and its refusal to engage in principled discussion. s/m lesbians have been forced into a struggle to maintain their membership in the movement and to defend themselves against slander. No major spokeswoman for lesbian s/m has argued for any kind of s/m supremacy or advocated that everyone should be a sadomasochist. In addition to self-defense, s/m lesbians have called for appreciation for erotic diversity and more open discussion of sexuality.[89] Trying to find a middle course between WAP and Samois is a bit like saying that the truth about homosexuality lies somewhere between the positions of the Moral Majority and those of the gay movement.

In political life, it is all too easy to marginalize radicals and to attempt to buy acceptance for a moderate position by portraying others as extremists. Liberals have done this for years to communists. Sexual radicals have opened up the sex debates. It is shameful to deny their contribution, misrepresent their positions, and further their stigmatization.

In contrast to cultural feminists, who simply want to purge sexual dissidents, the sexual moderates are willing to defend the rights of erotic nonconformists to political participation. Yet this defense of political rights is linked to an implicit system of ideological condescension.[90] The argument has two major parts. The first is an accusation that sexual dissidents have not paid close enough attention to the meaning, sources, or historical construction of their sexuality. This emphasis on meaning appears to function in much the same way that the question of etiology has functioned in discussions of homosexuality. That is, homosexuality, sadomasochism, prostitution, or boy-love are taken to be mysterious and problematic in some way that more respectable sexualities are not. The search for a cause is a search for something that could change so that these "problematic" eroticisms would simply not occur. Sexual militants have replied to such exercises by maintaining that although the question of etiology or cause is of intellectual interest, it is not high on the political agenda and that, moreover, the privileging of such questions is itself a regressive political choice.

The second part of the "moderate" position focuses on questions of consent. Sexual radicals of all varieties have demanded the legal and social legitimation of consenting sexual behavior. Feminists have criticized them for ostensibly finessing questions about "the limits of consent" and "structural constraints" on consent.[91] Although there are deep problems with the political discourse of consent, and although there are certainly structural constraints on sexual choice, this criticism has been consistently misapplied in the sex debates. It does not take into account the very specific semantic content that consent has in sex law and sex practice.

As I mentioned earlier, a great deal of sex law does not distinguish between consensual and coercive behavior. Only rape law contains such a distinction. Rape law is based on the assumption, correct in my view, that heterosexual activity may be freely chosen or forcibly coerced. One has the legal right to engage in heterosexual behavior as long as it does not fall under the purview of other statutes and as long as it is agreeable to both parties.

This is not the case for most other sexual acts. Sodomy laws, as I mentioned above, are based on the assumption that the forbidden acts are an "abominable and detestable crime against nature." Criminality is intrinsic to the acts themselves, no matter what the desires of the participants. "Unlike rape, sodomy or an unnatural or perverted sexual act may be committed between two persons both of whom consent, and, regardless of which is the aggressor, both may be prosecuted."[92] Before the consenting-adults statute was passed in California, in 1976, lesbian lovers could have been prosecuted for committing oral copulation. If both participants were capable of consent, both were equally guilty.[93]

Adult-incest statutes operate in a similar fashion. Contrary to popular mythology, the incest statutes have little to do with protecting children from rape by close relatives. The incest statutes themselves prohibit marriage or sexual intercourse between adults who are closely related. Prosecutions are rare, but two were reported recently. In 1979, a nineteen-year-old Marine met his forty-two-year-old mother, from whom he had been separated at birth. The two fell in love and got married. They were charged and found guilty of incest, which under Virginia law carries a maximum ten-year sentence. During their trial, the Marine testified, "I love her very much. I feel that two people who love each other should be able to live together."[94] In another case, a brother and sister who had been raised separately met and decided to get married. They were arrested and pleaded guilty to felony incest in return for probation. A condition of probation was that they not live together as husband and wife. Had they not accepted, they would have faced twenty years in prison.[95]

In a famous s/m case, a man was convicted of aggravated assault for a whipping administered in an s/m scene. There was no complaining victim. The session had been filmed, and he was prosecuted on the basis of the film. The man appealed his conviction by arguing that he had been involved in a consensual sexual encounter and had assaulted no one. In rejecting his appeal, the court ruled that one may not consent to an assault or battery "except in a situation involving ordinary physical contact or blows incident to sports such as football, boxing, or wrestling."[96] The court went on to note that the "consent of a person without legal capacity to give consent, such as a child or insane person, is ineffective," and that "it is a matter of common knowledge that a normal person in full possession of his mental faculties does not freely consent to the use, upon himself, of force likely to produce great bodily injury."[97] Therefore, anyone who would consent to a whipping would be presumed *non compos mentis* and legally incapable of consenting. s/m sex generally involves a much lower level of force than the average football game, and results in far fewer injuries than most sports. But the court ruled that football players are sane, whereas masochists are not.

Sodomy laws, adult-incest laws, and legal interpretations such as the one above clearly interfere with consensual behavior and impose criminal penalties on it. Within the law, consent is a privilege enjoyed only by those who engage in the highest-status sexual behavior. Those who enjoy low-status sexual behavior do not have the legal right to engage in it. In addition, economic sanctions, family pressures, erotic stigma, social discrimination, negative ideology, and the paucity of information about erotic behavior all serve to make it difficult for people to make unconventional sexual choices. There certainly are structural constraints that impede free sexual choice, but they hardly operate to coerce anyone into being a pervert. On the contrary, they operate to coerce everyone toward normality.

The "brainwash theory" explains erotic diversity by assuming that some sexual acts are so disgusting that no one would willingly perform them. Therefore, the reasoning goes, anyone who does so must have been forced or fooled. Even constructivist sexual theory has been pressed into the service of explaining away why otherwise rational individuals might engage in variant sexual behavior. Another position that is not yet fully formed uses the ideas of Foucault and Weeks to imply that the "perversions" are an especially unsavory or problematic aspect of the construction of modern sexuality.[98] This is yet another version of the notion that sexual dissidents are victims of the subtle machinations of the social system. Weeks and Foucault would not accept such an interpretation, since they consider all sexuality to be constructed, the conventional no less than the deviant.

Psychology is the last resort of those who refuse to acknowledge that sexual dissidents are as conscious and free as any other group of sexual actors. If deviants are not responding to the manipulations of the social system, then perhaps the source of their incomprehensible choices can be found in a bad childhood, unsuccessful socialization, or inadequate identity formation. In her essay on erotic domination, Jessica Benjamin draws upon psychoanalysis and philosophy to explain why what she calls "sadomasochism" is alienated, distorted, unsatisfactory, numb, purposeless, and an attempt to "relieve an original effort at differentiation that failed."[99] This essay substitutes a psychophilosophical inferiority for the more usual means of devaluing dissident eroticism. One reviewer has already construed Benjamin's argument as showing that sadomasochism is merely an "obsessive replay of the infant power struggle."[100]

The position which defends the political rights of perverts but which seeks to understand their "alienated" sexuality is certainly preferable to the WAP-style bloodbaths. But for the most part, the sexual moderates have not confronted their discomfort with erotic choices that differ from their own. Erotic chauvinism cannot be redeemed by tarting it up in Marxist drag, sophisticated constructivist theory, or retro-psychobabble.

Whichever feminist position on sexuality—right, left, or center—eventually attains dominance, the existence of such a rich discussion is evidence that the feminist movement will always be a source of interesting thought about sex. Nevertheless, I want to challenge the assumption that feminism is or should be the privileged site of a theory of sexuality. Feminism is the theory of gender oppression. To automatically assume that this makes it the theory of sexual oppression is to fail to distinguish between gender, on the one hand, and erotic desire, on the other.

In the English language, the word *sex* has two very different meanings. It means bodies differentiated by reproductive anatomy, and gender and gender identity, as in "the female sex" or "the male sex." But sex also refers to sexual activity, lust, intercourse, and arousal, as in "to have sex." This semantic merging reflects a cultural assumption that sexuality is reducible to sexual intercourse and that it is a function of the relations between women and men. The cultural fusion of gender with sexuality has given rise to the idea that a theory of sexuality may be derived directly out of a theory of gender.

In an earlier essay, "The Traffic in Women," I used the concept of a sex/gender system, defined as a "set of arrangements by which a society transforms biological sexuality into products of human activity."[101] I went on to argue that "sex as we know it—gender identity, sexual desire and fantasy, concepts of childhood—is itself a social product."[102] In that essay, I did not distinguish between lust and gender, treating both as modalities of the same underlying social process.

"The Traffic in Women" was inspired by the literature on kin-based systems of social organization. It appeared to me at the time that gender and desire were systemically intertwined in such social formations. This may or may not be an accurate assessment of the relationship between sex and gender in tribal organizations. But it is surely not an adequate formulation for sexuality in Western industrial societies. As Foucault has pointed out, a system of sexuality has emerged out of earlier kinship forms and has acquired significant autonomy. "Particularly from the eighteenth century onward, Western societies created and deployed a new apparatus which was superimposed on the previous one, and which, without completely supplanting the latter, helped to reduce its importance. I am speaking of the deployment of *sexuality.* . . . For the first [kinship], what is pertinent is the link between partners and definite statutes; the second [sexuality] is concerned with the sensations of the body, the quality of pleasures, and the nature of impressions."[103]

The development of this sexual system has taken place in the context of historically specific gender relations. Part of the modern ideology of sex is that lust is the province of men, purity that of women. It is no accident that pornography and the perversions have been considered part of the male domain. In the sex industry, women have been excluded from most production and consumption, and allowed to participate primarily as workers. In order to participate in the "perversions," women have had to overcome serious limitations on their social mobility, their economic resources, and their sexual freedoms. Gender affects the operation of the sexual system, and the sexual system has had gender-specific manifestations. But although sex and gender are related, they are not the same thing, and they form the basis of two distinct arenas of social practice.

In contrast to my perspective in "The Traffic in Women," I am now arguing that it is essential to separate gender and sexuality analytically to more accurately reflect their separate social existence. This goes against the grain of much contemporary feminist thought, which treats sexuality as a derivation of gender. For instance, lesbian feminist ideology has mostly analyzed the oppression of lesbians in terms of the oppression of women. However, lesbians are also oppressed as queers and perverts, by the operation of sexual, not gender, stratification. Although it pains many lesbians to think about it, the fact is that lesbians have shared many of the sociological features and suffered from many of the same social penalties as have gay men, sadomasochists, transvestites, and prostitutes.

Catharine MacKinnon has made the most explicit theoretical attempt to subsume sexuality under feminist thought. According to MacKinnon, "Sexuality is to feminism what work is to Marxism.... [T]he molding, direction, and expression of sexuality organizes society into two sexes, women and men."[104] This analytic strategy in turn rests on a decision to "use sex and gender relatively interchangeably."[105] It is this definitional fusion that I want to challenge.[106]

There is an instructive analogy in the history of the differentiation of contemporary feminist thought from Marxism. Marxism is probably the most supple and powerful conceptual system extant for analyzing social inequality. But attempts to make Marxism the sole explanatory system for all social inequalities have been dismal exercises. Marxism is most successful in the areas of social life for which it was originally developed—class relations under capitalism.

In the early days of the contemporary women's movement, a theoretical conflict took place over the applicability of Marxism to gender stratification. Since Marxist theory is relatively powerful, it does in fact detect important and interesting aspects of gender oppression. It works best for those issues of gender most closely related to issues of class and the organization of labor. The issues more specific to the social structure of gender were not amenable to Marxist analysis.

The relationship between feminism and a radical theory of sexual oppression is similar. Feminist conceptual tools were developed to detect and analyze gender-based hierarchies. To the extent that these overlap with erotic strati-fications, feminist theory has some explanatory power. But as issues become less those of gender and more those of sexuality, feminist analysis becomes misleading and often irrelevant. Feminist thought simply lacks angles of vision that can encompass fully the social organization of sexuality. The criteria of relevance in feminist thought do not allow it to see or assess critical power re-lations in the area of sexuality.

In the long run, feminism's critique of gender hierarchy must be incorpo-rated into a radical theory of sex, and the critique of sexual oppression should enrich feminism. But an autonomous theory and politics specific to sexuality must be developed.

It is a mistake to substitute feminism for Marxism as the last word in social theory. Feminism is no more capable than Marxism of being the ultimate and complete account of all social inequality. Nor is feminism the residual theory that can take care of everything to which Marx did not attend. These critical tools were fashioned to handle very specific areas of social activity. Other areas of social life, their forms of power, and their characteristic modes of oppres-sion need their own conceptual implements. In this essay, I have argued for theoretical as well as sexual pluralism.

Conclusion

> . . . these pleasures which are lightly called physical . . .
> —**Colette,** *The Ripening Seed*[107]

Like gender, sexuality is political. It is organized into systems of power, which reward and encourage some individuals and activities, while punishing and suppressing others. Like the capitalist organization of labor and its distribution of rewards and powers, the modern sexual system has been the object of politi-cal struggle since it emerged and as it has evolved. But if the disputes between labor and capital are mystified, sexual conflicts are completely camouflaged.

The legislative restructuring that took place at the end of the nineteenth century and in the early decades of the twentieth was a refracted response to the emergence of the modern erotic system. During that period, new erotic communities formed. It became possible to be a male homosexual or a lesbian in a way it had not been previously. Mass-produced erotica became available, and the possibilities for sexual commerce expanded. The first homosexual rights organizations were formed, and the first analyses of sexual oppression were articulated.[108]

The repression of the 1950s was in part a backlash to the expansion of sexual communities and possibilities which took place during the Second World War.[109] During the 1950s, gay-rights organizations were established, the Kinsey reports were published, and lesbian literature flourished. The 1950s were a formative as well as a repressive era.

The current right-wing sexual counteroffensive is in part a reaction to the sexual liberalization of the 1960s and early 1970s. Moreover, it has brought about a unified and self-conscious coalition of sexual radicals. In one sense, what is now occurring is the emergence of a new sexual movement, aware of new issues and seeking a new theoretical basis. The sex wars out on the streets have been partly responsible for provoking a new intellectual focus on sexuality. The sexual system is shifting once again, and we are seeing many symptoms of its change.

In Western culture, sex is taken all too seriously. A person is not considered immoral, is not sent to prison, and is not expelled from her or his family for enjoying spicy cuisine. But an individual may go through all this and more for enjoying shoe leather. Ultimately, of what possible social significance is it if a person likes to masturbate over a shoe? It may even be nonconsensual, but since we do not ask permission of our shoes to wear them, it hardly seems necessary to obtain dispensation to come on them.

If sex is taken too seriously, sexual persecution is not taken seriously enough. There is systematic mistreatment of individuals and communities on the basis of erotic taste or behavior. There are serious penalties for belonging to the various sexual occupational castes. The sexuality of the young is denied, adult sexuality is often treated like a variety of nuclear waste, and the graphic representation of sex takes place in a mire of legal and social circumlocution. Specific populations bear the brunt of the current system of erotic power, but their persecution upholds a system that affects everyone.

The 1980s have already been a time of great sexual suffering. They have also been a time of ferment and new possibilities. Those who consider themselves progressive need to examine their preconceptions, update their sexual educations, and acquaint themselves with the existence and operation of sexual hierarchy. It is time to recognize the political dimensions of erotic life.

Afterword to "Thinking Sex: Notes for a
Radical Theory of the Politics of Sexuality" | **6**

Since "Thinking Sex" was published in 1984, the world has changed quite profoundly. The context in which this essay was conceived has shifted in significant, tectonic ways. To call for more academic work and political thought around sexuality seems quaintly anachronistic as I write this in 1992, when so much concern with sex has been thought, written, legislated, taken to the streets, and wound up in court. When "Thinking Sex" was written, there was no Act Up, no Queer Nation, no PoMo Homos, no Boy with Arms Akimbo, and no generation of young lesbians with "Bad Girl" identities. There were gay scholars and there was gay scholarship. But the gay-studies explosion, the critiques of gay identity politics, and much of what has become postmodern sex politics, style, and academic work were yet to come.[1]

When I wrote "Thinking Sex," there had been no Attorney General's Commission on Pornography (the Meese Commission), no Supreme Court decision upholding sodomy laws, no Helms Amendment restricting funding by the National Endowment for the Arts (NEA). *Roe v. Wade* and women's right to terminate unwanted pregnancies were secure. There was no Parents Music Resource Center denouncing the content of rock-and-roll lyrics. Judas Priest had not been sued. Members of 2 Live Crew had not been arrested, and their rap album had not been found obscene. A Cincinnati art museum and its director had not been tried for obscenity because of an exhibit of photographs by

Chapter 6 was originally published in Linda S. Kauffman, *American Feminist Thought at Century's End: A Reader* (Oxford: Blackwell, 1993), 1–64.

Robert Mapplethorpe. The mayor of Minneapolis had just vetoed a so-called "civil rights antiporn ordinance" coauthored by Catharine MacKinnon and Andrea Dworkin.[2] The Mayor of Indianapolis would sign a similar ordinance into law in May of 1984.[3]

The Centers for Disease Control (CDC) had not banned "explicit sex" from AIDS education literature. Jesse Helms had not passed an amendment prohibiting federal funds for gay-related safe-sex materials. The Senate had not voted to make it a federal crime for any HIV-positive health worker to perform invasive procedures. The campaign to close the gay baths was about to erupt.

Many of the things I feared have not only come to pass, they are now commonplace features of the political and social landscape. The politics of sexuality in the United States have swerved far to the right after over a decade of unrelenting right-wing mobilization and religious fundamentalist pressure. The impact of conservative domination of the federal government has become substantial and devastating. The costs of sex—especially for those outside of the married, heterosexual family—have escalated.

The Road to Ruin

Sex panics over pornography, children, homosexuality, AIDS, popular music, and sadomasochism have occurred with alarming frequency in the last decade. The symbolic themes of these panics have been intertwined and mutually reinforcing. Pornography is seen as a threat to children, homosexuality is confused with AIDS, sadomasochism is conflated with AIDS and homosexuality, rock-and-roll and rap music are portrayed as bringing sex and AIDS and sadomasochism and pornography to children. Such witchy brews have ignited public hysteria, legislative reform, and regulatory adjustment. The social and personal repercussions of these changes have yet to be catalogued.

Pornography has been, along with AIDS, one of the most symbolically potent flash points. Right-wing politicians, officials, and religious fundamentalists have become the primary force fueling antipornography activity. In 1985, President Reagan's attorney general, Edwin Meese, impaneled a commission to study pornography and make recommendations for federal policy and legislation. The Meese Commission was packed with conservatives who duly concluded that pornography is harmful and a social menace. Their report recommended increased obscenity prosecution and included an ambitious wish list of draconian legislation, policy, and funding toward that end.[4]

The Meese Commission recommended that federal obscenity laws be amended to enact forfeiture provisions for persons convicted of obscenity, to eliminate the necessity to prove interstate commerce as a requirement for federal jurisdiction, to proscribe obscene programming on cable television, and to prohibit any telephone transmission of obscene material. The report recommended that state legislatures tighten state obscenity laws to conform to the federal "Miller" standard, make all second offenses felonies instead of misdemeanors, enact forfeiture provisions for obscenity offenses, and enact Racketeer Influenced Corrupt Organizations (RICO) provisions for obscenity cases.

The report recommended that the U.S. Department of Justice direct U.S. attorneys to step up obscenity prosecutions, establish an Obscenity Task Force, create an obscenity enforcement database linking federal, state, and local law enforcement agencies, employ federal RICO provisions in obscenity cases, and provide training to U.S. attorneys in legal procedures for a more successful obscenity conviction rate. The commission went on to suggest that the Federal Communications Commission be used to control sexual communication via telephone, cable television, and satellite TV.[5]

The report included fifty-five recommendations to control child pornography in spite of the fact that by 1986 there was no commercial child pornography in the United States. The report recommended that states make possession of child pornography a felony. Child pornography is now often defined as a sexually explicit visual depiction of a child, that is, a person under the age of eighteen.[6]

A gruesome number of the Meese Commission's recommendations have been put into practice. The U.S. Department of Justice did establish an obscenity unit and exponentially increased the number of U.S. attorneys working to prosecute obscenity cases (our tax dollars hard at work).[7] The government has used the confiscatory powers of RICO to seize assets of individuals convicted of obscenity.[8] The Supreme Court has upheld restrictions on telephone transmission of sexually explicit speech (in a recent "Dial-A-Porn" decision). A newly passed bill regulating cable television has a little noticed Helms amendment prohibiting sexually explicit programming on cable television.[9] Many states have revamped their obscenity laws to conform to the Miller standard.

The tsunami of panic about child pornography and child sexual abuse continues to overwhelm considered approaches to the genuine issues of protecting young children from abusive treatment. Public concern and law-enforcement priorities have been deflected from the ordinary adult heterosexual men who are responsible for most of the sexual abuse of children and from the ordinary families where most child abuse (sexual and otherwise) occurs. Instead, police, media, and public hysteria have targeted strangers and weirdos: day-care workers, gay men, pedophiles, readers of porn, and Satanists, real and imagined.[10]

Many states have criminalized simple possession of "child pornography," and federal law now makes possession of three or more publications or videos containing sexually explicit images of persons under eighteen a felony.[11] Obscenity legislation is now routinely called child-pornography legislation. For example, the "Child Pornography and Obscenity Enforcement Act of 1988" was only marginally concerned with child pornography, although it did increase penalties for existing offenses. The act was primarily concerned with expanding forfeiture provisions in obscenity cases. The bill also contained some nifty attempts to prohibit the distribution of obscene material via cable or subscription television and to make it a felony to possess obscene material on federal property. In 1991, the Justice Department Obscenity Unit was retitled the Child Exploitation and Obscenity Section even though there is virtually no child pornography for it to prosecute.[12]

As the consequences of antiporn legislation and enforcement have become more glaringly apparent, antiporn politics have lost their glitter among feminists. But feminist antiporn rhetoric has been thoroughly assimilated into conservative sexual discourse. Those feminists who still pursue an antiporn agenda increasingly do so by cooperating with right-wing politicians and crusaders in pursuing common goals to restrict or eliminate sexually explicit media.

Catharine MacKinnon, Andrea Dworkin, and Dorchen Leidholdt are prominent antiporn feminists who testified before the Meese Commission and who publicly lauded its report. Leidholdt even brought the Women Against Pornography (WAP) slide show for the delectation of the commissioners. One of the commissioners, Park Deitz, was moved to tears by Dworkin's testimony.[13]

In 1986, feminist antiporn strategy had two legislative goals, embodied in the MacKinnon-Dworkin civil-rights antiporn ordinance. The first goal was to make "pornography" a cause for civil action. The second was to codify into law an ostensibly "feminist" definition of pornography as a practice of sex discrimination. "Pornography" would then be a legal entity distinct from "obscenity," which is presently the only category of proscribed sexually explicit material featuring adults. Feminist antiporn activists were attempting to create a new category of illicit sexual material.

Unlike obscenity, this new legal definition of pornography was declared unconstitutional by the U.S. Supreme Court. The Meese Commission endorsed a version of the civil-rights approach that might hold up to constitutional scrutiny. The report recommended making pornography a cause of civil action, but only if the material were legally obscene.[14] MacKinnon, Dworkin, and Women Against Pornography all praised the commission, but condemned its endorsement of obscenity law.[15]

Many antiporn feminists have now adopted the position of the Meese Commission. While they still aim to make pornography a cause of civil action, they have largely abandoned their attempts to create a new category of legally vulnerable sexual materials. They are relying on the existing legal categories of obscenity and child pornography, precisely because the courts have held these to be unprotected by the First Amendment.

This strategy is codified in Senate Bill 1521, the Pornography Victims Compensation Act, currently poised to pass out of the Senate Judiciary Committee and go before the full Senate. The Pornography Victims Compensation Act is supported by both right-wing conservatives and antiporn feminists. The bill makes obscene material a cause of civil action. It would allow victims of sex crimes to sue the producers and distributors of obscene materials for damages if the plaintiff could show that such materials "caused" the crime. The bill would establish third-party liability for obscene material, and would enable a victim to sue not the perpetrator of a crime, but third parties whose only involvement was the production and distribution of written or visual material in which the actual perpetrator may have found some inspiration.

Such liability would apply only to sexual materials found to be legally obscene or to materials that fit the definition of child pornography. It would not apply to slasher movies, detective fiction, religious writings, romantic novels, mainstream advertising, military training manuals, or any other nonobscene material that may be equally provocative to a violent criminal. Antiporn feminists are supporting this bill despite its reliance on old-fashioned nonfeminist obscenity as the category of illicit representation.[16]

Life in Unimaginable Times

Although it is fashionable to blame feminists for most of what is wrong with sexual politics, feminists have also sounded the alarm about the burgeoning menace of misdirected sex panics and politics since the late 1970s and early 1980s. Many feminists have repeatedly cautioned progressives to leave that wooden horse alone. But like Cassandra's pronouncements at Troy, our warnings seemed like wild ravings, febrile nightmares, a soap opera from the Twilight Zone. Who could have anticipated the following incidents?

In 1989, the far-right Senator Jesse Helms stunned the art world by success-fully passing an amendment restricting the funding process of the National Endowment for the Arts. The infamous "Helms Amendment" prohibited NEA grants to any "obscene materials including but not limited to depictions of sadomasochism, homoeroticism, the sexual exploitation of children, or indi-viduals engaged in sex acts." The imbroglio leading up to the passage of these restrictions was sparked in large part by a retrospective exhibit of the work of the gay photographer Robert Mapplethorpe, who was dying of AIDS. His work included images of homosexual men, sadomasochistic erotic activities, many beautiful black male nudes, a few partially undressed children, and dozens of flower arrangements. The NEA controversy was an overdetermined nexus of a decade of enhanced sex phobias, old-fashioned racism, and the long-held determination of right-wing politicians to reduce or eliminate public funding for the arts.[17]

Another incident that shook the art world was the April 1990 raid on the San Francisco photographer Jock Sturges, a highly respected artist whose work includes many nude studies of minors. Photo labs are now required by law and FBI policy to report any material which may qualify as "child pornography." Acting on such a report, FBI agents and San Francisco police officers raided Sturges's home. They seized his computer, his photographic equipment, and thousands of negatives and prints. Although Sturges was never indicted, he was subjected to accusations in the press of being a "child pornographer," his home was ravaged, his livelihood was damaged, and he did not get back his equipment until a federal judge ordered the government to return his property in February of 1991.[18]

In January 1991, single mother Denise Perrigo lost custody of her two-year-old child after calling a community center to obtain the phone number of La Leche League, a local breast-feeding advocacy and support group. She also asked if it was normal to become aroused while nursing her infant. According to La Leche, such feelings are not unusual. But Perrigo was referred to a Rape Crisis Center, where her question was interpreted as evidence of sexual abuse. Perrigo was arrested and her daughter taken away.

Although no criminal charges were filed, social services filed sexual abuse and neglect charges against Perrigo in family court and refused to return her daughter. Perrigo's parents filed for custody, but the department of social ser-vices ruled them unacceptable since they "did not believe any abuse had taken place."[19] After the family-court judge ruled that no abuse had taken place, the county filed new charges. "Among these were allegations that Perrigo had in-serted foreign objects in the girl's vagina; later, it was decided that this was the child's description of having her temperature taken rectally."[20] A second judge found no abuse, but ruled that the child had been neglected because, among other things, Perrigo had subjected her daughter to all this state intervention by making her original phone call. Perrigo's daughter was returned home in January 1992, traumatized by a year of separation from her mother.

In the early 1990s, publishers and distributors of gay and lesbian books are encountering mounting obstacles. Increasing numbers of print shops are unwilling to produce gay books and books on sex. Eighteen printers turned down Alyson Publications's *Gay Sex: A Manual for Men Who Love Men*. A printer turned down *Wanting Women*, a collection of erotic lesbian poetry. Several printers refused to work on *How Do I Look?*, a collection on gay and lesbian images in film.[21] Even an academic study on the history of gay male pornography remains unpublished because of its inclusion of sexually explicit but historically significant photographs.[22]

In 1991, U.S. Customs seized copies of *Love Bites*, a book of erotic lesbian photography published in England and on its way to a U.S. distributor. Customs declared the book obscene and intended to destroy all copies. After *Publishers Weekly* contacted the U.S. Attorney's office on behalf of the publishing industry, all charges against the book were dropped and the book was released.[23]

In 1992, the Oregon Citizens Alliance (OCA) is attempting to place an initiative on the ballot that would declare homosexuality, sadomasochism, and pedophilia unconstitutional in the state of Oregon.

In 1991, the U.S. government was poised to conduct a five-year survey of teenage sexual behavior. The study was intended to explore factors that "put adolescents at risk of either pregnancy or sexually transmitted diseases, particularly AIDS." After pressure from conservatives, particularly Jesse Helms, Secretary of Health and Human Services Louis Sullivan suspended the study. Helms and other conservatives denounced the study as a way to "legitimize the homosexual lifestyle." A spokesperson for the American Psychological Association stated, "This is probably the most profound defeat to AIDS prevention efforts since the first Helms amendment [banning] the 'promotion of homosexuality' in [AIDS] educational programs [in 1987]." The funds for the sex study were eventually transferred to a program that encourages sexual abstinence for teenagers.[24]

The policies controlling the accumulation and availability of sexual information are not trivial. The suppression of sexual information in AIDS educational materials and the suppression of sexual information that could lead to AIDS education are callous policies that have killed people. It is amazing to contemplate the politicians who pontificate about the need to protect the lives of unborn babies and who also actively promote murderous policies toward homosexuals, sexually active teenagers, and drug addicts.

We Told You So

These are but a few vignettes taken from the events, incidents, and consequences of the sexual politics of the last decade. It is a pretty grim picture. Those of us who warned of the dangers of antiporn and other antisex politics may get some faint pleasure from vindication. But on the whole, I would rather have been wrong.

Postscript to "Thinking Sex: Notes for a Radical Theory of the Politics of Sexuality"

7

Only four months ago I prepared a lengthy afterword to accompany another reprint of "Thinking Sex" (Linda Kauffman, *American Feminist Thought, 1982–1992*, Oxford: Basil Blackwell, 1993).[1] In that afterword I detailed a few of the ways in which sex politics and thought have shifted since the essay was published. I need not reiterate them here. Nevertheless, since I mailed off the afterword in mid-February there have been several developments that illustrate what is at stake in conflicts over sex and the increasingly giddy pace at which they occur. Three areas of critical activity are the codification of antipornography ideas into law, the growing criminalization of sadomasochistic representation and practice, and the alarming level of political gay-bashing taking place in the 1992 U.S. elections.

Late in February, the Canadian Supreme Court upheld Canada's obscenity law in a decision (*Butler v. Her Majesty the Queen*) which redefined obscenity along the lines pursued by antipornography feminists since the late 1970s.[2] The Canadian court adopted language similar to the definitions in the MacKinnon-Dworkin so-called "civil-rights antipornography" ordinances. In Canada, the legal definition of obscenity is now based, in part, on depictions of sexual behavior considered to be "degrading and dehumanizing." This approach was rejected by the U.S. Supreme Court as a violation of the First Amendment. Canada has nothing comparable to the Bill of Rights and has fewer legal protections for speech and political expression.

Chapter 7 was originally published in Henry Abelove, Michéle Aina Barale, and David M. Halperin, eds., *The Lesbian and Gay Studies Reader* (New York: Routledge, 1993), 41–44.

Although the Canadian legal situation is different from that of the United States, the increasingly right-wing U.S. Supreme Court may be influenced by the Canadian decision when it next considers similar legal wording. The logic of Senate Bill 1521 (the Pornography Victims Compensation Act) is based on the same flawed assumptions as the Butler decision. This bill was just passed out of the Senate Judiciary Committee late in June and now heads to the Senate floor.[3]

In addition, it appears that the Butler decision was facilitated by the slow accumulation of legal precedent in lesser cases. In the United States, antiporn activists and attorneys are attempting to build a similar body of precedent in cases which might initially appear tangential to obscenity law. Anticensorship feminist and civil-rights lawyers should be alert to language that treats pornography as inherently "harmful" or "anti-woman" in, for example, sexual-harassment cases (pornography, like Coke cans or any number of other objects, may in fact be used to harass; but it is far more tempting to think of pornography as harmful regardless of context than it is to make similar assumptions about less demonized items).

Many gay activists in Canada warned that the new obscenity definitions would be used differentially against gay and lesbian media. Glad Day Books, the gay and lesbian bookstore in Toronto, has already suffered through a decade of police harassment, and customs confiscations have already made many gay and lesbian publications unobtainable in Canada. Emboldened by the Butler definitions, police raided Glad Day on 30 April and charged the store manager with violating obscenity law for selling *Bad Attitude*, a U.S. lesbian sex magazine which contained depictions of bondage and penetration. On 4 May, the owner and corporation were also charged with obscenity.[4]

The new criteria for obscenity effectively make s/m erotica illegal in Canada, since such materials most closely resemble the category of "degrading and dehumanizing" pornography.[5] Moreover, gay male s/m materials appear to have played a key role in persuading the court to adopt the new obscenity standards. One news article praising the Canadian decision contains a disturbing claim by one of the victorious attorneys. She is quoted as attributing the success of their litigation to showing the justices "violent and degrading *gay* movies. We made the point that the abused men in these films were being treated like women—*and the judges got it*. Otherwise, men can't put themselves in our shoes."[6] If this report is accurate, feminist lawyers sold their analysis by using depictions of gay male sex to elicit the predictably defensive responses and homophobic repugnance such films were likely to produce among heterosexual men. For many years, feminist antiporn activists have exploited ignorance and bigotry toward sadomasochism to substitute for their lack of evidence; in exploiting ignorance and bigotry toward male homosexuality they have sunk to new depths of political irresponsibility and opportunism.

This is particularly distressing in the wake of a recent court decision in England, and in the context of significant gay-baiting in the 1992 U.S. elections. In England in 1990, sixteen men were convicted on various charges arising from consensual homosexual sadomasochistic activities. Many were given prison sentences, some up to four-and-a-half years. None of the participants complained or brought charges; the men were arrested after police confiscated homemade sex videos which documented their activities.[7] The case was appealed. In late February, the Court of Appeal upheld the convictions, ruling that "the question of consent was immaterial," and effectively confirming that s/m sexual activity is illegal in England.[8] While the decision is based on earlier rulings, such prosecutions have been extremely rare. The fact that so many gay men were given lengthy prison sentences for private consensual adult sexual activities is ominous.

In the United States, homophobia has become a major political tactic in this year's elections. In February the presidential primary season was just heating up. As the elections have progressed, the National Endowment for the Arts (NEA), the Public Broadcasting System (PBS), representations of homosexuality, and homosexuality itself have all become hot buttons and hot targets. Funding for PBS has been attacked, and the former chair of the NEA has been sacked (for believing in the Constitution and the Bill of Rights). From Patrick Buchanan's neo-Nazi rantings to Dan Quayle's euphemistic emphasis on "family values," both overt and covert attacks on homosexuality have been prominent tactics in the 1992 election campaigns.[9]

In Oregon, the right-wing Oregon Citizens Alliance (OCA) is attempting to pass two initiatives which would amend the state constitution to define homosexuality, sadomasochism, pedophilia, bestiality, and necrophilia as "abnormal, wrong, unnatural, and perverse" *by law*. If passed, these initiatives would prevent such groups from using public facilities, would prohibit any civil-rights legislation to protect sexual minorities, and would forbid teaching positive views of such behaviors in any state-funded school, college, or university.[10]

While the OCA claims its initiative would not change the criminal law or increase criminal penalties for these behaviors, the initiative is reminiscent of several aspects of National Socialist legislation. The OCA initiatives would, if passed, deprive sexual minorities of equal citizenship, make them "inferior" by law and public policy, mandate teaching such inferiority in all state-supported educational institutions, and suppress the promulgation of opinions or evidence that would contravene such legally dictated inferiority.[11]

I am now preparing to mail this postscript in early July. Four months remain until the 1992 elections. Who know what hysterias will be elicited, what fears drummed upon, what hostilities and antagonisms enticed, and to what base levels the political process will plunge in order to keep power, wealth, and privilege as concentrated as possible? Who knows how many more harmless people will be jailed, ostracized, harassed, financially destroyed, or physically assaulted? Who knows why ostensibly progressive and well-intentioned people continue to fail to oppose regressive policies with serious and devastating consequences? By now they should all know better.

Tune in next year for another exciting episode.

Blood under the Bridge

Reflections on "Thinking Sex"

8

*To the incomparable Eve Sedgwick, whose absence
has been so acutely felt and sadly noted.*

The Fight against Forgetting

Twenty-five years after its publication, I have been asked to reflect on my essay "Thinking Sex." A quarter of a century is a long time. One indicator of time's passage is the technology of textual production. I bought my first computer a year after "Thinking Sex" went to the publisher. "Thinking Sex" was thus written the old-fashioned way: on a typewriter. It was edited when "cut and paste" still meant slicing up paper with real scissors and reassembling the pieces with actual glue.[1] Reading back through the reams of material generated by the controversies of the early feminist sex wars, I was continually reminded that almost all of the innumerable flyers, leaflets, articles, broadsides, and letters to the editor were done without computers. In the early 1980s there was an Internet, but it was still mostly the preserve of military personnel, scientists, and computer programmers. Most communication was still by way of landline telephones and snail mail.

Another indicator of change is the status of the essay itself. Although the paper resulted from the intersection of several different intellectual agendas

Chapter 8 was originally published in Heather Love, Ann Cvetkovich, and Annamarie Jagose, eds., "Rethinking Sex," special issue, GLQ 17, no. 1 (November 2010): 15–48.

and political concerns, its initial reception was filtered through the acrimonious controversies of the feminist sex wars. These conflicts have at times obscured the essay's intellectual concerns and scholarly contributions. As a result, many of the early responses to "Thinking Sex" fluctuated between patronizing condescension and hostile indignation.[2] As these conflicts within feminism have cooled, the essay's academic aspects have become more visible and salient. Its reception has shifted from the scholarly to the scandalous and back again.

"Thinking Sex" was first published in Carole Vance's 1984 book *Pleasure and Danger*, the anthology of papers from the 1982 Barnard Sex Conference where I had given a version of "Thinking Sex" as a workshop.[3] The Barnard conference has become famous, in large part because it was the occasion of one of the most volcanic battles in the feminist sex wars. What actually happened at Barnard has been widely misunderstood. In her opening remarks at the "Rethinking Sex" conference, Heather Love commented that she, who was not in attendance at Barnard, had a fear of having missed something. I, on the other hand, nurse the horror of having been there. The attack on the Barnard conference was a particularly repellent episode in what was unfortunately a repetitive pattern of conduct. Some antipornography advocates have consistently resorted to *ad feminem* attacks and character assassination instead of debating substantive issues. They have routinely attempted to excommunicate from the feminist movement anyone who disagreed with them, and they aggressively sabotaged events that did not adhere to the antiporn party line. Their conduct left a bitter legacy for feminism. Like many others involved in the sex wars, I was thoroughly traumatized by the breakdown of feminist civility and the venomous treatment to which dissenters from the antiporn orthodoxy were routinely subjected.[4]

I had been working on the ideas presented at my Barnard workshop for several years prior to the conference. I had lectured on these subjects at the University of California, Berkeley; the University of California, Los Angeles; the University of California, Santa Cruz; and the New York Institute for the Humanities. In all of these venues, audience responses were unremarkable, and the discussions that ensued were typical of academic events: spirited and engaged, at times argumentative, yet always polite.

Once I had been identified as a public enemy by early feminist antipornography activists, however, my appearances became occasions for protests against my speaking, not just on pornography but on any topic at all. The protest against my participation at the Barnard conference generated the most press of any of these attempts at silencing and intimidation, but it was neither the first such occurrence nor the last. The opposition began a few years before the Barnard conference and continued for more than a decade thereafter. There were some early and, in comparison with later events, relatively mild episodes in the Bay Area in the late 1970s. They were like small foreshocks that portend a larger seismic jolt.

For example, around 1979, I was scheduled to make a presentation about Michel Foucault for an informal Marxist-Feminist discussion group in Berkeley. Several antiporn members of the group felt I should not be allowed to speak. After a campaign to have me removed from the panel failed, those opposing my participation boycotted the discussion. In another incident, a local group of gay and lesbian leftists imploded over having invited me to participate on a panel discussion of political differences and similarities between lesbians and gay men. These kinds of situations proliferated and became increasingly vitriolic.

Nor was I the only target. The list of ostensibly unacceptable feminists expanded over time, and eventually included, among many others, Dorothy Allison, Pat Califia, Lisa Duggan, Dierdre English, Amber Hollibaugh, Nan Hunter, Joan Nestle, Cindy Patton, Carole Vance, and Ellen Willis. Revisiting those days is at best bittersweet. Nonetheless, this is an occasion to situate my essay in the context in which it was produced and to remember the historical conditions that shaped it. Jonathan Ned Katz, one of the founders of the modern field of gay, lesbian, bisexual, and transgender history, ends his e-mails with the slogan "Fight Against Forgetting."[5] While these memories can be painful, I am happy to be a foot soldier in the fight against forgetting.

Shifting Paradigms of Sex

With all due respect to the organizers of the "Rethinking Sex" conference, I do not believe that my essay "inaugurated the field of contemporary sexuality studies."[6] My own work was a product of a broader set of intellectual transformations in the study of gender and sexuality that were well under way in the 1970s. My work resulted from many of the same developments that influenced writers and scholars such as Allan Bérubé, George Chauncey, Madeline Davis, John D'Emilio, Martin Duberman, Jeffrey Escoffier, Estelle Freedman, Eric Garber, Jonathan Ned Katz, Liz Kennedy, Joan Nestle, Esther Newton, Jim Steakley, Martha Vicinus, and Jeffrey Weeks, just to name a handful of people working on what would eventually become the field of gay and lesbian studies. This burst of scholarly activity was produced largely by social movements—feminism and gay liberation—taking place both inside and outside the academy. The early 1970s were the heady days of the first Berkshire Conference on the History of Women, the conferences of the Gay Academic Union, and the founding of journals such as *Feminist Studies* and *Signs*. By the mid-1970s, the cross-pollination of concepts and data from anthropology, sociology, and history had resulted in a new theoretical formation. By 1977 Weeks drew from his training in both sociology and history to articulate a framework for gay history that would come to be labeled "the social construction of sex."[7]

A great deal of nonsense has been written about the "social construction of sex" paradigm. Critics often argue against a caricature and seem to think that social constructionists believe that prior to the 1890s no one ever engaged in same-sex desire, orgasmic connection, or cross-gender behavior.[8] I am not aware of anyone who makes such ludicrous claims.

Social construction simply situates homosexuality and sexuality within the histories of everyday and intimate life: things such as marriage, childhood, and table manners. No one assumes that historians of childhood think that physical immaturity itself is a modern invention. Historians of marriage note that, like homosexuality, *marriage* is not a universal term or concept. They do not claim that no couples ever mated, lived together, had children, shared property, or were granted special legal status. They do point to the discontinuities between different ways of doing so and the distinct constellations of behavior, custom, and emotion involved.[9]

Social construction treats sexual conduct the way historians and anthropologists have long treated other social phenomena. Thus a farmer in twentieth-century Nebraska is not the same as a peasant in czarist Russia even though both cultivate the soil and grow food. The cattle barons of Texas are not the same as the cattle herders of the Nuer, although both are involved in economies of beef. Slaves in ancient Athens were not the same kind of property as slaves in the antebellum American South.[10] Property is socially constructed and widely variable, and it is those diverse forms of ownership and bundles of rights to which entire literatures in anthropology, history, and law are addressed. Why should sexuality be exempt from the ordinary processes of social-scientific inquiry and legal history?

Social construction is simply the insistence that sexuality be subjected to the same set of methodological tactics and theoretical principles as any other topic or aspect of human conduct. What seemed so radical was in many respects the application of a conventional set of approaches to an unconventional and highly stigmatized subject. As Vance has often observed in conversation, what is most odd is not that social-constructionist theories of sexuality were developed, but how long it took. By showing that same-sex eroticisms and cross-gender behavior were historically and culturally specific, social construction cleared away obsolete assumptions, generated new research programs, and legitimized new topics. Despite initial controversy and some persistent arguments, the major assumptions of social construction now form the familiar ground on which most queer scholarship takes place. It is easy to forget what the field was like before that paradigm shift, when, among other things, much of gay history was the search for glorious ancestors, and male homosexuality and lesbianism were understood to be stable and largely unchanging phenomena. The accumulation of data within the old paradigm was incredibly valuable, however, and provided the foundation for social construction to emerge. "Thinking Sex" was part of the intellectual ferment reshaping the study of sexuality in the late 1970s.[11] Generated by the excitement of my initial encounters with the social-constructionist framework, the essay was an attempt to work out some of its implications, especially with respect to my own ethnographic research on urban sexual populations and locations.

I have previously complained in print about the amnesia that obscures the early strata of homophile and gay-liberation scholarship.[12] I do want to note, at least in passing, that the neglect of this body of work stemmed in part from the paucity of institutional support for it. Some who did this work were not affiliated with any university.[13] Those within academia who studied gay topics were, to put it mildly, not well rewarded.[14] Many were graduate students whose advisers told them bluntly that they were committing academic suicide, and these warnings were not unrealistic. Many others who did this early work of queer scholarship endured systematic unemployment or underemployment in the academy.

These kinds of subjects, and the scholars who studied them, were generally treated as disreputable within their disciplines, and such research was not deemed appropriate for publication in the prestigious academic journals. Some of the most important work in gay history, such as D'Emilio's study of the homophile movement, Steakley's revelations of the Nazi persecution of homosexuals, and Bérubé's early research on gay San Francisco, was published not in academic journals but in programs for gay-pride celebrations; in the *Body Politic*, a Canadian gay-liberation newspaper; and in *Gay Community News*, the gay-liberation newspaper from Boston.[15] One of Bérubé's first essays on gay men and lesbians in the Second World War was published in *Mother Jones*.[16] These were great periodicals, but they did not count toward tenure. There was a sea change in the 1990s, when queer and sexuality scholarship (especially for junior scholars in some fields) was no longer a career killer. This change occurred earlier in the humanities and more slowly in the social sciences, where LGBTQ studies are still struggling to establish a durable institutional presence.

While academia did not nurture the early gay and sexuality scholarship, there was nevertheless a dense intellectual and social network that did. When we did not have departments, we had study groups where community-based and university-affiliated researchers could share their discoveries. Two such informal groups were extremely important to me. One was an intensely educational and stimulating "feminism and the history of sex" study group with participants such as Nancy Chodorow, Ellen DuBois, Barbara Epstein, Michelle Rosaldo, Mary Ryan, Judith Stacey, Kaye Trimberger, and Martha Vicinus. The second was the San Francisco Lesbian and Gay History Project. The History Project was founded by Bérubé, Escoffier, and Garber. Amber Hollibaugh, Estelle Freedman, and I soon joined. As Freedman recalls, "Around 1978, I joined the fledgling San Francisco Lesbian and Gay History Project, a small and intensely stimulating group of scholars, lay historians and filmmakers committed to making gay history accessible to the public."[17] The membership was fluid and changed over time, but Bérubé, Garber, Escoffier, Freedman, Hollibaugh, D'Emilio, and I were among the active long-term participants. Many others, such as Bert Hansen and Judith Schwartz, visited when they came to San Francisco.[18] Bérubé's research provided an anchor. He discovered archival data on women who passed as men in early San Francisco.[19] He found documentation on the surveillance of gay bars in California conducted by the Alcoholic Beverage Commission, as well as the court cases that established the legal rights for homosexuals to drink in public.[20] I remember the first time he spoke of a box of letters written by gay men during the Second World War; these letters started the project that resulted in his pathbreaking book *Coming Out Under Fire*.[21] I first heard Garber speak of his work on African American gay men and lesbians in Harlem in the early twentieth century at a meeting of the History Project.[22]

I cannot say enough about the intellectual excitement and impact of the History Project. Nevertheless, it was not insulated from the early phases of the sex wars. In 1979, "Allan Bérubé gave the first presentation of his slide show about women who had passed as men in early San Francisco, *Lesbian Masquerade*, before a packed audience at the Women's Building. It was a grand celebration, and immediately netted the history project new recruits to our collective cultural enterprise."[23] Unfortunately, some of those new recruits came with ideological commitments that led them to try to expel me, both because of my research, which was on the gay male leather and s/m population, and because of my involvement in the then nascent lesbian s/m community. In the end, I was able to stay, and those who were most opposed to my presence left the History Project. I maintained my membership, but it was, in Erving Goffman's terms, "spoiled."[24] I was sufficiently radioactive that for many years after I was not asked to share my research at any of our public presentations.

Speaking Bitterness: The Feminist Sex Wars

The name "Barnard Sex Conference" is actually shorthand for "The Scholar and the Feminist IX: Towards a Politics of Sexuality," the ninth iteration of "The Scholar and the Feminist" conference held annually at Barnard College since 1974. The Barnard Sex Conference's concept paper was titled "Towards a Politics of Sexuality." The planning committee for the conference included Barnard faculty, graduate students from Columbia University, and New York feminist intellectuals and activists, who responded to an open letter calling for participation. The invitation letter, written by Vance, the conference's academic coordinator, was sent to Barnard College faculty, all members of previous Scholar and Feminist planning committees, and academics and activists who worked on sexuality.[25] The planning committee met every two weeks for eight months, functioning as a study group on sexuality. Minutes of the meetings of the planning committee and comments by each member of the planning group were included in a seventy-two-page booklet, *Diary of a Conference on Sexuality*.

Like the conference itself, the *Diary* was innovative, ambitious, and fresh. It was to be distributed to attendees, and since it was intended to serve as the conference program, it included the schedule of events and the list of speakers. However, it was much more than a program. It was designed to be an archival document, not only of the planning process, but also of the day itself. There were even blank pages so attendees could take notes. Each workshop was given a page containing a description of the workshop, a list of the presenters, and often a suggested bibliography. The workshop pages featured faux postcards that were used to list the presenters' credentials. The speakers were asked to send in some kind of graphic to be used as the image on the front of the postcard. The image could reference the workshop topic, but, in the spirit of a diary, it could also be something personal or even merely something each speaker found meaningful, interesting, visually compelling, or amusing.[26]

Plenary speakers for the opening and closing sessions included DuBois, Alice Echols, Linda Gordon, Hollibaugh, Hortense Spillers, and the poets hattie gossett, Cherríe Moraga, and Sharon Olds. The eighteen afternoon workshops featured diverse topics and presenters. Workshop leaders included Allison, Meryl Altman, Dale Bernstein, Mary Calderone, Arlene Carmen, Muriel Dimen, Oliva Espin, Elsa First, Roberta Galler, Faye Ginsburg, Bette Gordon, Diane Harriford, Susan Hill, Shirley Kaplan, Barbara Kruger, Maire Kurrik, Kate Millett, Carole Munter, Nestle, Newton, Mirtha Quintanales, Pat Robinson, Kaja Silverman, Sharon Thompson, Shirley Walton, and Paula Webster. Topics addressed in the workshops included Jacques Lacan, abortion rights, gay and lesbian rights, pornography, teen romance, popular sex advice literature, creativity and theater, artistic vision, butch/femme roles in both gay and straight relationships, class, race, psychotherapy, politically correct and incorrect sex, body image, disability, the sexuality of infancy and childhood, prostitution, and psychoanalysis. My workshop was "Concepts for a Radical Politics of Sex."

The conference's reputation, however, bears almost no relationship to the substance of the event. A small number of antipornography activists from New York were outraged by the conference, or what they imagined it to be. As recounted in Vance's detailed epilogue to *Pleasure and Danger*, these antagonists staged a noisy protest outside the conference, distributed leaflets denouncing it as antifeminist, and thoroughly spooked the Barnard administration.[27] As Vance noted, the leaflet was "a masterpiece of misinformation" that served "as a template for subsequent reaction to the conference."[28] She observed, "The leaflet, along with the rumors and distorted newspaper reporting it inspired, depicted a phantom conference, restricted to but a few issues which matched the anti-pornographers' tunnel vision concerns about sexuality.... That such diversity of thought and experience should be reduced to pornography, s/M, and butch/femme—the anti-pornographers' counterpart to the New Right's unholy trinity of sex, drugs, and rock 'n' roll—is an example of the effective use of symbols to instigate a sex panic."[29]

Ironically, the conference's major theme, reflected in workshops, the concept paper, and the resulting anthology, was that sexuality is for women both a means of pleasure and a source of danger. To be sure, there was no deference at Barnard to the specific claims of antipornography feminism. There was a workshop on pornography. As noted in the description recorded in the *Diary*, "This workshop will situate pornography within the context of a number of other discourses which construct sexual difference and the female subject in similar ways, most notably advertising and dominant cinema. We will also argue that pornography cannot be isolated from a larger critique of the existing symbolic order, or from such seemingly diverse structures as the family or the church."[30] Such nuance was anathema to the leadership of the antiporn movement, whose ideology situates pornography as a major engine of female subordination and a uniquely pernicious institution of male supremacy.

One of the architects of the Barnard protest was Dorchen Leidholdt, from New York's Women Against Pornography (WAP). Leidholdt's response is captured by Susan Brownmiller, a fellow antiporn activist: "'Then,' Dorchen recalls with a shudder, 'came the Barnard conference.'"[31] Brownmiller's description typifies the antiporn account of the conference.

> The ninth annual "The Scholar and the Feminist" conference at Barnard College on Saturday, April 24, 1982, proclaimed "Towards a Politics of Sexuality" as its groundbreaking theme. Months of planning by Carole Vance, a Columbia anthropologist, and a team of advisers of her choosing had gone into the day's proceedings, intended to produce a joyful exploration of "politically incorrect" sexual behavior, to counter the "fascist" and "moralistic" tendencies of WAP. The bizarre result was a somewhat nervous, somewhat giddy, occasionally tearful exposition of the pleasures of s/m.... Not every speaker at Barnard that day addressed s/m or butch-femme roles. A few invitees read academic papers.[32]

In actuality, none of the eighteen workshops specifically focused on s/M and only one on butch/femme. Although these topics certainly did come up during various discussions—probably drawing even more attention than they otherwise would have after attendees had been handed leaflets specifically denouncing them—they were hardly the dominant focus. With three workshops, psychotherapy and psychoanalysis got far more attention than s/M, and abortion rights were more heavily emphasized than butch/femme. The common denominator of the workshops was, in fact, people reading academic papers. The account of the conference promulgated by antipornography crusaders had a few grains of reality swirling in a noxious brew of hyperbole and misinformation. Vance did not assemble a group of "advisors of her choosing." She had issued an open call to which interested parties had responded. All of this was documented in the *Diary*. But no one saw the *Diary* on the day of the conference, because the *Diary* had been confiscated by the panicked Barnard administration.[33]

Instead, the some eight hundred attendees arriving at the Barnard College gates were confronted by a small group of protesters who wore T-shirts emblazoned with "For a Feminist Sexuality" on the front and "Against s/M" on the back.[34] They were handing out leaflets that accused the conference organizers of endorsing "the backlash against radical feminism" and of having "thrown their support to the very sexual institutions and values that oppress all women."[35] The leaflet singled out several participants for special condemnation because of their allegedly "un-feminist" sexual behaviors or political opinions. These included Allison and two unnamed proponents of "butch femme roles," presumably Nestle, Hollibaugh, or Moraga. The leaflet complained about the participation of Brett Harvey because of her involvement with No More Nice Girls, a reproductive-rights group characterized as "a group of women writers who publish in the *Village Voice* and who contend that pornography is liberating." The leaflet's rationale for the objection to No More Nice Girls was that one of its founders was Willis, who did write for the *Voice* and who was one of the first feminists to publicly take issue with the antipornography analysis.[36] My participation was attacked because of my association with Samois, a lesbian s/m group from San Francisco. Califia, also a member of Samois, was denounced in the leaflet despite having no role at all in the conference beyond that of an attendee. The leaflet claimed I was there "representing" Samois, which I was not.[37] Leidholdt would later claim in *off our backs* that "we weren't protesting the exclusion of WAP but of the whole sexual violence part of the movement. It's particularly dangerous when you're including someone like Gayle Rubin."[38]

There were actually two contradictory versions of the WAP complaint: the first was that the Barnard conference was a blatant celebration of s/m. The second was that the perverted agenda was all the more insidious because it was a hidden one. Leidholdt told a reporter from *off our backs* that "the bias was so hidden at the Barnard conference," and she complained that "nowhere in the program were workshop leaders' affiliations with Samois or LSM (New York's Lesbian Sex Mafia) given."[39] This complaint bears some scrutiny. Of the almost forty speakers and workshop leaders, only two were members of either organization. But in any case, of what relevance were such memberships? Should all participants in academic events list all of their recreational, social, and political associations? I was a graduate student at the University of Michigan speaking at an academic conference, so I listed my academic affiliation, as was appropriate. Evidently, I should have had the decency to wear a black leather triangle or perhaps a scarlet letter.

Whether people supported or opposed the conference's aims, the exaggerated and inaccurate characterizations promulgated by the leaflet and subsequent press coverage remain to this day the conference's dominant legend. While there were arguments over the conference's legitimacy, these rarely challenged the accuracy of the phantom conference narratives. For example, a decade after Barnard, Leidholdt still proclaimed that "along with waging a no holds barred attack on radical feminists and our politics, conference speakers, organizers, and workshop leaders promoted and defended the sexuality of dominance and submission. And at times thinly disguised, at times overt defense of sadomasochism was an underlying theme."[40] Even Jane Gerhard's largely sympathetic account of the conference describes it as composed of "sessions on sexual practice, s/M, butch/femme roles, pornography, children's sexuality, and sexual therapies."[41] While they differ in their evaluations, Leidholdt's and Gerhard's descriptions substantially agree on the conference's ostensible emphasis and fail to mention the majority of topics discussed.

There are many reasons for the persistence of the conference's image as a venue to celebrate kinky sex. But one was surely the confiscation of the *Diary*. As Vance noted, "The unavailability of the *Diary* to registrants on that day made the conference's purpose more vulnerable to distortion. Leaflets were handed out before any papers or presentations were made, and registrants' perceptions of what occurred were colored by the leaflet's inflammatory and sensational charges."[42] By the time the *Diary* was finally republished and provided to participants several weeks later, the outlandish claims and febrile descriptions of the antiporn contingent's narrative had taken root.

As Vance recounts, in the week preceding the conference,

> anti-pornography feminists made telephone calls to Barnard College officials and trustees, as well as prominent local feminists, complaining that the conference was promoting anti-feminist views and had been taken over by "sexual perverts." Lunatic as these claims were, they had a galvanizing effect on the representatives of a sexually conservative women's college. . . . Within days, Ellen V. Futter, President of Barnard, interrogated the staff of the women's center, scrutinized the program, and—concerned about the possible reactions of funders to sexual topics and images—confiscated all copies of the conference booklet.[43]

Jane Gould, the director of the Barnard Women's Center, recounts being summoned to the president's office just prior to the conference. Gould later learned that "the president's office had been inundated with calls from Women Against Pornography attacking the conference, calling it pornography, and announcing their intention to picket on the day of the conference. One of the calls informed the president that the conference planning had been dominated by a California lesbian group called Samois, which supported sadomasochism."[44] I should note that no one from Samois was part of the planning group; those making such farfetched claims apparently failed to consider the logistical implausibility of a San Francisco group participating in meetings in New York every two weeks for eight months. But these myths persevere. Gerhard even lists me as a conference planner, which I was not. That she does so demonstrates the triumph of the narrative over the facts.[45]

When Gould entered the president's office, she found "Futter, the director of public relations, and the college lawyer . . . all with copies of the *Diary*. President Futter's expression said it all. She plunged right in, saying that she regarded the publication as a piece of pornography and that she was not going to tolerate its distribution to the conference participants and to the public. . . . She insisted that it must be destroyed, shredded immediately."[46] Vance notes that while the Barnard administration confiscated all fifteen hundred copies two days before the conference, she and members of the planning committee were not informed of the confiscation until less than twenty-four hours before the conference.[47] Barnard administrators directed Vance to say that the *Diary* was "delayed at the printers." She ignored this demand and informed participants that the president of Barnard College had confiscated and censored the *Diary*. After considerable pressure and legal threats, Barnard College agreed to pay to reprint the *Diary*, removing two lines of type with the names of Barnard College and the conference funder, the Helena B. Rubinstein Foundation, and to distribute the reprinted document to conference participants.[48]

The *Diary* was finally reprinted and mailed out to attendees in June. In August Andrea Dworkin sent out copies of the *Diary* with a cover letter stating,

> This is a copy of the so-called Diary put together by the planners of the recent conference on sexuality at Barnard College. . . . *Please read this Diary from beginning to end. Please do not skip any parts of it.* Please look at the pictures. Please read it right away: however busy you are please do not put off reading this. This Diary shows how the s&m and pro-pornography activists . . . are being intellectually and politically justified and supported. It shows too the conceptual framework for distorting and significantly undermining radical feminist theory, activism, and efficacy. There is no feminist standard, I believe, by which this material and these arguments taken as a whole are not perniciously anti-woman and anti-feminist. It is doubtful, in my view, that the feminist movement can maintain its political integrity and moral authority with this kind of attack on its fundamental and essential premises from within.[49]

The news coverage of the conference further enshrined the vision of the phantom conference. The periodical *off our backs* was the closest thing to a newspaper of record of the feminist movement. It was therefore extremely distressing that its coverage so closely mirrored the WAP accounts. There was an avalanche of letters to the editor from those of us with a different perspective: from me, Frances Doughty, Barbara Grier, Hollibaugh, Nestle, Newton, Vance, Walton, and Willis. There is a letter from Samois. There is even a letter from Cleveland Women Against Violence Against Women in which the organization distanced itself from the protest leaflet.[50] But while the articles from *off our backs* are readily available online, the letters are not. A digitized version of *off our backs* is available through Proquest, but the letters have not been included in the digital archives. The incomplete digitization of *off our backs* ensures that the one-sided and distorted picture of the events remains canonical. To get a sense of the full range of the discussion in *off our backs*, it is necessary to consult crumbling newsprint. As yet, there has been no comprehensive history of the feminist sex wars, and one challenge is that so many of the primary documents are not easily accessible.[51]

The West Coast Wars: WAVPM and Samois

The actual events of the Barnard conference demonstrate the absurdity of the claims that the conference was characterized by a single-minded devotion to s/m, butch/femme, and an uncritical promotion of pornography. The ease with which such distortions were treated as credible and their remarkable persistence call for both analytic attention and historical contextualization. Why were some feminists protesting a feminist conference, and why were they wearing T-shirts emblazoned with the slogan "Against s/m"? Why was Samois, then a small and obscure San Francisco lesbian s/m group, supposed to be involved in, much less responsible for, a conference three thousand miles away? Part of the explanation lies in events that took place prior to the Barnard Sex Conference and far from New York. Many people, particularly those from the East Coast, think that the Barnard conference initiated the feminist sex wars. But there were earlier episodes, and by 1978, one important battle front had already opened in the San Francisco Bay Area. The controversies that engulfed the Barnard conference are more intelligible with some knowledge of this prehistory.

The West Coast battles took place between Women Against Violence in Pornography and Media (WAVPM), the first feminist antipornography organization, and Samois, the first lesbian s/m organization, both active in the San Francisco Bay Area in the late 1970s. Their skirmishes generated many of the patterns and themes that characterized the early phases of the sex wars. "Pornography," a genre of media, and "sadomasochism," a sexual preference and practice, are different kinds of things. Yet the terms were quickly construed as equivalent and used to articulate a range of political differences.

Once pornography and sadomasochism were treated as indistinguishable, or at least as facets of the same ostensibly malign phenomena, then antipornography and sadomasochism could be considered antipoles: ontological opposites, as implacably incompatible as matter and antimatter, and unable to ever occupy the same political or moral space. The conflict between WAVPM and Samois helped establish "antipornography" and "sadomasochism" as critical positions, ideological frameworks, and antithetical worldviews that were then deployed throughout the sex wars.

Founded in the San Francisco Bay Area in 1976, WAVPM held the first national feminist conference on pornography in 1978.[52] Inspired by the conference, New York antiporn activists established Women Against Pornography (WAP) in 1979.[53] While WAP's name more explicitly demarcated the movement's focus, the groups were ideologically similar.

It is not widely understood how much the feminist antipornography movement was also, from its inception, a war against s/M imagery and practice. Diana Russell, one of the founders of WAVPM, articulated these fusions (and confusions) in a 1977 article in the feminist journal *Chrysalis*. Russell rarely gets the credit she clearly deserves for her contributions to the antiporn movement, which is often attributed instead to Catharine MacKinnon and Dworkin.[54] Yet Russell provided the early movement with most of its intellectual leadership, analytic language, and ideological coherence.

In the *Chrysalis* article, she asserts that pornography is "degrading" to women by nature, that it is inherently misogynist, and that it is vicious, antiwoman propaganda. Moreover, she used s/M porn to represent all that she found repugnant in pornography: "Before disagreeing with this statement, go see some of it! You might try a batch of movies regularly shown at the San Francisco Kearny Cinema (or its equivalent in other cities). The titles are self-explanatory: 'Lesson in Pain,' 'Corporal Punishment,' 'Slave Girl,' 'Golden Pain,' 'Club Brute Force,' and 'Water Power.'"[55] At the time of this writing, San Francisco had probably twenty or so porn film theaters, of which only two, the Kearny and the North Beach, showed films with bondage or s/M themes. Yet these two theaters are repeatedly singled out in San Francisco antiporn literature. Similarly, there were probably hundreds or thousands of porn movies shown annually, but the titles of the small number of kinky films were used as if these represented pornographic films as a whole. s/M materials in Russell's essay were used to persuade readers of the truth of the indictment against pornography, and their mere existence was taken both as representative of all porn and evidence confirming that porn is intrinsically foul.

Russell continues,

Pornography is not made to educate but to sell, and for the most part, what sells in a sexist society is a bunch of lies about sex and women. Women are portrayed as enjoying being raped, spanked, or beaten, tied up, mutilated, and enslaved, or they accept it as their lot as women to be victims in such experiences. In the less sadistic films, women are portrayed as turned on and sexually satisfied by doing anything and everything that men want or order them to do. . . . Some pornography I saw recently doesn't even include sex: Women are kidnapped, beaten, tied up, then hung upside down like pieces of meat. And that's the end of the movie. Domination and torture are what it is about.[56]

Several features of what would become recognizable as antipornography rhetoric are apparent in this passage. One common tactic is lists that mix some things that are clearly horrible, such as rape, with some other things that might be pleasurable, such as being spanked. Disgust mobilized by the front-loaded images of horror is then directed at things that might ordinarily be more difficult to get people upset about, for example, a woman finding pleasure in heterosexual intercourse.[57]

Describing a different film, Russell exclaims: "In another movie I saw, boiling candle wax was dripped onto a bound woman's breasts. Had she consented beforehand? Even if she had, this is a violent act—one which was followed by her acting the willing and adoring lover of her torturer. So, even where models have consented to participate, they don't necessarily know what they're in for, and often they are in no position to maintain control."[58] Russell assumes that no one could enjoy hot candle-wax dripping on bound breasts; that such experiences could not be part of legitimate lovemaking; and that the act is intrinsically violent. One implication is that any woman who might actually enjoy such a practice must have something wrong with her. While such tactics are routine to this literature, it is never explained by what standards erotic activities or desires are sorted into the inherently enjoyable or the invariably repugnant. Instead, the erotic preferences of the writer seem to be presumed as universal. Russell's analysis betrays a limited concept of human sexual variation and an assumption that s/m is intrinsically degrading and repulsive.

Such premises also allow her to make the more explicit claim that the models could have agreed to participate in such films only because they were uninformed, duped, or coerced. In other words, the image's content, and Russell's own revulsion, substitute for evidence that anyone was actually tricked, abused, or coerced in the making of the film. As I have pointed out elsewhere, there is confusion between the image's content and the conditions of its production;

if such criteria were consistently applied, we would have to assume that all of the actors blown up, murdered, shot, burned, drowned, or otherwise killed in movies were actual fatalities.[59]

Russell's arguments, assumptions, language, and rhetorical tactics were incorporated into the early WAVPM literature. For example, each issue of WAVPM's newsletter, *Newspage*, contained a statement, "Who Are We?" In the September 1977 issue, it reads,

> Women Against Violence in Pornography and Media is a core group of approximately 35 Bay Area women who are meeting because we share a common concern about the alarming increase of violent crimes against women. Media, including pornography, is our primary focus. We believe there is a relationship between what we see and hear in the media, and how we think and consequently act. *We want to put an end to all portrayals of women being bound, raped, tortured, mutilated, abused, or degraded in any way for sexual or erotic stimulation.*[60]

Like Russell, WAVPM was blaming pornography, and especially S/M imagery, for violence against women. Both Russell and WAVPM precluded the possibility of any legitimate S/M erotica, whose elimination is plainly stated as an explicit political goal of the organization. The mechanics of its abolition are left unspecified.

In a later *Newspage*, WAVPM published a list of frequently asked questions and their answers. Although the group's stated purpose was "to educate women and men about the hatred of women expressed in pornography and other media-violence to women," the entire document focuses on pornography. In WAVPM literature, other forms of "media-violence" quickly became a subsidiary theme and an occasional afterthought, unless their objectionable aspects could be blamed on pornography.

Q: What kinds of images are you talking about when you say you are opposed to "violence in pornography and media"?

A: We are talking about books and magazines which depict women being bound, beaten, and abused. We are protesting the message of these images—that beating and raping women, urinating and defecating on women, is erotic and pleasurable for men; and that women desire this kind of treatment, or at least expect it. We are talking about record-album photos, fashion and men's magazine lay-outs, department-store window displays and billboards, in which women are shown bound, gagged, beaten, whipped, and chained.

Q: But not all pornography is violent. So you object to pornography in which there is no violence.

A: *Yes.* Not all pornography is violent, but even the most banal pornography objectifies women's bodies.[61]

While WAVPM's critique was ostensibly directed against pornography, assumptions about sadomasochism in word, deed, and representation were integral to its analysis. WAVPM swept all S/M erotica up into its category of images that should not exist, and its program demanded the elimination of all S/M imagery or at least its banishment from public visibility. When WAVPM began to stage public protests in the spring of 1977, its focus was on S/M as much as porn, or rather on this confused composite target made up of porn, S/M, violence against women, and female subordination.

It was not surprising that WAVPM's rhetoric, program, and targets of protest alarmed local S/M activists, particularly the feminist ones. S/M activism had been inaugurated in 1971 with the formation of the Eulenspiegel Society in New York, which was followed by San Francisco's Society of Janus in 1974. Eulenspiegel and Janus were initially mixed-gender and mixed-orientation groups, but by the late 1970s they were predominantly heterosexual. Ferment over S/M had begun to appear in the lesbian feminist press in the mid-1970s. There were attempts to form lesbian S/M organizations at least as early as 1975, but Samois, founded in 1978, was the first ongoing lesbian S/M organization. The group articulated an ideological defense of S/M as a legitimate eroticism, even for feminists. Samois never claimed that S/M was particularly feminist, only that there was no intrinsic contradiction between feminist politics and S/M practice. Nor did Samois claim that S/M was an inherently liberatory practice, only that it was not inherently oppressive.[62]

Since Samois was a lesbian group, many of whose members, including me, had already been active in the women's movement, it was attuned to developments in feminism in a way that the more heterosexually oriented Eulenspiegel and Janus were not. Several of us quickly perceived that WAVPM's program was as much anti-S/M as antipornography. We naïvely assumed that the members of WAVPM were uneducated about S/M and would welcome dialogue and discussion. As it turned out, WAVPM had no interest in discussing issues with any feminist who disagreed with them, much less with people who engaged without apparent guilt in forms of sexuality they felt exemplified the worst manifestations of patriarchy.[63]

Shortly after Samois was formed, we started sending letters to WAVPM asking to meet to discuss their position on S/M. These requests were consistently rebuffed. The tensions between the two groups, however, escalated in April 1980 when flyers suddenly appeared around the Bay Area announcing a WAVPM fundraiser: a forum on sadomasochism in the lesbian community.[64] Since WAVPM had refused all previous efforts to discuss S/M, Samois objected to the forum and responded with a leaflet. One of WAVPM's favorite slogans was that "pornography was a lie about women." The Samois leaflet, titled "This Forum Is a Lie about S/M," expressed three objections to the forum.

1. WAVPM, without taking an "official" position on S/M has nonetheless promoted false image of S/M sexuality and helped to create a climate that is oppressive and dangerous to S/M-identified people. WAVPM's most obvious error is the equation of consensual S/M with violence. . . .

2. Panelists have made . . . public statements that equate S/M with self destruction, male supremacy, fascism, misogyny, or mental illness. The anti-S/M arguments you will hear at this forum are as biased and bigoted as homophobic attacks on lesbians and gay men or right-wing attacks on independent feminist women. These arguments are based on biological determinism, conventional morality, and psychiatric notions of sexual perversion. We protest the promulgation of negative stereotypes of S/M.

3. Consensual S/M is not anti-feminist or anti-woman. S/M people are a stigmatized sexual minority, and as such are subjected to street harassment, job and housing discrimination, violence, and other forms of persecution.[65]

All of the speakers at the forum denounced S/M. Eventually, many of their talks became articles in the anthology *Against Sadomasochism: A Radical Feminist Analysis.*[66] After the forum, WAVPM had an internal debate on whether to take an official position on S/M. When the organization declined to do so, several disgruntled members decided to edit and publish the anti-S/M anthology.

One of the biggest successes of the feminist antipornography movement has been to intensify a shift in the locus of legal and social concern about sexual imagery away from genital proximity and toward kinkiness. The movement helped transform popular conceptions of "hard core," and legal definitions have shifted as well. The distinction between hard- and soft-core porn once had mainly to do with whether there was genital exposure and contact. Increasingly, "hard core" refers to something the viewer finds repugnant or considers "way out there," and all too often consists of depictions of kinky or S/M sexuality. As Linda Williams notes, this shift is reflected in the enforcement of obscenity laws. She traces "a major change taking place in American obscenity law and the prosecution of sex crimes as they have moved away from

the notion of explicit sex and toward the targeting of scapegoatable 'deviants.'
. . . [I]n the definition of obscenity, explicitness has given way to the deviant
sexuality of the 'other,' defined in relation to a presumed heterosexual, non-
sadomasochistic norm that excludes both fellatio and cunnilingus."[67]

s/m continued to be a potent flashpoint throughout the feminist sex wars,
in part because the antipornography argument depended on its indictment of
s/m, its contention that pornography overwhelmingly featured s/m content,
and its use of s/m imagery as an effective tool of persuasion. wavpm pioneered
a characteristic fusion of anti-s/m and antiporn propositions that shaped subsequent feminist antiporn ideology and activity. Opposition to s/m has always
been a major subtext of the feminist antiporn movement: indispensable to its
analytic coherence, the source of its most rhetorically potent examples, and
a primary target of its prescriptions for social change. Samois challenged the
fundamental credibility of both the logical structure and empirical claims of
wavpm's case against porn. Thus the disputes between Samois and wavpm prefigured much of the subsequent struggle in feminism over sexual practice and
sexual representation. They help explain why s/m (engaged in by a relatively
small proportion of the population, feminist or otherwise) was such an incen-
diary topic, and why the name of Samois became such a significant talisman.

By the time of the Barnard conference, the specific confrontation between
wavpm and Samois had been generalized. s/m had become a code for any
feminist opposition to the antipornography creed. Since antiporn feminists
seemed unable to accept that there might be any rational basis for disagree-
ment, s/m also functioned as an explanation for behavior they apparently considered both inexplicable and despicable. Given the stigma of s/m, it was also
a convenient slur with which to try to discredit any opposition. Feminists
who did not go along with the antiporn program were accused of being tools
of the patriarchy, dupes of the pornographers, sadomasochists and other sex
perverts, leftists, Marxists, bourgeois academics, liberals, libertarians, heterosexuals, lesbians, and antifeminists. Some of these characterizations were of
course true. Some of us were, after all, academics, heterosexuals, lesbians, liberals, leftists, and even the occasional sadomasochist. It was not made clear,
however, how these categories of identity, belief, or behavior invalidated our
arguments and empirical claims. Name calling and smear tactics replaced debate, logic, and evidence. Some characterizations were erroneous, some were
debatable, and many were completely idiotic. All were deployed to impugn our
right to speak on the issues and to excommunicate us from the ranks of legitimate feminists. Feminists who opposed antiporn dogma were often called
sadomasochists or supporters of sadomasochism, whatever their actual sexual

preferences.[68] All of this history came into play not only at Barnard but also well beyond. These legacies haunt us still.

Barnard Redux

The Barnard Sex Conference, it turned out, was the opening act for a series of similar conflicts. As Vance perceptively noted in the Barnard aftermath, "Some feminists decried these tactics, but the fact that the people who had deployed them were not totally discredited guaranteed that they would be repeated. The principle was established: Zealotry and unprincipled behavior were acceptable in the service of 'protecting' women."[69] In 1986 they were indeed repeated when the Five College Women's Studies Project held a conference called "Feminism, Sexuality, and Power" at Mount Holyoke. I had been invited to give the keynote, on new theories of sexuality. The organizers experienced something quite different from what they had planned, as Margaret Hunt reported in *Gay Community News*.

> More than a hundred feminist activists met at Mt. Holyoke College for a symposium intended . . . to explore the variety of ideas about the ways that sexual practices are affected by history, culture and politics. . . . [T]he conference organizers had in mind a quite broad based approach to sexuality and power. They planned a program which included a substantial amount of material on the ways class and race interacted with gender in the organization of sexuality and they took care to represent a variety of erotic lifestyles to avoid the prevalent Western bias of much scholarship on sexuality. What they got was a pitched battle over the question of lesbian SM, an issue which so dominated the conference as to make all other matters fade into the polished neo-gothic Mt. Holyoke woodwork.[70]

After this debacle, Meryl Fingrudt, one of the organizers, lamented,

> Radical feminism, as it was presented at our conference, has a very narrow range of vision. . . . [I]t was at the level of intellectual and personal freedoms that these radical feminists threw me into despair. The speakers refused to be moved off the issues of pornography and SM and they were downright nasty to their sisters. . . . They refused to debate or sit on the same panel with anyone who held another point of view. . . . Above all, it was unnerving to see, with each successive presentation, incredibly narrow and specific lines drawn around sexual practices that were permissible if one wanted to be a real feminist. . . . [A]ny inquiry that proposes to raise questions about the

content of these categories or even argue that these are dangerously limiting is labeled non-feminist, anti-feminist, or fascistic.[71]

The Five Colleges conference ended up feeling like Barnard, Act 2.[72]

Act 3 played out in Australia, in 1993, when several American scholars whose work dealt with sexuality and LGBT studies were invited to the Humanities Research Centre (HRC) at the Australian National University (ANU). Among the visiting fellows from the United States were Henry Abelove, D'Emilio, Duggan, David Halperin, Patton, Vance, Vicinus, and me. Several Australian radical feminists, including Sheila Jeffreys, Denise Thompson, and Renate Klein, sent a letter to the university's vice chancellor to protest our presence and attack the HRC for having invited us. "Some of the women invited," said the letter, "hold what can only be described as anti-feminist positions. . . . In particular we want to protest in the strongest possible terms against the HRC's bias in inviting Gayle Rubin, Cindy Patton and Carol [sic] Vance to be conference participants. . . . The work of these women from the U.S. displays a zeal in defence of male supremacist meanings and values that amounts to an outright anti-feminism."[73]

A few days later, the *Sydney Star Observer* ran an article with the headline "ANU Denies Conferences Showcase Anti-feminism." Thompson is quoted in the article as saying, "Not only do these women from the U.S. lack any ability to think through questions of sex and power, they are also anti-feminist." Thompson also blasted the ANU for "importing tenth-rate yanks."[74] The HRC and ANU politely but firmly stood by their invitations and continued with their plans. Some of us among the visiting fellows took to calling ourselves the Tenth-Rate Yanks. It would have been a great name for a band.

Over the years, there have been plenty of mini-Barnards. Many of those who were involved in the attacks on Barnard, the Five Colleges conference, and the HRC are still actively working in pursuit of the same, or closely related, agendas. They continue to dismiss anyone who disagrees with them as antifeminist, sadomasochists, and supporters of patriarchal violence.[75] We might hear less about them these days because so many of them have left the women's movement as their arena of action to work in the federal government and international nongovernmental organizations, where they influence decisions with great public impact. Most now describe their target as "sex trafficking," to which they are bringing the same agenda they brought to pornography and which they hope to codify in international law and policy.[76] For example, Dorchen Leidholdt helped found the Coalition Against Trafficking in Women (CATW) and has served as its co-director. Laura Lederer, one of the early organizers of WAVPM, served as senior advisor on trafficking in persons to the undersecretary of state during the Bush administration. These are large arenas, whose spheres of influence extend far beyond those of feminist academic conferences.

Rethinking "Thinking Sex"

Once I write a paper, I rarely reread it. But the "Rethinking Sex" conference seemed a good time to reacquaint myself with "Thinking Sex." I am often asked what I might have written differently. There is a part of me that always wants to go back and do yet another edit on any article that has left my hands, but any serious revision would require another article, one set in these different times. Yet there are certainly some things I would have done differently, had I known then what I know now. My remarks about transsexuality, sex work, and the sexuality of the young were far too sketchy for such complex topics. Nor is it possible here to redress those lacunae fully; a few brief comments will have to suffice.

Every theory has what Max Weber famously called "inconvenient facts," examples or data that stress the capabilities of any given intellectual scheme.[77] Both sex work and transsexuality are in a sense such "inconvenient facts," in that they reveal the limitations of the theoretical models and conceptual distinctions developed in "Thinking Sex." The essay had useful things to say about each, and I tried to note the ways in which each did not fit the argument's framework.[78] Nonetheless, both phenomena exceed the parameters the essay was so careful to construct.

Susan Stryker has gently taken "Thinking Sex" to task for having "clearly categorized transgender practices as sexual or erotic acts rather than expressions of gender identity or sense of self." This is a legitimate criticism, although transgender practices were initially grouped with the sexual perversions when modern sexological taxonomies took shape. In the early twentieth century, the category of "sexual inversion" referred to both sexual preferences and gender conduct. Over succeeding decades, gender identity and sexual orientation were slowly and unevenly disentangled.[79] When the first *Diagnostic and Statistical Manual* (*DSM*) was published in 1952, the category of sexual deviation specifically included transvestism along with homosexuality, pedophilia, fetishism, and sexual sadism.[80] In 1968, the second edition of the *DSM* added exhibitionism, voyeurism, and masochism, but still classified "transvestism" among the sexual deviations.[81] It was not until 1980 that *DSM-III* carved out a new class of "gender identity disorders" from the "paraphilias" (the new label for the old sexual deviations).

Gender inversions, moreover, had disaggregated over time. As sex change technologies became more available so did new identities, and "transsexualities" were increasingly distinguished from "transvestisms." "Transsexualism" appeared in the third DSM, where it was assigned to the new "gender identity disorders." At the same time, "transvestism" remained as a separate diagnostic entry, still classed as one of the "paraphilias."[82]

As Stryker notes, however, "Thinking Sex" inadvertently contributed to an analytic framework that transgender theories had to overcome: "As the transgender movement began to regather force in the early 1990s, it posed a challenge to the new queer theory similar to the one posed by sexuality to feminism—it asked whether the framework of queer sexuality could adequately account for transgender phenomena, or whether a new frame of analysis was required. These are the questions that led, in the years ahead, to the development of the new interdisciplinary academic field of transgender studies."[83]

Of course, Stryker is completely correct in her observation that "transgender phenomena are not intrinsically sexual (having more to do, more often than not, with regulatory schema of bodily integrity, visual coherence, and bureaucratic intelligibility than with wanton ways of fucking)."[84] The contrast between transgender studies now and the cruder tools available in the early 1980s illuminates some of the very positive changes that have occurred in the interim.

Since transgender studies did not yet exist when I was writing "Thinking Sex," I had limited resources with which to respond to the nasty vein of antitranssexual sentiment that had developed within feminism in the 1970s and was articulated most comprehensively by Janice Raymond.[85] Although I wanted to undermine the foundations on which such antitrans screeds were built, there were many alternative strategies I might have used. One approach would have been to ground my argument in feminism's own core critiques of gender roles and anatomical determinism, although that would have unduly complicated other agendas of the essay.

I should reiterate that antifeminism was not among my objectives. While the essay has sometimes been interpreted as a rejection of feminism, I saw it as completely within the best traditions of feminist discourse, particularly the constant self-critical striving toward more analytic clarity and descriptive precision about inequality and injustice. Unfortunately, as time erodes the details of context, such conversations, internal to feminism, are often seen as more oppositional than they were ever intended to be.

In addition, the caustic politics of the sex wars inflected interpretations of the essay. I had concluded "Thinking Sex" by proposing that sexuality and gender be analytically separated. At the time, these were commonly conflated, or sexuality was seen as merely a derivative of gender relations. A corollary was that feminism was often assumed to be the privileged theoretical and political framework with which to analyze all things sexual. I challenged that assumption and suggested that theoretical tools specific to sexuality be developed. And I noted that the concept of "sex/gender system," which I had introduced a decade previously in "The Traffic in Women," did not make these distinctions.

Some antiporn feminists jumped on these comments in their attempts to discredit me. The idea seemed to be that "Thinking Sex" was such a radical break from my earlier, presumably legitimate feminist contributions that I could now be safely quarantined. Hence a claim was often made that I had "repudiated" feminism along with my own previous work.[86]

I have always considered that changing one's mind and constantly reaching for better ways to think about our subjects were not only what scholars do, but something of a moral obligation of the craft. It is rather unremarkable that as we learn more, we modify our analyses. Moreover, the revision I suggested in "Thinking Sex," about the relationship between sex and gender, is well within the mainstream traditions of social theory. It was done in much the same spirit as Max Weber's analytic strategy for grappling with different kinds of social stratification.

Weber distinguished between class, status, and party, as well as ethnicity and caste. He commented

> The way in which social honor is distributed in a community between typical groups participating in this distribution we may call the "social order." The social and the economic order are, of course, similarly related to the "legal order." However, the social and the economic order are not identical. The economic order is for us merely the way in which economic goods and services are distributed and used. The social order is of course conditioned by the economic order to a high degree, and in its turn reacts upon it.[87]

Weber further distinguished "status groups" from classes, even though, "for all practical purposes, stratification by status goes hand in hand with a monopolization of ideal and material goods or opportunities."[88]

Nonetheless, status and class are distinguishable. "With some oversimplification, one might thus say that 'classes' are stratified according to their relations to the production and acquisition of goods; whereas 'status groups' are stratified according to the principles of their *consumption* of goods as represented by special 'styles of life.'"[89] Weber understood that class position and status are interconnected but not identical, related but distinguishable. I had proposed developing the kind of nuanced distinctions for gender and sexuality that Weber applied to hierarchies of status and class. This should hardly be controversial, and can only be taken as a "repudiation" of feminism if feminism is taken to be a static canon of ossified doctrine to which no further improvements are possible. Some would call that dogma.

Then there are the children. I clearly underestimated the staggering dimensions of the impending tsunami about the sexuality of the young. When I finished writing "Thinking Sex" in 1983, the outlines of the panics over children were clear, but their scale and duration were inconceivable.[90] The panics that seemed episodic in 1983 now are a permanent and colossal feature of our social and political landscape. When the history of the last quarter of a century is finally written, one of the distinguishing features of this period will be the extent to which legitimate concerns for the sexual welfare of the young have been vehicles for political mobilizations and policies with consequences well beyond their explicit aims, some quite damaging to the young people they are supposed to help.

There are certainly many positive aspects to the movements to protect children and make their lives better. The relentless focus on sexual perils and stranger danger, however, has had many collateral effects whose impact has yet to be fully recognized. Hysteria, fear, and political opportunism have inhibited careful analysis and empirical research. Instead, many issues pertaining to sexuality and the young are riddled with unexamined assumptions, unverified claims, definitional incoherence, and muddled categories.[91] Too often, scandal journalism has been a poor substitute for sober scholarship.

One consequence is that the rhetoric of child protection has anchored many conservative agendas. It has been utilized in campaigns to intensify women's subordinate status, reinforce hierarchical family structures, curtail gay citizenship, oppose comprehensive sex education, limit the availability of contraception, and restrict abortion, especially for young women and girls.[92]

Laws and policies that are supposed to protect children have been used to deprive young people of age-appropriate and eagerly desired sexual information and services. Laws intended to protect children and young people, such as very broadly drawn child-pornography statutes, have been used to prosecute them (such as the cases where minors have been charged with breaking the law by texting nude images of themselves). Almost anything, from promoting abstinence to banning gay marriage and adoption, can be and has been framed as promoting children's safety and welfare.[93] A critical evaluation of the details, impact, and scope of child-protection laws and policies is long overdue; yet people who try to engage in such analysis are often attacked and accused of supporting child abuse.

In the early 1980s one could still have a thoughtful discussion about the sexuality of the young. It has become increasingly perilous to address the many complex questions about children and sex that need to be thoroughly discussed and carefully vetted: these include what kind of sexual information, services, and behavior are appropriate for the young, and at what ages; what constitutes sexual abuse and how can it be prevented and minimized; how should young people learn about sex; what are the appropriate roles of adults in the sexual lives and learning of children; what kinds of representations of sexuality should be available to minors, and at what ages; should sexually active minors be treated in punitive ways, and where is the line between protection and punishment; in what ways do the policies, legal apparatus, and structures of fear that have been built over the last several decades enhance or damage the experience of growing up; what is pedophilia, and what is child molestation; who abuses children; what is child pornography; and for what offenses is someone labeled a "sex offender." I do not have answers to all of these questions, but it is tragic that discussion of most of these questions has been reduced to a collection of crude sound bites, stereotypes, and scare tactics, which have been cynically manipulated into stampeding the public and politicians into many ill-considered changes in law and policy that have not made the world a safer place for minors or more conducive to their development.

One example is California's 1994 initiative, Three Strikes and You're Out. This law was passed in the emotional wake of a horrible crime: the abduction, rape, and murder of a young girl. But the law was an example of bait-and-switch: rather than protect young people from serial rapists, the primary effect of the law has been to incarcerate tens of thousands of Californians, many on relatively minor charges, including petty theft, drug use, and drug possession. Three Strikes has contributed to the out-of-control expansion of a vast prison gulag and diverted critical resources from other needs, including one of the most important for children: primary, secondary, and higher education.[94]

The fear of sexual abduction, rape, and murder of children by strangers has substantially reshaped many areas of society. It is a major concern of parents, and haunts the young. Yet it is relatively rare. According to *Newsweek*, far more children drown in swimming pools each year than are abducted by strangers.[95] By a large margin, the leading cause of fatalities among teenagers is automobile accidents.[96] Yet most people are not terrified of cars, and few parents are as afraid of swimming pools as they are of "sex offenders," ostensibly lurking behind every bush and lamppost. Despite the facts that most sex abuse is perpetrated at home and by family members, most murdered children are killed by their parents, and most kidnapped children are abducted by noncustodial parents, the family is depicted as a place of safety threatened by dangerous strangers. The ever-growing apparatus of regulation and control adopted to address these issues is directed primarily toward such strangers, although the "sex offender" net is capacious and snares not only family members but even a growing number of minors.[97] "Child protection" is a bit like the defense budget, the intelligence bureaucracy, and the endless wars on terror: these address genuine issues and real problems, but much of the response to them consists of uncontrolled institutional expansion, escalating expenditure of resources, poorly defined targets, and few effective ways to measure success.[98]

Finally, as Steven Angelides has so eloquently argued, "the discourse of child sex abuse has expanded at the expense of a discourse of child sexuality."[99] In her statement about her Barnard workshop on the sexuality of infancy and childhood, Kate Millett observed: "There is, in short, a great deal of sexual politics frustrating the sexual expression of children and the young. You and I will live to see this discussed, almost for the first time in history. Considering we were all children once, and if we are very good, we're children still — we all have a stake in this. The emancipation of children is our emancipation in retrospect, and that of the future as well."[100] Millett's comments (and some of mine in "Thinking Sex") now seem hopelessly naïve and unrealistically optimistic. But she was right to emphasize that all of us who have reached adulthood are former children. Much of my concern in these areas is that of an ex-child, one who grew up in the 1950s. That past has made me hope for and work toward a better sexual future for the young.

Like most other girls, I had plenty of experience with both "pleasures and dangers." I had to contend with my share of unwanted sex, but I also encountered obstacles to aspects of sexual experience and information that I avidly sought. Contraception was unavailable (and largely illegal), abortion was illegal, and the stigmatization of sexually active young women was ferocious. Sex education in my school consisted of a film about menstruation, enhanced by surreptitious reading of disreputable novels like *The Catcher in the Rye* and gleaning sexual terms from the rare unabridged copies of *Webster's* dictionary. Getting pregnant was ruinous: when I was in high school, girls who got pregnant were summarily expelled. They lost their chance at further education and became pariahs.

Knowledge of homosexuality and the conditions of homosexual life varied widely, depending on factors such as local politics, police conduct, and city size. But while gay people were more visible in New York City than in the rural South of my youth, they were hardly safe even there. This was the period of a sustained, unprecedented, and systematic war on homosexual citizens: barred from federal employment, banned from the military, investigated by Congress and the FBI, hounded by police, incarcerated in prisons, registered as sex offenders, and treated as sexual psychopaths.[101] Queer people built viable lives and thriving communities in the teeth of such repression, but many simply tried to stay well under the radar and escape notice. Where I grew up, gay men and women were exceedingly discreet. Looking back years later, it was clear that there were plenty of gay men and lesbians in my home town, and that I had encountered many of them among the librarians and schoolteachers. But lacking a language for homosexuality, I did not interpret the signals. I only heard references to homosexuality as part of a string of epithets: commie, pinko, atheist, queer. The sexual connotations were there, but sexual, political, and religious dissent were only indistinctly differentiated.

Second-wave feminism and gay liberation were in part a reaction to this punitive sexual regime. Social conservatives, on the other hand, seek to reconstitute such repressive systems, or construct something even worse. They often justify their program as necessary to protect a sentimentalized notion of childhood innocence.

It is long past time to reopen broad ranging conversations about sexuality and the young, and to gauge the dissonant legacies of three decades of intense mobilization around this complicated tangle of issues. As Joel Best has commented, "A society which is mobilized to keep child molesters, kidnappers, and Satanists away from innocent children is not necessarily prepared to protect children from ignorance, poverty, and ill health. Inevitably, some campaigns succeed in the social problems marketplace. Whether the most significant issues come to the fore is another question."[102] Writing "Thinking Sex," I dimly saw the outlines of the shape of things to come, but badly miscalculated their reach, persistence, and consequences. My comments on sex and children were made in a different context, in which I assumed (wrongly, as it turned out) that no one would imagine that I supported the rape of pre-pubescents. Even now, as I write this, I am aware that whatever I say will be interpreted in the worst possible way by someone, and misconstructions are inevitable. Children are not, in fact, a major area of my interest or expertise. But why should even an exploration of such issues need to be done so gingerly and feel so dangerous? That it does is an indication of something deeply wrong.

The parts of "Thinking Sex" that are most germane to my current work concern issues of urban space, which have been the most enduring aspects of my research. I am completing a long term ethnographic project on gay men in San Francisco, and am even more focused now than I was then on topics such as geographies of sexual location, and the formation and dissipation of gay neighborhoods. While the term *gentrification* had been coined in the 1960s, the study of gentrification was just becoming a coherent field in the late 1970s and early 1980s, and there were only a handful of studies exploring the relationships of gentrification, gay populations, and gay territoriality.[103] My field research had made it clear, however, that the location of gay populations and institutions was enmeshed in conflicts over land use and that homosexuals were convenient scapegoats for the crisis in affordable housing in San Francisco.[104]

It was even more obvious that large redevelopment projects threatened existing gay enclaves and that sexual stigma was a readily exploitable resource for making land available for capital-intensive development. In 1984 I commented that areas such as Times Square in New York and San Francisco's Tenderloin, North Beach, and South of Market were on the verge of being "made safe for convention centers, international hotels, corporate headquarters, and housing for the rich."[105] There is now a sizable literature on the transformation of Times Square, including Samuel Delany's elegiac *Times Square Red, Times Square Blue*.[106] In San Francisco, the Tenderloin and North Beach have not yet been conquered, but South of Market, the location of my research, has been substantially rebuilt and socially reconstructed. Blocks that once housed maritime union halls and places where gay men congregated are now the sites of luxury condominium towers. My work on South of Market built upon and added a sexual dimension to a story of neighborhood transformation so brilliantly chronicled by Chester Hartman and Paul Groth, and so movingly photographed by Ira Nowinski.[107]

Moreover, the other gay neighborhoods of San Francisco from the 1960s and 1970s are either gone or shrinking. In "Thinking Sex," I observed that the gay neighborhoods that we could take for granted in the early 1980s might prove temporary.[108] The attrition of urban gay concentrations in the early twenty-first century has become a serious challenge for gay social life and political aspirations, and its potential consequences have not yet been fully articulated.

One aspect of the essay of which I am most proud is its "protoqueerness." I wanted to move the discussion of sexual politics beyond single issues and single constituencies, from women and lesbians and gay men to analyses that could incorporate and address with more intricacy the cross-identifications and multiple subject positions that most of us occupy. There has been in the interim a vast outpouring of wonderful scholarship that has exceeded all of my expectations. My delight in how far we have come is often tempered by my bitterness about the feminist sex wars, particularly one of their most unfortunate legacies: the sex wars made it difficult for feminists to form a united opposition to the reactionary sexual and gender agendas of social conservatives. Mimeograph machines are long gone, and tweets seem to have replaced leafleting. But the battles of the early eighties are still smoldering. Many contemporary conflicts are rooted in the disputes that overwhelmed the Barnard conference and shaped "Thinking Sex." Yet I continue to believe that our best political hopes for the future lie in finding common ground and building coalitions based on mutual respect and appreciation of differences, and that the best intellectual work is able to accommodate complexity, treasure nuance, and resist the temptations of dogma and oversimplification.

The Catacombs / **9**

A Temple of the Butthole

When I first heard of the Catacombs, the name conjured up images of the underground tombs of ancient Rome, where early Christians fled to escape state persecution and practice their illegal religion in as much privacy as they could find. San Francisco's Catacombs was a similarly underground establishment where twentieth-century sexual heretics could practice their own rites and rituals in a situation that was insulated, as much as possible, from the curious and the hostile.[1]

The Catacombs played a distinctive role in the sexual history of San Francisco. As one of the world's "capital cities" of leather, San Francisco got off to a somewhat late start. The earliest gay male leather bars and motorcycle clubs appeared in the mid-fifties, in New York, Los Angeles, and Chicago. San Francisco's first dedicated leather bar, the Why Not, opened in 1962 in the Tenderloin neighborhood and closed soon thereafter. The first really successful local leather bar was another early-sixties place, the Tool Box. Located at 399 Fourth Street at Harrison, the Tool Box was also the first San Francisco leather bar located in South of Market.

San Francisco never had leather populations as large as those in bigger cities such as New York, Los Angeles, and Chicago. But a serendipitous combination of local factors — including traditions of sexual license and social tolerance, the demographics of city elections, and the singular economic and

Chapter 9 was originally published in Mark Thompson, ed., *Leatherfolk: Radical Sex, People, Politics, and Practice* (Boston: Alyson, 1991), 119–41.

physical characteristics of certain neighborhoods—contributed to the emergence in San Francisco of one of the most extensive, diverse, and visible leather territories in the world.

In the mid-sixties, other leather bars followed the Tool Box into the South of Market neighborhood. When several opened along a three-block strip of Folsom Street, they established a core area which anchored a burgeoning leather economy that continued to develop and expand in the seventies. While there were important institutions of the leather community in other neighborhoods, few were very far away, and South of Market functioned as a "town square" for the local leather population.[2]

Leather development surged during the seventies. In the decade after Stonewall and before AIDS, gay communities generally underwent explosive growth in terms of population, economic power, and political self-confidence. Leather communities were similarly robust. In San Francisco, the leather occupation South of Market reached its maximum density and expansion by the late seventies and early eighties. Leather establishments flourished in an area that sprawled between Howard and Bryant Streets, from Sixth to Twelfth. At night, leathermen owned those streets, prowling easily among the bars, sex clubs, bathhouses, and back alleys.

In the seventies, new kinds of leather/s/m social structures emerged, and older organizational forms were infused with fresh vitality. The first explicitly political s/m organizations were formed in the seventies, as were the first publicly accessible groups for heterosexually oriented s/m and leather women and men. The Eulenspiegel Society held its first meetings in New York in 1971, and the Society of Janus began in San Francisco in 1974.[3] Networking among s/m lesbians began in the mid-seventies. Samois, the first successful lesbian s/m organization, was founded in 1978.[4] But one of the most distinctive characteristics of the seventies decade was the efflorescence of the Great Parties.

Sex parties had been critical to the development of leather social life at least as far back as the late forties. Before there were leather bars, there were s/m parties. These parties were usually held in private homes and apartments, hosted by one or two individuals, and populated by means of informal networks of referral. The parties in turn helped the early gay s/m networks to diversify and grow. The contacts made through these networks in the late forties and early fifties led to the establishment of the first leather bars. Parties have continued ever since to be important mechanisms for building and maintaining leather and s/m communities.

In the seventies, gay men's s/m and leather parties reached new pinnacles of organization, sophistication, and capital investment. The Great Parties of the seventies were intelligently planned, skillfully executed, and durable over time. They were locally run but internationally known and attended. Several of these seventies Great Parties were especially influential. One of the best known was New York's Mineshaft, an after-hours sex club that hosted nightly play. It was perhaps the preeminent on-going leather sex establishment from the time it opened in 1976 until it was closed in 1985.[5] Another renowned party is the Inferno run, a weekend encampment for s/M play held annually since 1976 by the Chicago Hellfire Club. Attendance at Inferno is by invitation only, and those treasured invitations are extended only to highly regarded players. Finally, the Catacombs opened in 1975 and quickly became a fine and famous venue for fist-fucking parties.[6] The Catacombs was a Mecca of handballing. Fisters from all over the Western world made the pilgrimage to San Francisco to attend parties at the Catacombs.

The Catacombs was primarily a place for gay male fisting parties. It was also a place for s/M, and over time, the Catacombs was shared with other groups — kinky lesbians, heterosexuals, and bisexuals. While it never lost its identity as a fister's paradise, over the years it increasingly took on a role as a community center for the local s/M population. It was a beloved institution. When the Catacombs became a casualty not only of AIDS but of the misguided witch hunts of AIDS hysteria, its closure occasioned a deluge of mourning.

The Catacombs did not begin as one of the world's premier sex clubs. It began more humbly as a birthday present from Steve McEachern to his lover. When Steve decided to convert the back of the basement of his San Francisco Victorian into a dungeon, the Catacombs began to take shape.

Steve was an audacious, bright, moody, stubborn, difficult, irascible, and utterly endearing person. He was a sexual visionary who made it his life's business to create an environment in which he could comfortably indulge in the kind of sexual intensity he liked. He was one of those rare individuals whose selfish determination to do what he wanted created a world of pleasure for those around him.[7]

Steve came to San Francisco as a teenager and eventually found his way into the sixties leather crowd. He used to sneak into the Tool Box when he was underage. He met Tony Tavarossi, who had managed the short-lived Why Not and who would later become a Catacombs regular. Steve became involved with the local Fist Fuckers of America (FFA). With some creative financing, he managed to buy a large, two-flat, Mission District Victorian house at a tax auction.

The house was located on the south side of Twenty-First Street between Valencia and Guerrero. Steve lived in the first-floor flat and ran a typing business out of the basement before he began to build the dungeon that eventually became the Catacombs. By the mid-seventies, Steve's basement had become the gathering spot for one group of local fisting aficionados. The Catacombs opened officially for weekly Saturday night fisting parties in May of 1975, and Steve held an anniversary party each year thereafter to commemorate the founding of the club.

Although the Catacombs generated the kind of camaraderie and loyalty associated with clubs, it was not a club in the usual sense. It was a privately owned space, and the events there were private parties. Steve ran the Catacombs with an eagle eye and an iron grip. He applied his considerable intelligence to figuring out what made sex parties work and what made them hot. The party technology he developed was so successful that it was adopted by others. Many kinky San Francisco parties are still run along similar lines.

It was not easy to get into the Catacombs. As a good host, Steve knew that a successful party depended on having "the right people." Like the Chicago Hellfire Club's Inferno, the Catacombs was exclusive. To be invited to the parties, you had to be on Steve's list. To get on Steve's list, you had to be recommended by someone he knew, and often had to be interviewed by him as well.

You did not have to be a handsome hunk with drop-dead pecs or a huge dick to get on Steve's list. Physical beauty did not go unappreciated there, but the Catacombs was not about being pretty. It was about intense bodily experiences, intimate connection, male fellowship, and having a good time. To get into the parties, a person had to be a serious player or a seriously interested novice. And he had to know how to behave at a sex party or show some ability and willingness to learn appropriate etiquette. Steve ruthlessly eighty-sixed anyone who was rude, unable to handle his drugs, or who infringed unduly on the ability of others to have fun.

Even if you were on Steve's list, you did not just drop in at the Catacombs. You made an advance reservation to be admitted to the party. A sign on the door said, "If you didn't call first, don't ring now." Guests were admitted only from 9:00 p.m. to 11:00 p.m., or a few minutes thereafter. Steve felt that a party would come together better and scale higher levels of exhilaration if everyone was inside and getting settled by 11:30. He did not want the celebrants to be alarmed by the sound of the doorbell ringing all night, or distracted by the arrival of new people with strange energy and different timetables for joining the festivities.

Once you made it to the Catacombs, you entered an environment that was both intensely sexual and positively cozy. The door was usually opened by a smiling naked man who let you into a little anteroom which shielded the main room from cold air and prying eyes. You went into the main room and stepped up to Steve's command post at the end of the bar. There you checked in and paid your money and your respects to Steve.

Next you looked for an area under the benches to stash your gear, your toys, and your clothes. Nudity was the norm at the Catacombs. People wore leather harnesses, arm bands, jocks, socks, cockrings, or nothing at all. Steve always had the heat turned up. He deliberately kept the temperature warm enough so that naked people would be comfortable and anyone in clothes miserably hot. Steve himself usually started out the evening in a pair of leather shorts with a removable codpiece. I remember him most vividly as a tall, very thin, angular presence, snorting poppers and holding court at the end of the bar, wearing those tight leather shorts.

The front room was the social area of the Catacombs. It looked and felt a lot like a leather bar, except that it was more intimate and everyone was nude. An extraordinary collection of male erotic art graced its walls. Fisting was a major theme, as was the history of the local leather community. Many of the pieces were artifacts of leather bars, by then already old and gone—the Why Not, the Tool Box, and the Red Star Saloon. Steve had a profound sense of the history of his community. After I expressed an interest, he took me around and lovingly explained the significance of each relic.

The front room contained a "bar," although no alcohol was sold at the Catacombs. Patrons stashed their beer in the refrigerator and helped themselves to the ice, soft-drink, and coffee machines behind the bar. The lights were low, the music soft, and the men plentiful. The front was where people would come in, sit down, greet their friends, do their drugs, finish their manicures, and make the transition from the everyday world into "play space."

"Out front" was distinguished from "the back." In the front room, people socialized, smoked, drank, flirted, negotiated, and came up for air. Although there was sometimes sex play in the front, it was uncommon and generally more lighthearted than sex in the back. When two or more people had made a connection and were ready for serious play, they headed for the back. There was no smoking, eating, or drinking permitted in the back rooms. The back was not for casual socializing. The back was for sex.

The back consisted of two rooms, the "Bridal Suite" and the dungeon. The Bridal Suite was given its name and a commemorative brass plaque after the consummation of one particularly notable union on a huge four-poster water bed that dominated the room. Many other affairs commenced—or were announced—on that bed. Stereo speakers had been positioned to aim music directly at the bed. The water bed was readily visible to much of the party, yet its immensity afforded its occupants some physical distance from others. It was thus the ideal spot for those public displays of special intimacy.

Built-in benches lined the other walls of the Bridal Suite. These were about three feet wide, covered with foam pads, and comfortable to play on. Just past the water bed was one of Steve's favorite pieces of equipment. It was the top part of a hospital gurney, covered with a foam mattress and hung from the ceiling by chains and large springs. Leather stirrups were available for the bottom's legs and the whole thing could bounce up and down and swing back and forth. Steve loved to sit there with his hand buried in the ass of his current favorite, hooting and hollering and jumping up and down.

Finally, all the way in the back, was the dungeon. Just walking into that room could put a person in a leathery mood. The dungeon had big exposed wood beams and posts. It had a wood plank floor sanded smooth as baby skin and covered at all times with a thin sheen of Crisco. There were mirrors on the walls and ceilings. Victorian gaslights added a suggestion of nineteenth-century mystery to the general ambience.

A black iron cage about seven feet tall and about two feet wide stood directly opposite the doorway into the dungeon. The cage was bolted to the dungeon floor and fitted with padlocks. The key was kept up at the front of the bar until someone wanted to use the cage. To the left of the cage was a suspension hoist. No one was allowed to use the hoist until Steve was satisfied that the person knew how to do so safely.

In the middle of the room, a large wooden bondage cross had been fashioned by adding horizontal beams to one of the support pillars of the house. The cross was a favorite spot for whipping. A uniquely designed padded bondage table stood along the right-hand wall. A U-shaped cut from the foot of the table enabled the top to step right up to the bottom's dick and butt. The usual stirrups were hanging above to help the bottom keep his legs in the air.

In the far back were two operating tables, perfect for medical scenes or precision torture. Mattress pads lined the outside walls. The back half of the dungeon was occupied by two rows of commodious black leather slings, one row along each side of the room. Steve had made most of the slings himself. Each sling was fitted with the ubiquitous stirrups. To hold cans of Crisco, big empty coffee cans were hung by chains next to each sling.

The doorless entrance to the bathroom was off to the side near the front of the dungeon. Long towel racks had been installed and the shower was fitted with a douche hose. Patrons were expected to douche at home, but the hose was available for touch ups and emergencies. There were often several people in the bathroom at the same time. One might be sitting on the hose, another using the john, a third washing up his hands and forearms, and a few more standing around waiting and talking. As a result, the bathroom sometimes had a lighter and more social atmosphere than the rest of "the back."

Sex without Friction

Fisting is an art that involves seducing one of the jumpiest and tightest muscles in the body. The Catacombs was designed to help the butthole open up, relax, and feel good. The space was set up to minimize any distractions from the quest for deep penetration and other extreme bodily pleasures. It was thoughtfully constructed to enhance the ability to focus on intense physical sensation. At the Catacombs, a person could experience a hand in his butt or the exquisite agonies of s/m in total, absolute comfort.

The environment was kept as clean, safe, and warm as possible. The equipment was well-built and sturdy. Surfaces were smooth. Floors were kept unobstructed. No one needed to worry about stubbing toes on bags of gear, getting splinters from the wood, or whether the equipment would hold a body's weight. Once the doors closed and the bell stopped ringing, awareness of the outside world and its troubles receded into distant recesses of the mind.

The play stations were designed to reduce unnecessary stress on the body. Most surfaces were soft or padded. The leg stirrups allowed a player to lie back with his (and later, her) legs in the air for a long time. One could concentrate on assholes, genitals, nipples, or one's partner rather than on cramping thighs or lumbar back strain.

Much of the equipment was built for movement. The slings, waterbed, gurney, and suspension hoist provided feelings of floating and weightlessness. Their specific motions enabled a top to swing, wiggle, bounce, or rock the bottom without much expenditure of energy or force. This saved wear and tear on many an arm.

Vast quantities of Crisco were essential to the Catacombs experience. Crisco was the lube of choice. Nothing ever removed the pervasive layer of Crisco that coated every surface. Fresh cans were put out before every party and strategically placed within easy reach of every possible play station. Sometimes Steve initiated Crisco fights just to loosen up the party. Crisco greased the asshole. It greased whole bodies. It greased the walls. It greased the way for smooth and easy contact.

Lube reduced friction. Dirt and grit created unwanted abrasion. They were anathema. Steve's insistence on cleanliness helped to maintain a smooth environment. As one regular put it, sex at the Catacombs was about "fit, comfort, rhythm, and grease." Sex at the Catacombs meant different things to different people at different times. The Catacombs was dedicated to adult recreation and having a good time, but for many, the sheer intensity of the activities in which they engaged added other dimensions to their experience. Good fisting and s/m require a great deal of attention, intimacy, and trust. Because of this, even casual encounters could lead to deep affection and enduring friendships. Moreover, in many cultures the application of carefully chosen physical stress is a method for inducing transcendental mental and emotional states. People came to the Catacombs to do prodigious things to their bodies and minds, and some habitués reported having the kinds of transformational experiences more often associated with spiritual disciplines.

Catacombs sex was often intense and serious, but it also had a playful, kids-in-the-sandbox quality. There was a lot of humor at the parties, from the Crisco fights to the poppers-sniffing contests to the endless practical jokes that Steve liked to play. The Catacombs enabled people to indulge in wild excess by providing the protection of many social and physical safety nets. The extravagant surface prodigality was buttressed by a number of systems designed to prevent or break falls. The Catacombs environment enabled adults to have an almost child-like wonder at the body. It facilitated explorations of the body's sensate capabilities that are rarely available in modern, Western societies.

Music to Fuck By

Music was an essential ingredient of the Catacombs experience. An excellent sound system delivered music to every corner of the place. Steve was a brilliant DJ. He recorded a series of music tapes that he used to enhance, intensify, and manipulate the party mood. By changing the soundtrack, Steve could charge up the party, change its direction, or bring it down.

For the first couple of hours while the doors were open and guests arriving, he played a variety of songs designed to get people relaxed and excited. After the doors shut and the party was ready to take off, Steve generally put on specially selected, high-energy, sexually suggestive disco. This kind of music got people into "the back," enthusiastically pumping or whipping to its insistently sensual beat. Later in the evening, Steve usually switched to moodier, darker, and sometimes menacing electronic music that worked better for slow deep fucking and intense pain trips.

Steve had a talent for finding music with lyrics that spoke directly to the experience of the players. While many were written with different contexts in mind, in the middle of a Catacombs party they all seemed to have been penned for a gay male sex club (and some undoubtedly were). Imagine a man standing in front of a sling, gently rocking another man whose life he holds on his arm. The top is pulling the bottom down on his hand by using the chain that connects the bottom's nipple rings. Imagine the man who is lying in that sling; his poppers hit and his resistance dissolves. Lines such as these flit through their minds and evoke their awareness of one another: "And now, I'm gonna take you to Heaven." "Feel the need, feel the need in me." "You need a strong love, to keep you warm, you need a man's love." "I need a man." "In and out, in and out, in and out." "I was made for loving you, baby." "It took me twenty years to learn how to swim; fear of flying's gonna do me in." "Can you feel it, can you feel it; feel it in your body, let your body move." "I need you, I need you, I need you, I need you right now."

Some of the Catacombs's hits were gay leather anthems such as Bette Midler's "Knight in Black Leather" or the Skatt Brothers' "Walk the Night." Sometimes Steve let out his wicked sense of humor. In the middle of one tape, with no warning, was the sudden sound of a toilet flushing. Steve often commissioned original songs for special parties such as birthdays or New Year's Eve. One memorable New Year's, at the stroke of twelve, the guests were serenaded to the tune of Auld Lang Syne with verses of "A Fist in Your Behind, My Love, A Fist in Your Behind."

An Oasis of Kink

At the regular Saturday night Catacombs parties, there was some divergence between fisting play and s/m. This in turn reflected a division in the men's leather community at large. Despite the considerable overlap between fisters and sadomasochists, they comprised separate groups with distinctive social patterns throughout most of the 1970s.

Many of the serious sadomasochists thought of Crisco as something that ruined leather, and some were scandalized by what they perceived as a lack of decorum and formality among fisters. On the other hand, many fisters were disinterested in s/m and some were openly hostile. To many fisters, s/m was at worst a form of brutality, and at best a noisy intrusion into the peaceful meditative atmosphere they sought.

While the Catacombs crowd was primarily interested in fisting, Steve himself was a devotee of both fisting and s/m. s/m was always part of the Catacombs, and it became more prevalent as the space became accessible to women and mixed-gender populations.

Cynthia Slater was the person responsible for other groups gaining access to the Catacombs. By the time she died of AIDS, in October 1989, Cynthia had changed the shape of the San Francisco leather community.[8] In 1974, she co-founded the Society of Janus, which quickly became a point of connection between straight, bisexual, and gay sadomasochists in the Bay Area. Through Janus, a lot of very different sorts of kinky people have found some common ground.

Through Janus, Cynthia also made contact with Steve and the Catacombs. By 1977, she and Steve were lovers. Steve eventually decided to allow Cynthia into the Saturday night parties. Some of the regulars were appalled by a woman's presence, but Steve's attitude about this and many other circumstances was that "they would get over it." Cynthia was bisexual. She introduced a couple of her female lovers into the space, and they in turn brought other lovers and friends. By the summer of 1978, there were usually from one to five women mingling among sixty to eighty men. As Steve had predicted, most of the men got over it, and many of them came to enjoy the presence of a few women as yet another twist on an already wild situation.

Pat Califia was one of those whom Cynthia brought to the Catacombs.[9] Pat noticed that the Catacombs was unused on Friday nights. She had the inspired idea of approaching Steve about renting the Catacombs on a Friday night for a women's s/m play party. Steve agreed. On 1 June 1979, the first of what would be many women's parties at the Catacombs was held. Steve was generally present at the women's parties, as was his lover, Fred Heramb, who had succeeded Cynthia as Steve's consort. So the women's parties usually consisted of about thirty women and two men.[10]

In a very real sense, s/m lesbians learned how to party at the Catacombs. Lesbian sadomasochists were just getting organized, and Steve's generosity made it possible for them to encounter a world of party and play technology that would have otherwise been inaccessible. The Catacombs quickly became a home and clubhouse for the nascent San Francisco lesbian s/m community. Because the local group was instrumental in the emergence of organized lesbian s/m nationally, the lessons of the Catacombs were transmitted to a generation of kinky gay women.[11]

In 1980, Cynthia Slater and Susan Thorner, another of her friends, decided to rent the Catacombs on a Friday night for a big mixed-gender/mixed-orientation s/m party. The event, held on 21 March, was the first time significant numbers of kinky gay men, lesbians, bisexuals, and heterosexuals partied together in the Bay Area. The party was so successful that Cynthia and her co-conspirator rented the top two floors of the Hothouse, another gay male leather sex place, for two more gigantic mixed parties.[12] There were also smaller mixed parties at Cynthia's home and private dungeon.

The successors to these early mixed parties would eventually become a local tradition. While the mixed parties included both men and women, they included too many gay men and lesbians to be "straight," and too many heterosexuals to be gay. Although they provided opportunities for experimentation, they were not about getting people to abandon their different orientations. On the contrary, by fostering an attitude of respect for difference, the parties created a comfortable atmosphere in which diverse populations could observe one another, appreciate their mutual interest in kink, and discover what they did have in common.

The Beginning of the End

The golden age of the Catacombs ended abruptly in the early morning hours of 28 August 1981. Steve and Fred had been happily cavorting on the waterbed in the Bridal Suite when Steve had a sudden heart attack and died in Fred's arms. Fred was in a disconsolate state of shock and grief. For all practical purposes, the Catacombs had vanished.

Steve left no will. The house was in the name of close friends, a heterosexual couple who had helped him finance the building. His other possessions reverted to his family of origin. They had no interest in the Catacombs, and seemed anxious to have it disappear as quickly as possible. They authorized Fred to sell the moveable equipment. One of the old regulars paid $500 for all the slings, tables, stirrups, cage, hoist, and gurney. Various friends came by to claim pieces of the artwork. I spoke to Fred of my concern that a historically significant collection of material would be scattered and difficult to trace. He said to take the rest of the art, which ended up stored for several months in my apartment. To keep the music tapes, Fred purchased them from Steve's family. Within two days of Steve's death, the basement was stripped of everything that had been the Catacombs. It had been completely dismantled.

The Catacombs crowd still needed a place to gather. The man who had bought the equipment acquired some partners, and they opened the San Francisco Catacombs II, at 736 Larkin, on 30 October 1981. The San Francisco Catacombs II invited women to its grand opening but excluded them thereafter. It had designer grey walls and a hot tub. Many of the regulars grumbled that the Crisco would stain the walls and muck up the hot tub. The San Francisco Catacombs II never caught on and closed within three months.

In January of 1982, I got an excited call from Fred. He had bought a house on Shotwell Street, just off Folsom in an area of the Mission district a few blocks from the main leather neighborhood. Fred planned to convert the house into a party and living space. He had the tapes and he had the party list. He had two partners, one of whom was the man who owned the equipment. They were going to reopen the Catacombs on Shotwell.

The Shotwell house was smaller than the old Catacombs building. It consisted of one flat over a large garage and basement. Fred and his friends went to work. They walled over the garage door. They installed a wooden floor. They put in heating and plumbing and a sound system. Fred came and got the artwork he had left with me, and he was eventually able to recover all but one piece of the rest of the art. The Catacombs reopened on 13 February 1982.

Fred restored the Catacombs in precise and exacting detail. The floor plan was different at Shotwell, and this dictated some changes in the layout of the dungeon. There was no place for a waterbed, but there was room for several additional slings. Fred somehow reassembled virtually every moveable piece of the old place—equipment, artwork, music tapes, and even a metal stool used by shorter persons (mostly women) to get in and out of equipment designed for taller ones (mostly men). The Shotwell Catacombs was Fred's farewell gift to Steve. Fred built a monument to Steve by painstakingly reconstructing the environment Steve had built and loved.

Fred also added some innovations of his own. One of the most popular was a motorcycle bolted to the floor. He added new art work and found people to do new music tapes. When Mark Joplin took over the music, the soundtrack changed. There was more new wave and Euro-rock, more electronic music, and less disco. There was, however, a very long disco version of Handel's Hallelujah chorus that became the anthem of the Shotwell Catacombs. When the Hallelujah chorus came on, usually at midnight, people would start slapping and whipping and pumping in unison, shouting Hallelujah and celebrating their ecstasy, their freedom, and their shared sacraments of communion. The revived Catacombs was a marvelous club, faithful to the original and wonderful in its own right.

At Shotwell, the sociology of the Catacombs changed. Ultimately, the different genders and sexual populations mingled more successfully at this location than they had at the original. Ironically, this came about in part because women were once again excluded from the Saturday parties.

Women were admitted to the parties for the first few months at Shotwell. But there was only one woman, named Carla, who consistently attended them.

Carla had been introduced to the Catacombs by Mark Joplin, her lover. After several months, an antiwoman faction persuaded Fred to bar women on Saturday nights. Women were still admitted to a Tuesday party, but as they were in the middle of the work week, these parties were considerably more subdued.

Mark and Carla therefore decided to throw regular mixed "Down and Dirty" parties one Friday a month. As a result, mixed-gender parties became an ongoing and stable institution. The mixed parties have continued since that time. They have been treated as a precious legacy in the local s/m community. They have been passed on from one group to another, and have survived AIDS, the closing of the baths, many deaths (including those of Fred and Mark), and the final disappearance of the Catacombs. The parties still run, heirs to the traditions established by Cynthia at her mixed parties a decade ago, and by Steve at the Catacombs over fifteen years ago.

The Bitter End

If I were asked what ultimately destroyed the Catacombs, I would have to say AIDS, even though that is too simple a response. There were other factors, and the impact of AIDS was felt in complex and unanticipated ways. But directly and indirectly, AIDS took the Catacombs and the lives of many of the individuals who called it home.

The first hint of what was in store came in the summer of 1981, about a month before Steve's heart attack. Tony Tavarossi suddenly died of pneumonia. I remember his friends being so puzzled, since people did not generally die of pneumonia or go as quickly as he did. In retrospect, it became clear that Tony had been one of the earliest San Francisco victims of pneumocystis. At that time there were health problems around the Catacombs—familiar things like intestinal parasites and hepatitis. But no one then even knew that AIDS existed.

When the Catacombs reopened in 1982, AIDS was still a distant cloud. As it moved in, information was scarce and inconclusive. There was a great deal of confusion about what was happening and how to deal with it. Epidemiologists suspected that AIDS was caused by a microorganism, and they theorized that it was sexually transmitted. But no one knew what the organism was, or the actual means of its transmission.

The first safe-sex guidelines appeared only in 1983, and these early recommendations were based on educated guesswork. Safe-sex practices spread slowly at first, and began to take hold among gay men in 1984. One of the problems faced by the Catacombs crowd in adopting safe-sex practices was that all the guidelines listed fisting as unsafe, which left fisters with no alternative but to abandon what they were doing.

There is something deeply irrational in the way fisting has been treated in safe-sex recommendations. Many health professionals simply assumed that fisting was inherently "unsafe," regardless of its relationship to AIDS. This assumption kept fisting in the category of unsafe acts in the AIDS education literature and hindered the development of AIDS risk-reduction guidelines for fisting.

It is true that one of the first cluster studies of AIDS included many fisters, and that there was an early statistical correlation between fisting and AIDS. Nevertheless, the causal mechanisms proposed to explain this correlation were unpersuasive. One common explanation was that fisting might cause microscopic tears in the rectum that could facilitate the entry of AIDS-infected semen from anal intercourse into the bloodstream. But if this were the case, transmission of the organism would result from anal intercourse rather than from fisting itself.

The early epidemiological data indicated that AIDS was difficult to catch and required some kind of direct contact between the blood or mucosa of two individuals. It was unclear how a hand could efficiently transmit or receive the presumed organism, unless there were breaks in the skin. For such situations, it would have been logical to recommend rubber gloves as a barrier to infection. During this same period of early confusion, condoms were often recommended for anal sex, which was a far more likely vector for disease transmission.

As more data accumulated and the correlation between AIDS and fisting became weaker, lists of unsafe practices continued to include fisting. When anal intercourse became seen as the major risk factor associated with AIDS, unprotected anal intercourse was listed as unsafe, but anal sex with condoms was considered possibly (or probably) safe. Why health guidelines from the same era never suggested fisting with opera-length rubber gloves as a method of risk reduction is still a mystery to me. The failure to develop risk-reduction guidelines for fisting endangered those who engaged in the practice.[13]

During 1983 and 1984, the Catacombs responded as quickly and responsibly as possible when information about AIDS began to trickle in. Fred welcomed visits by representatives from the Centers for Disease Control (CDC). According to Fred, they told him the Catacombs was the cleanest sex club they had seen. As the presence of a deadly communicable disease became more evident, the cleaning protocol became ever more elaborate. After each party, the Catacombs was washed down with industrial strength disinfectants. The towels were laundered in germicidal potions. Surgical scrub and mouthwash were put next to the sinks. Signs were prominently posted encouraging patrons to "Wash Hands After Every Fuck."

When the CDC recommended using condoms, Fred immediately provided them. One man looked at him and asked, "What am I supposed to do with these, put one on each finger?" At a subsequent party, Fred handed out shoulder-length veterinary gloves, with inches marked up the arm.

A volatile political campaign to close the baths and sex clubs erupted in the spring of 1984. The safe-sex campaigns worked on the premise that what you did was important, not where you did it. While some of the local baths and sex clubs resisted dealing with AIDS and refused to distribute safe-sex materials, others actively promoted safe-sex information. The Cauldron hosted safe-sex programs, and both the Cauldron and the Catacombs provided safe-sex updates to their respective clienteles.

The attempts to close the baths represented an alternative strategy for dealing with AIDS. Rather than promoting changes in sexual behavior to reduce the risk of transmission, the move to close the baths emphasized reducing the opportunities for gay men to have sex at all. Proponents of closure argued that their program was an obvious measure to save lives. They portrayed the debate about bathhouse closure as one that pitted public-health needs against civil-rights concerns.

This perspective oversimplified and distorted the situation. The closure efforts set dangerous precedents for state harassment of gay businesses and gay behavior. Wholesale closure eliminated opportunities for sex education along with opportunities for sex. Closure drove men to the streets and alleys and parks, which were arguably less safe and clean than the clubs they lost.

Moreover, the advantages of closing the baths were not balanced with a realistic assessment of the losses involved. Those who pushed for closure appeared to assume that nothing important or good occurred in the sex palaces. They placed little value on the baths and clubs and failed to recognize them as important institutions that served many needs in the gay male community.[14]

It took another year of bureaucratic and legal maneuvering for the crusade against the baths to succeed. Nevertheless, the handwriting on the wall was large and glaring. Many club owners took opportunities to get out before they were forced out.

Fred decided to close the Catacombs. He did not want to police what people did. He did not want to be closed by legal fiat. Above all, he saw the grim realities that in 1984 made the future of running a gay sex club a dubious enterprise.

He scheduled a final round of parties and a garage sale of the club contents. As it had been after Steve's death, the Catacombs was dismantled once again, this time permanently. Many who loved the Catacombs came to the sale to take home a piece of it to keep and cherish.

At one of the final parties, there was a big cake that said "Farewell Catacombs, Fuck You World." The last Catacombs party was held on Saturday night, 21 April 1984. The discovery of the human immunodeficiency virus (HIV, but then called HTLV-3) was officially announced to the press on the following Monday morning.

Not Forgotten

Although the Catacombs is gone, it has left a considerable legacy. In addition to its now widely imitated "recipes for a successful sex party," a set of Catacombs attitudes have taken root in a larger community. The Catacombs expressed a very deep love for the physical body. A place that could facilitate so much anal pleasure could make any part of the body feel happy. For the most part, our society treats the pursuit of physical pleasure as something akin to taking out the garbage. At the Catacombs, the body and its capacities for sensory experience were valued, celebrated, and loved. I learned some precious lessons there, and feel very lucky to have had the privilege of sharing in that experience. Even though its focus was on the male body, the Catacombs gave me a greater appreciation for my own, female body.

When reading descriptions in the straight press (and often in the gay press as well) of the places where gay sex, fisting, and s/M occur, I am often stunned by their utter lack of comprehension. Places devoted to sex are usually depicted as harsh, alienated, scary environments, where people have only the most utilitarian and exploitative relationships. The Catacombs could not have been more different. It was not a perfect utopia where nothing bad ever happened. It had its share of melodrama, heartache, and the human condition. But it was essentially a friendly place. It was a sexually organized environment where people treated each other with mutual respect, and where they were lovingly sexual without being in holy wedlock.

At the Catacombs, even brief connections were handled with courtesy and care. And there was a particular kind of love that emerged from the slings. Sometimes that love only happened in "the back." Just as often, it extended out into the everyday world. The Catacombs facilitated the formation of important friendships and lasting networks of support. Many of the men who frequented the Catacombs found relationships there that have sustained them through time, nurtured them with affection, cared for them in sickness, and buried them in sorrow.

The creation of well-designed and deftly managed sexual environments is as much an achievement as the building of more "respectable" institutions. The individuals who have built them should be recognized for their accomplishments. The influence of the Mineshaft, Inferno, and the Catacombs extends far beyond their local communities. They have all become widely recognized models for conducting successful leather sex parties. They will continue to provide inspiration to other times and other places.

AIDS will not last forever. The gay community is already recovering its balance and its strength. There will be a renaissance of sex. There will be new clubs, new parties, and new horizons. The best of these will have some of the grace and verve and spunk of the Catacombs.

Of Catamites and Kings

Reflections on Butch, Gender, and Boundaries

10

What Is Butch? Conceptions and Misconceptions of Lesbian Gender

Attempting to define terms such as *butch* and *femme* is one of the surest ways to incite volatile discussion among lesbians. Butch and femme are important categories within lesbian experience, and as such they have accumulated multiple layers of significance. Most lesbians would probably agree with a definition from *The Queen's Vernacular*, that a butch is a "lesbian with masculine characteristics."[1] But many corollaries attending that initial premise oversimplify and misrepresent butch experience. In this essay, I approach butch from the perspective of gender in order to discuss, clarify, and challenge some prevalent lesbian cultural assumptions about what is butch.

Many commentators have noted that the categories butch and femme have historically served numerous functions in the lesbian world. Describing the lesbian community in Buffalo from the 1930s through the 1950s, Elizabeth Kennedy and Madeline Davis comment,

> These roles had two dimensions: First, they constituted a code of personal behavior, particularly in the areas of image and sexuality. Butches affected a masculine style, while fems appeared characteristically female. Butch and fem also complemented one another in an erotic system in which the butch was expected to be both the doer and the giver; the fem's passion was the butch's fulfillment. Second, butch-fem roles were what we call a social im-

---

Chapter 10 was originally published in Joan Nestle, ed., *The Persistent Desire* (Boston: Alyson, 1992), 466–82.

perative. They were the organizing principle for this community's relation to the outside world and for its members' relationships to one another.[2]

While I do not wish to deny or underestimate the complexity of its functions, I will argue that the simplest definition of butch is the most helpful one. Butch is most usefully understood as a category of lesbian gender that is constituted through the deployment and manipulation of masculine gender codes and symbols.

Butch and femme are ways of coding identities and behaviors that are both connected to and distinct from standard societal roles for men and women.[3] Among lesbian and bisexual women, as in the general population, there are individuals who strongly identify as masculine or feminine as well as individuals whose gender preferences are more flexible or fluid. Femmes identify predominantly as feminine or prefer behaviors and signals defined as feminine within the larger culture; butches identify primarily as masculine or prefer masculine signals, personal appearance, and styles. There are also many lesbians (and bisexual women) with intermediate or unmarked gender styles. In the old days, terms such as *ki-ki* indicated such intermediate or indeterminate gender styles or identities. We appear to have no contemporary equivalent, although at times, *lesbian* and *dyke* are used to indicate women whose gender messages are not markedly butch or femme.[4]

Butch is the lesbian vernacular term for women who are more comfortable with masculine gender codes, styles, or identities than with feminine ones. The term encompasses individuals with a broad range of investments in "masculinity." It includes, for example, women who are not at all interested in male gender identities, but who use traits associated with masculinity to signal their lesbianism or to communicate their desire to engage in the kinds of active or initiatory sexual behaviors that in this society are allowed or expected from men. It includes women who adopt "male" fashions and mannerisms as a way to claim privileges or deference usually reserved for men. It may include women who find men's clothing better made or who consider women's usual clothes too confining, uncomfortable, or who feel it leaves them vulnerable or exposed.[5]

Butch is also the indigenous lesbian category for women who are gender *dysphoric*. *Gender dysphoria* is a technical term for individuals who are dissatisfied with the gender to which they were assigned (usually at birth) on the basis of their anatomical sex. Within the psychological and medical communities, gender dysphoria is considered a disorder, as were lesbianism and male homosexuality before the American Psychiatric Association removed them from its official list of mental diseases in 1973.[6] I am not using *gender dysphoria* in the clinical sense, with its connotations of neurosis or psychological impairment. I am using it as a purely descriptive term for persons who have gender feelings and identities that are at odds with their assigned gender status or their physical bodies. Individuals who have very powerful gender dysphoria, particularly those with strong drives to alter their bodies to conform to their preferred gender identities, are called transsexuals.[7]

The lesbian community is organized along an axis of sexual orientation, and comprises women who have sexual, affectional, erotic, and intimate relations with other women. It nevertheless harbors a great deal of gender dysphoria.[8] Drag, cross-dressing, passing, transvestism, and transsexualism are all common in lesbian populations, particularly those not attempting to meet constricted standards of political virtue.[9]

In spite of their prevalence, issues of gender variance are strangely out of focus in lesbian thought, analysis, and terminology. The intricacies of lesbian gender are inadequately and infrequently addressed. *Butch* is one of the few terms currently available with which to express or indicate masculine gender preferences among lesbians, and it carries a heavy, undifferentiated load.[10] The category of butch encompasses a wide range of gender variation within lesbian cultures.

Within the group of women labeled butch, there are many individuals who are gender dysphoric to varying degrees. Many butches have partially male gender identities. Others border on being, and some are, female-to-male transsexuals (FTMs), although many lesbians *and* FTMs find the areas of overlap between butchness and transsexualism disturbing.[11] Saying that many butches identify as masculine to some degree does not mean that all, even most butches "want to be men," although some undoubtedly do. Most butches enjoy combining expressions of masculinity with a female body. The coexistence of masculine traits with a female anatomy is a fundamental characteristic of "butch" and is a highly charged, eroticized, and consequential lesbian signal.[12]

By saying that many lesbians identify partially or substantially as masculine, I am also not saying that such individuals are "male identified" in the political sense. When the term *male identified* was originally used in early-seventies second-wave feminism, it denoted nothing about gender identity. It described a political attitude in which members of a category of generally oppressed persons (women) failed to identify with their self-interest as women, and instead identified with goals, policies, and attitudes beneficial to a group of generally privileged oppressors (men). Though such women were sometimes butch or masculine in style, they might as easily be femme or feminine. One typical manifestation of male identification in this sense consisted of very feminine heterosexual women who supported traditional male privilege. On a more contemporary note, some of the feminine right-wing women whose political aims include strengthening male authority in conventional family arrangements could also be called male identified.

There are many problems with the notion of male identified, not the least of which are questions of who defines what "women's interests" are in a given situation and the assumption of a unitary category of "women" whose interests are always the same. But the point here is not a political critique of the concept of male identification. It is simply to register that a similarity in terminology has often led to a conflation of political positions with gender identities. A strongly masculine butch will not necessarily identify politically with men. In fact, it is sometimes the most masculine women who confront male privilege most directly and painfully and are the most enraged by it.[13]

Varieties of Butch

The iconography in many contemporary lesbian periodicals leaves a strong impression that a butch always has very short hair, wears a leather jacket, rides a Harley, and works construction. This butch paragon speaks mostly in monosyllables, is tough yet sensitive, is irresistible to women, and is semiotically related to a long line of images of young, rebellious, sexy, white, working-class masculinity that stretches from Marlon Brando in *The Wild One* (1954) to the character of James Hurley on *Twin Peaks* (1990). She is usually accompanied by a half-dressed, ultrafeminine creature who is artfully draped on her boots, her bike, or one of her muscular tattooed forearms.[14]

These images originate in the motorcycle and street gangs of the early fifties. They have been powerful erotic icons ever since, and lesbians are not the only group to find them engaging and sexy. Among gay men, the figure of the outlaw leather biker (usually with a heart of gold) has symbolically anchored an entire subculture. During the late seventies, similar imagery dominated even mainstream male homosexual style and fashion. There are many rock-and-roll variants, from classic biker (early Bruce Springsteen) to futuristic road warrior (Judas Priest, Billy Idol) to postmodern punk (Sex Pistols). The contemporary *Act-Up* and Queer Nation styles so popular among young gay men and women are lineal descendants of those of the punk rockers, whose torn jackets and safety pins fractured and utilized the same leather aesthetic.

Within the lesbian community, the most commonly recognized butch styles are those based on these models of white, working-class, youthful masculinity. But in spite of the enduring glamour and undeniable charm of these figures of rebellious individualism, they do not encompass the actual range of lesbian masculinity. Butches vary in their styles of masculinity, their preferred modes of sexual expression, and their choices of partners.

There are many different ways to be masculine. Men get to express masculinity with numerous and diverse cultural codes, and there is no reason to assume that women are limited to a narrower choice of idioms. There are at least as many ways to be butch as there are ways for men to be masculine; actually, there are more ways to be butch, because when women appropriate masculine styles the element of travesty produces new significance and meaning. Butches adopt and transmute the many available codes of masculinity.[15]

Sometimes lesbians use the term *butch* to indicate only the most manly women.[16] But the equation of butch with hypermasculine women indulges a stereotype. Butches vary widely in how masculine they feel, and consequently, in how they perceive and present themselves. Some butches are only faintly masculine, some are partly masculine, some "dag" butches are very manly, and some "drag kings" pass as men.

Butches vary in how they relate to their female bodies. Some butches are comfortable being pregnant and having kids, while for others the thought of undergoing the female component of mammalian reproduction is utterly repugnant. Some enjoy their breasts while others despise them. Some butches hide their genitals and some refuse penetration. There are butches who abhor tampons, because of their resonance with intercourse; other butches love getting fucked. Some butches are perfectly content in their female bodies, while others may border on or become transsexuals.

Forms of masculinity are molded by the experiences and expectations of nationality, class, race, ethnicity, religion, occupation, age, subculture, and individual personality. Socially and culturally distinct populations differ widely in what constitutes masculinity, and each has its own system for communicating and conferring "manhood." In some cultures, physical strength and aggression are the privileged signals of masculinity. In other cultures, manliness is expressed by literacy and the ability to manipulate numbers or text. The travails of Barbara Streisand's character in *Yentl* occurred because scholarship was considered the exclusive domain of men among traditional Orthodox Jews of Eastern Europe. Myopia and stooped shoulders from a lifetime of reading were prized traits of masculinity. Some butches play rugby; some debate political theory; some do both.

Manliness also varies according to class origin, income level, and occupation. Masculinity can be expressed by educational level, career achievement, emotional detachment, musical or artistic talent, sexual conquest, intellectual style, or disposable income. The poor, the working classes, the middle classes, and the rich all provide different sets of skills and expectations that butches as well as men use to certify their masculinity.[17]

The styles of masculinity executive and professional men favor differ sharply from those of truckers and carpenters. The self-presentations of marginally employed intellectuals differ from those of prosperous lawyers. Classical musicians differ from jazz musicians who are distinguishable from rock-and-roll musicians. Short hair, shaved heads, and Mohawks did not make eighties punk rockers more studly than today's long-haired heavy-metal headbangers. All of these are recognizably male styles, and there are butches who express their masculinity within each symbolic assemblage.

Butches come in all the shapes and varieties and idioms of masculinity. There are butches who are tough street dudes, butches who are jocks, butches who are scholars, butches who are artists, rock-and-roll butches, butches who have motorcycles, and butches who have money. There are butches whose male models are effeminate men, sissies, drag queens, and many different types of male homosexuals. There are butch nerds, butches with soft bodies and hard minds.

Butch Sexualities

Thinking of butch as a category of gender expression may help to account for what appear to be butch sexual anomalies. Do butches who prefer to let their partners run the sex become "femme in the sheets"? Are butches who go out with other butches instead of femmes "homosexuals"? Does that make femmes who date femmes "lesbians"?

Butchness often signals a sexual interest in femmes and a desire or willingness to orchestrate sexual encounters. However, ideas that butches partner exclusively with femmes or that butches always "top" (that is, "run the sex") are stereotypes that mask substantial variation in butch erotic experience.[18]

Historically, butches were expected to seduce, arouse, and sexually satisfy their partners, who were expected to be femmes. During similar eras, men were expected to inaugurate and manage sexual relations with their female partners. Both sets of expectation were located within a system in which gender role, sexual orientation, and erotic behavior were presumed to exist only in certain fixed relationships to one another. Variations existed and were recognized, but considered aberrant.

Though we still live in a culture that privileges heterosexuality and gender conformity, many of the old links have been broken, bent, strained, and twisted into new formations. Perhaps more important, configurations of gender role and sexual practice that were once rare have become much more widespread. In contemporary lesbian populations there are many combinations of gender and desire.

Many butches like to seduce women and control sexual encounters. Some butches become aroused only when they are managing a sexual situation. But there are femmes who like to stay in control, and there are butches who prefer their partners to determine the direction and rhythms of lovemaking. Such butches may seek out sexually dominant femmes or sexually aggressive butches. Every conceivable combination of butch, femme, intermediate, top, bottom, and switch exists, even though some are rarely acknowledged. There are butch tops and butch bottoms, femme tops and femme bottoms. There are butch-femme couples, femme-femme partners, and butch-butch pairs.

Butches are often identified in relation to femmes. Within this framework, butch and femme are considered as an indissoluble unity, each defined with reference to the other; butches are invariably the partners of femmes. Defining butch as the object of femme desire, or femme as the object of butch desire presupposes that butches do not desire or partner with other butches, and that femmes do not desire or go with other femmes.

Butch-butch eroticism is much less documented than butch-femme sexuality, and lesbians do not always recognize or understand it. Although it is not uncommon, lesbian culture contains few models for it. Many butches who lust after other butches have looked to gay male literature and behavior as sources of imagery and language. The erotic dynamics of butch-butch sex sometimes resemble those of gay men, who have developed many patterns for sexual relations between different kinds of men. Gay men also have role models for men who are passive or subordinate in sexual encounters yet retain their masculinity. Many butch-butch couples think of themselves as women doing male homosexual sex with one another. There are "catamites" who are the submissive or passive partners of active "sodomites." There are "daddies" and "daddy's boys." There are bodybuilders who worship one another's musculature and lick each other's sweat. There are leather dudes who cruise together for "victims" to pleasure.[19]

No system of classification can successfully catalogue or explain the infinite vagaries of human diversity. To paraphrase Foucault, no system of thought can ever "tame the wild profusion of existing things."[20] Anomalies will always occur, challenging customary modes of thought without representing any actual threat to health, safety, or community survival. However, human beings are easily upset by exactly those "existing things" that escape classification, treating such phenomena as dangerous, polluting, and requiring eradication.[21] Female-to-male transsexuals present just such a challenge to lesbian gender categories.

Although important discontinuities separate lesbian butch experience and female-to-male transsexual experience, there are also significant points of connection. Some butches are psychologically indistinguishable from female-to-male transsexuals, except for the identities they choose and the extent to which they are willing or able to alter their bodies. Many FTMs have lived as butches before adopting transsexual or male identities. Some individuals explore each identity before choosing one that is more meaningful for them, and others use both categories to interpret and organize their experience. The boundaries between the categories of butch and transsexual are permeable.[22]

Many of the passing women and diesel butches so venerated as lesbian ancestors are also claimed in the historical lineages of female-to-male transsexuals. There is a deep-rooted appreciation in lesbian culture for the beauty and heroism of manly women. Accounts of butch exploits form a substantial part of lesbian fiction and history; images of butches and passing women are among our most striking ancestral portraits. These include the photographs of Radclyffe Hall as a dashing young gent, the Berenice Abbott photo of Jane Heap wearing a suit and fixing an intimidating glare at the camera, and Brassai's pictures of the nameless but exquisitely cross-dressed and manicured butches who patronized Le Monocle in 1930s Paris.

Some of these women were likely as much transsexual as butch, although transsexual identities had not yet taken their modern forms. For example, several years ago the San Francisco Lesbian and Gay History Project produced a slide show on passing women in North America.[23] One of those women was Babe Bean, also known as Jack Bee Garland. Bean/Garland later became the subject of a biography by Louis Sullivan, a leader and scholar in the FTM community until his recent death from AIDS. Sullivan's study highlighted Garland's gender deviance rather than his sexual relationships, repositioning him within a transgender lineage.[24] It is interesting to ponder what other venerable lesbian forebears might be considered transsexuals; if testosterone had been available, some would undoubtedly have seized the opportunity to take it.

In spite of the overlap and kinship between some areas of lesbian and transsexual experience, many lesbians are antagonistic toward transsexuals, treating male-to-female transsexuals as menacing intruders and female-to-male transsexuals as treasonous deserters. Transsexuals of both genders are commonly perceived and described in contemptuous stereotypes: unhealthy, deluded, self-hating, enslaved to patriarchal gender roles, sick, antifeminist, antiwoman, and self-mutilating.

Despite theoretically embracing diversity, contemporary lesbian culture has a deep streak of xenophobia. When confronted with phenomena that do not neatly fit our categories, lesbians have been known to respond with hysteria, bigotry, and a desire to stamp out the offending messy realities. A "country club syndrome" sometimes prevails in which the lesbian community is treated as an exclusive enclave from which the riffraff must be systematically expunged. Everyone has a right to emotional responses. But it is imperative to distinguish between emotions and principles. Just as "hard cases make bad law," intense emotions make bad policy. Over the years, lesbian groups have gone through periodic attempts to purge male-to-female transsexuals, sadomasochists, butch-femme lesbians, bisexuals, and even lesbians who are not separatists. FTMs are another witch hunt waiting to happen.[25]

For many years, male-to-female transsexuals (MTFS) have vastly outnumbered female-to-male individuals. A small percentage of MTFS are sexually involved with women and define themselves as lesbian. Until recently, lesbian discomfort was triggered primarily by those male-to-female lesbians, who have been the focus of controversy and who have often been driven out of lesbian groups and businesses. Discrimination against MTFS is no longer monolithic, and many lesbian organizations have made a point of admitting male-to-female lesbians.

However, such discrimination has not disappeared. It surfaced in 1991 at the National Lesbian Conference, which banned "nongenetic women."[26] Transsexual women became the cause célèbre of the 1991 Michigan Womyn's Music Festival. Festival organizers expelled a transsexual woman, then retroactively articulated a policy banning all but "womyn-born-womyn" from future events.[27] After decades of feminist insistence that women are "made, not born," after fighting to establish that "anatomy is not destiny," it is astounding that ostensibly progressive events can get away with discriminatory policies based so blatantly on recycled biological determinism.

The next debate over inclusion and exclusion will focus on female-to-male transsexuals. Transsexual demographics are changing. FTMS still comprise only a fraction of the visible transsexual population, but their numbers are growing and awareness of their presence is increasing. Female-to-male transsexuals who are in, or in the process of leaving, lesbian communities are becoming the objects of controversy and posing new challenges to the ways in which lesbian communities handle diversity. A woman who has been respected, admired, and loved as a butch may suddenly be despised, rejected, and hounded when s/he starts a sex change.[28]

Sex changes are often stressful, not only for the person undergoing change but also for the network in which that person is embedded. Individuals and local groups cope with such stress well or badly, depending on their level of knowledge about gender diversity, their relationships with the person involved, their willingness to face difficult emotions, their ability to think beyond immediate emotional responses, and the unique details of local history and personality. As a community goes through the process of handling a sex change by one of its members, it evolves techniques and sets precedents for doing so.

Though some lesbians are not disturbed by FTMS, and some find them uniquely attractive, many lesbians are upset by them. When a woman's body begins to change into a male body, the transposition of male and female signals that constitutes "butch" begins to disintegrate. A cross-dressing, dildo-packing, bodybuilding butch may use a male name and masculine pronouns, yet still have soft skin, no facial hair, the visible swell of breasts or hips under male clothing, small hands and feet, or some other detectable sign of femaleness. If the same person grows a mustache, develops a lower voice, binds his breasts, grows a beard, or begins to bald, his body offers no evidence to contravene his social signals. When he begins to read like a man, many lesbians no longer find him attractive and some want to banish him from their social universe. If the FTM has lesbian partners (and many do), they also risk ostracism.

Instead of another destructive round of border patrols, surveillance, and expulsion, I would suggest a different strategy. Lesbians should instead relax, wait, and support the individuals involved as they sort out their own identities and decide where they fit socially.

A sex change is a transition. A woman does not immediately become physically male as soon as she begins to take hormones. During the initial states of changing sex, many FTMS will not be ready to leave the world of women. There is no good reason to harass them through a transitional period during which they will not quite fit as women or men. Most FTMS who undergo sex reassignment identify as men and are anxious to live as men as soon as possible. They will leave lesbian contexts on their own, when they can, when they are ready, and when those environments are no longer comfortable. It is not necessary for gender vigilantes to drive them out. Some FTMs will experiment with sex change and elect to abandon the effort. They should not be deprived of their lesbian credentials for having explored the option.

The partners of FTMs do not necessarily or suddenly become bisexual or heterosexual because a lover decides on a sex change, although some do eventually renegotiate their own identities. An attraction to people of intermediate sex does not automatically displace or negate an attraction to other women. Dealing with their sex-changing partners is difficult and confusing enough for the lovers of transsexuals without having to worry about being thrown out of their social universe. Friends and lovers of FTMs often have intense feelings of loss, grief, and abandonment. They need support for handling such feelings, and should not be terrorized into keeping them secret.

In the past, most FTMs were committed to a fairly complete change, a commitment that was required for an individual to gain access to sex-change technologies controlled by the therapeutic and medical establishments. To obtain hormones or surgery, transsexuals (of both directions) had to be able to persuade a number of professionals that they were determined to be completely "normal" members of the target sex (that is, feminine heterosexual women and masculine heterosexual men). Gay transsexuals had to hide their homosexuality to get sex-change treatment. This has begun to change, and transsexuals now have more freedom to be gay and less traditionally gender stereotyped after the change.

More transsexuals also now exist who do not pursue a complete change. Increasing numbers of individuals utilize some but not all of the available sex-change technology, resulting in "intermediate" bodies, somewhere between female and male. Some FTMs may be part women, part men—genetic females with male body shapes, female genitals, and intermediate gender identities. Some of these may not want to leave their lesbian communities and they should not be forced to do so. They may cause confusion, repelling some lesbians and attracting others. But if community membership were based on universal desirability, no one would qualify. Our desires can be as selective, exclusive, and imperious as we like; our society should be as inclusive, humane, and tolerant as we can make it.

In writing this essay, I have wanted to diversify conceptions of butchness, to promote a more nuanced conceptualization of gender variation among lesbian and bisexual women, and to forestall prejudice against individuals who use other modes of managing gender. I also have an underlying agenda to support the tendencies among lesbians to enjoy and celebrate our differences. Lesbian communities and individuals have suffered enough from the assumption that we should all be the same, or that every difference must be justified by a claim of political or moral superiority.

We should not attempt to decide whether butch-femme or transsexuality are acceptable for anyone or preferable for everyone. Individuals should be allowed to navigate their own trails through the possibilities, complexities, and difficulties of life in postmodern times. Each strategy and each set of categories has its capabilities, benefits, and drawbacks. None are perfect, and none work for everyone all the time.

Early lesbian-feminism rejected butch-femme roles out of ignorance of their historical context and because their limitations had become readily obvious. Butch and femme were brilliantly adapted for building a minority sexual culture out of the tools, materials, and debris of a dominant sexual system. Their costs included obligations for each lesbian to choose a role, the ways such roles sometimes reinforced subservient status for femmes, and the sexual frustrations often experienced by butches.

The rejection of butch-femme was equally a product of its time. Feminism has often simply announced changes already in progress for which it has taken credit and for which it has been held responsible. The denunciation of butch-femme occurred in part because some of its premises were outdated and because lesbian populations had other tools with which to create viable social worlds. Yet wholesale condemnation of butch-femme impoverished our understandings, experiences, and models for lesbian gender. It subjected many women to gratuitous denigration and harassment, and left a legacy of confusion, lost pleasures, and cultural deprivation. As we reclaim butch-femme, I hope we do not invent yet another form of politically correct behavior or morality.

Feminism and lesbian-feminism developed in opposition to a system that imposed rigid roles, limited individual potential, exploited women as physical and emotional resources, and persecuted sexual and gender diversity. Feminism and lesbian-feminism should not be used to impose new but equally rigid limitations, or as an excuse to create new vulnerable and exploitable populations. Lesbian communities were built by sex and gender refugees; the lesbian world should not create new rationales for sex and gender persecution.

Our categories are important. We cannot organize a social life, a political movement, or our individual identities and desires without them. The fact that categories invariably leak and can never contain all the relevant "existing things" does not render them useless, only limited. Categories like "woman," "butch," "lesbian," or "transsexual" are all imperfect, historical, temporary, and arbitrary. We use them, and they use us. We use them to construct meaningful lives, and they mold us into historically specific forms of personhood. Instead of fighting for immaculate classifications and impenetrable boundaries, let us strive to maintain a community that understands diversity as a gift, sees anomalies as precious, and treats all basic principles with a hefty dose of skepticism.

Misguided, Dangerous, and Wrong

An Analysis of Antipornography Politics

11

For those who believe in God, in His absolute supremacy as the Creator and Lawgiver of life, in the dignity and destiny which He has conferred upon the human person, in the moral code that governs sexual activity—for those who believe in these "things" no argument against pornography should be necessary. Though the meaning of pornography is generally understood, reference is seldom made to the root meaning of the term itself. This seems important to me. The Greeks had a word for it, for many "its." And the Greek word for pornography is highly significant. It comes from two Greek words, in fact: "prostitute" and "write." So, the dictionary defines pornography as "originally a description of prostitutes and their trade." Pornography is not merely associated in this historical sense with prostitution, but it is actually a form of prostitution because it advertises and advocates "sex for sale," pleasure for a price. . . . A person is much more than a body, and any form of sexual activity which is impersonal, which uses the body alone for pleasure, violates the integrity of the person and thereby reduces him to the level of an irrational and irresponsible animal.
—**Statement by Charles H. Keating Jr.,** *The Report of the Commission on Obscenity and Pornography*

Chapter 11 was originally published in Alison Assiter and Avedon Carol, eds., *Bad Girls and Dirty Pictures: The Challenge to Reclaim Feminism* (London: Pluto, 1993), 18–40.

The Empress Has No Clothes

The targeting of pornography as a focus of feminist rage and political effort has been a dangerous, costly, and tragic mistake. Feminists should be aware of the potentially disastrous consequences of this misguided crusade. It is important for feminists to realize that the arguments against pornography are incredibly flimsy, and that there is little intellectual justification for a feminist antiporn position.

Antipornography politics surfaced as a volatile flashpoint in the women's movement in the United States in the late 1970s.[1] Although criticisms of pornography had previously occurred in feminist writing, pornography did not become a major focus of feminist agitation until after the emergence of a group in the San Francisco Bay Area in 1976 called Women Against Violence in Pornography and Media (WAVPM). In 1978, WAVPM held a "Feminist Perspectives on Pornography Conference" in San Francisco. This gathering quickly sparked the formation of New York City's Women Against Pornography (WAP) and marked the eruption of pornography as a popular feminist issue.[2]

By 1978 feminists had already spent a decade identifying and criticizing the ideologies that justified male supremacy and that permeated virtually all of Western literature, high art, popular media, religion, and education. Ideas of male dominance were deeply embedded in children's reading material, in medicine and psychiatry, and in all the academic disciplines. Similar attitudes were endemic to advertising, television, movies, and fiction. Feminists denounced cultural expressions of male supremacy and began to produce new art, fiction, children's literature, film, and academic work with different values. Feminists demanded changes in medical and psychological practice and in popular media such as advertising, television, and film.[3]

In all of these areas, feminists attempted to reform existing practice and to agitate for nonsexist attitudes. In no case did feminists call for the abolition of the area or domain in question. There were never groups called Women Against Film, Women Against Television, or Women Against the Novel, even though most film, television, and fiction were demonstrably sexist. When pornography became an issue, it was treated in an entirely unique fashion. Instead of criticizing the sexist content of sexually explicit media and calling for the production of nonsexist, pro-feminist, or woman-oriented sexual materials, feminists concerned with porn simply demanded that it be eliminated altogether.[4] Unlike any other category of media or representation, pornography was treated as beyond feminist salvage. The singularity of this position and its underlying premises have too often been overlooked.

Advocates of the antiporn position commonly declared it to be self-evident and undebatable.[5] They insisted that opposition to pornography was essential to feminism and that by definition a feminist could not dispute the antiporn position. Those of us who did disagree were dismissed as not being true feminists or smeared with accusations of promoting violence against women.[6]

With little debate, antiporn ideas became a coercive dogma and a premature orthodoxy. Ungrounded and often outlandish assertions became unquestioned assumptions. Important distinctions, such as those between sex and violence, image and act, harmless fantasy and criminal assault, the sexually explicit and the explicitly violent, were hopelessly blurred. The words *violence* and *pornography* began to be used interchangeably, as though they were synonymous. Pornography was often simply equated with violence. This muddled terminology and its conceptual confusions became widespread in the feminist media. Even women who had reservations about the antiporn position or its consequences often expressed these within the terms set by the language of antiporn proponents.[7]

It is well known to students of rhetoric that people may become convinced of a false premise or an illogical conclusion if it is merely asserted loudly enough, often enough, or with sufficient conviction. This has occurred in the porn "debates." A common tactic of demagogues is to use inflammatory images to drive people into fear and hate beyond the reach of rational discussion. This has occurred in the porn "debates." When any discourse is polarized, those not directly involved in the conflict tend to assume that the truth of the matter lies in the middle between the extremes of opinion expressed. This is a dangerous tendency that has often resulted in giving more credibility to the messages of hate-mongering groups than they deserve.[8] This too has occurred in the porn "debates."

Many feminists have accepted the notions that pornography is an especially odious expression of male supremacy, that pornography is violent, or that pornography is synonymous with violent media. They merely disagree about what should be done about it. For example, there are many feminists who think of porn as disgusting sexist propaganda, but who nevertheless are concerned about defending the First Amendment and who are cautious about invoking censorship. I certainly agree that concerns over censorship and freedom of expression are valid and vital. However, my purpose here is not to argue that pornography is antiwoman speech which unfortunately deserves constitutional protection. My goal is to challenge the assumptions that pornography is, per se, particularly sexist, especially violent or implicated in violence, or intrinsically antithetical to the interests of women.

The "pornography problem" is a false problem, at least as it is generally posed. There are legitimate feminist concerns with regard to sexually explicit media and the conditions under which it is produced. However, these are not the concerns that have dominated the feminist antiporn politics. Instead, pornography has become an easy, pliant, and overdetermined scapegoat for problems for which it is not responsible. To support this contention, I will examine the fundamental propositions and structure of antiporn argument.

Premises, Presuppositions, and Definitions

The Conflation of Pornography and Violence

One of the most basic claims of the antiporn position is that pornography is violent and promotes violence against women.[9] Two assertions are implicit or explicit to this claim. One is that pornography is characteristically violent and/or sexist in what it depicts, and the other is that pornography is more violent and/or sexist in content than other media. Both of these propositions are demonstrably false.

Very little pornography actually depicts violent acts. Pornography does depict some form of sexual activity, and these sexual activities vary widely. The most common behavior featured in porn is ordinary heterosexual intercourse (although it is a convention of porn movies that male orgasm must be visible to the viewer, so ejaculation in porn films generally takes place outside the body). Nudity, genital close-ups, and oral sex are also prevalent. Anal sex is far less common, but some magazines and films specialize in depicting it. While some films and magazines attempt to have "something for everyone," a lot of porn is fairly specialized, and many porn shops group their material according to the primary activity it contains, with separate sections featuring oral sex, anal sex, or gay male sex.

There is also "lesbian" material designed to appeal to heterosexual men rather than to lesbians. Until the last decade, there was very little porn produced by or actually intended for lesbian viewers. This has been changing with the advent of some small circulation, low-budget sex magazines produced by and for lesbians. Ironically, this nascent lesbian porn is endangered by both right-wing and feminist antiporn activity.[10]

There are several subgenres of porn designed to cater to minority sexual populations. The most successful example of this is gay male porn. There are many specialized shops serving the gay male market. Much male homosexual pornography is produced by and for gay men, and its quality is relatively high. Transsexual porn is rarer and found in fewer shops. It is designed to appeal to transsexuals and those who find them erotic. Many of the models seem to be transsexuals who are working in the sex industry, either because discrimination against them makes employment elsewhere difficult, or in order to raise money for sex-change treatment.

Another specialized subgenre is s/m porn. s/m materials have been used as the primary "evidence" for the alleged violence of porn as a whole. s/m materials are only a small percentage of commercial porn, and they are hardly representative. They appeal primarily to a distinct minority, and they are not as readily available as other materials. For example, in San Francisco only two of the dozen or so adult theaters of the late 1970s and early 1980s regularly showed bondage or s/m movies. These two theaters, however, have always been prominently featured in local antiporn invective.[11]

Many of the local porn shops have small sections of bondage material, but only a couple have extensive collections and are therefore favored by connoisseurs. Mainstream porn magazines such as *Playboy* and *Penthouse* rarely contain any bondage or s/m photographs. When they do, however, these again are emphasized in antiporn arguments. Some bondage photos in the December 1984 *Penthouse* are a case in point. They have often been used as examples in slide shows and displays by antiporn activists who invariably neglect to mention that the occurrence of such spreads in *Penthouse* is exceedingly unusual and quite unrepresentative.[12]

s/m materials are aimed at an audience that understands a set of conventions for interpreting them. Sadomasochism is not a form of violence, but is rather a type of ritual and contractual sex play whose aficionados go to great lengths in order to do it and to ensure the safety and enjoyment of one another. s/m fantasy does involve images of coercion and sexual activities that may appear violent to outsiders. s/m erotic materials can be shocking to those unfamiliar with the highly negotiated nature of most s/m encounters. This is compounded by the unfortunate fact that most commercial s/m porn is produced by people who are not practicing sadomasochists and whose understanding of s/m is not unlike that of the antiporn feminists. Thus commercial s/m porn often reflects the prejudices of its producers rather than common s/m practice.[13]

Torn out of context, s/m material is upsetting to unprepared audiences and this shock value has been mercilessly exploited in antiporn presentations. s/m porn is itself misrepresented, its relationship to s/m activity is distorted, and it is treated as though it is representative of porn as a whole.

Pioneered by wavpm and adopted by wap, slide shows have been a basic organizing tool of antiporn groups. Slides of images are used to persuade audiences of the alleged violence of pornography. The antiporn movie *Not a Love Story* follows a format similar to the slide shows and utilizes many of the same techniques.[14] The slide shows and the movie always display a completely unrepresentative sample of pornography in order to "demonstrate" its ostensible violence. s/m imagery occupies a much greater space in the slide shows and in *Not a Love Story* than it does in actual adult bookstores or theaters.

In addition to s/m materials, the presentations utilize images from porn that are violent or distasteful, but that are again unrepresentative. An example of this is the notorious *Hustler* cover showing a woman being fed into a meat grinder. This image is upsetting and distasteful, but it is not even legally obscene. It is also unusual. *Hustler* is a magazine that strives to be in bad taste. It is as different from other comparable mass-circulation sex magazines as the *National Lampoon* is from *Esquire* or *Harpers*.

Arguing from bad examples is effective but irresponsible. It is the classic method for promulgating negative stereotypes and is one of the favored rhetorical tactics for selling various forms of racism, bigotry, hatred, and xenophobia. It is always possible to find bad examples—of, for example, women, gay people, transsexuals, blacks, Jews, Italians, Irish, immigrants, the poor—and to use them to construct malicious descriptions to attack or delegitimize an entire group of people or an area of activity.

For example, in the 1950s, homosexuals were commonly perceived as a criminal population, not just in the sense that homosexual activity was illegal but also in the sense that homosexuals were thought to be disproportionately prone to engage in criminal behavior in addition to (criminal) homosexual acts. This stereotype has been revived by Paul Cameron, one of the most virulent antigay ideologues in the United States, whose Institute for the Scientific Investigation of Sexuality (ISIS) publishes vitriolic antigay pamphlets.[15]

One of his most extraordinary pamphlets is "Murder, Violence, and Homosexuality," in which Cameron argues that homosexuality is linked to a disposition for serial violent crime. He claims that "You are *15 times* more apt to be killed by a gay than a heterosexual during a sexual murder spree" and that "most victims of sex murderers died at the hands of gays." Cameron employs a great deal of imaginative license and creative interpretation to make his case. He also uses the undeniable existence of homosexual murderers to jump to the absurd, malicious, and unsustainable conclusion that there is an "association between brutal murder and homosexual habits."[16]

A great deal of antiporn analysis is argued in a similar format. It jumps from examples of undeniably loathsome porn to unwarranted assertions about pornography as a whole. It is politically reprehensible and intellectually embarrassing to target pornography on the basis of inflammatory examples and manipulative rhetoric.

Is pornography any more violent than other mass media? While there are no reliable comparative studies on this point, I would argue that there are fewer images or descriptions of violence in pornography, taken as a whole, than in mainstream movies, television, or fiction. Our media are all extremely violent, and it is also true that their depictions of violence against women are often both sexualized and gender specific. An evening in front of the television is likely to result in viewing multiple fatal automobile accidents, shootings, fistfights, rapes, and situations in which women are threatened by a variety of creepy villains. Prostitutes and sex workers are frequently victims of violence in police and detective shows where they are killed off with relentless abandon. There are dozens of slasher movies characterized by hideous and graphic violence, disproportionately directed at women.

While much of this media is sexualized, very little is sexually explicit or legally obscene. Consequently, it would be completely unaffected by any new legal measures against pornography. If the problem is violence, why single out sexually explicit media? What is the justification for creating social movements and legal tools aimed at media that are sexually explicit rather than media that are explicitly violent?

In addition, in their efforts to condemn pornography, antiporn presentations such as the slide shows and *Not a Love Story* often include non–sexually explicit images such as record album covers and high-fashion ads. The justification for including nonpornographic images in antiporn presentations is not always clear. Sometimes it is implied or stated that these images display a "pornographic" attitude toward women. While it is true that some of the conventional imagery of porn has become more common in the mass media, it is absurd to blame pornography for the sexism or violence of advertising and other forms of popular media.

There is an implicit theory of causality in antiporn analysis in which a wildly exaggerated role is attributed to pornography in the creation, maintenance, and representation of women's subordination. Gender inequality and contemptuous attitudes toward women are endemic to this society and are consequently reflected in virtually all our media, including advertising and pornography. They do not originate in pornography and migrate from there into the rest of popular culture. It is important to recall that rape, violence against women, oppression and exploitation of women, and the attitudes which encouraged and justified these activities have been present throughout most of human history and predate the emergence of commercial erotica by several millennia.

The inclusion of nonpornographic imagery in the antiporn slide shows is also justified simply by redefining them as pornography or pornographic. This raises the issue of the inconsistent ways in which pornography is defined throughout the antiporn discourse.

Definitions: What Is Pornography?

The issue of definition—what is pornography and who defines it—haunts the entire discussion and is rarely addressed. This is especially interesting since the definitions of pornography employed within antiporn rhetoric are circular, vague, arbitrary, and inconsistent.

It is difficult to arrive at a precise definition of pornography, but at least the complexities can be better situated. According to the *American Heritage Dictionary of the English Language* (1973), pornography is "written, graphic, or other forms of communication intended to excite lascivious feelings." The term *pornography* was adopted in the middle of the nineteenth century to categorize rediscovered sexually explicit artifacts from the Greco-Roman world.[17] In the late nineteenth century, sexually frank books and graphic art were rare, expensive, and accessible primarily to wealthy and educated men. Although the term *pornography* was originally used to refer to all kinds of explicitly sexual writing and art, it has increasingly been associated with the phenomenon of inexpensive commercial erotica. Particularly since the Second World War, the term has acquired connotations of the "cheap stuff," mass-market, commercial materials distinct from more expensive, artistic, or sophisticated "erotica."

According to the same dictionary, erotica is "literature or art concerning or intended to arouse sexual desire." Erotica has had the connotations of being softer, classier, better produced, less blatant, and often less bluntly explicit than pornography.

Neither erotica nor pornography is illegal per se. "Obscenity" is the category of legally restricted sexual speech or imagery. It is important to note that until recently pornography has not been a legal category in the United States. For over a century, sexually explicit materials were illegal only if they were found to be obscene. Although the criteria for obscenity have shifted over time, they have had specific legal parameters. *Pornographic* was a term of judgment but not of law.

This has now begun to shift and a new category of illegal sexual material that is "pornographic" but not necessarily "obscene" is evolving. For example, "child pornography" is now a well-established legal category in the United States, and the criteria for conviction are broader and less stringent than in obscenity cases. The antiporn ordinance authored by Catharine MacKinnon and Andrea Dworkin and passed in Indianapolis, Indiana, was an attempt, among other things, to create a new legal category of "pornography" distinct from "obscenity." This new category of "pornography" would have codified a feminist antiporn description into law.

Both right-wingers and antiporn feminists have at times favored this "pornography" strategy as a means to circumvent those court decisions on obscenity which have resulted in greater legal protection for some types of sexually explicit material. However, since the Indianapolis ordinance was declared unconstitutional by the United States Supreme Court, subsequent efforts to make pornography a cause of civil action have relied on traditional legal categories of obscenity rather than on the so-called feminist definition.[18]

Within feminism, the debates on pornography have hinged on the definition of pornography. More crucially, its definition has often functioned as a substitute for argument or proof in antiporn analysis. Feminists have approached other media with the intention of changing them for the better rather than by striving to eliminate them altogether. What distinguishes pornography from other media is the level of sexual explicitness, not the quantity of violence in its imagery or the quality of its political consciousness. Why, then, has pornography alone been considered beyond feminist redemption and its eradication posited as a condition for female freedom? This breathtaking leap of logic has been accomplished simply by redefining pornography so that it is sexist and violent *by definition*.

For example, in *Take Back the Night*, the following definitions are found.

> Pornography, then, is verbal or pictorial material which represents or describes sexual behavior that is degrading or abusive to one or more of the participants in such a way as to endorse the degradation. . . . [I]t is material that explicitly represents or describes degrading and abusive sexual behavior so as to endorse and/or recommend the behavior as described. . . . What is wrong with pornography, then, is its degrading and dehumanizing portrayal of women (and not its sexual content). Pornography, *by its very nature*, requires that women be subordinate to men and mere instruments for the fulfillment of male fantasies.[19]

This is argument by tautology. If pornography is simply defined as that which is inherently degrading to women, then by definition it cannot be reformed and must be extirpated. This tactic completely finesses the necessity of providing some demonstration that what is generally thought of as pornography is accurately denoted by such a definition.

A similar definition is at the heart of MacKinnon and Dworkin's so-called "civil rights antipornography ordinance."[20] Catherine MacKinnon has argued that her proposed civil-rights ordinance does not hinge on the prevalence of violent imagery within pornography. She has stated that the way a legal definition works is that whatever it would define as pornography would be pornography, so that her ordinance would simply cover whatever fits its definition.[21] This is true, but again the reasoning is circular. It completely avoids the question of why such an ordinance *should* cover pornography, however defined, whether such a definition has any relation to pornography in the usual sense, and why any feminist-supported law should single out sexually explicit materials in the first place.

Moreover, the various definitions of porn employed in antiporn discourse are not consistently applied. When the targets of antiporn agitation are identified, they are the things more commonly associated with the term *pornography*, that is, X-rated videos and films, *Playboy* and *Penthouse*, the magazines sold in adult bookstores, lesbian sex magazines, gay male one-handed reading — in short, smut in the more usual sense. If pornography is that which is violent and/or intrinsically degrading to women in one sentence, it cannot be sexually explicit popular media in the next, unless a plausible argument is made that sexually explicit popular media is indeed distinctively violent and/or intrinsically and differentially degrading to women.

Furthermore, the category of "pornography" seems conveniently expandable. As mentioned above, ads and other media images that are sexually suggestive or particularly sexist are routinely included and called pornographic. Sometimes even sex toys are incorporated into the category. For example, in one of the opening sequences of *Not a Love Story*, as the narrator is describing the ostensible growth and size of the porn industry, the image on the screen shows the crafting of leather wristbands and collars. Whatever one thinks of such items, they are articles of dress and display, not media. In a nonfeminist context, the Meese Commission on Pornography has discussed laws prohibiting the sale of sex toys such as vibrators and dildos.[22]

Since few feminists would support the suppression of all sexually explicit media, many antiporn statements include a disclaimer that not all sexually explicit material is pornography. The residual category is "erotica." A distinction is made between "pornography" (the objectionable stuff against which feminists ought to fight) and "erotica" (the remaining sexual stuff of which feminists could approve). However, the problems with this approach become apparent as soon as anyone tries to define just exactly what separates erotica from pornography. Early in this debate, Ellen Willis noted with her customary dry wit that most attempts to define erotica and pornography amount to a statement of "What I like is erotica, and what you like is pornographic."[23]

For example, the cover of the November 1978 *Ms.* magazine inquires, "Erotica and Pornography: Do You Know the Difference?" Inside, Gloria Steinem purports to detail the "clear and present difference." Erotica, she tells us, "is rooted in eros or passionate love, and thus in the idea of positive choice, free will, the yearning for a particular person," whereas in pornography "the subject is not love at all, but domination and violence against women."[24]

In July of 1979, WAVPM's *Newspage* grappled the issue. Acknowledging that "the question of the differences between erotica and pornography cannot be totally resolved," *Newspage* published a list of distinctions. Among other things, erotica is characterized by this list: personal, emotional, has lightness, refreshing, rejuvenating, creative, natural, fulfilling, circular, and "just there." Pornography's list includes: defined by penis, for male titillation, having power imbalance, producing violence, suggesting violence, unreal, elements of fear, mindlessness, heavy, contorted bodies, voyeuristic, linear, and "something you buy and sell."[25] Admittedly, these lists were summaries of a discussion and not intended as a coherent final statement. But no one has ever been able to come up with a more definitive delineation. These lists are revealing of the arbitrary quality of the distinction. Indeed, one of the few points upon which both Andrea Dworkin and I agree is that the distinction between pornography and erotica is not a useful one for these discussions.[26]

Some antiporn groups have also exempted sex-education materials from condemnation. However, Dworkin has been quoted as wondering "whether some of the films made specifically for educational purposes contained material as offensive as that found in commercial porn."[27] In fact, many of the sex-education movies are made by heterosexual men whose attitudes toward women are similar to the heterosexual men who dominate the production of commercial porn. This does not mean they all promote violence; it does mean that few of them are paragons of feminist consciousness. To me, these similarities suggest that we should encourage more women to enter both fields as producers, writers, and directors. To some antiporn activists, however, these similarities will be an excuse to include sex-education films in their general condemnation of pornography and to subject them to whatever legal penalties and liabilities result from antiporn campaigns.

Most of the prominent spokespeople for the antiporn position have also stated publicly that the lesbian sex magazines, such as *On Our Backs*, *Bad Attitude*, and *Outrageous Women*, fit their definitions of pornography (indeed, I have heard some of them describe these magazines as "heterosexual"). Since many of these antiporn individuals support the passage of legislation to make pornography a cause of civil action, one may infer that they would support bringing civil suits against these magazines.

Despite constant assertions about how porn is "big business," most of the really interesting porn and all of these lesbian publications are small, low-budget affairs. While *Playboy* and *Penthouse* could survive repeated lawsuits, legal action would put the lesbian sex magazines out of business. Who is going to decide what is "pornographic," what forms lesbian sexuality must take, and what a lesbian may choose to read? If "erotica" cannot be agreed upon, if sex-education films fit the definitions of "pornography," and if indigenous lesbian sex magazines are "heterosexual pornography," what sexual imagery is sufficiently "nonpornographic" to be acceptable to feminists and exempt from legal harassment?

The "Harm" of Porn: Allegations, Assertions, and Creative Causality

The Research

Supporters of antiporn politics have argued that recent research in experimental psychology proves that pornography causes violence against women. The research does nothing of the sort.[28] There are many methodological cautions associated with the kind of research on which the antiporn position is based. Those studies of pornography show *at most* some changes in attitudes in artificial settings which may or may not have implications for behavior in real-life situations. The classic experiments, such as those of Edward Donnerstein, used materials that were both sexually explicit and violent, but which were not at all representative of most commercial pornography. At most, the conclusions of such studies pertain only to such materials and cannot be applied to pornography as a whole.[29]

Virtually all the recent studies have exonerated nonviolent porn, with the exception of those conducted by Dolf Zillman and Jennings Bryant. However, among the negative effects attributed to porn by Zillman and Bryant are less belief in marriage, greater dissatisfaction with one's present sex life, and greater tolerance for homosexuality and sexual variety.[30] If these are legitimate reasons for condemnation, then feminism and feminist literature are also culpable.

In studies in which subjects appeared more willing to express hostile behavior after exposure to violent sexual materials, they were asked to decide whether to shock or not to shock a "victim" after viewing the materials. They were given no other options. For example, they could not choose to be alone, do nothing, or masturbate. In real-life situations, pornography is most frequently used for masturbation or as a prelude to sexual activity with a partner. It would be revealing to compare how many experimental subjects would choose to shock someone if they were allowed masturbation as an alternative.

Finally, none of the published studies thus far have compared levels of aggression after viewing violent sexual material with those after viewing violent nonsexual material. However, Donnerstein is reported to be working on a new study in which it has been found that images of women being beaten but which contain *no* sexual content elicit higher levels of aggression in experimental subjects than images of sexual violence. Donnerstein has publicly cautioned against overinterpretation of his earlier findings, spoken against censorship, and has stated that it is probably violence in media rather than sex which has a negative impact.[31]

The available data are, at the present time, inconclusive, and certainly do not constitute anything resembling proof of broad assertions about the alleged responsibility of pornography in causing violence against women.[32] There is substantial evidence that violence in media is a problem. While there would be serious First Amendment problems to consider in any attempts legally to control violent media, there is more justification for feminist concern in that area. Currently in the United States there are no legal prohibitions on violence in media, while there are many legal constraints on representations of sex in media. What possible justification can there be for seeking more restrictions on the sexually explicit, while leaving the vast quantities of media violence unmolested?

Is Porn a "Documentary of Abuse"?

Catharine MacKinnon has argued that pornography is a literal photographic record of women being abused. She has listed various images found in porn, such as women being bound, tortured, humiliated, battered, urinated upon, forced to eat excrement, killed, or "merely taken and used."[33] She has then concluded that a woman had to have had these things done to her in order for the pornography to have been made; thus for each such image some woman had been bound, tortured, humiliated, battered, urinated upon, forced to eat excrement, murdered, or "merely taken and used."[34] Or as Andrea Dworkin puts it, "Real women are tied up, stretched, hanged, fucked, gang-banged, whipped, beaten, and begging for more. In the photographs and films, real women are used."[35] In this view, pornography is a photographic record of horrible abuse perpetrated upon the models and actors who appear in it. Several points may be made about this theory of pornographic harm.

The items on such lists are not all equivalent nor are they equally prevalent. I would guess that the "merely taken and used" is in reference to ordinary, non-kinky sexual activities, while the items bound, tortured, humiliated, urinated upon, and forced to eat excrement may refer to kinky porn. Porn featuring the eating of excrement is extraordinarily rare. Images of bondage, pain, humiliation, and urination are found in porn but again are absent from the majority of pornography. I have heard references to porn showing women mutilated or murdered but have never seen any except some rare drawings — *not* photographs — in European materials not available in the United States. I hate to belabor the point, but there are more women battered and murdered on prime-time television and Hollywood films than in pornographic materials.[36]

Perhaps more significantly, in this model of porn there is no concept of the role of artifice in the production of images. We do not assume that the occupants of the vehicles routinely destroyed in police chases on television are actually burning along with their cars, or that actors in fight scenes are actually being beaten to a pulp, or that western movies result in actual fatalities to cowboys and native Americans. It is ludicrous to assume that the level of coercion in an image is a reliable guide to the treatment of the actors involved. Yet this is precisely what is being asserted with regard to pornographic images.

In their characterizations of pornography as a documentary of abuse, both Dworkin and MacKinnon appear to think that certain sexual activities are so inherently distasteful that no one would do them willingly, and therefore the models are "victims" who must have been forced to participate against their wills. Since s/m often involves an appearance of coercion, it is especially easy to presume that the people doing it are victims. However, as I noted above, this is simply a false stereotype and does not reflect social and sexual reality. Sadomasochism is part of the erotic repertoire, and many people are not only willing but eager participants in s/m activity.[37]

However, sadomasochism is not the only behavior subjected to condescending and insulting judgments. For example, MacKinnon has also described porn in which someone was "raped in the throat where a penis cannot go."[38] There are plenty of gay men, and even a good number of heterosexual women, who enjoy cock-sucking. There are even lesbians who relish going down on dildos. Obviously, oral penetration is not an activity for everyone, but it is presumptuous to assume that it is physically impossible or necessarily coercive in all circumstances. Embedded in the idea of porn as a documentary of abuse is a very narrow conception of human sexuality, one lacking even elementary notions of sexual diversity.

The notion of harm embodied in the MacKinnon-Dworkin approach is based on a fundamental confusion between the content of an image and the conditions of its production. The fact that an image does not appeal to a viewer does not mean that the actors or models experienced revulsion while making it. The fact that an image depicts coercion does not mean that the actors or models were forced into making it.

One can infer nothing from the content of an image about the conditions of its production. Any discussion of greater protections for actors and models should focus on whether or not they have been coerced and on the conditions under which their work is performed *regardless of the nature of the image involved*. Any standards considered for the health, safety, or cleanliness of working conditions in the sex industry should conform to those pertaining to similar occupations such as fashion modeling, filmmaking, stage acting, or professional dancing. The content of the image produced, whether or not it is sexual, and whether or not it is violent or distasteful to a viewer, is irrelevant.

While antiporn activists often claim to want to protect women in (and from) the sex industry, much of their analysis is based on condescension and contempt toward sex workers. The notion that pornography is a documentary of sexual abuse assumes that the women who work in the sex industry (as strippers, porn models, or prostitutes) are invariably forced to do so and that such women are merely victims of "pornographers." This is a malignant stereotype and one that is especially inappropriate for feminists to reinforce.

There are, of course, incidents of abuse and exploitation in the sex industry, as there are in all work situations. I am not claiming that no one has ever been coerced into appearing in a porn movie or that in such cases the perpetrators should not be prosecuted. I am saying that such coercion is not the industry norm. Furthermore, I am not promoting a simple "free choice" model of employment, in which structural forces and limited choices have no influence on what decisions individuals make about how to earn a living. But those who choose sex work do so for complex reasons, and their choices should be accorded the same respect granted to those who work in less stigmatized occupations.

Indeed, the degree to which sex workers are exposed to more exploitation and hazardous working conditions is a function of the stigma, illegality, or marginal legality of sex work. People in stigmatized or illegal occupations find it difficult to obtain the same protections, privileges, and opportunities available for those in other jobs. Prostitutes, porn models, and erotic dancers have less recourse to police, courts, medical treatment, legal redress, or sympathy when they are subjected to criminal, violent, or unscrupulous behavior. It is more difficult for them to unionize or mobilize for protection as workers.

We need to support women wherever they work. We need to realize that more stigma and more legal regulation of the sex industry will merely increase the vulnerability of the women in it. Feminists who want to support sex workers should strive to decriminalize and legitimize sex work. Sex workers relieved of the threat of scandal or incarceration are in a better position to gain more control over their work and working conditions.[39]

Contempt toward sex workers, especially prostitutes, is one of the most disturbing aspects of the antiporn invective. Throughout her book *Pornography*, Dworkin uses the stigma of prostitution to convey her opprobrium and make her argument against pornography. She says, "Contemporary pornography strictly and literally conforms to the word's root meaning: the graphic depiction of *vile whores*, or in our language, *sluts, cows* (as in: *sexual cattle, sexual chattel*), *cunts*."[40] This is a degrading and insulting description of prostitutes. Feminists should be working to remove stigma from prostitution, not exploiting it for rhetorical gain.

Is Porn at the Core of Women's Subordination?

Porn is often described as "at the center" or "at the core" of women's subordination. Andrea Dworkin makes the following statement in *Right-Wing Women*: "At the heart of the female condition is pornography: *it is the ideology that is the source of all the rest*; it truly defines what women are in this system—and how women are treated issues from what women are. Pornography is not a metaphor for what women are; it is what women are in theory and in practice."[41] This rather extraordinary statement is accompanied by several diagrams in which pornography is first placed literally "at the center" of women's condition, then diagrammed as the underlying ideology of women's condition, and finally depicted as the surface phenomenon with prostitution the underlying system.[42] These are breathtaking claims, and they are made with little supporting evidence and not a single citation.

Since the 1960s, feminist theorists and academics have explored a multitude of explanations for female subordination and the oppression of women. There are hundreds of articles, essays, and books debating the merits of various factors in the creation and maintenance of female subordination. These have included, for example, private property, the formation of state societies, the sexual division of labor, the emergence of economic classes, religion, educational arrangements, cultural structures, family and kinship systems, psychological factors, and control over reproduction, among others. I cannot think of a single attempt prior to the porn debates to derive women's subordination from either pornography or prostitution. There is no credible historical, anthropological, or sociological argument for such a position.

It would be difficult to argue that pornography or prostitution had played such critical roles in women's subordination since women are quite dramatically oppressed in societies which have neither (for example, many sedentary horticulturalists in the South Pacific and in South America). Furthermore, pornography and prostitution as they now exist in the West are modern phenomena. The institutional structures of prostitution in, for example, ancient Greece were entirely different from those that obtain today.

Pornography in the contemporary sense did not exist before the nineteenth century.[43] Other cultures have certainly produced visual art and crafts depicting genitalia and sexual activity (e.g., the ancient Greeks, the Egyptians, and the Moche Indians from pre-Columbian coastal Peru). But there is no systematic correlation between low status for women and cultures in which sexually explicit visual imagery exists, or high status for women and societies in which it does not. Moreover, such images are not pornography unless porn is to be defined as all sexually explicit imagery, in which case antiporn ideology would posit the impossibility of any acceptable explicit depictions of sex and few feminists would support it.

Pornography could be thought of as being at the heart of women's condition if it is conceptualized as a transhistorical category existing throughout human history and culture. In *Pornography*, Dworkin states that the word *pornography* comes from Greek words meaning "writing about whores." She goes on to discuss the place of the "whores" in Greek society and concludes that "the word pornography does not have any other meaning than the one cited here, the graphic depiction of the lowest whores." From this discussion, and similar accounts by others, it has often been inferred that the term *pornography* was used by the Greeks and that it refers to categories of Greek experience.[44]

However, the term *pornography* was not used by the ancient Greeks, did not refer to their painted vases, and should not be treated as evidence that the Greeks felt about porn the way Dworkin does. The term was coined *from Greek roots* in the nineteenth century, when many of the sex terms still in use (such as *homosexuality*) were assembled from Greek and Latin root words. It embodies not the prejudices of the Greeks, but those of the Victorians.[45]

There is one further sense in which it might be argued that pornography is "the ideology that is the source of all the rest" of women's oppression and that is if pornography is conceived of as the quintessence of all ideologies of female inferiority. What then are we to make of all the religious and moral and philo-sophical versions of male superiority? Is the Koran pornography? The Bible? Psychiatry? And what has any of this to do with modern, contemporary com-mercial porn? What has it to do with adult bookstores or *Playboy*?

Why Has Opposition to Pornography Been So Acceptable in Feminism?

One may wonder why such sloppy definitions, unsupported assertions, and outlandish claims have gained so much credibility within the feminist move-ment. There are several explanations.

1. Pornography is already highly stigmatized in this society. This stigma cer-tainly predates feminist attention to the subject. Most people in this society are already uncomfortable with pornography and a little afraid of being contami-nated with its aura of disrepute. For well over a century, the safest and most respectable attitude toward sexually explicit media has been one of condem-nation. This stigma of pornography also makes it easier for people to accept false statements about it. One could assemble all the most grotesque slasher films or offensive paperback fiction and try to incite feminist frenzy against movie-houses or bookstores, but few feminists would take such a campaign seriously.

2. It is often easy for women to accept hyperbolic descriptions of pornog-raphy because most women who do not work in the sex industry are unfamil-iar with pornographic materials and their conventions of meaning and inter-pretation. Traditionally, pornography has been male territory. "Respectable" women did not get much opportunity to go into porn shops and theaters or to view pornography.

Men's behavior around porn—often embarrassed, furtive, and uncomfort-able—has done little to change this situation or to reassure women about what might be going on in those male enclaves. Many women are angry and re-sentful about men's privileged access to sexually explicit material. All of this is changing, as the women who work in the sex industry are becoming more outspoken and as the industry itself evolves. The video revolution has enabled women to rent movies and view them in the comfort of their own homes. More women are becoming comfortable in adult theaters and bookstores.

3. Most pornography *is* sexist. Traditionally, it has been aimed at a male audience and at the values of mainstream men. Consequently, the women in most commercial porn really are there to represent what the average male con-sumer wants to think about when he is masturbating. Most pornography does

Misguided, Dangerous, and Wrong   271

misrepresent women's sexuality and does not encourage men to learn the arts of seduction or to think of their sex partners as independent people with their own needs.

However, this sexism is no more intrinsic to pornography than it is to fiction. It is already changing as more women have become involved with the production of porn. Furthermore, the porn industry is beginning to recognize women as potential consumers and to design products intended to appeal to a female audience.

4. Commercial porn does not pretty-up sex the way Hollywood movies do. Most porn is poorly produced, badly acted, too brightly lit, and shot on too low a budget. It looks cheap. In spite of all the tripe about porn being a multibillion dollar megalith, most porn movies are shot on budgets that would barely dent the cosmetic allowance for a major Hollywood film. The actors are not always well trained, and few have the impeccably good looks of major film stars. Many people come to porn expecting it to have the visual appearance of big screen romance, and it quite regularly fails to meet such expectations.

5. In this society we do not often get to view people who are nude or engaging in fornication or other sex acts. Most people consequently feel that sex looks kind of silly, and are afraid they must look ridiculous when they do it. Antiporn ideology manipulates such feelings and reinforces the message that unadorned sex is ugly, undignified, and shameful.

6. Due to the stigma historically associated with sexually explicit materials, we already use the words *obscene* and *pornographic* to express many kinds of intense revulsion. For example, war may be "obscene" and Reagan's policies "pornographic." However, neither is customarily found in adult bookstores. Since the terms are commonly used to convey profound and extreme disapproval, it is all too easy to utilize them to invoke anxiety, disgust, and repulsion.

7. There are legitimate feminist concerns with regard to sexually explicit materials. Although pornography should not be singled out, it should not be immune from feminist criticism. Porn is certainly not uniformly pleasing, well produced, artistically edifying, or politically advanced. There is plenty of room for improvement and for porn that is well made, creative, more diverse, more attuned to women's fantasies, and more infused with feminist awareness. This will only happen as more women and more feminists become involved in the production of sexually explicit material. A feminist politics on pornography should be aimed at making it easier—not more difficult—for this to occur.

As I mentioned above, the women who work in the sex industry are more vulnerable to harassment, violence, and exploitation because they are denied many of the protections readily available to others. A feminist politics on the sex industry should demand immediate decriminalization of prostitution and pornography, equal protection under the law for sex workers, and an end to the punitive stigma inflicted upon people in the industry.

Costs and Dangers of Antiporn Politics

The focus on pornography trivializes real violence and ignores its gravity. Experiences of being raped, assaulted, battered, or harassed are dramatic, devastating, and qualitatively different from the ordinary insults of everyday oppression. Violence should never be conflated with experiences that are merely upsetting, unpleasant, irritating, distasteful, or even enraging.

Antiporn activity distracts attention and drains activism from more fundamental issues for women. Porn is a sexier topic than the more intractable problems of unequal pay, job discrimination, sexual violence and harassment, the unequal burdens of childcare and housework, increasing right-wing infringements on hard-won feminist gains, and several millennia of unrelenting male privilege vis-à-vis the labor, love, personal service, and possession of women. Antiporn campaigns are pitifully misdirected and ineffective. They cannot solve the problems they purport to address.

If antiporn politics were only a trivial diversion from more important concerns, they would not deserve so much critical attention. This is unfortunately not the case. There are real costs to these campaigns that will be paid by whole new classes of victims. The scapegoating of pornography will create new problems, new forms of legal and social abuse, and new modes of persecution. A responsible and progressive political movement has no business pursuing strategies that will result in witch hunts.

Antiporn politics scapegoat innocent but despised behaviors, media, and individuals for problems for which they are not responsible. Antiporn politics are intended to result in increased stigma and increased legal persecution of pornography, prostitution, and perversion. But these are neither abstractions nor monsters. The consequences of more criminalization of sexually explicit materials and of increased stigmatization of sexual variation are very real. They mean police abuse and bureaucratic harassment for women and men who have done nothing wrong but express unfashionable desires, create illicit imagery, or engage in disreputable occupations.

It is a terrible thing to bring down the police, public hatred, and bureaucratic intervention upon innocent communities or individuals. It is inappropriate and shameful for feminism to collude in establishing policies, attitudes, and law that will deprive innocent women and men of their liberty, livelihoods, and peace of mind. Feminists are under the same obligations as everyone else to remember that just because something seems strange or frightening does not mean it is dangerous or a menace to public safety.

Antiporn feminists are playing into the hands of the right wing and its reactionary agenda. There may not be a direct conspiracy, but there is certainly a convergence of aims and intentions. At best, antiporn feminists seem naïve about the political context in which they are operating. The Right has already adopted feminist antiporn rhetoric, concepts, and language, conveniently stripped of its already marginal progressive content.

The women's movement lacks the political capacity to enact any legislative program on pornography at this time. The Right is suffering no such limitation. The Right is more powerfully entrenched in the political structure of the United States than it has been in decades. It wields the formidable power of the federal bureaucracy and has enormous influence on legislative activity at all levels of government. We can expect a wave of conservative legislation on pornography to pass at the local, state, and federal levels in the next few years. It is especially likely that laws loosely modeled on the concepts of the MacKinnon-Dworkin ordinance but wedded to traditional obscenity standards will become common.[46] Moreover, everything we have seen so far will have been a prelude to the legislative avalanche we can expect once the Meese Commission on pornography reports.[47]

These are times of great danger. We are in a period in which the social attitudes and legal regulation of sexuality are undergoing massive transformation. The laws, policies, and beliefs that are established in this era will haunt feminism, women, sex workers, lesbians, gay men, and other sexual minorities for decades.

Feminism and Sexual Politics

It is tragic that the feminist movement has already fed the gathering sexual storm. The antiporn ideology in all its manifestations has damaged the women's movement as a progressive voice in sexual politics. It has far too often paralyzed feminist response to right-wing encroachments. It is critical that the women's movement mobilize to oppose any further depredations on sexual freedoms.

Instead of fighting porn, feminism should oppose censorship, support the decriminalization of prostitution, call for the abolition of all obscenity laws, support the rights of sex workers, support women in management positions in the sex industry, support the availability of sexually explicit materials, support sex education for the young, affirm the rights of sexual minorities, and affirm the legitimacy of human sexual diversity. Such a direction would begin to redress the mistakes of the past. It would restore feminism to a position of leadership and credibility in matters of sexual policy. And it would revive feminism as a progressive, visionary force in the domain of sexuality.

Sexual Traffic

Interview with Gayle Rubin by Judith Butler

12

Judith Butler: The reason I wanted to do this interview is that some people would say that you set the methodology for feminist theory, then the methodology for lesbian and gay studies. And I think it would be interesting, as a way to understand the relation between these two fields, for people to understand how you moved from your position in "The Traffic in Women" to your position in "Thinking Sex." But then also it would be interesting to hear a bit about the kind of work you are doing now. So, I thought I might begin at one of the beginnings, namely "The Traffic in Women," and ask you to elaborate a little bit about the context in which you wrote it, and also to ask you when you began to take distance from the position you elaborated there.

Gayle Rubin: Well, I guess I have a different sense of the relationship of those papers to feminist thought and lesbian and gay studies. Each was part of an ongoing process, a field of inquiry developing at the time. "Traffic in Women" had its origins in early second-wave feminism when many of us who were involved in the late 1960s were trying to figure out how to think about and articulate the oppression of women. The dominant political context at that time was the New Left, particularly the antiwar movement and the opposition to militarized U.S. imperialism. The dominant paradigm among progressive intellectuals was Marxism, in various forms. Many of the early second-wave feminists came out of the New Left and were Marxists of one sort or another.

Chapter 12 was originally published in *differences* 6, nos. 2–3 (1994): 62–99.

I don't think one can fully comprehend early second-wave feminism without understanding its intimate yet conflicted relationship to New Left politics and Marxist intellectual frameworks. There is an immense Marxist legacy within feminism, and feminist thought is greatly indebted to Marxism. In a sense, Marxism enabled people to pose a whole set of questions that Marxism could not satisfactorily answer.

Marxism, no matter how modified, seemed unable to fully grasp the issues of gender difference and the oppression of women. Many of us were struggling with—or within—that dominant framework to make it work or figure out why it didn't. I was one of many who finally concluded that one could only go so far within a Marxist paradigm and that while it was useful, it had limitations with regard to gender and sex.

I should add that there were different kinds of Marxist approaches. There were some pretty reductive formulations about the "woman question," and some especially simplistic strategies for women's liberation. I remember one group in Ann Arbor, which I think was called the Red Star Sisters. Their idea of women's liberation was to mobilize women's groups to fight imperialism. There was no room in their approach to specifically address gender oppression; it was only a precipitate of class oppression and imperialism, and presumably would wither away after the workers' revolution.

There were a lot of people working over Engels's *The Origin of the Family, Private Property, and the State*. Engels was part of the Marxian canon, and he *did* talk about women, so his work was granted special status. There were dozens of little schemas about the ostensible overthrow of the supposed early matriarchy and the invention of private property as the source of women's oppression. In retrospect some of this literature seems quaint, but at the time it was taken very seriously. I doubt people who weren't there could begin to imagine the intensity with which people fought over whether or not there was an original matriarchy, and whether its demise accounted for class differences and the oppression of women.

Even the best of Marxist work at that time tended to focus on issues that were closer to the central concerns of Marxism, such as class, work, relations of production, and even some very creative thinking about the social relations of reproduction. There was a wonderful, very interesting literature that came up around housework, for example. There was good work on the sexual division of labor, on the place of women in the labor market, on the role of women in the reproduction of labor. Some of this literature was very interesting and very useful, but it could not get at some core issues which concerned feminists: gender difference, gender oppression, and sexuality. So there was a general effort to differentiate feminism from that political context and its dominant preoccupations. There were a lot of people looking for leverage on the problem of women's oppression, and searching for tools with which one could get different angles of vision on it. "Traffic in Women" was a part of that effort and is an artifact of that set of problems. There were many other articles dealing with similar issues; one of my favorites was "The Unhappy Marriage of Marxism and Feminism," by Heidi Hartmann.

The immediate precipitating factor of "Traffic" was a course on tribal economics given by Marshall Sahlins at the University of Michigan, about 1970. That course changed my life. I had already been involved with feminism, but this was my first experience of anthropology, and I was smitten. I was utterly seduced by Sahlins's theoretical approach, as well as the descriptive richness of the ethnographic literature. I was co-writing a term paper with two friends on the status of women in tribal societies. Sahlins suggested that I read Lévi-Strauss's *The Elementary Structures of Kinship*. To use the vernacular of the time, "It completely blew my mind." So did some of the other literature of French structuralism. I read the Althusser article on Freud and Lacan from *New Left Review* right around the time I was reading *The Elementary Structures of Kinship* and there was just some moment of revelation that these approaches had a relationship.[1] Then I read most of the classic psychoanalytic essays on "femininity." The confluence of those things was where "The Traffic in Women" came from. I was very excited about all these connections and wanted to incorporate them into the term paper for Sahlins's class. One of my coauthors was reluctant to include this wild stuff in the body of the paper, so I wrote the first version of "Traffic" as an appendix for the paper. Then I kept reading and thinking about it.

At that time, the University of Michigan allowed students to declare an independent major through the honors program. I had taken advantage of the program to construct a major in Women's Studies in 1969. At that time there was no Women's Studies program at Michigan, so I was the first Women's Studies major there. The independent major required a senior honors thesis, so I did half on lesbian literature and history, and half on this analysis of psychoanalysis and kinship. I finished the senior thesis in 1972 and kept reworking the "Traffic" part until Rayna Rapp (then Reiter) extracted the final version for *Toward an Anthropology of Women*. A penultimate version was published in an obscure Ann Arbor journal called *Dissemination* in 1974.

Something that people now probably forget is how little of the French structuralist and poststructuralist literature was available then in English. While Lévi-Strauss, Althusser, and Foucault were very well translated by 1970,

Lacan was not readily available. Besides the Althusser essay on him, Lacan was mostly represented in English by a handful of books, such as Anthony Wilden's *The Language of the Self* and a book by Maud Mannoni.[2] I remember seeing maybe one or two articles by Derrida. Most of Derrida, as well as Lyotard, Kristeva, Irigaray, and Bourdieu were still pretty much restricted to those fluent in French. This kind of thinking was relatively unknown in the United States. When I wrote the version of "Traffic" that was finally published, one of my friends edited it. She thought only ten people would read it. I thought maybe two hundred people would read it, and I think we agreed on fifty.

JB: You were saying that in some ways you wanted to make an intervention in Marxist feminism and make feminism something other than a kind of subsidiary movement in Marxism. Would you elaborate on that?

GR: I felt that if people privileged Marxism as the theory with which to approach the oppression of women, then they were going to miss a lot, and they did. I think of "Traffic" as a neo-Marxist, proto-pomo exercise. It was written on the cusp of a transition between dominant paradigms, both in progressive intellectual thought in general, and feminist thought in particular. But the basic problem was that Marxism had a weak grasp of sex and gender, and had intrinsic limitations as a theoretical framework for feminism. There were other issues, such as the whole problem of trying to find some theoretical basis for lesbianism.

JB: It seemed to me that you based much of what you say about sexuality and gender in "The Traffic in Women" in an understanding of kinship that you were taking from Lévi-Strauss. To the extent that you could show that kinship relations were in the service of compulsory heterosexuality you could also show that gender identities were in some sense derived from kinship relations. You then speculated that it might be possible to get beyond gender— maybe "gender identity" is the better word—if one also could do something like overthrow kinship. . . .

GR: Right, and the cultural residue and the symbolic manifestations and all of the other aspects of that system, and the inscription and installation of those structures and categories within people.

JB: It was a utopian vision of sorts.

GR: Well, we were all pretty utopian in those days. I mean this was about 1969 to 1974. I was young and optimistic about social change. In those days there was a common expectation that utopia was around the corner. I feel very differently now. I worry instead that fascism in our time is around the corner. I am almost as pessimistic now as I was optimistic then.

JB: Yes. So could you narrate something about the distance you took from that particular vision and what prompted the writing of "Thinking Sex"?

GR: There was a different set of concerns that generated "Thinking Sex." I suppose the most basic differences were that, theoretically, I felt that feminism dealt inadequately with sexual practice, particularly diverse sexual conduct; and practically, the political situation was changing. "Thinking Sex" came from the late 1970s, when the New Right was beginning to be ascendant in U.S. politics, and when stigmatized sexual practices were drawing a lot of repressive attention. Nineteen seventy-seven was the year of Anita Bryant and the campaign to repeal the Dade County gay-rights ordinance. Such campaigns are now, unfortunately, the common stuff of gay politics, but at that time the bigotry and homophobia that emerged in that fight were shocking. This period was when Richard Viguerie's direct-mail fund-raising operation was underwriting a new era of radical right-wing political organizing. By 1980 Reagan was in office. This shifted the status, safety, and legal positions of homosexuality, sex work, sexually explicit media, and many other forms of sexual practice.

"Thinking Sex" wasn't conceived in a direct line or as a direct departure from the concerns of "Traffic." I was trying to get at something different, which had some implications for my previous formulations. But I think those last few pages have been overinterpreted as some huge rejection or turnabout on my part. I saw them more as a corrective, and as a way to get a handle on another group of issues. I wasn't looking to get away from "Traffic in Women." I was trying to deal with issues of sexual difference and sexual variety. And when I use "sexual difference" I realize from reading your paper "Against Proper Objects" that you are using it in a very different way than I am. I am using the term to refer to different sexual practices. You seem to be using it to refer to gender.

JB: You mean I am using "sexual difference" in the way that you were using "gender" in "Traffic in Women"?

GR: Well, I'm not sure. Tell me how you are using "sexual difference," because I'm not clear on it.

JB: Yes, well, I think that for the most part that people who work in a "sexual difference" framework actually believe in some kind of symbolic position of the masculine and the feminine, or believe there is something persistent about sexual difference understood in terms of masculine and feminine. At the same time they tend to engage psychoanalysis or some theory of the symbolic. And what I always found interesting in "The Traffic in Women" was that you used the term *gender* to track that same kind of problem that came out of Lacan and Lévi-Strauss, but that you actually took a very different direction than most of the—what I would call—sexual-difference feminists, who now work almost exclusively within psychoanalytic domains. And what interested me in "The Traffic in Women" was that you, by using a term that comes from American sociological discourse—*gender*—by using that term, you actually made gender less fixed, and you imagined a kind of mobility to it which I think would be quite impossible in the Lacanian framework. So I think that what you produced was an amalgamation of positions which I very much appreciated, and it became one of the reasons I went with gender myself in *Gender Trouble*.

GR: Well, I didn't want to get stuck in the Lacanian trap. It seemed to me, and with all due respect to those who are very skilled at evading or manipulating the snares, that Lacan's work came with a dangerous tendency to create a kind of deep crevasse from which it would be hard to escape. I kept wanting to find ways not to get caught in the demands of certain systems, and Lacanian psychoanalysis both provided leverage and posed new challenges. Lacanian psychoanalysis is very useful in dealing with structures of gender and desire, but it comes with a price. I was concerned with the totalizing tendencies in Lacan, and the nonsocial qualities of his concept of the symbolic.

JB: Yes. This is actually an interesting problem. My sense is that in British feminism, for instance in the seventies, there was a belief that if you could reconfigure and change your kinship arrangements that you could also reconfigure your sexuality and your psyche, and that psychic transformation really followed directly from the social transformation of kinship arrangements. And then when everybody had done that and found out that their psyches were still in the same old pits that they had always been in, I think that the Lacanian position became very popular. I guess the problem became how to describe those constraints on sexuality which seem more persistent than what we can change through the transformation of social and kinship relations. Maybe there is something intractable, maybe there is something more persistent . . .

GR: Leaving aside such issues as how much these social and kinship relations have actually been transformed at this point, the magnitude of such changes and the time spans required to make them, and the fact that most of our psyches were long since formed and are resistant to such swift re-education, what is the something that is *intractable*? One of the nifty things about psychoanalytic approaches is that they explain both change and intractability. But there is something about the particular intractability of what is called the symbolic that I don't understand. Is there supposed to be something in the very nature of the structure of the brain and the way it creates language?

JB: I would say the structure of language, the emergence of the speaking subject through sexual differentiation, and how language subsequently creates intelligibility.

GR: . . . that makes it somehow necessary to have a masculine and a feminine?

JB: As you know from some of the reading of Lacan that you have done, there is a tendency to understand sexual difference coextensive with language itself. And that there is no possibility of speaking, of taking a position in language outside of differentiating moves, not only through a differentiation from the maternal which is said to install a speaker in language for the first time, but then further differentiations among speakers positioned within kinship, which includes the prohibition on incest. To the extent that is done within the constellation of, say, Mother-Father as symbolic positions . . .

GR: There is something intrinsically problematic about any notion that somehow language itself or the capacity for acquiring it requires a sexual differentiation as a primary differentiation. If humans were hermaphroditic or reproduced asexually, I can imagine we would still be capable of speech. A specific symbolic relation that precedes any social life whatsoever—I have a problem with that. One of the problems I have with Lacan was that his system didn't seem to allow quite enough latitude for the social structuring of the symbolic.

JB: Right. I agree with you on this. But I think that it is one of the reasons why the social doesn't have such a great name and is really not of interest for many who work in the Lacanian domain. I guess what I always found really great about "The Traffic in Women" is that it actually did give us a way to understand psychic structures in relationship to social structures.

GR: Well, that is what I wanted to do, and I didn't want to get entangled in a symbolic that couldn't be socially accessed in some way. People often assume that if something is social it is also somehow fragile and can be changed quickly. For example, some right-wing antigay literature now argues that since homosexuality is socially constructed, people can (and should) easily change their sexual orientation. And as you were saying earlier, frustration with the enduring quality of certain things sometimes leads people to think that they can't be socially generated. But the kind of social change we are talking about takes a long time, and the time frame in which we have been undertaking such change is incredibly tiny.

Besides, the imprint of kinship arrangements on individual psyches is very durable. The acquisition of our sexual and gender programming is much like the learning of our native cultural system or language. It is much harder to learn new languages, or to be as facile in them as in our first language. As Carole Vance has argued, this same model can be useful for thinking about gender and sexual preferences.[3] As with languages, some people have more gender and erotic flexibility than others. Some can acquire secondary sexual or gender languages, and even fewer will be completely fluent in more than one position. But most people have a home language and home sexual or gender comfort zones that will not change much. This doesn't mean these things are not social, any more than the difficulties of acquiring other languages means that languages are not social. Social phenomena can be incredibly obdurate. Nonetheless, I wanted in "Traffic" to put gender and sexuality into a social framework, and I did not want to go completely in the direction of the Lacanian symbolic and be stuck with a primary category of gender differences which might as well be inscribed in granite.

JB: So, if you would, talk about the theoretical and political circumstances that made you turn toward "Thinking Sex."

GR: "Thinking Sex" was part of a movement away from an early structuralist focus on the binary aspects of language, such as the binary oppositions you see very much in Lévi-Strauss and Lacan, toward the more discursive models of later poststructuralism or postmodernism. If you are really going to take seriously that social life is structured like language, then you need complex models for how language is structured. I think these binary models seemed to work better for gender, because our usual understandings posit gender as in some ways binary; even the continuums of gender differences often seem structured by a primary binary opposition. But as soon as you get away from the presumptions of heterosexuality, or a simple hetero-homo opposition, differences in sexual conduct are not very intelligible in terms of binary models. Even the notion of a continuum is not a good model for sexual variations; one needs one of those mathematical models they do now with strange topologies and convoluted shapes. There needs to be some kind of model that is not binary, because sexual variation is a system of many differences, not just a couple of salient ones.

We were talking earlier about the ostensible relationship of "Thinking Sex" to MacKinnon's work. Retrospectively, many people have interpreted "Thinking Sex" as a reaction to MacKinnon's work against pornography.

JB: I'm doubtless guilty of that . . .

GR: While the early feminist antipornography movement was an issue, most of the work for "Thinking Sex" was done before MacKinnon became a visible figure in that movement. To many, MacKinnon has come to represent the feminist antiporn movement, but actually she was a relative latecomer to it. She became visible as an important actor in the porn wars about 1984, after the passage of the so-called "civil rights" antiporn ordinances, first in Minneapolis late in 1983, and subsequently in Indianapolis. Her fame tends to eclipse the early history of the feminist antiporn movement, which is represented better by the anthology *Take Back the Night*. I mostly knew about MacKinnon from those two articles in *Signs*. The first was published in 1982, and I had seen an earlier version. I had already been working on versions of "Thinking Sex" for some time. But I could see where MacKinnon was heading, at least at the theoretical level, and I was going in a different direction. She wanted to make feminism the privileged site for analyzing sexuality and to subordinate sexual politics not only to feminism, but to a particular type of feminism. On the grand chessboard of life, I wanted to block this particular move. But it was not the impetus for the paper. At some level, I think there were some underlying social and political shifts that produced "Thinking Sex," the feminist antiporn movement, MacKinnon's approach, and the right-wing focus on homosexuality and other forms of variant sexual conduct, among other things.

JB: You are referring to MacKinnon's "Marxism, Feminism, Method and the State."[4]

GR: Yes. "Thinking Sex" had its roots back in 1977–78, and I started doing lecture versions of it in 1979. I think you were at one of these, at the Second Sex Conference at the New York Institute for the Humanities.

JB: Right. The first time I saw a copy of Michel Foucault's *The History of Sexuality* . . .

GR: Was I waving it around?

JB: Yes. You introduced it to me.

GR: I was really, just totally hot for that book.

JB: Yes, you made me hot for it too . . . [laughter]

GR: The paper actually began before I ran into Foucault, but his work clarified issues and inspired me. In any event, the sources of this paper were earlier, and a little different. First of all, I started to get more and more dissatisfied with what were then the stock feminist explanations for certain kinds of sexual behaviors. A number of different debates, incidents, and issues forced me to start questioning the wisdom, if not the relevance, of feminism as the privileged political movement or political theory for certain issues of sexuality and sexual difference. One was the debate on transsexuality. Even before that debate hit print toward the late 1970s, the discussion really flipped me out because it was so biologically deterministic. When it finally erupted into print over the hiring of Sandy Stone, a male-to-female transsexual, by Olivia Records, there were a number of articles in the lesbian press about how women were born and not made,[5] which I found rather . . .

GR and JB: [in unison] distressing.

GR: To say the least. And then there were other issues that came up. Around 1977–78, there was a repression, to use an old-fashioned term, going on in Michigan, directed against gay male public sex. All of a sudden men were being arrested in a much more aggressive way for sex in parks and tea rooms. There were a couple of old cruising areas on the Michigan campus, one in the Union and the other in Mason Hall. The cops came in and arrested some people. There was a truck stop on I-94 between Ann Arbor and Detroit where a number of men were arrested, and in one park sweep I think one of the officials of the Detroit public-school system was nabbed and subsequently fired. And as these stories started to percolate through the feminist and lesbian communities, the most common opinion I heard was that these were just men doing horrible masculine, patriarchal things, and they probably should be arrested. This was not a position I could accept. No one was going around arresting all the people having heterosexual sex in parks and automobiles. To support or rationalize the arrests of anyone for engaging in consensual homosexual sex was abhorrent to me.

There was another set of incidents that happened, again in Ann Arbor in the late 1970s, around sex work and prostitution. There was a really interesting woman named Carol Ernst. We had disagreed on many things over the years; she was very involved with ideas for which I had little patience, like matriarchy theory and the patriarchal revolt as an explanation for women's oppression, and the idea that women had political power in societies that worshiped female deities. But you know how in small communities people tend to talk to each other even if they disagree or have really different perspectives. That was the case there, and we were friends. Carol did a number of things which were very important in that community. At one point she went to work for a local massage parlor. She ended up trying to unionize the sex workers, and sometime in the early 1970s she spearheaded a labor action against the parlor management. There were hookers with picket signs on the street in front of this dirty bookstore in downtown Ann Arbor, and the striking sex workers even filed an unfair labor practice complaint with the Michigan Labor Relations Board. It was amazing.

Then Carol left the massage parlor and went to work for the bus company, where she was also deeply involved in labor issues and unionization. Many Ann Arbor lesbians ended up working either at the massage parlor or the bus company, which we fondly referred to as "dial-a-dyke." During the mid-1970s, the three major employers of the lesbian community in Ann Arbor were the university, the bus company, and the massage parlor. It's pretty comic but that's how it was.

Then the massage parlor where many of the dykes worked was busted. One of the arrested women was a really wonderful, good-looking, athletic butch who happened to be the star left-fielder of the lesbian softball team. The local lesbian-feminist community suddenly had to deal with the fact that many of their friends and heroes had been arrested for prostitution.

JB: Fabulous.

GR: Most of the rest of us initially had a stock response, which was that they shouldn't be doing this work and that they were upholding the patriarchy. The arrested women and their supporters formed an organization, called PEP, the Prostitution Education Project. They put the rest of us through quite an educational process. They asked how what they did was so different from what anyone else did for a living. Some said they liked the work more than other kinds of work available to them. They asked why it was more feminist to work as secretaries and for longer hours and less money. Some said they liked the working conditions; the busted parlor even had a weight room where the jocks worked out while waiting for clients. They demanded that we deal with prostitution as a work issue rather than a moralistic one. They brought in Margo St. James and had a big hookers' ball to raise funds for the legal defense.

Carol Ernst was later tragically killed in an automobile accident. But she was a visionary, and her peculiar combination of feminist and labor politics really left an imprint. She challenged me on my rhetorical use of prostitution to make debating points about the horror of women's oppression. I used to convince people to feel moral outrage by comparing the situation of women in marriage and similar sexual/economic arrangements to prostitution. Carol argued that I was using the stigma of prostitution as a technique of persuasion, and that in so doing I was maintaining and intensifying such stigma at the expense of the women who did sex work. She was right. I finally realized that the rhetorical effectiveness came from the stigma, and decided that my rhetorical gain could not justify reinforcing attitudes which rationalized the persecution of sex workers. All of these incidents began to eat away at some of my preconceptions about how to think about power and sex, and the politics of sex.

I was also getting more and more alarmed at the way the logic of the woman-identified-woman picture of lesbianism had been working itself out. By defining lesbianism entirely as something about supportive relations between women, rather than as something with sexual content, the woman-identified-woman approach essentially evacuated it—to use a popular term—of any sexual content. It made it difficult to tell the difference between a lesbian and a nonlesbian. These were tendencies of thought common in local lesbian communities. Adrienne Rich in a way codified a certain approach that was widespread at the time, in which people didn't want to distinguish very much between lesbians and other women in close supportive relationships. And I found this both intellectually and politically problematic. A lot of things that were not by any stretch of the imagination lesbian were being incorporated into the category of lesbian. And this approach also diminished some of what was interesting and special about lesbians. I had initially been incredibly excited about the woman-identified-woman ideas, but I was starting to get a sense of their limitations.

JB: Is it that you objected to calling "lesbian" the whole domain of female friendship?

GR: In part. I objected to a particular obfuscation of the categories, and of taking the limited world of nineteenth-century romantic friendship, bound as it was by rigid sex-role segregation and enmeshed in marriage relations, as some kind of ideal standard for lesbian existence. I objected to the master narrative that was then developing in lesbian historiography, in which the shifts which undermined that world were seen as entirely negative, a fall from grace, an expulsion from Eden engineered by nasty sexologists with their knowledge of carnal desires. I did not like the way in which lesbians motivated by lust, or lesbians who were invested in butch-femme roles, were treated as inferior residents of the lesbian continuum, while some women who never had sexual desire for women were granted more elevated status. This narrative and its prejudices were expressed in the title of the Nancy Sahli article, which was called "Smashing: Women's Relationships before the Fall." It is highly developed in Lillian Faderman's *Surpassing the Love of Men*. Caroll Smith-Rosenberg's original 1975 essay deliberately blurred some of the distinctions between categories of lesbianism as a sexual status and other types of female intimacy, but she refrained from using romantic friendship as the standard by which lesbianism should be measured.[6] I suppose the most vulgar reduction of this "paradise lost" narrative of lesbian history can be found in Sheila Jeffreys's work.

JB: But then Rich's notion of the continuum, I take it you . . .

GR: Rich's piece shares many of the same elements and assumptions that turn up in the historical work. I was not opposed to historical research on these relationships, but thought it was a mistake to privilege them in defining the category of "lesbian," either historically or in a contemporary context, and to judge other forms of lesbianism as wanting, degraded, or inferior. For example, from reading *Surpassing the Love of Men*, you might conclude that "mannish lesbians" were concocted by the sexologists as a plot to discredit romantic friendship. In addition, both Sahli's and Faderman's analyses imply that the conditions which enable the emergence of sexually aware lesbians, conscious lesbian identities, and lesbian subcultures in the late nineteenth century are regrettable, because they undermined the old innocent passions and pure friendships. Then nothing much good happened for lesbians until the emergence of lesbian feminism in the early 1970s. Unfortunately, this ostensible dark age happens to coincide with much of the early development of lesbian cultures, literatures, identities, self-awareness, and politics.

This narrative structure oversimplified the complexities of these friendships, obscured their class components, and obliterated many important distinctions. This is a much longer discussion than we can have here, but the point I want to make is just that this categorical system submerged many historical and social complexities in a romantic, politicized, and limited notion of lesbianism. It, moreover, displaced sexual preference with a form of gender solidarity. The displacement was both moral and analytical. While female intimacy and solidarity are important and overlap in certain ways with lesbian erotic passions, they are not isomorphic and they require a finer set of distinctions.

Another problem in the late 1970s was presented by gay male politics. Feminism was also used quite a bit as the political theory of gay male politics, and it didn't work very well. Very little gay male behavior actually was granted the feminist seal of approval. Most of the actual practice of gay male culture was objectionable to many feminists, who mercilessly condemned drag and cross-dressing, gay public sex, gay male promiscuity, gay male masculinity, gay leather, gay fist-fucking, gay cruising, and just about everything else gay men did. I could not accept the usual lines about why all this stuff was terrible and antifeminist, and thought they were frequently an expression of reconstituted homophobia. By the late 1970s, there was an emerging body of gay male political writing on issues of gay male sexual practice. I found this literature fascinating, and thought it was not only helpful in thinking about gay male sexuality, but also that it had implications for the politics of lesbian sexual practice as well.

And then there was just the whole issue of sexual difference. I am using the terminology of "sexual difference" here to refer to what has otherwise been called perversion, sexual deviance, sexual variance, or sexual diversity. By the late 1970s, almost every sexual variation was described somewhere in feminist literature in negative terms with a feminist rationalization. Transsexuality, male homosexuality, promiscuity, public sex, transvestism, fetishism, and sadomasochism were all vilified within a feminist rhetoric, and some causal primacy in the creation and maintenance of female subordination was attributed to each of them. Somehow, these poor sexual deviations were suddenly the ultimate expressions of patriarchal domination. I found this move baffling: on the one hand, it took relatively minor, relatively powerless sexual practices and populations and targeted them as the primary enemy of women's freedom and well-being. At the same time, it exonerated the more powerful institutions of male supremacy and the traditional loci for feminist agitation: the family, religion, job discrimination and economic dependency, forced reproduction, biased education, lack of legal rights and civil status, etc.

JB: OK. Well let's go back for a minute. You spoke earlier about how you were forced to rethink the notion of prostitution, and I gather that it became for you something very different. You spoke about rethinking prostitution both as a labor question and a question of women's work. You then talked about the desexualization of the lesbian, and you also talked about how gay male politics had feminism as its theory, and yet that theory didn't really fit with the kinds of practices that gay men were engaged in.

GR: Toward the late seventies and early eighties, just before AIDS hit and changed everyone's preoccupations, there was an emergent literature of gay male political theory of sexuality. Much of this appeared in North America's two best gay/lesbian newspapers at the time, the *Body Politic*, and GCN [*Gay Community News*]. There were articles on public sex, fist-fucking, man-boy love, promiscuity, cruising, public sex, and sex ads. Gay men were articulating an indigenous political theory of their own sexual cultures. This body of work evaluated gay male sexual behavior in its own terms, rather than appealing to feminism for either justification or condemnation.

Looking back, it seems clear to me now that many things were happening almost at once. Somehow, the political conditions of sexual practice were undergoing a shift in the late 1970s, and the emergence of creative gay male sexual political theory was part of that. A major development was the phenomenal growth of the New Right. By the late 1970s it was mobilizing explicitly and successfully around sexual issues. The New Right had a strong sexual agenda: to raise the punitive costs of sexual activity for the young, to prevent homosexuals (male and female) from obtaining social and civic equality, to coerce women to reproduce, and so forth. Then the antiporn movement erupted into feminism in the late 1970s. WAVPM [Women Against Violence in Pornography and Media] was founded around 1976–77, and WAP [Women Against Pornography] followed in 1979. Samois, the first lesbian s/m organization, was founded in 1978. There was something profound going on; some larger underlying shift in how sexuality was experienced, conceptualized, and mobilized. "Thinking Sex" was just one response to this change in the social and political weather. I think my work shifted because something different was happening, and my set of operating assumptions and tools was not adequate for helping me navigate the shifts.

JB: I gather that you also objected to the available language in which so-called sexual deviants were described. . . .

GR: I looked at sex "deviants," and frankly they didn't strike me as the apotheosis of patriarchy. On the contrary, they seemed like people with a whole set of problems of their own, generated by a dominant system of sexual politics that treated them very badly. They did not strike me as the avatars of political and social power in this society. So I asked myself, What's wrong with this picture? It seemed to me that many feminists had simply assimilated the usual stigmas and common hatreds of certain forms of non-normative sexual practice which they then rearticulated in their own framework.

I was also becoming dissatisfied with the dominance of certain kinds of psychoanalytic interpretations of variant sexualities, and the common presumption that psychoanalysis was the privileged site for interpreting differences of sexual conduct. Despite its limitations and its problems, psychoanalysis has a certain power and utility for thinking about issues of gender identity and gender difference. By contrast, much of the psychoanalytic approach to sexual variation, also known as perversion, struck me as incredibly reductionist and oversimplified. Moreover, many of these traditional approaches to "perversion" had come into feminism almost uncriticized. For me, the explanatory potency of psychoanalysis seemed much more limited with regard to sexual variation.

For example, to look at something like fetishism and say it has to do with castration and the lack, or maybe it's the knowledge of castration, or maybe it's the denial of the knowledge of castration, or maybe it is the foreclosure of the knowledge of, or the displacement of the knowledge . . . well, it says very little to me about fetishism.

When I think about fetishism I want to know about many other things. I do not see how one can talk about fetishism, or sadomasochism, without thinking about the production of rubber, the techniques and gear used for controlling and riding horses, the high polished gleam of military footwear, the history of silk stockings, the cold authoritative qualities of medical equipment, or the allure of motorcycles and the elusive liberties of leaving the city for the open road. For that matter, how can we think of fetishism without the impact of cities, of certain streets and parks, of red-light districts and "cheap amusements," or the seductions of department-store counters, piled high with desirable and glamorous goods?[7] To me, fetishism raises all sorts of issues concerning shifts in the manufacture of objects, the historical and social specificities of control and skin and social etiquette, or ambiguously experienced body invasions and minutely graduated hierarchies. If all of this complex social information is reduced to castration or the Oedipus complex or knowing or not knowing what one is not supposed to know, I think something important has been lost.

I want to know about the topographies and political economies of erotic signification. I think that we acquire much of our grammar of eroticism very early in life and that psychoanalysis has very strong models for the active acquisition and personalized transformations of meanings by the very young. But I do not find the conventional preoccupations of psychoanalysis to be all that illuminating with regard to the shifting historical and social content of those meanings. So much of the input gets—to borrow some phrasing—foreclosed, denied, or displaced. There is a lot of very interesting and creative and smart psychoanalytic work. But when I wanted to think about sexual diversity, psychoanalytic approaches seemed less interesting to me. They seemed prone to impoverish the rich complexity of erotic meaning and conduct.

Moreover, it seemed that many psychoanalytically based approaches made a lot of assumptions about what certain variant erotic practices or preferences meant. These interpretations, mostly derived a priori from the literature, were then applied to living populations of individual practitioners, without any concern to check to see if such interpretations had any relevance or validity.

There has also been a kind of degradation of psychoanalytic approaches, when the language and concepts are applied with great enthusiasm and little discrimination. Instead of vulgar Marxism, we now have a kind of vulgar Lacanianism. Even the best ideas from truly creative minds can be overused and beaten into the ground. I remember sitting in the audience of one conference and thinking that there was now a "phallus ex machina," a kind of dramatic technique for the resolution of academic papers. I was remembering an image from a famous Japanese print, where the men have these very large cocks, and one man has a member so huge that he rolls it around in a wheelbarrow. I had this image of the phallus being brought up to the podium on a cart. I have heard a few too many papers where the phallus, or the lack, were brought in as if they provided profound analysis or sudden illumination. On many of these occasions, they did neither.

At some point, I went back and read some of the early sexology and realized that Freud's comments on the sexual aberrations were a brilliant, but limited, intervention into a preexisting literature that was very dense, rich, and interesting. His brilliance and fame, and the role of psychoanalytic explanation within psychiatry, have given his comments on sexual variation a kind of canonical status.[8] Even though many of his successors ignored or reversed his insights, Freud's prestige has been used to legitimate the later psychoanalytic literature as the privileged discourse on the "perversions." This has eclipsed a vast sexological enterprise that was roughly contemporary with Freud and which was actually more directly concerned with the sexual "aberrations" than he was.

Early sexology has many problems of its own. Besides being sexist and anti-homosexual, the earliest sexology treated pretty much all sexual practice other than procreative heterosexuality as a pathology. Even oral sex was classified as a perversion. The dominant models were drawn from evolutionism, particularly a kind of Lamarckian social evolutionism that was deeply embedded in ideologies of the ostensible superiority of the societies of white Europeans. But sexology, particularly after Krafft-Ebing, actually *looked* at sexual variety, taking sexual "aberrations" or "perversions" as its primary subject.[9] Sexologists began to collect cases, and to record studies of living, breathing, speaking inverts and perverts. Their data collecting was very uneven—some were better at it than others. And many historians are pointing out the limitations of their empirical practices. For example, from her work on the Alice Mitchell trial, Lisa Duggan has discussed how sexologists unskeptically treated newspaper reports or reports from other sexologists as primary data.[10] Robert Nye and Jann Matlock have analyzed assumptions and prejudices, especially about men and women, which shaped the early configurations of the categories of sexual fetishism and perversion.[11] Nonetheless, early sexological compendia are incredible sources to mine. Even Krafft-Ebing is useful.[12] For example, actual "inverts" and "perverts" read his early work and wrote him. They sent him their life histories, their anguished self-examinations, and their angry social critiques. Some of these were duly published in the later editions of *Psychopathia Sexualis*. So there are these amazing voices, like the early activist invert who eloquently denounces the social and legal sanctions against homosexuality. Or there is an account of what was called the "woman-haters" ball, but was actually a drag ball in turn-of-the-century Berlin. The detailed description notes that the dancing was accompanied by "a very fine orchestra" and that many beautifully bedecked "women" suddenly lit up cigars or spoke in a deep baritone.[13]

JB: Who were the other sexologists you were thinking of?

GR: Well Havelock Ellis is one of the best of them. Magnus Hirschfeld was also very important. Ellis and Hirschfeld probably did the most, before Freud, to normalize and destigmatize homosexuality and other sexual variations. An indication of Ellis's power as a polemicist can be seen in the famous letter Freud wrote to an American mother who was worried about her homosexual son. Freud assured her that many great individuals were homosexual, and that homosexuals should not be persecuted. He advised her, if she didn't believe him, to go "read the books of Havelock Ellis."[14]

Ellis and Freud both acknowledge a considerable debt to Hirschfeld. Virtually everyone who writes about homosexuality at the turn of the century cites Hirschfeld's journal, the *Jahrbuch für sexuelle Zwischenstufen* [*The Journal for Intermediate Sexual Stages*]. Other important sexologists included Albert Moll, Albert Eulenberg, and Iwan Bloch. In the first footnote to his famous essay on the sexual aberrations, Freud lists several of the most influential sexologists. These are the writers with whom he is in dialogue. They each have their own approach, and some are more interesting than others. Despite a limited theoretical apparatus, there is a rich social, historical, and cultural complexity reflected in this literature that gets lost in much of the later psychoanalytic writings.[15]

My sense is that Freud was not all that interested in "perverts" or "inverts"; he seemed much more excited by neurosis and the psychic costs of sexual "normality." Yet his interventions into turn-of-the-century sexology have overshadowed the context in which he was writing and the memory of that substantial and fascinating literature. In any event, instead of just taking off from Freud or later psychoanalysis, I thought it would be a good idea to go back to that literature before the psychoanalytic branch became so dominant, and see what could be learned from the issues and materials that were salient to those who first looked at sexual diversity as their main object of study.

JB: And Foucault, I presume he offered you an alternative to psychoanalysis. You were reading the first volume of Foucault's *History of Sexuality* somewhere around this time as well.

GR: Yes. That was published in English in 1978. I immediately gravitated to it. As you can see from my copy here it is very marked up and dog-eared. That was a very important book. I do think that because of his undoubted stature, other work in the field of sexuality is retrospectively credited to him. There was a debate recently on one of the gay studies lists on the Internet, in which Foucault was credited as the originator of "social construction" theory. The key roles of people like Mary McIntosh, Jeffrey Weeks, Kenneth Plummer, and a host of other historians, anthropologists, and sociologists were completely erased in the context of this discussion. It astonishes me how quickly people forget even recent history, and how much they are willing to project current attitudes back as a fictive chronological sequence. I was influenced by Jeffrey Weeks as much as Foucault. In my opinion, Weeks is one of the great under-appreciated figures in gay studies and the social theory of sexuality. He published the basic statement of social construction of homosexuality in 1977, the year before Foucault's *History of Sexuality* was translated.[16]

Many others who were working in the field of gay or lesbian history were rapidly coming to the same kinds of conclusions. I had been researching the history of lesbianism in the early 1970s, and quickly became aware that there was some discontinuity in the type of available data and the kinds of characteristic persons called "lesbian" before and after the late nineteenth century. There were earlier records of women who had relationships with women, and records of cross-dressing or passing women. But it seemed there was little evidence of self-conscious, self-identified lesbians, or lesbian communities, or a kind of lesbian political critique, until the late 1800s.

In 1973, I took another course that changed my life. It was "The Urbanization of Europe, 1500–1900," and was given by Charles Tilly [also at the University of Michigan]. Tilly described how industrialization resulted in massive transfers of population from countryside to cities, how urban life was subsequently transformed, and how the forms of voluntary association available to city-dwellers differed from those in peasant villages. Another major theme of the course was how the language and repertoire of political action changed in different historical periods. We spent a lot of time on different structures of revolutionary action and political protest in France, and how these changed over time and were specific to particular historical circumstances. Another theme of the course was the way in which forms of individual consciousness changed in the course of all these developments. We discussed E. P. Thompson's work on shifts in how people experienced time, and I was already familiar with the discussions of different forms of historical individuality in Althusser and Balibar.[17] It was a short jump from the impact of urbanization and industrialization on repertoires of political protest, the conventions of time, and forms of historical individuality, to thinking about how different forms of sexual identity and subjectivity might have resulted from the same large-scale social changes. These ideas seemed to make sense of what I was finding in my explorations of lesbian history. I didn't label any of this as "social construction," but I was reaching for ways to think about such issues. Many different scholars were taking the common approaches of social history, anthropology, and sociology, and applying these in a consistent way to homosexuality. There was a widespread convergence of this kind of thinking about male and female homosexuality, and a sudden paradigm shift, in the mid-1970s.

I was unaware of the extent of Foucault's involvement in this emerging paradigm, but I had some idea that he was doing research on sexuality and homosexuality. I had met Foucault earlier, when I was studying in France in the summers of 1972 and 1973. One of my friends was a wonderful man named Larry Shields. We were both completely obsessed with "structuralism," which was what we then called most of the contemporary French thought. We had read Lévi-Strauss and what there was of Lacan, and books of Foucault's such as *The Order of Things*. But there was so little of this material around, and we wanted to go to the source. We got grants to go off to Paris to do research on structuralism. Well, Larry dutifully sat in the main reading room at the Bibliothèque Nationale reading Godelier, Lyotard, Kristeva, and Baudrillard.

But I found that my French was inadequate to this task. As a game to find my way through the labyrinthine catalogue of the Bibliothèque Nationale, I started looking for some obscure lesbian novels that I had not been able to get my hands on for the part of my senior thesis on lesbian literature. When I found that they had Liane de Pougy's *Idylle Sapphique*, her roman à clef about her affair with Natalie Barney, I went up to the Réserve room to read it. I found a whole deposit of books by the Natalie Barney and Renée Vivien crowd, with penciled marginalia containing incredible biographical information on the cast of characters. So I ended up spending the summer in the Réserve, clutching my dictionary and verb book, reading dirty lesbian novels.

GR/JB: [in unison] My/*Your* French was good enough for that!

GR: Well, one day Larry spotted Foucault in the main reading room, and we got up our nerve and asked him out for coffee. We were totally dumbfounded when he accepted. So we went out for coffee, and he asked us what we were doing. Larry enthusiastically reported on his explorations of cutting-edge theorists. When Foucault asked me what I was doing, I very sheepishly admitted that I was reading lesbian novels upstairs in the Réserve. To my surprise, he seemed completely nonplussed, and just said, "Oh, I've been studying sodomy convictions." He explained that while sodomy laws were on the books for most of European history, they were only sporadically enforced. He was curious about what determined such patterns of enforcement. This was totally unexpected; I was astonished.

He was incredibly friendly and approachable, and gave us his address and phone number. I thought no more about it until I saw *The History of Sexuality* in 1978. I was just starting my research on the gay male leather community in San Francisco. I was going to France for a feminist conference. I mailed Foucault the very rough draft of my dissertation proposal and told him how much I loved his new book. I thought my work might interest him at a theoretical level, but I expected him to be put off by specific things, like the focus on gay male s/m. Once again he surprised me by inviting me to dinner. It was not until I got to the dinner that I finally realized that he was homosexual, that he seemed perfectly comfortable about s/m, and that I could stop worrying about offending him.

JB: So what was it in Foucault that you found useful to your thinking about sexual practices and sexuality in general?

GR: I thought his discussion of the emergence of a new relationship between systems of alliance and sexuality, at least in certain Western industrial countries, was incredibly insightful. You know, I said earlier that many people seem to have overinterpreted the last few pages of "Thinking Sex." I was not arguing there that kinship, gender, feminism, or psychoanalysis no longer mattered in any way. Rather, I was arguing that there were systems other than kinship which had assumed some kind of relative autonomy and could not be reduced to kinship, at least in the Lévi-Straussian sense. When I wrote about that, I very much had in mind the section from *The History of Sexuality* where Foucault says: "Particularly from the eighteenth century onwards, Western societies created and deployed a new apparatus which was superimposed on the previous one."[18] He never says it *replaces*, he says "superimposed."

JB: Right, right.

GR: "And which, without completely supplanting the latter helped reduce its importance." That is the actual phrase. It does not supplant, it simply reduces its importance. "I am speaking of the deployment of sexuality: like the deployment of alliances it connects up with the circuit of sexual partners, but in a different way. The systems can be contrasted term by term." And then he says, "For the first"—that is, alliance—"what is pertinent is the link between partners and definite statutes. The second is concerned with the sensations of the body, the quality of the pleasures, and the nature of impressions, however tenuous or imperceptible these may be." Then, on the next page, he goes on to explain that "it is not exact to say that the deployment of sexuality supplanted the deployment of alliance."[19] He writes, "One can imagine that one day it will have replaced it, but as things stand at present, while it does tend to cover up the deployment of alliance, *it has neither obliterated the latter, nor rendered it useless. Moreover, historically it was around, and on the basis of the deployment of alliance that the deployment of sexuality was constructed.*"[20] And then he goes on to write, "Since then it has not ceased to operate in conjunction with a system of alliance on which it had depended for support."[21] He even says the family is the "interchange" of sexuality and alliance. "It conveys the law in the juridical dimension in the deployment of sexuality, and it conveys the economy of pleasure, and the intensity of sensations in the regime of alliance." He calls the family "the most active site of sexuality."[22] Echoing this discussion, it never occurred to me that anyone would think I was arguing that kinship or the family, and their respective dynamics, have ceased to have any relevance. What he was saying helped me to think about the outlines of another system that had different dynamics, a different topography, and different lines of force. In this whole section by Foucault, you can hear the echoes of his conversations with Lévi-Strauss and Lacan. I felt that his assessment of those relationships was novel, insightful, and accurate.

There were so many things I loved about this book—the brilliance and descriptive richness of his writing, his rearrangement of the dominant concepts of sexuality, his interpretations of Freud, Lacan, Reich, and Lévi-Strauss, the dazzling insights, his models for social power, his ideas about resistance and revolution, the depth of his commitment to social and historical causality.

He generated many wonderful phrases—such as the proliferation of perversions. It gave me new ideas, provided some really clear and vivid language, and confirmed that my own preoccupations at the time were not completely absurd. I had given a couple talks on the emergence of modern lesbianism and homosexuality, and many people who heard them probably thought, politely, that I was out of my mind. Finding out that Weeks in *Coming Out* and Foucault in *The History of Sexuality* had already come to similar conclusions and had a similar understanding of a set of historical and theoretical issues was immensely reassuring and helped shape my subsequent approach.

JB: I realize that you don't want to discount the force of kinship altogether, but isn't there another issue here, namely, developing a vocabulary to articulate contemporary configurations of kinship. I guess another question for me is whether various supportive networks within the lesbian and gay community can't also be understood as contemporary forms of kinship.

GR: You can understand them that way, but then you are using kinship in a really different way. When people talk about gay kinship, for example, they are using a different model of kinship. Instead of Lévi-Strauss, it is based more on the work of David Schneider, who wrote about kinship in America.[23] You have to be specific about how the term is used. In a Lévi-Straussian sense, kinship is a way of generating a social and political structure from manipulations of marriage and descent. In a more vernacular sense, particularly in complex societies like this one, kinship can mean simply the social relations of support, intimacy, and enduring connection. This use of kinship is very different from the Lévi-Straussian notion of kinship.

JB: Well, of course it is. But doesn't that mark the conservatism of the Lévi-Straussian notion?

GR: Yes, but I'm saying that the terms are not quite commensurate. In feminist theory, a lot rides on that Lévi-Straussian notion of kinship, which can't just be switched into a more fluid notion of modern or gay-type kinship systems. So one has to be careful about what one is then saying about kinship in this different sense. A system of voluntary association is very different from a system in which obligatory marriages create dynastic systems or other forms of political organization.

Lévi-Strauss is talking about societies in which those relations of marriage and descent *are* the social structure. They either organize almost all of the social life, or they are the most important and visible institutional apparatus. In modern systems, kinship is already a structure that is much reduced in institutional importance. It is not radical to say, in anthropology, that kinship doesn't do in modern urban societies what it used to do in premodern cultures. Furthermore, gay kinship closely resembles what anthropologists would call "fictive" or "informal kinship." Such systems of informal or fictive kinship are even less institutionalized and structurally stable than those relationships which are reinforced by state authority.[24]

JB: Right. Well, I would certainly say that kinship can't possibly be the predominant way in which we try to take account of the complexity of contemporary social or sexual life. I mean, that seems clear. On the other hand, it seems to me that the Foucauldian historiography that you have just noted takes for granted the Lévi-Straussian account of kinship and presumes that this form of kinship is itself something in the past.

GR: No. I don't mean to suggest that. Again, one issue is how we are defining kinship.

JB: OK. Because if we understand kinship as obligatory relations, or we think about societies that are governed by obligatory kinship relations, then certainly we would be able to say that is not commensurate with social life as we live it. On the other hand, it seems to me that kinship itself may have lost some of that obligatory status, or is in the process of losing it. And I am wondering if there is some value in holding on to the term "kinship" precisely in order to document that shift in the way in which the social life of sexuality is reconfigured and sustained.

I guess this becomes important when people want to say that feminism, especially in its psychoanalytic or structuralist mode, could talk about kinship. But that particular discourse can't possibly describe the complexity of more modern arrangements or regulatory powers that are governing sexuality. And I think that the problem has been that some people have taken this distinction to be the basis of the distinction between what feminism ought to do, namely look at kinship and gender and psychoanalysis, and what sexuality studies ought to do. And then some people, I think, have taken that a step further and have said that sexuality is the proper "object," as it were, of gay and lesbian studies, and have based the whole methodological distinction between feminism and gay and lesbian studies on the apparent autonomy of those two domains. So maybe it would be better if I just asked you to address that question now.

GR: You have several different issues here. To take one pertinent at the time I wrote "Traffic," there was still a kind of naïve tendency to make general statements about the human condition that most people, including me, would now try to avoid. When you read Lévi-Strauss or Lacan, they make pretty grandiose generalizations. Plus, they never hesitate to call something *the* theory of this and *the* theory of that. I often wonder if that usage reflects a grandiosity that is no longer possible or if it is only an artifact of the translation. In French everything has an article in front of it. So "*la theorie*" in French can mean something quite different from *the* theory in English. In "Traffic," I simply absorbed the idioms and innocent universalism of the time. By the time I wrote "Thinking Sex," I wanted to make more modest claims. That was part of why, in "Thinking Sex," I noted that the Lévi-Straussian–Lacanian formulations might or might not be accurate for other societies, even as I was certain that they had limited applicability to our own. I had acquired some skepticism about the universality of those models.

As for this great methodological divide you are talking about, between feminism and gay/lesbian studies, I do not think I would accept that distribution of interests, activities, objects, and methods. I see no reason why feminism has to be limited to kinship and psychoanalysis, and I never said it should not work on sexuality. I only said it should not be seen as the privileged site for work on sexuality. I cannot imagine a gay and lesbian studies that is not interested in gender as well as sexuality and, as you note in your paper, there are many other sexualities to explore besides male homosexuality and lesbianism. But I am not persuaded that there is widespread acceptance of this division of intellectual labor between feminism, on the one hand, and gay and lesbian studies on the other. And it was certainly never my intention to establish a mutually exclusive disciplinary barrier between feminism and gay and lesbian studies. That was not an issue I was dealing with. I was trying to make some space for work on sexuality (and even gender) that did not presume feminism as the obligatory and sufficient approach. But I was not trying to found a field. For one thing, at that time the institutionalization of gay and lesbian studies was a fond dream that seemed far removed from the realm of immediate possibility. And yet, on the other hand, gay and lesbian studies as an enterprise was well under way. "Thinking Sex" was part of that ongoing process.

Some of the context for "Thinking Sex" was the developing project of gay and lesbian studies, especially gay and lesbian history and anthropology. There now seems to be a certain amnesia about the early work of lesbian and gay studies, as if the field only just started in the early or mid-1980s. This just isn't true. There are whole strata of work in lesbian and gay scholarship which date from the early 1970s and which came out of the gay-liberation movement. These in turn built on even earlier research based in the homophile movement. Gay scholarly work was not institutionalized in academia, and many of the people who did that work in the 1970s have paid a high price in terms of their academic careers. But lesbian and gay studies certainly didn't start with me, or at such a late date.

For example, the San Francisco Lesbian and Gay History Project started in 1978. A lot of work was begun in the excitement of that time: Allan Bérubé's work on gays in the military, Liz Kennedy's and Madeline Davis's work on the Buffalo lesbian community, and my research on gay male leather were all undertaken then.[25] By that time, there were many other scholars involved, and most of us were in communication and dialogue with one another and with one another's work.

Jonathan Ned Katz's *Gay American History*, John D'Emilio's *Sexual Politics, Sexual Communities*, Jim Steakley's *The Homosexual Emancipation Movement in Germany*, and Jeffrey Weeks's *Coming Out: Homosexual Politics in Britain* were from an even earlier period. There was another book on the German gay-rights movement by John Lauritsen and David Thorstad published in 1974.[26] By the very early 1970s, lesbian scholars were starting to build on the earlier, pathbreaking bibliographic studies by Jeannette Foster and Barbara Grier.[27] I bring this work up to note that gay and lesbian studies preceded "Thinking Sex" and that it was a thriving scholarly enterprise long before it began to be institutionalized.

JB: Well, tell us what you had in mind then when you wanted to designate the provisionally autonomous status of sexuality as a field.

GR: I wanted to have better scholarship on sexuality, and a richer set of ideas about it than were readily available. I wanted to be able to articulate a sexual politics that did not assume that feminism was the last word and holy writ on the subject. Just as I had a decade earlier wanted a way to think about gender oppression as distinct from class oppression (though not necessarily unrelated or in opposition), I later wanted to be able to think about oppression based on sexual conduct or illicit desire that was distinct from gender oppression (although, again, not necessarily unrelated or in opposition to it). I felt that we had to be able to articulate the structures of sexual stratification and make them visible in order to contest them. I thought that if we did not, progressive constituencies would unwittingly play into a very reactionary sexual agenda, which has, alas, too often been the case. I was afraid that if there were no independent analysis of sexual stratification and erotic persecution, well-intentioned feminists and other progressives would support abusive, oppressive, and undeserved witch hunts.

I think by then a certain kind of feminist orthodoxy had become an edifice with some of the same problems that had earlier plagued Marxism. Instead of class, gender was often supposed to be the primary contradiction from which all social problems flowed. There was an attitude that feminism now had the answers to all the problems for which Marxism was found wanting. I remember that one Marxist scholar made a wonderful comment about a certain approach to Marxism, which I thought was beginning to be applicable to a certain kind of feminism as well. I cannot recall who made the comment, although I think it was Martin Nicolaus. But the comment criticized those Marxists who treated *Capital* as if it were a lemon, as if by squeezing it hard enough all the categories of social life would come dripping out. By the early 1980s, there were many people who approached feminism in the same way. For some, feminism had become the successor to Marxism and was supposed to be the next grand theory of all human misery. I am skeptical of any attempt to privilege one set of analytical tools over all others, and all such claims of theoretical and political omnipotence.

I approach systems of thought as tools people make to gain leverage and control over certain problems. I am skeptical of all universal tools. A tool may do one job brilliantly, and be less helpful for another. I did not see feminism as the best tool for the job of getting leverage over issues of sexual variation.

I certainly never intended "Thinking Sex" as an attack on feminism, any more than I intended "Traffic" as an attack on Marxism. "Traffic" was largely addressed to an audience drenched in Marxism, and can be easily misunderstood in an era whose preoccupations are so different. I find the current neglect of Marx a tragedy, and I hope to see a revival of interest in his work. Marx was a brilliant social thinker, and the failure to engage important and vital issues of Marxist thought has weakened social and political analysis.

"Thinking Sex" similarly assumed a largely feminist readership. It was delivered at a feminist conference, aimed at a feminist audience, and written within the context of feminist discussion. I do not consider it an attack on a body of work to say that it cannot do everything equally well.

Finally, I wanted to add sexual practice to the grand list of social stratifications, and to establish sexuality as a vector of persecution and oppression. In the 1960s, the important stratifications were pretty much understood to be caste, class, and race. One of the great contributions of feminism was to add gender to that list. By the early 1980s, it had become clear to me that adding gender did not take care of the issues of sexual persecution, and that sexuality needed to be included as well.

JB: Your own work has become descriptively very rich, especially the ethnographic work, and earlier, with respect to the sexologists, you applaud their efforts for being full of valuable descriptive data. You mention as well that they "looked at" cases and practices. Is "looking at" in this sense a theoretical activity? In other words, don't we look with or through certain kinds of theoretical suppositions? And are certain kinds of practices "seeable" or "unseeable" depending on which theoretical presuppositions are used? Perhaps you would like to take this opportunity to speak a bit more about the relationship between descriptive and theoretical work?

GR: Yes, of course; whenever we look at anything we are already making decisions at some level about what constitutes the "seeable," and those decisions affect how we interpret what it is that we "see." The paradigms that informed early sexology produced a certain set of interpretations and explanations which I would reject, particularly the presumption that sexual diversity equals sexual pathology. The assumptions of sexology structured many of the categories and presuppositions that we are still dealing with today, for example, the idea that women are less capable of, less prone to, and less adept at sexual perversions than men. At the same time, their approach enabled sexologists to bring sexual diversity, however misperceived, into their field of view. It is, as it were, at the center of their lens, at the focal point of their enterprise. While Freud had, in general, a lens with better optics and higher resolution, sexual diversity was more at the edge of his field of view. In a way, it remains there in much subsequent work, including large parts of feminism.

But your question raises another issue for me, and that is the way in which empirical research and descriptive work are often treated as some kind of low-status, even stigmatized, activity that is inferior to "theory." There needs to be a discussion of what exactly is meant, these days, by "theory," and what counts as "theory." I would like to see a less dismissive attitude toward empirical work. There is a disturbing trend to treat with condescension or contempt any work that bothers to wrestle with data. This comes, in part, from the quite justified critiques of positivism and crude empiricism. But such critiques should sharpen the techniques for gathering and evaluating information rather than becoming a rationalization for failing to gather information at all.

One friend of mine likes to say, "All data are dirty." I take this to mean that data are not just things out there waiting to be harvested, with intrinsic meanings that are readily or inevitably apparent. Data, too, are socially constructed, and there are always perspectives that determine what constitutes data or affect evaluations of what can be learned from data. Nonetheless, it is a big mistake to decide that since data are imperfect, it is better to avoid the challenges of dealing with data altogether. I am appalled at a developing attitude that seems to think that having no data is better than having any data, or that dealing with data is an inferior and discrediting activity. A lack of solid, well-researched, careful descriptive work will eventually impoverish feminism, and gay and lesbian studies, as much as a lack of rigorous conceptual scrutiny will. I find this galloping idealism as disturbing as mindless positivism.

I also find preposterous the idea that empirical work is always easy, simple, or unanalytical. Unfortunately, virtuoso empirical work often goes unrecognized. Good empirical research involves as much thought and is as intellectually challenging as good conceptual analysis. In many ways, it is more challenging. I know this is a completely heretical opinion, but it is often more difficult to assemble, assimilate, understand, organize, and present original data than it is to work over a group of canonical texts which have been, by now, cultivated for so long by so many that they are already largely digested. There is plenty of "theory" in the best empirical studies, even if such studies often fail to cite the latest list of twenty-five essential authorizing or legitimizing "theorists."

Moreover, many people who deal with data are trained to be sophisticated about how to evaluate empirical material. Some who proclaim the supremacy of theory and who are contemptuous of empirical research can be quite naïve about the material used in their own "theoretical" work. Often, data come in, as it were, by the back door. In the absence of empirical research or training, some ostensibly theoretical texts end up relying on assumptions, stereotypes, anecdotes, fragments of data that are out of context, inaccurate details, other people's research, or material that is recycled from other so-called theoretical texts. So some extremely dirty data get enshrined as "theory." The opposition between "theoretical" and "empirical" work is a false, or at least, distorted one; the imbalance between conceptual analysis and data analysis needs some redress. In short, I would like to see more "interrogation" of the contemporary category of "theory," and of the relationships between such "theory" and empirical or descriptive research.

There is another specific problem I see with regard to sexuality. There is a common assumption that certain kinds of conceptual analysis or literary and film criticism provide descriptions or explanations about living individuals or populations, without establishing the relevance or applicability of such analyses to those individuals or groups. I have no objection to people performing dazzling analytic moves upon a body of assumptions or texts in order to say interesting things about those assumptions or texts. I have nothing against philosophy, literary analysis, or film criticism per se. But I have a problem with the indiscriminate use of such analyses to generate descriptions of living populations or explanations of their behaviors.

For example, there is a trend to analyze sexual variance by mixing a few privileged "theoretical" texts with literary or film criticism to produce statements about either the thing (e.g., "masochism") or the population (e.g., "masochists"). The currently fashionable "theory" of sadomasochism is Deleuze's long 1971 essay on "masochism." Despite the fact that Deleuze based much of his analysis on fiction, primarily Sacher-Masoch's novel *Venus in Furs* and some texts of de Sade, he is taken to be an authority on sadism and masochism in general. Since he is known as a theorist, his comments on sadism and masochism are surrounded with the penumbra of "Theory."

Deleuze treats differences in the literary techniques of Sade and Sacher-Masoch as evidence for ostensible differences between "sadism" and "masochism." But what are the "sadism" and "masochism" of which he speaks? Are they literary genres? Desires of living sadists and masochists? Floating formations of desire? He makes sweeping generalizations about "sadism" and "masochism," such as, "Sadism negates the mother and inflates the father; masochism disavows the mother and abolishes the father. . . . There is an aestheticism in masochism, while sadism is hostile to the aesthetic attitude."[28] I find statements like these fairly meaningless, intelligible only because of a psychoanalytic tradition that has equated particular constellations of sexual desire with alleged universals of childhood development. What troubles me is that such generalizations are and will be taken as descriptive statements about those persons and populations who might be considered "masochistic" or "sadistic."

Deleuze is very smart, and it also seems clear from his text that he had some acquaintance with practicing perverts. But his empirical knowledge enters primarily as anecdote. He seems familiar with female dominance, particularly by professional Mistresses. He seems to generalize from some literature and some kind of personal knowledge to make statements about "masochism" and "sadism" in a broader context. This essay is fascinating, yet hardly definitive. It is nonetheless becoming an authoritative text for writing about masochism and sadism.

There are now discussions which draw on Deleuze to analyze the "masochistic aesthetic," "the masochistic text," "masochism's psychodynamics," or "masochistic narrativity." Such usage implies that masochism is an "it," a unitary phenomenon whose singular psychodynamic, text, aesthetic, or narrativity are not only knowable but known. Leaving aside the issue of what terms like this mean, I see a danger that statements about what "masochism" in this sense "is" or "does" or "means" will be taken as descriptions or interpretations of what actual masochists are, do, or mean. Yet the authority of these statements is not derived from any systematic knowledge of masochism as it is practiced by masochists. It is derived from an analytic apparatus balanced precariously upon Deleuze's commentary, Sade's fiction and philosophical writings, Sacher-Masoch's novels, psychoanalytic writings on the etiology of masochism, various other texts and films, and personal anecdote.

I have this quaint, social-science attitude that statements about living populations should be based on some knowledge of such populations, not on speculative analysis, literary texts, cinematic representations, or preconceived assumptions. And I can hear the objection to what I'm saying already: "But Deleuze," someone is bound to say, "is Theory."

JB: So tell us more about the kind of work you are currently doing, and how it negotiates this tension between conceptual and descriptive domains. You just completed your study on the gay male leather community in San Francisco. What is it that you sought to find there?

GR: Well, when I started this project I was interested in the whole question of sexual ethnogenesis. I wanted to understand better how sexual communities form. This question came out of work I had done in lesbian history, and initially I was trying to figure out where lesbian communities came from, or how they come to exist. I became curious about gay male as well as lesbian communities. Then I realized that many sexualities were organized as urban populations, some quite territorial. I started to wonder about what stork brought all of these sexual populations, and how it happened. This was all part of reorienting my thinking about such categories as lesbianism, homosexuality, sadism, masochism, or fetishism. Instead of seeing these as clinical entities or categories of individual psychology, I wanted to approach them as social groups with histories, territories, institutional structures, modes of communication, etc.

As an anthropologist, I wanted to study something contemporary. There were a number of reasons why I picked this community, but one was that it had crystallized since World War Two. There were still individuals around who were involved then, from the late 1940s on. I had access to them, and could study this fascinating process whereby some sexual practice or desire that was once completely stigmatized, hidden, and despised could actually be institutionalized in a subculture in which it was considered normal and desirable. The building of subcultural systems designed to facilitate nonnormative sexualities is an interesting process.

And in many ways, the gay male leather community is a textbook case of sexual social formation, although the sexualities within it are more complex than I initially thought. For one thing, "leather" does not always mean "s/M." Leather is a broader category that includes gay men who do s/M, gay men who are into fisting, gay men who are fetishists, and gay men who are masculine and prefer masculine partners. Leather is a multivalent symbol that has different meanings to different individuals and groups within such communities. Among gay men, leather and its idioms of masculinity have been the main framework for gay male s/M since the late 1940s. Other groups organize similar desires in different social and symbolic constellations. For example, heterosexual s/M for most of the same period was not organized around the symbol of leather, idioms of masculinity, or urban territories. "Leather" is a historically and culturally specific construct in which certain forms of desire among gay men have been organized and structured socially.

I also did not know when I began this research that at least one sexual activity, fist-fucking, seems to have been a truly original invention. As others have pointed out, fisting is perhaps the only sexual practice invented in this century. It may have been practiced earlier. But it really became popular in the late 1960s and early 1970s, and then spawned its own unique subcultural elaboration and institutionalization.

Within the gay male leather community, you get this particular unity of the kinky and the masculine in a way that you don't see among heterosexuals or lesbians, where those things are mapped out differently. It is a very unique and interesting way of putting certain sexual practices together.

JB: What is the significance of the combination of masculinity and kinkiness?

GR: That is a huge subject, and requires a much longer discussion than we can have here. Among gay men, the adoption of masculinity is complicated, and has a lot to do with rejecting the traditional equations of male homosexual desire with effeminacy. Since the mid-nineteenth century, there has been a slowly evolving distinction between homosexual object choice and cross-gender or transgender behavior. A masculine homosexual (like a feminine lesbian) was once considered an oxymoron; such persons existed but were "unthinkable" in terms of the hegemonic models of sexuality and gender. The development of the leather community is part of a long historical process in which masculinity has been claimed, asserted, or reappropriated by male homosexuals. Gay male leather, including gay male s/M, codes both desiring/desired subjects and desired/desiring objects as masculine. In this system, a man can be overpowered, restrained, tormented, and penetrated, yet retain his masculinity, desirability, and subjectivity. There are also symbolics of effeminate homosexual s/m, but these have been a relatively minor theme in the fifty years of gay male leather.

Other communities don't combine these things in the same way. During most of the same time period, heterosexual s/m was organized more through sex ads, professional dominance, and some private social clubs. For heterosexual s/m, leather was a fetish, but not the core symbol which anchored institutionalization. Straight s/m was not territorial, and if anything, the dominant stylistic idioms were feminine.

The imagery of heterosexual s/m and fetishism draws on a lot of feminine symbolism. s/m erotica aimed at male heterosexuals often has mostly female characters, and the few male characters are often effeminized. There are many reasons for this, including the idiosyncrasies of the history of legal regulation of s/m erotica. But evidently many heterosexual men have fantasies of being lovely young ladies. Most of the better-equipped houses of dominance have a special room for cross-dressing male clients who pay handsomely for the privilege. These "fantasy" rooms are distinguished from "dungeons" or "medical" rooms. They are often decorated in pink frills and ruffles. One typical heterosexual s/m coupling may involve a woman dressed in feminine attire, dominating a man who may be overtly or covertly "effeminized."

I do not mean to imply that there are no "masculine" heterosexual male masochists or sadists. Moreover, this feminine imagery is not as hegemonic for heterosexual s/m as is masculine imagery for gay male s/m. But a visible and common style of heterosexual s/m involves a feminine woman and an effeminized man, a sort of fantasy "lesbian" couple. Meanwhile, among actual lesbian sadomasochists, there seems to be a pretty even distribution of masculine and feminine styles, genders, and symbolism.

JB: I'd like to bring us back to gender . . .

GR: You would! I will only say that I never claimed that sexuality and gender were always unconnected, only that they are not identical. Moreover, their relationships are situational, not universal, and must be determined in particular situations. I think I will leave any further comments on gender to you, in your capacity as the reigning "Queen" of Gender!

Studying Sexual Subcultures

Excavating the Ethnography of Gay

Communities in Urban North America

13

Anthropology and Homosexuality

Our own society disapproves of any form of homosexual behavior for males and females of all ages. In this it differs from the majority of human societies. Some people resemble us in this respect, but a larger number condone or even encourage homosexuality for at least some members of the population. Despite social and legal barriers to such behavior, homosexual activities do occur among some American men and women.
—**Clellen S. Ford and Frank A. Beach,** *Patterns of Sexual Behavior*

Over the past several decades, anthropology has played a prominent yet inconsistent role in the study of sexual communities and erotic populations. Anthropology has been a major force in contemporary theories of sexuality, particularly in the critiques of gender and heterosexuality as naturalized universals.[1] Comparative ethnographic data have helped undercut the moral legitimacy of antihomosexual bias.[2] Anthropologists have made substantial contributions to the social-science literature on homosexuality.[3] Anthropological work has helped to undercut the intellectual foundations of "perversion" models of sexual variation.

For much of the twentieth century, sexual practice that varied from a

Chapter 13 was originally published in Ellen Lewin and William Leap, eds., *Out in Theory: The Emergence of Lesbian and Gay Anthropology* (Urbana: University of Illinois Press, 2002), 17–68.

norm of fairly straightforward, generally monogamous, and preferably marital heterosexuality with a possibility of procreation was cast not only as undesirable but also physically unhealthy, socially inferior, or symptomatic of psychological impairment. Such perversion models presumed the pathology of sexual variety. These assumptions of disease and dysfunction could be explicit or implicit, but they were ubiquitous. They were particularly characteristic of medical and psychiatric literatures, which in turn were hegemonic professional discourses of sexuality.

The social sciences—particularly anthropology, sociology, and history—can often articulate a countervailing intellectual tendency toward accepting the moral equality of social diversity. Anthropology has facilitated potent shifts toward ideological leveling in many registers, including the sexual, by refusing to accept Western industrial civilizations as the measure of human achievement, by treating different cultural systems as equally legitimate, by attacking the foundations of racial ranking and the concept of race itself, by situating epistemological assumptions within culturally specific frameworks, and by showing how systems of moral value are produced by particular social contexts. In the second half of the twentieth century, anthropology and the other social sciences contested medicine for control over the study of sexuality and helped displace perversion-based models with frameworks grounded in the appreciation of the diversity of human cultural practice.

Nonetheless, anthropology remains enmeshed in its own social locations, and has been considerably less self-reflective about the resulting implications for sexual bias than other forms of rationalized condescension. It is ironic that so influential a discipline has also been oddly parochial in resisting the study of sexuality. In particular, the institutions of the discipline have often failed to encourage, and have in some respects obstructed, research on homosexuality, especially in Western urban contexts. The resulting discrepancy between anthropology's strong intellectual contributions and weak institutional presence in contemporary scholarship on homosexuality and other sexual populations has had significant repercussions. Many scholars who work on gay, lesbian, bisexual, or transgender issues, for example, assume that such research began in the 1990s, is derived almost entirely from French theory, and is primarily located in fields such as modern languages and literature, philosophy, and film studies.[4] Many anthropologists, in turn, are unaware of the extensive history of social-science attention to sexualities and may think of gay research as something accomplished mainly in the ethereal realms of aesthetic critique.

Nonetheless, the study of homosexuality and other nonnormative sexualities has a long and distinguished lineage in the social sciences. This essay is an attempt to excavate some of that history, specifically in terms of the ethnographic study of gay, lesbian, and other minority sexual populations in the metropolitan areas of North America, and suggest some of the ways in which that body of work contributed to the articulation of new theories and paradigms of sexuality in the early to mid-1970s.[5]

The Urban Problem

> Anthropology . . . has been mainly concerned up to the present with the study of primitive peoples. But civilized man is quite as interesting as an object of investigation, and at the same time his life is more open to observation and study. . . . The same patient methods of observation which anthropologists like Boas and Lowie have expended on the study of the life and manners of the North American Indian might be even more fruitfully employed in the investigation of the customs, beliefs, social practices, and general conceptions of life prevalent in Little Italy on the lower North Side in Chicago, or in recording the more sophisticated folkways of the inhabitants of Greenwich Village and the neighborhood of Washington Square, New York.
> —**Robert E. Park**, **Ernest W. Burgess**, and **Roderick McKenzie**, *The City*

As a neophyte graduate student in anthropology in the early 1970s I spent many hours in the library at the University of Michigan, looking for material on the anthropology of homosexuality. There were rich data about same-sex contact in some non-Western societies, the most obvious of which included extensive literature on ritualized semen exchanges among males in New Guinea and nearby Pacific Island cultures, and institutionalized roles for intermediate genders, principally among indigenous people of North America. There were also the occasional reports of homosexual practice or same-sex unions, for example in some African societies.[6] Data on contemporary sexual communities such as gay Greenwich Village, Fire Island, or West Hollywood, however, were scarce, and anthropological interest in such populations difficult to detect.

The two major compendia then available on the anthropology of sexuality were Ford's and Beach's *Patterns of Sexual Behavior* (1951) and Marshall's and Suggs's *Human Sexual Behavior* (1971). *Patterns of Sexual Behavior* was an indispensable text in comparative sexology. It was widely cited and highly influential in establishing the extent of cultural variation in sexual practices. Ford and Beach included a chapter on homosexuality in which material was presented chiefly in terms of whether societies approved or disapproved of homosexual conduct. By noting that the level of disapproval that obtained in the

United States in the 1950s was not universal and was even somewhat extreme, Ford and Beach expressed an implied, if muted, criticism of the prevailing intolerance. Their overview and references provided a wonderfully useful finding guide for locating data on same-sex contact in the ethnographic literature for other societies, especially in the Human Relations Area Files.

For the United States, however, Ford and Beach relied on the major sex surveys available at that time, notably the first volume of the Kinsey report from 1948, George Henry's two-volume opus on sex variants (1941), and Katherine Bement Davis's survey of the sex lives of twenty-two hundred women (1929). The discussion in Ford and Beach reflects those sources by focusing on individuals and types of sexual activity. It reiterates, for example, how many of Kinsey's respondents had practiced "mutual handling of the penis" or what percentage had engaged in anal copulation. Given that social groups are the more customary units of anthropological interest, the absence of any awareness of organized communities of homosexuals in the United States is striking. Ford and Beach brought to the study of homosexuality a strong measure of cultural relativism, but little recognition of the social complexity of urban sexual populations.

By contrast, when *Human Sexual Behavior* was published two decades later, Marshall and Suggs were well versed in the social life of urban homosexuals, yet considerably less adept at maintaining a consistent stance of ethnographic relativism. They noted that "some homosexuals congregate or regularly visit for residence or recreation specific districts that have shown more tolerance for deviant behavior" and that "some Western homosexuals have developed entire subcultures, with their own patterned behavior."[7]

Despite their recognition of homosexual social life, Marshall and Suggs still invoked the classification of homosexuality as a mental disease and a symptom of severe psychological malfunction. "Just as the homosexual advertisements in the *Berkeley Barb* appear with those of the voyeur, the sadist, the masochist, and the fetishist," they stated, "so it is difficult to interpret such behavioral manifestations as the 'fairy balls,' or the transvestite 'beauty contests' of some urban areas as anything more exalted than sociopathic manifestations of personality disturbances *complicated by membership in a pervasive subculture*."[8]

Furthermore, according to Marshall and Suggs, "Medical and psychiatric data together with interpretations by some analysts and by logic indicate that some contemporary Western sexual deviants must be regarded as socially and personally maladjusted, in some cases so very ill as to endanger society."[9] A scant two years before homosexuality was officially reclassified as nonpathological and removed from the list of psychosexual disorders by the American Psychiatric Association, they could flatly state, "Social approval of active homosexuality is tantamount to declaring that society has no interest in, or obligation to make well, the sociopsychologically deviant so as to prevent a disturbing behavior pattern from spreading in its midst—or that the society is not concerned with its own survival."[10]

Marshall and Suggs concluded by claiming a new level of ethnographic objectivity and scientific neutrality in the study of sexuality: "With all the effort devoted to the study of manifold aspects of sex throughout the decades since Ellis, Krafft-Ebing, Freud, and others, *only now have we begun to arrive at a relatively culture-free perspective of this most basic aspect of human behavior.*"[11] Their laudable attempt to approach sexual variation with an open mind and a minimum of cultural baggage, however, floundered on the presumption of homosexuality as intrinsically pathological. Far from establishing a non-ethnocentric study of human sexuality, *Human Sexual Behavior* demonstrates the extent to which ethnographic reflexes were still trumped by common prejudice and psychiatric hegemony as late as 1971. It is ironic that during the two decades bracketed by these two anthropological texts the work of establishing a social-science approach to sex, of producing ethnographic studies of contemporary sexual populations, and of challenging the privileged role of psychiatry in the study of human sexuality was mostly accomplished by sociologists.

The University of Chicago and the Discovery of Sexual Worlds

> The refashioning of homosexuality as a social phenomenon, rather than a purely psychological one, was established by two means—first by the definition of *homosexuality as a social problem* (ambiguously framed as one of either a problem of the social adjustment of homosexuals or the elimination of prejudice against homosexuals), and second, the public recognition of *the existence of a homosexual world*. Starting in the immediate postwar period and up through the sixties homosexuality as a social issue emerged in a number of different bodies of discourse.
> —**Jeffrey Escoffier**, "Reading the Social"

The idea that sexuality was social and an appropriate object of social-science inquiry was powerfully articulated during the 1950s and 1960s in a small literature in the sociology of deviance.[12] The assumptions, questions, and implications of this body of work challenged those of psychiatry, displacing interest in the etiologies of individual disorders with curiosity about the institutional structures and socialization mechanisms of deviant subcultures. As Jeffrey Escoffier has observed, the "discovery" of homosexual social worlds was central to the reclassification of homosexuality as a social rather than a medical issue. Ethnographic attention to homosexual subcultures shifted attention from individuals to communities and from illness to routine.

Many key scholarly figures of this transition were trained in sociology at the University of Chicago, including John Gagnon, William Simon, Albert Reiss, William Westley, and less directly, Howard Becker and Erving Goffman. There were, of course, many other notable researchers who also contributed to this process, especially Evelyn Hooker, a psychologist, and Alfred Kinsey, whose background was in biological science. And in addition to Chicago, there were other institutions, such as UCLA, where Hooker was on the faculty, and Indiana University, where the Kinsey Institute was located, that served as major intellectual loci for redefining sexuality and resituating sexual deviance.[13] Nonetheless, the centrality of urban ethnography, the sociology of deviance, and the peculiar concentration of individuals trained in social science at Chicago deserve attention.

Social research at the University of Chicago had been famous for its pioneering work in urban sociology since the publication of *The Polish Peasant in Europe and America* (1918–20) by W. I. Thomas and Florian Znanieki. Thomas is perhaps best known for his role in establishing urban research based on detailed field observation, but he also published a sexological treatise in 1907. His *Sex and Society: Studies in the Social Psychology of Sex* (1907) assembled a collection of earlier journal articles. *Sex and Society* is not grounded in original research but is primarily a commentary based on previously published data, much of it ethnographic. Thomas extensively cites many of the familiar turn-of-the-century anthropological tomes, such as those of Westermarck, Tyler, Spencer, Lubbock, and Morgan; he also invokes early sexological compendia such as the work of Havelock Ellis. *Sex and Society* is a reminder that data on sexual practice were central to late-nineteenth-century anthropology and social theory; similarly, anthropological concerns, findings, and scholarship powerfully shaped early sexology. The overlap between these fields was substantial and their differentiation still embryonic.

W. I. Thomas had also served on the Chicago Vice Commission, one of several investigatory bodies established as a result of interrelated anti-vice crusades that flourished in the United States in the early part of the twentieth century. In addition to the temperance movement, there were also enormous social mobilizations against prostitution (the "social evil") and "white slavery" as well as active campaigns to raise the age of consent for girls and curb the social freedoms of young working-class women.[14] It is ironic that much of what we know about "vice" in U.S. cities in the early twentieth century results from data collected to assist in attempts at its elimination.

Moreover, the surveillance of prostitution by anti-vice organizations produced observational data on homosexuality. New York's Committee of Fifteen (founded in 1900) documented prostitution in New York City, as did its successor, the Committee of Fourteen, "an anti-prostitution society whose investigators kept much of the city's nightlife and streetlife under surveillance from 1905 to 1932. . . . In the course of their search for prostitutes, they [investigators for the Committee of Fourteen] regularly encountered gay men. . . . The reports they filed about those encounters provide exceptionally rich evidence about the haunts of gay men, gay street culture, and the social conventions that governed gay men's interactions with other men and the reactions of the investigators themselves to them."[15] Like its New York counterparts, the Vice Commission of Chicago documented the existence of homosexual underworlds in Chicago as it gathered intelligence on female prostitution.[16]

Despite his service on the Chicago Vice Commission and his position on the faculty at the University of Chicago, W. I. Thomas was a casualty of these turn-of-the-century, anti-vice crusades. He was fired in 1918 after being arrested in a hotel with a woman to whom he was not married and charged with violating the Mann Act. The Mann Act, enacted in 1910 and also known as the White Slave Traffic Act, prohibited the interstate transportation of women or girls for "immoral purposes." Although its ostensible purpose was to protect women from coerced prostitution, in practice the Mann Act resulted in restrictions on female travel, harassment of unmarried heterosexual couples, and the establishment of the FBI as a permanent office of the federal bureaucracy.[17]

Although the case against Thomas was dropped, publicity about the morals charge ended his career at Chicago. "His dismissal was . . . a cruel and considered blow, which was pushed through with thoroughness. The University of Chicago Press, which had published the first two volumes of *The Polish Peasant*, was ordered by the president to terminate the contract and cease distribution of the volumes published. . . . Thomas's name was to be expunged from the university."[18] Thomas never again held a regular academic appointment, spending the rest of his career as a freelance researcher.

Despite Thomas's departure, however, urban ethnography continued to thrive at Chicago throughout the 1920s and 1930s under Robert E. Park and

Ernest Burgess. Recreation and leisure activities were an inescapable element of the urban landscape. Indeed, in a 1915 essay on the urban environment,[19] Park devoted considerable attention to the relationship between the dynamics of metropolitan life and "vice," noting that "commercialized vice is indigenous" to cities and that conditions peculiar to city life "make the control of vice especially difficult."[20] Indeed, the city drew individuals who did not fit into the life of small towns and rural areas.

> The attraction of the metropolis is due in part . . . to the fact that in the long run every individual finds somewhere among the varied manifestations of city life the sort of environment in which he expands and feels at ease; finds, in short, the moral climate in which his peculiar nature obtains the stimulations that bring his innate dispositions to full and free expression. It is, I suspect, motives of this kind . . . which draw many, if not most, of the young men and young women from the security of their homes in the country into the big, booming confusion and excitement of city life. In a small community it is the normal man, the man without eccentricity or genius, who seems most likely to succeed. The small community often tolerates eccentricity. The city, on the contrary, rewards it. . . . In the city many of these divergent types now find a milieu in which, for good or for ill, their dispositions and talents parturiate and bear fruit.[21]

The concentration of specializations made possible by city size and gravitational pull result in what Park famously called "moral regions" of a city.

> The population tends to segregate itself, not merely in accordance with its interests, but in accordance with its tastes or its temperaments. The resulting distribution of the population is likely to be quite different from that brought about by occupational interests or economic conditions. Every neighborhood, under the influences which tend to distribute or segregate city populations, may assume the character of a "moral region." Such, for example, are the vice districts, which are found in most cities. A moral region is not necessarily a place of abode. It may be a mere rendezvous, a place of resort. . . . We must then accept these "moral regions" and the more or less eccentric and exceptional people who inhabit them, in a sense, at least, as part of the natural, if not the normal, life of a city. It is not necessary to understand by the expression "moral region" a place or a society that is either necessarily criminal or abnormal. It is intended rather to apply to regions in which a divergent moral code prevails, because it is a region in which the people who inhabit it are dominated, as people are ordinarily

not dominated, by a taste or a passion or by some interest. . . . It may be an art, like music, or a sport, like horse-racing. . . . Because of the opportunity it offers, particularly to the exceptional and abnormal types of man, a great city tends to spread out and lay bare to the public view in a massive manner all the human characters and traits which are ordinarily obscured and suppressed in smaller communities.[22]

In these comments, Park notes the existence of populations organized around nonnormative sexualities, observes that they are spatially located and socially distinct, recognizes their idiosyncratic criteria for moral legitimacy, and provides a rationale for their study.

Students of Park and Burgess fanned out into Chicago to study saloons, speakeasies, gangs, slums, hobos, and a wide range of urban activity, life, and leisure.[23] None of the published work of this period was primarily focused on homosexuality, but as Chad Heap observes, "Students also examined the increasing presence of homosexuality in the city, chronicling a wide range of same-sex relations and networks associated with specific urban locations and populations."[24] Heap singles out Nels Anderson's *The Hobo* and Zorbaugh's *The Gold Coast and the Slum* as two published works that contained descriptions of same-sex activities and networks.[25] Fortunately, much of the unpublished research on homosexuality has been preserved in the Burgess Papers at the University of Chicago. Contemporary scholars such as Allen Drexel, Chad Heap, David K. Johnson, and Kevin Mumford have been exploring the Burgess archives and finding extraordinarily rich documentation on homosexual life in Chicago before the Second World War.[26]

The traditions of urban ethnography continued at Chicago after the Second World War. Joseph Gusfield conveys something of the spirit of this work with the following comment: "We used to say that a thesis about drinking written by a Harvard student might well be entitled 'Modes of Cultural Release in Western Social Systems'; by a Columbia student it would be entitled, 'Latent Functions of Alcohol Use in a National Sample'; and by a Chicago student as, 'Social Interaction at Jimmy's: A 55th St. Bar.'"[27] But the post–Second World War cohort did more than add to the literature on diverse concentrations of urban delinquents. Several of its members also developed a pervasive critique of the prevailing assumption that something was intrinsically wrong with deviants and misfits. They showed how such populations became morally discredited within dominant social systems, and how they constructed alternative structures of community and meaningful lives within them.

Dismantling Deviance

> The attitudes we normals have toward a person with a stigma, and the actions we take in regard to him, are well known, since these responses are what benevolent social action is designed to soften and ameliorate. By definition, of course, we believe the person with a stigma is not quite human. On this assumption we exercise varieties of discrimination, through which we effectively, if often unthinkingly, reduce his life chances. We construct a stigma theory, an ideology to explain his inferiority and account for the danger he represents, sometimes rationalizing an animosity based on other differences, such as those of social class. . . . We tend to impute a wide range of imperfections on the basis of the original one.
>
> —**Erving Goffman,** *Stigma*

> When do we accuse ourselves and our fellow sociologists of bias? I think an inspection of representative instances would show that the accusation arises . . . when the research gives credence, in any serious way, to the perspective of the subordinate group in some hierarchical relationship. The superordinate parties in the relationship are those who represent the forces of approved and official morality; the subordinate parties are those who, it is alleged, have violated that morality. . . . We provoke the suspicion that we are biased in favor of the subordinate parties . . . when we tell the story from their point of view.
>
> —**Howard Becker,** "Whose Side Are We On?"

In an essay called "Chicago's Two Worlds of Deviance Research: Whose Side Are They On?," John Galliher details the impact of a cohort of sociologists who did their graduate work at Chicago after the Second World War and proceeded to significantly reshape studies of deviance and crime. One of the key figures in repositioning "deviance" was Howard Becker.[28] Becker's influence was due to many factors: his choices of research topics, his bold reconceptualizations of the field, his work as an editor of the journal *Social Problems* in the early 1960s, and his service as president of the Society for the Study of Social Problems. His 1966 presidential address, later published in *Social Problems*, was the famous "Whose Side Are We On?"[29]

In it Becker challenges social researchers to include the perspectives of all parties, not only those of the accepted authorities. "It is easily ascertained that a great many more studies are biased in the direction of the interests of responsible officials than the other way around."[30] A key concept was what Becker dubbed "the hierarchy of credibility." He noted that "In any system of ranked groups, participants take it as a given that members of the highest group have the right to define the way things really are. . . . [T]hus credibility and the right to be heard are differentially distributed through the ranks of the system. As sociologists, we provoke the charge of bias . . . by refusing to give credence and deference to an established order, in which knowledge of truth and the right to be heard are not equally distributed."[31]

In his research and theoretical writings, Becker in various ways declines to observe that moral hierarchy and engages instead in what might be called a project of "moral leveling."[32] He comments, for example, "In the course of our work . . . we fall into deep sympathy with the people we are studying, so that while the rest of the society views them as unfit in one or another respect for the deference ordinarily accorded a fellow citizen, we believe that they are at least as good as anyone else."[33] Giving equal consideration to the opinions of disreputable deviants, respectable citizens, and authoritative officials was extraordinarily subversive.

Although Becker's early research on "outsiders" focused on marijuana users and jazz musicians, he discussed homosexuality in the context of deviance and "deviant careers."[34] In *Stigma: Notes on the Management of Spoiled Identity* (1963), Erving Goffman also uses homosexuality to exemplify the broader workings of stigma. His interest was in how individuals and groups become discredited, tainted, and discounted, and how they construct or learn to participate in alternative values, social affiliations, and "moral careers."

It was John Gagnon and William Simon, two other Chicago-trained sociologists, who would undertake the most comprehensive rethinking of specifically sexual deviance, including a sweeping reevaluation of homosexuality. After their graduate work, they were hired to conduct research at the Institute for Sex Research at Bloomington, Indiana. Gagnon arrived in 1959, and Simon followed in 1964. The confluence of the intellectual heritage of Chicago social research and the Kinsey Institute's focus on sexuality was fortuitous. Gagnon and Simon quickly grasped the implications of their sociological perspectives for the conduct of sex research and the reshaping of sexual theory. During the course of the 1960s and early 1970s, they produced a body of work that virtually reinvented sex research as social science. They also aggressively contested the hegemony of psychiatry and the paucity of its interests. Reminiscing about this period years later, Gagnon commented, "Each of the research projects [undertaken by them] was an attempt to bring the field of sexuality under the control of a sociological orientation. The novelty of what we did then was to lay a sociological claim to an aspect of social life that seemed determined by biology or psychology. . . . The research project on gay men . . . began with a distrust of etiological theories and a vision of sexual lives as determined by social factors."[35]

This insistence on treating sexuality in all its forms as a social phenomenon addressable by social science was perhaps their most influential and breathtaking accomplishment. Simon and Gagnon promoted the application of ordinary sociological questions and techniques to the study of homosexuals as well as to a range of other sexual populations and topics. Kenneth Plummer observed, "One of the central ideological thrusts in their writings is their wish to take the study of human sexuality out of the realm of the extraordinary and replace it where they believe it belongs: in the world of the ordinary."[36] Simon and Gagnon reformulated the research project to ask not why a particular individual was homosexual, but how that person became socialized into homosexual life and the social content of that particular "deviant career."

The researchers were critical of etiological obsessions and the naturalization of heterosexuality.

> The study of homosexuality today, except for a few rare and relatively recent examples, suffers from two major defects: (1) it is ruled by a simplistic and homogeneous view of the psychological and social contents of the category "homosexual," (2) At the same time it is nearly exclusively interested in the most difficult and least rewarding of all questions, that of etiology. . . . It is this nearly obsessive concern with the ultimate causes of adult conditions which has played a major role in structuring our concerns about beliefs and about attitudes toward the homosexual. Whatever the specific elements that make up an etiological theory, the search for etiology has its own consequences for research methodology and the construction of theories about behavior. . . . [T]he problem of finding out how people become homosexual requires an adequate theory of how they become heterosexual; that is, one cannot explain homosexuality in one way and leave heterosexuality as a large residual category labeled "all other."[37]

They also highlight the arbitrary quality of the assumption of homosexual pathology.

> In practically all cases, the presence of homosexuality is seen as prima facie evidence of major psychopathology. When the heterosexual meets these minimal definitions of mental health, he is exculpated; the homosexual—no matter how good his adjustment in nonsexual areas of life is—remains suspect. . . . Obviously, the pursuit of a homosexual commitment—like most forms of deviance—makes social adjustment more problematic than

it might be for a conventional population. What is important to understand is that consequences of these sexual practices are not necessarily direct functions of such practices. It is necessary to move away from an obsessive concern with the sexuality of the individual, and to attempt to see the homosexual in terms of broader commitments that he must make in order to live in the world around him. Like the heterosexual, the homosexual must come to terms with the problems which are attendant upon being a member of the society: he must find a place to work, learn to live with or without his family, be involved or apathetic in political life, find a group of friends to talk to and live with, fill his leisure time usefully or frivolously, handle all the common and uncommon problems . . . and in some manner socialize his sexual interests.[38]

In short, a sociological approach to homosexuality would "trace out the patterns of living in their pedestrian aspects as well as those which are seemingly exotic."[39]

Gagnon and Simon also conducted and promoted social research, including ethnographic studies, on other sexual populations. They wrote widely on many sexual topics, including pornography and lesbianism, coauthored two influential anthologies, *Sexual Deviance* (1967), *The Sexual Scene* (1970), and produced a magisterial summation of their social and theoretical approach to sexuality in *Sexual Conduct* (1973).[40]

Sexual Deviance is an extraordinary collection of classics that have almost been lost, and the anthology should be brought back into print. In addition to sections on sex offenses, lesbians, and prostitutes, *Sexual Deviance* contains most of the key originating articles on the ethnography of contemporary homosexual life. Among these are Evelyn Hooker's "The Homosexual Community" (first presented as a paper in 1961); Maurice Leznoff and William A. Westley's article by the same name (first published in *Social Problems* in 1956); Albert J. Reiss's study of teenage hustlers, "The Social Integration of Peers and Queers" (also originally published in *Social Problems*, in 1961); and Nancy Achilles's remarkable article on San Francisco gay bars, "The Development of the Homosexual Bar as an Institution" (based on her unpublished 1964 master's thesis for the Committee on Human Development at the University of Chicago).

The three essays that provide overviews of urban gay populations span a period of observation from roughly the mid-1950s to the early 1960s, and three cities: Los Angeles, San Francisco, and an unspecified "large Canadian city" (presumably Montreal). Leznoff's and Westley's study was the earliest and in some respects the most rudimentary. It documented that there were "known homosexual meeting places within the city such as specific bars, hotel lobbies, street corners, and lavatories," and discussed the way in which "queens" (whose homosexuality was open and somewhat flagrant) exercised social leadership functions.[41]

The most interesting aspects of the article are the authors' observations about the relationships among social status, economic location, community participation, and homosexual disclosure. Leznoff and Westley observed two basic strategies for managing homosexual stigma and the attendant legal and social sanctions. Some number of their research population "passed" as heterosexuals, both at work and in social relationships. Others who were openly homosexual in mid-1950s Canada tended to "work in occupations where the homosexual is tolerated, withdraw from uncompromising heterosexual groups, and confine most of their social life to homosexual circles."[42]

Leznoff and Westley called these two crowds the "secret" and the "overt." They noted an inverse relationship between overt disclosure of the stigmatized homosexual identity and class status and social mobility. "The overt homosexual tends to fit into an occupation of low status rank; the secret homosexual into an occupation with a relatively high status rank."[43] Furthermore, "the homosexual tends to change his orientation from 'overt' to 'covert' as he becomes upwardly mobile."[44] In the intervening decades, as the punitive costs of overt homosexuality have diminished, this relationship has undoubtedly altered, but it still can be discerned in muted and mutated forms. A larger arena of economic and social practice now permits open disclosure of homosexuality, although acknowledged homosexuality is still hazardous for individuals in a wide range of careers and positions, such as military personnel, politicians, members of the judiciary, entertainers, professional athletes, teachers and educators, and the clergy of most denominations.

Hooker's research depicts a slightly later, larger, more differentiated, and evidently less anxious community. She noted a much more developed territoriality. Although the Los Angeles homosexual community of the late 1950s and early 1960s lacked "a territorial base with primary institutions serving a residential population," homosexuals were "nevertheless, not randomly distributed throughout the city, nor are the facilities of institutions which provide needed services and functions as focal gathering places. . . . [H]eavy concentrations of homosexuals result in large cluster formations. In these sections, apartment houses on particular streets may be owned by, and rented exclusively to, homosexuals. . . . The concentrated character of these areas is not generally known except in the homosexual community, and in many instances by the police."[45]

Hooker also noted the central importance of the "gay bar" among the public institutions of homosexual social life, and the relationship of this importance to antigay stigma: "Because most homosexuals make every effort to conceal their homosexuality at work, and from heterosexuals, the community activities are largely leisure time or recreational activities. The most important of these community gathering places is the 'gay bar' . . . but there are also steam baths catering almost exclusively to homosexuals, 'gay' streets, parks, public toilets, beaches, gyms, coffee houses, and restaurants. Newsstands, bookstores, record shops, clothing stores, barber shops, grocery stores, and launderettes may become preferred establishments for service or for a rendezvous, but they are secondary in importance."[46] Hooker counted sixty gay bars in Los Angeles around 1960 and observed in passing the harassment of these bars by police and the alcoholic beverage control authorities.[47]

The essay by Nancy Achilles explores the institutional centrality of the gay bars of the early 1960s in greater depth. The most important service of the gay bars, she comments, consisted of

> the provision of a setting in which social interaction may occur; without such a place to congregate, the group would cease to be a group. . . . Articulating with various commercial and political institutions of the larger society, the bar may obtain legitimate and illegitimate goods and services for its clientele. As each bar develops a "personality" of its own and becomes an institution in its own right, it fulfills more specialized and nonsocial functions. A particular bar, for example, may serve as a loan office, restaurant, message reception center, telephone exchange, and so forth. . . . The bar is the homosexual equivalent of the USO or the youth club.[48]

This institutional importance of the gay bars made their control by police and the state alcohol authorities politically significant. "If there is one particular issue which calls forth a unified protest from the homosexual Community, it is that of police activity. Many homosexuals remain passive until a favorite bar or close friend is threatened by the police. . . . The greatest sense of group cohesion in the homosexual Community is expressed in reaction to the police."[49]

Moreover, as Achilles notes, some of the important legal battles to establish the right of homosexuals to congregate in public were fought over regulations governing liquor licenses. Consequently, in attempting to retain their licenses and serve a homosexual clientele, "it is often the bars themselves which make the most salient plea for the homosexual's civil rights, for it is most often the bars which undertake a defense in cases involving the law."[50]

Considerable bar specialization was evident by the early 1960s.

> The gay world is one marked by a galaxy of social types, each one comprising a sub-group within the Community. Often a bar will cater to one particular sub-group, and the bartender will be representative of its social type. For example, one bar will be known as a "leather bar," where the customers are the exaggeratedly masculine type, sporting motorcycle jackets and boots. Another bar may be popular with the effeminate "queens." .... A female behind the bar indicates a primarily Lesbian clientele. The same applies to more subtle distinctions; in the discreet gilt and mahogany bars of the financial district, the bartenders wear black ties and speak with Oxford accents.[51]

Some of the spatial distribution of gay sites could be specified by the early 1960s. Achilles noted that several bars were "located in the Tenderloin district of San Francisco, and several others in the industrial section and its adjacent waterfront," likely South of Market, which was largely industrial, and the old Embarcadero, where gay men patronized many of the establishments along the wharves.[52] Her research was undertaken a decade before the Castro became a significant location in the city's homosexual geography and when local gay sites were indeed heavily concentrated in the Tenderloin/Polk area, the port, and the South of Market.

Finally, Achilles utilized the notion of a "gay bar system," noting that "the individual bars may open and close rapidly and regularly, but the system and its participants remain the same."[53] Achilles's study was evidently conducted during a period of relative stability in the system, and perhaps that led her to overestimate its permanence. "The bars come and go, like a chain of lights blinking on and off over a map of the city, but the system remains constant."[54] This observation is insightful if unduly functionalist and overly generalized to other periods. Within a decade of Achilles's research, gay settlements in major North American metropoles would undergo substantial and visible expansions of territory, economic diversification, and institutional proliferation. Certainly in San Francisco, the "gay bar system" was not stable. It underwent explosive growth, and then, during the mid-1980s it contracted and shrank. Such changes are significant, result from changes in the urban environment, and indicate new kinds of institutional formation or attrition within urban gay populations.[55] Nonetheless, Achilles's research remains an invaluable description of a vanished time. Yesterday's sociology has become today's history.

One of the very real problems of the ethnographic work on gay communities from the 1950s and 1960s (a problem shared with most other ethnography from the period) is a lack of temporal awareness and the consequent misidentification of transient conditions as universal ones. For example, Simon and Gagnon stated, "In contrast to ethnic and occupational subcultures the homosexual community—as well as other deviant subcommunities—has very limited content."[56] That view, common at the time, made perfect sense when gay life was both more secretive and less institutionally elaborated than it would become in the 1970s. Writing from a later vantage point, Harry and DeVall could observe, "The Gagnon and Simon thesis of cultural impoverishment was a time-bound hypothesis that had a measure of validity for certain gay settings . . . and for earlier decades. However, the growth of gay institutions during the last fifteen years, the rise of a sense of collective identity, the creation of a sophisticated political culture, and the efflorescence of a variety of gay recreational styles has significantly expanded the content of that culture."[57]

Such debates demonstrate the importance of longitudinal observation, sensitivity to the diachronic dimensions of social structures, and the hazards of elevating contingencies into principles. But these discussions and their resulting refinements would not have even been possible without the kind of data on homosexual settlements found in *Sexual Deviance*. *Sexual Deviance* also included Albert Reiss's fascinating article on commercial sexual transactions between adult homosexual men and young "hustlers" who do not consider themselves "queer." "The adult male client pays a delinquent boy prostitute a sum of money in order to be allowed to act as a fellator. The transaction is limited to fellation and is one in which the boy develops no self-conception as a homosexual person or sexual deviator, although he perceives adult male clients as sexual deviators, 'queers' or 'gay boys.'"[58] This pattern of conduct lead Reiss to distinguish between "homosexual behavior" and the "homosexual role" and to think about the mechanisms by which boundaries between "homosexual acts" and "homosexual identities" were maintained by the rules governing these transactions.[59]

The exchange of money, for example, demarcated "queers" (who paid) from "peers" (whose heterosexual masculinity was protected by being paid). The sexual acts were limited, at least in principle, to oral sex, with boy as penetrator and the homosexual, penetrated. The sexual acts should be "affectively neutral," and only the homosexual participants could acknowledge sexual gratification as a goal. "It should be kept in mind that self-gratification is permitted in the sexual act. Only the motivation to sexual gratification in the transaction is tabooed. But self-gratification must occur without displaying either positive or negative affect toward the queer. In the prescribed form of the role relationship, the boy sells a service for profit and the queer is to accept it without show of emotion."[60]

Finally, violence could be used to reassert boundaries should any of these expectations be violated. Should the "queer" fail to pay, treat the "boy" with overt affection, or attempt penetration, the boy is entitled or even required to defend his masculinity and heterosexuality by beating up the client.

> Put another way, a boy cannot admit that he failed to get money from the transaction unless he used violence toward the fellator and he cannot admit that he sought it as a means of sexual gratification. . . . [T]he *violence is a means of enforcing the peer entrepreneurial norms of the system.* . . . The fellator risks violence, therefore, if he threatens the boy's self-conception by suggesting that the boy may be homosexual and treats him as if he were. . . . The prescriptions that the goal is money, that sexual gratification is not to be sought as an end in the relationship, that affective neutrality be maintained toward the fellator and that only mouth-genital fellation is permitted, all tend to insulate the boy from a homosexual self-definition. So long as he conforms to these expectations, *his "significant others" will not define him as homosexual*; and this is perhaps the most crucial factor in his own self-definition.[61]

In this system of sexual signification, an individual could engage in homosexual acts without assuming the identity of a homosexual. Moreover, the borders between "gay" and "nongay" were maintained by purely conventional means that included a set of customary expectations regarding money, sexual position, emotional affect, and physical violence. In retrospect, the categories of heterosexual and homosexual were already demonstrably arbitrary and thoroughly destabilized in this 1961 account, decades before "queer theory." Reiss's essay is yet another example of how work in what was then called "sexual deviance" had already incorporated several conceptual innovations, the implications of which would eventually contribute to major shifts in the theoretical paradigms governing research on sexuality.[62]

By dismembering deviance in general and sexual deviance in particular, and by producing ethnographic studies of urban gay life, this small sociological literature would have many reverberations. It would be a major influence in the earliest ethnographic research conducted by anthropologists on gay communities in urban North America. In the mid-1970s it would also help instigate a profound, extensive, and aggressive reappropriation of sexuality as a topic by sociologists, historians, and anthropologists.

From Sexual Deviance to Social Construction

> The development of a social-constructionist interpretation of homosexual history is one of the major intellectual achievements of the Stonewall generation of lesbian and gay scholars.
>
> —**Jeffrey Escoffier,** "Inside the Ivory Closet"

> Michael J. Sweet: "But many of Boswell's critics are truly dogmatic in their social constructionism. . . . The response of the rabid constructionists seems to be to ignore anything that doesn't fit their schemata. . . ."
>
> Gayle Rubin: "As I am curious to read what you are calling 'rabid constructionists,' perhaps you could provide some citations?"
>
> Michael J. Sweet: "Well, 'rabid' was polemical of course. Foucault, who started it all, and his epigones—Jeffrey Weeks, David Greenberg, Ken Plummer, David Halperin, just to mention the Anglo-Americans—who have done fine work all, but seem to have this persistent theoretical bias."
>
> —Posts to Queer Studies List at State University of New York, Buffalo, 28–29 July 1994

> It is frustrating for those of us who have been toiling in this particular vineyard since the turn of the 1960s and 1970s to have our early efforts in understanding sexuality in general, and homosexuality in particular, refracted . . . through post-Foucauldian abstractions . . . and then taken up as if the ideas are freshly minted. I am struck . . . by the reception of queer theorists . . . in recent writing about the body and sexuality (especially in literary studies) in the Anglo-Saxon world, when . . . they are not saying anything fundamentally different from what some of us have been trying to say for twenty-five years or so, inspired in large part by a reading of Mary McIntosh's 'The Homosexual Role,' which was first published in 1968.
>
> —**Jeffrey Weeks,** "The 'Homosexual Role' after Thirty Years"

Despite considerable controversy, "social construction of sex theories" became an indispensable paradigm for social-science research on sexuality in the last decades of the twentieth century.[63] The persistence of its attribution primarily to the work of Michel Foucault, particularly volume one of his *The History of Sexuality*, is as puzzling as it is frustrating, given the very clear lineages and citational trails that link early social-construction scholarship to previous work in sociology, anthropology, and social history. Two sociologists, Kenneth Plummer and Mary McIntosh, were significant conduits through which the sociology of sexual deviance was absorbed into emerging work in gay history.

Plummer is a major figure. When *Sexual Stigma: An Interactionist Account* was published in 1975, it joined Gagnon's and Simon's *Sexual Conduct* as a consummate reappraisal of the sociology of sex. Plummer was aware of and cited all the individuals discussed earlier, although he seemed to take much inspiration more directly from Blumer's *Symbolic Interactionism* (1969), Berger's and Luckmann's *The Social Construction of Reality* (1967), and Goffman's *Stigma*. Plummer applied their approaches directly to sexuality, particularly male homosexuality. He later edited two important anthologies — *The Making of the Modern Homosexual* (1981) and *Modern Homosexualities* (1992) — and currently edits the journal *Sexualities*. In his introductory essay in *The Making of the Modern Homosexual*, Plummer provides a brief history of some of the key ideas of social construction, singling out the work of Kinsey, Simon and Gagnon, and Mary McIntosh as particularly formative. A reprint of the McIntosh essay originally published in 1968 in *Social Problems* is also included in the volume.

Mary McIntosh's "The Homosexual Role" is a pivotal essay that links pre-existing work in sociology to the evolving gay histories, social theories, and sexual political activism of the early 1970s.[64] McIntosh provides a dazzling synthesis of the theoretical implications of Kinsey's research, cross-cultural data on homosexuality from anthropology, and the sociological literature on sexual deviance. She notes, for example, the difficulty in studying homosexuality because "behavior patterns cannot be conveniently dichotomized into heterosexual and homosexual," a perspective brilliantly elucidated by Kinsey in *Sexual Behavior in the Human Male*, particularly the extensive and subversive chapter on male homosexuality.[65] Moreover, because homosexuality had been understood as a "condition," "the major research task has been seen as the study of its aetiology." In a particularly memorable formulation, McIntosh comments, "One might as well try to trace the aetiology of 'committee chairmanship' or 'Seventh Day Adventism' as of 'homosexuality.' The vantage point of comparative sociology enables us to see that the conception of homosexuality as a condition is, in itself, a possible object of study."[66]

McIntosh proposes "that the homosexual should be seen as playing a social role rather than as having a condition."[67] In addition, the social role itself is culturally and historically specific. McIntosh reviews ethnographic data on homosexuality (drawn primarily from the Human Relations Area Files and other cross-cultural data discussed in Ford's and Beach's *Patterns of Sexual Behavior*) to establish the cultural specificity of the "homosexual role." "In all these societies," she notes, "there may be much homosexual behavior, but there are no 'homosexuals.'"[68]

McIntosh's greatest contribution, however, was to historicize this "homosexual role." A social role involving a type of person we could call "a homosexual," she maintains, is a fairly recent phenomenon: "Thus a distinct, separate, specialized role of 'homosexual' emerged in England at the end of the seventeenth century, and the conception of homosexuality as a condition which characterized certain individuals and not others is now firmly established in our society."[69] That claim opened a new field of historical inquiry into the conditions and mechanisms and specifications of the development of new kinds of sexual practice, identity, and meaning. This key insight—that homosexuality itself had a history—was profound in its implications. The "discovery" of homosexual social worlds had led to a reconsideration of homosexuality as a social rather than a medical problem. Similarly, the "discovery" of the extent of historical change in what we think of as homosexuality helped precipitate the articulation of a new theoretical framework, what we now call "social construction of sexuality."

Jeffrey Weeks was quick to grasp the implications of McIntosh's sketchy historical outline as well as the ideas developed in the work of Plummer, Gagnon, and Simon. A generation of gay historians and anthropologists met these thinkers and the perspectives embedded in their work through Weeks's early articles and his first book, *Coming Out: Homosexual Politics in Britain, from the Nineteenth Century to the Present* (1977). The first bibliographic entry of *Coming Out* reads: "My general approach has been influenced by the following: Mary McIntosh, 'The Homosexual Role', *Social Problems*, vol. 16, no. 2, Fall 1968; Kenneth Plummer, *Sexual Stigma*, London 1975; J. J. Gagnon and William Simon, *Sexual Conduct: The Social Sources of Human Sexuality*, London 1973."[70]

Coming Out was the first major social history of homosexuality and was also one of the earliest crystallizations of the premises of the social construction of sex paradigm. It was a comprehensive treatment of the position that homosexuality was not a transhistorical category, but rather was a form of same-sex behavior that involved particular types of historically specific persons, identities, and communities. As Weeks put it in his introduction,

> We tend to think now that the word "homosexual" has had an unvarying meaning, beyond time and history. In fact it is itself a product of history, a cultural artifact designed to express a particular concept. . . . The term "homosexuality" was not even invented until 1869. . . . and it did not enter English currency until the 1890s. . . . They [new terms such as *homosexuality* and "*gay*"] are not just new labels for old realities: they point to a changing reality.[71]

One such shift was the emergence of urban homosexual subcultures. *Coming Out* highlighted the historical and theoretical significance of such developments.

> Homosexuality has everywhere existed, but it is only in some cultures that it has become structured into a sub-culture. . . . A sub-culture does not arise in a vacuum. There needs to be both the felt need for a collective solution to a problem (group access to sexuality in this case) and the possibility of its satisfaction. And it is the growth of towns with large groupings of people and relative anonymity which provides the possibility of both. . . . By the mid-century [nineteenth] the sub-culture is much more complex and variegated. The records of the court cases from this period show the spread of a homosexual underworld in the major cities (especially London and Dublin) and the garrison and naval towns. In the 1840s, London had brothels that supplied young boys as well as young girls. . . . A network of meeting-places developed, often located around public lavatories after the mid-century, the occasional public bath, private meeting places and clubs, and straightforward cruising areas. In London, the Regent's Street Quadrant, the Haymarket and areas toward Trafalgar Square and the Strand were favourite haunts for male (as for female) prostitutes, while in the 1880s, the circle of the Alhambra Theatre was a well-known picking-up area, as was part of the Empire Music Hall, the Pavilion, the bar of the St James's and a skating rink in Knightsbridge.[72]

The notion that homosexuality had a history was one of the central insights grounding the early articulations of social-construction frameworks. Previous work in gay history had tended to assume an unvarying homosexuality subjected to variable legal sanctions and cultural assessments. The new gay history, of which Weeks's work was so exemplary, discovered instead a mutable homosexuality that had discontinuities sufficient to make problematic even the application of labels such as "lesbian," "gay," or "homosexual" to persons in other historical periods or cultural contexts. That which we might be tempted to identify as "homosexual" might refer to an assemblage of institutional elements and social relations alien to a modern or Western notion of sexual, much less "homosexual," conduct.

Gay history was recast from the history of homosexuals, or even a unitary notion of homosexuality, to histories of homosexualities or homoerotic sexual practice whose precise social and cultural relationships and valences had to be determined in particular contexts rather than assumed on the basis of those obtaining in modern Western industrialized societies. In addition, the realization that homosexuality was historically and culturally protean had broader implications: a corollary was that other sexualities also had histories.[73] Volume 1 of Michel Foucault's *The History of Sexuality*, entitled *An Introduction*, was published in France in 1976 and in English translation in the United States in 1978. In it, Foucault proposed an expansive model in which all of the sexual "perversions," as well as the concept of sexual perversion, had histories. Eventually, Jonathan Katz, who previously had done trailblazing work in gay history, published an essay and a book on "the invention of heterosexuality."[74]

Like Weeks, I have profound appreciation for Foucault's work. I do not intend to impugn his originality and brilliance or to suggest that his innovations should be situated in some lineage of Anglo-American sociology. There were innumerable theoretical currents within French academia and politics that comprised the intellectual context for Foucault.[75] Nor do I wish to imply a rigid separation between French, British, and U.S. academic developments. Clearly there was a great deal of cross-fertilization as well as convergent theoretical evolution. Moreover, much French "theory" in the 1960s and 1970s was rooted in disciplines such as anthropology, linguistics, and history, even if many of the ideas therein were most successfully introduced into U.S. contexts through philosophy or literary criticism.[76]

I do wish to caution, however, against an all-too-common and oversimplified attribution of many ideas, including social construction of sexuality, to a short list of French thinkers or to a sudden revelatory flash circa 1978. Most component parts that led to social construction and then to queer theory had been in circulation for decades and across a broad range of disciplines, although much of that history appears to be forgotten or seems to be remembered by only a few sociologists. It is interesting in this regard to peruse the citations and index entries of two more recent books on queer theory, Annamarie Jagose's *Queer Theory: An Introduction* (1996) and William Turner's *A Genealogy of Queer Theory* (2000).

Both volumes give accounts of the origins, sources, and development of queer theory, although Turner's is more explicitly historical and more conversant with the role of gay history in the evolution of the queer-theory conceptual apparatus. Jeffrey Weeks is cited and discussed in both books, although Foucault receives more attention. The entries for Weeks in Turner's index fit on one line, whereas the entries for Foucault take up almost an entire page. The bibliographies of both books include Kenneth Plummer and Mary McIntosh, although Plummer is not discussed in the text and there is only a single brief mention of McIntosh.[77] The names of John Gagnon and William Simon do not appear in either bibliography, nor do any of the other authors in *Sexual Deviance*. It seems that the acknowledged debt of Weeks and Plummer to McIntosh has insured her inclusion in lineages of queer theory, but then the trail goes completely cold. The entire sociological tradition in which her own work can be situated is absent.[78]

Turner comments that "Foucault acquired an unearned reputation as the originator of 'work on the social construction of sex' because *The History of Sexuality* had the effect of helping to legitimize the historical study of sex."[79] I tend to agree with that assessment. Foucault's legitimating effect stemmed not only from the undoubted quality of his work but also from his reputation as a major thinker and the fact that in the mid- to late 1970s his homosexuality was little known in the United States. Concurrent developments within gay history were sexually stigmatized, intellectually segregated, and more readily ignored by mainstream academicians.

Turner perceptively observes that "the similarities in the accounts of Weeks and Foucault stemmed from their coincident movement in the same direction, not from Weeks' following Foucault. The relationship among the writings of Weeks, Katz, and Foucault suggested epistemic change, the intellectual manifestation and perpetuation of social, political, and economic changes that produced similar results at disparate locations for disparate scholars."[80] Many scholars were arriving independently at similar formulations within a short period around the mid-1970s, drawing on the available data and applying existing theoretical frameworks to sexuality. As Simon and Gagnon had done a decade earlier in sociology, the theoretical move of "social construction" was to treat sexuality as ordinary and to assume it could be productively addressed using conventional tools, notably those of social history and cultural anthropology. A few short additional examples illustrate some of the preexisting work that made the emergence of "social construction of sexuality" theories not only possible but also highly likely. The question is not why so many people began to approach the study of sexuality in this way at that time, but why they did not do so sooner and with less controversy. As Carole Vance observed, "The specialness of sex is highlighted by this comparison, since a quite ordinary and accepted insight about cultural construction in most areas of human life seems very difficult to understand without distortion when applied to sexuality."[81]

The arguments between social constructionism and essentialism vis-à-vis sexuality are conceptually similar to those in economic anthropology between substantivism and formalism. As Polanyi argued in the 1950s, economic formalism presumed a consistent type of economic actor who could be found in all human societies, a universal set of economic motivations always shaping economic behavior, and an economic domain that in all cases acted upon the societies in which it was located. "Approaching the economy in any of its widely varied aspects, the social scientist is still hampered by an intellectual heritage of man as an entity with an innate propensity to truck, barter and exchange one thing for another. This remains so in spite of all the protestations against 'economic man' and the intermittent attempts to provide a social framework for the economy."[82]

Polanyi observed that such assumptions about economic action were instead a specific product of a particular social form: "This view of the economy . . . grew out of the Western milieu of the eighteenth century and it is admittedly relevant under the institutional arrangements of the market system, since actual conditions here roughly satisfy the requirements set by the economistic postulate. But does this postulate allow us to infer the generality of a market system in the realm of empirical fact? The claim of formal economics to a historically universal applicability answers in the affirmative."[83]

Polanyi argued the negative. He proposed instead that economic motivations were a product of social institutions and varied accordingly. Moreover, economies are what he famously called "instituted processes," that is, human economies are "embedded and enmeshed in institutions, economic and noneconomic. . . . The study of the shifting place occupied by the economy in society is therefore no other than the study of the manner in which the economic process is instituted at different times and places."[84] The decentering of "economic man" and the insistence on economic motivations as structurally produced and specific to the societies in which they are located is conceptually similar to the subsequent process of thinking about how sexuality is socially structured, institutionally shaped, and widely variable. If the psychology of economic decision making was not universal, why not the psychologies of desire? If "the economy" is an instituted process, why not sexuality?

Marxist-inflected British social history was also influential in shaping ways of thinking that were applied first to gender and then to sexuality. E. P. Thompson, in his preface to *The Making of the English Working Class*, comments,

> This book has a clumsy title, but it is one which meets its purpose. *Making*, because it is a study in an active process, which owes as much to agency as to conditioning. The working class did not rise like the sun at an appointed time. It was present at its own making. *Class*, rather than classes. . . . By class

I understand an historical phenomenon, unifying a number of disparate and seemingly unconnected events, both in the raw material of experience and in consciousness. I emphasize that it is an *historical* phenomenon. I do not see class as a "structure," nor even as a "category," but as something which in fact happens . . . in human relationships.[85]

Thompson's insistence on class as a historically constructed formation rather than a universal classification and his emphasis on the produced quality of what appear to be unvarying human experiences prefigure subsequent approaches to gender and sexuality. A superb example is his essay on "Time, Work-Discipline, and Industrial Capitalism," which was first published in 1967. There, Thompson "deconstructed" our modern experience of time, and showed the ways in which the requirements and accomplishments of industrialization profoundly reshaped something as timeless as "time."[86]

By the early 1970s, feminist anthropologists and historians were among those actively dismantling the prevailing notions of gender along similar lines, and a tendency to extend such analyses to sexuality was immanent in much of this material.[87] One example is the work of Judith Walkowitz on the social history of Victorian prostitution. In her work, prostitution is no longer an unchanging and universal vice, the "oldest profession," but rather a shifting institutional complex. An entire chapter of *Prostitution and Victorian Society* is devoted to "The Making of an Outcast Group: Prostitutes and Working Women in Plymouth and Southampton."[88] The emphasis is on changing social formations, and on how they are produced by social action in specific historical conditions and cultural parameters.

These examples could be readily multiplied. Throughout the 1970s a number of works created a new theoretical paradigm by applying, with increasing consistency and effectiveness, the ordinary tools of history, anthropology, and sociology to sexualities. By the summer of 1979, the *Radical History Review* put out a special issue on "Sexuality in History" that included two theoretical essays articulating the emergent "social construction" perspective: Bert Hansen's "The Historical Construction of Homosexuality" and Robert Padgug's "Sexual Matters: On Conceptualizing Sexuality in History."[89] As Carole Vance observed, "Social construction theory in the field of sexuality proposed an extremely outrageous idea. It suggested that one of the last remaining outposts of the 'natural' in our thinking was fluid and changeable, the product of human action and history rather than the invariant result of the body, biology, or an innate sex drive."[90] Social construction work has refined the theoretical bases for social approaches to sexual behavior. Although it built upon developments in history, anthropology, and sociology, social construction insisted on more thoroughly social approaches than its predecessors.[91]

Since then, this new theoretical consolidation has inspired a vast outpouring of work that has continuously destabilized universal sexual categories, and increasingly placed sexualities into history, society, and culture.[92] Yet it is important to remember that such perspectives were grounded in older literatures, and have grounded in turn a newer body of work that includes what is now called queer theory.

From Sociology to Anthropology

> Anthropologists have ignored homosexuality in Western societies, and, what is worse, have barely taken note of it as it manifests itself in primitive groups. . . . Ford and Beach (1951) could only generally distill from anthropologists' reports societies which simply (1) have homosexuality present or not (as ethnographers saw it) and (2) have condoned or condemned it. Such has been the Science of Man's attention to a most obvious aspect of human behavior.
>
> —**David Sonenschein**, "Homosexuality as a Subject of Anthropological Inquiry"

When John Gagnon and William Simon were at Indiana University in the 1960s, they hired David Sonenschein, a graduate student in the anthropology department, to conduct a study on the gay male community in Chicago. Sonenschein wrote the earliest articles from within anthropology that pointed to the need to do research on contemporary homosexual populations in industrialized countries. His essay on "Homosexuality as a Subject of Anthropological Inquiry," written in 1966, is a remarkably prescient document. It reviewed the state of anthropological research on the subject, sketched out a program for future work, and summarized many of the repetitive themes and problems that have bedeviled ethnographic work in this area.

Like virtually all social scientists who ventured into the area of sex before the early 1970s, Sonenschein had to confront the hegemonic models.

> Rather than to establish a claim of validity or rationale that would enable an anthropologist to professionally approach the subject of homosexuality (or to make him feel more comfortable in doing so), this paper is presented more as a simple plea for research and as a departure point for discussion. . . . Quite obviously, homosexuality has traditionally and predominantly been considered as a research problem for psychology. . . . The three

main considerations in dealing with homosexuality by psychologists have been (1) its origin or cause (2) its ongoing operation, and (3) its treatment and ultimate cure. All research has assumed the locus of the individual as the basic, final, and exclusive unit of study.[93]

Sonenschein went on to observe the existence of the small but important sociological literature that had appeared by the mid-1960s and which would be anthologized in *Sexual Deviance*, the first of the Simon and Gagnon collections, published the year after Sonenschein's essay.

> Stemming from recent attention to delinquency and the development of a sociology of delinquent behavior, various writers have had occasion to use, for example, theories relating to reference group behavior and to consider homosexuals as forming a minority group. . . . With these newer considerations, later writings have assumed a somewhat greater depth and broadness of scope. . . . The dynamics of social roles and interactions within and among homosexual communities provide excellent opportunities for the applications of small group . . . methods.[94]

Sonenschein pointed to the relative neglect of the subject within anthropology. In reviewing the literature available on the subject, he noted behaviors in non-Western cultures that were "homosexual-like" or "would appear in our society as homosexual tendencies," but he stopped short of describing shamans or berdache as homosexuals. He distinguished between homosexual behavior and cross-gender practices, a distinction that is still too often neglected.

Sonenschein noted that "homosexuality emerges as being in reality a group phenomenon as well as an individual one" and called for

> the application of an anthropological investigation of homosexuality in contemporary Western society . . . [T]he anthropological approach assumes that homosexual groups and individuals transmit, learn, share, create, and change the content of various forms (such as speech, dress, behavior, artifacts) so as to establish and maintain what can be called a relatively distinct "culture." . . . Here, all the interests of cultural and social anthropologists would prevail: social organization, economics, communication, social control and norms, world-views and myths, demography, social and cultural change, material culture, enculturation and socialization.[95]

Sonenschein concluded with the observation that most previous data on homosexuals were based on a population of *patients*, many of whom were in therapy by court order, and that anthropological research would result in a different perspective on homosexuality. He advised attention to homosexual subcultures. "Among humans," he noted, "at least in the Western Urban tradition, homosexual behavior manifests itself in special kinds of culturally distinct groups and artifacts."[96]

Virtually all the major points in this essay with regard to homosexuality can be applied to many other forms of contemporary erotic diversity. During the 1960s, Sonenschein had set out a research program for the anthropological study of homosexuality and, by extension, other sexual populations in modern, Western, urban societies. With one equally extraordinary exception—Esther Newton's *Mother Camp*—it would take quite awhile for Sonenschein's insights to have an impact on the field of anthropology.

Mother Camp

> It should be noted that by "women" I mean the signs and symbols, some obvious and some subtle, of the socially defined category in American Culture. On the cross-cultural level, it is obvious that female impersonators look like American "women," not like Hopi "women" or Chinese peasant "women." What is not so obvious is the relationship *within* American culture between biology, concepts of biology ("nature"), and sex-role symbols. It seems self-evident that persons classified as "men" would have to create artificially the image of a "woman," but of course "women" create the image "artificially" too.
>
> On the one hand there is the "gentleman deviant." . . . At this pole we find the "masculine," "respectable" homosexuals, the leaders of most homophile organizations and so on. At the opposite pole there are the persons who most visibly and flagrantly embody the stigma, "drag queens," men who dress and act "like women." Professional drag queens are, therefore, professional homosexuals; they represent the stigma of the gay world. Not surprisingly, as professional homosexuals, drag queens find their occupation to be a source of dishonor, especially in the relation to the straight world. Their situation in the gay world is more complex. The clever drag queen possesses skills that are widely distributed and prized in the gay world: verbal facility and wit, a sense of "camp" (homosexual humor and taste). . . . In exclusively gay settings such as bars and parties, drag queens may be almost lionized.
>
> —**Esther Newton,** *Mother Camp*

In the early 1970s only two anthropologists—Sonenschein and Esther Newton—could be found among the slightly more numerous sociologists producing ethnographic work on gay populations. Newton's 1972 *Mother Camp*, a monograph on female impersonators, was the first book-length ethnography of a modern, Western, urban gay population. *Mother Camp* focuses on the more specialized subgroup of professional female impersonators, but Newton's observations of gay community life, social structure, and economics were insightful, original, and foundational.

Mother Camp was based on Newton's 1968 dissertation for the department of anthropology at the University of Chicago, where her advisor was David Schneider. Newton was fortunate to be at Chicago and especially to work with Schneider. She has recalled the extraordinary and unusual quality of Schneider's support for graduate students with then unconventional demographics. Schneider was

> a blessing for those of his students like me who were marginal and offbeat, for in addition to the white males whom everyone thought would succeed, Schneider was attracted to students like closet gays and struggling women who could not easily attract the support of the powerful. I well recall when Schneider reported to me on the year-end departmental review of my progress; the professors relayed to me through Schneider that my wearing pants manifested a lack of commitment to the anthropological vocation. . . . In the Schneiders' living room, by contrast, I was told that wearing dresses was neither here nor there on the ultimate scale of value.[97]

Schneider was also supportive of unconventional research topics.

> When I showed David some field notes and my excitement, he encouraged me to make female impersonators the subject of my doctoral dissertation. . . . He helped me to develop the intellectual tools to do the work, and just as important, he was prepared to back me up with his departmental clout. . . . Gays were then looked on within social science as the object solely of psychological, medical, or even criminological study. . . . What he [Schneider] imparted to me, more in his office and his home than in the classroom, was that female impersonators (about whom he knew nothing more than what I told him) were a group of human beings and so necessarily had a culture worth studying. The insight that gays were not just a category of sick isolates, but a group, and so had a culture, was a breathtaking leap whose daring is hard to recapture now.[98]

Newton noted in her discussion of field methods in *Mother Camp*, there was "to date no full ethnography of the homosexual community, much less the drag world, so that from the beginning I was 'flying blind.' Moreover, very few ethnographies (except for the early community studies) have been attempted in America, so that my model of field work procedure was largely based on non-urban precedents."[99] When Newton began to discuss her work with Schneider, however, he directed her to the literature in the sociology of deviance dealing with sexuality.[100] There was little anthropological literature upon which to draw, but Newton cites and productively used the ethnographic work of Hooker and Sonenschein, the perspective on stigma of Goffman, the sex research of Kinsey, the general theoretical orientation of Simon and Gagnon, the economic observations of Leznoff and Westley, and the notion of a "deviant career" developed with such thoroughness by Becker and others. If there was little direct help in anthropology, there was a great deal in the extant sociology of "deviance."

Mother Camp is a deceptively straightforward book whose sophistication and subtlety becomes more remarkable with each reading. It is laden with astute observations about the social organization of gay life in the 1960s, the social and physical architecture of gay performance, and the internal stylistic and sexual differentiation of gay populations as well as specific theatrical techniques of professional female impersonation. But *Mother Camp* is most profoundly effective in three areas. It prefigures notions of gender as "performed"; provides an analysis of the political economies of homosexuality in the 1960s; and links types of performance to economic stratification, political orientation, and hierarchies of social status.

Newton's work focused on a small group of female impersonators who were paid, worked on stage and in theaters, and considered themselves to be entertainment professionals. Thus there was always a performance aspect to their drag. Newton broadened this notion of gender performance by observing that all drag, "whether formal, informal, or professional, has a theatrical structure and style."[101] This distinguishing characteristic of drag, she argued, was its "group character." The performance of gender required an audience. Moreover, she saw how the gender reversal of drag "questions the 'naturalness' of the sex-role system in toto; if sex-role behavior can be achieved by the 'wrong' sex, it logically follows that it is in reality also achieved, not inherited, by the 'right' sex."[102] Moreover, "drag implies that sex role, and by extension, role in general is something superficial, which can be manipulated."[103]

It is fascinating that Newton used stage performance to make points about ordinary activities that anticipate the more refined formulations in contemporary work on gender, particularly that of Judith Butler. Butler uses more philosophically developed notions of performativity, drawn in part from speech-act theory. But she cites Newton's *Mother Camp* and also uses drag and gender inversion to make points about the way gender is interactively produced.[104]

Although Butler's work has facilitated a contemporary reevaluation of Newton's early articulations of the relationships of gender to drag and performance, *Mother Camp*'s contributions to the political economies of sexualities have been largely ignored. Newton built on the observations of Leznoff and Westley to take exploration of the relationships between sexual disclosure and economic position to new levels of intricacy. She elaborated on their distinction between secret and overt homosexuals, but used the slightly modified terminology of "overt" and "covert."

> The overts live their entire lives within the context of the [gay] community; the coverts live their entire nonworking lives within it. That is, the coverts are "straight" during working hours, but most social activities are conducted with and with reference to other homosexuals. . . . Overt-covert distinctions correlate to some extent with social class, but by no means invariably. . . . Covert means only that one cannot be publicly identified by the straight world and its representatives, such as bosses, co-workers, family, landladies, teachers, and the man on the street. One hides, or attempts to hide, one's homosexual identity *from straight people*. In Goffman's terminology, one attempts to manage one's discreditability through control of personal front and restriction about one's personal life.[105]

At the time of Newton's study in the late 1960s, gay communities in North America were less economically developed and institutionally differentiated than they would become in the 1970s. Thus she observed that the gay community "has an economics but no economy. Strictly speaking, the gay world has no class system. Nevertheless, gay life has recognizable social strata that are accorded differential value. People speak about 'high-class,' 'middle-class,' and 'low-class' bars, parties, clothes and people."[106] And the category of "low-class" was not a purely economic designation; rather, "low status homosexuals who [were] socially avoided and morally despised by the middles and uppers" were often those who, "in their flamboyant stylization and distinctive adaptations to extreme alienation," were extremely overt in self-presentation.[107] There was a set of assumed relationships between class, stigma, and overtness, and a resulting set of mechanisms intended to create social boundaries and manage the dangers of proximity to economic or social ruin.

All of these vectors intersect in the large status difference between two kinds of drag performers: professional impersonators, on the one hand, and "street fairies" on the other. "Street fairies are jobless young homosexual men who publicly epitomize the homosexual stereotype and are the underclass of the gay world. . . . The stage pattern, on the other hand, *segregates* the stigma from the personal by limiting it to the stage context as much as possible. The work is viewed as a profession with goals and standards."[108] Female impersonators were, in effect, "professional homosexuals," who could make a living from overt expression of stigmatized identities. On the one hand, they represented the stigma of homosexuality; on the other, they were public figures celebrated for their glamour, and occupied a relatively high-status position among those performing drag.

Professional performers looked down on street fairies and attempted to maintain social distance from them. Street drag was "tacky," meaning "cheap, shoddy, or of poor quality. . . . 'Tacky' is a pejorative term. No single word was used more consistently by the older, more show-business oriented performers to describe the appearance of lower-status street oriented performers. . . . 'Tacky' is thus indirectly a class descriptive term."[109]

Such disapproval of obvious expressions of stigmatized and discrediting homosexuality was situational and mobile.

> This may be viewed as a hierarchy of stigmatization, or "obviousness." Any particular group will tend to draw the line just below itself. For instance, female impersonators are considered by most homosexuals to be too overt. They are consistently placed on the low end of the continuum of stigmatization, and one of the first things that female impersonators must learn is not to recognize anyone on the street or in any other public place unless they are recognized first. Yet female impersonators who believe themselves to be less overt try to avoid public association with female impersonators whom they consider "too obvious," and very few female impersonators will associate publicly with "street fairies," boys who wear make up on the street, because "there's no point in wearing a sign. I believe I can pass." Those on the low end resent those above them.[110]

The marginal conditions of the pre-Stonewall gay economy made the maintenance of a high-status performing career somewhat perilous. The performance venues themselves were stratified. At the low end was the gay bar, always vulnerable to the police. "Any gay bar is living on borrowed time, and neither the owners nor clientele can count on permanence. Therefore, gay bars operate by and large on a quick-money policy. This is most extreme where police pressure is most intense and less pronounced where owners can count on some degree of stability. But quick-money policy means that owners invest little in plant, keep overhead and operating expenses low, and try to reap quick profits."[111] As a result, the bars tended to be small facilities in poor condition, the salaries for performers low, and "job tenure [was] nil" because the "bar could be closed at any time."[112]

Higher up on the scale of status, facility, and compensation was the "tourist club," where a mostly straight clientele comes to see "exotic" entertainment. Such clubs have a larger base of customers and are subject to far less punitive police attention; they "are stable institutions by gay bar standards. The stability . . . allows the tourist bar to be at least three times the size of the average gay bar. Not only is the stage larger to accommodate a larger and more lavish show, but the floor space is larger to pack in more people. . . . From the point of view of the performer, working in a tourist club means working in a bigger and more elaborate show. . . . In terms of physical amenities (dressing room), stage facilities (lighting, curtains, band), and actual time spent on stage, the show at the tourist club is probably easier on the performers. However, performers in a tourist club are freaks or clowns up for display to a hostile audience."[113] Thus tourist bars offer greater compensation and conditions of work at the cost of potentially damaged self-esteem.

The social marginality and scarcity of job sites for impersonators meant that even the higher-status performers often lived precariously close to disaster. "The manager is the man the impersonators most fear," Newton observes, "for he has a great deal of control over them, ultimately hiring and firing. The impersonators have no way to fight back; no way to appeal. . . . None of the performers worked under contract, so that they could be (and were) fired at a moment's notice. No one knew when the ax might fall. Requirements for job holding were nowhere formalized or even made explicit, although performers knew that seriously antagonizing the manager in any way could mean dismissal."[114] As a result, the actual line of demarcation between the more respectable and prosperous impersonators and the more disreputable and impoverished street fairies was perilously thin. Many professionals had been street fairies before becoming impersonators, and "if they lost their jobs or quit, they had no place to go but back to the street. When stage impersonators talked about quitting, they said they wanted to 'go legit.' But when I asked a street performer what drag queens do when they are out of work, he said, 'They get their butts out on the street, my dear, and they sell their little twats for whatever they can get for them.'"[115] The actual economic instability and permeable boundaries contrast with the carefully cultivated symbolic differentiation between stage and street.

Newton's descriptive richness and analytic elegance wove together and elaborated on many of the themes of the work that preceded her own. These include Park's observations on the importance of cities for sexual subcultures, Hooker's and Achilles's emphasis on the social centrality of bars to gay communities and the role of the police in setting the parameters of homosexual social institutions, and the political economies of the closet and sexual disclosure first articulated by Leznoff and Westley. Newton explores in much more luxuriant detail the complex internal differentiation of gay populations noted by previous observers. She productively expands on Goffman's and Becker's dismemberment of the moral hierarchies of deviance, Simon's and Gagnon's appropriation of the study of sexuality into the disciplinary reach of the social sciences, and the prefiguring of social-construction theories implicit in Simon, Gagnon, and Reiss. *Mother Camp* cites Becker, Goffman, Hooker, Gagnon, Simon, Sonenschein, Leznoff, and Westley. Newton skillfully brought their tools and tactical moves to bear in what is ultimately a masterful synthesis linking gender, class, stigma, self-presentation, and the political economies of marginal sexualities in the period before Stonewall.

Newton's work is situated within a long sociological tradition and stands at the beginning of a newer lineage of anthropologists. Although *Mother Camp* should have signaled a new wave of work on homosexuality within anthropology, it was instead largely ignored and followed by thundering silence for a painfully long hiatus. For many years, *Mother Camp* stood alone, an exceptional document with no apparent successors or company. It would be almost two decades before there was much anthropological literature on urban gay communities in the United States.[116]

In 1979, Deborah Goleman Wolf's study of *The Lesbian Community* was published. The same year, Stephen Murray's important essay on homosexuals as "quasi-ethnic" communities was published, albeit in a journal of sociology. In 1980, Kenneth Read's *Other Voices: The Style of a Male Homosexual Tavern* appeared. A great deal of important work was published during the 1980s, for example, Blackwood's edited collection *The Many Faces of Homosexuality* (1986) and a burgeoning literature on AIDS. Gilbert Herdt's *Guardians of the Flutes* (1981) was a milestone in the anthropology of homosexual practice, although not about a modern urban population.

It was only in the 1990s, however, almost two decades after the publication of *Mother Camp*, that a substantial literature began to accumulate. Just how sudden that shift was can be seen by two articles in the *Annual Review of Anthropology*. In 1987 a review essay on "The Cross-Cultural Study of Human Sexuality" could still comment that "the most glaring omission in professional research on sexual practice is certainly in the area of homosexuality. Although early attempts were made to describe same sex patterns of arousal and attraction, this topic quickly went 'underground' and is only today receiving the serious attention it deserves."[117]

By 1993, the growth of lesbian and gay research within anthropology was so dramatic that the journal included Kath Weston's review essay on the subject, a mere six years after the 1987 review complained about the paucity of such material.

Publications since 1990 would include Weston's *Families We Choose: Lesbians, Gays, Kinship* (1991) and Gilbert Herdt's edited collection *Gay Culture in America* (1992). Three landmark studies by anthropologists were finally published in 1993, after many years of anticipation: *Boots of Leather, Slippers of Gold: The History of a Lesbian Community* (in Buffalo) by Elizabeth Kennedy and Madeline Davis; *Lesbian Mothers* by Ellen Lewin; and Esther Newton's study of *Cherry Grove, Fire Island*. Since 1993, an exponential increase has occurred in the number of publications, resulting in a rich and substantial ethnographic literature on gay, lesbian, bisexual, transgender, and other erotically demarcated populations.

Legacies and Lessons

My own work is deeply indebted to scholars such as Esther Newton, John Gagnon, and William Simon. They allowed me to contemplate doing ethnographic work on sexual communities in urban North America at a time when such projects were outside the accepted parameters of anthropological research. The corpus of ideas they conveyed had sources I did not know, but provided intellectual frameworks for thinking as a social scientist about marginal and stigmatized erotic populations. When I finally did encounter Robert Park and Howard Becker, for example, they were shockingly familiar, because their fingerprints were all over other texts I had read.

My research on urban gay communities has given me an ever-greater appreciation of the older ethnographic texts, and I continue to be impressed by their conceptual sophistication and descriptive richness. The importance of bars to gay and lesbian social life in the mid-twentieth century may not seem at first glance very interesting or exciting. Gay bars are so familiar that it is easy to forget that bars in the modern sense did not really exist in the United States until after the repeal of Prohibition, when taverns and cafés were restructured as licensed premises; that liquor-license regulations have powerfully shaped urban social practice; and that the escalating price of urban real estate and increasing availability of Internet-based contact may be undermining the viability and centrality of bars as gay social institutions. Gay bars may be vanishing or at least eclipsed institutions, but they have been as characteristic of mid-twentieth-century homosexuality as were Big Men to political systems of highland New Guinea or large-scale trading circuits to the indigenous peoples of the South Pacific. Knowing this about gay bars and thinking about their shifting significance is not as trivial as it may first appear. Similarly, the complicated intersections of class, race, social status, income, sexual orientation, gender identity, job segregation, and stylistic expression beg for further exploration.

Because the idioms of previous decades may seem dated, their theoretical subtlcty and originality is often underestimated. Many ideas articulated in these texts continue to resonate in contemporary scholarship, however, even when their sources are obscured. The work of these authors permeates social construction paradigms and helped to assemble them. This literature has been key in wresting intellectual authority over sexuality from its monopolization by medicine and psychiatry, firmly establishing the intellectual (if not institutional) claims of social science in the field of sexual studies. Finally, in both theoretical innovations and ethnographic contributions, the texts discussed here have been major forces in displacing "perversion" models of sexual variation, which presume pathology, with "diversity" models, which imply moral equality and leveled legitimacy.

It is common to mistake the place where we first encounter a theoretical revelation as its original manifestation, and to confuse one's own intellectual biography with some more public sequence of events. In this essay, I hope that I am not inadvertently making the same error and confusing my paths of discovery with a general history. I certainly do not want to be proposing some new, oversimplified tale of origin for those I have criticized. Nonetheless, much of what we now take for granted in the anthropology of sexuality and homosexuality owes a great deal to an odd assortment of urban sociologists, historians of homosexuality, and brave, pioneering ethnographers who went where almost no one had gone before and undertook considerable risks to do so. There is a great deal to learn from looking back and seeing how much they did. If their contributions have been so readily forgotten, this is less a commentary on the work itself than on the extraordinary limitations of the intellectual and institutional circumstances in which they operated.

Geologies of Queer Studies

It's Déjà Vu All Over Again

14

I thought I would use the occasion of this lecture to think about queer knowledges and the conditions of their production. I want to use an experience I keep having with GLBTQ (gay, lesbian, bisexual, transgender, and queer) knowledges to accentuate the continuing need to build stable institutional forms that can insure the ongoing development, preservation, and transmission of such knowledge. This is the déjà vu to which my title refers: the more I explore these queer knowledges, the more I find out how much we have already forgotten, rediscovered, and promptly forgotten again. I myself have attempted to reinvent the wheel on several occasions. I want to think about why this has happened with such annoying regularity. A major problem is that we still lack sufficient organizational resources to routinize the conservation of previously attained knowledges and their conveyance to new generations.

So if you will indulge me, I'll play Mr. Peabody and invite you into my personal Way Back Machine. It is around 1970, and I am a brand-new baby dyke. The first thing I want to do is to seduce the object of my desire; the second is to read a good lesbian novel. Having little luck with the former project, I head over to the graduate library at the University of Michigan and look up lesbianism in the card catalogue (this was before the advent of computerized catalogues). There were two entries under the subject heading of "lesbian." One

Chapter 14 was an excerpt from the Twelfth Annual David R. Kessler Lecture delivered at the Graduate Center, City University of New York, 5 December 2003, and published in *CLAGS News* 14, no. 2 (summer 2004): 6–10.

was Radclyffe Hall's *The Well of Loneliness*. The other was a book by Jess Stern called *The Grapevine*, a semi-sensational account of the Daughters of Bilitis (DOB), the San Francisco-based lesbian-rights organization founded in the early period of homophile activism in the mid-1950s.[1] I did not yet know that DOB had produced a small journal called *The Ladder*, nor that *The Ladder* was still being published, albeit not by DOB.

Since the library at the University of Michigan was (and is) one of the greatest in North America, I concluded that there was very little written on the topic or else there was a screaming need for a lesbian bibliography. I decided to produce such a bibliography for my senior honors thesis, and spent the next few months of my life consumed with trying to locate any and all written sources on lesbianism.

The first step was to inquire at the reference desk why there was so little listed on lesbianism and ask if anyone had suggestions for finding more. I was met with blank stares. But over the next few weeks, as I was working in the card catalogue, I'd sense a presence at my shoulder. This would be some discreet reference librarian quietly whispering that I might be interested in the section on women philanthropists, or the books on women in prisons. The books on philanthropy were indeed full of accounts of wealthy bisexual women romancing their way through the distaff side of the social register. The literature on incarceration was full of reports of prison passion written by middle-class social workers scandalized by the erotic lives of the mostly poor and working-class women under their supervision (interracial liaisons provoking special consternation).

However, my big research breakthrough occurred accidentally on a visit to Boston. I stumbled across a copy of *The Ladder* in a small bookshop near Harvard Square. I immediately wrote a letter to *The Ladder*, explaining that I was working on a bibliography of lesbian literature and asking if anyone there could help. The editor was one Gene Damon, who was of course Barbara Grier. She replied with a sharp rebuke, informing me that such a bibliography already existed. This was *The Lesbian in Literature*, by Gene Damon (Grier's pseudonym) and Lee Stuart, published in 1967. I was also duly chastised for my ignorance of Jeannette Foster's even earlier book, *Sex Variant Women in Literature* (1956). Grier's mighty typewriter could have taken the hide off a rhino, and it certainly knocked some of the wind out of my youthful enthusiasm. I am happy to report that after this initially testy encounter, Barbara relented, generously sharing her extraordinarily detailed and vast knowledge of the hidden riches of lesbian texts. However, the point of this tale is how difficult it was circa 1970 to find such publications. The work had been done, but it was largely inaccessible. The mechanisms for systematic impartation and acquisition of lesbian knowledge were at best rudimentary.

After hearing that there were existing lesbian bibliographies, I returned to the reference desk to see if I could get them through interlibrary loan. A few days later, one of those probably queer reference librarians led me to another gateway into the hidden world of LGBTQ scholarship. He suggested I go up to Special Collections and ask for the Labadie Collection. Since the holdings of Labadie were catalogued separately they did not appear in the main catalogue. But he thought some of the materials for which I was searching were up with the rest of the rare books on the seventh floor. I followed this breadcrumb trail upstairs to the desk of Ed Weber.

The Labadie Collection was founded in 1911 by a Detroit anarchist named Joseph Labadie. The collection was initially focused on anarchist writings, but had gradually expanded to include social-protest literatures, especially those considered "extremist." When Ed Weber was hired as curator, in 1960, he began to collect homophile publications and gay materials. As a result, Labadie became one of the most extensive repositories of homosexual publications in the country at a time when most university and public libraries dismissed them as pornographic trash. It turned out that almost everything for which I had been searching was indeed upstairs in Labadie, a wonderland of homophile scholarship. The collection had it all: Damon's and Stuart's *The Lesbian in Literature*, Foster's *Sex Variant Women in Literature*, some early bibliographies compiled by Marion Zimmer Bradley, and an almost complete run of *The Ladder*.

I pretty much moved into Labadie for the remainder of my undergraduate career in order to devour these documents. It still astonishes me how much these women knew about lesbian history and how difficult it was for me to find out what they knew. At the time I was fairly oblivious to gay male publications, so I did not explore Labadie's equally impressive collections of *Mattachine Review*, *One*, and the *One Institute Quarterly*. But I discovered later, when my interests broadened, that these too contained huge compilations of gay history, bibliography, social analysis, and political critique.

I was also unaware that my own interests were part of a large wave of scholarship emerging out of the gay-liberation movement. I have only understood in retrospect how much my cohort built on the trails charted by our homophile predecessors, even as we often dismissed them for ostensibly lacking theoretical sophistication or terminological precision. While I was preparing these remarks, I emailed several of my old friends who were also doing gay research at the time to ask how they found direction and source material.

Everyone acknowledged significant debts to homophile scholarship, organizational records, and individual collections.

It is not surprising that much of the material for John D'Emilio's early book on the homophile movement came from publications such as *Mattachine Review*, *The Ladder*, and the records of the New York chapter of the Mattachine Society. But it is interesting where John found these periodicals and other documentary evidence. Many of the records he consulted had been amassed and preserved by individuals, mainly Jim Kepner in his Los Angeles apartment and Don Lucas in his San Francisco garage. John also consulted the vertical files at the Kinsey Institute, and he visited Ann Arbor to utilize Labadie's collection of periodicals. For his magisterial *Gay American History* (1976), Jonathan Ned Katz also relied heavily on the bibliographic largesse produced by the early homophile press. When I queried Jonathan about his treasure maps, he mentioned *The Lesbian in Literature*, *Mattachine Review*, *One*, and several gay male bibliographies, especially those of Noel Garde.

Jonathan's email made me want to take a closer look at Garde, and I had already decided in preparation for this lecture to spend some time with the old homophile publications. I was fortuitously back at Michigan and able to return to my undergraduate haunt to try to squeeze out more insight from the voices of queer scholars past. I had missed much of their significance thirty years ago because of a lack of context. I read these texts differently now, because I know so much more than I did then, and can filter them through the lens of work such as that of Jonathan Katz, John D'Emilio, Allan Bérubé, Jim Steakley, Estelle Freedman, and William Eskridge (among others). There are certain common themes and repetitive subjects. An individual who read through *The Ladder*, *One*, *Mattachine Review*, and the *One Institute Quarterly* would have had a pretty firm grasp of the important issues, legal cases, government reports, and polemics affecting gay life in the 1950s and 1960s.

Bibliography was a central shared obsession. In addition to Marion Zimmer Bradley's detailed and thoughtful review of Jeannette Foster in its May 1957 issue, *The Ladder* featured Bradley's regular bibliographic column called "Lesbiana." Barbara Grier eventually took on the "Lesbiana" column, the contents of which provided much of the material for *The Lesbian in Literature*. Similarly, in 1957 the *Mattachine Review* started a serial "Bibliography on Homosexual Subjects." In 1959 Noel Garde published *The Homosexual in Literature*, billed as a "chronological bibliography circa 700 B.C.–1958," and in 1964 Vantage Press brought out his book *From Jonathan to Gide: The Homosexual in History*. At the time of their publication, the Garde and Damon/Stuart compendia were the state of the art in gay bibliography. While my younger self would have critiqued this kind of work for its failure to interrogate the category of "homosexual," I now understand such texts as a considerable achievement. Moreover, such compilations made possible the application of the theoretical armamentaria of late 1960s social history, cultural anthropology, and urban sociology to GLBTQ subject matter.

But what were their sources? How did researchers such as Garde and Grier find out what they knew? Both obviously were passionate in their bibliographic zeal, and both also were able to build on previous work. Grier and Bradley drew heavily on Jeannette Foster. Foster, in turn, was a reference librarian by trade who worked at the Kinsey Institute from 1948 to 1952.[2] She was thus able to utilize the incomparable collection amassed by Kinsey. Foster followed many leads, but it is clear from her own citations that she also carefully mined the sexological texts of Havelock Ellis and Magnus Hirschfeld, as well as the contemporaneous writings of John Addington Symonds and Edward Carpenter. In many respects, Foster's book is a kind of hinge text, linking the homophile generation to earlier accumulations of queer knowledge in the late-nineteenth and early-twentieth centuries.

Similarly, Donald Webster Cory's 1951 book *The Homosexual in America* is a major conduit of literature produced before the First World War to the post–Second World War cohort of homophile intellectuals. Noel Garde explicitly acknowledges Cory's references, as well as a bibliography produced by the New York chapter of the Mattachine Society. *The Homosexual in America* has many problematic aspects, but it also set an agenda for much of the homophile scholarship it preceded and prefigured.[3] Cory included every major U.S. government document pertaining to homosexuality, including "The Employment of Homosexuals and Other Sex Perverts in Government" and the Veterans Administration regulations dealing with military personnel dishonorably discharged for homosexuality. *The Homosexual in America* also listed the legal statutes regulating homosexual activities in what were then all forty-eight states. Cory's own bibliography and list of sources is still remarkable, and he included as a special appendix a "Check List of Novels and Dramas" pertaining to homosexuality. Foster too had read, used, and cited Cory, and I suspect the bibliographies printed in *Mattachine Review* began by updating Cory's work.

Cory, in turn, drew a great deal of his material from another of the great sedimentary layers of queer knowledge, the one that accumulated in Britain and in continental Europe in the late-nineteenth and early-twentieth centuries. I often call this layer "late-nineteenth-century sexology," but that shorthand does not do justice to the complex ways in which the medically credentialed sexologists, the stigmatized homosexual intellectuals, and the mostly anonymous but active members of the burgeoning queer communities engaged in a complicated tango of communication and publication, as detailed in Harry Oosterhuis's brilliant work on Richard von Krafft-Ebing.[4] It might be better to think of this large body of work as a fusion of medical texts with the writings of homosexual (or invert) intellectuals who assembled polemical resources with which to articulate early critiques of sexual injustice and persecution. These resources included biographies of famous homosexuals, material gleaned from the Greek and Latin classics, personal testimony about the effects of blackmail and sexual deprivation, ethnographic reports, data on animal behavior, observations about homosexual community life, and some of the earliest modern compilations of queer bibliography. Taken as a whole, the body of work we call sexology is an intensely collaborative enterprise between the doctors and the perverts. It resulted in a massive consolidation of a major stratum of queer knowledge—sometimes fruitfully mined, sometimes ignored, dismissed, or forgotten. But one thing has become abundantly clear: just as my gay-liberation cohort built on the publications and archival resources assembled by our immediate predecessors, homophile-era researchers drew on previous strata, particularly the "sexological" one.

Among the most important sexologists were Richard von Krafft-Ebing, Havelock Ellis, and Magnus Hirschfeld. The key polemics included the writings of Karl Heinrich Ulrichs, Edward Carpenter, and John Addington Symonds.[5] Magnus Hirschfeld was, like Ellis and Krafft-Ebing, a credentialed physician. He was also a brilliant polemicist, whose own homosexuality was sometimes used to undermine his medical authority. Ulrichs and Carpenter lacked medical credentials but were heavily cited in the medical texts. Symonds's role is especially complex. His name was removed from *Sexual Inversion* at the insistence of his estate, but he contributed a great deal of the historical information and much of the analysis that we attribute to Ellis.[6] Symonds's own work contains incisive reviews of the medical literature, in which he is cited in turn.[7]

Magnus Hirschfeld's thousand-page tome, *The Homosexuality of Men and Women* (1914), is emblematic of the attainments of this period. Hirschfeld intended a complete account of everything known on the topic of homosexuality. He incorporated the work of other medical sexologists, lay writers such as Symonds, Carpenter, and Ulrichs, and his own primary research. The second part of the book, called "The Homosexuality of Men and Women as Sociological Occurrence," is particularly compelling. It includes the results of one of the first statistical surveys of homosexuals, as well as chapters on homosexuality at different class levels and in different countries. Hirschfeld's book also contains an extraordinary report on urban gay life in the early twentieth century. John Addington Symonds noted that the homosexual passion "throbs in our huge cities. The pulse of it can be felt in London, Paris, Berlin, Vienna, no less than in Constantinople, Naples, Teheran, and Moscow."[8] Hirschfeld proceeded to detail the sociology of this heartbeat in the chapter on community life and meeting places of homosexual men and women (mainly in Berlin), including circles of friends, private clubs, political clubs, sports clubs, and a complicated network of bars catering to different subsets of the population. He documented the homosexual use of public theaters, a group of homosexual bathhouses, drag balls for both men and women, hotels and guest houses favored by homosexuals, cruising in public parks and toilets, and the use of personal advertisements to find partners.[9] And the significance of this city-based subculture is shown, he noted, by the "many, who day after day have seldom been able to remove their masks, and feel here as if liberated. People have seen homosexuals from the provinces set foot in such bars for the first time and burst into violently emotional tears."[10] Hirschfeld also devoted considerable space to the legal and social victimization, persecution, and prosecution of homosexuals. He included a detailed history of the organized movement against this persecution as well as a list of antigay laws around the world.

Hirschfeld's intellectual significance has often been underestimated as a consequence of the paucity of reliable translations of his magnificent oeuvre.[11] A few excerpts of *The Homosexuality of Men and Women* were translated by Henry Gerber and published in the *One Institute Quarterly* in the early 1960s, but a complete translation by Michael Lombardi-Nash has only been available since 2000. I had not read *The Homosexuality of Men and Women* when I first encountered *The Homosexual in America*. Now, having read both, I can see their kinship. Cory had read Hirschfeld in the German and was able to draw on Hirschfeld's bibliographic compilations, historical data, and rhetorical tactics. Cory discussed what he called the "Hirschfeld movement" and the "Carpenter movement" in the late-nineteenth and early-twentieth centuries, lamenting that there had been nothing similar since their decline. He probably could not know that a major revival of such activism was about to erupt, nor that his elaborations on the pre–First World War corpus of knowledge would be further embellished by an emerging group of homophile researchers.

The layer of queer knowledge generated from roughly the late 1880s to the 1920s, mostly in England and continental Europe, has continued to inspire new work as scholars excavate its resources in the service of more contemporary projects. For example, Jeffrey Weeks's early work, especially his *Coming Out: A History of Homosexual Politics in Britain* (1977), is in many ways an extended meditation on Havelock Ellis, Edward Carpenter, and John Addington

Symonds, inflected with considerable knowledge of Krafft-Ebing. Foucault's *The History of Sexuality: Volume 1* is in large part a brilliant reading of Krafft-Ebing and late-nineteenth-century French psychiatry. Lisa Duggan's work on the Alice Mitchell case and Harry Oosterhuis's biography of Krafft-Ebing make whole new readings of sexology possible. Nonetheless, I believe both the sexological texts and the homophile corpus are underutilized and could still launch a thousand dissertations.

It is this sense of queer knowledges in sedimented layers that I hoped to convey with my title tonight. In the geologic record, certain strata are fossil rich, partly because of the conditions that produce luxuriant life forms and partly because of the conditions that favor their preservation in fossil form. Similarly, there seem to be periods in which social and political conditions have favored the abundant proliferation of queer knowledges, while other conditions dictate their preservation or destruction. And it is up to succeeding generations to ensure that such sedimentary formations are identified, excavated, catalogued, and utilized to produce new knowledge. Unfortunately, because of the lack of durable structural mechanisms to secure the reliable transfer of queer knowledges, they are often instead lost, buried, and forgotten.

For example, it is difficult to teach material that is only available in photocopied course packs or in special collections with limited access. Most of the books to which I referred tonight are out of print or hard to find. Many were briefly available in reprint editions during the 1970s as a consequence of the 1975 Arno Press series *Homosexuality: Lesbians and Gay Men in Society, History, and Literature*. These reprints of primary texts were among the most important achievements of the early wave of gay-liberation scholarship. The series consisted of fifty-four books and two periodicals, including the early homophile bibliographies by Damon, Stuart, Bradley, and Garde; several key U.S. government documents relating to homosexuality; reprints of important books by Edward Carpenter, Xavier Mayne, Natalie Barney, Earl Lind, Mercedes de Acosta, Blair Niles, Renée Vivien, and Donald Webster Cory; lesbian classics and pulp novels; texts from the gay-rights movement in Germany; and reprints of complete runs of *The Ladder* and *Mattachine Review*.[12] This extraordinary series was three decades too early. Sadly, it, too, is now out of print, and the Arno editions are almost as rare as the originals. Both Krafft-Ebing's *Pychopathia Sexualis* and Havelock Ellis's *Sexual Inversion* were recently re-released in cheap paperback editions, but when I tried to order them as textbooks this year they were already once again unobtainable.

I want to use this brief review to make a few points. The first is the prevalence of amnesia about Queer Studies's past. I am continually shocked at the assumption that GLBTQ studies only got started sometime in the 1990s. I chose the metaphor of geology because it helps us think about longer time frames and pull our focus away from the present. In geologic time, the present is a blip. Our sense of what is important in queer scholarship should not be distorted by the glitter of the current, the trendy, and the new. I want us to think about longer processes that have shaped the present and in which the present is deeply rooted. Any scholarly project can benefit from an accumulation of knowledge that can be evaluated, validated, criticized, updated, polished, improved, or used to provide new trails to investigate. We need to be more conscious about including the older material in the contemporary canon of Queer Studies.

However, the causes of limited memory are more structural than stylistic, and are produced less by curricular decisions than by institutional impediments. My main point is that we need to do more to overcome the institutional deficiencies that constrict access to older knowledge. We must continue to develop organizational structures to guarantee the conservation, transmission, and development of queer knowledges. As a discipline, GLBTQ studies is still very rudimentarily institutionalized in the universities, and this is a challenge to its continued viability. Clearly, there is much greater institutionalization now than there was even a decade ago, as events such as this lecture series and the existence of institutions such as CLAGS demonstrate. But the number of departments of GLBTQ studies is minuscule in comparison to the number of, for example, departments of sociology or political science. The infrastructures of knowledge require physical space and durable organizational structures — offices, buildings, libraries, archives, departments, programs, centers, faculty lines, staff positions, and paychecks. We must work to accumulate more resources and build better bureaucracies.

Many of us instinctively recoil at the idea of bureaucratization and consider it distasteful. Bureaucracy has many drawbacks, including staleness, boredom, pointless procedures, and petty bureaucrats. Bureaucracies almost by nature lack excitement, glamour, or charisma. We often live for fleeting intensities and charged moments, and celebrate marginality as a kind of permanent desideratum. But if bureaucracy and routinization have their costs, so do marginality and charisma. Marginality and momentary excitements are intrinsically fragile, evanescent, and unstable. Part of the reason for our impaired memory of the older strata of queer knowledges is that the institutions and organizations that produced them are gone. Queer life is full of examples of fabulous explosions that left little or no detectable trace, or whose documentary and artifactual remains were never systematically assembled or adequately conserved.

Those of you who know me will understand the ambivalence with which I recall one such set of vanished institutions: the "women's community" that rose up out of feminism and radical lesbianism in the 1970s. By the late 1970s, there were dozens of feminist and lesbian newspapers, at least a dozen journals, several thriving feminist presses, and a network of local communities with significant public territory. In San Francisco, much of this women's territory was along Valencia Street where there were lesbian bars, feminist coffeehouses, the women's bookstore, and several women's collectives and businesses. There were similar settlements in western Massachusetts, in Iowa City, and across the San Francisco Bay in Oakland. Today, there is almost nothing left of that world. Most of the newspapers, journals, bookstores, coffeehouses, and businesses are gone, despite a few stubborn survivors such as *Lesbian Connection*. There are complicated reasons for the collapse of these communities, but one of them was their infrastructural fragility. In San Francisco, for example, most of the shops were in rented storefronts along a low-rent business corridor. When commercial rents began to skyrocket, these shops were driven out. The only remnant of this once vibrant women's neighborhood is the Women's Building, and the only reason it is still there is because it was purchased, not rented. But the built environment is expensive to obtain and challenging to maintain. Stability is resource intensive.

Queer populations have an overabundance of marginality and an insufficiency of stability. Max Weber noted that bureaucracy, once fully established, is among the hardest social structures to destroy.[13] That can be a curse. But we could use some of that stability, and the resources required to sustain it, in Queer Studies. New theoretical frameworks, new data, and new discoveries will always force rethinking of our premises and assumptions. We must count on periodic rebellions, reformations, and upheavals to bring refreshment and renewal. But to paraphrase Marx and Marshall Berman, all that seems solid can vanish in a heartbeat, and to mangle Santayana, those who fail to secure the transmission of their histories are doomed to lose them.

Notes

Introduction: Sex, Gender, Politics

1. This is true even in the physical library. The digital library can exacerbate these tendencies. The material qualities of a book, periodical, piece of ephemera, or archival document can communicate something about its age, place of origin, and conditions of production; these are often lost in digital translation.

2. Tilly, *Durable Inequality*. Charles Tilly was one of my professors in graduate school and he has had a profound influence on my work, even when it strayed far from the topics he studied.

3. I say "Nerd out of Carolina" with a tip of the hat to Dorothy Allison.

4. For examples of some of the groups that did not fit, see Berry, *Almost White*; and Trillin, "U.S. Journal: Sumter County, SC Turks."

5. In contrast to the Klan, the White Citizens Councils admitted Catholics and Jews. It has been fascinating in recent years to watch politicians who have dealt with the current Citizens Councils try to deny their racist history and *raison d'etre*.

6. I do not intend to imply by this that the racist and religious Right was an exclusively Southern phenomenon. Clearly it was not. The *Dearborn Independent, National Socialist World*, Father Charles Coughlin, Carl McIntire, the apex of the Ku Klux Klan's political reach, the Aryan Nations, the militias, the Posse Comitatus, and the origins and luxuriant growth of Christian Identity all occurred well outside of Dixie. Detroit is currently the official headquarters of the National Socialist Movement. But I would guess that there are few parts of the United States where public discourse and institutions have such a pronounced and pervasive lurch to the right end of the theological, cultural, and political spectrum as they do in the South. See Aho, *The Politics of Righteousness*; Applebome, *Dixie Rising*; Barkun, *Religion and the Racist Right*; Bennett, *The Party of Fear*; Chalmers, *Hooded Americanism*; Crawford, *Thunder on the Right*; Ford, *The International Jew*; Kaplan, *Encyclopedia of White Power*; Klassen, *The White Man's Bible*; Levitas, *The Terrorist Next Door*; Lipset and Raab, *The Politics of Unreason*; Martin, *With God on Our Side*; Quarles, *Christian Identity*; Ridgeway, *Blood in the Face*; Stern, *A Force upon the Plain*; Walters, *One Aryan Nation under God*; and Zeskind, *Blood Politics*, and *The "Christian Identity" Movement*. For other perspectives, see Lassiter and Crespino, *The Myth of Southern Exceptionalism*.

7. McGreevy, *Catholicism and American Freedom*, 7.

8. Ibid., 8.

9. One of the significant changes in the political landscape of conflict over "social issues" was the truce hammered out in the late twentieth century between Catholic and Protestant conservative activists, who had previously engaged in so many mutual hostilities.

10. Many years after I left South Carolina, the children of the local rabbi did finally successfully protest public-school prayers, which were still occurring.

11. This vice-principal was unmarried, tough as nails, and most of the students found her terrifying. I thought she was fabulous. She used to call me into her office to chat and was always friendly and supportive. I stayed in touch with her after I left for college and until she died.

12. It was not until 1983 that the United States sent its first female, Sally Ride, into space. The Soviet space program had sent up a woman in 1963.

13. There was a whole genre of dance and romance tunes called "Beach Music." Pat Conroy wrote a book with this title (Conroy, *Beach Music*). See also Bryan, *Shag*; Hook, *Shagging in the Carolinas*; and Richardson and Chase, *Pawleys Island Historically Speaking*.

14. Two songs catch the impact of the music at that time: The Velvet Underground/ Lou Reed's "Rock 'n' Roll" and Jonathan Richman's "Roadrunner."

15. Mauss, *The Gift*.

16. "In 1961, the U.S. Court of Appeals for the Fifth Circuit decided *Dixon v. Alabama*, a landmark ruling that presaged a new definition of student rights. The case arose after Alabama State College (now Alabama State University) expelled six black students who had participated in civil-rights demonstrations. . . . The appellate court deemed such rules unconstitutional. . . . 'This was the first time a court had ever said anything remotely like that,' says Peter F. Lake, a law professor at Stetson University. Dixon doomed *in loco parentis*, explains Mr. Lake, who directs the Center for Excellence in Higher Education Law and Policy at Stetson. Courts would recast students as adults, or 'nonminors,' with constitutional rights. Colleges, in turn, would no longer have near-limitless power to govern and punish them." *Chronicle of Higher Education*, 5 September 2008, A1. It took a while for the consequences of this decision to materialize, but it contributed to the ultimate success of the movement for greater student freedom later in the 1960s.

17. Thorne, "Women in the Draft Resistance Movement."

18. For more on early women's liberation and its relationship to New Left, see Baxandall and Gordon, *Dear Sisters*; Freeman, *Politics of Women's Liberation*; Morgan, *Sisterhood Is Powerful*; Redstockings of the Women's Liberation Movement, *Feminist Revolution*; Koedt, Levine, and Rapone, *Radical Feminism*; Evans, *Personal Politics*; Cell 16, *No More Fun and Games* and *Female Revolution*; Echols, *Daring to Be Bad*.

19. I wrote my first published essay for the *Argus*, but it is such a piece of juvenilia that I have not included it in this collection.

20. I do not think anyone kept lists of attendance, much less minutes, of this

group. We generated articles, but no archives. The years have dimmed my memories of the participants, but I do know that they included the following: Rayna Rapp (then Rayna Reiter), now a professor of anthropology at New York University; Beth Schneider, a professor of sociology at the University of California, Santa Barbara; Joanne Parent, a cofounder of the Feminist Federal Credit Union and the Feminist Economic Network in Detroit and one of the signatories to the "Fourth World Manifesto" (see Echols, *Daring to Be Bad*); and Elli Meeropol, a writer living in western Massachusetts.

21. See my essay "Sites, Settlements, and Urban Sex" for a longer account of the impact of archaeology on my subsequent research project.

22. Darwin, *The Origin of Species*, chapter 11, "Geographical Distribution."

23. Continental drift explained why only the Old World had great apes.

24. See Livingstone, "On the Non-Existence of the Human Races"; Brace, *"Race" Is a Four Letter Word*.

25. See Bordin, *Women at Michigan: The "Dangerous Experiment," 1870s to the Present*; and McGuigan, *A Dangerous Experiment: 100 Years of Women at the University of Michigan*.

26. As the grader for Sahlins, Rayna was the first person to read any version of the paper. See her account of this period and these events in Kulick, "Anthropologists are Talking About Feminist Anthropology."

27. Harding, "Why Has the Sex/Gender System Become Visible Only Now?" Harding cites my essay, but only as one of several criticizing the shortfalls of Marxism for feminist analysis.

28. Germon, *Gender: A Genealogy of an Idea*, 1. See also Jordan-Young, *Brainstorm*, 12–15.

29. Ibid., 102. Although flattering, this attribution is not entirely correct. I cannot know the extent to which gender appeared in the entire anthropological literature of the period, but it was present. For example, Esther Newton used the term several times in her book *Mother Camp* (1972). However, it is true that her use was more descriptive than theoretical. "Sex role" bears more of the analytic weight than gender in Newton's text.

30. Ibid., 103.

31. This was of course a double edged blade: it helped justify making surgical reassignment available to transsexuals, while also helping to rationalize the surgical excision of anomalous infant genitalia.

32. Germon, *Gender*, 85–86.

33. Ibid., 86–87.

34. The relationship of these texts to French feminism is complicated, and I do not wish to imply that "Psych et Po" is representative of feminism in France. On the contrary, as Christine Delphy points out, "what is taught as 'French Feminism' has in fact little to do with what is happening in France on the feminist scene, either from a theoretical or from an activist's point of view." She specifically notes that "in constructing 'French Feminism,' Anglo-American authors favored a certain overtly anti-

feminist political trend called 'Psych et po,' to the detriment of what is considered, by Anglo-American as well as French feminist historians, to be the core of the feminist movement; and their bias has contributed to weakening the French movement" ("The Invention of French Feminism," 167–68). See also Moses, "Made in America." I cannot claim any expertise on feminism in France, although my intellectual and political predilections are probably closer to Delphy's than to Psych et Po, despite a shared interest in Lacan. But that is part of my point. I am indebted to Rostom Mesli for calling my attention to the essay by Delphy. See also Chodorow, *The Reproduction of Mothering*, *Feminism and Psychoanalytic Theory*, and *Femininities, Masculinities, Sexualities*.

35. Marion Zimmer Bradley was the major bibliographer of lesbian texts in the time between Foster's and Damon/Grier and Stuart's publications. Bradley assembled two early lesbian bibliographies shortly after the publication of Foster's book. These were *Astra's Tower: Special Leaflet #2* (1958) and *Astra's Tower: Special Leaflet #3* (1959). In the early 1960s, Bradley and Grier collaborated on a *Checklist* ("a complete, cumulative checklist of lesbian, variant, and homosexual fiction, in English, or available in English translation, with supplements of related material, for the use of collectors, students, and librarians"), and two supplements to the *Checklist*. All of these were reprinted, along with *The Lesbian in Literature*, Noel Garde's *The Homosexual in Literature*, and William Parker's *Homosexuality in A Gay Bibliography*, part of the massive 1975 Arno Press series on homosexuality.

36. When John D'Emilio was doing his research on the homophile movement in 1976, he came to Ann Arbor to consult the resources Weber had compiled in the Labadie collection.

37. They have of course by now been processed, and well used. But not by me.

38. See Benstock, *Women of the Left Bank Paris, 1900–1940*; Hawthorne, "Natalie Barney and Her Circle"; Jay, *The Amazon and the Page*; Latimer, *Women Together/Women Apart*; Livia, *A Perilous Advantage*; Rodriguez, *Wild Heart*; Schenkar, *Truly Wilde*; and Weiss, *Paris Was a Woman*.

39. I was delighted to find that Emily Apter had complimented my footnotes, which were compiled under such challenging conditions, and also that she credited my having written "this introduction early in her career, consulting Vivien and Barney archives that had attracted little notice by critics at the time." Apter, "Reflections on Gynophobia," 118.

40. Marks, *Marrano As Metaphor*.

41. Ibid., 46, 50, 56. See also Livia, "The Trouble with Heroines."

42. Ibid., 44.

43. Ibid., 56–57.

44. The seminar, titled "The Aryans: Politics, Language, Religion, and Race from Sanskrit Philology to the Neo-Nazis," was taught with Thomas Trautmann and Tomoko Masuzawa in 2007 at the University of Michigan. In the course of doing the reading that led to this class, I found out much more about Salomon Reinach, a figure of significance to Vivien and Barney. He was "a scholar of extraordinary breadth

and depth," whose major contributions were in classics, archaeology, and anthropology, and who was deeply involved in debates about race, language, and "the Aryans" (Bernal, *Black Athena*, 371; see also Poliakov, *The Aryan Myth*, and Masuzawa, *The Invention of World Religions*). Reinach's involvement in two such distinct areas of my own interest is quite a coincidence. I now understand, however, why his marginal notes on the Vivien and Barney crowd were so meticulous and erudite (see chap. 3, n. 9 of this book). It was an unexpected gift that he turned such cultivated scholarly habits to figuring out who was sleeping with whom in this group of generally privileged and educated women in early-twentieth-century Paris. Of course, when I was doing the research on Vivien and Barney, I knew almost as little about Reinach as I did about Maurras.

45. I could quibble with Marks in one respect. She is viewing my piece through the lens of her vast knowledge of French literature, culture, and history, as well as from a much later vantage point. My article might look rather different if considered in its own time frame and context, and especially in comparison with the lesbian feminist historical and theoretical writing with which it was roughly contemporaneous. See, for example, Sahli, "Smashing"; Faderman, *Surpassing the Love of Men*; and Rich, "Compulsory Heterosexuality and Lesbian Existence." By the time these were published, I had moved in a different direction.

46. Other speakers on the panel, sponsored by the Gay Socialist Caucus, included Jonathan (Ned) Katz, Joan Nestle, James Steakley, and David Thorstad. Reporting on the conference, Dan Tsang summarized my comments: "UM graduate student Gayle Rubin discussed her research on lesbians in Paris at the turn of the century. She made the point that homosexuality assumed its modern form (in which, among other things, the concept meant who you *were* instead of just what you *did*) only by the end of the 19th century, and warned against uncritical application of this concept to other cultures and times." Tsang, "Gay Academics Reflect on Movement Role," 2B.

47. This shift of perspective was also noted in an afterword I wrote, in 1979, for the second edition of *A Woman Appeared to Me*. See chap. 3 below.

48. Weeks, "'Sins and Diseases.'"

49. Newton had, however, noted the existence of the "leather queens" (*Mother Camp*, 33n21). Brief mentions were also in Hooker, "The Homosexual Community," and Achilles, "The Development of the Homosexual Bar as an Institution."

50. See chaps. 12 and 13.

51. Nye, "The Medical Origins of Sexual Fetishism"; Singy, "A History of Violence," and "Sadism at the Limits."

52. See Oosterhuis, *Step-Children of Nature*; Weeks, *Sex, Politics, and Society*; Rosario, *Science and Homosexualities*; Bland and Doan, *Sexology in Culture*; Davidson, *The Emergence of Sexuality*.

53. Foucault, *History of Sexuality*, 104–5.

54. Ibid., 106–13.

55. Ibid., 106–7.

56. See Polanyi, *The Great Transformation*.

57. See chap. 8. The origin dates of the history project are somewhat murky. In their biographical introduction to a collection of Bérubé's essays (*My Desire for History*), John D'Emilio and Estelle Freedman deal with this chronological ambiguity by stating, "By early 1979, at least, Bérubé was no longer working alone" ("Allan Bérubé and the Power of Community History," 10). I think we were meeting by late 1978, but it is not clear at what point we had a name. I would concur with John and Estelle that we were definitely an entity by early 1979.

58. D'Emilio and Freedman, "Allan Bérubé and the Power of Community History," 13.

59. White, *Pre-Gay L.A.*; Koskovich, "Lesbian, Gay, Bisexual and Transgender Archives and Libraries in the United States."

60. Koskovich, "Lesbian, Gay, Bisexual and Transgender Archives and Libraries in the United States"; D'Emilio and Freedman, "Introduction," 18.

61. See Kinsella, *Covering the Plague.*

62. See Rubin, "Sites, Settlements, and Urban Sex," "The Miracle Mile," "Elegy for the Valley of the Kings," "The Valley of the Kings: Leathermen in San Francisco, 1960–1990," and *Valley of the Kings.*

63. See Crimp, AIDS; Fee and Fox, AIDS: *The Burdens of History*, and AIDS: *The Making of a Chronic Disease*; Levine, Nardi, and Gagnon, *In Changing Times*; Nardi, *Journal of Sociology and Social Work*; Patton, *Inventing AIDS*; Treichler, *How to Have Theory in an Epidemic*; and Watney, *Imagine Hope, Policing Desire*, and *Practices of Freedom.*

64. See Burlein, *Lift High the Cross*; Hardisty, *Mobilizing Resentment*; Herman, *The Antigay Agenda*; LaHaye, *The Unhappy Gays*; Bransford, *Gay Politics vs. Colorado and America*; Bryant, *The Anita Bryant Story*; Bull and Gallagher, *Perfect Enemies*; Callahan and Payton, *"Shut Up Fag"*; Cameron, *Exposing the AIDS Scandal* and *The Gay Nineties*; Cobb, *God Hates Fags*; Cohen, *Coming Out Straight*; Dannemeyer, *Shadow in the Land*; Decter, *The New Chastity and Other Arguments against Women's Liberation*; Dobson, *The New Dare to Discipline*; du Mas, *Gay Is Not Good*; Eichel and Nobile, *The Perfect Fit*; Engel, *Sex Education*; Erzen, *Straight to Jesus*; Gilder, *Sexual Suicide*; Himmelfarb, *The De-Moralization of Society*; Irvine, *Talk about Sex*; Klatch, *Women of the New Right*; Levine, *Harmful to Minors*; Lively, *Seven Steps to Recruit-Proof Your Child*; Marrs, *Big Sister Is Watching You* and *Ravaged by the New Age*; Martin, *With God on Our Side*; Minkowitz, *Ferocious Romance*; Noebel, *The Homosexual Revolution*; Noebel, Lutton, and Cameron, AIDS; Peters, *The Death Penalty for Homosexuals Is Prescribed in the Bible*; Reisman, Eichel, Court, and Muir, *Kinsey, Sex, and Fraud*; Rekers, *Growing Up Straight*; Smith, *New Right Discourse on Race and Sexuality*; Smith and Windes, *Progay/Antigay*; Socarides, *Homosexuality*; Sprigg, *Outrage*; and Wolfe, *Homosexuality and American Public Life.*

65. See Vance, *Pleasure and Danger*, 434–36.

66. See House and Cowan, "Can Men Be Women?"; Raymond, *The Transsexual Empire*; Stone, "The 'Empire' Strikes Back"; and Riddell, *Divided Sisterhood*. These were mainly directed at male to female transsexuality. The issue of female to male

transsexuals has roiled many lesbian communities in the interim since I wrote "Catamites and Kings." As far as I know, transsexuals are still banned from the Michigan Womyn's Music Festival, but other "women's" events and lesbian populations have quietly adjusted to full transgender participation. Apart from holdouts such as the Michigan Festival, the gender boundaries seem to be more sharply contested now among gay men, where the presence or female to male transsexuals has become controversial. For example, the Chicago Hellfire Club will not admit FTMs to its annual Inferno run. On the other hand, FTMs have competed for major men's leather titles, and the 2010 International Mr. Leather was a female to male transsexual.

67. See chaps. 5, 6, 7 and 8.

68. "Blood Under the Bridge" was first delivered as a lecture at the "Rethinking Sex" conference, held at the University of Pennsylvania, in 2009. It was published as a journal article in 2010, and was again revised for this collection.

69. Chast, "In the Nostalgia District," 4.

70. For one example of many, see Dean and Lane, *Homosexuality & Psychoanalysis*.

71. Johnson, *The Lavender Scare*. See also chap. 4, n. 1.

72. Johnson, *The Lavender Scare*, 210.

73. Bayer, *Homosexuality and American Psychiatry*; Drescher and Merlino, *American Psychiatry and Homosexuality*; and Engelhardt and Caplan, *Scientific Controversies*.

74. *Lawrence v. Texas*, 539 U.S. 558 (2003).

75. Bérubé, *Coming Out Under Fire*; D'Emilio and Freedman, "Allan Bérubé and the Power of Community History."

76. Frank Rich, "The Culture Warriors Get Laid Off," *New York Times*, 14 March 2009.

77. Frank Rich, "It Still Felt Good the Morning After," *New York Times*, 9 November 2008.

78. Dan Balz, "The GOP Takeover in the States," *Washington Post*, 13 November 2010.

79. Laura Bassett and Tyler Kingkade, "State-Level Assaults on Abortion Rights," *Huffington Post*, 17 June 2011.

80. See Chauncey, *Why Marriage?*

81. Susan Stryker is my source for that wonderful term, "bureaucratic unintelligibility."

82. There is also too little attention paid to the history of the involvement of religious authorities with marriage. Marriage has not always been under the jurisdiction of religious authorities; this may actually be more the exception than the rule over the course of human history. Even in Christian Europe, the sacralization of marriage was a much later development than is commonly assumed. For example, Christopher Brooke argues in *The Medieval Idea of Marriage* that the establishment of clerical control over marriage was "a long and disputed process" (127). While the codification of religious marriage rituals was well under way in the eleventh and twelfth centuries,

"not until the sixteenth century did marriage in church become a legal necessity—and then by the edict of the Council of Trent, which was mandatory for Roman Catholics, ignored by the Protestant churches" (139). See also Witte, *From Sacrament to Contract*; Witte and Kingdon, *Sex, Marriage, and Family in John Calvin's Geneva*; Cairncross, *After Polygamy was Made a Sin*; Mair, *Marriage*; and Westermarck, *The History of Human Marriage*.

83. Phillips, *The Politics of Rich and Poor*; Harvey, *A Brief History of Neoliberalism*; Johnston, *Free Lunch*; Dollars and Sense, *The Wealth Inequality Reader*; Henwood, *The State of the U.S.A Atlas*; Wolff, *Top Heavy*; Frank, *Richistan*; Bernstein and Swan, *All the Money in the World*; Bartels, *Unequal Democracy*; Leopold, *The Looting of America*; "The Forbes Four Hundred"; "Forbes 400" (2007, 2008, and 2009); "The Billionaires: The World's Richest People"; "Billionaires: The Richest People in the World" (2008, 2009, and 2010).

84. Frank, *What's the Matter With Kansas?*

Chapter 1. The Traffic in Women

Acknowledgments are an inadequate expression of how much this paper, like most, is the product of many minds. They are also necessary to free others of the responsibility for what is ultimately a personal vision of a collective conversation. I want to free and thank the following persons: Tom Anderson and Arlene Gorelick, with whom I coauthored the paper from which this one evolved; Rayna Reiter, Larry Shields, Ray Kelly, Peggy White, Norma Diamond, Randy Reiter, Frederick Wyatt, Anne Locksley, Juliet Mitchell, and Susan Harding for countless conversations and ideas; Marshall Sahlins for the revelation of anthropology; Rod Aya for elucidating Marx; Lynn Eden for merciless editing; the members of Women's Studies 340/004 for my initiation into teaching; Sally Brenner for heroic typing; Susan Lowes for incredible patience; and Emma Goldman for the title.

1. Tiger and Fox, *The Imperial Animal*.
2. Marx, *Wage-Labor and Capital*, 28.
3. On this, see Althusser and Balibar, *Reading Capital*, 11–69.
4. Moving between Marxism, structuralism, and psychoanalysis produces a certain clash of epistemologies. In particular, structuralism is a can from which worms crawl out all over the epistemological map. Rather than trying to cope with this problem, I have more or less ignored the fact that Lacan and Lévi-Strauss are among the foremost living ancestors of the contemporary French intellectual revolution (see Foucault, *The Order of Things*). It would be fun, interesting, and, if this were France, essential to start my argument from the center of the structuralist maze and work my way out from there, along the lines of a "dialectical theory of signifying practices" (see Hefner, "The *Tel Quel* Ideology").
5. Benston, "The Political Economy of Women's Liberation"; Dalla Costa, *The Power of Women and the Subversion of the Community*; Larguia and Dumoulin,

"Towards a Science of Women's Liberation"; Gerstein, "Domestic Work and Capitalism"; Vogel, "The Earthly Family"; Secombe, "Housework under Capitalism"; Gardiner, "Political Economy of Female Labor in Capitalist Society"; Rowntree and Rowntree, "More on the Political Economy of Women's Liberation."

6. Marx, *Theories of Surplus Value, Part 1*, 399.

7. Marx, *Capital*, 572.

8. Ibid., 171.

9. A lot of the debate on women and housework has centered around whether or not housework is "productive" labor. Strictly speaking, housework is not ordinarily "productive" in the technical sense of the term (Gough, "Marx and Productive Labour"; Marx, *Theories of Surplus Value, Part 1*, 387–413). But this distinction is irrelevant to the main line of the argument. Housework may not be "productive," in the sense of directly producing surplus value, capital, and yet be a crucial element in the production of surplus value and capital.

10. Murphy, "Social Structure and Sex Antagonism," 195.

11. Marx, *Capital*, 171, emphasis added.

12. Engels, *The Origin of the Family, Private Property, and the State*, 71–72, emphasis added.

13. That some of them are pretty bizarre from our point of view only demonstrates the point that sexuality is expressed through the intervention of culture (see Ford and Beach, *Patterns of Sexual Behaviour*). Some examples may be chosen from among the exotica in which anthropologists delight. Among the Banaro, marriage involved several socially sanctioned sexual partnerships. When a woman is married, she is initiated into intercourse by the sib-friend of her groom's father. After bearing a child by this man, she begins to have intercourse with her husband. She also has an institutionalized partnership with the sib-friend of her husband. A man's partners include his wife, the wife of his sib-friend, and the wife of his sib-friend's son (Thurnwald, "Banaro Society"). Multiple intercourse is a more pronounced custom among the Marind Anim. At the time of marriage, the bride has intercourse with all of the members of the groom's clan, the groom coming last. Every major festival is accompanied by a practice known as *otiv-bombari*, in which semen is collected for ritual purposes. A few women have intercourse with many men, and the resulting semen is collected in coconut-shell buckets. A Marind male is subjected to multiple homosexual intercourse during initiation (Van Baal, *Dema*). Among the Etoro, heterosexual intercourse is taboo for between 205 and 260 days a year (Kelly, "Witchcraft and Sexual Relations"). In much of New Guinea, men fear copulation and think that it will kill them if they engage in it without magical precautions (Glasse, "The Mask of Venery"; Meggitt, "Male-Female Relationships in the Highlands of Australian New Guinea"). Usually, such ideas of feminine pollution express the subordination of women. But symbolic systems contain internal contradictions, whose logical extensions sometimes lead to inversions of the propositions on which a system is based. In New Britain, men's fear of sex is so extreme that rape appears to be feared by men rather than women. Women run after men, who flee from them, women are the sexual aggressors,

and it is bridegrooms who are reluctant (Goodale and Chowning, "The Contaminating Woman"). Other interesting sexual variations can be found in Yalmon, "On the Purity of Women in the Castes of Ceylon and Malabar," and Gough, "The Nayars and the Definition of Marriage."

14. See Enga, Maring, Bena Bena, Huli, Melpa, Kuma, Gahuku-Gama, Fore, Marind Anim, ad nauseam. See Berndt, *Excess and Restraint*; Langness, "Sexual Antagonism in the New Guinea Highlands"; Rappaport, *Pigs for the Ancestors*; Read, "The Nama Cult of the Central Highlands, New Guinea"; Meggitt, "Male-Female Relationships in the Highlands of Australian New Guinea"; Glasse, "The Mask of Venery"; Strathern, *Women in Between*; Reay, *The Kuma*; Van Baal, *Dema*; Lindenbaum, "A Wife Is the Hand of the Man."

15. Engels thought men acquired wealth in the form of herds and, wanting to pass this wealth to their own children, overthrew "mother right" in favor of patrilineal inheritance. "The overthrow of mother right was the *world historical defeat of the female sex*. The man took command in the home also; the woman was degraded and reduced to servitude; she became the slave of his lust and a mere instrument for the production of children" (Engels, *The Origin of the Family, Private Property, and the State*, 120–21). As has been often pointed out, women do not necessarily have significant social authority in societies practicing matrilineal inheritance (Schneider and Gough, *Matrilineal Kinship*).

16. Sahlins, "The Origin of Society"; Livingstone, "Genetics, Ecology, and the Origins of Incest and Exogamy"; Lévi-Strauss, *The Elementary Structures of Kinship*.

17. Fee, "The Sexual Politics of Victorian Social Anthropology."

18. See also Sahlins, *Stone Age Economics*, chap. 4.

19. Arapesh, cited in Lévi-Strauss, *The Elementary Structures of Kinship*, 27.

20. Malinowski, *The Sexual Life of Savages*.

21. Sahlins, *Stone Age Economics*, 169, 175.

22. Lévi-Strauss, *The Elementary Structures of Kinship*, 51, 481.

23. Best, cited in ibid., 481.

24. "What, would you like to marry your sister? What is the matter with you? Don't you want a brother-in-law? Don't you realize that if you marry another man's sister and another man marries your sister, you will have at least two brothers-in-law, while if you marry your own sister you will have none? With whom will you hunt, with whom will you garden, whom will you go visit?" (Arapesh, cited in ibid., 485).

25. Ibid., 115. This analysis of society as based on bonds between men by means of women makes the separatist responses of the women's movement thoroughly intelligible. Separatism can be seen as a mutation in social structure, as an attempt to form social groups based on unmediated bonds between women. It can also be seen as a radical denial of men's "rights" in women, and as a claim by women of rights in themselves.

26. Strathern, *Women in Between*, 161.

27. For this sense of production, see Marx, *Pre-capitalist Economic Formations*, 80–99.

28. "In studying women we cannot neglect the methods of a science of the mind, a theory that attempts to explain how women become women and men, men. The borderline between the biological and the social which finds expression in the family is the land psychoanalysis sets out to chart, the land where sexual distinction originates" (Mitchell, *Women's Estate*, 167). "What is the *object* of psychoanalysis? . . . but the '*effects*,' prolonged into the surviving adult, of the extraordinary adventure which from birth the liquidation of the Oedipal phase transforms a small animal conceived by a man and a women into a small human child . . . the 'effects' still present in the survivors of the forced 'humanization' of the small human animal into a *man* or a *woman*" (Althusser, "Freud and Lacan," 57, 59).

29. The psychoanalytic theories of femininity were articulated in the context of a debate which took place largely in the *International Journal of Psychoanalysis* and *The Psychoanalytic Quarterly*, in the late 1920s and early 1930s. Articles representing the range of discussion include: Freud, "Female Sexuality," "Some Psychical Consequences of the Anatomical Distinction between the Sexes," "Femininity"; Lampl de Groot, "Problems of Femininity," "The Evolution of the Oedipus Complex in Women"; Deutsch, "On Female Homosexuality," "The Significance of Masochism in the Mental Life of Women"; Horney, "The Denial of the Vagina"; Jones, "The Phallic Phase." Some of my dates are of reprints; for the original chronology, see Chasseguet-Smirgel (*Female Sexuality*, introduction).

The debate was complex, and I have simplified it. Freud, Lampl de Groot, and Deutsch argued that femininity developed out of a bisexual, "phallic" girl-child; Horney and Jones argued for an innate femininity. The debate was not without its ironies. Horney defended women against penis envy by postulating that women are born and not made; Deutsch, who considered women to be made and not born, developed a theory of feminine masochism whose best rival is *Story of O*. I have attributed the core of the "Freudian" version of female development equally to Freud and to Lampl de Groot. In reading through the articles, it has seemed to me that the theory is as much (or more) hers as it is his.

30. Freud, "Femininity," 119.

31. Ibid., 116

32. Lacan, *The Language of Self: The Function of Language in Psychoanalysis*, 48.

33. Ibid., 126.

34. Ibid., 40.

35. [Erotic desires and gender identities may of course deviate from their proscribed destinations. But even deviance is shaped within historically and socially available parameters.—G. R.]

36. Thompson, *The Making of the English Working Class*.

37. See also the discussion of different forms of "historical individuality" in Althusser and Balibar, *Reading Capital*, 112, 251–53.

38. I have taken my position on Freud somewhere between the French structuralist interpretations and the American biologistic ones, because I think that Freud's wording is similarly somewhere in the middle. He does talk about penises, about

the "inferiority" of the clitoris, and about the psychic consequences of anatomy. The Lacanians, on the other hand, argue from Freud's text that he is unintelligible if his words are taken literally, and that a thoroughly nonanatomical theory can be deduced as Freud's intention (see Althusser, "Freud and Lacan"). I think that they are right; the penis is walking around too much for its role to be taken literally. The detachability of the penis and its transformation in fantasy (e.g., penis = feces = child = gift) argue strongly for a symbolic interpretation. Nevertheless, I don't think that Freud was as consistent as either I or Lacan would like him to have been, and some gesture must be made to what he said, even as we play with what he must have meant.

39. Laplanche and Pontalis, in Mehlman, *French Freud*, 198–99, emphasis added.

40. Wilden, "Lacan and the Discourse of the Other, 271.

41. Jakobson and Halle, *Fundamentals of Language*, on distinctive features.

42. Wilden, "Lacan and the Discourse of the Other," 303–5.

43. The pre-Oedipal mother is the "phallic mother"; she is believed to possess the phallus. The Oedipal-inducing information is that the mother does not possess the phallus. In other words, the crisis is precipitated by the "castration" of the mother, by the recognition that the phallus only passes through her but does not settle on her. The "phallus" must pass through her, since the relationship of a male to every other male is defined through a woman. A man is linked to a son by a mother, to his nephew by virtue of a sister, and so on. Every relationship between male kin is defined by the woman between them. If power is a male prerogative, and must be passed on, it must go through the women-in-between. Marshall Sahlins (personal communication) once suggested that the reason women are so often defined as stupid, polluting, disorderly, silly, profane, or whatever, is that such categorizations define women as "incapable" of possessing the power which must be transferred through them.

44. See Sahlins, *Stone Age Economics*, chap. 4.

45. Lampl de Groot, "Problems of Femininity," 497, emphasis added.

46. Lampl de Groot, "The Evolution of the Oedipus Complex in Women," 213.

47. Freud, "Some Psychical Consequences of the Anatomical Distinction between the Sexes," 239.

48. Freud, "Femininity," 131.

49. Horney, "The Denial of the Vagina," 148–49.

50. Deutsch, "On Female Homosexuality," 228.

51. Ibid., 231.

52. See also Mitchell, *Women's Estate* and *Psychoanalysis and Feminism*; Lasch, "Freud and Women."

53. Derrida, "Structure, Sign, and Play in the Discourse of the Human Sciences," 250.

54. Parts of Wittig's *Les Guérillères* (1973) appear to be tirades against Lévi-Strauss and Lacan. For instance: "Has he not indeed written, power and the possession of women, leisure and the enjoyment of women: He writes that you are currency, an item of exchange. He writes, barter, barter, possession and acquisition of women and merchandise. Better for you to see your guts in the sun and utter the death rattle than

to live a life that anyone can appropriate. What belongs to you on this earth? Only death. No power on earth can take that away from you. And—consider explain tell yourself—if happiness consists in the possession of something, then hold fast to this sovereign happiness—to die" (Wittig, *Les Guérillères*, 115–16; see also 106–7, 113–14, 134). The awareness by French feminists of Lévi-Strauss and Lacan is most clearly evident in a group called Psychoanalyse et Politique, which defined its task as a feminist use and critique of Lacanian psychoanalysis.

55. Lévi-Strauss, *The Elementary Structures of Kinship*, 496, emphasis added.

56. Freud, *A General Introduction to Psychoanalysis*, 376–77, emphasis added.

57. "Every woman adores a fascist" (Plath, "Daddy").

58. One clinician, Charlotte Wolff (*Love between Women*) has taken the psychoanalytic theory of womanhood to its logical extreme and proposed that lesbianism is a healthy response to female socialization: "Women who do not rebel against the status of object have declared themselves defeated as persons in their own right" (65). "The lesbian girl is the one who, by all means at her disposal, will try to find a place of safety inside and outside the family, through her fight for equality with the male. She will not, like other women, play up to him: indeed, she despises the very idea of it" (ibid., 59). "The lesbian was and is unquestionably in the avant-garde of the fight for equality of the sexes, and for the psychical liberation of women" (ibid., 66). It is revealing to compare Wolff's discussion with the articles on lesbianism in Marmor, *Sexual Inversion*.

59. Scott, "The Role of Collegiate Sororities in Maintaining Class and Ethnic Endogamy."

60. Goody and Tambiah, *Bridewealth and Dowry*, 2.

61. Douglas, *The Lele of Kasai*.

62. Reay, *The Kuma*.

63. Strathern, *Women in Between*.

64. Bulmer, "Political Aspects of the Moka Ceremonial Exchange System among the Kyaka People of the Western Highlands of New Guinea," 11.

65. Another line of inquiry would compare bridewealth systems to dowry systems. Many of these questions are treated in Goody and Tambiah, *Bridewealth and Dowry*.

66. Leach, *Rethinking Anthropology*, 90.

67. Ibid., 88.

68. Ibid., 89.

69. Malinowski, "The Primitive Economics of the Trobriand Islanders."

70. Henry Wright, personal communication.

Chapter 2. The Trouble with Trafficking

This essay was originally presented as a paper on the panel "Ethnography and Policy: What Do We Know about 'Trafficking'?," American Anthropological Association, 22 November 2002, New Orleans, organized by Carole S. Vance. Another version was presented at the Symposium, "The Traffic in Women, Thirty Years Later," University of Michigan, 2005, organized by David Halperin. I am exceedingly grateful to Carole Vance, who is an endless and generous font of wisdom, precise information, editorial suggestions, and bibliographic mastery. Any mistakes or misconceptions are my own.

1. This essay was included in her collection, *Anarchism and Other Essays*, which was initially published in 1910. I am using a small reprint brought out in 1970 by the Times Change Press that cites an edition of *Anarchism and Other Essays* from 1917. That apparently was the third edition and it is cited as such as the source for the Dover reissue of 1969. In her introduction to *Red Emma Speaks*, Alix Kates Shulman says that *Anarchism and Other Essays* was published in 1911 (104). However, there was an earlier publication in 1910. My pagination is from the Times Change Press edition.

2. Rubin, *Surveiller et Jouir*.

3. Vance, "Thinking Trafficking," 138.

4. United Nations, "Protocol to Prevent, Suppress and Punish Trafficking in Persons."

5. Vance, "Thinking Trafficking," 139. See also Miller, "Sexuality, Violence against Women, and Human Rights," 33–34.

6. Bristow, *Prostitution and Prejudice*, 35.

7. Ibid., 36–37.

8. Ibid., 39–40.

9. Ibid., 37; Gorham, "The 'Maiden Tribute of Modern Babylon'"; Walkowitz, *City of Dreadful Delight*, *Prostitution and Victorian Society*, and "Male Vice and Feminist Virtue."

10. Bristow, *Vice and Vigilance*, 86. See also Jordan, *Josephine Butler*.

11. Bristow, *Prostitution and Prejudice*.

12. Bartley, *Prostitution*, 172–73.

13. Ibid., 173.

14. Walkowitz, *Prostitution and Victorian Society*, 247.

15. Bristow, *Vice and Vigilance*, 173.

16. Vance, "Thinking Trafficking," 141; see also Limoncelli, *The Politics of Trafficking*; Doezema, *Sex Slaves and Discourse Masters*. For U.S. law, see Trafficking Victims Protection Act, U.S. Code 22 (2011), §7101 (Purposes and findings); and U.S. Code 22 (2011), §7102 (Definitions). See also Chuang, "The United States as Global Sheriff"; DeStefano, *The War on Human Trafficking*; and Haynes, "(Not) Found Chained to a Bed in a Brothel."

17. Langum, *Crossing Over the Line*, 15.

18. Connelly, *The Response to Prostitution in the Progressive Era*, 12.

19. Langum, *Crossing Over the Line*, 27.

20. Ibid., 7.

21. Ibid., 27. See also Donovan, *White Slave Crusades*.

22. Connelly, *The Response to Prostitution in the Progressive Era*, 114.

23. Ibid.

24. Ibid., 115

25. See also Guterl, *The Color of Race in America*; Baum, *The Rise and Fall of the Caucasian Race*; Jacobson, *Whiteness of a Different Color*; Barkun, *Retreat of Scientific Racism*; Brace, *"Race" Is a Four-Letter Word*; Hankins, *The Racial Basis of Civilization*; Brodkin, *How the Jews Became White Folks*; Ignatiev, *How the Irish Became White*. On the Dillingham Commission, see Zeidel, *Immigrants, Progressives, and Exclusion Politics*; Zolberg, *A Nation by Design*. On Madison Grant, see Spiro, *Defending the Master Race*. See also Stocking, "Turn of the Century Concept of Race."

26. These quotas were in turn based on the number of immigrants from each country who were already in the United States in 1890, as recorded in the census of that year. One of the crucial debates leading up to the passage of the law was on which census to base these quotas. Since immigration from southern and eastern Europe had risen dramatically after 1890, using a later census would have meant allowing larger numbers of new immigrants from those areas. Quotas based on the 1890 census insured that immigration from those countries would virtually halt. Note that these measures were aimed at "non-favored" groups of Europeans. Asian immigration was eliminated after a longer and different political and legal trajectory. Jacobson, *Whiteness of a Different Color*, 83–84.

27. Carole Vance noted, in "Thinking Trafficking," the melodramatic structure of much current antitrafficking film and literature. For more detailed analysis of antitrafficking melodramas, see also Vance, "'Juanita/Svetlana/Geeta' Is Crying," and "Hiss the Villain."

28. Connelly, *The Response to Prostitution in the Progressive Era*, 118.

29. Langum, *Crossing Over the Line*.

30. Ibid., 261.

31. Ibid., 49.

32. Ibid., 55.

33. Ibid., 56.

34. Ibid., 65.

35. Ibid., 145–47. The Federal Industrial Institution for Women at Alderson was the first federal prison for women. Billie Holiday, Elizabeth Gurley Flynn, and Martha Stewart are among its famous alumnae.

36. Bulmer, *The Chicago School of Sociology*, 59–60.

37. "Sexual slavery" is now a common term. See Barry, *Female Sexual Slavery*.

38. Feingold, "Trafficking in Numbers," 62. For critical perspectives on the elision of prostitution and trafficking, see Kempadoo and Doezema, *Global Sex Workers*, and Kempadoo et al., *Trafficking and Prostitution Reconsidered*.

39. Wijers and Lap-Chew, *Trafficking in Women*, 45.

40. See the "About" section of CATW's official website, www.catwinternational .org/.

41. Many others have made similar points about the lingering resonances of the nineteenth- and early-twentieth-century campaigns. See for example, Soderlund, "Running from the Rescuers," and Doezema, "Loose Women or Lost Women?"

42. Best, *Threatened Children*, 60.

43. Ibid., 61–62.

44. Ibid. 62.

45. Such fictitious numbers contributed to the antihomosexual witch hunts conducted by the federal government in the early 1950s. Roy Blick, a lieutenant in the Washington vice squad, testified before a Senate committee that there were 5,000 homosexuals in the District of Columbia, of whom 3,750 were federal employees. But when interviewed about the source of his numbers, Blick "suggested that he derived the 5,000 figure by extrapolating from the number of people arrested on homosexual charges in Washington," which he then multiplied by the number of friends he assumed each person had. His number of homosexual federal employees was the result of similarly inventive statistical speculation. Nonetheless, these numbers were accepted as official, endlessly repeated in the press, and used as the basis of a claim that "the real menace facing the capital was perversion." Johnson, *The Lavender Scare*, 86.

46. Connelly, *The Response to Prostitution in the Progressive Era*, 17–18.

47. Ibid., 18.

48. Both quoted in ibid., 18.

49. Ibid., 20–21.

50. Ibid., 21.

51. Ibid., 20. These numbers seem suspect even to a casual reader.

52. Ibid., 21–21.

53. Ibid., 21.

54. Feingold, "Trafficking in Numbers," 47, 52. See also the United States Government Accountability Office, *Human Trafficking*, which is a comprehensive review of the questionable nature of the data on prevalence, along with suggestions for obtaining better numbers.

55. Feingold, "Trafficking in Numbers," 51.

56. Ibid., 55.

57. Ibid., 57. See also Soderlund, "Covering Urban Vice."

58. Best, *Threatened Children*, 28.

59. Emma Goldman, "The Traffic in Women," 19–20.

60. Ibid., 20–21.

61. Ibid., 25.

62. Ibid., 24, 25.

63. See, for example, Barry, *Female Sexual Slavery* and *The Prostitution of Sexuality*; Jeffreys, *The Idea of Prostitution*; Dworkin, *Right-Wing Women*.

64. See Vance, "Thinking Trafficking"; Davidson, "Will the Real Sex Slave Please Stand Up?"; Sayeed, "Making Political Hay of Sex and Slavery."

65. See Bernstein, "The Sexual Politics of the 'New Abolitionism,'" and "Militarized Humanitarianism Meets Carceral Feminism."

66. Walkowitz, *Prostitution and Victorian Society*, 250. For the details of her assessment, see her epilogue, 246–56.

67. Walkowitz, "Male Vice and Female Virtue," 434. See also her epilogue in *City of Dreadful Delight*.

68. Walkowitz, "Male Vice and Female Virtue," 434.

69. It was first published in *History Workshop* under a slightly different title. I have used the revised version from *Powers of Desire*, published a year later.

Chapter 3. *A Woman Appeared to Me*

Numerous individuals and institutions made this essay possible. Grants from the Center for Western European Studies at the University of Michigan funded two seasons of research in Paris. The Michigan Society of Fellows has funded further study. François Chapon gave generously of his knowledge and his skill, and identified the Reinach notes for me. [In the summer of 1973, M. Chapon kindly accompanied me to the Réserves at the Bibliothèque Nationale to see the marginalia and verify that they were in Reinach's hand. At that time, the staff at the BN were unable to do so.— G. R.] Jean Chalon carries on the tradition of his friendship with Natalie Barney in his helpfulness to those who study her. Berthe Cleyrergue regaled me with stories and with cookies "just like the ones I made Mademoiselle." George Wickes has been generous beyond words with his time, his knowledge, and his galleys. Conversations with Robert Phelps and Gregory Pearson were extremely helpful. Marilyn Young indirectly sparked my interest by telling me to read *Nightwood*. Denise Blue, Hélène Francès, Barbara Grier, Bertha Harris, Margaret A. Porter, Robert Sklar, Vicki Sork, Jack Thomas, Ed Weber, and Harriet Whitehead all gave encouragement at the critical moments. The librarians in the Salle de la Réserve and the Salle des Manuscrits of the Bibliothèque Nationale produced miracles of library science. I am grateful for having been permitted to see the treasures in storage at the National Collection of Fine Arts. Without the editing heroics of Lynn Eden and Itsie Hull, the manuscript would never have been completed. The translations from French were done by Lynn Hunt, with a little help from me.

1. Reinach, untitled [Query]; Cooper, *Women Poets of the Twentieth Century in France*.

2. L'Autre, "Twenty-four Poems by Renée Vivien."

3. Harris, "The More Profound Nationality of their Lesbianism," 87.

4. These urban homosexual communities may in fact have appeared earlier. They seem to be an established fact of life by the last part of the nineteenth century, and are described in literature from that period. There is a discussion of such literary evidence for lesbian communities in Foster, *Sex Variant Women in Literature*, 99–115.

5. Phelps, *Earthly Paradise*, 144–50.

6. Colette, *The Pure and the Impure*, 67–69.

7. The source material for Renée Vivien's life is scarce. Most of the literature on her is concerned with her writing. The only full-length biography (Germain, *Renée Vivien*) uses pseudonyms and seems to be based largely on *A Woman Appeared to Me*. There are biographical discussions of varying lengths in Foster, *Sex Variant Women in Literature*; Klaich, *Woman Plus Woman*; Maurras, *L'Avenir de l'intelligence*; and

Cooper, *Women Poets of the Twentieth Century in France*. Lacretelle (*L'Amour sur la place*) published several of Vivien's letters, most of them to Natalie Barney in 1904. Colette's lovely memoir, *The Pure and the Impure*, remains one of the most revealing and sympathetic portraits. Wickes's "A Natalie Barney Garland" includes Romaine Brooks's memory of her encounter with Vivien. Natalie Barney's memoirs (*Aventures de l'esprit*; *Souvenirs indiscrets*) contain extensive sections on Vivien. Charles Brun taught Vivien Greek, and Salomon Reinach became the self-appointed curator of her memory. An exchange between the two men (Reinach, untitled [Query]; Brun, "Untitled [Response to Salomon Reinach]") provides a few of the relatively meager facts of Vivien's early life.

Primary source material on Vivien is problematic. Both Foster and Cooper say that Salomon Reinach acquired Vivien's papers after her death and gave them to the Bibliothèque Nationale, to be released in the year 2000. A letter by Reinach in Barney's *Aventures de l'esprit* says only that he *planned* to give the papers to the Bibliothèque Nationale. In fact, Vivien's papers are not in that library, and their whereabouts remain mysterious. [This may no longer be accurate. I was told in the early 1970s by various staff members that the Bibliothèque Nationale did not have these papers. However, they may only have been unprocessed. My intelligence is woefully out of date.—G. R.] Reinach was also rumored to have written a manuscript of a biography of Vivien, but I have been unable to confirm its existence. If anyone knows more about Reinach's alleged manuscript or the missing Vivien archive, I would like to hear from them.

Reinach did, however, possess a collection of Vivien's books, Barney's books, and some miscellaneous articles pertaining to Vivien. He gave this collection to the Bibliothèque Nationale when he died, and it is now housed in the Salle de la Réserve. Reinach recorded much of his own research on Vivien in the pages of the books of this collection, and his marginalia remain one of the best sources on her life and its relationship to her work. (See Reinach Salomon's unpublished marginalia in a collection of books by Renée Vivien, Natalie Barney, and others, plus miscellaneous articles and manuscripts. The collection is in the Salle de la Réserve of the Bibliothèque Nationale and is primarily catalogued under the number: 8° Z. Don 593, numbers 1–48. As this collection is highly irregular, anyone trying to consult it is advised to ask for a shelf list of the legacy of Salomon Reinach, 21 May 1933.) [When I wrote about the Reinach marginalia, they had not yet been identified by the Bibliothèque Nationale and the planned volume of an updated catalogue which would have contained the entries for Pauline Tarn/Renée Vivien had not yet been published. When I briefly returned to the BN some years later, the volume with the Vivien entries had been completed. The marginalia were clearly catalogued and attributed to Reinach, so perhaps it is no longer necessary to consult the shelf list.—G. R.]

Natalie Barney's archive (see note 9 below) may contain letters and other papers of Vivien. I have recently been informed that Paul Lorenz is preparing a biography of Renée Vivien (Gregory Pearson, personal communication) [See Lorenz, *Sapho*

1900. — G. R.]. Rodin's bust of Vivien may be seen in the Rodin Museum in Paris. For published photographs, see note 9.

8. To avoid confusion, I have used the name Renée Vivien throughout the essay, although she did not begin to use the name until around 1900.

9. The literature on Natalie Barney is extensive and growing rapidly. Barney's own memoirs are one of the most important sources, and I have relied heavily on her chapter on Renée Vivien from *Souvenirs indiscrets*, which recounts Barney's early life. Rogers's *Ladies Bountiful* is primarily an amusing summary of that chapter. Gregory Pearson is preparing and editing an English translation of Barney's memoirs. Bertha Harris's "The More Profound Nationality of Their Lesbianism" has the best discussion of the relevance to the women's movement of Barney, Vivien, and the other women associated with them. The recent book on Romaine Brooks (Secrest, *Between Me and Life*) contains a long section on Barney. Chalon's recent and intimate biography of Barney, *Portrait d'une séductrice*, could only have been written by a close friend, and will soon be translated into English. Natalie Barney left an enormous archive to the Bibliothèque Doucet, under the direction of Françios Chapon. Unfortunately, these papers were not ready for public scrutiny when I was doing this research. I understand that at least some of them are now available to be read, and that the Doucet is preparing to publish various letters and papers. Jean Chalon generously permitted me to see some of his own considerable collection of Barney memorabilia. George Wickes's biography of Barney, *The Amazon of Letters*, will be published in 1977. He has enabled me to consult much of the book as it progressed, and his biography promises to be definitive.

Many photographs of Barney, Vivien, and the other women of their circle have been published, most notably in Secrest, *Between Me and Life*; Chalon, "La Maison de Natalie Barney" and *Portrait d'une séductrice*; Blume, "Natalie Barney, Legendary Lady of the Rue Jacob"; and Wickes, "A Natalie Barney Garland." Wickes's *The Amazon of Letters* will also contain photographs. Alice Pike Barney painted Natalie Barney, Eva Palmer, and Renée Vivien. The portraits of Barney and Palmer can be seen in a published catalogue of Alice Barney's work (Smithsonian Institution, *Alice Pike Barney*). Romaine Brooks painted herself, Barney, Elizabeth de Gramont, and others. These can be seen in Breeskin, *Romaine Brooks, "Thief of Souls"* and Whitworth, "Romaine Brooks." See also notes 11 and 13 below.

10. Barney attended Les Ruches some years after the events described in *Olivia* (Strachey, *Olivia*), and the personnel had changed. For the background information of Olivia's Les Ruches, see Holroyd, *Lytton Strachey*, 36–41.

11. Alice Pike Barney left the Barney home in Washington (Studio House) and much of her work to the Smithsonian. The Barney family retained their connections to the Smithsonian, and Natalie Barney arranged for the Smithsonian to acquire the great bulk of Romaine Brooks's work. Several of Brooks's portraits are displayed at the National Collection of Fine Arts, and many more of them are in storage. The museum also has some pieces of jewelry which belonged to Natalie and her sister Laura.

12. Barney, *Souvenirs indiscrets*, 30.

13. Natalie Barney's love of costume, and this costume in particular, are referred to in *A Woman Appeared to Me*. The Duran portrait is now in storage at the National Collection of Fine Arts. It has been reproduced in Blume, "Natalie Barney, Legendary Lady of the Rue Jacob," and Chalon, "La Maison de Natalie Barney."

14. Grindea, "The Amazon of Letters," 10.

15. In this fictional (?) account of the seduction, Natalie appeared before the object of her desires wearing a gray velvet doublet with Liane's initials, and demanded to be her beloved's page (Pougy, *Idylle Saphique*)!

16. Ibid., 277.

17. Ibid., 57.

18. Lauritsen and Thorstad, *The Early Homosexual Rights Movement*.

19. Foster, *Sex Variant Women in Literature*, 81–115.

20. Vivien, *A Woman Appeared to Me*, 53.

21. Vivien, *Brumes de fjords*, 115–18.

22. Vivien, "Le Voile de Vashti," 131–44.

23. *Book of Esther*, I:17–18. King James Version.

24. Vivien, "Le Voile de Vashti," 140.

25. Ibid., 143–44.

26. Vivien, *Du vert au violet*, 89–90.

27. Vivien, "Brune comme une Noisette," 145–64.

28. Colette, *The Pure and the Impure*, 91.

29. Vivien, "Paroles a l'Amie," *Poèsies completes*, 58–60.

30. Hall, *The Well of Loneliness*, 352.

31. After their reconciliation, Renée Vivien rewrote *A Woman Appeared to Me*, bringing the story up to date and changing Natalie's name from Vally to Lorely. Both versions were published, the first in 1904 and the second in 1905. Foster's translation is of the earlier text. It is not surprising that Natalie disliked both versions, and felt that neither did her justice. However, the 1905 version is less hard on Natalie.

32. Vivien, *A Woman Appeared to Me*, 39.

33. Reinach's notes in *Evocations* (Vivien, *Du vert au violet*) say that both Eva and Natalie told him that the poem "To the Sunset Goddess" (ibid.) referred to Eva Palmer. The "Eva" in *A Woman Appeared to Me* is called the Sunset Goddess. In the same margin, Reinach says that Liane de Pougy and Natalie confirmed that Eva Palmer was "never very intimate" with Vivien (Reinach, unpublished marginalia, in the Salle de la Réserve, Bibliothèque Nationale, 8° Z. Don 593, numbers 1–48).

34. In *Souvenirs indiscrets* (67) Natalie says that she spent much of her time at Bryn Mawr at the feet of one professor, "Miss G." Given the date of the Bryn Mawr excursion, "Miss G." was probably Miss Mary Gwinn, whose triangular relationship with M. Carey Thomas and Alfred Hodder appears in some of Gertrude Stein's early writings. The events at Bryn Mawr and their relationship to Stein's work are discussed in Leon Katz, introduction to *Fernhurst, Q.E.D., and Other Early Writings*, xxxi–xxxviii.

35. Chalon, *Portrait d'une Seductrice*, 107.

36. Reinach, unpublished marginalia, in the Salle de la Réserve, Bibliothèque Nationale, 8° Z. Don 593, numbers 1–48. This note in *Cendres et poussières* was copied by Reinach from a book which had belonged to Natalie, who also had a habit of writing in margins. Natalie commented on the poems and then gave the book to Renée, who may also have written in it. The copy was sold after Renée died. It was found by a bookseller, who gave it back to Natalie. In 1917, she showed it to Reinach, who copied all of the earlier notes and added his own. When Natalie died, the book was either sold again or else was sent to the Doucet.

37. After Dolly Wilde's death, Natalie assembled a volume of memorial essays (Barney, *In Memory of Dorothy Irene Wilde*). The book also contains a number of Dolly Wilde's letters. Some of these are to an unidentifiable friend, and many of them are to a lover (Natalie). They provide an unusual glimpse into the interior of the seraglio. The following excerpt is from a letter to the friend.

> The fifteen days of motoring was wonderful in many ways, altho' the arrival of R. [Romaine Brooks] on the scene was the herald of unimaginable suffering to me. I must tell you all the story when I see you. It contains all but the obvious ingredients. Dear Madame de C.-T. [Elizabeth de Clermont-Tonnerre] was with us, exquisite, wonderful and so sensitive to someone she likes, that after an outwardly amusing evening she got up in the middle of the night and came to my room because she felt I was feeling sad—and indeed I was in tears! Such sweet rough comforting! . . .
>
> Gradually I perceive S. [Natalie Barney] to be of transcendental intelligence—without sensibilities in the weaker meaning of the word—altho' alive through her intelligence to that quality in others. Thus, she is not tender—but will assume tenderness like a cloak—is not romantic but if needs be will pander to romanticism, etc. A week of charming companionship with her has left me like a refreshed martyr gathered up in new strength! forgetful of the pangs of torture. (ibid., 115–17)

Dolly Wilde later discussed the letter above in a letter to Natalie, retracting much of her earlier response: "I was *amazed* reading it. . . . You are the only serious thing in my life emotionally. I remember in those days feeling as if you overshadowed me like a great mountain—that all at once uplifted me and awed me. I blush now at my description of your character (though parts of it *are* very true)—but I retract 'no tenderness' darling! You don't assume it 'like a cloak'; your tenderness seems my very security now" (ibid., 117).

One of Dolly's letters even indicates that Natalie was quite capable of jealousy: "Why did you take such a stern attitude towards me this morning. As you have no jealousy I am left to think logic and reason inspired you. *Why Why*? . . . I have not fallen in love with anyone. . . . I meant my wire and when you telephoned from Marseilles I immediately arranged for 'my present love' to leave—without a pang. You cut short explanations by ringing off. And then telephoning all day yesterday with such bewildering results. From tomorrow at 12 I am alone. *Please* understand. LOVE ME DARLING" (ibid., 127–28).

Nevertheless, this letter from Dolly indicates that Natalie continued to claim her own freedom: "I could have wished your kindness to have gone even further and not left evidences of your love in the book by my bed—amongst the writing paper, etc. Horrid stabs—unnecessary hurt. Tout Paris pours endless stories into my ears—but acceptance of the rhythm of destiny becomes easier and easier" (ibid., 132). Dolly continues: "I'd like to shout a friendly warning to your harem: 'Take care!'" (ibid., 137).

38. Chalon, *Portrait d'une Séductrice*, 112–15.

39. Renée must have found out about Natalie's affair with Delarue-Mardrus after her own reconciliation with Natalie in 1904. In the 1905 version of *A Woman Appeared to Me*, Petrus is gone, and Lucie Delarue-Mardrus appears as Dorianne, another rejected lover of Lorely-Natalie. The poems in *Nos secrètes amours* (Delarue-Mardrus, *L'Ange et les pervers*) were apparently inspired by Natalie.

40. Music was one of Renée's most intense passions. All the chapters of *A Woman Appeared to Me* were originally preceded by selections of music (see translator's notes, Vivien, *A Woman Appeared to Me*, 64). In the novel, San Giovanni speaks for Renée when she says, "To my eternal sorrow, I am not a musician" (ibid., 16).

41. George Wickes (personal communication) supplied the information that Natalie stayed in Washington, probably for several months to a year. Natalie was accompanied on her journey by Eva Palmer and a young man named Freddy (Barney, *Souvenirs indiscrets*, 74). Natalie had met Freddy through Olive Custance. Freddy may not have been his real name. It is possible that this young man is the "Prostitute" in *A Woman Appeared to Me*.

42. These prose poems were published, in 1910, as *Je me souviens*, and describe the relationship with Renée from Natalie's perspective.

43. Colette, *The Pure and the Impure*, 93.

44. Violet Shilleto had lived at 23, Ave. du Bois with her family when she was a child. Renée moved to another apartment at the same address in 1901.

45. Romaine Brooks therefore had met Renée before she met Natalie in 1915. Romaine says in the same piece: "Renée Vivien had often spoken to me of Natalie Barney and I found little interest in listening to those endless love grievances which are so often devoid of any logical justification" (Wickes, "A Natalie Barney Garland," 104).

46. Cited in ibid., 102.

47. Colette, *The Pure and the Impure*, 84.

48. Letter to Lèon Hammel, in Phelps, *Earthly Paradise*, 164.

49. In his notes, Reinach says that the Riversdale poems were largely the work of the Baroness (Reinach, unpublished marginalia, in the Salle de la Réserve, Bibliothèque Nationale, 8° Z. Don 593, numbers 1–48). Hélène de Zuylen de Nyevelt published non-lesbian poems under her own name.

50. On the flyleaf to the copy of Vivien's *A l'heure des mains jointes*, Reinach wrote out a fairly complete chronology of the last years of her life. He indicates three liaisons in 1908 (Reinach, unpublished marginalia, in the Salle de la Réserve, Bibliothèque Nationale, 8° Z. Don 593, numbers 1–48). There are three love letters from Renée to "Une Dame Turque" dated 1905–1906 (in Lacretelle, *L'Amour sur la place*, 382–83).

51. Colette, *The Pure and the Impure*, 85.

52. Ibid., 95.

53. Ibid., 96.

54. Vivien, "Ainsi je parlerai . . ." *Poèsies completes*, 52–55.

55. Katz, *Gay American History*, 518–20.

56. Hansen, "The Historical Construction of Homosexuality," 67.

Chapter 4. The Leather Menace

I have benefited immensely from innumerable conversations about sex, politics, and s/M with Pat Califia. The work that Allan Bérubé, John D'Emilio, and Daniel Tsang have done to exhume the story of gay persecution in the fifties has taught me how sex repression works. My sense of the politics of sex in the nineteenth century evolved during conversations with Ellen Dubois, Mary Ryan, and Martha Vicinus. My sense of the context for the politics of sex during the Cold War is largely due to input from Lynn Eden. Conversations with Jeff Escoffier and Amber Hollibaugh have sparked many lines of thought about the social relations of sexuality. I have been taught much of the recent history and many of the fine points of s/M by I. B., Camilla Decarnin, Jim Kane, Jason Klein, Terry Kolb, the Illustrious Mistress LaLash, Steve McEachern, Bob Milne, Cynthia Slater, Sam Steward, Louis Weingarden, and Doric Wilson. While responsibility for the opinions expressed in this essay is mine, I want to express my thanks to all these individuals for their insights, their information, and their generosity.

This essay was revised somewhat for the second edition of *Coming to Power*.

1. [The historical and critical literatures on the Cold War–era sexual regimes have changed dramatically in the three decades since this article was written. A small sample of the scholarship that emerged in the interim would include Corber, *Homosexuality in Cold War America*, and *In the Name of National Security*; Chauncey, "The Postwar Sex Crime Panic"; D'Emilio, "The Homosexual Menace"; Eskridge, "Privacy Jurisprudence and the Apartheid of the Closet, 1946–1961"; Freedman, "Uncontrolled Desires: The Response to the Sexual Psychopath, 1920–1960"; Graves, *And They Were Wonderful Teachers*; Higgins, *Heterosexual Dictatorship*; Johnson, *The Lavender Scare*; Robbins, "The Library of Congress and Federal Loyalty Programs, 1947–1956"; and Werth, *The Scarlet Professor.*—G. R.]

2. I am indebted to Allan Bérubé, John D'Emilio, and Daniel Tsang for much of what I know about the antigay repression of the Cold War period. Each of them has generously shared his research in progress. For published sources, see the following:

D'Emilio, "Radical Beginnings, 1950–51," "Dreams Deferred," and "Gay Politics, Gay Community"; Bérubé, "Behind the Spectre of San Francisco"; Katz, *Gay American History*, 91–119 and 406–20. See also Gerassi, *The Boys of Boise.*

3. For further details, see Califia, "The Age of Consent"; Mitzel, *The Boston Sex Scandal*; Moody, *Indecent Assault.*

4. Meanwhile, Dan White got seven years for the cold-blooded murder of two public officials, one of them gay, and Ronald Crumpley was acquitted of the murder of two gay men (and the wounding of several others) by reason of insanity.

5. [When I wrote this essay, there were a small number of legal cases in which tops or dominants had been arrested, prosecuted, and convicted of assault for consensual SM. I was aware that bottoms and submissives could in principle be arrested under the assault statutes and charged with aiding and abetting their own assaults. This seemed far-fetched, however, and I found no documentation that such charges had ever been brought. Some years later, this unlikely scenario did in fact occur in England in the Spanner case. In 1990, sixteen gay men were sentenced for consensual SM activities in a private home and some had been convicted of abetting the "assaults" upon their own persons. See *Regina v. Brown*; Thompson, *Sadomasochism.*—G. R.]

6. Lest I be misunderstood, the point is not that the Jaguar should not be supported. It should. But the contrast in community response to the troubles of the Jaguar and the troubles of the Bootcamp was stunning.

7. Randy Alfred, text of complaint against *Gay Power, Gay Politics*, lodged with the National News Council, 10 July 1980, 4 (on file with the author).

8. Ibid., 5.

9. Ibid.

10. Pearl Stewart, "Safety Workshops for S.F. Masochists," *San Francisco Chronicle*, 12 March 1981.

11. Marshall Kilduff, "Angry Mayor Cuts Off Coroner's S&M Classes," *San Francisco Chronicle*, 14 March 1981.

12. *San Francisco Chronicle*, 11–14 July 1981.

13. [*On Homosexuality* was a position paper issued by the Revolutionary Union (RU) in the early 1970s. In 1975, an unnamed anarchist group in Ann Arbor printed the statement in its entirety along with critical commentary in the form of position papers of the Front Homosexuel d'Action Revolutionnaire, an appendix on the treatment of homosexuals in communist Cuba, and assorted news items on homosexuality in China, Korea, and the Soviet Union. The most effective critical perspectives, however, were conveyed by several hilarious cartoons in the style of Roy Lichtenstein. The cartoons featured stereotypical heterosexual couples whose dialog was taken from the RU statement. So, for example, one panel shows a male figure resembling Clark Gable, staring down at the upturned face of an expectant woman, eyes closed, awaiting his kiss. The dialog box for the man says, "Male homosexuality reinforces male chauvinism in its refusal to deal with relationships with women." In another panel, the man says, "The only road to real happiness for homosexuals is to eliminate

the . . ." and the woman finishes with "system that drives them to homosexuality." Note that the RU statement was referring to both lesbians and gay men. Pamphlet on file with author. Copies are available in the Labadie Collection, Hatcher Graduate Library, University of Michigan.—G. R.]

14. Karr, "Susan Griffin."

15. [Samois was a lesbian feminist SM support group in the San Francisco Bay Area from 1978 to 1983. The organization published *What Color Is Your Handkerchief?* and *Coming to Power.*—G. R.]

16. Correspondence and other documentation of the interactions between Samois and various feminist institutions (including the Women's Building and *off our backs*) are on file at the Lesbian Herstory Archives in New York City. The Women's Building adopted a formal policy banning the rental of meeting space to any s/m group. The policy was finally rescinded almost a decade later, in 1989, largely as a result of agitation by a subsequent organization, the Outcasts.

17. After nearly two decades of futile attempts to change this language, a successful campaign by the s/m Policy Reform Project of the National Coalition for Sexual Freedom finally resulted in its removal in 1999.

18. [The Institute for Sex Research in Bloomington, Indiana, is popularly known as the Kinsey Institute. I did not know at the time this essay was written that the barriers to using the institute's library were not adopted voluntarily by the institute, but were imposed by court order in 1957. The same decision that allowed the institute to amass its collections also restricted access to them to "qualified scholars." Yamashiro, "In the Realm of the Sciences," 32–33.]

19. The phenomenon of feminism as a closet for lesbianism is discussed by Chris Bearchell in "The Cloak of Feminism."

20. I should add that the term has also simply become an all-purpose insult whose meaning is simply that the speaker does not approve of the person or activity to which it is applied.

21. An excellent historical study of some of these shifts in feminist ideology can be found in Echols, "Cultural Feminism."

22. There is a certain amount of bad faith around sex in all this. There is plenty of sex in the women's movement, and most feminists are just as obsessed with it as anyone else. But it has gotten hard to call things by their real names, or acknowledge lust as an end in itself. There is rampant euphemism, and a self-centered notion that "feminist sex" is a higher form of erotic expression. And the boundaries of what can be "feminist sex" shrink by the day.

23. Among the histories which shed light on the relationship between nineteenth-century feminism and various sexual populations and issues are these: Gordon, *Woman's Body, Woman's Right*; Walkowitz, "The Politics of Prostitution" and *Prostitution and Victorian Society*; Weeks, *Coming Out.*

24. Bannon, *I Am a Woman.*

25. Cited in D'Emilio, "Radical Beginnings, 1950–51," 24.

It is always a treat to get to the point in a paper when I can thank those who contributed to its realization. Many of my ideas about the formation of sexual communities first occurred to me during a course given by Charles Tilly on "The Urbanization of Europe from 1500–1900." Few courses could ever provide as much excitement, stimulation, and conceptual richness as did that one. Daniel Tsang alerted me to the significance of the events of 1977 and taught me to pay attention to sex law. Pat Califia deepened my appreciation for human sexual variety and taught me to respect the much maligned fields of sex research and sex education. Jeff Escoffier shared his powerful grasp of gay history and sociology, and I have especially benefited from his insights into the gay economy. Allan Bérubé's work-in-progress on gay history has enabled me to think with more clarity about the dynamics of sexual oppression. Conversations with Ellen Dubois, Amber Hollibaugh, Mary Ryan, Judy Stacey, Kay Trimberger, Rayna Rapp, and Martha Vicinus have influenced the direction of my thinking.

I am very grateful to Cynthia Astuto for advice and research on legal matters, and to David Sachs, book-dealer extraordinaire, for pointing out the right-wing pamphlet literature on sex. I am grateful to Allan Bérubé, Ralph Bruno, Estelle Freedman, Kent Gerard, Barbara Kerr, Michael Shively, Carole Vance, Bill Walker, and Judy Walkowitz for miscellaneous references and factual information. I cannot begin to express my gratitude to those who read and commented on versions of this paper: Jeanne Bergman, Sally Binford, Lynn Eden, Laura Engelstein, Jeff Escoffier, Carole Vance, and Ellen Willis. Mark Leger both edited and performed acts of secretarial heroism in preparing the manuscript. Marybeth Nelson provided emergency graphics assistance.

I owe special thanks to two friends whose care mitigated the strains of writing. E.S. kept my back operational and guided me firmly through some monumental bouts of writer's block. Cynthia Astuto's many kindnesses and unwavering support enabled me to keep working at an absurd pace for many weeks.

None of these individuals should be held responsible for my opinions, but I am grateful to them all for inspiration, information, and assistance.

1. Gordon and Dubois, "Seeking Ecstasy on the Battlefield"; Marcus, *The Other Victorians*; Ryan, "The Power of Women's Networks"; Pivar, *Purity Crusade*; Walkowitz, *Prostitution and Victorian Society*, and "Male Vice and Feminist Virtue"; Weeks, *Sex, Politics, and Society*.

2. Barker-Benfield, *The Horrors of the Half-Known Life*; Marcus, *The Other Victorians*; Weeks, *Sex, Politics, and Society*, especially pages 48–52; Zambaco, "Onanism and Nervous Disorders in Two Little Girls."

3. [The literature on the history of antimasturbation ideas and crusades has proliferated since this essay was written. It includes Laqueur, *Solitary Sex*; Bennett and Rosario, *Solitary Pleasures*; Stengers and Van Neck, *Masturbation*; and Mason, *The Secret Vice.*—G. R.]

4. Beserra, Franklin, and Clevenger, *Sex Code of California*, 113.

5. Ibid., 113–17.

6. A note on definitions: Throughout this essay, I use terms such as *homosexual*, *sex worker*, and *pervert*. I use *homosexual* to refer to both women and men. If I want to be more specific, I use terms such as *lesbian* or *gay male*. *Sex worker* is intended to be more inclusive than *prostitute* in order to encompass the many jobs of the sex industry. *Sex worker* includes erotic dancers, strippers, porn models, nude women who will talk to a customer via telephone hook-up and can be seen but not touched, phone partners, and the various other employees of sex businesses such as receptionists, janitors, and barkers. Obviously, it also includes prostitutes, hustlers, and "male models." I use the term *pervert* as a shorthand for all the stigmatized sexual orientations. It used to cover male and female homosexuality as well, but as these become less disreputable, the term has increasingly referred to the other "deviations." Terms such as *pervert* and *deviant* have, in general use, a connotation of disapproval, disgust, and dislike. I am using these terms in a denotative fashion, and do not intend them to convey any disapproval on my part.

7. Walkowitz, "Male Vice and Feminist Virtue," 83. Walkowitz's entire discussion of *The Maiden Tribute of Modern Babylon* and its aftermath (83–85) is illuminating. [An expanded treatment of the Maiden Tribute in Walkowitz, *City of Dreadful Delight*, provides additional details of the events of this period.—G. R.]

8. Ibid., 85–88.

9. Beserra, Franklin, and Clevenger, *Sex Code of California*, 106–7. [For an excellent book length treatment of the Mann Act, see Langum, *Crossing Over the Line.*—G. R.]

10. Commonwealth of Massachusetts, *Preliminary Report of the Special Commission Investigating the Prevalence of Sex Crimes*, 1947; State of New Hampshire, *Report of the Interim Commission of the State of New Hampshire to Study the Cause and Prevention of Serious Sex Crimes*, 1949; City of New York, *Report of the Mayor's Committee for the Study of Sex Offences*, 1939; State of New York, *Report to the Governor on a Study of 102 Sex Offenders at Sing Sing Prison*, 1950; Samuel Hartwell, *A Citizen's Handbook of Sexual Abnormalities and the Mental Hygiene Approach to Their Prevention*, State of Michigan, 1950; State of Michigan, *Report of the Governor's Study Commission on the Deviated Criminal Sex Offender*, 1951. This is merely a sampler.

11. Freedman, "'Uncontrolled Desire.'" [The published version of this talk is "Uncontrolled Desires."—G. R.]

12. Bérubé, "Behind the Spectre of San Francisco," and "Marching to a Different Drummer"; D'Emilio, *Sexual Politics, Sexual Communities*; Katz, *Gay American History*.

13. D'Emilio, *Sexual Politics, Sexual Communities*; Bérubé, personal communications. See also chap. 4, n. 1.

14. Gerassi, *The Boys of Boise*, 14. I am indebted to Allan Bérubé for calling my attention to this incident.

15. Bérubé, personal communication; D'Emilio, *Sexual Politics, Sexual Communities*.

16. The following examples suggest avenues for additional research. A local

crackdown at the University of Michigan is documented in Tsang, "Gay Ann Arbor Purges," parts 1 and 2. At the University of Michigan, the number of faculty dismissed for alleged homosexuality appears to rival the number fired for alleged communist tendencies. It would be interesting to have figures comparing the number of professors who lost their positions during this period due to sexual and political offenses. On regulatory reform, many states passed laws during this period prohibiting the sale of alcoholic beverages to "known sex perverts" or mandating that bars which catered to "sex perverts" be closed. Such a law was passed in California in 1955 and declared unconstitutional by the state Supreme Court in 1959 (Allan Bérubé, personal communication). It would be of great interest to know exactly which states passed such statutes, the dates of their enactment, the discussion that preceded them, and how many are still on the books. On the persecution of other erotic populations, evidence indicates that John Willie and Irving Klaw, the two premier producers and distributors of bondage erotica in the United States from the late 1940s through the early 1960s, encountered frequent police harassment and that Klaw, at least, was affected by a congressional investigation conducted by the Kefauver Committee. I am indebted to personal communication from J. B. Rund for information on the careers of Willie and Klaw. Published sources are scarce, but see Willie, *The Adventures of Sweet Gwendoline*; Rund, preface to *Bizarre Comix*, preface to *Bizarre Fotos*, and preface to *Bizarre Katalogs*. It would be useful to have more systematic information on legal shifts and police activity affecting nongay erotic dissidence.

17. "Chicago Is Center of National Child Porno Ring: The Child Predators," "Child Sex: Square in New Town Tells It All," "U.S. Orders Hearings on Child Pornography: Rodino Calls Sex Racket an 'Outrage,'" "Hunt Six Men, Twenty Boys in Crackdown," *Chicago Tribune*, 16 May 1977; "Dentist Seized in Child Sex Raid: Carey to Open Probe," "How Ruses Lure Victims to Child Pornographers," *Chicago Tribune*, 17 May 1977; "Child Pornographers Thrive on Legal Confusion," "U.S. Raids Hit Porn Sellers," *Chicago Tribune*, 18 May 1977.

18. [Since this essay was written, the expansion of child porn laws has been exponential. I have not followed these developments closely, but it seems that simple possession of child porn is now illegal in most jurisdictions. Even viewing an online image classified as child porn is legally hazardous. — G. R.]

19. For more information on the "kiddie porn panic," see Califia, "The Great Kiddy Porn Scare of '77 and Its Aftermath," and "A Thorny Issue Splits a Movement"; Mitzel, *The Boston Sex Scandal*; Rubin, "Sexual Politics, the New Right, and the Sexual Fringe." On the issue of cross-generational relationships, see also Moody, *Indecent Assault*; O'Carroll, *Paedophilia*; Tsang, *The Age Taboo*; and Wilson, *The Man They Called a Monster*.

20. "House Passes Tough Bill on Child Porn," *San Francisco Chronicle*, 15 November 1983, 14.

21. Stambolian, "Creating the New Man"; "Jacqueline Livingston." [Since the travails of Livingston, several other female and feminist photographers have run afoul of the child porn laws. See, for example, Powell, *Framing Innocence*. — G. R.]

22. [This assessment was, to say the least, overly optimistic. Moreover, the context in which these comments were written has changed beyond recognition. To reconstruct that context and deal with all of the complexities of this issue would require a major rewrite or another article. Since that cannot be undertaken here, let me be clear that I was primarily referring to consensual male homosexual relationships between adult men and teenagers at a time when many of the adult partners were being prosecuted over the objections of their younger lovers. In some cases the young partners clearly felt abused not by their lovers but by the legal process that was supposed to be protecting them.—G. R.]

23. Gebhard, "The Institute."

24. Courtney, *The Sex Education Racket*; Drake, SIECUS.

25. [For a comprehensive history of activism against sex education, see Irvine, *Talk About Sex*.—G. R.]

26. Podhoretz, "The Culture of Appeasement."

27. Wolfe and Sanders, "Resurgent Cold War Ideology."

28. Jimmy Breslin, "The Moral Majority in Your Motel Room," *San Francisco Chronicle*, 22 January 1981, 41; Gordon and Hunter, "Sex, Family, and the New Right"; Gregory-Lewis, "The Neo-Right Political Apparatus," "Right Wing Finds New Organizing Tactic," and "Unraveling the Anti-Gay Network"; Andrew Kopkind, "America's New Right," *New Times*, 30 September 1977; Petchesky, "Anti-abortion, Antifeminism, and the Rise of the New Right."

29. Rhonda Brown, "Blueprint for a Moral America."

30. [Not to belabor the point, but in the twenty-five years since this essay was published, anti-abortion, antigay, and pro-abstinence constituencies have expanded their spheres of influence in national, state, and local politics.—G. R.]

31. This insight was first articulated by McIntosh, "The Homosexual Role"; the idea has been developed in Weeks, *Coming Out*, and *Sex, Politics and Society*; see also D'Emilio, *Sexual Politics, Sexual Communities*; and Rubin, introduction to *A Woman Appeared to Me* (chap. 3 in this volume).

32. Hansen, "The Historical Construction of Homosexuality."

33. Walkowitz, *Prostitution and Victorian Society*, and "Male Vice and Feminist Virtue."

34. Foucault, *The History of Sexuality*.

35. A very useful discussion of these issues can be found in Padgug, "Sexual Matters.

36. Lévi-Strauss, "A Confrontation." In this conversation, Lévi-Strauss calls his position "a Kantianism without a transcendental subject."

37. ["The doubts I would like to oppose to the repressive hypothesis are aimed less at showing it to be mistaken than at putting it back within a general economy of discourses on sex in modern societies since the seventeenth century." Foucault, *The History of Sexuality*, 11.—G. R.]

38. Weeks, *Sex, Politics, and Society*.

39. Ibid., 22.

40. [My comments here are overly simple, and a large body of excellent scholarship that has emerged in the interim highlights the complexities of the history of sexuality and Christianity. Much of what is often assumed to date from the Bible or early Christianity was developed at later dates and retrospectively attributed to biblical and other older sources. See, for example, Mark Jordan, *The Invention of Sodomy.*—G. R.]

41. See, for example, "Pope Praises Couples for Self-Control," *San Francisco Chronicle*, 13 October 1980, 5; "Pope Says Sexual Arousal Isn't a Sin If It's Ethical," *San Francisco Chronicle*, 6 November 1980, 33; "Pope Condemns 'Carnal Lust' As Abuse of Human Freedom," *San Francisco Chronicle*, 15 January 1981, 2; "Pope Again Hits Abortion, Birth Control," *San Francisco Chronicle*, 16 January 1981, 13; and "Sexuality, Not Sex in Heaven," *San Francisco Chronicle*, 3 December 1981, 50.

42. Sontag, *Styles of Radical Will*, 46.

43. [Much more detailed histories of sodomy regulation have been published since 1984, and they have refined the chronologies and enforcement patters of sodomy laws in Europe. These include Rugiero, *The Boundaries of Eros*; Gerard and Hekma, *The Pursuit of Sodomy*; and Puff, *Sodomy in Reformation Germany and Switzerland*. Of course, sodomy laws in the United States were declared unconstitutional in 2003 in *Lawrence v. Texas.*—G. R.]

44. Foucault, *The History of Sexuality*, 106.

45. American Psychiatric Association, *Diagnostic and Statistical Manual of Mental Disorders*, 3rd edn.

46. Throughout this essay I treated transgender behavior and individuals in terms of the sex system rather than the gender system, although transvestites and transsexuals are clearly transgressing gender boundaries. I did so because transgendered people are stigmatized, harassed, persecuted, and generally treated like sex "deviants" and perverts. But clearly this is an instance of the ways in which my classificatory system does not quite encompass the existing complexities. The schematic renderings of sexual hierarchies in figures 1 and 2 were oversimplified to make a point. Although the point remains valid, the actual power relationships of sexual variation are considerably more complicated.

47. Kinsey, Pomeroy, and Martin, *Sexual Behavior in the Human Male*; Kinsey, Pomeroy, Martin, and Gebhard, *Sexual Behavior in the Human Female*.

48. Gagnon and Simon, *Sexual Deviance*, and *The Sexual Scene*; Gagnon, *Human Sexualities*.

49. [Krafft-Ebing, *Psychopathia Sexualis*; Hirschfeld, *The Homosexuality of Men and Women*; Ellis, *Studies in the Psychology of Sex*. Hirschfeld, Krafft-Ebing, Ellis, and other early sexologists are increasingly recognized as important figures who, despite their late-nineteenth and early-twentieth-century scientific language, made important contributions to the study of human sexuality. Paul Robinson's wonderful *Modernization of Sex* was an early reappraisal and was especially generous in its treatment of Ellis. See also Rosario, *Science and Homosexualities*; Oosterhuis, *Stepchildren of*

Nature; Steakley, "Per scientiam ad justitiam"; Bland and Doan, *Sexology in Culture*, and *Sexology Uncensored*; Sulloway, *Freud: Biologist of the Mind.*—G. R.]

50. Herdt, *Guardians of the Flutes*; Kelly, "Witchcraft and Sexual Relations"; Rubin, "Coconuts," and "Review of *Guardians of the Flutes*"; Van Baal, *Dema*; Williams, *Papuans of the Trans-Fly.*

51. Bingham, "Seventeenth-Century Attitudes toward Deviant Sex," 465.

52. Harry and DeVall, *The Social Organization of Gay Males*; Murray, "The Institutional Elaboration of a Quasi-Ethnic Community."

53. [I did not intend to imply here that gay and lesbian concentrations did not exist earlier in some cities.—G. R.]

54. For further elaboration of these processes, see: Bérubé, "Behind the Spectre of San Francisco," and "Marching to a Different Drummer"; D'Emilio, "Gay Politics, Gay Community," and *Sexual Politics, Sexual Communities*; Foucault, *The History of Sexuality*; Hansen, "The Historical Construction of Homosexuality"; Katz, *Gay American History*; Weeks, *Coming Out*, and *Sex, Politics and Society.*

55. Walkowitz, *Prostitution and Victorian Society.*

56. Vice cops also harass all sex businesses, be these gay bars, gay baths, adult bookstores, the producers and distributors of commercial erotica, or swing clubs.

57. [I did not intend to imply here that the naming of perversions in the medical literature created the social groups; on the contrary, the emergence of identifiable groups provoked medical classification. This remark referred instead to social and political mobilization, and a kind of ideological self-confidence, when such populations are able to contest their relegation to the categories of mental disease and assert their social legitimacy.—G. R.]

58. McLellan, *The Grundrisse*, 94.

59. Clark Norton's "Sex in America" is a superb summary of much current sex law and should be required reading for anyone interested in sex.

60. Beserra, Franklin, and Clevenger, *Sex Code of California*, 165–67.

61. Beserra, Jewel, Matthews, and Gatov, *Sex Code of California*, 163–68. This earlier edition of the *Sex Code of California* preceded the 1976 consenting-adults statute and consequently gives a better overview of sodomy laws. [Incest is a tricky term, whose meaning has undergone significant redefinition in recent decades. It is often used to indicate the sexual abuse of children within families. However, incest statutes generally prohibit sex or marriage between close relatives who are adults. As such, incest is an area of law that is distinct from that pertaining to sexual abuse of children by adults either within or outside of families. See note 94.—G. R.]

62. [For the decision that state sodomy laws are unconstitutional, see note 43. Despite the decriminalization of sodomy, many laws used to arrest homosexuals are still in place and enforced, and there is still a great deal of legal inequality for gay sex.—G. R.]

63. For a wonderful historical study of the relationship between gays and the military, see Bérubé, *Coming Out Under Fire*. [This section was written almost a decade

before "Don't Ask, Don't Tell" modified what had been a total ban on gay military service, when attempts to repeal the ban failed.—G. R.]

64. [Much of the struggle for gay civil equality is now being played out over exactly these issues: marriage, military service, immigration, confiscatory taxation, and discriminatory distribution of benefits. As this book goes to press, "Don't Ask, Don't Tell," the residue of the ban on homosexual military service, is slated for elimination but still technically in force. The conflicts over same-sex marriage have put in sharp relief the impact of state bans and the federal Defense of Marriage Act on issues of citizenship, health care, and taxation. For an excellent overview of the issues of same-sex marriage, see Chauncey, *Why Marriage?*—G. R.]

65. Newton, *Mother Camp*, 21.

66. ["Pedophile" is another term whose meaning has shifted since this piece was written. Pedophile is now used almost interchangeably with, or instead of, "child molester." Molestation is an illegal act. Pedophilia is technically a psychological state and indicates nothing about what a person does.—G. R.]

67. D'Emilio, *Sexual Politics, Sexual Communities*, 40–53, has an excellent discussion of gay oppression in the 1950s which covers many of the areas I have mentioned. The dynamics he describes, however, are operative in modified forms for other erotic populations, and in other periods. The specific model of gay oppression needs to be generalized to apply, with appropriate modifications, to other sexual groups.

68. [I am no longer certain that statutory rape should be eliminated as an area of law, but I am still convinced that it is in dire need of a thorough reexamination.—G. R.]

69. [Now, of course, the Internet has opened the informational flood gates. The present problem is less the quantity of information than its quality.—G. R.]

70. [The redevelopment of Times Square has been largely accomplished and has generated an extensive literature. A few examples would include Delaney, *Times Square Red, Times Square Blue*; Papayanis, "Sex and the Revanchist City"; and Eeckhout, "The Disneyfication of Times Square."—G. R.]

71. I have adopted this terminology from the very useful discussion in Weeks, *Sex, Politics, and Society*, 14–15.

72. See Spooner, *Vices Are Not Crimes*, 25–9. Feminist antiporn discourse fits right into the tradition of justifying attempts at moral control by claiming that such action will protect women and children from violence.

73. "Pope's Talk on Sexual Spontaneity," *San Francisco Chronicle*, 13 November 1980, 8. See also Foucault, *The History of Sexuality*, 106–7. Julia Penelope argues that "we do not need anything that labels itself purely sexual" and that "fantasy, as an aspect of sexuality, may be a phallocentric 'need' from which we are not yet free" ("And Now For the Really Hard Questions," 103).

74. See especially Walkowitz, *Prostitution and Victorian Society*, and Weeks, *Sex, Politics, and Society*.

75. *Moral Majority Report*, July 1983. I am indebted to Allan Bérubé for calling my attention to this image.

76. Cited in Bush, "Capitol Report," 60.

77. The literature on AIDS and its social consequences has mushroomed since this essay was published. A few of the important texts are Crimp, *AIDS*; Crimp and Rolston, *AIDS Demographics*; Fee and Fox, *AIDS: The Burdens of History* and *AIDS: The Making of a Chronic Disease*; Patton, *Sex and Germs* and *Inventing AIDS*; Watney, *Policing Desire*; Carter and Watney, *Taking Liberties*; Boffin and Gupta, *Ecstatic Antibodies*; Kinsella, *Covering the Plague*.

78. See for example Lederer, *Take Back the Night*; Dworkin, *Pornography*. The *Newspage* of San Francisco's Women Against Violence in Pornography and Media and the *Newsreport* of New York: Women Against Pornography are excellent sources.

79. Barry, *Female Sexual Slavery,* and "Sadomasochism"; Raymond, *The Transsexual Empire*; Linden, Pagano, Russell, and Starr, *Against Sadomasochism*; Rush, *The Best Kept Secret*.

80. "On the other hand, there is homosexual patriarchal culture, a culture created by homosexual men, reflecting such male stereotypes as dominance and submission as modes of relationship, and the separation of sex from emotional involvement—a culture tainted by profound hatred for women. The male 'gay' culture has offered lesbians the imitation role-stereotypes of 'butch' and 'femme,' 'active' and 'passive,' cruising, sado-masochism, and the violent, self-destructive world of 'gay' bars." Adrienne Rich, *On Lies, Secrets, and Silence*, 225. See also Rich, "Compulsory Heterosexuality and Lesbian Existence"; Pasternak, "The Strangest Bedfellows"; Gearhart, "An Open Letter to the Voters in District 5 and San Francisco's Gay Community."

81. Penelope, "And Now For the Really Hard Questions."

82. Jeffreys, *The Spinster and Her Enemies*. See especially chap. 7, "Antifeminism and Sex Reform before the First World War," and chap. 8, "The Decline of Militant Feminism." A further elaboration of this tendency can be found in Pasternak, "The Strangest Bedfellows."

83. Califia, "Among Us, Against Us," "Feminism vs. Sex," "The Great Kiddy Porn Scare of '77 and Its Aftermath," *Sapphistry*, "A Thorny Issue Splits a Movement," "Feminism and Sadomasochism," "What Is Gay Liberation," "Public Sex," "Response to Dorchen Leidholdt," "Doing It Together," "Gender-Bending," and "The Sex Industry"; English, Hollibaugh, and Rubin, "Talking Sex"; Hollibaugh, "The Erotophobic Voice of Women"; Holz, "Porn"; O'Dair, "Sex, Love, and Desire"; Orlando, "Bad Girls and 'Good' Politics"; Russ, "Being against Pornography"; Samois, *What Color Is Your Handkerchief*; Samois, *Coming to Power*; Sundahl, "Stripping for a Living"; Wechsler, "Interview with Pat Califia and Gayle Rubin"; Willis, *Beginning to See the Light*. For an excellent overview of the history of the ideological shifts in feminism which have affected the sex debates, see Echols, "Cultural Feminism." [I do not particularly like the term "pro-sex," although I often resort to it for lack of a better one. The group of activists and thinkers assembled under that label are not uncritical about sex or the issues of social power involved in sexuality.—G. R.]

84. Orlando, "Bad Girls and 'Good' Politics"; Willis, "Who Is a Feminist?"

85. Willis, *Beginning to See the Light*, 146. I am indebted to Jeanne Bergman for calling my attention to this quote.

86. See, for example Benjamin, "Master and Slave," 297; and Rich, review of *Powers of Desire*.

87. The label "libertarian feminist" or "sexual libertarian" continues to be used as a shorthand for feminist sex radicals. The label is erroneous and misleading. It is true that the Libertarian Party opposes state control of consensual sexual behavior. We agree on the pernicious qualities of state activity in this area, and I consider the Libertarian program to repeal most sex legislation as superior to that of any other organized political party. However, there the similarity ends. Feminist sex radicals rely on concepts of systemic, socially structured inequalities, and differential powers. In this analysis, state regulation of sex is part of a more complex system of oppression that it reflects, enforces, and influences. The state also develops its own structures of interest, powers, and investments in sexual regulation.

As I have explained in this essay and elsewhere, the concept of consent plays a different role in sex law than it does in the social contract or the wage contract. The qualities, quantity, and significance of state intervention and regulation of sexual behavior need to be analyzed in context, and not crudely equated with analyses drawn from economic theory. Certain basic freedoms that are taken for granted in other areas of life do not exist in the area of sex. Those that do exist are not equally available to members of different sexual populations and are differentially applied to various sexual activities.

88. Rich, review of *Powers of Desire*, 76.

89. Samois, *What Color Is Your Handkerchief* and *Coming to Power*; Califia, "The Great Kiddy Porn Scare of '77 and Its Aftermath," and "Feminism and Sadomasochism."

90. My favorite recent expression of ideological condescension is this one: "The Sadomasochists are not entirely 'valueless,' but they have resisted any values that might limit their freedom rather than someone else's judgment; and in this they show themselves as lacking in an understanding of the requirements of common life." It appears in Phelan, *Identity Politics*, 133.

91. Orlando, "Power Plays"; Wilson, "The Context of 'Between Pleasure and Danger,'" especially 35–41.

92. *Taylor v. State*, 214 Md. 156, 165, 133 A. 2d 414, 418. This quote is from a dissenting opinion, but it is a statement of prevailing law.

93. Beserra, Jewel, Matthews, and Gatov, *Sex Code of California*, 163–65.

94. "Marine and Mom Guilty of Incest," *San Francisco Chronicle*, 16 November 1979, 16.

95. Norton, "Sex in America," 18.

96. *People v. Samuels*, 250 Cal. App. 2d 501, 513, 58 Cal. Rptr. 439, 447 (1967).

97. *People v. Samuels*, 250 Cal. App. 2d. at 513–514, 58 Cal. Rptr. at 447.

98. Valverde, "Feminism Meets Fist-Fucking"; Wilson, "The Context of 'Between Pleasure and Danger.'"

99. Benjamin, "Master and Slave," 292, but see also 286, 291–97.

100. Ehrenreich, "What Is This Thing Called Sex," 247.

101. Rubin, "The Traffic in Women," 159, included as chap. 1 in this volume.

102. Ibid., 166.

103. Foucault, *The History of Sexuality*, 106.

104. MacKinnon, "Feminism, Marxism, Method and the State: An Agenda for Theory," 515–16.

105. MacKinnon, "Feminism, Marxism, Method and the State: Toward Feminist Jurisprudence," 635.

106. MacKinnon's published oeuvre has also burgeoned. See MacKinnon, *Feminism Unmodified* and *Toward a Feminist Theory of the State*.

107. On the second page of her introduction to *The Pure and the Impure*, Janet Flanner notes that this phrase, from *The Ripening Seed*, was going to be Colette's original title for the book.

108. Steakley, *The Homosexual Emancipation Movement in Germany*; Lauritsen and Thorstad, *The Early Homosexual Rights Movement*.

109. D'Emilio, *Sexual Politics, Sexual Communities*; Bérubé, "Behind the Spectre of San Francisco," and "Marching to a Different Drummer."

Chapter 6. Afterword to "Thinking Sex"

1. [This Afterword, and the Postscript that follows as chap. 7, were both written after twelve years of Republican control of the Federal Executive: Reagan's two terms as president, and the presidency of George H. W. Bush.—G. R.]

2. Page, "Minneapolis Mayor Vetoes Anti-Porn Law."

3. Page, "Indianapolis Enacts Anti-Pornography Bill."

4. Attorney General's Commission on Pornography, *Final Report*; Vance, "Meese Commission"; Vance, "Porn in the USA"; Vance, "Dubious Data, Blatant Bias"; Vance, "Negotiating Sex and Gender in the Attorney General's Commission on Pornography"; Vance, "The Pleasures of Looking"; Lynn, *Rushing to Censorship*; Lynn, *Polluting the Censorship Debate*; Duggan, "Of Meese and Women."

5. Attorney General's Commission on Pornography, *Final Report*, 433–42.

6. Ibid., 442–58.

7. ACLU Arts Censorship Project, *Above the Law*; Reyes, "Smothering Smut."

8. "Justice Department Targets Distributors of Porn," *San Francisco Chronicle*, 12 January 1988; Malcolm Glover, "U.S. Closes Five Porn Shops in Bay Area," *San Francisco Examiner*, 21 March 1991, A6; Jeff Boswell, "Polk Street Bookstores Are Seized," *Bay Area Reporter*, 21 March 1991, A1; Jim Doyle, "4 Tenderloin Sex Shops, Movie Houses Seized," *San Francisco Chronicle*, 21 March 1991, A3; "Feds Close Bookstores," *San Francisco Examiner*, 1 April 1991, A16; Keith Clark, "Smut, Art and the RICO Act," *Bay Area Reporter*, 28 March 1991, 14.

9. "Senate Votes to Limit Sex Programs on Cable," *San Francisco Chronicle*, 31 Janu-

ary 1992, D6; Paul Farhi, "Senate OKs Bill Allowing Renewed Cable TV Rules," *San Francisco Chronicle*, 1 February 1992, 1.

10. Nathan, *Women and Other Aliens*, 116–67; Andriette, "The Government's War on Child Pornography"; Stanley, "The Hysteria over Child Pornography and Paedophilia."

11. Andriette, "New Weapons for the Sex Police." As Andriette points out in his article, the law does not make fine distinctions, and even research collections such as the Institute for Sex Research (the Kinsey Institute) in Bloomington, Indiana, may be in violation of the law. Art museums, old *National Geographic* magazines, and collections of ethnographic film may also technically violate federal child-pornography law.

12. ACLU Arts Censorship Project, *Above the Law*, 1, 19. [The Internet has evidently changed this situation by providing new ways to distribute all pornography, including child porn. News stories reporting the successful busts of ostensibly huge online child porn rings are commonplace. However, it is difficult to get a handle on what is actually floating around in the cyberspace. Doing research on the topic may itself be illegal, since there are also reports of individuals being arrested for viewing such images online. The perilous legality of scholarship leaves the area largely unexamined, and knowledge of it coming mainly from police reports and press releases, along with lurid journalism.—G. R.]

13. Attorney General's Commission on Pornography, *Final Report*; Rollins, "When Conservatives Investigate Porn"; Dorries, "Feminists Differ at Chicago Porn Hearing"; Page, "Feminists Stand Divided on Meese Commission Report"; "Statement of Catharine A. MacKinnon and Andrea Dworkin," Women Against Pornography press release, 9 July 1986; "Statement by Dorchen Leidholdt on Behalf of Women Against Pornography," Women Against Pornography press release, 9 July 1986.

14. Attorney General's Commission on Pornography, *Final Report*, 391–96.

15. See "Statement of Catharine A. Mackinnon and Andrea Dworkin," Women Against Pornography press release, 9 July 1986, and "Statement by Dorchen Leidholdt on Behalf of Women Against Pornography," Women Against Pornography press release, 9 July 1986, for their positions on obscenity law.

16. [This bill did not pass. See also my discussion in "Misguided, Dangerous and Wrong," chap. 11 of this volume.—G. R.]

17. Vance, "The War On Culture," "Misunderstanding Obscenity," and "Reagan's Revenge."

18. Liz Lufkin, "Photographer's Life Put on Hold after Police Raid," *San Francisco Chronicle*, 25 May 1990, E3; Elizabeth Fernandez, "Film Developers Fear Porn Witchhunt," *San Francisco Examiner*, 8 July 1990, B1; Atkins, "Art Police Strike in S.F."; Mike Weiss, "The State vs. Jock Sturges"; Jim Doyle, "No Indictment in Child Porn Case," *San Francisco Chronicle*, 23 August 1991, A2; Jim Doyle, "U.S. Must Return Gear to Photographer," *San Francisco Chronicle*, 8 February 1991, A2.

19. Lisa Levitt Ryckman, "Nursing Mom's Inquiry Gets Child Taken Away," *San Francisco Chronicle*, 2 February 1992, A6.

20. Ibid.

21. Pela, "No Freedom of Gay Press."

22. Jeffrey Escoffier, personal communication.

23. Stamps, "Customs Releases Lesbian Erotica."

24. Cliff O'Neill, "Sex Survey Funds Transferred to Teen Abstinence Program," *Bay Area Reporter*, 19 September 1991, 19.

Chapter 7. Postscript to "Thinking Sex"

1. See chap. 6 in this volume.

2. Tamar Levin, "Canada Court Says Pornography Harms Women and Can Be Barred," *New York Times*, 28 February 1992, 1; Landsberg, "Canada."

3. [This bill did not ultimately pass.—G. R.]

4. Syms and Wofford, "Obscenity Crackdown."

5. Diaz, "The Porn Debates Reignite."

6. Landsberg, "Canada," 15, emphasis added.

7. "Sado-masochists Jailed for 'Degrading' Sex Acts," *Guardian*, December 1990; Rex Wockner, "SM Crackdown in London," *Bay Area Reporter*, 24 January 1991, 16; Rex Wockner, "London S/M Gays Fight Oppression," *Bay Area Reporter*, 21 February 1991, 20; "Taking Liberties"; Feldwebel, "Two Steps Backward"; "SM Gays—SM and the Law."

8. Chris Woods, "SM Sex Was a Crime, Court Rules," *Capital Gay*, 21 February 1992; Angus Hamilton, "Criminalizing Gay Sex," *Pink Paper*, 23 February 1992, 9; "S&M Is Illegal in England." [See also *Regina v. Brown*; and Thompson, *Sadomasochism*.—G. R.]

9. "Buchanan's New Anti-Bush Ad Shows Gay Scenes from PBS," *San Francisco Chronicle*, 27 February 1992, A2; Susan Yoachum, "Buchanan Calls AIDS 'Retribution,'" *San Francisco Chronicle*, 28 February 1992, 1; Elizabeth Kolbert, "Bitter G.O.P. Air War Reflects Competitiveness of Georgia Race," *New York Times*, 28 February 1992, A9; "Hitler's 'Courage' Etc.," *San Francisco Examiner*, 8 March 1992, A12; Dawn Schmitz, "Riggs, Buchanan Battle for Public TV," *Gay Community News*, 5–18 April 1992, 5; Jerry Roberts, "Quayle Blames Riots on Decline of Family Values," *San Francisco Chronicle*, 20 May 1992, 1; Carl Irving, "Quayle: Marriage Is Key to Ending Poverty," *San Francisco Examiner*, 20 May 1992, A14; Marsha Ginsburg and Larry D. Hatfield, "'Murphy Brown' Furor Grows," *San Francisco Examiner*, 20 May 1992, 1; Jerry Roberts, "Uproar over Comments by Quayle," *San Francisco Chronicle*, 21 May 1992, 1; George Raine, "Quayle Planned Attack on 'Murphy,'" *San Francisco Examiner*, 21 May 1992, A1; "Bush Links Big-City Woes to Collapse of the Family," *San Francisco Chronicle*, 10 March 1992, A4; Torie Osborn and David M. Smith, "Are Gays Being Made '92's Hate Symbol?," *San Francisco Chronicle*, 9 March 1992, A21; Elaine Herscher, "Gays Under Fire in Presidential Race," *San Francisco Chronicle*, 26 June 1992, 1. [*Plus ça change*: among the items of contention in this year's federal budget,

the NEA and PBS again loomed large. Homosexuality continues to be a potent political flashpoint, although much of the focus is now on preventing same-sex civil marriage and maintaining unequal benefits for same-sex partners.—G. R.]

10. Information about these initiatives based on flyers prepared by the Right to Privacy PAC and the Campaign for a Hate-Free Oregon in Portland, Oregon. [There is now a great deal more material about the OCA campaigns. See for example, Herman, *The AntiGay Agenda*; Stein, *The Stranger Next Door*; and the documentary film, *Ballot Measure 9*.—G. R.]

11. [The Oregon Citizens Alliance continues to have an impact in the early decades of the twenty-first century. One example is the antihomosexual law proposed in Uganda in 2009 (Bahati, "The Anti Homosexuality Bill, 2009"). The provisions in this legislation that would impose capital punishment for some homosexual acts have received the most attention, but there are many other harshly punitive clauses, including lengthy prison sentences even for failing to report homosexual acts to authorities. The impetus for drafting the law emerged from a 2009 Kampala conference at which several antigay activists from the United States spoke. Scott Lively was among them. Lively was active in the OCA campaigns of the early 1990s. He has become a dedicated antigay evangelical who is particularly well known for his inventive Holocaust revisionism, which involves outlandish claims linking homosexuality and gay rights to the Nazi party. Lively, *Seven Steps to Recruit Proof Your Child*; Lively and Abrams, *Pink Swastika*; Lively (and his early coauthor Kevin Abrams) recycled a notorious text by Samuel Igra, *Germany's National Vice*. Published in 1945, Igra's book blamed Nazism on homosexuality, which he called a "poisoned stream" in German history.

According to the dust jacket of *Germany's National Vice*,

> The book describes the moral background out of which German atrocities have arisen—the tortures of the concentration camps, the lethal chambers where thousands of Jews were gassed to death, the incinerators of Lublin, the horrors of Lidice, Oradure-Sure-Glane. . . . This German lust for wallowing in torture and destruction of human life is, according to the present author, attributable to one basic vice. It is a vice that has been raised almost to a social cult by the political leaders of Germany, and its poison has seeped down into the rank and file. . . . "The explanation for this outbreak of sadistic cruelty may be that sexual perversion, and in particular homosexuality, are very prevalent in Germany. . . . [M]ass sexual perversity may offer an explanation for this otherwise inexplicable outbreak." . . . [Igra] traces the development of homosexuality as a poisoned stream originating with the Teutonic Knights. . . . The stream . . . had reached flood-level under Kaiser William II, on the eve of the first world war. Under the Hitler regime it has overflowed its banks and inundated wide tracts of German character with its foul poison.

Lively later republished parts of *Germany's National Vice* under the title *The Poisoned Stream*. Videos of Lively's presentation in Uganda show him claiming that butch homosexuals were responsible for the worst Nazi crimes, and were probably also the perpetrators of the Rwandan genocide. Such videos can be found on YouTube under the titles "Pastor Scott Lively on what HE started in Uganda!," "Scott Lively in Uganda: Gay People," "Scott Lively in Uganda: What Causes Homosexuality?," and "Scott Lively preaches against homosexuality in Uganda." As this book goes to press, the Ugandan law is on hold, but not after having instigated a frenzy of antigay sentiment and activity. In January of 2011, Ugandan gay activist David Kato was bludgeoned to death in his home (Jeffrey Gettleman, "Ugandan Who Spoke Up for Gays Is Beaten to Death," *New York Times*, 27 January 2011). —G. R.]

Chapter 8. Blood under the Bridge

Thanks to Bob Schoenberg and Ann Matter, and to the many departments and units at the University of Pennsylvania that supported the conference "Rethinking Sex." Thanks to Steven Epstein, Sharon Holland, and Susan Stryker for their gracious and generous comments. Thanks especially to Heather Love, for having brought us all together, and for honoring my work. Thanks to Melanie Micir and Poulomi Saha for taking such good care of the logistics. For help on this essay, I am immensely grateful to Heather Love, Carole Vance, Claire Potter, Jill Julius Matthews, Andrew McBride, and Valerie Traub.

1. It was a rare privilege that Ellen Willis did the final edit on "Thinking Sex." Editing then was a more thorough overhaul of a text than the limited copyediting that is the current standard procedure, and Ellen was a brilliant practitioner of those almost lost editorial arts. I have very fond memories of sitting on the floor of her New York apartment cutting up the text and pasting it back together.

2. See, e.g., B. Ruby Rich, "Is There Anything New under the Covers?" In "Review: Feminism and Sexuality in the 1980s," Rich dismissed me without engaging at all with "Thinking Sex" in a review essay covering several books, including *Pleasure and Danger*. In *Sex, Power, and Pleasure* (16–18, 150–55, 198–203), Mariana Valverde managed to excoriate "Thinking Sex" while using conceptual language (such as the "Domino Theory") almost identical to mine, but without attribution. Like many others, she avoided addressing the complexities raised in my discussion of sexual consent by characterizing my approach as an "exclusive" focus on consent that lacked awareness of differential social power. See also Elizabeth Wilson, "The Context of 'Between Pleasure and Danger,'" although Wilson's comments were based on the lecture rather than the published version. Exemplary of the hostile reviews was Pauline B. Bart's "Review: Their Pleasure and Our Danger." See also Jeffreys, *Anti-Climax*; and Bar On, "The Feminist Sexuality Debates and the Transformation of the Political." A welcome exception was Michèle Aina Barale's thoughtful and engaged comments in "Review: Body Politic/Body Pleasured: Feminism's Theories of Sexuality, a Review Essay."

3. Rubin, "Thinking Sex: Notes for a Radical Theory of the Politics of Sexuality," included as chap. 5 in this volume.

4. See Robin Morgan, *The Anatomy of Freedom*, 115; and Ellen Willis, "Who Is a Feminist?"

5. The historian Jonathan Ned Katz coined this slogan, which now graces the website www.outhistory.org, a community-created, nonprofit site on lesbian, gay, bisexual, transgender, queer, and heterosexual history.

6. From the welcome statement of the "Rethinking Sex" conference brochure, available at the University of Pennsylvania School of Arts and Sciences website, www.sas.upenn.edu/.

7. Weeks, *Coming Out*. See also Hansen, "The Historical Construction of Homosexuality"; Padgug, "Sexual Matters."

8. Kramer, "Queer Theory's Heist of Our History"; Brass, "Kudos to Kramer on Queer Theory"; Champagne, "Queer Theory Deserves a Fair Hearing"; Schneiderman, "In Defense of Queer Theory"; Kramer, "Letter to the Editor"; Yaeger, "To the Editor"; Brass, "Essentialism vs. Constructionism Redux"; Allard, "To the Editor."

9. For children, see Aries, *Centuries of Childhood*; Fass, *Children of a New World*; and Mintz, *Huck's Raft*. For marriage, see Cott, *Public Vows*; Lawrence Stone, *The Family, Sex and Marriage in England 1500–1800*; Coontz, *Marriage, a History*; and Simmons, *Making Marriage Modern*.

10. See Thompson, "Time, Work-Discipline, and Industrial Capitalism," and *The Making of the English Working Class*; Finley, *Ancient Slavery and Modern Ideology*; and Kelly, *Etoro Social Structure*.

11. This paradigm shift happened across a broad swath of researchers more or less simultaneously. In addition to my own essay, see Walkowitz and Walkowitz, "'We Are Not Beasts of the Field'"; Foucault, *The History of Sexuality*; Padgug, "Sexual Matters"; Hansen, "The Historical Construction of Homosexuality"; Walkowitz, *Prostitution and Victorian Society*; Vance, "Social Construction Theory," and "Anthropology Discovers Sexuality"; Epstein, "A Queer Encounter"; and Rubin, "Studying Sexual Subcultures," included as chap. 13 in this volume.

12. Rubin and Butler, "Interview."

13. Two key independent scholars were Jonathan Ned Katz and Allan Bérubé. See Katz, *Gay American History*, and *Gay/Lesbian Almanac*; Bérubé, *Coming Out Under Fire*.

14. See Lewin and Leap, *Final Report of the Commission on Lesbian, Gay, Bisexual and Transgender Issues in Anthropology*.

15. D'Emilio, "Dreams Deferred: Part 1," and "Dreams Deferred: Part 2"; Steakley, "The Gay Movement in Germany Part One," "The Gay Movement in Germany Part Two," and "Homosexuals and the Third Reich"; Bérubé, "The First Stonewall," "Behind the Spectre of San Francisco," and "Lesbian Masquerade." For more on *Gay Community News*, see Amy Hoffman's wonderful memoir, *An Army of Ex-Lovers: My Life at the Gay Community News*.

16. Bérubé, "Coming Out Under Fire."

17. Freedman, *Feminism, Sexuality and Politics*, 15.

18. See D'Emilio, "Allan Bérubé's Gift to History."

19. Bérubé, "Lesbian Masquerade."

20. Bérubé, "The First Stonewall."

21. Bérubé, *Coming Out Under Fire.*

22. See Garber, "A Spectacle in Color," and "Gladys Bentley."

23. D'Emilio, *Making Trouble*, xl.

24. Goffman, *Stigma.*

25. Vance, "Invitation Letter."

26. A substantial number of pages from the *Diary of a Conference on Sexuality* were reprinted in "Diary of a Conference on Sexuality, 1982: The GLQ Archive."

27. Vance, epilogue to *Pleasure and Danger*, 434.

28. Vance, "More Danger, More Pleasure," xxii.

29. Vance, epilogue to *Pleasure and Danger*, 434. In the epilogue, Vance introduced the terminology of "sex panic" rather than that of "moral panic," which was used by Cohen, then Weeks, and me. See Stanley Cohen, *Folk Devils and Moral Panics*; Weeks, *Sex, Politics, and Society*, 14–15; and Rubin, "Thinking Sex," 297–98, included as chap. 5 in this volume.

30. Alderfer, Jaker, and Nelson, *Diary of a Conference on Sexuality*, 47.

31. Cited in Brownmiller, *In Our Time*, 314.

32. Ibid., 314–15.

33. See Alderfer, Jaker, and Nelson, *Diary of a Conference on Sexuality*; Vance, epilogue to *Pleasure and Danger*, and "More Danger, More Pleasure."

34. Vance, epilogue to *Pleasure and Danger*, 433–34.

35. Coalition for a Feminist Sexuality and against Sadomasochism, "We Protest," leaflet distributed at Barnard Sex Conference, April 1981. From the collection of Gayle Rubin.

36. Willis, "Feminism, Moralism, and Pornography."

37. For several lengthy responses to the leaflet, see Vance, "Letter to the Editor"; and Willis, "Letter to the Editor"; and Rubin, "Letter to the Editor."

38. Quoted in Dejanikus, "Charges of Exclusion and McCarthyism at Barnard Conference," 5.

39. Quoted in Ibid.

40. Leidholdt, "Back to Barnard," 30.

41. Gerhard, *Desiring Revolution*, 188.

42. Vance, epilogue to *Pleasure and Danger*, 434.

43. Vance, "More Danger, More Pleasure," xxi.

44. Gould, *Juggling*, 200.

45. Gerhard, *Desiring Revolution*, 184. The actual members of the planning committee were listed in the *Diary* and also in Vance, *Pleasure and Danger*, xvii. Lynn Chancer provides yet another inventive version of the role of Samois in the Barnard conference. While she does not think that Samois was involved in the conference planning, she instead makes Samois responsible for igniting the conflict. According to Chancer, "the core of the dispute was the claim of a West Coast lesbian group called Samois . . . that Samois, like any other feminist participants, was entitled to represen-

tation on conference panels. . . . The outcome was that the planners of the Barnard conference defended Samois's right to participate, on sexual libertarian grounds." (Chancer, *Reconcilable Differences*, 207). Although the specter of Samois was relentlessly invoked, the organization had made no claims on the conference, was not represented at the conference, and had no prior relationship to the conference. It was WAP, not Samois, that generated the controversies. Among other things, the WAP protesters effectively demanded a blacklist by insisting that no member or supporter of Samois be allowed to speak on any topic at all. Moreover, the disputes were over a broader set of issues than Samois and sadomasochism. They were also about pornography, butch/femme lesbianism, and disparate visions of feminism itself. Chancer provides no citations to any source that would verify her account. Her bibliography does not include the *Diary*, *Pleasure and Danger*, or even the slanted press coverage.

46. Gould, *Juggling*, 200.

47. Vance, epilogue to *Pleasure and Danger*, 431–32.

48. Carole Vance, personal communication, June 2010.

49. Andrea Dworkin, memo, circulated but unpublished, August 1981, author's personal collection. Dworkin's assessment of the *Diary* can now more easily be compared with a substantial sample of the contents, which were reprinted in a special issue of GLQ. See "Diary of a Conference on Sexuality, 1982: The GLQ Archive."

50. Letters to the editor, *off our backs* 12.7 (1982): Gayle Rubin, 24; Amber Hollibaugh, 25; Shirley Walton, 25; Esther Newton, 25; Francis Doughty, 26. Letters to the editor, *off our backs* 12.8 (1982): Ellen Willis, 32; Joan Nestle, 32; Barbara Grier, 33. Letters to the editor, *off our backs* 12.10 (1982): Samois, 26; Cleveland WAVAW, 26.

51. But see Feminist Anti-Censorship Taskforce et al., *Caught Looking*; *Heresies: The Sex Issue* 12 (1981); and Duggan and Hunter, *Sex Wars*, for a useful chronology and incisive commentary.

52. See Lederer, *Take Back the Night*. This is the most representative collection of essays from the early feminist antiporn movement.

53. Brownmiller, *In Our Time*, 301–3.

54. MacKinnon mentioned pornography in passing in her 1982 and 1983 *Signs* articles, but did not become a prominent figure in the antiporn movement until the 1983 Minneapolis ordinance. See MacKinnon, "Feminism, Marxism, Method, and the State: An Agenda for Theory," and "Feminism, Marxism, Method, and the State: Toward Feminist Jurisprudence." See also Gayle Rubin, "Misguided, Dangerous, and Wrong," included as chap. 11 in this volume.

55. Russell and Griffin, "On Pornography," 11.

56. Ibid., 12. Russell appears to be unaware that the relative lack of explicit sex in some S/M films often resulted from attempts to avoid prosecution. The threshold of explicitness for bringing obscenity charges was often lower for S/M materials.

57. Carole Vance has a particularly lucid analysis of the rhetorical tactics involved in such "laundry lists" in an essay on the 1989 imbroglio over the National Endowment for the Arts (NEA). See Vance, "Misunderstanding Obscenity." See especially her discussion of the language of the Helms Amendment to restrict NEA funding (ibid.,

51). In addition, one must be careful to understand how potentially loaded terms are used in antiporn literature, and how their meaning can slip. One example, found in the Russell passage cited here, is mutilation. We generally think of mutilation as some terrible injury that inflicts permanent damage, but mutilation in antiporn texts often refers to practices of body modification such as genital piercing, nipple rings, or even tattoos. One person's idea of mutilation is another's idea of personal adornment.

58. Russell and Griffin, "On Pornography," 13.

59. See, for instance, Rubin, "Misguided, Dangerous, and Wrong," included as chap. 11 in this volume.

60. Women Against Violence in Pornography and Media, "Who Are We?"

61. Women Against Violence in Pornography and Media, "Questions We Get Asked Most Often," emphasis added.

62. Samois, *What Color Is Your Handkerchief*, and the organization's carefully worded statement of purpose printed on the inside of the back cover of the first edition of *Coming to Power*. See also Rubin, "Samois," and "The Leather Menace" (included as chap. 4 in this volume).

63. Califia, "History of Samois."

64. Women Against Violence in Pornography and Media, "A Forum on s&m in the Women's Community," leaflet, 1980. Collection of Gayle Rubin.

65. Samois, "This Forum Is a Lie About s/m," leaflet. Collection of Gayle Rubin.

66. Linden, Pagano, Russell, and Starr, *Against Sadomasochism*. Lynn Chancer erroneously states that *Against Sadomasochism* was written after Barnard and in response to it (Chancer, *Reconcilable Differences*, 207). Chancer provides no documentation to support her chronology. Since *Against Sadomasochism* came out in 1982, the same year as the conference, truly heroic measures would have been required to generate such a rapid response. Moreover, all of the individual articles were copyrighted between 1975 and 1981. *Against Sadomasochism* was well under way before Barnard, and was rooted in the antecedent Bay Area disputes.

67. Williams, "Second Thoughts on *Hard Core*," 47, 49.

68. Leidholdt and Raymond, *The Sexual Liberals and the Attack on Feminism*. See also Leidholdt, "A Small Group"; Hunter, "Sex-Baiting and Dangerous Bedfellows," and "Modern McCarthyism"; and Duggan, "The Binds that Divide."

69. Vance, "More Danger, More Pleasure," xxi.

70. Hunt, "Discord in the Happy Valley."

71. Fingrudt, ". . . An Organizer," 24.

72. It was at this conference that I first met Eve Sedgwick. Eve's paper was called "Spanking and Poetry: Starting with the Fundamentals." Eve, too, was attacked in some of the press coverage for ostensibly participating in the s/m conspiracy.

73. Multiple authors, "A Protest at the Emphasis of the Humanities Research Centre's 1993 Conferences," Australian National University, 9 March 1993, 1. See Sheila Jeffreys's account in *The Lesbian Heresy*, 95–97.

74. Barbara Farrelly, "ANU Denies Conferences Showcase Anti-feminism," *Sydney Observer*, 19 March 1993.

75. Leidholdt and Raymond, *The Sexual Liberals and the Attack on Feminism*.

76. CATW campaigns against decriminalizing prostitution, supports the Mann Act, and supports the federalization of antiprostitution enforcement. See Dorchen Leidholdt, "'Successfully Prosecuting Sex Traffickers': Testimony before the Committee on the Judiciary, House of Representatives, United States" and "Biography of Dorchen A. Leidholdt," both available on the CATW website, http://www .catwinternational.org/. Jeffreys is also currently involved in feminist antitrafficking and antiprostitution activism. See Vance, "Thinking Trafficking"; and Rubin, "The Trouble with Trafficking," included as chap. 2 in this volume.

77. Gerth and Mills, *From Max Weber*, 147.

78. For my comments on prostitution, see Rubin, "Thinking Sex," 157–58, included as chap. 5 in this volume. For comments on transsexuality, see "Thinking Sex," 386, n. 46.

79. Chauncey, "From Sexual Inversion to Homosexuality."

80. American Psychiatric Association, *Diagnostic and Statistical Manual*.

81. American Psychiatric Association, *Diagnostic and Statistical Manual*, 2nd Edition.

82. American Psychiatric Association, *Diagnostic and Statistical Manual*, 3rd Edition.

83. Stryker, *Transgender History*, 130–31.

84. Stryker, "Thoughts on Transgender Feminism and the Barnard Conference on Women," 218.

85. Raymond, *The Transsexual Empire*. See also House and Cowan, "Can Men Be Women?" For responses to Raymond, see Stone, "The 'Empire' Strikes Back"; and Riddell, *Divided Sisterhood*. Raymond has also moved into antiprostitution activism and was the co-executive director of the Coalition Against Trafficking in Women (CATW) from 1994 to 2007.

86. See, for example, Sheila Jeffreys's *The Lesbian Heresy*: "Gayle Rubin . . . remains famous in women's studies circles for a seventies article called *The Traffic in Women*. Rubin *repudiates* this article in the volume *Pleasure and Danger* in which she explains that she used to think that sex and gender were inevitably connected but now accepts the existence of a separate system of sexual oppression . . . a system which cannot be analyzed by feminists whose theory has only limited usefulness for looking at sex" (128; emphasis added). See also Jeffreys, *AntiClimax*, 274. For a contrasting assessment, see Annamarie Jagose's careful and detailed discussion of the relationship of queer theory to feminism, in which she correctly notes that the gulf between queer theory and feminism has been exaggerated, and comments that my essay was "a resolutely feminist intervention" ("Feminism's Queer Theory," 165).

87. Gerth and Mills, *From Max Weber*, 181.

88. Ibid., 190.

89. Ibid., 193.

90. Best, *Threatened Children*, 23–24. See also Fass, *Kidnapped*; and Mintz, *Huck's Raft*, 335–71.

91. As Steven Angelides notes in a comment on the literature on child sexual abuse, "The category of 'child' is only loosely defined in this body of work, and a child of five is rarely distinguished theoretically from a child of fifteen or sixteen." "Feminism, Child Sexual Abuse, and the Erasure of Child Sexuality," 149.

92. See, for example, Greslé-Favier, "*Raising Sexually Pure Kids.*"

93. See Burlein, *Lift High the Cross*; Irvine, *Talk about Sex*; and Levine, *Harmful to Minors.*

94. See *The Legacy*, directed by Michael J. Moore; Gilmore, *Golden Gulag*; and Domanick, *Cruel Justice.*

95. "What Should You Really Be Afraid Of?"

96. Quindlen, "Driving to the Funeral."

97. For a very thoughtful analysis of the expanding classification of sex offenders and its implications, see Fischel, "Transcendent Homosexuals and Dangerous Sex Offenders." For juvenile offenders, see Okami, "'Child Perpetrators of Sexual Abuse'"; and Levine, "A Question of Abuse."

98. Fischel, "Transcendent Homosexuals and Dangerous Sex Offenders."

99. Angelides, "Feminism, Child Sexual Abuse, and the Erasure of Child Sexuality," 142.

100. Alderfer, Jaker, and Nelson, *Diary of a Conference on Sexuality*, 59.

101. Corber, *Homosexuality in Cold War America*, and *In the Name of National Security*; Chauncey, "The Postwar Sex Crime Panic"; D'Emilio, "The Homosexual Menace"; Eskridge, "Privacy Jurisprudence and the Apartheid of the Closet, 1946–1961"; Freedman, "Uncontrolled Desires"; Gerassi, *The Boys of Boise*; Graves, *And They Were Wonderful Teachers*; Higgins, *Heterosexual Dictatorship*; Johnson, *The Lavender Scare*; Miller, *Sex-Crime Panic*; Robbins, "The Library of Congress and Federal Loyalty Programs, 1947–1956"; and Werth, *The Scarlet Professor*. Also see *The Fall of '55*, dir. by Seth Randall.

102. Best, *Threatened Children*, 184.

103. Castells, *The City and the Grassroots*; and Castells and Murphy, "Organization of San Francisco's Gay Community."

104. For the escalating costs of housing in the early 1980s, see Fainstein, Fainstein, and Armistead, "San Francisco."

105. Rubin, "Thinking Sex," 296–97, included as chap. 5 in this volume.

106. Delany, *Times Square Red, Times Square Blue*. Also on the development of Times Square, see Papayanis, "Sex and the Revanchist City"; and Eeckhout, "The Disneyfication of Times Square."

107. See Hartman et al., *Yerba Buena*; Hartman, *Transformation of San Francisco*; Hartman with Carnochan, *City for Sale*; Nowinski, *No Vacancy*, and *Ira Nowinski's San Francisco*; also note some of Nowinski's photos in Solnit and Schwartzenberg, *Hollow City*. Also see Groth, *Living Downtown*, for accounts of displacement of residents.

108. Rubin, "Thinking Sex," 296, included as chap. 5 in this volume.

9. The Catacombs

This essay is a revision of an article that appeared in *Drummer* 139 (May 1990).

1. For further reading on the Catacombs, see Jack Fritscher's knowledgeable and affectionate memoir of the Twenty-First Street Catacombs in *Drummer* 23 (1978). The article is accompanied by priceless photographs of the interior. Geoff Mains was a Catacombs regular whose experiences there are often reflected in his writing. See especially *Urban Aboriginals* (1984), chap. 6; "View from a Sling"; and *Gentle Warriors* (1989).

2. For more detail on the leather history of South of Market, see Rubin, "Elegy for the Valley of the Kings," "The Miracle Mile," "The Valley of the Kings," and "Requiem for the Valley of the Kings."

3. An interview with Pat Bond discussing the founding of the Eulenspiegel Society can be found in the introductory issue of the society's publication *Prometheus* (1973). For a history of the mixed-gender s/m community in San Francisco, see Truscott, "San Francisco."

4. For an account of the early days of organized lesbian s/m, see Califia, "A Personal View of the Lesbian s/m Community and Movement in San Francisco."

5. For fictional stories based on the Mineshaft, and some introductory remarks describing the place, see Cardini, *Mineshaft Nights*.

6. Fist-fucking is also known as fisting or handballing. It is a sexual technique in which the hand and arm, rather than a penis or dildo, are used to penetrate a bodily orifice. Fisting usually refers to anal penetration, although the terms are also used for the insertion of a hand into a vagina. Among gay men, fisters are a particular subgroup who have developed a rich set of behaviors and terminologies around their sexual practices. Among these are the following.

> The *manicure*: Well before AIDS, fisters took great pains to minimize injury. This required a very complete manicure to insure that fingernails did not tear rectal tissue. The fister's manicure involved cutting the nails very short, then filing down the remaining nail until no sharp edges protruded. Smooth fingertips were always de rigueur among fisters.
> The *douche*: For both aesthetic and health reasons, fisters developed a habit of cleaning out the rectum and colon with a particularly thorough enema, and this lengthy and repetitive enema was referred to as a douche.
> *Lube*: Comfortable anal sex requires some form of artificial lubrication, abbreviated as "lube." Comfortable fisting requires vast quantities of lube.
> *Top* and *bottom*: Fisters refer to the person providing the hand as the "top," and the person providing the orifice as the "bottom."

7. [Much of the gay world was built by such small businesses, where an individual or small group with limited capital and a small base of customers could establish some kind of alternative public space. It should also be noted, however, that while the small business format has been a source of community strength, it also has intrinsic

weaknesses. Because so many gay and lesbian "public goods" are privately owned, the communities they serve have little control over how, when, or even if they continue to operate. Such institutions are subject to various regulatory regimes, but they are primarily controlled by owners, license holders, and landlords. Gay bars and sex clubs are in this respect somewhat like professional sports teams in that their fans identify with and feel possessive about them, but it is the actual owners who decide whether to stay in town, or leave for a more prosperous market or a better stadium package.—G. R.]

8. See Truscott, "San Francisco." Also, the December 1989 *Growing Pains*, the newsletter of the Society of Janus, is a memorial issue dedicated to Cynthia Slater.

9. [Pat is now Patrick Califia.—G. R.]

10. Reminiscences of Fred Heramb can be found in the August 1989 issue of *Growing Pains*, newsletter of the Society of Janus.

11. [For a lovely memoir of these women's parties, see Due, "Blackbeard Lost."—G. R.]

12. The Hothouse was another remarkable leather-oriented sexual place. Located South of Market at 374 Fifth Street, between Folsom and Harrison, from 1979 to 1983 the Hothouse occupied a four-story building and had many specialized "fantasy" rooms. Louis Gaspar was the primary force behind the Hothouse, but many other individuals helped to design and build the customized fantasy rooms. Like the Catacombs, the Hothouse was a labor of love, embodied a great deal of personalized vision, and had its own group of devoted followers.

13. More recent AIDS risk-reduction guidelines have finally begun to suggest using rubber gloves for fisting, and current safe-sex guidelines from the AIDS Foundation in San Francisco no longer even mention fisting as a risky practice for catching AIDS. But as late as 1987, fisting without a glove was listed in one set of guidelines as moderately risky, although the only reference cited for this assessment was a study dating from 1983.

14. For the significance of the baths in gay male social life, see Bérubé, "The History of Gay Bathhouses."

Chapter 10. Of Catamites and Kings

I am indebted to Jay Marston for the conversations and encouragement that led me to write this essay, and to Jay Marston, Nilos Nevertheless, Allan Bérubé, Jeffrey Escoffier, Jeanne Bergman, Carole Vance, and Lynn Eden for reading the drafts and making innumerable helpful suggestions. Kath Weston kindly shared some of her work in progress. Thanks to Lynne Fletcher for ruthless editing (my favorite kind). I am, of course, responsible for any errors or misconceptions. I am out on this particular limb all by myself, but I am grateful to them all for helping me get here.

1. "**Butch**. 1. lesbian with masculine characteristics, see **dyke**. 2. non-homosexual man whose virile appearance both draws and repels the [male] homosexual. Syn: **all**

man; butch number . . . stud. 3. [gay male who is] manly in speech, in fashions and in bed; submission impossible. **Butch it up**. warning [to gay man] to act manly in the presence of friends who 'don't know' or the police who do. **Butch queen**. homosexual man whose virile activities and responsibilities make him hard to detect." Rodgers, *The Queen's Vernacular*, 39; see also **dyke**, 70–71.

2. Kennedy and Davis, "The Reproduction of Butch-Fem Roles."

3. In this essay, I am taking for granted a number of things that I will not directly address. I am assuming two decades worth of sustained critique of categories of sex and gender, including the argument that gendered identities, roles, and behaviors are social constructs rather than properties intrinsic to or emanating from physical bodies. Gender categories and identities are, nevertheless, deeply implicated in the ways in which individuals experience and present themselves. I also am aware of the many critiques that make straightforward use of terms like *identities* difficult. In this article, however, I am less interested in a rigorous use of terminology or theory than I am in exploring lesbian folk beliefs regarding gender, and aspects of gender experience among lesbian and bisexual women. I do not intend to exclude bisexual women by speaking mostly of lesbians. Many bisexuals have similar issues and experiences.

In addition, I am not interested in engaging the argument that butch-femme roles are a noxious residue of patriarchal oppression or the claim that butch-femme roles are uniquely situated "outside ideology" and embody an inherent critique of gender. For a statement of the first position, see Jeffreys, "Butch and Femme," 65–95; for the later see Case, "Towards a Butch-Femme Aesthetic," 55–73. For Jeffreys, lesbianism is a royal road to philosophical or political salvation, although this can be accomplished only by the lesbian couple who "make love without roles" (90). Case argues that it is the butch-femme couple that lends "agency and self-determination to the historically passive [female] subject" (65).

Case's approach is far preferable to that of Jeffreys. However, both analyses place an undue burden of moral gravity on lesbian behavior. Like lesbianism itself, butch and femme are structured within dominant gender systems. Like lesbianism, butch and femme can be vehicles for resisting and transforming those systems. Like lesbianism, butch and femme can function to uphold those systems. And nothing — not "mutual, equalitarian lesbianism" and not butch-femme — escapes those systems completely. More important, butch and femme should not be judged, justified, evaluated, held accountable, or rejected on the basis of such attributions of significance.

4. *Androgynous* is also sometimes used to indicate women somewhere between butch and femme. Androgynous used to mean someone who was intermediate between male and female, and many traditional and classic butches were androgynous in the sense that they combined highly masculine signals with detectably female bodies. Those who cross-dressed enough to successfully pass as men were not androgynous. This older meaning of *androgynous* is lost when the term is used to refer to individuals whose self-presentation falls somewhere between butch and femme.

5. I should make it clear that I do not consider any behavior, trait, or mannerism to be inherently "male" or "female," and that my operating assumption is that cultures

assign behaviors to one or another gender category and then attribute gendered significance to various behaviors. Individuals can then express gender conformity, gender deviance, gender rebellion, and many other messages by manipulating gender meanings and taxonomies.

6. Bayer, *Homosexuality and American Psychiatry*. There was opposition to classifying homosexuality as a disease before the 1973 decision, and there are still some therapists who consider homosexuality a pathology and would like to see the 1973 decision revoked. Nevertheless, the removal of homosexuality from the *Diagnostic and Statistical Manual III* remains a watershed.

7. For an overview of gender issues, including some aspects of transsexuality, see Kessler and McKenna, *Gender*. For female-to-male transsexuals, see Sullivan, *Information for the Female to Male Cross Dresser and Transsexual*; and Scheiner, "Some Girls Will Be Boys," 20–22, 38–43.

8. Not all lesbians are gender dysphoric, and not all gender-dysphoric women are lesbian or bisexual. For example, there are manly heterosexual women who sometimes attract (and confuse) lesbians. There are female-to-male transsexuals who are erotically drawn to women and identify as heterosexual men (even when they have women's bodies), and there are female-to-male transsexuals who are attracted to men and consider themselves male homosexuals.

9. For a discussion of "mannish lesbians" in the historical context of the early twentieth century, see Newton, "The Mythic Mannish Lesbian."

10. Older lesbian culture had many terms in addition to *butch*. *Bull, bull dyke, bull-dagger, dagger, dag, diesel dyke, drag butch*, and *drag king* are among the expressive terms that were once more commonly in circulation. See Rodgers, *The Queen's Vernacular*, 70–71.

11. For discomfort with the association of female-to-male transsexuals (FTMs) with butch lesbians, see a fascinating exchange that appeared in several issues of *FTM*, a newsletter for female-to-male transsexuals and cross-dressers. It began with an article in issue 12 (June 1990, 5), and continued in the letters columns in issues 13 (September 1990, 3), and 14 (December 1990, 2). A related exchange appeared in issue 15 (April 1991, 2–3).

12. See Butler, *Gender Trouble*, especially 23. For a study of butch-femme that contains a critique of Butler, although not on this point, see Weston, "Do Clothes Make the Woman?"

13. The concept *woman identified* explicitly links sexual orientation and certain kinds of "political" behavior (Radicalesbians, "The Woman Identified Woman"). The concept of the woman-identified-woman presents problems beyond the scope of this discussion. But while it equated feminism with lesbianism, "woman identified" did not at that time mean femininity or female gender identity. In contrast to "male identification" it is rarely taken as a synonym for "femme," although it has often been used as a synonym or euphemism for lesbianism. Although the apparent relationships between feminism and lesbianism were exciting and trailblazing when this essay first appeared in 1970, much of what has gone awry within feminist politics of sex can be

traced to a failure to recognize the differences between sexual orientations, gender identities, and political positions. Sexual preference, gender role, and political stance cannot be equated and do not directly determine or reflect one another.

14. See, for example, *On Our Backs* (1984–91), *Outrageous Women* (1984–88), and *Bad Attitude* (1984–91). For a look at the evolution of lesbian styles in the eighties, see Stein, "All Dressed Up, but No Place to Go?"

15. See Butler, *Gender Trouble*, 31. In addition, it is not only butches who play with symbols of masculinity. Lesbian femmes can play with male attire, as do heterosexual women, for a variety of reasons. A suit and tie do not necessarily "make the butch."

16. This is similar to gay male usage. Gay men use *butch* to refer to especially masculine men (Rodgers, *The Queen's Vernacular*). For a humorous send-up of gay male notions of butch, see Henley, *The Butch Manual*.

17. Several well-known butches of classic lesbian fiction exhibit some of the class spectrum of butch masculinity. Beebo Brinker is exemplary of white, working-class butchness (Bannon, *I Am a Woman*, *Women in the Shadows*, *Journey to a Woman*, and *Beebo Brinker*). Randy Salem's Christopher "Chris" Hamilton is an educated, middle-class white butch (Salem, *Chris*). Two of the upper-class, aristocratic cross-dressers are Jesse Cannon (Salem, *The Unfortunate Flesh*) and, of course, Stephen Gordon from *The Well of Loneliness* (Hall). And butch takes many more forms than these few examples can express.

18. For a discussion of the differences between erotic roles such as "top" and "bottom," and gender roles such as butch and femme, see Newton and Walton, "The Misunderstanding."

19. Lesbians, in turn, provide models for other permutations of gender, sex, and role. I know a technically heterosexual couple that consists of a lesbian-identified woman whose primary partner is an effeminate, female-identified mostly gay man. The woman once told me she has "lesbian sex" with the "girl" in him.

20. Foucault, *The Order of Things*.

21. Douglas, *Purity and Danger*.

22. Transgender organizations directly address issues of variant gender and how to live with it, understand it, and customize it. Some lesbian and bisexual women gravitate to such groups to sort out their gender questions in a context that provides a more sophisticated awareness of the subtleties of gender diversity than is currently available within most lesbian communities.

23. San Francisco Lesbian and Gay History Project, "'She Even Chewed Tobacco.'"

24. Sullivan, *From Female to Male*. In addition to the Garland biography, Sullivan wrote prolifically on transsexual issues and edited the FTM newsletter from 1987 to 1990.

25. It is interesting to speculate about how gay men will deal with FTMs who are gay male identified. Traditionally, gay male communities have dealt relatively well with male-to-female transvestites and transsexuals, while lesbian communities have not. But gay men are now faced with women becoming men, who may or may not

have male genitals whose origins are undetectable. I hope gay men meet the challenge of accepting gay FTMs with balance and good grace.

26. See "Genetic Lesbians."

27. See "Festival Womyn Speak Out." It is interesting to note that s/M was not a big issue at Michigan in 1991, nor was there controversy over s/M at the National Lesbian Conference. It saddens me that lesbians, from whom I expect better, appear so prone to need a target for horizontal hostility.

28. And if a woman who was disliked starts a sex change, the sex change becomes a convenient pretext to get rid of her/him. Obnoxious behavior that would be tolerated in a butch will often be considered intolerable in an FTM. Like other groups of stigmatized individuals, transsexuals are often subjected to particularly stringent standards of conduct.

Chapter 11. Misguided, Dangerous, and Wrong

[This essay has grown by sedimentary accretion, pushed together at various times by the geologic forces of publication. The resulting formation, like a folded ancient seabed, suffers from some vertiginous moments of anachronism. It would require major surgery to adequately update the article, so here I will only add the merest new layer, and try to give some historical context to the previous strata. The article was initially a revision of remarks submitted as testimony to hearings on pornography held by the National Organization for Women (NOW) in San Francisco, California, on 26 March 1986. These hearings were inspired by and more or less contemporaneous with the hearings of the Attorney General's Commission on Pornography. Shortly after the hearings, I sent a written version to NOW for inclusion in a spiral bound collection of statements from these hearings. The collection was available from the national NOW office, but I do not know for how long. When the version here was edited for publication in 1992, I tried to minimize the revisions, although some changes were made to update the references and reflect what was then recent history. Another two decades have now passed. For the present volume, I choose again to make some minimal adjustments to reflect the passage of time and add some references, while leaving the essay as close to its original form as possible. While the political terrain and regulatory apparatus have undergone significant evolution, the basic feminist arguments against pornography have not changed much and are still too often treated as tenable, with minimal attention to their evidentiary and logical insufficiencies. So I leave the article as a period piece unfortunately more prophetic than I knew. Its usefulness lies not in a state of the art bibliography, which it does not have, or in an up to date assessment of the political conditions for sexual representation, but rather in its challenges to the analytic structure and empirical claims of the feminist antipornography faction. That Empress still has no clothes. — G. R.]

1. There is a discussion of the early roots of antipornography analysis in feminism in Echols, *Daring to Be Bad*, 288–291, 360–364n.

2. Lederer, *Take Back the Night*, 15–16, 23.

3. Emblematic anthologies from this period of feminism include such classics as Gornick and Moran, *Women in Sexist Society*; Miller, *Psychoanalysis and Women*; Mitchell and Oakley, *The Rights and Wrongs of Women*; Koedt, Levine and Rapone, *Radical Feminism*; Morgan, *Sisterhood Is Powerful*.

4. See Russell and Lederer, "Questions We Are Asked Most Often," 23–29.

5. I have attended many educational presentations by WAVPM, and in none of them was any questioning of their basic assumptions permitted. Questions were restricted to inquiries about implementing their program, and those who tried to raise other issues were ignored or dismissed. For similar experiences, see two accounts of WAP's slide show and tour, in Webster, "Pornography and Pleasure," 48–51; and D'Emilio, "Women Against Pornography," 19–26.

6. The rhetorical attacks have heated up in the interim. Now feminists who reject antiporn dogma are called "Uncle Toms," accused of supporting male supremacy, and described as attacking feminism.

In this regard, exemplary texts are Jeffreys, *AntiClimax*, 260–86; and Leidholdt and Raymond, *The Sexual Liberals and the Attack on Feminism*. In *Pornography and Civil Rights: A New Day for Women's Equality*, Catharine MacKinnon and Andrea Dworkin state, "There is no viable propornography feminism. Our legitimate differences center on *how* to fight pornography" (83). See also MacKinnon, *Feminism Unmodified*, 146: "A critique of pornography is to feminism what its defense is to male supremacy." I disagree. In MacKinnon's work and that of other antiporn feminists, the critique of pornography has been substituted for a critique of male supremacy.

7. Such terminological confusions continue to bedevil feminist discourse. The more updated version is to use pornography as a synonym for the subordination of women itself, and to equate opposition to pornography with opposition to male supremacy.

8. Willis, *Beginning to See the Light*, 145–46. As Willis wryly puts it, "The feminist bias is that women are equal to men and the male chauvinist bias is that women are inferior. The unbiased view is that the truth lies somewhere in between." I often rephrase her comment as follows: the view of gay activism is that homosexuals deserve equality and respect. The view of neofascist homophobes is that homosexuals are diseased and should be incarcerated, punished, or exterminated. What, pray tell, is the position in the middle?

9. In addition to the Lederer collection, other major antiporn texts include Dworkin, *Pornography* and *Right-Wing Women*; Griffin, *Pornography and Silence*; Dworkin and MacKinnon, *Pornography and Civil Rights*; MacKinnon, *Feminism Unmodified* and *Toward a Feminist Theory of State*; Brownmiller, *Against Our Will*; Barry, *Female Sexual Slavery*.

10. San Francisco's *On Our Backs*, Boston's *Bad Attitude* and *Outrageous Women*, Britain's *Quim*, and Australia's *Wicked Women* are a few of these lesbian-oriented sexual publications. All have encountered governmental or community censorship.

11. Russell and Lederer, "Questions We Are Asked Most Often," 24. The Kearny

and the North Beach were the two theaters that catered to the bondage crowd. When asked "what kinds of images are you talking about when you say you are opposed to 'violence in pornography and media'" the response was "We are talking about films like the ones shown in the Kearny Cinema in San Francisco."

12. Dworkin is referring to this spread when she complains that "*Penthouse* hangs Asian women from trees." Dworkin and MacKinnon, *Pornography and Civil Rights*, 63.

13. There was a movement in the early eighties to produce commercial s/M erotica made by and for s/M practitioners, which resulted in successful and now classic films such as *Story of K.* (Film Company, 1980) and *Journey into Pain* (Loving s/M Productions, 1983). Ironically, none of these films are currently available due to the increasingly harsh legal climate for sexual materials in the United States.

14. For the slide shows, see Webster, "Pornography and Pleasure," and D'Emilio, "Women Against Pornography." *Not a Love Story: A Film about Pornography* purports to be a documentary of pornography. It was directed by Bonnie Sherr Klein and produced by Dorothy Todd Henaut, Studio D., National Film Board of Canada, 1981.

15. See for instance Cameron, *The Psychology of Homosexuality*; *AIDS, the Blood Supply, and Homosexuality* (*What Homosexuals Do in Public Is Offensive, What They Do in Private Is Deadly*); *What Homosexuals Do* (*Its More than Merely Disgusting*); *Criminality, Social Disruption, and Homosexuality* (*Homosexuality Is a Crime against Humanity*); *Homosexuality and the AIDS threat to the Nation's Blood Supply*; *Child Molestation and Homosexuality* (*Homosexuality Is a Crime against Humanity*).

16. Cameron, *Murder, Violence, and Homosexuality* (*What Homosexuals Do in Public Is Offensive, What They Do in Private Is Deadly!*). In the same pamphlet, Cameron claims that the Nazis "started out as a gay rights party."

17. Kendrick, *The Secret Museum*.

18. As I prepare this manuscript for publication, there is proposed federal legislation along these lines. See note 26, below.

19. Longino, "Pornography, Oppression, and Freedom," 40–54, especially 42–46, emphasis added.

20. Dworkin and MacKinnon, *Pornography and Civil Rights*, 36; MacKinnon, *Feminism Unmodified*, 148.

21. National Organization for Women, *Hearings on Pornography*.

22. Attorney General's Commission on Pornography, *Final Report*; Vance, "Porn in the USA: The Meese Commission on the Road," "The Pleasures of Looking: The Attorney General's Commission on Pornography vs. Visual Images," and "Negotiating Sex and Gender in the Attorney General's Commission on Pornography"; Segal and McIntosh, *Sex Exposed*. Some states have now banned dildos and artificial vaginas, and in a 1985 decision the Supreme Court of Canada ruled that penis-shaped vibrators and inflatable dolls were "obscene."

23. Ellen Willis, untitled columns, *Village Voice*, 15 October 1979, 8, and 12 November 1979, 8. These two splendid pieces were reprinted as "Feminism, Moralism, and Pornography," in Willis, *Beginning to See the Light*.

24. Steinem, "Erotica and Pornography," 53–54, 75, 78.

25. Scope, "Erotica Versus Pornography: An Exploration."

26. Indeed, Dworkin could not have said it better: "Erotica is simply high-class pornography: better produced, better conceived, better executed, better packaged, designed for a better class of consumer." *Pornography*, second page of unpaginated preface.

27. Rob Stein, "Medical School Sex Film Wars," *San Francisco Examiner*, 15 January 1986, AA-55.

28. McCormack, "Appendix 1"; Henry, "Porn Is Subordination?," 20, 24. Prior to her 1984 article, Alice Henry had often expressed support of antiporn politics in the pages of *off our backs*, but in this incisive essay even she expressed skepticism of the claims about empirical research (as well as the wisdom of new antiporn legislation).

29. Donnerstein, "Aggressive Erotica and Violence against Women"; Malamuth and Donnerstein, *Pornography and Sexual Aggression*.

30. Zillman and Bryant, "Effects of Massive Exposure to Pornography." See also "X-Rated Flicks Cool People to Real-Life Sex," *San Francisco Examiner*, 23 April 1986, A7.

31. Donnerstein and Linz, "The Question of Pornography"; Daniel Goldman, "Researchers Dispute Pornography Report on Link to Violence," *New York Times*, 17 May 1986, 1, 7; Donnerstein, "Interview." This entire section of the essay is extremely out of date, and would have required complete revision to fix. I elected to leave it alone; however, there has been a deluge of material on this point. Among the most germane is Donnerstein, Linz, and Penrod, *The Question of Pornography*, particularly chapter 6, "Is It the Sex or Is It the Violence?" The book also contains a critique of the misuse of the research data by the Meese Commission. Two of the female members of the Meese Commission, Dr. Judith Becker and Ellen Levine, included harsh criticisms of the conclusions of the commission and the process by which these conclusions were reached. In their dissenting report, they noted that "it is essential to state that the social science research has not been designed to evaluate the relationship between exposure to pornography and the commission of sexual crimes; therefore efforts to tease the current data into proof of a causal link between these acts simply cannot be accepted. Furthermore, social science does not speak to harm, on which this Commission report focuses" (Attorney General's Commission on Pornography, *Final Report*, 204).

32. For a completely different perspective from that of the antipornography movement on the relationship between violence and women's subordination, see Baron, "Pornography and Gender Equality," 363–80.

33. MacKinnon, *Feminism Unmodified*, 53–54, 146–50, 198–201; *Toward a Feminist Theory of the State*, 138–44, 197–99.

34. National Organization for Women, *Hearings on Pornography*.

35. [Since its earliest incarnations, antiporn rhetoric has referred to "snuff movies" as if these were an actual genre, and as if they documented actual killings. But the snuff movies were an urban legend. In *Hard Core*, Linda Williams devotes several

pages (189–95) to deconstructing the mythology, noting that the original film, *Snuff*, "does not belong in the pornographic genre" at all, and moreover that the murder it depicted was, like most movie violence, a product of special effects. "The outcry over *Snuff* forced the New York City district attorney to investigate the circumstances of the film's making and to interview the actress who was supposedly killed in the final sequence. Even after the hoax was revealed, though, the idea of snuff continued to haunt the imagination." Williams, *Hard Core*, 193.—G. R.]

36. Dworkin, *Pornography*, 201.

37. Samois, *Coming to Power*; Weinberg and Kamel, *S and M*; Mains, *Urban Aboriginals*; Stoller, *Pain and Passion*; Thompson, *Leatherfolk*; Grumley and Gallucci, *Hard Corps*; Rosen, *Sexual Magic* and *Sexual Portraits*.

38. I recall this language from several oral presentations in the mid-1980s. I believe one was the National Organization for Women, *Hearings on Pornography*, although this phraseology is absent from MacKinnon's written remarks (National Organization for Women, *Hearings on Pornography: Materials on the Personal Testimony of NOW Activists on Pornography*).

39. Delacoste and Alexander, *Sex Work*; Jaget, *Prostitutes*; Pheterson, *A Vindication of the Rights of Whores*; James et al., *The Politics of Prostitution*.

40. Dworkin, *Pornography*, 200, emphasis added.

41. Dworkin, *Right-Wing Women*, 223, emphasis added.

42. Ibid., 222, 228–29.

43. [Since this essay was written there has been an explosion of superb historical work on early modern European forms of erotic representation. Hunt, *The Invention of Pornography*, Peakman, *Mighty Lewd Books*, Cryle, *Geometry of the Boudoir*, and McCalman, *Radical Underworld*, are but a few. This work raises many issues of chronology and taxonomy that cannot be addressed here, but which do not, I think, affect my brief against the feminist indictment of porn. Whether we call the erotica of the eighteenth century pornography or libertine literature, it is abundantly clear these genres have complex and historically specific characteristics that do not readily fit into the analytic framework of the antiporn movement. As Lynn Hunt notes, "Pornography did not constitute a wholly separate and distinct category of written or visual representation before the early nineteenth century. . . . [P]ornography was almost always an adjunct to something else until the middle or end of the eighteenth century. Pornography nevertheless slowly emerged as a distinct category. . . . [P]ornography as a legal and artistic category seems to be an especially Western idea with a specific chronology and geography" (*The Invention of Pornography*, 9–10).—G. R.]

44. Dworkin, *Pornography*, 199–200. This dubious history and phony etymology appears repeatedly throughout the antiporn literature, where it is often used as a key argument against pornography. In *Pornography and Civil Rights*, MacKinnon and Dworkin state that "we can trace pornography without any difficulty back as far as ancient Greece in the West. Pornography is a Greek word. . . . It refers to writing, etching, or drawing of women who, in real life, were kept in female sexual slavery in ancient Greece. Pornography has always, as far back as we can go, had to do with ex-

ploiting, debasing, and violating women in forced sex" (74). In the *Ms.* article "Erotica and Pornography," Gloria Steinem employs it as the basis of her erotica-pornography distinction.

45. Actually, as Kendrick points out (*The Secret Museum*, 11), the term did exist in ancient Greece. But it appears so rarely in the surviving Greek texts that it could not have been indicative of a significant category of ancient experience, let alone one that so closely approximates the opinions of sexual materials expressed by Dworkin or those held by nineteenth-century scholars (John J. Winkler, personal communication, 1986).

[Some years after writing this essay, I found the same rhetorical tactic—of attributing a modern antiporn position to the ancient Greeks—in the dissenting opinion of Charles Keating to the 1970 *Report of the Commission on Obscenity and Pornography*, and include it as an epigraph to begin this essay in the present volume. Did Dworkin, Steinem, MacKinnon, and other antiporn feminists get their etymological analysis from Keating? If so, did they consider the source?—G. R.]

46. [This has indeed been the case. When I submitted the earlier version of this essay in 1986, I enclosed California Assembly Bill No. 3645, in which the diffusion of antiporn ideas into legal initiatives was already apparent. AB 3645 did not pass. But as this essay went to press in 1993, Senate Bill 1521, the Pornography Victims Compensation Act, was poised to become federal law. As initially proposed, the bill made pornography a cause of civil action, as was proposed in the MacKinnon-Dworkin ordinance, and allowed "victims" to sue not their perpetrators but the makers and distributors of any obscene material that may have influenced their perpetrators. In contrast to the original MacKinnon-Dworkin approach, this bill was based on a traditional legal definition of obscenity rather than the so-called feminist definition in the Indianapolis ordinance.

The bill did not pass. It is worth thinking, however, about what it would have made legal and what would not have been affected by its passage. Had the bill become law, when some lunatic who has read porn or seen a pornographic film went on a rampage, the producers and distributors of his reading material would be held accountable for his behavior and sued in federal court. The bill established third-party liability, but only for the producers and distributors of sexual media. The same kind of liability has been ruled unconstitutional in the case of non-obscene media. But since obscenity is not constitutionally protected speech, SB 1521 might have been upheld in the courts.

If that same lunatic, after reading his Bible, went out and murdered a bunch of prostitutes (not an altogether unusual occurrence), no similar liability would be incurred by religious publishers and bookstores. There is a horrific tale in Judges (19–21) about the Levite's Concubine, who is brutally murdered and dismembered after being raped. This event is followed by a war of near extermination, and the abduction and forced marriages of four hundred young virgins. While producers and bookstores could be taken to court if someone was inspired by a scenario in a porn magazine, the invocation of biblical authority to commit murder, violate corpses, engage in genocidal warfare, or instigate mass rape and force the victims to marry their rapists would bring no grief to those who printed and sold copies of the Old Testament.—G. R.]

47. This has also come to pass. The Meese Commission released its *Final Report* in July of 1986. The report included a long wish list of new obscenity legislation and suggested procedures to increase enforcement of existing law at the local, state, and federal levels. Much of the antiporn agenda articulated in the report has become law, policy, and common practice. The U.S. Department of Justice duly created an obscenity enforcement unit, increased obscenity prosecutions, began to bring forfeiture proceedings against those convicted of obscenity offenses, and started a national computerized databank on producers, distributors, and consumers of sexually explicit material (ACLU Arts Censorship Project, *Above the Law*).

The obscenity unit was recently renamed the Child Exploitation and Obscenity Unit. The irony of this new title is that there has been no commercial child pornography available in the United States since the late 1970s. In its efforts to entrap suspected pedophiles, the federal government has become the largest (and only) distributor of child pornography in the United States. [This was apparently true in the early 1990s, when print was still a dominant medium for porn. With the explosion of Internet access, production and distribution of almost all porn has undergone a radical transformation.—G. R.] For a longer discussion of the right-wing war on porn and of the collaboration of antiporn feminists, see my "Afterword to 'Thinking Sex: Notes for a Radical Theory of the Politics of Sexuality,'" included as chap. 6 in this volume.

Chapter 12. Sexual Traffic

1. Althusser, "Freud and Lacan."

2. Mannoni, *The Child, His "Illness" and the Others*.

3. Vance, "Social Construction Theory: Problems in the History of Sexuality," and "Anthropology Rediscovers Sexuality: A Theoretical Comment."

4. MacKinnon's "Marxism, Feminism, Method and the State: Toward Feminist Jurisprudence."

5. House and Cowan, "Can Men Be Women?"

6. Smith-Rosenberg, "The Female World of Love and Ritual."

7. Walkowitz, *City of Dreadful Delight*; Peiss, *Cheap Amusements*; Matlock, "Masquerading Women, Pathologized Men."

8. Freud, "The Sexual Aberrations."

9. Krafft-Ebing, *Psychopathia Sexualis, with Special Reference to the Contrary Sexual Instinct*.

10. Duggan, "The Trials of Alice Mitchell."

11. Nye, "The Medical Origins of Sexual Fetishism"; Matlock, "Masquerading Women."

12. Krafft-Ebing, *Psychopathia Sexualis, with Special Reference to the Contrary Sexual Instinct*.

13. Oosterhuis, *Stepchildren of Nature*.

14. Abelove, "Freud, Male Homosexuality, and the Americans," 381.

15. Sulloway, *Freud: Biologist of the Mind*, chap. 8, "Freud and the Sexologists." See also Davidson, "How to Do the History of Psychoanalysis."

16. Weeks, *Coming Out*.

17. Thompson, "Time, Work-Discipline, and Industrial Capitalism"; Althusser and Balibar, *Reading Capital*, 251–53.

18. Foucault, *The History of Sexuality*, 106.

19. Ibid., 107.

20. Ibid., emphasis added by Gayle Rubin.

21. Ibid., 108.

22. Ibid., 109.

23. Schneider, *American Kinship* and *Critique of the Study of Kinship*.

24. [I misspoke somewhat in this discussion of kinship and should have noted that one of David Schneider's points is that "all kinship is fictive," in the sense that even kin statuses ostensibly based in biology are cultural constructs. It is cultural systems that determine what kinds of biological relationships are significant, or not. I also was well behind Butler in thinking about gay and lesbian kinship. I had not yet grappled with the issues raised by gay marriage, and had no idea of the bureaucratic and legal issues with which gay couples having children have to contend. I have since come to appreciate in excruciating detail how gay families are, to use Susan Stryker's term, "bureaucratically unintelligible," as well as legally disenfranchised and economically despoiled. —G. R.]

25. Bérubé, *Coming Out Under Fire*; Kennedy and Davis, *Boots of Leather, Slippers of Gold*.

26. Lauritsen and Thorstad, *The Early Homosexual Rights Movement*.

27. Foster, *Sex Variant Women in Literature*; Grier, *The Lesbian in Literature*.

28. Deleuze, *Masochism*, 115.

Chapter 13. Studying Sexual Subcultures

Although this essay is rooted in the literature chapter of my dissertation ("The Valley of the Kings"), I have delivered several versions as lectures. These include papers at the 1996 annual meeting of the American Anthropological Association and the 1998 annual meeting of the American Sociological Association and invited lectures at the University of California, Los Angeles (1997); California State University, Northridge (1997); and the University of Missouri, St. Louis (1995).

I am indebted to many individuals who have contributed to this essay and the ideas behind it. Conversations with Jeffrey Escoffier, John Gagnon, William Simon, Barrie Thorne, Howard Becker, and Esther Newton have been particularly informative about the context of social research at the University of Chicago and its importance to contemporary studies of sexuality. Barrie Thorne directed me to some helpful articles and provided me with copies, and when she found out about my interest in his work, she introduced me to Howard Becker. My editors, Ellen Lewin and William Leap, have exhibited patience and encouragement beyond the call of duty. Mitchell Duneier, Jeffrey Escoffier, John Gagnon, Esther Newton, PJ McGann, and Carole Vance all read earlier drafts and I am deeply grateful for their suggestions and comments. Jay Marston has been a constant source of support and inspiration. The writing of this essay was assisted by a fellowship from the Sexuality Research Fellowship Program of the Social Science Research Council with funds provided by the Ford Foundation.

1. Reiter, *Toward an Anthropology of Women*; Rosaldo and Lamphere, *Women, Culture, and Society*.

2. Ford and Beach, *Patterns of Sexual Behavior*; Ortner and Whitehead, *Sexual Meanings*.

3. For an excellent overview, see Weston, "Lesbian/Gay Studies in the House of Anthropology."

4. Jagose (*Queer Theory*) and Turner (*A Genealogy of Queer Theory*) both provide excellent overviews of queer theory, although neither discusses most of the literature discussed in this essay.

5. Since this essay was originally drafted, several publications have appeared that address some of these same issues. See, for example, Epstein, "A Queer Encounter"; Stein and Plummer, "'I Can't Even Think Straight'"; Gagnon, "Sexual Conduct"; Nardi and Schneider, "Kinsey" and *Social Perspectives in Lesbian and Gay Studies*; Rubin with Butler, "Interview" (chap. 12 in this volume); Schneider and Nardi, "John H. Gagnon and William Simon's *Sexual Conduct*"; Simon, "*Sexual Conduct* in Retrospective Perspective"; Weeks, "The 'Homosexual Role' after Thirty Years"; and Weston, *Long Slow Burn*.

6. For New Guinea and Oceania, see for example Herdt, *Guardians of the Flutes* and *Ritualized Homosexuality in Melanesia*; Kelly, "Witchcraft and Sexual Relations"; and Williams, *Papuans of the Trans-Fly*. For North America, see, for example, Brown, *Two Spirit People*; Devereaux, "Institutionalized Homosexuality among Mohave Indians"; Jacobs, Thomas, and Lang, *Two-Spirit People*; McMurtrie, "A Legend of Lesbian Love among North American Indians"; Roscoe, *The Zuni Man-Woman*; Whitehead, "The Bow and the Burden Strap"; Williams, *The Spirit and the Flesh*. See also Evans-Pritchard, "Sexual Inversion among the Azande"; and Herskovitz, "A Note on 'Woman Marriage' in Dahomey."

7. Marshall and Suggs, *Human Sexual Behavior*, 234.

8. Ibid., 235.

9. Ibid., 231.

10. Ibid., 236; see also American Psychiatric Association's *Diagnostic and Statistical Manuals of Mental Disorders*, 1st–4th editions (1952, 1968, 1980, 1987, and 1994); and Bayer, *Homosexuality and American Psychiatry*.

11. Marshall and Suggs, *Human Sexual Behavior*, 242, emphasis added.

12. On the refashioning of homosexuality as a social phenomenon, see also Escoffier, *American Homo*, 79–98.

13. I do not mean to underestimate the enormity of the contributions of Kinsey and Hooker, both of whom deserve a much more extensive treatment beyond the scope of this essay. Many others have of course written on Kinsey's impact, with Paul Robinson's analysis (*The Modernization of Sex*) among the most insightful. In 1998 the first issue of the journal *Sexualities* devoted a special section to a symposium on the fiftieth anniversary of the publication of the first Kinsey report (Nardi and Schneider, "Kinsey"). One of the best overviews of Hooker's impact is *Changing Our Minds: The Story of Dr. Evelyn Hooker*, a documentary film directed by Richard Schmiechen. Most of Hooker's work was in article form, and it is unfortunate that these have so far not been assembled and published as a collection.

14. Detailed studies of various aspects of the sexual politics of the period can be found in Brandt, *No Magic Bullet*; Connelly, *The Response to Prostitution in the Progressive Era*; D'Emilio and Freedman, *Intimate Matters*; Langum, *Crossing Over the Line*; Odem, *Delinquent Daughters*; and Peiss, *Cheap Amusements*. For "white slavery," see especially Connelly and Langum.

15. Chauncey, *Gay New York*, 367. Chauncey's entire note on sources (366–70) provides a useful overview of such material, particularly for New York.

16. Heap, *Homosexuality in the City*, 16; Vice Commission of Chicago, *The Social Evil in Chicago*.

17. Langum, *Crossing Over the Line*. "The Mann Act," Langum comments, "resulted in the Bureau's first major field office, in Baltimore, and a dramatic increase in manpower.... [T]he Mann Act provided the real takeoff for the FBI. One historian of the FBI wrote that 'the enforcement of the Mann Act began the transformation of the Justice Department's police bureau from a modest agency concerned with odds and ends of Federal law enforcement to a nationally recognized institution, with agents in every State and every large city'" (ibid., 49).

18. Bulmer, *The Chicago School of Sociology*, 60, but see 59–60. Other famous targets of Mann Act prosecution included Jack Johnson, Chuck Berry, and Charlie Chaplin (Langum, *Crossing Over the Line*).

19. Park, Burgess, and McKenzie, *The City*, 32–33.

20. Park's essay had appeared in journal form in 1915.

21. Ibid., 41–42.

22. Ibid., 43, 45–46.

23. Anderson, *On Hobos and Homelessness*; Creesey, *The Taxi-Dance Hall*; Reckless, *Vice in Chicago*; Zorbaugh, *The Gold Coast and the Slum*.

24. Heap, *Homosexuality in the City*, 17.

25. Ibid.

26. Drexel, "Before Paris Burned"; Heap, *Homosexuality in the City*; Johnson, "The Kids of Fairytown"; Mumford "Homosex Changes" and *Interzones*.

27. Cited in Galliher, "Chicago's Two Worlds of Deviance Research," 183. Barrie Thorne (in a personal communication) has conveyed something of this tradition in noting its "unshockability," which allowed for virtually anything to be studied, no

matter how disreputable the topic or population. This unshockability opened research vistas that criteria of respectability would have made inaccessible.

28. Becker points out the difficulty in assigning such shifts in intellectual frameworks to any individual. "I wasn't the only one interested in saying things about deviance. Kai Erikson (1962) had been saying the same thing. John Kitsuse (1962) was saying the same things. Lemert had said it years before. There were a number of people whose ideas were in the air. Probably what I did was to make a very clear and simple statement as to what it was about. At least I think it's a clear and simple statement" (Becker with Debro, "Dialogue with Howard S. Becker [1970]," 33). Although I think Becker is unduly modest (and characteristically generous), most such conceptual innovations do have complex genealogies and multiple origins. I risk in this essay an unintended oversimplification, particularly as I am trained in neither sociology nor intellectual history. Nonetheless, the writings of Becker (and Goffman) seem to have been particularly effective in communicating this body of ideas. My larger point is that there was an intellectual culture whose tendencies were absorbed and creatively applied by a number of thinkers and which ultimately had an impact on reevaluating homosexuality.

Chapoulie credits much of that culture to Everett Hughes: "More than a dozen years after his death in 1983, Everett C. Hughes is generally recognized as one of the links between the founders of 'The Chicago School'—W. I. Thomas and Robert E. Park, to whom we might add Ernest W. Burgess and the philosopher George Herbert Mead—and the group of sociologists trained at the University of Chicago in the 1940s and 1950s, who are often labeled collectively as symbolic interactionists. This group, notable for its studies of institutions, work and the professions, art, deviance, and medicine, includes such researchers as Erving Goffman, Howard S. Becker, Anselm Strauss, and Eliot Freidson, who have also contributed to making fieldwork—the ethnographic method—one of the most fruitful research approaches in the social sciences" ("Everett Hughes and the Chicago Tradition," 3). Chapoulie also notes that by the end of the 1950s, the ethnographic approach had become unpopular at Chicago, resulting in the departures of Hughes and many of his students (ibid., 19). See also Reinharz, "The Chicago School of Sociology and the Founding of the Graduate Program in Sociology at Brandeis University."

Chapoulie also notes the importance of journals such as *Social Problems* and *Urban Life and Culture*, which were associated with this group of scholars and published extremely important work in the sociology of sexuality during the 1960s and 1970s. I leave fuller exploration of the role of these individuals and journals to those more qualified to produce histories of sociological work. My point here is to help insure greater appreciation of their contributions by anthropologists, queer theorists, and others whose training, like my own, may not have provided exposure to this material. See also Becker, *The Other Side*.

29. Galliher, "Chicago's Two Worlds of Deviance Research," 169.

30. Becker, "Whose Side Are We On?," 127.

31. Ibid., 126–27.

32. The phrase *moral leveling* is indebted to Paul Robinson, who uses the phrase *sexual leveling* in his discussion of Kinsey (*The Modernization of Sex*, 58–59).

33. Becker, "Whose Side Are We On?," 124; see also Goffman, *Stigma*, for a similar leveling effect.

34. Becker, *Outsiders*, 30–38, 167–68.

35. Gagnon, "An Unlikely Story," 231.

36. Plummer, *The Making of the Modern Homosexual*, 24.

37. Simon and Gagnon, "Homosexuality," 14–16.

38. Ibid., 17–19, 24.

39. Ibid., 24.

40. It is notable that *Sexual Conduct* was published in the Observations series edited by Howard Becker for Aldine.

41. Leznoff and Westley, "The Homosexual Community," 195–96, 194–95.

42. Ibid., 189.

43. Ibid., 191.

44. Ibid., 192.

45. Hooker, "The Homosexual Community," 171–72.

46. Ibid., 173.

47. Ibid. Of relevance to my own research on gay male leather communities (but not to this particular essay) is the fact that Hooker was aware of a particular "motor-cycle crowd, or leather set" which resisted stereotypical gay "effeminacy" (ibid., 182).

48. Achilles, "The Development of the Homosexual Bar as an Institution," 230–31.

49. Ibid., 234–35.

50. Ibid., 235.

51. Ibid., 230.

52. Ibid., 242.

53. Ibid., 239.

54. Ibid., 244.

55. Garber, "A Historical Directory of Lesbian and Gay Establishments in the San Francisco Bay Area"; Garber and Walker, "Queer Sites in San Francisco," database, Gay, Lesbian, Bisexual, Transgender Historical Society of Northern California, 2000; Rubin, "The Valley of the Kings," "Elegy for the Valley of the Kings," "The Miracle Mile," "Sites, Settlements, and Urban Sex."

56. Simon and Gagnon, "Homosexuality," 21.

57. Harry and DeVall, *The Social Organization of Gay Males*, 154. Steve Murray makes similar points. He notes that "insofar as 'community' is a technical term in the social sciences and insofar as there can be said to be 'communities' in North American cities, there are 'gay communities'" ("The Institutional Elaboration of a Quasi-Ethnic Community," 165).

58. Reiss, "The Social Integration of Peers and Queers," 199.

59. Ibid., 225.

60. Ibid., 214–19.

61. Ibid., 224–25.

62. Some of these theoretical strategies in turn are rooted in Kinsey's, Pomeroy's, and Martin's *Sexual Behavior in the Human Male*, published in 1948, and in which the distinction between sexual acts and named sexual identities was widely used. Kinsey's role was critical and should not be underestimated, although his contributions lie outside the main line of argument in this particular essay. His work, however, clearly had an impact on the sociologists discussed here.

63. Escoffier, "Inside the Ivory Closet," "Generations and Paradigms," and *American Homo*; Hansen, "The Historical Construction of Homosexuality"; Katz, *Gay/Lesbian Almanac*; Padgug, "Sexual Matters"; Plummer, *Sexual Stigma, The Making of the Modern Homosexual,* and *Modern Homosexualities*; Rubin, "Thinking Sex" (chap. 5 in this volume); Vance, "Social Construction Theory," and "Anthropology Rediscovers Sexuality"; Weeks, *Coming Out, Sex, Politics, and Society, Sexuality and Its Discontents, Sexuality,* and *Against Nature,* "The 'Homosexual Role' after Thirty Years," and *Making Sexual History*.

64. McIntosh, "The Homosexual Role"; Plummer, *Sexual Stigma,* and *The Making of the Modern Homosexual*; Weeks, *Coming Out,* "The 'Homosexual Role' after Thirty Years," and *Making Sexual History*.

65. Kinsey, Pomeroy, and Martin, *Sexual Behavior in the Human Male,* 610–66. Some of Kinsey's many insightful comments are worth remembering: "Concerning patterns of sexual behavior, a great deal of the thinking done by scientists and laymen alike stems from the assumption that there are persons who are 'heterosexual' and persons who are 'homosexual,' that these two types represent antitheses in the sexual world, and that there is only an insignificant class of 'bisexuals' who occupy the intermediate position between the other groups. It is implied that every individual is innately—inherently—either heterosexual or homosexual. It is further implied that from the time of birth one is fated to be one thing or the other, and that there is little chance for one to change his pattern in the course of a lifetime" (*Sexual Behavior in the Human Male,* 636–37). Moreover, "Males do not represent two discrete populations, heterosexual and homosexual. The world is not divided into sheep and goats. Not all things are black nor all things white. It is a fundamental of taxonomy that nature rarely deals with discrete categories. Only the human mind invents categories and tries to force facts into separated pigeon-holes. The living world is a continuum in each and every one of its aspects. The sooner we learn this concerning human sexual behavior the sooner we shall reach a sound understanding of the realities of sex" (ibid., 639).

66. McIntosh, "The Homosexual Role," 183.

67. Ibid., 33.

68. Ibid., 187.

69. Ibid., 188–89.

70. Weeks, *Coming Out,* 239.

71. Ibid., 3.

72. Ibid., 35–37.

73. For less abbreviated versions of this history of the development of social construction theory, see Vance ("Social Construction Theory," "Anthropology Rediscovers Sexuality") and Escoffier ("Inside the Ivory Closet," "Generations and Paradigms").

74. Katz, *Gay American History*, *Gay/Lesbian Almanac*, "The Invention of Heterosexuality," and *The Invention of Heterosexuality*.

75. A very small example can be seen in Althusser's and Balibar's *Reading Capital*, published in France in 1968 and in English translation in 1970. Balibar elaborates on the concept of the "*differential forms of historical individuality*" (251). "We can say that each relatively autonomous practice thus engenders forms of historical individuality which are peculiar to it. . . . For each practice and for each transformation of that practice, they are the different forms of individuality which can be defined on the basis of its combination structure" (ibid., 252). The production of subjectivity was a major concern of many French intellectuals throughout the 1960s, and it is not a huge leap from the production of subjectivity in general to the production of sexual subjectivity in particular. See also Eribon, "Michel Foucault's Histories of Sexuality" and, more broadly, Dosse, *History of Structuralism*, volumes 1 and 2.

76. In his preface to *The Order of Things*, Foucault commented: "This book first arose out of a passage in Borges, out of the laughter that shattered, as I read the passage, all the familiar landmarks of my thought—*our* thought, the thought that bears the stamp of our age and our geography—while breaking up all the ordered surfaces and all the places with which we are accustomed to tame the wild profusion of existing things. . . . This passage quotes a 'certain Chinese encyclopaedia' in which it is written that 'animals are divided into: (a) belonging to the Emperor, (b) embalmed, (c) tame, (d) sucking pigs, (e) sirens, (f) fabulous, (g) stray dogs, (h) included in the present classification, (i) frenzied, (j) innumerable, (k) drawn with a very fine camel-hair brush, (l) *et cetera*, (m) having just broken the water pitcher, (n) that from a long way off look like flies.' In the wonderment of this taxonomy, the thing we apprehend in one great leap, the thing that, by means of the fable, is demonstrated as the exotic charm of another system of thought, is the limitation of our own" (xv). This is a deeply anthropological moment, albeit generated by fiction rather than the equally startling details of ethnoclassification.

77. Turner, *A Genealogy of Queer Theory*, 66.

78. Although this essay addresses the amnesia in queer studies of its social-science antecedents, it is also important to note a similar memory lapse within sociology with respect to its contributions to sex research. For example, in Gary Alan Fine's edited collection on post–Second World War Chicago sociology, neither John Gagnon nor William Simon are mentioned at all. This absence is striking, given the significance of their work on human sexuality. Reiss and Westley are mentioned, but only in connection with work on criminology, deviance, and methodology. Their forays into the ethnographic study of homosexuals are not noted. This suggests that despite their critical perspectives on stigma, sociologists, too, are not immune to the undertow of sexual discreditization.

79. Turner, *A Genealogy of Queer Theory*, 63.

80. I have made a similar point (Rubin with Butler, "Interview"). I also concur with Turner: "The almost complete triumph of the social constructionist position, in turn, would contribute crucially to the conditions of possibility for queer theory, which assumes the radical historical variability of sexual identity categories" (*A Genealogy of Queer Theory*, 69).

81. Vance, "Social Construction Theory," 17.

82. Polanyi, Arensberg, and Pearson, *Trade and Market in the Early Empires*, 239.

83. Ibid., 240.

84. Ibid., 250; see also Sahlins, *Stone Age Economics*.

85. Thompson, *The Making of the English Working Class*, 9.

86. I am grateful to Charles Tilly for bringing this wonderful essay to my attention.

87. A fuller discussion of the issue lies outside the scope of this essay, but feminism and various forms of Marxism were significant areas in which these larger epistemic shifts had been developing. See also Stein and Plummer, "'I Can't Even Think Straight.'"

88. Walkowitz, *Prostitution and Victorian Society*, 192–213. Judith and Daniel Walkowitz were making a similar argument as early as 1973.

89. This entire issue constitutes a watershed in scholarly journal publication. In addition to Padgug and Hansen, there are essays on families by E. P. Thompson and Ellen Ross, an article on lesbian history by Blanche Wiesen Cook, Ann Barr Snitow's essay on romance novels, a piece on sexual meanings and gay identities by Jeffrey Weeks, a critique of sociobiology in the context of the history of biological science by Donna Haraway, and several other distinguished contributions.

90. Vance, "Social Construction Theory," 13.

91. Vance ("Anthropology Rediscovers Sexuality") contrasts social construction with some of the earlier anthropological literature on sexuality, which was less consistent in its application of social analysis and retained certain biomedical assumptions.

92. A small sample of the relevant work would include the following: Altman et al., "Homosexuality, Which Homosexuality?"; Bérubé, *Coming Out Under Fire*, "'Dignity for All,'" and "The History of the Bathhouses"; Chauncey, "From Sexual Inversion to Homosexuality," *Gay New York*, and "Christian Brotherhood or Sexual Perversion?"; D'Emilio, "Capitalism and Gay Identity," *Sexual Politics, Sexual Communities*, "Gay Politics and Community in San Francisco," "The Homosexual Menace," and *Making Trouble*; D'Emilio and Freedman, *Intimate Matters*; Duberman, Vicinus, and Chauncey, *Hidden from History*; Duggan, "The Trials of Alice Mitchell," and *Sapphic Slashers*; Escoffier, "Inside the Ivory Closet," "Generations and Paradigms," and *American Homo*; Foucault, *The History of Sexuality*; Freedman, "Uncontrolled Desires"; Halperin, *One Hundred Years of Homosexuality*; Halperin, Winkler, and Zeitlin, *Before Sexuality*; Katz, *Gay/Lesbian Almanac*, "The Invention of Heterosexuality," and *The Invention of Heterosexuality*; Kennedy and Davis, *Boots of Leather, Slippers of Gold*; Peiss and Simmons, with Padgug, *Passion and Power*; Plummer, *The Making of the Modern Homosexual*, and *Modern Homosexualities*; Rubin, "Thinking

Sex"; Snitow, Stansell, and Thompson, *Powers of Desire*; Vance, *Pleasure and Danger*, "Social Construction Theory," "The War on Culture," "Misunderstanding Obscenity," "Negotiating Sex and Gender in the Attorney General's Commission on Pornography," "Reagan's Revenge," "The Pleasures of Looking," and "Anthropology Rediscovers Sexuality"; Vicinus, "Sexuality and Power," and "'They Wonder to Which Sex I Belong'"; Walkowitz, "The Politics of Prostitution," *Prostitution and Victorian Society*, "Male Vice and Feminist Virtue," and *City of Dreadful Delight*; Weeks, *Coming Out*, *Sexuality and Its Discontents*, *Against Nature*, "The 'Homosexual Role' after Thirty Years," *Making Sexual History*, and *Sex, Politics, and Society*; and Winkler, *The Constraints of Desire*.

93. Sonenschein, "Homosexuality as a Subject of Anthropological Inquiry," 73.

94. Ibid., 75.

95. Ibid., 76–77.

96. Ibid., 80.

97. Newton, *Margaret Mead Made Me Gay*, 217.

98. Ibid., 216.

99. Newton, *Mother Camp*, 132.

100. Esther Newton, personal communication.

101. Newton, *Mother Camp*, 37.

102. Ibid., 103.

103. Ibid., 109.

104. Butler, *Gender Trouble*, especially 136–37, and *Bodies That Matter*.

105. Newton, *Mother Camp*, 21–22.

106. Ibid., 28.

107. Ibid., 29.

108. Ibid., 8.

109. Ibid., 49.

110. Ibid., 25.

111. Ibid., 115.

112. Ibid., 116.

113. Ibid., 118.

114. Ibid., 123–24.

115. Ibid., 10.

116. Since 1970 sociologists have undertaken a number of important ethnographic and analytic projects. The first and most famous of these was Laud Humphreys's *Tearoom Trade: Impersonal Sex in Public Places*. During the late 1970s several books appeared almost simultaneously. Joseph Harry's and William DeVall's *The Social Organization of Gay Males*, John Allan Lee's *Getting Sex*, and Barbara Ponse's *Identities in the Lesbian World* all appeared in 1978. The following year saw the publication of Martin Levine's wonderful anthology *Gay Men: The Sociology of Male Homosexuality*. Also published in 1978 was Bell's and Weinberg's *Homosexualities*. Although that volume was mostly based on survey research, it included as an appendix, "Ethnography

of the Bay Area Homosexual Scene." In 1983, Susan Kreiger's *The Mirror Dance* appeared.

117. Davis and Whitten, "The Cross-Cultural Study of Human Sexuality," 71.

Chapter 14. Geologies of Queer Studies

All notes were added in 2011.

1. For Daughters of Bilitis, see Gallo, *Different Daughters*.

2. For Foster's biography, see Passet, *Sex Variant Woman*.

3. Jeffrey Escoffier first alerted me to the significance of Cory's book.

4. Oosterhuis, *Stepchildren of Nature*.

5. Krafft-Ebing, *Psychopathia Sexualis*; Ellis, *Sexual Inversion*; Hirschfeld, *The Homosexuality of Men and Women*; Ulrichs, *The Riddle of "Man-Manly" Love*; Carpenter, *The Intermediate Sex*; Symonds, *A Problem in Greek Ethics*, and *A Problem in Modern Ethics*. Excellent essays on Ulrichs, Krafft-Ebing, and Hirschfeld are included in the splendid collection edited by Vernon Rosario, *Science and Homosexualities*. Also see Crozier's critical edition of *Sexual Inversion*; Bland and Doan, *Sexology and Culture*, and *Sexology Uncensored*. Biographies include Kennedy, *Ulrichs*; Rowbotham, *Edward Carpenter*; Wolff, *Magnus Hirschfeld*; Grosskurth, *Havelock Ellis*, and *The Woeful Victorian*. Additional work on Hirschfeld includes Steakley, *The Homosexual Emancipation Movement in Germany*, and Mancini, *Magnus Hirschfeld*.

6. Bristow, "Symond's History, Ellis's Heredity."

7. See especially Symonds, *A Problem in Modern Ethics*.

8. Ibid., 2.

9. Hirschfeld, *The Homosexuality of Men and Women*, 776–803.

10. Ibid., 785.

11. Steakley, "Per scientiam ad justitiam," 133–34.

12. The catalogue of the Arno series, *Homosexuality: Lesbians and Gay Men in Society, History, and Literature*, is itself a remarkable research document. Jonathan Katz was the general editor, Louis Crompton, Barbara Gittings, James Steakley, and Dolores Noll were the editorial board, and J. Michael Siegelaub was the research assistant.

13. Gerth and Mills, *From Max Weber*, 228.

Bibliography

Abelove, Henry. "Freud, Male Homosexuality, and the Americans." *The Lesbian and Gay Studies Reader*, ed. Henry Abelove, Michèle Barale, and David Halperin, 381–93. New York: Routledge, 1993.

Achilles, Nancy. "The Development of the Homosexual Bar as an Institution." *Sexual Deviance*, ed. John Gagnon and William Simon, 228–44. New York: Harper and Row, 1967.

ACLU Arts Censorship Project. *Above the Law: The Justice Department's War against the First Amendment*. Medford, N.Y.: American Civil Liberties Union, 1991.

Aho, James A. *The Politics of Righteousness: Idaho Christian Patriotism*. Seattle: University of Washington Press, 1990.

Alcoff, Linda Martin. "Dangerous Pleasures: Foucault and the Politics of Pedophilia." *Feminist Interpretations of Michel Foucault*, ed. Susan Hekman, 99–136. University Park: Pennsylvania State University Press, 1996.

Alderfer, Hannah, Beth Jaker, and Marybeth Nelson, eds. *Diary of a Conference on Sexuality*. New York: Faculty Press, 1982.

Allard, Ed. "To the Editor." *Gay and Lesbian Review Worldwide* 17, no. 3 (2010): 7.

Allison, Dorothy. *Bastard out of Carolina*. New York: Dutton, 1992.

Althusser, Louis. "Freud and Lacan." *New Left Review* 55 (May–June 1969): 48–66.

Althusser, Louis, and Etienne Balibar. *Reading Capital*. London: New Left, 1970.

Altman, Dennis, et al. *Homosexuality, Which Homosexuality? International Conference on Gay and Lesbian Studies, Amsterdam*. London: Gay Men's Press, 1989.

American Psychiatric Association. *Diagnostic and Statistical Manual, Mental Disorders*. Washington: American Psychiatric Association, 1952.

———. *Diagnostic and Statistical Manual of Mental Disorders*. 2nd edn. Washington: American Psychiatric Association, 1968.

———. *Diagnostic and Statistical Manual of Mental Disorders*. 3rd edn. Washington: American Psychiatric Association, 1980.

———. *Diagnostic and Statistical Manual of Mental Disorders*. 3rd edn., rev. Washington: American Psychiatric Association, 1987.

———. *Diagnostic and Statistical Manual of Mental Disorders*. 4th edn. Washington: American Psychiatric Association, 1994.

Anderson, Nels. *The Hobo: The Sociology of the Homeless Man*. Chicago: University of Chicago Press, 1923.

———. *On Hobos and Homelessness*. 1923; reprint, Chicago: University of Chicago Press, 1998.

Andriette, Bill. "The Government's War on Child Pornography: Who Are the Real Targets?" *Guide to the Gay Northeast*, September 1988: 1–6.

———. "New Weapons for the Sex Police." *Guide to the Gay Northeast*, February 1991: 1–7.

Angelides, Steven. "Historicizing Affect, Psychoanalyzing History: Pedophilia and the Discourse of Child Sexuality." *Journal of Homosexuality* 46, nos. 1–2 (2003): 79–109.

———. "Feminism, Child Sexual Abuse, and the Erasure of Child Sexuality." GLQ: *A Journal of Gay and Lesbian Studies* 10, no. 2 (2004): 141–77.

Applebome, Peter. *Dixie Rising: How the South Is Shaping American Values, Politics and Culture*. San Diego: Harcourt Brace, 1996.

Apter, Emily. "Reflections on Gynophobia." *Coming Out of Feminism?*, ed. Mandy Merck, Naomi Segal, and Elizabeth Wright, 102–22. Oxford: Blackwell, 1998.

Apter, Emily, and William Pietz, eds. *Fetishism as Cultural Discourse*. Ithaca: Cornell University Press, 1993.

Aries, Philippe. *Centuries of Childhood: A Social History of Family Life*. 1960; reprint, New York: Vintage, 1962.

Atkins, Robert. "Art Police Strike in S.F." *Village Voice*, 12 June 1990, 75–76.

Attorney General's Commission on Pornography. *Final Report*. Washington: U.S. Department of Justice, July 1986.

l'Autre, Gabrielle (Margaret A. Porter). "Twenty-four Poems by Renée Vivien." *The Ladder* 13 (1969): 11; 12 (1969): 9–17.

Bahati, David. "The Anti Homosexuality Bill, 2009." *Bills Supplement to the Uganda Gazette* 102, no. 47 (2009).

Ballot Measure 9. Directed by Heather MacDonald. Oregon Tape Project, 1995.

Bannon, Ann. *Beebo Brinker*. Greenwich, Conn.: Fawcett Gold Medal, 1962.

———. *I Am a Woman*. Greenwich, Conn.: Fawcett Gold Medal, 1959.

———. *Journey to a Woman*. Greenwich, Conn.: Fawcett Gold Medal, 1960.

———. *Women in the Shadows*. Greenwich, Conn.: Fawcett Gold Medal, 1959.

Barale, Michéle Aina. "Review: Body Politic/Body Pleasured: Feminism's Theories of Sexuality, a Review Essay." *Frontiers* 9 (1986): 80–89.

Barker-Benfield, G. J. *The Horrors of the Half-Known Life*. New York: Harper Colophon, 1976.

Barkun, Elazar. *The Retreat of Scientific Racism: Changing Concepts of Race in Britain and the United States between the World Wars*. Cambridge: Cambridge University Press, 1993.

Barkun, Michael. *Religion and the Racist Right*. Chapel Hill: University of North Carolina Press, 1997.

Barnes, Djuna. *Ladies Almanack*. Paris: Titus, 1928.

Barney, Natalie Clifford. *Aventures de l'esprit*. Paris: Emile-Paul, 1929.

———. *In Memory of Dorothy Irene Wilde*. Dijon: Darantière, 1951.

———. *Je me souviens*. Paris: Sansot, 1910.

———. *Pensées d'une Amazone*. Paris: Emilie-Paul, 1920.

———. *Souvenirs indiscrets*. Paris: Flammarion, 1960.

Bar On, Bat-Ami. "The Feminist Sexuality Debates and the Transformation of the Political." *Adventures in Lesbian Philosophy*, ed. Claudia Card, 51–63. Bloomington: Indiana University Press, 1994.

Baron, Larry. "Pornography and Gender Equality: An Empirical Analysis." *Journal of Sex Research* 27, no. 3 (1990): 363–80.

Barr, James. *Quatrefoil*. New York: Greenberg, 1950.

Barry, Kathleen. *Female Sexual Slavery*. Englewood Cliffs, N.J.: Prentice-Hall, 1979.

———. *The Prostitution of Sexuality*. New York: New York University Press, 1995.

———. "Sadomasochism: The New Backlash to Feminism." *Trivia* 1 (fall 1982): 77–92.

Bart, Pauline B. "Review: Their Pleasure and Our Danger," *Contemporary Sociology* 15 (1986): 832–35.

Bartels, Larry M. *Unequal Democracy: The Political Economy of the New Gilded Age*. New York: Russell Sage Foundation, 2008.

Bartley, Paula. *Prostitution: Prevention and Reform in England, 1860–1914*. New York: Routledge, 1999.

Baum, Bruce David. *The Rise and Fall of the Caucasian Race: A Political History of Racial Identity*. New York: New York University Press, 2006.

Baxandall, Rosalyn, and Linda Gordon, eds. *Dear Sisters: Dispatches from the Women's Liberation Movement*. New York: Basic, 2000.

Bayer, Ronald. *Homosexuality and American Psychiatry: The Politics of Diagnosis*. New York: Basic, 1981.

Bearchell, Chris. "The Cloak of Feminism." *Body Politic* 53 (1979): 20.

Becker, Howard S. *Outsiders: Studies in the Sociology of Deviance*. New York: Free Press, 1973.

———, ed. *The Other Side: Perspectives on Deviance*. New York: Free Press, 1964.

———. "Whose Side Are We On?" *Sociological Work: Method and Substance*, ed. Howard S. Becker, 123–34. 1967; reprint, New Brunswick: Transaction, 1970.

Becker, Howard S., with Julius Debro. "Dialogue with Howard S. Becker (1970): An Interview Conducted by Julius Debro." *Doing Things Together: Selected Papers*, ed. Howard S. Becker, 25–46. Evanston: Northwestern University Press, 1986.

Bell, Alan P., and Martin S. Weinberg. *Homosexualities: A Study in Diversity among Men and Women*. New York: Simon and Schuster, 1978.

Benjamin, Jessica. "Master and Slave: The Fantasy of Erotic Domination." *Powers of Desire: The Politics of Sexuality*, ed. Ann Snitow, Christine Stansell, and Sharon Thompson, 280–99. New York: Monthly Review Press, 1983.

Bennett, David H. *The Party of Fear: The American Far Right from Nativism to the Militia Movement*. Rev. edn. New York: Vintage, 1995.

Bennett, Paula, and Vernon A. Rosario II, eds. *Solitary Pleasures: The Historical, Literary, and Artistic Discourses of Autoeroticism.* New York: Routledge, 1995.

Benstock, Shari. *Women of the Left Bank Paris, 1900–1940.* Austin: University of Texas Press, 1986.

Benston, Margaret. "The Political Economy of Women's Liberation." *Monthly Review* 21, no. 4 (1969): 13–27.

Berger, Peter, and Thomas Luckman. *The Social Construction of Reality: A Treatise in the Sociology of Knowledge.* Garden City: Doubleday, 1967.

Bernal, Martin. *Black Athena: The Afroasiatic Roots of Classical Civilization.* London: Free Association Books, 1987.

Berndt, Ronald. *Excess and Restraint.* Chicago: University of Chicago, 1962.

Bernstein, Elizabeth. "Militarized Humanitarianism Meets Carceral Feminism: The Politics of Sex, Rights, and Freedom in Contemporary Antitrafficking Campaigns." *Signs* 36, no. 1 (2010): 45–71.

———. "The Sexual Politics of the 'New Abolitionism.'" *differences: A Journal of Feminist Cultural Studies* 18, no. 3 (2007): 128–51.

Bernstein, Peter W., and Annalyn Swan, eds. *All the Money in the World: How the Forbes 400 Make—and Spend—Their Fortunes.* New York: Alfred A. Knopf, 2007.

Berry, Brewton. *Almost White.* New York: Macmillan, 1963.

Bérubé, Allan. "Behind the Spectre of San Francisco." *Body Politic* 72 (April 1981): 25–27.

———. "Coming Out Under Fire." *Mother Jones,* February–March 1983, 45.

———. *Coming Out Under Fire: The History of Gay Men and Women in World War Two.* New York: Free Press, 1990.

———. "'Dignity for All': The Role of Homosexuality in the Marine Cooks and Stewards Union (1930s–1950s)." Paper delivered at the "Reworking American Labor History: Race, Gender, and Class" conference, Madison, Wisconsin, 1993.

———. "The First Stonewall." *San Francisco Lesbian and Gay Freedom Day Program* 27 (1983).

———. "The History of Gay Bathhouses." *Coming Up* (December 1984).

———. "The History of the Bathhouses." *Policing Public Sex: Queer Politics and the Future of AIDS Activism,* ed. Dangerous Bedfellows, 187–220. Boston: South End, 1996.

———. "Lesbian Masquerade." *Gay Community News,* 17 November 1979.

———. "Marching to a Different Drummer." *Advocate,* 15 October 1981.

———. *My Desire for History: Essays in Gay, Community, and Labor History.* Edited with an introduction by John D'Emilio and Estelle B. Freedman. Chapel Hill: University of North Carolina Press, 2011.

Beserra, Sarah Senefeld, Sterling G. Franklin, and Norma Clevenger, eds. *Sex Code of California.* Sacramento: Planned Parenthood Affiliates of California, 1977.

Beserra, Sarah Senefeld, Nancy M. Jewel, Melody West Matthews, and Elizabeth R. Gatov, eds. *Sex Code of California.* Sacramento: Public Education and Research Committee of California, 1973.

Best, Joel. *Threatened Children: Rhetoric and Concern about Child-Victims*. Chicago: University of Chicago Press, 1990.

"Billionaires: The Richest People in the World." *Forbes*, 30 March 2009.

"Billionaires: The Richest People in the World." *Forbes*, 24 March 2008.

"Billionaires: The World's Richest People." *Forbes*, 29 March 2010.

"The Billionaires: The World's Richest People." *Fortune*, 12 October 1987.

Bingham, Caroline. "Seventeenth-Century Attitudes toward Deviant Sex." *Journal of Interdisciplinary History* (spring 1971): 447–68.

Blackwood, Evelyn, ed. *The Many Faces of Homosexuality: Anthropological Approaches to Homosexual Behavior*. New York: Harrington Park, 1986.

Bland, Lucy, and Laura Doan. *Sexology in Culture: Labelling Bodies and Desires*. Chicago: University of Chicago Press, 1998.

———. *Sexology Uncensored: The Documents of Sexual Science*. Chicago: University of Chicago Press, 1998.

Blume, Mary. "Natalie Barney, Legendary Lady of the Rue Jacob." *Realités* 183 (1966): 20–23.

Blumer, Herbert. *Symbolic Interactionism: Perspective and Method*. Englewood Cliffs, N.J.: Prentice-Hall, 1969.

Boffin, Tessa, and Sunil Gupta. *Ecstatic Antibodies*. London: Rivers Oram, 1990.

Bordin, Ruth. *Women at Michigan: The "Dangerous Experiment," 1870s to the Present*. Ann Arbor: University of Michigan Press, 1999.

Brace, C. Loring. *"Race" Is a Four-Letter Word: The Genesis of the Concept*. Oxford: Oxford University Press, 2005.

Bradley, Marion Zimmer. *Astra's Tower: Special Leaflet #2*. Rochester, Tex.: 1958.

———. *Astra's Tower: Special Leaflet #3*. Rochester, Tex.: 1959.

———. "Variant Women in Literature." *The Ladder* 1, no. 8 (1957): 8–10.

Bradley, Marion Zimmer, and Gene Damon. *Checklist: A Complete, Cumulative Checklist of Lesbian, Variant, and Homosexual Fiction, in English, or Available in English Translation, with Supplements of Related Material, for the Use of Collectors, Students, and Librarians*. Rochester, Tex.: s.n., 1960.

Brandt, Allan M. *No Magic Bullet: A Social History of Venereal Disease in the United States since 1880*. New York: Oxford University Press, 1985.

Bransford, Stephen. *Gay Politics vs. Colorado and America: The Inside Story of Amendment 2*. Cascade, Colo.: Sardis, 1994.

Brass, Perry. "Essentialism v. Constructionism Redux." *Gay and Lesbian Review Worldwide* 17, no. 3 (2010): 7.

———. "Kudos to Kramer on Queer Theory." *Gay and Lesbian Review Worldwide* 16, no. 6 (2009): 7–8.

Breeskin, Adelyn. *Romaine Brooks, "Thief of Souls."* Washington: Smithsonian, 1971.

Bristow, Edward J. *Prostitution and Prejudice: The Jewish Fight against White Slavery 1870–1939*. Oxford: Oxford University Press, 1982.

———. "Symond's History, Ellis's Heredity: Sexual Inversion." *Sexology in Culture:*

Labelling Bodies and Desires, ed. Laura Doan and Lucy Bland, 79–99. Chicago: University of Chicago Press, 1998.

———. *Vice and Vigilance: Purity Movements in Britain Since 1700*. London: Gill and Macmillan, 1977.

Brodkin, Karen. *How the Jews Became White Folks and What that Says about Race in America*. New Brunswick: Rutgers University Press, 1998.

Brooke, Christopher N. L. *The Medieval Idea of Marriage*. Oxford: Oxford University Press, 1989.

Brown, Lester K. *Two Spirit People: American Indian Lesbian Women and Gay Men*. New York: Harrington Park, 1997.

Brown, Rhonda. "Blueprint for a Moral America." *Nation*, 23 May 1981.

Brownmiller, Susan. *Against Our Will: Men, Women, and Rape*. New York: Bantam, 1976.

———. *In Our Time: Memoir of a Revolution*. New York: Dial, 1999.

Brun, Charles. "Untitled (Response to Salomon Reinach)." *Notes and Queries* 10 (1914): 151.

Bryan, Bo. *Shag: The Legendary Dance of the South*. Beaufort: Foundation Books for Fast Dance, 1995.

Bryant, Anita. *The Anita Bryant Story: The Survival of Our Nation's Families and the Threat of Militant Homosexuality*. Old Tappan, N.J.: Fleming H. Revell, 1977.

Bull, Chris, and John Gallagher. *Perfect Enemies: The Religious Right, the Gay Movement, and the Politics of the 1990s*. New York: Crown, 1996.

Bulmer, Martin. *The Chicago School of Sociology: The Institutionalization, Diversity, and the Rise of Sociological Research*. Chicago: University of Chicago Press, 1984.

Bulmer, Ralph. "Political Aspects of the Moka Ceremonial Exchange System among the Kyaka People of the Western Highlands of New Guinea." *Oceania* 31, no. 1 (1960): 1–13.

Burlein, Ann. *Lift High the Cross: Where White Supremacy and the Christian Right Converge*. Durham: Duke University Press, 2002.

Bush, Larry. "Capitol Report." *Advocate*, 8 December 1983.

Butler, Judith. *Bodies That Matter: On the Discursive Limits of "Sex."* New York: Routledge, 1993.

———. *Gender Trouble: Feminism and the Subversion of Identity*. New York: Routledge, 1990.

Cairncross, John. *After Polygamy was Made a Sin: The Social History of Christian Polygamy*. London: Routledge and Kegan Paul, 1974.

Califia, Pat. "The Age of Consent." *Advocate*, 16 October 1980; 30 October 1980.

———. "Among Us, Against Us—The New Puritans." *Advocate*, 17 April 1980.

———. "Doing It Together: Gay Men, Lesbians, and Sex." *Advocate*, 7 July 1983.

———. "Feminism and Sadomasochism." *Co-Evolution Quarterly* 33 (spring 1981): 33–40.

———. "Feminism vs. Sex: A New Conservative Wave." *Advocate*, 21 February 1980.

———. "Gender-Bending." *Advocate*, 15 September 1983.

———. "The Great Kiddy Porn Scare of '77 and Its Aftermath." *Advocate*, 16 October 1980.

———. "History of Samois." 1982. *Coming to Power*, ed. Samois, 243–81. Boston: Alyson, 1987.

———. "A Personal View of the Lesbian s/M Community and Movement in San Francisco." 1982. *Coming to Power*, ed. Samois, 243–81. Boston: Alyson, 1987.

———. "Public Sex." *Advocate*, 30 September 1982.

———. "Response to Dorchen Leidholdt." *New Women's Times* (October 1982).

———. *Sapphistry*. Tallahassee: Naiad, 1980.

———. "The Sex Industry." *Advocate*, 13 October 1983.

———. "A Thorny Issue Splits a Movement." *Advocate*, 30 October 1980.

———. "What Is Gay Liberation." *Advocate*, 25 June 1981.

Callahan, Nathan, and William Payton, eds. *"Shut Up Fag": Quotations from the Files of Congressman Bob Dornan*. Irvine: Mainstreet Media, 1994.

Cameron, Paul. *AIDS, the Blood Supply, and Homosexuality* (*What Homosexuals Do in Public Is Offensive, What They Do in Private Is Deadly*). Lincoln: ISIS, 1985.

———. *Child Molestation and Homosexuality* (*Homosexuality Is a Crime against Humanity*). Lincoln: ISIS, 1985.

———. *Criminality, Social Disruption, and Homosexuality* (*Homosexuality Is a Crime against Humanity*). Lincoln: ISIS, 1985.

———. *Exposing the AIDS Scandal*. Lafayette, La.: Huntington House, 1988.

———. *The Gay Nineties: What the Empirical Evidence Reveals about Homosexuality*. Franklin, Tenn.: Adroit, 1993.

———. *Homosexuality and the AIDS Threat to the Nation's Blood Supply*. Lincoln: ISIS, 1985.

———. *Murder, Violence, and Homosexuality* (*What Homosexuals Do in Public Is Offensive, What They Do in Private Is Deadly!*). Lincoln: ISIS, 1985.

———. *The Psychology of Homosexuality*. Lincoln: ISIS, 1984.

———. *What Homosexuals Do* (*Is More than Merely Disgusting*). Lincoln: ISIS, 1985.

Cardini, Leo. *Mineshaft Nights*. Teaneck, N.J.: First Hand, 1990.

Carpenter, Edward. *The Intermediate Sex: A Study of Some Transitional Types of Men and Women*. New York: Kennerly, 1912.

———. *Selected Writings: Edward Carpenter*. London: Gay Men's Press, 1984.

Carter, Erica, and Simon Watney. *Taking Liberties: AIDS and Cultural Politics*. London: Serpent's Tail, 1989.

Case, Sue-Ellen. "Towards a Butch-Femme Aesthetic." *Discourse* 11, no. 1 (1988–89): 55–73.

Castells, Manuel. *The City and the Grassroots*. Berkeley: University of California Press, 1983.

Castells, Manuel, and Karen Murphy. "Organization of San Francisco's Gay Community." *Urban Policy Under Capitalism*, ed. Norman I. Fainstein and Susan S. Fainstein, 237–59. Beverly Hills: Sage, 1982.

Cell 16. *No More Fun and Games* (*Untitled*) 1 (October 1968).

————. *No More Fun and Games: The Dialectics of Sexism* 3 (November 1969).

Chalmers, David M. *Hooded Americanism: The History of the Ku Klux Klan.* 3rd edn. Durham: Duke University Press, 1987.

Chalon, Jean. "La Maison de Natalie Barney." *Connaissance des Arts* 165 (1965): 82–87.

————. *Portrait d'une séductrice.* Paris: Stock, 1976.

————. *Portrait of a Seductress: The World of Natalie Barney.* Translated by Carol Barko. New York: Crown Publishers, 1979.

Champagne, Eric. "Letter to the Editor: Queer Theory Deserves a Fair Hearing." *Gay and Lesbian Review* 17, no. 1 (2010): 7.

Chancer, Lynn. *Reconcilable Differences: Confronting Beauty, Pornography, and the Limits of Feminism.* Berkeley: University of California Press, 1998.

Changing Our Minds: The Story of Dr. Evelyn Hooker. Directed by Richard Schmiechen. Frameline, 1991.

Chapoulie, Jean-Michel. "Everett Hughes and the Chicago Tradition." Translated by Howard S. Becker. *Sociological Theory* 14, no. 1 (1996): 3–29.

Chasseguet-Smirgel, J. *Female Sexuality.* Ann Arbor: University of Michigan Press, 1970.

Chast, Roz. "In the Nostalgia District." *New Yorker,* May 16, 2001.

Chauncey, George Jr. "Christian Brotherhood or Sexual Perversion? Homosexual Identities and the Construction of Sexual Boundaries in the World War One Era." *Journal of Social History* 19 (winter 1995): 189–211.

————. "From Sexual Inversion to Homosexuality: Medicine and the Changing Conceptualization of Female Deviance." In "Homosexuality: Sacrilege, Vision, Politics," ed. Robert Boyers and George Steiner, special issue of *Salmagundi* 58–59 (fall–winter 1982–83): 114–46.

————. *Gay New York: Gender, Urban Culture, and the Making of the Gay World, 1890–1940.* New York: Basic, 1994.

————. "The Postwar Sex Crime Panic." *True Stories from the American Past,* ed. William Graebner, 160–78. New York: McGraw-Hill, 1993.

————. *Why Marriage?: The History Shaping Today's Debate Over Gay Equality.* Cambridge: Basic Books, 2004.

Chodorow, Nancy. *Femininities, Masculinities, Sexualities: Freud and Beyond.* Lexington: University of Kentucky Press, 1990.

————. *Feminism and Psychoanalytic Theory.* New Haven: Yale University Press, 1991.

————. *The Reproduction of Mothering: Psychoanalysis and the Sociology of Gender.* Berkeley: University of California Press, 1978.

Chuang, Janie. "The United States as Global Sheriff: Unilateral Sanctions and Human Trafficking." *Michigan Journal of International Law* 27 (winter 2006): 437–94.

City of New York. *Report of the Mayor's Committee for the Study of Sex Offences.* New York: City of New York, 1939.

Cobb, Michael. *God Hates Fags: The Rhetorics of Religious Violence.* New York: New York University Press, 2006.

Cohen, Richard. *Coming Out Straight: Understanding and Healing Homosexuality*. Winchester, Va.: Oakhill, 2000.

Cohen, Stanley. *Folk Devils and Moral Panics: The Creation of the Mods and Rockers*. 1972; reprint, Oxford: Martin Robertson, 1980.

Colette. *The Pure and the Impure*. New York: Farrar, Straus, and Giroux, 1967.

Commonwealth of Massachusetts. *Preliminary Report of the Special Commission Investigating the Prevalence of Sex Crimes*. House Report no. 1169. Boston: Wright and Potter, 1947.

Connelly, Mark Thomas. *The Response to Prostitution in the Progressive Era*. Chapel Hill: University of North Carolina Press, 1980.

Conroy, Pat. *Beach Music*. New York: Bantam, 1996.

Constantine, L. L. "Child Sexuality: Recent Developments and Implications for Treatment, Prevention, and Social Policy." *Medicine and Law* 2 (1983): 55–67.

Coontz, Stephanie. *Marriage, a History: How Love Conquered Marriage*. 2005; reprint, New York: Penguin, 2006.

Cooper, Clarissa. *Women Poets of the Twentieth Century in France*. New York: King's Crown, 1943.

Corber, Robert J. *Homosexuality in Cold War America: Resistance and the Crisis of Masculinity*. Durham: Duke University Press, 1997.

———. *In the Name of National Security: Hitchcock, Homophobia, and the Political Construction of Gender in Postwar America*. Durham: Duke University Press, 1993.

Cory, Donald Webster. *The Homosexual in America*. New York: Greenberg, 1951.

Cott, Nancy F. *Public Vows: A History of Marriage and the Nation*. 2000; reprint, Cambridge: Harvard University Press, 2002.

Courtney, Phoebe. *The Sex Education Racket: Pornography in the Schools (An Expose)*. New Orleans: Free Men Speak, 1969.

Crawford, Alan. *Thunder on the Right: The "New Right" and the Politics of Resentment*. New York: Pantheon, 1980.

Creesey, Paul G. *The Taxi-Dance Hall: A Sociological Study in Commercialized Recreation and City Life*. 1932. New York: Greenwood, 1968.

Crimp, Douglas. *AIDS: Cultural Analysis, Cultural Activism*. 1987; reprint, Cambridge: Massachusetts Institute of Technology Press, 1988.

Crimp, Douglas, and Adam Rolston. *AIDS Demographics*. Seattle: Bay Press, 1990.

Cryle, Peter. *Geometry in the Boudoir: Configurations of French Erotic Narrative*. Ithaca: Cornell University Press, 1994.

Dalla Costa, Mariarosa. *The Power of Women and the Subversion of the Community*. Bristol: Falling Wall, 1972.

Damon, Gene, and Lee Stuart. *The Lesbian in Literature: A Bibliography*. San Francisco: Daughters of Bilitis, 1967.

Dannemeyer, William. *Shadow in the Land: Homosexuality in America*. San Francisco: Ignatius, 1989.

Davidson, Arnold. *The Emergence of Sexuality: Historical Epistemology and the For-mation of Concepts*. Cambridge: Harvard University Press, 2001.

———. "How to Do the History of Psychoanalysis." *The Emergence of Sexuality: His-torical Epistemology and the Formation of Concepts*, 66–92. Cambridge: Harvard University Press, 2001.

Davidson, Julia O'Connell. *Prostitution, Power, and Freedom*. Ann Arbor: University of Michigan Press, 1998.

———. "Will the Real Sex Slave Please Stand Up?" *Feminist Review* no. 83 (2005): 4–23.

Davis, D. L., and R. G. Whitten. "The Cross-Cultural Study of Human Sexuality." *Annual Reviews in Anthropology* 16 (1987): 69–98.

Dean, Tim, and Christopher Lane, eds. *Homosexuality and Psychoanalysis*. Chicago: University of Chicago Press, 2001.

Decter, Midge. *The New Chastity and Other Arguments against Women's Liberation*. New York: Coward, McCann and Geoghegan, 1972.

dejanikus, tacie. "Charges of Exclusion and McCarthyism at Barnard Conference." *off our backs* 12, no. 6 (1982): 5.

———. "Our Legacy." *off our backs* 10, no. 10 (1980): 17.

Delacoste, Frederique, and Priscilla Alexander. *Sex Work: Writings by Women in the Sex Industry*. San Francisco: Cleis, 1987.

Delany, Samuel R. *Times Square Red, Times Square Blue*. New York: New York Uni-versity Press, 1999.

Delarue-Mardrus, Lucie. *L'Ange et les pervers*. Paris: Ferenczi, 1930.

———. *Nos secrètes amours*. Paris: Les Isles, 1951.

Deleuze, Gilles. *Masochism: An Interpretation of Coldness and Cruelty*. New York: George Braziller, 1971.

Delphy, Christine. "The Invention of French Feminism: An Essential Move." *Yale French Studies* 97 (2000): 166–97.

D'Emilio, John. "Allan Bérubé's Gift to History." *Gay and Lesbian Review Worldwide* 15, no. 3 (2008): 10–13.

———. "Capitalism and Gay Identity." *Powers of Desire*, ed. Ann Snitow et al., 100–113. New York: Monthly Review Press, 1983.

———. "Dreams Deferred, Part One." *Body Politic* 48 (November 1978): 19.

———. "Dreams Deferred, Part Two: Public Actions, Private Fears." *Body Politic* 49 (December–January 1978–1979): 24–29.

———. "Dreams Deferred, Part Three: Reaction, Redbaiting, & 'Respectability.'" *Body Politic* 50 (February 1979): 22–27.

———. "Gay Politics and Community in San Francisco since World War II." *Hidden from History: Reclaiming the Gay and Lesbian Past*, ed. Martin Bauml Duberman, Martha Vicinus, and George Chauncey Jr., 456–73. New York: New American Library, 1989.

———. "Gay Politics, Gay Community: The San Francisco Experience." *Socialist Re-view* (January–February 1981): 77–104.

―――. "The Homosexual Menace: The Politics of Sexuality in Cold War America." *Passion and Power: Sexuality in History*, ed. Kathy Peiss, Christina Simmons, and Robert Padgug, 226–40. Philadelphia: Temple University Press, 1989.

―――. *Making Trouble: Essays on Gay History, Politics, and the University*. New York: Routledge, 1992.

―――. "Radical Beginnings, 1950–51." *Body Politic* 48 (November 1978): 20–24.

―――. *Sexual Politics, Sexual Communities: The Making of a Homosexual Minority in the United States, 1940–1970*. Chicago: University of Chicago Press, 1983.

―――. "Women Against Pornography." *Christopher Street* (May 1980): 19–26.

D'Emilio, John, and Estelle B. Freedman, eds. *Intimate Matters: A History of Sexuality in America*. New York: Harper and Row, 1988.

―――. "Allan Bérubé and the Power of Community History." Introduction to *My Desire for History: Essays in Gay, Community, and Labor History*. Edited with an introduction by John D'Emilio and Estelle B. Freedman, 1–40. Chapel Hill: University of North Carolina Press, 2011.

Derrida, Jacques. "Structure, Sign, and Play in the Discourse of the Human Sciences." *The Structuralist Controversy*, ed. R. Macksey and E. Donato, 247–72. Baltimore: Johns Hopkins University Press, 1972.

DeStefano, Anthony. *The War on Human Trafficking: U.S. Policy Assessed*. New Brunswick, N.J.: Rutgers University Press, 2008.

Deutsch, Helene. "On Female Homosexuality." *The Psychoanalytic Reader*, ed. R. Fleiss, 237–60. New York: International Universities Press, 1948.

―――. "The Significance of Masochism in the Mental Life of Women." *The Psychoanalytic Reader*, ed. R. Fleiss, 223–36. New York: International Universities Press, 1948.

Devereaux, George. "Institutionalized Homosexuality among Mohave Indians." *Human Biology* 9, no. 4 (1937): 498–529.

"Diary of a Conference on Sexuality, 1982: The GLQ Archive." *GLQ* 17, no. 1 (2011): 49–78.

Diaz, Kathryn E. "The Porn Debates Reignite." *Gay Community News*, 6–19 June 1992, 3, 5.

Dobson, James. *The New Dare to Discipline*. 1970. Wheaton, Ill.: Tyndale House, 1992.

Doezema, Jo. "Loose Women or Lost Women? The Re-emergence of the Myth of White Slavery in Contemporary Discourses of Trafficking in Women." *Gender Issues* 18, no. 1 (2000): 23–50.

―――. *Sex Slaves and Discourse Masters: The Construction of Trafficking*. London: Zed, 2010.

Dollars and Sense, United for a Fair Economy, eds. *The Wealth Inequality Reader*. Cambridge, Mass.: Dollars and Sense, Economic Affairs Bureau, 2004.

Domanick, Joe. *Cruel Justice: Three Strikes and the Politics of Crime in America's Golden State*. Berkeley: University of California Press, 2004.

Donnerstein, Edward. "Aggressive Erotica and Violence against Women." *Journal of Personality and Social Psychology* 39, no. 2 (1990): 269–77.

———. "Interview." *Penthouse*, September 1985, 165–68, 180–81.

Donnerstein, Edward I., and Daniel G. Linz. "The Question of Pornography: It Is Not Sex, but Violence, that Is an Obscenity in Our Society." *Psychology Today*, December 1986, 56–59.

Donnerstein, Edward, Daniel Linz, and Steven Penrod. *The Question of Pornography: Research Findings and Policy Implications*. New York: Free Press, 1987.

Donovan, Brian. *White Slave Crusades: Race, Gender, and Anti-Vice Activism, 1887–1917*. Chicago: University of Illinois Press, 2006.

Dorries, Pam. "Feminists Differ at Chicago Porn Hearing." *Gay Community News*, 17 August 1985, 1, 6.

Dosse, François. *History of Structuralism*. Vol. 1, *The Rising Sign, 1945–1966*. Minneapolis: University of Minnesota Press, 1997.

———. *History of Structuralism*. Vol. 2, *The Sign Sets, 1967–Present*. Minneapolis: University of Minnesota Press, 1997.

Douglas, Mary. *The Lele of Kasai*. London: Oxford University Press, 1963.

———. *Purity and Danger: An Analysis of the Concepts of Pollution and Taboo*. Boston: Routledge and Kegan Paul, 1966.

Drake, Gordon V. SIECUS: *Corrupter of Youth*. Tulsa: Christian Crusade, 1969.

Drescher, Jack, and Joseph P. Merlino. *American Psychiatry and Homosexuality: An Oral History*. New York: Harrington Park Press, 2007.

Drexel, Allen. "Before Paris Burned: Race, Class, and Male Homosexuality on the Chicago South Side, 1935–1960." *Creating a Place for Ourselves*, ed. Brett Beemyn, 119–44. New York: Routledge, 1997.

Duberman, Martin Bauml, Martha Vicinus, and George Chauncey Jr., eds. *Hidden from History: Reclaiming the Gay and Lesbian Past*. New York: New American Library, 1989.

Duggan, Lisa. "The Binds that Divide." *off our backs* 15, no. 11 (1985): 26.

———. "Of Meese and Women: Porn Panic's New Face." *Village Voice*, 3 December 1985, 33–35.

———. *Sapphic Slashers: Sex, Violence, and American Modernity*. Durham: Duke University Press, 2000.

———. "The Trials of Alice Mitchell: Sensationalism, Sexology, and the Lesbian Subject in Turn-of-the-Century America." *Signs* 18, no. 4 (1993): 791–814.

Duggan, Lisa, and Nan D. Hunter. *Sex Wars: Sexual Dissent and Political Culture*. New York: Routledge, 1995.

du Mas, Frank M. *Gay Is Not Good*. Nashville: Thomas Nelson, 1979.

Dworkin, Andrea. *Pornography: Men Possessing Women*. New York: Perigee, 1981.

———. *Right-Wing Women*. New York: Perigee, 1983.

Dworkin, Andrea, and Catharine A. MacKinnon. *Pornography and Civil Rights: A New Day for Women's Equality*. Minneapolis: Organizing Against Pornography, 1988.

Echols, Alice. "Cultural Feminism: Feminist Capitalism and the Anti-Pornography Movement." *Social Text* 7 (spring–summer 1983): 34–53.

———. *Daring to Be Bad: Radical Feminism in America 1967–1975*. Minneapolis: University of Minnesota Press, 1989.

Eeckhout, Bart. "The Disneyfication of Times Square: Back to the Future?" *Critical Perspectives on Urban Redevelopment*, ed. Kevin Fox Gotham, 379–428. Oxford: Elsevier Science, 2001.

Ehrenreich, Barbara. "What Is This Thing Called Sex." *Nation*, 24 September 1983.

Eichel, Edward, and Philip Nobile. *The Perfect Fit: How to Achieve Fulfillment and Monogamous Passion through the New Intercourse*. New York: Donald I. Fine, 1992.

Ellis, Havelock. *Sexual Inversion*. Philadelphia: F. A. Davis Company, 1915.

———. *Studies in the Psychology of Sex*. New York: Random House, 1936.

Ellis, Havelock, and John Addington Symonds. *Sexual Inversion: A Critical Edition*. Edited by Ivan Crozier. Houndsmill: Palgrave Macmillan, 2008.

Engel, Randy. *Sex Education: The Final Plague*. Gaithersburg, Md.: Human Life International, 1989.

Engelhardt, H. Tristram, Jr., and Arthur L. Caplan, eds. *Scientific Controversies: Case Studies in the Resolution and Closure of Disputes in Science and Technology*. Cambridge: Cambridge University Press, 1987.

Engels, Friedrich. *The Origin of the Family, Private Property, and the State*. 1942. Introduction by Eleanor Burke Leacock. New York: International Publishers, 1972.

English, Deirdre, Amber Hollibaugh, and Gayle Rubin. "Talking Sex." *Socialist Review* (July–August 1981): 43–62.

Epstein, Steven. "A Queer Encounter: Sociology and the Study of Sexuality." *Queer Theory/Sociology*, ed. Steven Seidman, 145–67. Cambridge: Blackwell, 1996.

Eribon, Didier. "Michel Foucault's Histories of Sexuality." Translated by Michael Lucey. GLQ 7, no. 1 (2001): 31–86.

Erzen, Tanya. *Straight to Jesus: Sexual and Christian Conversions in the Ex-Gay Movement*. Berkeley: University of California Press, 2006.

Escoffier, Jeffrey. *American Homo: Community and Perversity*. Berkeley: University of California Press, 1998.

———. "Generations and Paradigms: Mainstreams in Lesbian and Gay Studies." *Gay and Lesbian Studies*, ed. Henry Minton, 112–27. New York: Harrington Park, 1992.

———. "Inside the Ivory Closet: The Challenges Facing Lesbian and Gay Studies." *Outlook* 10 (fall 1990): 2–26.

———. "Reading the Social: Homosexuality and the Sociological Imagination in the Fifties and Sixties." Paper delivered at the Center for Lesbian and Gay Studies, City University of New York, 1993.

Eskridge, William N. "Privacy Jurisprudence and the Apartheid of the Closet, 1946–1961." *Florida State University Law Review* 24 no. 4 (1997): 703–838.

Evans, Sara. *Personal Politics: The Roots of Women's Liberation in the Civil Rights Movement and the New Left*. New York: Vintage, 1980.

Evans-Pritchard, E. E. "Sexual Inversion among the Azande." *American Anthropologist* 72 (1970): 1428–34.

Faderman, Lillian. *Surpassing the Love of Men: Romantic Friendship and Love between Women from the Renaissance to the Present*. New York: Morrow, 1981.

Fainstein, Susan S., Norman I. Fainstein, and P. Jefferson Armistead. "San Francisco: Urban Transformation and the Local State." *Restructuring the City: The Political Economy of Urban Redevelopment*, rev. edn., ed. Susan S. Fainstein, Norman I. Fainstein, Richard Child Hill, Dennis R. Judd, and Michael Peter Smith, 202–44. 1983; reprint, New York: Longman, 1986.

The Fall of '55. Directed by Seth Randal. Produced by Louise Luster and Seth Randal. Entendre Pictures, 2006.

Fass, Paula. *Children of a New World: Society, Culture, and Globalization*. New York: New York University Press, 2007.

———. *Kidnapped: Child Abduction in America*. New York: Oxford University Press, 1997.

Fee, Elizabeth. "The Sexual Politics of Victorian Social Anthropology." *Feminist Studies* 1 (winter–spring 1973): 23–29.

Fee, Elizabeth, and Daniel M. Fox. *AIDS: The Burdens of History*. Berkeley: University of California Press, 1988.

———. *AIDS: The Making of a Chronic Disease*. Berkeley: University of California Press, 1992.

Feingold, David A. "Trafficking in Numbers: The Social Construction of Human Trafficking Data." *Sex, Drugs, and Body Counts: The Politics of Numbers in Global Crime and Conflict*, ed. Peter Andreas and Kelly M. Greenhill, 46–74. Ithaca: Cornell University Press, 2010.

Feldwebel, T. A. "Two Steps Backward." *DungeonMaster* 43 (1991): 3.

Feminist Anti-Censorship Taskforce et al., eds. *Caught Looking: Feminism, Pornography, and Censorship*. East Haven, Conn.: Long River, 1992.

"Festival Womyn Speak Out." *Gay Community News*, 17–23 November 1991, 4.

Field, Andrew. *Djuna, The Formidable Miss Barnes*. Austin: University of Texas Press, 1985.

Fingrudt, Meryl. ". . . An Organizer." *off our backs* 17, no. 3 (1987): 24.

Finkelhor, David. "What's Wrong with Sex between Adults and Children? Ethics and the Problem of Sexual Abuse." *American Journal of Orthopsychiatry* 49, no. 4 (1979): 692–97.

Finley, Moses I. *Ancient Society and Modern Ideology*. New York: Penguin, 1980.

Fischel, Joseph. "Per Se or Power? Age and Sexual Consent." *Yale Journal of Law and Feminism* 22, no. 2 (2010): 279–342.

———. "Transcendent Homosexuals and Dangerous Sex Offenders: Sexual Harm and Freedom in the Judicial Imaginary." *Duke Journal of Gender, Law, and Policy* 17, no. 2 (2010): 277–311.

Flanner, Janet. Introduction to *The Pure and the Impure*, by Colette. New York: Farrar, Straus, and Giroux, 1967.

"Forbes 400." *Forbes*, 19 October 2009.

"Forbes 400." *Forbes*, 6 October 2008.

"Forbes 400." *Forbes*, 8 October 2007.

"The Forbes Four Hundred." *Forbes*, 13 September 1982.

Ford, Clellen S., and Frank A. Beach. *Patterns of Sexual Behavior*. New York: Harper and Row, 1951.

Ford, Henry, Sr. *The International Jew: The World's Foremost Problem*. 1921. Honolulu: University Press of the Pacific, 2003.

Foster, Jeannette D. *Sex Variant Women in Literature*. New York: Vantage, 1956.

Foucault, Michel. *The History of Sexuality*. Vol. 1, *An Introduction*. Translated by Robert Hurley. New York: Pantheon, 1978.

————. *Madness and Civilization: A History of Insanity in the Age of Reason*. Translated by Richard Howard. New York: Pantheon, 1965.

————. *The Order of Things*. New York: Pantheon, 1970.

Frank, Robert H. *Richistan: A Journey Through the American Wealth Boom and the Lives of the New Rich*. Old Saybrook: Tantor Audio, 2007.

Frank, Robert H., and Phillip J. Cook. *The Winner-Take-All Society: Why the Few at the Top Get So Much More Than the Rest of Us*. New York: Penguin, 1995.

Frank, Thomas. *What's the Matter with Kansas?: How Conservatives Won the Heart of America*. New York: Metropolitan Books, 2004.

Freedman, Estelle. *Feminism, Sexuality, and Politics: Essays*. Chapel Hill: University of North Carolina Press, 2006.

————. "'Uncontrolled Desire': The Threat of the Sexual Psychopath in America, 1935–1960." Paper presented at the annual meeting of the American Historical Association, San Francisco, December 1983.

————. "Uncontrolled Desires: The Response to the Sexual Psychopath, 1920–1960." *Journal of American History* 74, no. 1 (1987): 83–106.

Freeman, Jo. *The Politics of Women's Liberation*. New York: Longman, 1975.

Freud, Sigmund. "Female Sexuality." *The Complete Works of Sigmund Freud*. Vol. 21, ed. James Strachey, 223–43. London: Hogarth, 1961.

————. "Femininity." *New Introductory Lecture in Psychoanalysis*, ed. James Strachey, 139–67. New York: Norton, 1965.

————. *A General Introduction to Psychoanalysis*. Garden City: Garden City, 1943.

————. "The Sexual Aberrations." 1905. *Three Essays on the Theory of Sexuality*. Vol. 17 of *The Standard Edition of the Complete Psychological Works of Sigmund Freud*, trans. and ed. James Strachey, 135–72. London: Hogarth, 1960.

————. "Some Psychical Consequences of the Anatomical Distinction between the Sexes." *The Complete Works of Sigmund Freud*, vol. 21, ed. James Strachey. London: Hogarth, 1961.

Fulton, John S. "The Medical Statistics of Sex Hygiene; Such as They Are." *American Journal of Public Health* 3, no. 7 (1913): 661–76.

————. "Addenda to Dr. John S. Fulton's Article Entitled 'The Medical Statistics of Sex Hygiene; Such as They Are,' which Appeared in the June Journal, p. 661." *American Journal of Public Health* 3, no. 8 (1913): 793–94.

Gagnon, John. *Human Sexualities*. Glenview, Ill.: Scott, Foresman, 1977.

―――. "Sexual Conduct: As Today's Memory Serves." *Sexualities* 2, no. 1 (1999): 115–26.

―――. "An Unlikely Story." *Authors of Their Own Lives: Intellectual Autobiographies of Twenty American Sociologists*, ed. Bennett M. Berger, 213–34. Berkeley: University of California Press, 1992.

Gagnon, John, and William Simon. *Sexual Deviance*. New York: Harper and Row, 1967.

―――, eds. *Sexual Conduct: The Social Sources of Human Sexuality*. Chicago: Aldine, 1973.

―――. *The Sexual Scene*. Chicago: Aldine / Trans-Action, 1970.

Galliher, John F., ed. "Chicago's Two Worlds of Deviance Research: Whose Side Are They On?" *A Second Chicago School? The Development of a Postwar American Sociology*, ed. Gary Alan Fine, 164–87. Chicago: University of Chicago Press, 1995.

Gallo, Marcia M. *Different Daughters: A History of the Daughters of Bilitis and the Rise of the Lesbian Rights Movement*. New York: Carroll and Graf, 2006.

Garber, Eric. "Gladys Bentley: The Bulldagger Who Sang the Blues." *OUTLook: National Lesbian and Gay Quarterly* 1 (ca. 1998): 52–61.

―――. "A Historical Directory of Lesbian and Gay Establishments in the San Francisco Bay Area." Unpublished manuscript, Gay and Lesbian Historical Society of Northern California, 1990.

―――. "A Spectacle in Color: The Lesbian and Gay Subculture of Jazz Age Harlem." *Hidden from History: Reclaiming the Gay and Lesbian Past*, ed. Martin B. Duberman, Martha Vicinus, and George Chauncey Jr., 318–31. New York: New American Library, 1991.

Garde, Noel. *From Jonathan to Gide: The Homosexual in History*. New York: Vantage, 1964.

―――. *The Homosexual in Literature: A Chronicle Bibliography Circa 700 B.C.–1958*. New York: Village Press, 1959.

Gardiner, Jean. "Political Economy of Female Labor in Capitalist Society." Paper delivered at the "Sexual Divisions and Society" conference, British Sociological Association, 1974.

A Gay Bibliography: Eight Bibliographies on Lesbian and Male Homosexuality. New York: Arno Press, 1975.

Gearhart, Sally. "An Open Letter to the Voters in District 5 and San Francisco's Gay Community from Sally Gearhart." San Francisco: Lesbians and Gays with Kay. Leaflet, 1979. Collection of the Author.

Gebhard, Paul H. "The Institute." *Sex Research: Studies from the Kinsey Institute*, ed. Marlin S. Weinberg, 10–22. New York: Oxford University Press, 1976.

"Genetic Lesbians." *Gay Community News*, 19–25 May 1991, 4.

Gerard, Kent, and Gert Hekma, eds. *The Pursuit of Sodomy: Male Homosexuality in Renaissance and Enlightenment Europe*. New York: Haworth Press, 1989.

Gerassi, John. *The Boys of Boise*. New York: Collier, 1966.

Gerhard, Jane F. *Desiring Revolution: Second-Wave Feminism and the Rewriting of*

American Sexual Thought, 1920 to 1982. New York: Columbia University Press, 2001.

Germain, André. *Renée Vivien*. Paris: Crès, 1917.

Germon, Jennifer. *Gender: A Genealogy of an Idea*. New York: Palgrave Macmillan, 2009.

Gerstein, Ira. "Domestic Work and Capitalism." *Radical America* 7, no. 4–5 (1973): 101–28.

Gerth, H. H., and C. Wright Mills, eds. *From Max Weber: Essays in Sociology*. New York: Oxford University Press, 1958.

Gettleman, Jeffrey. "Ugandan Who Spoke Up for Gays Is Beaten to Death." *New York Times*, 27 January 2011.

Gilder, George F. *Sexual Suicide*. New York: Quadrangle / New York Times Book Review, 1973.

Gilmore, Ruth Wilson. *Golden Gulag: Prisons, Surplus, Crisis, and Opposition in Globalizing California*. Berkeley: University of California Press, 2007.

Glasse, R. M. "The Mask of Venery." Paper presented at seventieth annual meeting of the American Anthropological Association, New York City, 1971.

Glickman, Neil. "Letter to the Editor." *Gay Community News*, 22 August 1981.

Global Rights: Partners for Justice. *Annotated Guide to the Complete UN Trafficking Protocol*. Washington: Global Rights, 2002.

Goffman, Erving. *Stigma: Notes on the Management of Spoiled Identity*. Englewood Cliffs, N.J.: Prentice-Hall, 1963.

Goldman, Emma. "The Traffic in Women." 1910. *Anarchism and Other Essays*. New York: Dover, 1969.

———. "The Traffic in Women." 1917. *The Traffic in Women and Other Essays on Feminism*, 19–32. New York: Times Change Press, 1970.

Goodale, Jane, and Ann Chowning. "The Contaminating Woman." Paper presented at the seventieth annual meeting of the American Anthropological Association, New York City, 1971.

Goody, Jack, and S. J. Tambiah. *Bridewealth and Dowry*. Cambridge: Cambridge University Press, 1973.

Gordon, Linda. *Woman's Body, Woman's Right*. New York: Penguin, 1976.

Gordon, Linda, and Ellen Dubois. "Seeking Ecstasy on the Battlefield: Danger and Pleasure in Nineteenth Century Feminist Sexual Thought." *Feminist Studies* 9.1 (1983): 7–25.

Gordon, Linda, and Allen Hunter. "Sex, Family, and the New Right." *Radical America* (winter 1977–78): 9–26.

Gorham, Deborah. "The 'Maiden Tribute of Modern Babylon' Re-Examined: Child Prostitution and the Idea of Childhood in Late-Victorian England." *Victorian Studies* 21, no. 3 (1978): 353–79.

Gornick, Vivien, and Barbara K. Moran. *Women in Sexist Society: Studies in Power and Powerlessness*. New York: Basic, 1971.

Gough, Ian. "Marx and Productive Labour." *New Left Review* 76 (1972): 47–72.

Gough, Kathleen. "The Nayars and the Definition of Marriage." *Journal of the Royal Anthropological Institute* 89 (1959): 23–24.

Gould, Jane. *Juggling: A Memoir of Work, Family, and Feminism*. New York: Feminist Press at the City University of New York, 1997.

Grant, Madison. *The Passing of the Great Race or The Racial Basis of European History*. New York: Charles Scribner's Sons, 1918.

Graves, Karen. *And They Were Wonderful Teachers: Florida's Purge of Gay and Lesbian Teachers*. Urbana: University of Illinois Press, 2009.

Green, Richard. "Is Pedophilia a Mental Disorder?" *Archives of Sexual Behavior* 31, no. 6 (2002): 467–71.

Gregory-Lewis, Sasha. "The Neo-Right Political Apparatus." *Advocate*, 8 February 1977.

———. "Right Wing Finds New Organizing Tactic." *Advocate*, 23 June 1977.

———. "Unraveling the Anti-Gay Network." *Advocate*, 7 September 1977.

Greslé-Favier, Claire. *"Raising Sexually Pure Kids": Sexual Abstinence, Conservative Christians and American Politics*. New York: Rodopi, 2009.

Grier, Barbara [Gene Damon]. *The Lesbian in Literature*. 1967. Tallahassee: Naiad, 1981.

Griffin, Susan. *Pornography and Silence: Culture's Revenge against Nature*. New York: Harper Colophon, 1981.

Grindea, Miron, ed. "The Amazon of Letters: A World Tribute to Natalie Clifford Barney," special issue of *Adam International Review* 29 (1961).

Groth, Paul. *Living Downtown: The History of Residential Hotels in the United States*. Berkeley: University of California Press, 1994.

Grumley, Michael, and Ed Gallucci. *Hard Corps: Studies in Leather and Sadomasochism*. New York: Dutton, 1977.

Guterl, Matthew Pratt. *The Color of Race in America, 1900–1940*. Cambridge: Harvard University Press, 2001.

Hall, Radclyffe. *The Well of Loneliness*. New York: Permabooks, 1959.

Halperin, David. *One Hundred Years of Homosexuality and Other Essays on Greek Love*. New York: Routledge, 1990.

Halperin, David M., John J. Winkler, and Froma I. Zeitlin, eds. *Before Sexuality: The Construction of Erotic Experience in the Ancient Greek World*. Princeton: Princeton University Press, 1990.

Hankins, Frank H. *The Racial Basis of Civilization: A Critique of the Nordic Doctrine*. New York: Knopf, 1926.

Hansen, Bert. "The Historical Construction of Homosexuality." *Radical History Review* 20 (spring–summer 1979): 66–75.

Harding, Sandra. "Why Has the Sex/Gender System Become Visible Only Now?" *Discovering Reality: Feminist Perspectives on Epistemology, Metaphysics, Methodology, and Philosophy of Science*, 311–24. 2nd edn. Dordrecht: Kluwer Academic Publishers, 2003.

Hardisty, Jean. *Mobilizing Resentment: Conservative Resurgence from the John Birch Society to the Promise Keepers*. Boston: Beacon, 1999.

Harris, Bertha. "The More Profound Nationality of Their Lesbianism: Lesbian Society in Paris in the 1920's." *Amazon Expedition: A Lesbian Feminist Anthology*, ed. Phyllis Birkby et al., 77–88. New York: Times Change Press, 1973.

Harry, Joseph, and William B. DeVall. *The Social Organization of Gay Males*. New York: Praeger, 1978.

Hartman, Chester. *The Transformation of San Francisco*. Totowa, N.J.: Rowman and Allanheld, 1984.

Hartman, Chester, et al. *Yerba Buena: Land Grab and Community Resistance in San Francisco*. San Francisco: Glide, 1974.

Hartman, Chester, with Sarah Carnochan. *City for Sale: The Transformation of San Francisco*. Berkeley: University of California Press, 2002.

Hartmann, Heidi. "The Unhappy Marriage of Marxism and Feminism." *Women and Revolution*, ed. Lydia Sargent, 1–41. Boston: South End, 1981.

Hartwell, Samuel. *A Citizen's Handbook of Sexual Abnormalities and the Mental Hygiene Approach to Their Prevention*. Lansing: State of Michigan, 1950.

Harvey, David. *A Brief History of Neoliberalism*. Oxford: Oxford University Press, 2006.

Hawthorne, Melanie, ed. "Natalie Barney and Her Circle," special issue of *South Central Review* 22, no. 3 (2005).

Haynes, Dina Francesca. "(Not) Found Chained to a Bed in a Brothel: Conceptual, Legal, and Procedural Failures to Fulfill the Promise of the Trafficking Victims Protection Act." *Georgetown Immigration Law Journal* 21 (spring 2007): 337–68.

Heap, Chad C. *Homosexuality in the City: A Century of Research at the University of Chicago*. Exhibition catalogue. Chicago: University of Chicago Library, 2000.

Hefner, Robert. "The *Tel Quel* Ideology: Material Practice upon Material Practice." *Substance* 8 (1974): 127–38.

Henley, Clark. *The Butch Manual*. New York: Sea Horse, 1982.

Henry, Alice. "Porn Is Subordination?" *off our backs* (November 1984): 20, 24.

Henry, George. *Sex Variants: A Study of Homosexual Patterns*. 2 vols. New York: Paul B. Hoeber, 1941.

Henwood, Doug. *The State of the U.S.A. Atlas: The Changing Face of American Life in Maps and Graphics*. New York: Simon and Schuster, 1994.

Herdt, Gilbert, ed. *Gay Culture in America: Essays from the Field*. Boston: Beacon, 1992.

———. *Guardians of the Flutes: Idioms of Masculinity*. New York: McGraw-Hill, 1981.

———. *Ritualized Homosexuality in Melanesia*. Berkeley: University of California Press, 1984.

Heresies: The Sex Issue 12 (1981).

Herman, Didi. *The Antigay Agenda: Orthodox Vision and the Christian Right*. 1997; reprint, Chicago: University of Chicago Press, 1998.

Herring, Phillip. *Djuna: The Life and Work of Djuna Barnes*. New York: Viking, 1995.

Herskovitz, Melville. "A Note on 'Woman Marriage' in Dahomey." *Africa* 10, no. 3 (1937): 335–41.

Higgens, Patrick. *Heterosexual Dictatorship: Male Homosexuality in Post-War Britain.* London: Fourth Estate, 1996.

Himmelfarb, Gertrude. *The De-Moralization of Society: From Victorian Virtues to Modern Values.* 1994; reprint, New York: Vintage, 1996.

Hirschfeld, Magnus. *The Homosexuality of Men and Women.* 1914. Translated by Michael Lombardi-Nash. Amherst, N.Y.: Prometheus, 2000.

Hoffman, Amy. *An Army of Ex-Lovers: My Life at the Gay Community News.* Amherst: University of Massachusetts Press, 2007.

Hollibaugh, Amber. "The Erotophobic Voice of Women: Building a Movement for the Nineteenth Century." *New York Native* (26 September–9 October 1983): 32–35.

Holroyd, Michael. *Lytton Strachey.* New York: Holt, Rinehart, and Winston, 1968.

Holz, Maxine. "Porn: Turn On or Put Down, Some Thoughts on Sexuality," *Processed World* 7 (spring 1983): 38–52.

Hook, 'Fessa John. *Shagging in the Carolinas.* Charleston: Arcadia, 2005.

Hooker, Evelyn. "The Homosexual Community." 1961. *Sexual Deviance*, ed. John Gagnon and William Simon, 167–84. New York: Harper and Row, 1967.

Horney, Karen. "The Denial of the Vagina." *Feminine Psychology*, 147–61. Edited by Harold Kelman. New York: Norton, 1973.

House, Penny, and Liza Cowan. "Can Men Be Women? Some Lesbians Think So! Transsexuals in the Women's Movement." *Dyke* 5 (fall 1977): 29–35.

Humphreys, Laud. *Tearoom Trade: Impersonal Sex in Public Places.* New York: Aldine, 1979.

Hunt, Lynn. Introduction to *The Invention of Pornography: Obscenity and the Origins of Modernity, 1500–1800*, ed. Lynn Hunt, 9–45. New York: Zone Books, 1993.

Hunt, Margaret. "Discord in the Happy Valley: Report of a Conference on Feminism, Sexuality, and Power." *Gay Community News* 14, no. 21 (1986): 8–9.

Hunter, Nan. "Modern McCarthyism." *off our backs* 15, no. 11 (1985): 26.

———. "Sex-Baiting and Dangerous Bedfellows." *off our backs* 15, no. 7 (1985): 33.

Hyde, H. Montgomery. *A History of Pornography.* New York: Dell, 1965.

Ignatiev, Noel. *How the Irish Became White.* New York: Routledge, 1995.

Igra, Samuel. *Germany's National Vice.* London: Quality Press, 1945.

Irvine, Janice. *Talk about Sex: The Battles over Sex Education in the United States.* Berkeley: University of California Press, 2002.

Jackson, Margaret. "Sex Research and the Construction of Sexuality: A Tool of Male Supremacy?" *Women's Studies Forum International* 7, no. 1 (1984): 43–51.

Jacobs, Sue-Ellen, Wesley Thomas, and Sabine Lang, eds. *Two-Spirit People: Native American Gender Identity, Sexuality, and Spirituality.* Urbana: University of Illinois Press, 1997.

Jacobson, Matthew Frye. *Whiteness of a Different Color: European Immigrants and the Alchemy of Race.* Cambridge: Harvard University Press, 1998.

"Jacqueline Livingston." *Clothed with the Sun* 3, no. 1 (May 1983): 33–39.

Jaget, Claude. *Prostitutes: Our Life.* Bristol: Falling Wall, 1980.

Jagose, Annamarie. "Feminism's Queer Theory." *Feminism and Psychology* 19, no. 2 (2009): 157–74.

———. *Queer Theory: An Introduction.* New York: New York University Press, 1996.

Jakobson, Roman, and Morris Halle. *Fundamentals of Language.* The Hague: Mouton, 1971.

James, Jennifer, et al. *The Politics of Prostitution.* Seattle: Social Research Associates, 1977.

Jay, Karla. *The Amazon and the Page: Natalie Clifford Barney and Renée Vivien.* Bloomington: Indiana University Press, 1988.

Jeffreys, Sheila. *AntiClimax: A Feminist Perspective on the Sexual Revolution.* London: Women's Press, 1990.

———. "Butch and Femme: Now and Then." *Gossip* 5 (1987): 65–95.

———. *The Idea of Prostitution.* Melbourne: Spinifex, 1997.

———. *The Lesbian Heresy: A Feminist Perspective on the Lesbian Sexual Revolution.* Melbourne: Spinifex, 1993.

———. *The Spinster and Her Enemies: Feminism and Sexuality.* Boston: Pandora, 1985.

———. "The Spinster and Her Enemies: Sexuality and the Last Wave of Feminism." *Scarlet Woman* 13, part 2 (July 1981): 22–27.

Johnson, David. "The Kids of Fairytown: Gay Male Culture on Chicago's Near North Side in the 1930s." *Creating a Place for Ourselves*, ed. Brett Beemyn, 97–118. New York: Routledge, 1997.

———. *The Lavender Scare: The Cold War Persecution of Gays and Lesbians in the Federal Government.* Chicago: University of Chicago Press, 2004.

Johnston, David Cay. *Free Lunch: How the Wealthiest Americans Enrich Themselves at Government Expense (and Stick You with the Bill).* New York: Portfolio, 2007.

Jones, Ernest. "The Phallic Phase." *International Journal of Psychoanalysis* 14 (1933): 1–33.

Jordan, Jane. *Josephine Butler.* London: Hambledon Continuum, 2001.

Jordan, Mark. *The Invention of Sodomy in Christian Theology.* Chicago: University of Chicago Press, 1997.

Kaplan, Jeffrey. *Encyclopedia of White Power: A Sourcebook on the Radical Racist Right.* Walnut Creek, Calif.: Altamira, 2000.

Karr, M. A. "Susan Griffin." *Advocate*, 20 March 1980.

Katz, Jonathan Ned. *Gay American History: Lesbians and Gay Men in the U.S.A.* New York: Thomas Crowell, 1976.

———. *Gay/Lesbian Almanac: A New Documentary.* New York: Harper and Row, 1983.

———, ed. *Homosexuality: Lesbians and Gay Men in Society, History, and Literature.* New York: Arno, 1975.

———. "The Invention of Heterosexuality." *Socialist Review* 20, no. 1 (1990): 7–34.

———. *The Invention of Heterosexuality.* New York: Plume, 1995.

Katz, Leon. Introduction to *Fernhurst, Q.E.D., and Other Early Writings*, by Gertrude Stein. New York: Liveright, 1973.

Kauffman, Linda. *American Feminist Thought, 1982–1992*. Oxford: Basil Blackwell, 1993.

Kelly, Raymond. *Etoro Social Structure: A Study in Structural Contradiction*. 1974; reprint, Ann Arbor: University of Michigan Press, 1977.

———. "Witchcraft and Sexual Relations: An Exploration of the Social and Semantic Implications of the Structure of Belief." Paper presented at the seventy-third annual meeting of the American Anthropological Association, Mexico City, 1974.

———. "Witchcraft and Sexual Relations: An Exploration of the Social and Semantic Implications of the Structure of Belief." *Man and Woman in the New Guinea Highlands*, ed. Paula Brown and Georgeda Buchbinder, 36–53. Washington: American Anthropological Association, 1976.

Kempadoo, Kamala, and Jo Doezema, eds. *Global Sex Workers: Rights, Resistance, and Redefinition*. New York: Routledge, 1998.

Kempadoo, Kamala, Jyoti Sanghera, and Bandana Pattanaik, eds. *Trafficking and Prostitution Reconsidered: New Perspectives on Migration, Sex Work, and Human Rights*. Boulder, Colo.: Paradigm Publishers, 2005.

Kendrick, Walter. *The Secret Museum: Pornography in Modern Culture*. New York: Viking, 1987.

Kennedy, Elizabeth Lapovsky, and Madeline D. Davis. *Boots of Leather, Slippers of Gold: The History of a Lesbian Community*. New York: Routledge, 1993.

———. "The Reproduction of Butch-Fem Roles: A Social Constructionist Approach." *Passion and Power: Sexuality in History*, ed. Kathy Peiss, Christina Simmons, with Robert A. Padgug, 241–56. Philadelphia: Temple University Press, 1989.

Kennedy, Hubert C. *Ulrichs: The Life and Works of Karl Heinrich Ulrichs, Pioneer of the Modern Gay Movement*. Boston: Alyson Publications, 1988.

Kessler, Suzanne J., and Wendy McKenna. *Gender: An Ethnomethodological Approach*. Chicago: University of Chicago Press, 1978.

Kinsella, James. *Covering the Plague: AIDS and the American Media*. New Brunswick: Rutgers University Press, 1989.

Kinsey, Alfred, Wardell B. Pomeroy, and Clyde E. Martin. *Sexual Behavior in the Human Male*. Philadelphia: W. B. Saunders, 1948.

Kinsey, Alfred, Wardell B. Pomeroy, Clyde E. Martin, and Paul H. Gebhard. *Sexual Behavior in the Human Female*. Philadelphia: W. B. Saunders, 1953.

Klaich, Dolores. *Woman Plus Woman*. New York: Simon and Schuster, 1974.

Klassen, Ben, P. M. *The White Man's Bible*. Otto, N.C.: Church of the Creator, 1981.

Klatch, Rebecca E. *Women of the New Right*. Philadelphia: Temple University Press, 1987.

Koedt, Anne, Ellen Levine, and Anita Rapone. *Radical Feminism*. New York: Quadrangle, 1973.

Koskovich, Gerard. "Lesbian, Gay, Bisexual and Transgender Archives and Libraries in the United States." *LGBTQ America Today: An Encyclopedia*, ed. John Hawley, 684–92. Westwood: Greenwood Press, 2009.

Krafft-Ebing, R. von. *Psychopathia Sexualis, with Special Reference to the Contrary Sexual Instinct: A Medico-Legal Study*. Philadelphia: Davis, 1899.

Kramer, Larry. "Letter to the Editor: Kramer on Theory: Rebuttal and a Defense." *Gay and Lesbian Review Worldwide* 17, no. 2 (2010): 6.

———. "Queer Theory's Heist of Our History." *Gay and Lesbian Review Worldwide* 16, no. 5 (2009): 11–13.

Kreiger, Susan. *The Mirror Dance: Identity in a Women's Community*. Philadelphia: Temple University Press, 1983.

Lacan, Jacques. *The Language of Self: The Function of Language in Psychoanalysis*. Translated by Anthony Wilden. Baltimore: Johns Hopkins University Press, 1968.

Lacretelle, Jacques de. *L'Amour sur la place*. Paris: Perrin, 1964.

LaHaye, Tim. *The Unhappy Gays: What Everyone Should Know about Homosexuality*. Carol Stream, Ill.: Tyndale House, 1978.

Lampl de Groot, Jeanne. "The Evolution of the Oedipus Complex in Women." *The Psychoanalytic Reader*, ed. R. Fleiss, 180–94. New York: International Universities Press, 1948

———. "Problems of Femininity." *Psychoanalytic Quarterly* 2 (1933): 489–518.

Landsberg, Michele. "Canada: Antipornography Breakthrough in the Law." *Ms.*, May–June 1992, 14–15.

Langness, L. L. "Sexual Antagonism in the New Guinea Highlands: A Bena Bena Example." *Oceania* 37, no. 3 (1967): 161–77.

Langum, David. *Crossing Over the Line: Legislating Morality and the Mann Act*. Chicago: University of Chicago Press, 1994.

Laqueur, Thomas. *Solitary Sex: A Cultural History of Masturbation*. New York: Zone Books, 2003.

Larguia, Isabel, and John Dumoulin. "Towards a Science of Women's Liberation." *NACLA Newsletter* 6, no. 10 (1972): 3–20.

Lasch, Christopher. "Freud and Women." *New York Review of Books* 21, no. 15 (1974): 12–17.

Lassiter, Matthew D., and Joseph Crespino. *The Myth of Southern Exceptionalism*. Oxford: Oxford University Press, 2010.

Latimer, Tirza True. *Women Together/Women Apart: Portraits of Lesbian Paris*. New Brunswick: Rutgers University Press, 2005.

Lauritsen, John, and David Thorstad. *The Early Homosexual Rights Movement*. New York: Times Change Press, 1974.

Lawrence v. Texas. 539 U.S. 558 (2003).

Leach, Edmund. *Rethinking Anthropology*. New York: Humanities, 1971.

Leahy, Terry. "Sex and the Age of Consent: The Ethical Issues." *Social Analysis* 39 (1996): 27–55.

Lederer, Laura, ed. *Take Back the Night: Women on Pornography*. New York: William Morrow, 1980.

Lee, John Allan. *Getting Sex: A New Approach, More Sex, Less Guilt.* Don Mills, Ontario: Musson, 1978.

The Legacy: Murder and Media, Politics and Prisons. Directed by Michael J. Moore. PBS, 2006.

Leidholdt, Dorchen. "Back to Barnard." *off our backs* 23, no. 9 (1993): 30.

———. "A Small Group," *off our backs* 15, no. 10 (1985): 26.

Leidholdt, Dorchen, and Janice G. Raymond. *The Sexual Liberals and the Attack on Feminism.* New York: Pergamon, 1990.

Leopold, Les. *The Looting of America: How Wall Street's Game of Fantasy Finance Destroyed Our Jobs, Pensions, and Prosperity, and What We Can Do About It.* White River Junction, Vt.: Chelsea Green, 2009.

Levine, Judith. "A Question of Abuse." *Mother Jones,* July-August 1996, 32–37, 67–70.

———. *Harmful to Minors: The Perils of Protecting Children from Sex.* Minneapolis: University of Minnesota Press, 2002.

Levine, Martin P. *Gay Men: The Sociology of Male Homosexuality.* New York: Harper Colophon, 1979.

Levine, Martin P., Peter M. Nardi, and John H. Gagnon, eds. *In Changing Times: Gay Men and Lesbians Encounter HIV/AIDS.* Chicago: University of Chicago Press, 1997.

Lévi-Strauss, Claude. "A Confrontation." *New Left Review* 62 (July–August 1970): 57–74.

———. *The Elementary Structures of Kinship.* Translated by James Harle Bell, John Richard von Strurmer, and Rodney Needham. Boston: Beacon, 1969.

Levitas, Daniel. *The Terrorist Next Door: The Militia Movement and the Radical Right.* New York: Thomas Dunne Books, St. Martin's Press, 2002.

Lewin, Ellen. *Lesbian Mothers.* Ithaca: Cornell University Press, 1993.

Lewin, Ellen, and William L. Leap. *Final Report of the Commission on Lesbian, Gay, Bisexual, and Transgender Issues in Anthropology.* Arlington, Va.: American Anthropological Association, 1999.

Leznoff, Maurice, and William A. Westley. "The Homosexual Community." *Sexual Deviance,* ed. John Gagnon and William Simon, 184–96. New York: Harper and Row, 1967.

Limoncelli, Stephanie. *The Politics of Trafficking: The First International Movement to Combat the Sexual Exploitation of Women.* Stanford: Stanford University Press, 2010.

Linden, Robin Ruth, Darlene R. Pagano, Diana E. H. Russell, and Susan Leigh Starr, eds. *Against Sadomasochism: A Radical Feminist Analysis.* East Palo Alto, Calif.: Frog in the Well Press, 1982.

Lindenbaum, Shirley. "A Wife Is the Hand of the Man." Paper presented at the seventy-second annual meeting of the American Anthropological Association, Mexico City, 1973.

Lipset, Seymour Martin, and Earl Raab. *The Politics of Unreason: Right-Wing Extremism in America, 1790–1970.* New York: Harper and Row, 1970.

Lively, Scott. *The Poisoned Stream: "Gay" Influence in Human History*. Keizer, Ore.: Founders Publishing Corportation, 1997.

———. *Seven Steps to Recruit-Proof Your Child*. Keizer, Ore.: Founders Publishing Corporation, 1998.

Lively, Scott, and Kevin Abrams. *The Pink Swastika: Homosexuality in the Nazi Party*. Keizer, Ore.: Founders Publishing Corporation, 1996.

Livia, Anna, ed. *A Perilous Advantage: The Best of Natalie Clifford Barney*. Norwich, Vt.: New Victoria, 1992.

———. "The Trouble with Heroines: Natalie Clifford Barney and Anti-Semitism." *A Perilous Advantage: The Best of Natalie Clifford Barney*, 181–93. Norwich, Vt.: New Victoria, 1992.

Livingstone, Frank. "Genetics, Ecology, and the Origins of Incest and Exogamy." *Current Anthropology* 10, no. 1 (1969): 45–61.

———. "On the Non-Existence of the Human Races." *Cultural Anthropology* 3, no. 3 (1962): 279–81.

Longino, Helen E. "Pornography, Oppression, and Freedom: A Closer Look." *Take Back the Night: Women on Pornography*, ed. Laura Lederer, 436–41. New York: William Morrow, 1980.

Lorenz, Paul. *Sapho 1900: Renée Vivien*. Paris: Julliard, 1977.

Lynn, Barry W. *Polluting the Censorship Debate: A Summary and Critique of the Attorney General's Commission on Pornography*. Washington: American Civil Liberties Union, 1986.

———. *Rushing to Censorship: An Interim Report on the Methods of Evidence Gathering and Evaluation by the Attorney General's Commission on Pornography*. Washington: American Civil Liberties Union, 1986.

MacKinnon, Catharine. "Feminism, Marxism, Method and the State: An Agenda for Theory." *Signs* 7, no. 3 (1982): 515–44.

———. "Feminism, Marxism, Method and the State: Toward Feminist Jurisprudence." *Signs* 8, no. 4 (1983): 635–58.

———. *Feminism Unmodified: Discourses on Life and Law*. Cambridge: Harvard University Press, 1987.

———. *Toward a Feminist Theory of the State*. Cambridge: Harvard University Press, 1989.

Mains, Geoff. *Gentle Warriors*. Stamford, Conn.: Knights, 1989.

———. *Urban Aboriginals*. San Francisco: Gay Sunshine, 1984.

———. "View From a Sling." *Drummer* 121 (1988).

Mair, Lucy. *Marriage*. Baltimore: Penguin Books, 1971.

Malamuth, Neal M., and Edward Donnerstein, eds. *Pornography and Sexual Aggression*. New York: Academic Press, 1984.

Malinowski, Bronislaw. "The Primitive Economics of the Trobriand Islanders." *Cultures of the Pacific*, ed. T. Harding and B. Wallace, 51–62. New York: Free Press, 1970.

———. *The Sexual Life of Savages*. London: Routledge and Kegan Paul, 1929.

Mannoni, Maud. *The Child, His "Illness" and the Others.* New York: Pantheon, 1970.

Marcus, Steven. *The Other Victorians.* New York: New American Library, 1974.

Marks, Elaine. *Marrano as Metaphor: The Jewish Presence in French Writing.* New York: Columbia University Press, 1996.

Marmor, Judd. *Sexual Inversion.* London: Basic, 1965.

Marrs, Texe. *Big Sister Is Watching You: Hillary Clinton and the White House Feminists Who Now Control America—and Tell the President What to Do.* Austin, Tex.: Living Truth, 1993.

———. *Ravaged by the New Age: Satan's Plan to Destroy Our Kids.* Austin, Tex.: Living Truth, 1989.

Marshall, Donald S., and Robert C. Suggs, eds. *Human Sexual Behavior: Variations in the Ethnographic Spectrum.* New York: Basic, 1971.

Martin, William. *With God on Our Side: The Rise of the Religious Right in America.* New York: Broadway, 1996.

Marx, Karl. *Capital.* New York: International Publishers, 1972.

———. *The Eighteenth Brumaire of Louis Bonaparte, with Explanatory Notes.* 1852. New York: International Publishers, 1963.

———. *Pre-capitalist Economic Formations.* New York: International Publishers, 1971.

———. *Theories of Surplus Value, Part 1.* Moscow: Progress, 1969.

———. *Wage-Labor and Capital.* New York: International Publishers, 1971.

Mason, Diane. *The Secret Vice: Masturbation in Victorian Fiction and Medical Culture.* Manchester: Manchester University Press, 2008.

Masuzawa, Tomoko. *The Invention of World Religions: Or, How European Universalism was Preserved in the Language of Pluralism.* Chicago: University of Chicago Press, 2005.

Matlock, Jann. "Masquerading Women, Pathologized Men: Cross-Dressing, Fetishism, and the Theory of Perversion, 1882–1935." *Fetishism as Cultural Discourse,* ed. Emily Apter and William Pietz, 31–61. Ithaca: Cornell University Press, 1993.

Maurras, Charles. *L'Avenir de l'intelligence.* Paris: Nouvelle Librarie Nationale, 1905.

Mauss, Marcel. *The Gift: Forms and Functions of Exchange in Archaic Societies.* New York: W. W. Norton, 1967.

McCalman, Iain. *Radical Underworld: Prophets, Revolutionaries and Pornographers in London, 1795–1940.* Cambridge: Cambridge University Press, 1988.

McClelland, Donald. *Where Shadows Live: Alice Pike Barney and Her Friends.* Exhibition catalogue. Washington: National College of Fine Arts, 1978.

McCormack, Thelma. "Appendix 1: Making Sense of the Research on Pornography." *Women against Censorship,* ed. Varda Burstyn, 181–205. Vancouver: Douglas and McIntyre, 1985.

McGreevy, John T. *Catholicism and American Freedom: A History.* New York: W. W. Norton, 2003.

McGuigan, Dorothy Gies. *A Dangerous Experiment: One Hundred Years of Women at the University of Michigan.* Ann Arbor: Center for Continuing Education of Women, 1970.

McIntosh, Mary. "The Homosexual Role." *Social Problems* 16, no. 2 (1968): 182–92.

McLellan, David, ed. *The Grundrisse.* New York: Harper and Row, 1971.

McMurtrie, Douglas. "A Legend of Lesbian Love among North American Indians." *Urologic and Cutaneous Review* (April 1914): 192–93.

Meggitt, M. J. "Male-Female Relationships in the Highlands of Australian New Guinea." *American Anthropologist* 66, no. 4, part 2 (1970): 204–24.

Mehlman, Jeffrey. *French Freud: Structural Studies in Psychoanalysis,* no. 48. New Haven: Yale French Studies, 1972.

Miller, Alice. "Sexuality, Violence Against Women, and Human Rights. Women Make Demands and Ladies Get Protection." *Health and Human Rights* 7, no. 2 (2004): 16–47.

Miller, Jean Baker. *Psychoanalysis and Women.* Baltimore: Penguin, 1973.

Miller, Neil. *Sex Crime Panic: A Journey to the Paranoid Heart of the 1950s.* Los Angeles: Alyson Books, 2002.

Minkowitz, Donna. *Ferocious Romance: What My Encounters with the Right Taught Me about Sex, God, and Fury.* New York: Free Press, 1998.

Mintz, Steven. *Huck's Raft: A History of American Childhood.* Cambridge: Harvard University Press, 2004.

Mitchell, Juliet. *Psychoanalysis and Feminism: Freud, Reich, Laing, and Women.* New York: Pantheon, 1974.

———. *Women's Estate.* New York: Vintage, 1971.

Mitchell, Juliet, and Ann Oakley. *The Rights and Wrongs of Women.* Middlesex: Harmondsworth, 1976.

Mitzel, John. *The Boston Sex Scandal.* Boston: Glad Day Books, 1980.

Money, John, and Anke A. Ehrhardt. *Man & Woman, Boy & Girl: The Differentiation and Dimorphism of Gender Identity from Conception to Maturity.* Baltimore: Johns Hopkins University Press, 1972.

Moody, Roger. *Indecent Assault.* London: Word Is Out, 1980.

Morgan, Lewis Henry. *Ancient Society, or Researches in the Lines of Human Progress from Savagery, through Barbarism to Civilization.* New York: Henry Holt, 1877.

Morgan, Robin. *The Anatomy of Freedom: Feminism, Physics, and Global Politics.* Garden City, N.Y.: Anchor Books / Doubleday, 1984.

———. *Sisterhood Is Powerful: An Anthology of Writings from the Women's Liberation Movement.* New York: Vintage, 1970.

Moses, Claire. "Made in America: 'French Feminism' in Academia." *Feminist Studies* 24, no. 2 (1998): 241–74.

Mumford, Kevin. "Homosex Changes: Race, Cultural Geography, and the Emergence of the Gay." *American Quarterly* 48, no. 3 (September 1996): 395–414.

———. *Interzones: Black/White Sex Districts in Chicago and New York in the Early Twentieth Century.* New York: Columbia University Press, 1997.

Murphy, Robert. "Social Structure and Sex Antagonism." *Southwestern Journal of Anthropology* 15, no. 1 (1959): 81–96.

Murray, Stephen O. "The Institutional Elaboration of a Quasi-Ethnic Community." *International Review of Modern Sociology* 9, no. 2 (1979): 155–75.

Nagle, Jill, ed. *Whores and Other Feminists*. New York: Routledge, 1997.

Nardi, Peter M., ed. *Journal of Sociology and Social Work: Perspectives on the Social Effects of AIDS* 11, nos. 1–2 (1988–89).

Nardi, Peter, and Beth Schneider, eds. "Kinsey: A Fiftieth-Anniversary Symposium," *Sexualities* 1, no. 1 (1998): 83–106.

——. *Social Perspectives in Lesbian and Gay Studies*. New York: Routledge, 1998.

Nathan, Debbie. *Women and Other Aliens: Essays from the U.S.-Mexican Border*. El Paso, Tex.: Cinco Puntos, 1991.

National Organization for Women. *Hearings on Pornography: Materials on the Personal Testimony of NOW Activists on Pornography*. Washington, 23 May 1986.

——. *Hearings on Pornography*. San Francisco, 26 March 1986.

Newton, Esther. *Cherry Grove, Fire Island: Sixty Years in America's First Gay and Lesbian Town*. Boston: Beacon, 1993.

——. *Margaret Mead Made Me Gay: Personal Essays, Public Ideas*. Durham: Duke University Press, 2000.

——. *Mother Camp: Female Impersonators in America*. Englewood Cliffs, N.J.: Prentice-Hall, 1972.

——. "The Mythic Mannish Lesbian: Radclyffe Hall and the New Woman." *Hidden from History: Reclaiming the Gay and Lesbian Past*, ed. Martin Bauml Duberman, Martha Vicinus, and George Chauncey Jr., 281–93. New York: New American Library, 1989.

Newton, Esther, and Shirley Walton. "The Misunderstanding: Toward a More Precise Sexual Vocabulary." *Pleasure and Danger*, ed. Carole Vance, 34–42. Boston: Routledge and Kegan Paul, 1984.

Noebel, David A. *The Homosexual Revolution*. 1977; reprint, Tulsa: American Christian College Press, 1978.

Noebel, David A., Wayne C. Lutton, and Paul Cameron. *AIDS: Acquired Immune Deficiency Syndrome Special Report*. Manitou Springs, Colo.: Summit Research Institute, 1986.

Norton, Clark. "Sex in America." *Inquiry* (5 October 1981): 11–18.

Not a Love Story: A Film about Pornography. Directed by Bonnie Sherr Klein. Produced by Dorothy Todd Henaut. Studio D., National Film Board of Canada, 1981.

Nowinski, Ira. *Ira Nowinski's San Francisco: Poets, Politics, and Divas*. Berkeley: Heyday, 2006.

——. *No Vacancy: Urban Renewal and the Elderly*. San Francisco: Carolyn Bean Associates, 1979.

Nye, Robert A. "The Medical Origins of Sexual Fetishism." *Fetishism as Cultural Discourse*, ed. Emily Apter and William Pietz, 13–30. Ithaca: Cornell University Press, 1993.

O'Carroll, Tom. *Paedophilia: The Radical Case*. London: Peter Owen, 1980.

O'Dair, Barbara. "Sex, Love, and Desire: Feminists Struggle over the Portrayal of Sex." *Alternative Media* (spring 1983).

Odem, Mary. *Delinquent Daughters: Protecting and Policing Adolescent Female Sexuality in the United States, 1885–1920*. Chapel Hill: University of North Carolina Press, 1995.

Okami, Paul. "'Child Perpetrators of Sexual Abuse': The Emergence of a Problematic Deviant Category." *Journal of Sex Research* 29, no. 1 (1992): 109–30.

Oosterhuis, Harry. *Stepchildren of Nature: Krafft-Ebing, Psychiatry, and the Making of Sexual Identity*. Chicago: University of Chicago Press, 2000.

Orlando, Lisa. "Bad Girls and 'Good' Politics." *Village Voice, Literary Supplement*, December 1982.

———. "Lust at Last! Spandex Invades the Academy." *Gay Community News*, 15 May 1982: 42–50.

———. "Power Plays: Coming to Terms with Lesbian S/M." *Village Voice*, 26 July 1983.

Ortner, Sherry B., and Harriet Whitehead, eds. *Sexual Meanings: The Cultural Construction of Gender and Sexuality*. New York: Cambridge University Press, 1981.

Padgug, Robert A. "Sexual Matters: On Conceptualizing Sexuality in History." *Radical History Review* 20 (spring–summer 1979): 3–23.

Page, Sharon. "Feminists Stand Divided on Meese Commission Report." *Gay Community News*, 3–9 August 1986, 1, 11.

———. "Indianapolis Enacts Anti-Pornography Bill." *Gay Community News*, 19 May 1984, 1, 3.

———. "Minneapolis Mayor Vetoes Anti-Porn Law." *Gay Community News*, 14 January 1984, 1, 6.

Papayanis, Nicholas. "Sex and the Revanchist City: Zoning Out Pornography." *Environment and Planning D: Space and Society* 18 (2000): 341–53.

Park, Robert E., Ernest W. Burgess, and Roderick McKenzie. *The City*. 1925. Chicago: University of Chicago Press, 1967.

Passet, Joanne. *Sex Variant Woman: The Life of Jeannette Howard Foster*. Cambridge: Da Capo Press, 2008.

Pasternak, Judith. "The Strangest Bedfellows: Lesbian Feminism and the Sexual Revolution." *Woman News* (October 1983).

Patton, Cindy. *Inventing AIDS*. New York: Routledge, 1990.

———. *Sex and Germs: The Politics of AIDS*. Boston: South End Press, 1985.

Pavlov's Children (They May Be Yours). Los Angeles: Impact, 1969.

Peakman, Julie. *Mighty Lewd Books: The Development of Pornography in Eighteenth-Century England*. New York: Palgrave Macmillan, 2003.

Peiss, Kathy. *Cheap Amusements: Working Women and Leisure in Turn-of-the-Century New York*. Philadelphia: Temple University Press, 1986.

Peiss, Kathy, and Christina Simmons, with Robert A. Padgug, eds. *Passion and Power: Sexuality in History*. Philadelphia: Temple University Press, 1989.

Pela, Robert L. "No Freedom of Gay Press: Publishers of Gay and Lesbian Books Faced Increased Printer Turndowns in 1991." *Advocate*, 14 January 1992, 84–85.

Penelope, Julia. "And Now for the Really Hard Questions." *Sinister Wisdom* 15 (fall 1980).

Petchesky, Rosalind Pollack. "Anti-abortion, Anti-feminism, and the Rise of the New Right." *Feminist Studies* 7, no. 2 (1981): 206–46.

Peters, Peter J. *The Death Penalty for Homosexuals Is Prescribed in the Bible*. 1992; reprint, LaPorte, Colo.: Scriptures for America, 1993.

Phelan, Shane. *Identity Politics: Lesbian Feminism and the Limits of Community*. Philadelphia: Temple University Press, 1989.

Phelps, Robert, ed. *Earthly Paradise*. New York: Farrar, Straus, and Giroux, 1966.

Pheterson, Gail. *A Vindication of the Rights of Whores*. Seattle: Seal, 1989.

Phillips, Kevin. *The Politics of Rich and Poor: Wealth and the American Electorate in the Reagan Aftermath*. New York: Random House, 1990.

———. *Wealth and Democracy: A Political History of the American Rich*. New York: Broadway Books, 2002.

Plath, Sylvia. "Daddy." *Ariel: The Restored Edition*, 64–66. New York: Harper Collins, 2004.

Plummer, Kenneth, ed. *The Making of the Modern Homosexual*. London: Hutchinson, 1981.

———, ed. *Modern Homosexualities: Fragments of Lesbian and Gay Experience*. New York: Routledge, 1992.

———. *Sexual Stigma: An Interactionist Account*. New York: Routledge and Kegan Paul, 1975.

Podhoretz, Norman. "The Culture of Appeasement." *Harper's*, October 1977.

Polanyi, Karl. *The Great Transformation*. New York: Farrar and Rinehart, 1944.

Polanyi, Karl, Conrad Arensberg, and Henry Pearson, eds. *Trade and Market in the Early Empires: Economies in History and Theory*. 1957. Chicago: Gateway, 1971.

Poliakov, Léon. *The Aryan Myth: A History of Racist and Nationalist Ideas in Europe*. Translated by Edmund Howard. New York: Basic Books, 1974.

Ponse, Barbara. *Identities in the Lesbian World: The Social Construction of Self*. Westport, Conn.: Greenwood, 1978.

Pougy, Liane de. *Idylle Sapphique*. Paris: La Plume, 1901.

Powell, Lynn. *Framing Innocence: A Mother's Photographs, a Prosecutor's Zeal, and a Small Town's Response*. New York: The New Press, 2010.

Puff, Helmut. *Sodomy in Reformation Germany and Switzerland, 1400–1600*. Chicago: University of Chicago Press, 2003.

Quarles, Chester L. *Christian Identity: The Aryan American Bloodline Religion*. Jefferson, N.C.: McFarland, 2004.

Quindlen, Anna. "Driving to the Funeral." *Newsweek*, 11 June 2007, 80.

Radicalesbians. "The Woman Identified Woman." *Radical Feminism*, ed. Anne Koedt, Ellen Levine, and Anita Rapone, 240–45. New York: Quadrangle, 1973.

Rappaport, Roy. *Pigs for the Ancestors: Ritual in the Ecology of a New Guinea People.* New Haven: Yale University Press, 1975.

Raymond, Janice. *The Transsexual Empire: The Making of the She-Male.* New York: Teachers College Press, 1979.

Read, Kenneth. "The Nama Cult of the Central Highlands, New Guinea." *Oceania* 23, no. 1 (1953): 1–25.

———. *Other Voices: The Style of a Male Homosexual Tavern.* Novato, Calif.: Chandler and Sharp, 1980.

Réage, Pauline. *Story of O.* New York: Grove, 1965.

Reay, Marie. *The Kuma.* London: Cambridge University Press, 1959.

Reckless, Walter C. *Vice in Chicago.* 1933. Montclair: Patterson Smith, 1969.

Redstockings of the Women's Liberation Movement. *Feminist Revolution: An Abridged Edition with Additional Writings.* New York: Random House, 1978.

Regina v. Brown. 2 All ER 75 (House of Lords, 1993).

Reinach, Salomon. Untitled (Query). *Notes and Queries* 9 (1914): 488.

Reinharz, Shulamit. "The Chicago School of Sociology and the Founding of the Graduate Program in Sociology at Brandeis University: A Case Study in Cultural Diffusion." *A Second Chicago School? The Development of a Postwar American Sociology,* ed. Gary Allan Fine, 273–321. Chicago: University of Chicago Press, 1995.

Reisman, Judith A., Edward W. Eichel, John H. Court, and J. Gordon Muir, eds. *Kinsey, Sex, and Fraud: The Indoctrination of a People.* Lafayette, La.: Huntington House, 1990.

Reiss, Albert. "The Social Integration of Peers and Queers." 1961. *Sexual Deviance,* ed. John Gagnon and William Simon, 197–227. New York: Harper and Row, 1967.

Reiter, Rayna R., ed. *Toward an Anthropology of Women.* New York: Monthly Review Press, 1975.

Rekers, George A. *Growing Up Straight: What Every Family Should Know about Homosexuality.* Chicago: Moody Press, 1982.

Revolutionary Union. *On Homosexuality: A Stalino-Leninist Guide to Love and Sex.* Ann Arbor: 1975.

Reyes, Nina. "Smothering Smut." *Outweek,* 26 September 1990, 37–42.

Rich, Adrienne. "Compulsory Heterosexuality and Lesbian Existence." *Signs* 5, no. 4 (1980): 631–60.

———. *On Lies, Secrets, and Silence.* New York: W. W. Norton, 1979.

Rich, B. Ruby. "Is There Anything New under the Covers?" *In These Times,* 20–26 February 1985, 19.

———. "Review: Feminism and Sexuality in the 1980s." *Feminist Studies* 12 (1986): 525–61.

———. Review of *Powers of Desire. In These Times,* 16–22 November 1983.

Richardson, Katherine H., and Eugene B. Chase Jr. *Pawleys Island Historically Speaking.* Pawleys Island, S.C.: Pawleys Island Civic Association, 1994.

Riddell, Carol. *Divided Sisterhood: A Critical Review of Janice Raymond's "The Transsexual Empire."* Liverpool: News from Nowhere, 1980.

Ridgeway, James. *Blood in the Face: The Ku Klux Klan, Aryan Nations, Nazi Skinheads, and the Rise of a New White Culture.* 1990; reprint, New York: Thunder's Mouth, 1995.

Robbins, Louise. "The Library of Congress and Federal Loyalty Programs, 1947–1956: No 'Communists or Cocksuckers.'" *The Library Quarterly* 64, no. 4 (1994): 365–85.

Robinson, Paul. *The Modernization of Sex.* New York: Harper and Row, 1976.

Rodgers, Bruce. *The Queen's Vernacular: A Gay Lexicon.* San Francisco: Straight Arrow, 1972.

Rodriguez, Suzanne. *Wild Heart: Natalie Clifford Barney's Journey from Victorian America to Belle Époque Paris.* New York: Ecco, 2002.

Rogers, William G. *Ladies Bountiful.* New York: Harcourt, Brace, and World, 1968.

Rollins, Chiquita. "When Conservatives Investigate Porn." *off our backs* 15.11 (1985): 1, 12–13.

Rosaldo, Michelle Zimbalist, and Lousie Lamphere, eds. *Women, Culture, and Society.* Stanford: Stanford University Press, 1974.

Rosario, Vernon A., ed. *Science and Homosexualities.* New York: Routledge, 1997.

Roscoe, Will. *The Zuni Man-Woman.* Albuquerque: University of New Mexico Press, 1991.

Rose, Stephen J. *Social Stratification in the United States: The American Profile Poster Revised and Expanded.* New York: New Press, 1992.

———. *Social Stratification in the United States: The American Profile Poster Revised and Updated Edition.* New York: New Press, 2000.

Rosen, Michael. *Sexual Magic: The s/m Photographs.* San Francisco: Shaynew, 1986.

———. *Sexual Portraits: Photographs of Radical Sexuality.* San Francisco: Shaynew, 1990.

Rowbotham, Sheila. *Edward Carpenter: A Life of Liberty and Love.* London: Verso, 2008.

Rowbotham, Sheila, and Jeffrey Weeks. *Socialism and the New Life: The Personal and Sexual Politics of Edward Carpenter and Havelock Ellis.* London: Pluto Press, 1977.

Rowntree, M., and J. Rowntree. "More on the Political Economy of Women's Liberation." *Monthly Review* 21, no. 8 (1970): 26–32.

Royére, Jean. "Sapho et Circé." *Le Pointe de vue de Sirius.* Paris: Messein, 1935.

Rubin, Gayle. "Afterword to 'Thinking Sex: Notes for a Radical Theory of the Politics of Sexuality.'" *American Feminist Thought, 1982–1992,* ed. Linda S. Kauffman. Oxford: Basil Blackwell, 1993.

———. "Coconuts: Aspects of Male/Female Relationships in New Guinea." Unpublished manuscript, 1974.

———. "A Contribution to the Critique of the Political Economy of Sex and Gender." *Dissemination* 1, no. 1 (1974): 6–13.

———. "A Contribution to the Critique of the Political Economy of Sex and Gender." *Dissemination* 1, no. 2 (1974): 23–32.

———. "Elegy for the Valley of the Kings: AIDS and the Leather Community in San Francisco, 1981–1996." *Changing Times: Gay Men and Lesbians Encounter HIV/ AIDS*, ed. Martin Levine, Peter Nardi, and John Gagnon, 101–44. Chicago: University of Chicago Press, 1997.

———. Introduction to *A Woman Appeared to Me*, by Renée Vivien. Weatherby Lake, Miss.: Naiad, 1979.

———. "The Leather Menace." *Coming to Power*, ed. Samois, 192–227. Boston: Alyson, 1982.

———. "Letter to the Editor." *Feminist Studies* 9, no. 3 (1983): 598–601.

———. "The Miracle Mile: South of Market and Gay Male Leather in San Francisco 1962–1996." *Reclaiming San Francisco: History, Politics, Culture*, ed. James Brook, Chris Carlsson, and Nancy Peters, 247–72. San Francisco: City Lights, 1998.

———. "Misguided, Dangerous, and Wrong: An Analysis of Anti-Pornography Politics." *Bad Girls and Dirty Pictures: The Challenge to Reclaim Feminism*, ed. Alison Assiter and Avedon Carol, 18–40. London: Pluto, 1993.

———. "Requiem for the Valley of the Kings." *Southern Oracle* (fall 1989).

———. "Review of *Guardians of the Flutes*." *Advocate*, 23 December 1982.

———. "Samois." *Encyclopedia of Lesbian, Gay, Bisexual, and Transgender History in America*, ed. Marc Stein, 67–69. New York: Scribner, 2004.

———. "Sexual Politics, the New Right, and the Sexual Fringe." *The Age Taboo*, ed. Daniel Tsang, 108–15. Boston: Alyson, 1981.

———. "Sites, Settlements, and Urban Sex: Archaeology and the Study of Gay Leathermen in San Francisco 1955–1995." *Archaeologies of Sexuality*, ed. Robert Schmidt and Barbara Voss, 62–88. London: Routledge, 2000.

———. "Studying Sexual Subcultures: The Ethnography of Gay Communities in Urban North America." *Out in Theory: The Emergence of Lesbian and Gay Anthropology*, ed. Ellen Lewin and William Leap, 17–68. Urbana: University of Illinois Press, 2002.

———. "Thinking Sex: Notes for a Radical Theory of the Politics of Sexuality." *Pleasure and Danger*, ed. Carole Vance, 267–319. New York: Routledge and Kegan Paul, 1984.

———. "The Traffic in Women: Notes on the 'Political Economy' of Sex." *Toward an Anthropology of Women*, ed. Rayna R. Reiter, 157–210. New York: Monthly Review Press, 1975.

———. "The Valley of the Kings." *Sentinel USA*, 13 September 1984.

———. "The Valley of the Kings: Leathermen in San Francisco, 1960–1990." Ph.D. diss., University of Michigan, 1994.

———. *Surveiller et Jouir: Anthropologie Politique du Sex*. Translated by Nicole-Claude Mathieu, Flora Bolter, Rostom Mesli, and Cristophe Broqua. Paris: Éditions Psychanalytiques de l'École Lacanienne, 2010.

————. *Valley of the Kings: Leathermen in San Francisco*. Durham: Duke University Press, forthcoming.

Rubin, Gayle, with Judith Butler. "Interview: Sexual Traffic." *differences* 6, no. 2–3 (1994): 62–99.

Ruggiero, Guido. *The Boundaries of Eros: Sex Crime and Sexuality in Renaissance Europe*. New York: Oxford University Press, 1985.

Rund, J. B. Preface to *Bizarre Comix*. Vol. 8. New York: Belier, 1977.

————. Preface to *Bizarre Fotos*. Vol. 1. New York: Belier, 1978.

————. Preface to *Bizarre Katalogs*. Vol. 1. New York: Belier, 1979.

Rush, Florence. *The Best Kept Secret: Sexual Abuse of Children*. New York: McGraw-Hill, 1980.

Russ, Joanna. "Being against Pornography." *Thirteenth Moon* 6, nos. 1–2 (1982): 55–61.

Russell, Diana. "Sadomasochism as a Contra-feminist Activity." *Plexus* (November 1980), 13.

Russell, Diana E. H., and Susan Griffin. "On Pornography: Two Feminists' Perspectives." *Chrysalis* 4 (1977): 11–17.

Russell, Diana E. H., and Laura Lederer. "Questions We Are Asked Most Often." *Take Back the Night: Women on Pornography*, ed. Laura Lederer, 23–29. New York: William Morrow, 1980.

ry. "s/m Keeps Lesbians Bound to the Patriarchy." *Lesbian Insider/Insighter/Inciter* (July 1981): 3, 16–17.

Ryan, Mary. "The Power of Women's Networks: A Case Study of Female Moral Reform in America." *Feminist Studies* 5, no. 1 (1979): 66–85.

"s&m Is Illegal in England." *Growing Pains* (May 1992): 1–2.

Sacher-Masoch, Leopold von. "Venus in Furs." *Masochism: An Interpretation of Coldness and Cruelty*, ed. Gilles Deleuze, 117–248. New York: George Braziller, 1971.

Sahli, Nancy. "Smashing: Women's Relationships before the Fall." *Chrysalis* 8 (1979): 17–27.

Sahlins, Marshall. "The Origin of Society." *Scientific American* 203 (1960): 76–87.

————. *Stone Age Economics*. Chicago: Aldine-Atherton, 1972.

Salem, Randy. *Chris*. New York: Softcover Library, 1959.

————. *The Unfortunate Flesh*. New York: Midwood Tower, 1960.

Samois, ed. *Coming to Power: Writings and Graphics on Lesbian s/m*. Berkeley: Samois, 1981.

————. *Coming to Power*. Boston: Alyson, 1982.

————. *What Color Is Your Handkerchief: A Lesbian s/m Sexuality Reader*. Berkeley: Samois, 1979.

San Francisco Lesbian and Gay History Project. "'She Even Chewed Tobacco': A Pictorial Narrative of Passing Women in America." *Hidden from History: Reclaiming the Gay and Lesbian Past*, ed. Martin Bauml Duberman, Martha Vicinus, and George Chauncey Jr., 183–94. New York: New American Library, 1989.

Sayeed, Almas. "Making Political Hay Out of Sex and Slavery: Kansas Conservatism,

Feminism and the Global Regulation of Sexual Moralities." *Feminist Review* no. 83 (2006): 119–31.

Scheiner, Marcy. "Some Girls Will Be Boys." *On Our Backs* 7, no. 4 (March–April 1991): 20–22, 38–43.

Schenkar, Joan. *Truly Wilde: The Unsettling Story of Dolly Wilde, Oscar's Unusual Niece.* New York: Basic, 2000.

Schneider, Beth, and Peter Nardi, eds. "John H. Gagnon and William Simon's *Sexual Conduct: The Social Sources of Human Sexuality.*" *Sexualities* 2, no. 1 (1999): 113–33.

Schneider, David M. *American Kinship: A Cultural Account.* Englewood Cliffs, N.J.: Prentice-Hall, 1968.

———. *Critique of the Study of Kinship.* Ann Arbor: University of Michigan Press, 1984.

Schneider, David M., and Kathleen Gough, eds. *Matrilineal Kinship.* Berkeley: University of California Press, 1961.

Schneiderman, Jason. "In Defense of Queer Theory." *Gay and Lesbian Review* 17, no. 1 (2010): 11–15.

Schwed, Fred, Jr. *Where Are the Customer's Yachts? Or, A Good Hard Look at Wall Street.* 1940. Springfield, Mass.: John Magee, 1960.

Scope, Sue. "Erotica Versus Pornography: An Exploration." *WAVPM Newspage* 3, no. 6 (1979): 1.

Scott, John Finley. "The Role of Collegiate Sororities in Maintaining Class and Ethnic Endogamy." *American Sociological Review* 30, no. 4 (1965): 415–26.

Secombe, Wally. "Housework under Capitalism." *New Left Review* 83 (1974): 3–24.

Secrest, Meryl. *Between Me and Life.* Garden City: Doubleday, 1974.

Segal, Lynne, and Mary McIntosh. *Sex Exposed: Sexuality and the Pornography Debate.* London: Virago, 1992.

Shorto, Russell. "Founding Father?" *New York Times Magazine,* 14 February 2002.

Shulman, Alix Kates, ed. *Red Emma Speaks: An Emma Goldman Reader.* Atlantic Highlands, N.J.: Humanity Books, 1996.

Simmons, Christina. *Making Marriage Modern: Women's Sexuality from the Progressive Era to World War II.* Oxford: Oxford University Press, 2009.

Simon, William. 1999. "*Sexual Conduct* in Retrospective Perspective." *Sexualities* 2, no. 1 (1999): 126–33.

Simon, William, and John Gagnon. "Homosexuality: The Formulation of a Sociological Perspective." *The Same Sex: An Appraisal of Homosexuality,* ed. Ralph Weltge, 14–24. 1967; reprint, Philadelphia: Pilgrim, 1969.

Singy, Patrick. "A History of Violence: Sadism and the Emergence of Sexuality." Unpublished, 2009.

———. *Sadism at the Limits: Sex, Violence, and the Historical Boundaries of Sexuality.* Unpublished manuscript.

"SM Gays—SM and the Law." *DungeonMaster* 43 (1991): 4.

Smith, Anna Marie. *New Right Discourse on Race and Sexuality*. New York: Cambridge University Press, 1994.

Smith, Ralph R., and Russel R. Windes. 2000. *Progay/Antigay: The Rhetorical War over Sexuality*. Thousand Oaks, Calif.: Sage, 2000.

Smith-Rosenberg, Caroll. "The Female World of Love and Ritual: Relations between Women in Nineteenth-Century America." *Signs* 1, no. 1 (1975): 1–29.

Smithsonian Institution. *Alice Pike Barney: Portraits in Oil and Pastel*. Washington: Smithsonian, 1957.

Snitow, Ann, Christine Stansell, and Sharon Thompson, eds. *Powers of Desire: The Politics of Sexuality*. New York: Monthly Review Press, 1983.

Socarides, Charles W. *Homosexuality: A Freedom Too Far*. Phoenix: Adam Margrave, 1995.

Soderlund, Gretchen. "Covering Urban Vice: The *New York Times*, 'White Slavery,' and the Construction of Journalistic Knowledge." *Critical Studies in Media Communication* 19, no. 4 (2002): 438–60.

———. "Running from the Rescuers: New U.S. Crusades Against Sex Trafficking and the Rhetoric of Abolition." *National Women's Studies Association Journal* 17, no. 3 (2005): 64–87.

Solnit, Rebecca, and Susan Schwartzenberg. *Hollow City: The Siege of San Francisco and the Crisis of American Urbanism*. New York: Verso, 2000.

Sonenschein, David. "Homosexuality as a Subject of Anthropological Inquiry." *Anthropological Quarterly* 2 (1966): 73–82.

Sontag, Susan. *Styles of Radical Will*. New York: Farrar, Straus, and Giroux, 1969.

Spiro, Jonathan. *Defending the Master Race: Conservation, Eugenics, and the Legacy of Madison Grant*. Burlington: University of Vermont Press, 2008.

Spooner, Lysander. *Vices Are Not Crimes: A Vindication of Moral Liberty*. Cupertino, Calif.: Tanstaafl, 1977.

Sprigg, Peter. *Outrage: How Gay Activists and Liberal Judges Are Trashing Democracy to Redefine Marriage*. Washington: Regency, 2004.

Stambolian, George. "Creating the New Man: A Conversation with Jacqueline Livingston." *Christopher Street* (May 1980).

Stamps, Wickie. "Customs Releases Lesbian Erotica." *Gay Community News*, 30 June–6 July 1991, 1, 6.

Stanley, Lawrence A. "The Hysteria over Child Pornography and Paedophilia." *Paidika* 1, no. 2 (1987): 13–34.

State of Michigan. *Report to the Governor's Study on the Deviated Criminal Sex Offender*. Detroit: G. Mennen Williams, 1951.

State of New Hampshire. *Report of the Interim Commission of the State of New Hampshire to Study the Cause and Prevention of Serious Sex Crimes*. Concord: Concord Press, 1949.

State of New York. *Report to the Governor on a Study of 102 Sex Offenders at Sing Sing Prison*. Albany: Department of Mental Hygiene, 1950.

Steakley, James. "The Gay Movement in Germany, Part One: 1860–1910." *Body Politic* 9 (1973): 12–17.

———. "The Gay Movement in Germany, Part Two: 1910–1933." *Body Politic* 10 (1973): 14–19.

———. *The Homosexual Emancipation Movement in Germany*. Salem, N.H.: Ayer, 1975.

———. "Homosexuals and the Third Reich." *Body Politic* 11 (1974): 1–3.

———. "Per scientiam ad justitiam: Magnus Hirschfeld and the Sexual Politics of Innate Homosexuality," *Science and Homosexualities*, ed. Vernon Rosario, 133–54. New York: Routledge, 1997.

Stein, Arlene. "All Dressed Up, but No Place to Go? Style Wars and the New Lesbianism." *Out/Look* 1, no. 4 (1989): 34–42.

———. *The Stranger Next Door: The Story of a Small Community's Battle Over Sex, Faith, and Civil Rights*. Boston: Beacon Press, 2001.

Stein, Arlene, and Kenneth Plummer. "'I Can't Even Think Straight': 'Queer' Theory and the Missing Sexual Revolution in Sociology." *Queer Theory/Sociology*, ed. Steven Seidman, 129–44. Cambridge: Blackwell, 1996.

Steinem, Gloria. "Erotica and Pornography: A Clear and Present Danger." *Ms.*, November 1978.

Stengers, Jean, and Anne Van Neck. *Masturbation: The History of a Great Terror*. Translated by Kathryn A. Hoffman. New York: Palgrave, 2001.

Stern, Jess. *The Grapevine: A Report on the Secret World of the Lesbian*. New York: Doubleday, 1964.

Stern, Kenneth S. *A Force upon the Plain: The American Militia Movement and the Politics of Hate*. New York: Simon and Schuster, 1996.

Stocking, George W. "Turn of the Century Concept of Race." *Modernism/Modernity* no. 1 (1994): 4–16.

Stoddard, Lothrop. *The Rising Tide of Color against White World-Supremacy*. New York: Charles Scribner's Sons, 1920.

Stoller, Robert. *Pain and Passion: A Psychoanalyst Explores the World of s&m*. New York: Plenum, 1991.

Stone, Lawrence. *The Family, Sex and Marriage in England 1500–1800*. New York: Harper and Row, 1977.

Stone, Sandy. "The 'Empire' Strikes Back: A Posttranssexual Manifesto." *Body Guards: The Cultural Politics of Gender Ambiguity*, ed. Kristina Straub and Julia Epstein, 280–304. New York: Routledge, 1991.

Strachey, Dorothy. *Olivia*. New York: Sloane, 1949.

Strathern, Marilyn. *Women in Between*. New York: Seminar, 1972.

Stryker, Susan. "Stray Thoughts on Transgender Feminism and the Barnard Conference on Women." *Communication Review* 11 (2008): 217–18.

———. *Transgender History*. Berkeley: Seal, 2008.

Sullivan, Louis. *From Female to Male: The Life of Jack Bee Garland*. Boston: Alyson, 1990.

————. *Information for the Female to Male Cross Dresser and Transsexual.* 3rd edn. Seattle: Ingersoll Gender Center, 1990.

Sulloway, Frank. *Freud, Biologist of the Mind: Beyond the Psychoanalytic Legend.* New York: Basic Books, 1979.

Sundahl, Deborah. "Stripping for a Living." *Advocate,* 13 October 1983.

Swinburne, Algernon. "Sapphics." *Poems and Ballads,* 235–38. London: James Camden Hotten, Piccadilly, 1868.

Symonds, John Addington. *A Problem in Greek Ethics: Being an Inquiry into the Phenomenon of Sexual Inversion: Addressed Especially to Medical Psychologists and Jurists.* London, 1901.

————. *A Problem in Modern Ethics: Being an Inquiry into the Phenomenon of Sexual Inversion: Addressed Especially to Medical Psychologists and Jurists.* London, 1896.

Syms, Shawn, and Carrie Wofford. "Obscenity Crackdown: Using Obscenity Laws, U.S. Customs Begins New Tactic of Seizing Gay Magazines; Toronto Police Raid a Gay Bookstore." *Gay Community News,* 22 May–4 June 1992, 1, 7.

"Taking Liberties." *Marxism Today* (March 1991): 16.

Thomas, W. I. *Sex and Society: Studies in the Social Psychology of Sex.* Chicago: University of Chicago Press, 1907.

Thomas, W. I., and Florian Znaniecki. *The Polish Peasant in Europe and America: Monograph of an Immigrant Group.* Chicago: University of Chicago Press, 1918–20.

Thompson, Bill. *Sadomasochism: Painful Perversion or Pleasurable Play?* London: Cassell, 1994.

Thompson, E. P. *Customs in Common.* New York: New Press, 1993.

————. *The Making of the English Working Class.* New York: Vintage, 1963.

————. "Time, Work-Discipline, and Industrial Capitalism." *Customs in Common: Studies in Traditional Popular Culture,* 352–403. 1967. New York: New Press, 1993.

Thompson, Mark. *Leatherfolk: Radical Sex, People, Politics, and Practice.* Boston: Alyson, 1991.

Thorne, Barrie. "Women in the Draft Resistance Movement: A Case Study of Sex Roles and Social Movements." *Sex Roles* 1, no. 3 (1998): 179–95.

Thurnwald, Richard. "Banaro Society." *Memoirs of the American Anthropological Association* 3, no. 4 (1916): 251–391.

Tiger, Lionel, and Robin Fox. *The Imperial Animal.* New York: Holt, Reinhart and Winston, 1971.

Tilly, Charles. *Durable Inequality.* Berkeley: University of California Press, 1998.

Treichler, Paula A. *How to Have Theory in an Epidemic: Cultural Chronicles of AIDS.* Durham: Duke University Press, 1999.

Trillin, Calvin. "U.S. Journal: Sumter County, SC Turks." *New Yorker,* 8 March 1969: 104–10.

Truscott, Carol. "San Francisco: A Reverent, Non-Linear, Necessarily Incomplete History of the S/M Scene." *Sandmutopia Guardian and Dungeon Journal* 8 (1990): 6–12.

Tsang, Daniel. "Gay Academics Reflect on Movement Role." *Michigan Free Press*, 19 December 1976, 2B.

———. "Gay Ann Arbor Purges." Part 1. *Midwest Gay Academic Journal* 1, no. 1 (1977): 13–19.

———. "Gay Ann Arbor Purges." Part 2. *Midwest Gay Academic Journal* 1, no. 2 (1977): 11–13.

———, ed. *The Age Taboo*. Boston: Alyson, 1981.

Turner, William B. *A Genealogy of Queer Theory*. Philadelphia: Temple University Press, 2000.

Ulrichs, Karl Heinrich. *The Riddle of "Man-Manly Love": The Pioneering Work on Male Homosexuality*. Translated by Michael A. Lombardi-Nash. Buffalo: Prometheus Books, 1994.

United Nations. "Protocol to Prevent, Suppress and Punish Trafficking in Persons, Especially Women and Children, Supplementing the United Nations Convention Against Transnational Organized Crime." G.A. Res. 25, annex II, U.N. GAOR, 55th Sess., Supp. No. 49, at 60, U.N. Doc. A/45/49. Vol. I (2001), *entered into force* 9 Sept. 2003.

United States Commission on Obscenity and Pornography. "Statement by Charles H. Keating, Jr." *The Report of the Commission on Obscenity and Pornography*, Vol. 1, 511–49. New York: Random House, 1971.

United States Government Accountability Office. *Human Trafficking: Better Data, Strategy, and Reporting Needed to Enhance U.S. Antitrafficking Efforts Abroad*. Washington: United States Government Accountability Office, 2006.

United States Immigration Commission. *Reports of the Immigration Commission*. 41 vols. Washington: Government Printing Office, 1911.

Valverde, Mariana. "Feminism Meets Fist-Fucking: Getting Lost in Lesbian S&M." *Body Politic* 60 (February 1980): 43.

———. *Sex, Power, and Pleasure*. Toronto: Women's Press, 1985.

Van Baal, J. *Dema*. The Hague: Nijhoff, 1966.

Vance, Carole. "Anthropology Rediscovers Sexuality: A Theoretical Comment." *Social Science and Medicine* 33.8 (1991): 875–84.

———. "Dubious Data, Blatant Bias." *Body Politic* 133 (18–19 December 1986): 18–19.

———. "Hiss the Villain: Depicting Sex Trafficking." Lecture delivered at the School for American Research, Santa Fe, N.M., May 2005.

———. "Invitation Letter." September 1981. *Diary of a Conference on Sexuality*, ed. Hannah Alderfer, Beth Jaker, Marybeth Nelson, 1. New York: Faculty Press, 1982.

———. "'Juanita/Svetlana/Geeta' Is Crying: Melodrama, Human Rights, and Anti-Trafficking Interventions." Owens Lecture, University of Rochester, Rochester, New York, 1 December 2006.

———. "Letter to the Editor." *Feminist Studies* 9, no. 3 (1983): 589–91.

———. "Meese Commission: The Porn Police Attack." *Gay Community News*, 27 July–2 August 1986, 3, 6, 12.

———. "Misunderstanding Obscenity." *Art in America*, May 1990, 49–55.

————. "More Danger, More Pleasure: A Decade after the Barnard Sexuality Conference." *Pleasure and Danger: Exploring Female Sexuality*, ed. Carole Vance, xvi–xxxix. 2nd edn. London: Pandora, 1992.

————. "Negotiating Sex and Gender in the Attorney General's Commission on Pornography." *Uncertain Terms: Negotiating Gender in American Culture*, ed. Faye Ginsburg and Anna L. Tsing, 118–34. Boston: Beacon, 1990.

————, ed. *Pleasure and Danger: Exploring Female Sexuality*. New York: Routledge, 1984.

————. "The Pleasures of Looking: The Attorney General's Commission on Pornography vs. Visual Images." *The Critical Image: Essays in Contemporary Photography*, ed. Carole Squiers, 38–58. Seattle: Bay Press, 1990.

————. "Porn in the USA: The Meese Commission on the Road." *The Nation*, 2–9 August 1986, 1, 76–82.

————. "Reagan's Revenge: Restructuring the NEA." *Art in America*, November 1990, 49–55.

————. "Social Construction Theory: Problems in the History of Sexuality." *Homosexuality, Which Homosexuality?*, ed. D. Altman, C. Vance, et al., 13–34. London: Gay Men's Press, 1989.

————. "Thinking Trafficking." GLQ 17, no. 1 (2010): 135–43.

————. "The War on Culture." *Art in America*. December 1989, 39–45.

Vice Commission of Chicago. *The Social Evil in Chicago: A Study of Existing Conditions*. Chicago: Gunthorp-Warren, 1911.

Vicinus, Martha. "Sexuality and Power: A Review of Current Work in the History of Sexuality." *Feminist Studies* 8, no. 1 (1982): 133–56.

————. "'They Wonder to Which Sex I Belong': The Historical Roots of the Modern Lesbian Identity." *Feminist Studies* 18, no. 3 (1992): 467–97.

Vivien, Renée. *Brumes de fjords*. Paris: Lemerre, 1902.

————. "Brune comme une Noisette." *La Dame à la louve*. Paris: Lemerre, 1904.

————. *Cendres et poussières*. Paris: Lemerre, 1902.

————. *La Dame à la louve*. Paris: Lemerre, 1904.

————. *Du vert au violet*. Paris: Lemerre, 1903.

————. *Evocations*. Paris: Lemerre, 1903.

————. *Une Femme m'apparut*. Paris: Lemerre, 1905.

————. *The Muse of the Violets*. Translated by Margaret Porter and Catherine Kroger. Tallahassee: Naiad, 1977.

————. *Poèsies completes*. Vol. 2. Paris: Lemerre, 1934.

————. "La Voile de Vashti." *La Dame à la louve*. Paris: Lemerre, 1904.

————. 1976. *A Woman Appeared to Me*. Reprint, Weatherby Lake, Miss.: Naiad, 1979.

Vogel, Lise. "The Earthly Family." *Radical America* 7, no. 4–5 (1973): 9–50.

Walkowitz, Judith R. *City of Dreadful Delight: Narratives of Sexual Danger in Late-Victorian London*. Chicago: University of Chicago Press, 1992.

————. "Male Vice and Feminist Virtue: Feminism and the Politics of Prostitution in Nineteenth-Century Britain." *Powers of Desire: The Politics of Sexuality*, edited by Ann Snitow, Christine Stansell, and Sharon Thompson, 419–38. New York: Monthly Review Press, 1983.

———. "The Politics of Prostitution." *Signs* 6, no. 1 (1980): 123–35.

———. *Prostitution and Victorian Society*. New York: Cambridge University Press, 1980.

Walkowitz, Judith, and Daniel Walkowitz. "'We Are Not Beasts of the Field': Prostitution and the Poor in Plymouth and Southampton under the Contagious Diseases Acts." *Feminist Studies* 1, no. 3–4 (1973): 73–106.

Walters, Jerome. *One Aryan Nation under God: How Religious Extremists Use the Bible to Justify Their Actions*. 2000; reprint, Naperville, Ill.: Sourcebooks, 2001.

Watney, Simon. *Imagine Hope: AIDS and Gay Identity*. New York: Routledge, 2000.

———. *Policing Desire: Pornography AIDS and the Media*. Minneapolis: University of Minnesota Press, 1987.

———. *Practices of Freedom: Selected Writings on HIV/AIDS*. Durham: Duke University Press, 1994.

Webster, Paula. "Pornography and Pleasure." In "The Sex Issue," special issue of *Heresies* 12 (1981): 48–51.

Wechsler, Nancy. "Interview with Pat Califia and Gayle Rubin," part 1. *Gay Community News*, 18 July 1981: 4–5.

———. "Interview with Pat Califia and Gayle Rubin," part 2. *Gay Community News*, 15 August 1981: 6–8.

Weeks, Jeffrey. *Against Nature: Essays on History, Sexuality, and Identity*. London: Rivers Oram, 1991.

———. *Coming Out: Homosexual Politics in Britain, from the Nineteenth Century to the Present*. London: Quartet, 1977.

———. "The 'Homosexual Role' after Thirty Years: An Appreciation of the Work of Mary McIntosh." *Sexualities* 1, no. 2 (1998): 131–52.

———. *Making Sexual History*. Cambridge: Blackwell, 2000.

———. *Sex, Politics, and Society: The Regulation of Sexuality since 1800*. London: Longman, 1981.

———. *Sexuality*. London: Tavistock, 1986.

———. *Sexuality and Its Discontents*. New York: Routledge and Kegan Paul, 1985.

———. "'Sins and Diseases': Some Notes on Homosexuality in the Nineteenth Century." *History Workshop* 1 (spring 1976): 211–19.

Weinberg, Thomas, and G. W. Levi Kamel. *S and M: Studies in Sadomasochism*. Buffalo: Prometheus, 1983.

Weiss, Andrea. *Paris Was a Woman: Portraits from the Left Bank*. San Francisco: Harper San Francisco, 1995.

Weiss, Mike. "The State vs. Jock Sturges." *Image*, 27 January 1991, 23–29.

Werth, Barry. *The Scarlet Professor*. New York: Doubleday (Nan Talese), 2001.

Westermarck, Edward. *This History of Human Marriage*. London: Macmillan, 1894.

Weston, Kath. "Do Clothes Make the Woman? Gender, Performance Theory, and Lesbian Eroticism." Unpublished manuscript, 1992.

———. *Families We Choose: Lesbians, Gays, Kinship*. New York: Columbia University Press, 1991.

———. "Lesbian/Gay Studies in the House of Anthropology." *Annual Review of Anthropology* 22 (1993): 339–67.

———. *Long Slow Burn: Sexuality and Social Science*. New York: Routledge, 1998.

"What Should You Really Be Afraid Of?" *Newsweek*, 24–31 May 2010, 64.

White, C. Todd. *Pre-Gay L.A.: A Social History of the Movement for Homosexual Rights*. Urbana: University of Illinois Press, 2009.

Whitehead, Harriet. "The Bow and the Burden Strap: A New Look at Institutionalized Homosexuality in Native North America." *Sexual Meanings: The Cultural Construction of Gender and Sexuality*, ed. Sherry B. Ortner and Harriet Whitehead, 80–115. New York: Cambridge University Press, 1981.

Whitworth, Sarah. "Romaine Brooks." *The Ladder* 16, no. 1–2 (1971): 39–45.

Wickes, George. *The Amazon of Letters: The Life and Loves of Natalie Barney*. New York: Putnam, 1977.

———. "A Natalie Barney Garland." *Paris Review* 61 (1975): 84–134.

Wijers, Marjan, and Lin Lap-Chew. *Trafficking in Women: Forced Labour and Slavery-like Practices in Marriage, Domestic Labour, and Prostitution*. Utrecht: Foundation against Trafficking in Women / Global Alliance against Traffic in Women, 1999.

Wilden, Anthony. "Lacan and the Discourse of the Other." *The Language of the Self: The Function of Language in Psychoanalysis*, by Jacques Lacan, 157–311. Baltimore: Johns Hopkins University Press, 1968.

Williams, F. E. *Papuans of the Trans-Fly*. New York: Oxford University Press, 1936.

Williams, Linda. "Second Thoughts on *Hard Core*: American Obscenity Law and the Scapegoating of Deviance." *Dirty Looks: Women, Pornography, and Power*, ed. Pamela Church Gibson and Roma Gibson, 46–61. London: British Film Institute, 1993.

———. *Hard Core: Power, Pleasure, and the "Frenzy of the Visible."* Berkeley: University of California Press, 1989.

Williams, Walter. *The Spirit and the Flesh: Sexual Diversity in American Indian Culture*. Boston: Beacon, 1986.

Willie, John. *The Adventures of Sweet Gwendoline*. New York: Belier, 1974.

Willis, Ellen. *Beginning to See the Light: Pieces of a Decade*. New York: Alfred Knopf, 1981.

———. "Feminism, Moralism, and Pornography." *Beginning to See the Light: Pieces of a Decade*, 219–27. New York: Alfred A. Knopf, 1981.

———. "Letter to the Editor." *Feminist Studies* 9, no. 3 (1983): 592–94.

———. "Who Is a Feminist? An Open Letter to Robin Morgan." *Village Voice Literary Supplement*, December 1982, 16–17.

Wilson, Elizabeth. "The Context of 'Between Pleasure and Danger': The Barnard Conference on Sexuality." *Feminist Review* 13 (spring 1983): 35–41.

Wilson, Paul. *The Man They Called a Monster*. New South Wales: Cassell Australia, 1981.

Winkler, John J. *The Constraints of Desire: The Anthropology of Sex and Gender in Ancient Greece*. New York: Routledge, 1990.

Witte, John, Jr. *From Sacrament to Contract: Marriage, Religion, and Law in the Western Tradition*. Louisville: Westminster John Knox Press, 1997.

Witte, John, Jr., and Robert M. Kingdon. *Sex, Marriage, and Family in John Calvin's Geneva*. Grand Rapids, Mich.: Eerdmans, 2005.

Wittig, Monique. *Les Guérillères*. New York: Avon, 1973.

Wolf, Deborah Goleman. *The Lesbian Community*. Berkeley: University of California Press, 1979.

Wolfe, Alan, and Jerry Sanders. "Resurgent Cold War Ideology: The Case of the Committee on the Present Danger." *Capitalism and the State in U.S.-Latin American Relations*, ed. Richard Fagen, 41–75. Stanford: Stanford University Press, 1979.

Wolfe, Christopher, ed. *Homosexuality and American Public Life*. 1999; reprint, Dallas: Spence, 2000.

Wolff, Charlotte. *Love between Women*. London: Duckworth, 1971.

Wolff, Edward N. *Top Heavy: The Increasing Inequality of Wealth in America and What Can Be Done about It*. New York: New Press, 1995.

Women Against Violence in Pornography and Media. "Questions We Get Asked Most Often." *wavpm Newspage* 1 no. 6 (November 1977): 1–4.

———. "Who Are We?" *wavpm Newspage* 1 no. 4 (September 1977): 3.

Yaeger, Marshall. "To the Editor." *Gay and Lesbian Review Worldwide* 17, no. 2 (2010): 6.

Yalmon, Nur. "On the Purity of Women in the Castes of Ceylon and Malabar." *Journal of the Royal Anthropological Institute* 93, no. 1 (1963): 25–58.

Yamashiro, Jennifer. "In the Realm of the Sciences: The Kinsey Institute's 31 Photographs." *Porn 101: Eroticism, Pornography, and the First Amendment*, ed. James Elias, et al., 32–52. Amherst: Prometheus Books, 1999.

Zambaco, Demetrius. "Onanism and Nervous Disorders in Two Little Girls." In "Polysexuality," ed. Francois Peraldi, special issue of *Semiotext(e)* 4, no. 1 (1981): 22–36.

Zeidel, Robert. *Immigrants, Progressives, and Exclusion Politics: The Dillingham Commission, 1900–1927*. DeKalb: Northern Illinois University Press, 2004.

Zeskind, Leonard. *Blood and Politics: The History of the White Nationalist Movement from the Margins to the Mainstream*. New York: Farrar, Straus and Giroux, 2009.

———. *The "Christian Identity" Movement: Analyzing Its Theological Rationalization for Racist and Anti-Semitic Violence*. 1986; reprint, Division of Church and Society of the National Council of the Churches of Christ in the U.S.A., 1987.

Zillman, Dolf, and Jennings Bryant. "Effects of Massive Exposure to Pornography."

Pornography and Sexual Aggression, ed. Neil M. Malamuth and Edward Donner-stein, 115–38. New York: Academic Press, 1984.

Zolberg, Aristide. *A Nation by Design: Immigration Policy in the Fashioning of America.* New York: Russell Sage Foundation and Harvard University Press, 2006.

Zorbaugh, Harvey Warren. *The Gold Coast and the Slum: A Sociological Study of Chicago's Near North Side.* 1929. Chicago: University of Chicago Press, 1976.

Index

Page numbers in *italics* refer to illustrations.

Becker, Judith, 409n31
Belboeuf, Missy, Marquise de, 89–90
Berger, Peter, 329
Berlin drag ball, 293–94
Berman, Marshall, 356
Bérubé, Allan, 199, 302, 361n57
Best, Joel, 78, 82
bibliographies, 15–16, 348–49. *See also*
  GLBTQ studies
Bibliothèque Nationale, 16, 296
biker images, 244
biology and essentialism, 146–48
Bloch, Iwan, 294
Blumer, Herbert, 329
border wars, 166–68
boy-lovers, 112–13, 143
Bradley, Marion Zimmer, 15, 350–51
brainwash theory, 177
bridewealth, 62–63
Bristow, Edward, 68
Britain: Contagious Diseases Acts, 169–70;
  Criminal Law Amendment Act (1885),
  139; s/m convictions in, 192; white
  slavery panics in, 68–70, 139
Britt, Harry, 117
Brooke, Christopher, 363n82
Brooks, Romaine, 101, 375n9, 375n11
"Brown like a Hazel-Nut" (Vivien), 95
Bryant, Anita, 25, 280
Bryant, Jennings, 265
Buchanan, Patrick, 192
bureaucracy, 162–63, 355–56
Burgess, Ernest W., 312, 317–18, 416n28
Burgess Papers, University of Chicago,
  318
Bush, George W., 30, 31
businesses, sex-oriented, 160–61. *See also*
  gay economy
butches: acceptance of variation and, 252–
  53; definitions and history of, 241–44;
  in fiction, 405n17; gay male usage of,
  405n16; gender dysphoria and, 242–43;
  rejection of butch-femme and, 252;
  sexualities and, 246–47; transsexuals
  and, 243, 248–51; varieties of, 244–46

Butler, Judith: Rubin interviewed by, 276–
  309; on performativity, 341
Butler v. Her Majesty the Queen (Canada),
  190–91

Califia, Pat, 203, 233
Cameron, Paul, 259
Canada, 114–15, 190–92
capitalism, 35–38, 160–61. *See also* gay
  economy
Carpenter, Edward, 352–53
Case, Sue-Ellen, 403n3
Castlehaven, Mervyn Touchet, Earl of, 156
castration complex, 49, 51–57, 291–92
Catacombs of San Francisco: AIDS and
  final closure of, 236–39; beginnings of,
  226–27; first closure of, 234; historical
  background of, 224–26; legacy of, 239–
  40; music and, 231–32; reopening on
  Shotwell Street of, 234–36; rooms and
  equipment in, 227–31; s/m and women
  in, 232–34
Catacombs of San Francisco II, 234
catamites, 247
Centers for Disease Control (CDC), 237–38
Chapon, François, 16
Chapoulie, Jean-Michel, 416n28
Chicago: Inferno, 226, 240; Leather Archives and Museum (LAM), 23; white
  slave hysteria in, 70–71
Chicago Vice Commission, 78–79, 315–16
Child Exploitation and Obscenity Unit,
  Justice Department, 185, 412n47
"child molester" vs. "pedophile," 387n66
Child Pornography and Obscenity Enforcement Act (1988), 185
children: as category, 400n91; child-porn
  panics, 141–43, 184–85, 391n12; sexual
  abuse panics, 184–85; sexuality of, 161,
  218–21; teenage sexual behavior study,
  188. *See also* family
Christianity, 106, 109, 148–49, 224
Chrysalis, 207
class: social construction of, 334–35; status
  vs., 217–18; stigma, overtness, and, 341

Cleveland Women against Violence against Women, 206

clothing: butch, 242, 244; concealing, 163; cross-dressing, 216, 242; drag, 338–44; leather, 115, 228, 263

Coalition against Trafficking in Women (CATW), 77, 214

Cohen, Stanley, 26

Cold War, 110–11

Colette, 89–90, 95, 103–4, 180

coming out, 123–24, 129–31, 132

Coming Out (Weeks), 18, 107, 302, 330–31

commodities, 36–37

communism, 143–44

Comstock, Anthony, 138–39

Comstock Act (1873), 138–39

conformity, 163–65

Congas, Lembi, 12–13

Connelly, Mark Thomas, 70–72, 79–81

consent: age-of-consent laws, 161; coerced, 129; freedom and, 389n87; legal interference with, 175–76; "moderate" feminism and, 175; s/M and, 129, 134, 176

consenting-adult statutes, 162

conservatives. *See* right wing conservatives

constitutional amendment campaigns, 188, 192

constructivism. *See* social construction of sexuality

Contagious Diseases Acts (England), 169–70

continuum, as problematic notion, 284

contract theory, 134

Cooke, McLaurin, 4–5

Cory, Donald Webster, 351, 353

coverts and overts, 163, 323

credibility, hierarchy of, 319–20

Crile, George, 117

Criminal Law Amendment Act (Britain, 1885), 139

Crisco, 230

cross-generational sex, 112–13, 143

Crumpley, Ronald, 379n7

cultural impoverishment thesis, 326

culture: biology and, 53; feminist denunciations of male supremacy in, 255; Lévi-Strauss on oppression of women and, 46; sexuality expressed through intervention of, 365n13

culture wars, 29–30

Custance, Olive, 98–99, 103

custody laws, 119–20, 161–62, 187–88

Dade County, Fla., 141–42

Damon, Gene (Barbara Grier), 15, 16–17, 302, 348, 350–51

Daughters of Bilitis (DOB), 348

Davis, Katherine Bement, 313

Davis, Madeline, 241–42, 302

definitional wars, 165

Deitz, Park, 185

dejanikus, tacie, 123

Delany, Samuel, 222

Delarue-Mardrus, Lucie, 97, 103

Deleuze, Gilles, 306–7

Delphy, Christine, 359n34

D'Emilio, John, 302, 350, 360n36, 361n57, 387n67

Derrida, Jacques, 279

descriptive and theoretical work, 304–7

Deutsch, Helene, 56, 60

DeVall, William B., 326

"Development of the Homosexual Bar as an Institution, The" (Achilles), 322, 324–25

Diagnostic and Statistical Manual of Mental Disorders (DSM), 150, 158, 215–16, 404n6

Diamond, Norma, 12–13

Diary of a Conference on Sexuality (Alderfer et al.), 200, 202, 204–5

difference. *See* sexual variation

Dillingham Commission and Report, 72

diversity. *See* sexual variation

Dixon v. Alabama, 10, 358n16

domino theory of sexual peril, 151

Donnerstein, Edward, 265–66

"Don't Ask, Don't Tell" policy, 387n64. *See also* military regulations double standard, 59–60, 83–84

Douglas, Alfred, 99

drag, 338–44

Duggan, Lisa, 293, 354

Duran, Carolus, 91

Dworkin, Andrea: Barnard Conference and, 205; civil-rights antipornography ordinance, 183, 262–63; on "documentary of abuse," 265–68; on erotica, 264; on female condition, 269; on feminism and pornography, 407n6; Meese Commission and, 185–86; on prostitution, 269

economy, gay. *See* gay economy

Ehrhardt, Anke A., 14

election politics, 192

Electra complex, 48

Elementary Structure of Kinship, The (Lévi-Strauss), 13, 42–47, 63

Elliott School Rebellion (Boston, 1859), 4–5

Ellis, Havelock, 155, 294, 352–54

empirical research, 304–5

Engels, Friedrich, 38–42, 65, 277, 366n15

Erikson, Kai, 416n28

Ernst, Carol, 286–87

erotica, 263–64

Escoffier, Jeffrey, 314–15, 328

essentialism, 146–48, 333–34

Esther, 93

"Eternal Slave, The" (Vivien), 94–95

ethnogenesis, sexual, 158, 307–8

ethnography of urban gay communities, 310–12, 344; dismantling of deviance and, 319–27; Ford's and Beach's *Patterns of Sexual Behavior*, 310, 312–13; Gagnon's and Simon's *Sexual Deviance*, 322–27; legacies and lessons of, 345–46; Marshall's and Sugg's *Human Sexual Behavior*, 313–14; Newton's *Mother Camp*, 338–44; social construction theory and, 328–36; Sonenschein's "Homosexuality as a Subject of Anthro-

pological Inquiry," 336–38; University of Chicago sociology and, 314–18

etiological theories, 321

Etoro, 365n13

Eulenberg, Albert, 294

Eulenspiegel Society, 210, 225

exchange of women concept, 44–47, 52

ex-gay ministries, 27

Faderman, Lillian, 288–89

fallacy of misplaced scale, 149

family: child abuse within, 184; Engels on, 38–42; Foucault on, 298; Oedipal complex, 50–58; as place of threatened safety, 220; Right's notion of, 25–26; sexual conformity in, 164. *See also* children; kinship; marriage

Family Protection Act (FPA), 144

Federal Bureau of Investigation (FBI), 74, 415n17

federal employment ban, 28

Feingold, David, 76, 77, 81–82

Feinstein, Dianne, 120

female impersonators, 338–44

female-to-male transsexuals (FTMs), 243, 248–51

feminine imagery, in heterosexual s/M, 309

"femininism," 127–28

feminism: antiprostitution movement and, 84–86; celebration of femininity and, 127–28; French, 359n34; Freud's theory of femininity and, 56–57; gender vs. sexuality and, 177–79; as grand theory, 303; male supremacy and, 255; Marxism and radical theory vs., 179–80; methodology of gay and lesbian studies vs., 300–301; need for dreaming of more, 61; as privileged site of sexuality theory, 177–78, 217, 284–85, 301; second-wave, 10–11, 276–78; separatism in, 366n25; sex in complex relationship with, 171–72; sexual difference and, 289–90; sexual hierarchy and, 135–36;

s/M and, 124–29, 169–70, 174; Vivien and Barney and, 93; warnings from, 186; "women's community" and, 356
"Feminism, Sexuality, and Power" conference (1986), 213–14
"feminism and the history of sex" study group, 199
"Feminist Perspectives on Pornography" conference (1978), 255
feminist sex wars: antipornography movement and, 169–70, 172–73, 185–86, 207–12; Australian HRC conference and, 214; Barnard Sex Conference and, 195–96, 200–206; Five Colleges conference and, 213–14; "moderate" position in, 174–77; rightward shift and, 127–28; sex panic concept and, 26–27; sex trafficking as new target in, 214–15; sexuality vs. gender and, 177–80, 216–18; sexual liberation and antisexual strains in, 172–74; on West Coast, 206–12. See also pornography and antiporn politics
femmes: butches and, 246–47; definition and history of, 241–42; rejection of role, 202–3, 252; sexuality in, 247. See also butches
fetishism, 291–92, 309. See also sadomasochism (s/M)
Fine, Gary Alan, 419n78
Fingrudt, Meryl, 213
fisting, 230–31, 237, 308, 401n6
Five College Women's Studies Project conference (1986), 213–14
Folk Devils and Moral Panics (Cohen), 26
Ford, Clellen S., 310, 312–13, 336
Foster, Jeannette, 15, 17–18, 88, 302, 348, 350–51
Foucault, Michel, 20, 354, 295, 328, 332–33; on alliance and sexuality, 21, 297–98; on constructivism, 146–48; Krafft-Ebing and, 354; "numberless family of perverts," 158; The Order of Things, 419n76; Rubin's meetings with, 296–97; on

sexual system, 178; on sodomy, 155; on "wild profusion," 248
Freedman, Estelle, 199, 361n57
freedom of speech, sexual, 110, 160
Freidson, Eliot, 416n28
French feminism, 359n34
Freud, Sigmund, 293; femininity theory of, 55–57; Hirschfeld and, 294; on homosexuality, 294; Lévi-Strauss's overlap with, 34–35, 57–61; on Oedipal complex, 51; as passé, 27; radical implications of, 47–48, 59
Fulton, John S., 80–81
Futter, Ellen V., 204–5

Gagnon, John J., 155, 320–27, 330, 336
Galliher, John, 319
Garber, Eric, 199
Garde, Noel, 350
Garland, Jack Bee (Babe Bean), 248
Gaspar, Louis, 402n12
Gay, Lesbian, Bisexual Transgender Historical Society (GLBTHS), 22–23
Gay Academic Union (GAU) conferences, 18
gay and lesbian studies. See GLBTQ studies; history, lesbian and gay
gay bars: history of, 130, 132; institutional importance of, 132, 324–25, 345–46, 353; leather, 116, 120–21, 132, 224–25, 325; lesbian, 132; police harassment of, 116, 140–41, 199, 324; quick-money policy of, 342–43; specialization in, 325; as system, 325
gay-bashing, 118, 141
gay economy: expansion of, 163–64; female impersonators and, 338–44; gay ghettos and, 167; small businesses in, 402n7
Gay Power, Gay Politics (CBS), 116–17
gay rights repeal campaigns, 141–42
gender: acceptance of variation and, 252–53; conceptual language of, 13–15; drag and, 340–41; Marxism's inability

gender (*continued*)

to grasp, 277, 279; as "sexual difference," 280–81; sexuality vs., 177–80, 216–18; transgender and sex system vs. gender system, 386n46. *See also* butches; transgender practices

Gender (Germon), 13–15

gender dysphoria, 242–43

"gender identity disorders," 215–16

Genealogy of Queer Theory, A (Turner), 332–33

genitals: castration complex, 49, 51–57, 291–92; Christian view of, 148; cultural stereotypes mapped onto, 55; Oedipal complex and, 51–57; "phallus ex machina," 292–93

geographies of sexual location. *See* urban space and migrations

geologic metaphors, 2

Gerber, Henry, 353

Gerhard, Jane, 204–5

Germon, Jennifer, 13–15

gift exchange and reciprocity, 7–8, 42–43

Glad Day Books, Toronto, 191

glass ceiling, 5–6

GLBTQ studies, 352–53; amnesia about, 301–2, 347, 354–55; community-based archives, 22–23; elusive resources in, 348–49; homophile layer of texts in, 349–51; methodology vs. feminism in, 300–301; organizational structures in, 355–56. *See also* history, lesbian and gay

Glickman, Neil, 129

Global Alliance against Trafficking in Women (GAATW), 76–77

Goffman, Erving, 200, 319, 320, 329, 416n28

Goldman, Emma, 66, 82–84

Gorelick, Arlene, 11

Gould, Jane, 204–5

Gramont, Elizabeth de, 97

Grant, Madison, 72

Great Parties, 225–26

Greece, ancient, 269

Grier, Barbara (Gene Damon), 15, 16–17, 302, 348, 350–51

Griffin, Susan, 123

Groth, Paul, 222

Guérillères, Les (Wittig), 42, 368n54

Guerin, J., 137

Gusfield, Joseph, 318

Gwinn, Mary, 376n34

Hall, Radclyffe, 92, 96–97, 248, 347–48

Hansen, Bert, 199, 335

"hard core," conceptions of, 211

Harding, Sandra, 13

Harris, Bertha, 87

Harry, Joseph, 326

Hartman, Chester, 222

Hartmann, Heidi, 278

Harvey, Brett, 203

Hawaii, 64

Hayden, Tom, 9

Heap, Chad, 318

Heap, Jane, 248

Helms, Jesse, 183, 187, 188

Helms Amendment, 183, 187

Henry, Alice, 409n28

Henry, George, 313

Heramb, Fred, 233–39

Herdt, Gilbert, 344–45

heterosexuality: child abuse and, 184; in hierarchy of sexual values, 149, 151, 172; hustlers and, 326–27; Oedipus complex and, 48–49, 53–55; pornography and, 257; sex laws and, 134; s/m and, 116, 131–32, 210, 308–9; sociological critiques of naturalized, 321–22; sodomy and, 162; transgender practices and, 251. *See also* kinship; marriage

hierarchy of credibility, 319–20

hierarchy of sexual behavior: consequences of, 164–65; feminist, 172; need for recognition of, 135–36; racist ideologies vs., 154; sexual value hierarchy, 149–51, 152, 153. *See also* stratification systems

hierarchy of stigmatization, 342

Livingston, Jacqueline, 142–43

Livingstone, Frank, 12

location, sexual. *See* urban space and migrations

Lombardi-Nash, Michael, 353

longitudinal observation, 326

Lorenz, Paul, 106

Los Angeles, 113, 323–24

Love, Heather, 195

Love and Pain (KPIX), 117–19

lube, 230–31

Lucas, Don, 350

Luckmann, Thomas, 329

Luhan, Mabel Dodge, 106–7

MacKinnon, Catharine: antipornography ordinance and, 183, 262–63; on "documentary of abuse," 265–68; on feminism and pornography, 407n6; as latecomer to antiporn movement, 284, 397n54; Meese Commission and, 185–86; sexuality subsumed under feminism by, 179

Madagascar, 65

Making of the English Working Class, The (Thompson), 334–35

"male identified," 127, 243–44

male-to-female transsexuals (MTFS), 249

Mann Act (1910), 73–76, 316, 415n17

Man & Woman, Boy & Girl (Money and Ehrhardt), 14

Mapplethorpe, Robert, 183, 187

Marind Anim, 365n13

Marks, Elaine, 17

marriage: exchange of women concept and, 44–47; Goldman on continuum of prostitution and, 83–84; history of religious authorities and, 363n82; political economy of, 61–65; same-sex, 30–32, 162, 387n64; social construction and, 197. *See also* kinship

Marshall, Donald S., 313–14

Marx, Karl: on influence of the past, 1; on market, 161; neglect of, 303; on "Negro slaves," 34; on working-class movement, 60

Marxism, 134, 179, 277, 279

masculinity: butch sterotype and, 242, 245–47; class and, 244–45; gay men and, 247, 308–9; hustlers and protection of, 327

masturbation, 20, 109, 128, 138–39, 149–51, 172, 166

Masuzawa, Tomoko, 360n44

Matlock, Jann, 293

Mattachine Review, 350

Mattachine Society, 124, 135

Maurras, Charles, 17

Mauss, Marcel, 8, 43

McCarthyism, 143–44

McClelland, Donald, 106

McEachern, Steve, 226–34

McIntosh, Mary, 328–30, 332–33

McKenzie, Roderick, 312

Mead, George Herbert, 416n28

media: child-porn panic and, 142; feminist, 124; gay and lesbian, 188, 191, 198; popular sexual hierarchy and, 150; on sexual-minority neighborhoods, 166; on s/m, 116–21; on trafficking, 67; violence in, 260

Meese Commission, 182–86, 263, 409n31, 412n47

Melpa, 45

memory: amnesia about gay and lesbian studies, 301–2, 347, 354–55; Vivien and, 87–88

Michigan, 285–86

Michigan Womyn's Music Festival (1991), 249

migrations. *See* urban space and migrations

military regulations, 162, 166–67, 387n64

Milk, Harvey, 24

Millett, Kate, 220

Mineshaft (New York), 226, 240

Mitchell, Alice, 293, 354

Mitchell, Juliet, 13, 15, 366n28

mode of reproduction, 39–40

Moll, Albert, 294

Money, John, 14–15

monogamy: in hierarchy of sexual values, 122, 149–54; lesbian, 125–27, 172; Vivien and Barney and, 101

Montgomery, Robert, 115

morality crusaders, 138–39, 173. *See also* laws and legal repression; pornography and antiporn politics

moral leveling, 311, 320

moral panics and sex panics: AIDS, 25, 170–71; as battleground, 168–69; child-porn, 141 43, 184–85, 391n12; child-protection, 218–20; "lavender scare," 28; origins of, 26; s/m, 169–70; symbolic themes of, 183; Vance on, 201; Weeks on, 165, 168; white slavery, 68–73, 139

"moral regions," 317–18

Morgan, Lewis Henry, 42

Moscone, George, 24–25

Moscone Center, San Francisco, 24–25

Mother Camp (Newton), 20, 338–44

mother right, 366n15

motorcycle images, 244

Mount Holyoke conference (1986), 213–14

"Murder, Violence, and Homosexuality" (Cameron), 259

Murray, Stephen, 344, 417n57

Naiad Press, 17

NAMBLA (North American Man/Boy Love Association), 112

National Endowment for the Arts (NEA), 187

National Lesbian Conference (1991), 249

National Organization of Women (NOW), 124–25

National Science Foundation (NSF), 8

neighborhoods. *See* urban space and migrations

New Britain, 365n13

New Guinea, 43, 63, 365n13

New Left, 10–11, 276–78

Newspage, 209, 264

Newton, Esther, 20, 163, 338–45

New York City: Eulenspiegel Society, 210, 225; Harlem Renaissance, 167; Mine-shaft club, 226, 240; prostitution sur-veillance in, 316; s/m community in, 116, 131; Times Square, 222, 388n70; Women against Pornography (WAP), 174, 185–86, 202, 255

New York Society for the Suppression of Vice, 138–39

Nicolaus, Martin, 303

No More Nice Girls, 203

North American Man/Boy Love Associa-tion (NAMBLA), 112

Not a Love Story (film), 259, 263

Nowinski, Ira, 222

Nuer, 41, 63

Nye, Robert, 293

obscenity: laws against, 139, 160, 183–86, 190–92, 211; pornography vs., 260–61

Oedipal complex, 50–58

off our backs, 203, 205–6

One, 350

One Institute Quarterly, 350

On Homosexuality (Revolutionary Union), 122

Oosterhuis, Harry, 352, 354

Order of Things, The (Foucault), 419n76

Oregon Citizens Alliance (OCA), 188, 192

Origin of the Family, Private Property, and the State (Engels), 38–42, 65, 277, 366n15

overts and coverts, 163, 323

Padgug, Robert, 335

Palmer, Eva, 91, 99, 103

panics. *See* moral panics and sex panics

Paris, lesbian society in, 16–18, 89–90

Park, Robert E., 312, 317–18, 416n28

passing women, 248

passivity: Freud on, 49; gay male roles and, 247; gender and, 59; Oedipal com-plex and, 54–55 patriarchy, 40–41, 388n80

Patterns of Sexual Behavior (Ford and Beach), 310, 312–13

pedophilia, 387n66. *See also* boy-lovers

Penelope, Julia, 169

penis envy, 49, 52

penis vs. phallus, 51–57

performativity, 341

Perrigo, Denise, 187–88

pervert, defined, 382n6

phallus, 51–57, 292–93

Phelan, Shane, 390n90

photography, 187

Planned Parenthood, 30

Plath, Sylvia, 58

Pleasure Chest, New York City, 131

Plummer, Kenneth, 18, 321, 328–29, 330, 332–33

Polanyi, Karl, 334

police harassment: of gay bars, 116, 140–41, 199, 324; in Michigan, 285–86; in 1950s, 140–41; of s/m, 113–16, 134. *See also* laws and legal repression

political theory, gay male, 289, 290

politics of sex, 110. *See also* feminist sex wars; "Thinking Sex" and politics of sexuality

popular sexual ideology hierarchy, 150

pornography, 255; in Canada, 190–91; changes in, 28; child-porn panics and, 141–43, 184–85; costs of opposing, 273–74; definitions of, 185, 254, 261–65; degradation or subordination argument against, 207–8, 269–71; erotica vs., 263–64; feminism and, 274–75; feminist movement against, 169–70, 172–73, 185–86, 207–12, 271–73; "hard core," 211; harm claims and, 265–71; Internet and, 391n12; lesbian sex magazines and, 191, 257, 265; Meese Commission and, 183–86; s/m conflated with, 169–70; standard presentation of, 258–61; subgenres of, 257–58; violence conflated with, 256, 257–61; workshop at Barnard Conference on, 200–201

Pornography Victims Compensation Act, 186, 191, 411n46

Pougy, Liane de, 91, 296

production, reproduction vs., 38–41

"Profane Genesis, The" (Vivien), 93

prostitutes and sex workers: crackdowns on, 141; definitions of, 79, 382n6; feminist and conservative campaigns and, 84–86; Goldman on, 83–84; moral arguments and, 287, 335; purported mortality rates among, 79–80; sex commerce prohibitions and, 160; surveillance and, 74; trafficking elided with prostitution, 66–67, 76–84; victim assumption and, 268–69; "white slavery" crusades and, 68–71; as workers, 157–58

Prostitution Education Project (PEP), 287

Protestantism, 4–5

protoqueerness, 222–23

Psychanalyse et Politique, 15

psychoanalytic approach: Benjamin on s/m and, 177; change and intractability in, 282; decline of, 27; degradation of, 292–93; ex-gay ministries and, 27; failure of self-criticism in, 47–48, 58–60; on sexual variation, 291–92; theories of femininity, 48–57

Public Broadcasting System (PBS), 192

Quayle, Dan, 192

queer-bashing, 118, 141

queer studies. *See* GLBTQ studies

Queer Theory (Jagose), 332–33

race: critique of, 12; Mann Act and, 75; Marx on "Negro slaves," 34; sexual hierarchy vs. ideologies of, 154; in the South, 3–4

Radical History Review, 335

Rapp (Reiter), Rayna, 12–13, 15

Read, Kenneth, 344

Reading Capital (Althusser and Balibar), 419n75

real-estate politics, 167–68

reciprocity, 42–43

Red Star Sisters, 277

Reinach, Salomon, 105, 360n44, 373n7, 376n33, 376n36

Reiss, Albert J., 322, 326–27, 419n78

Reiter (Rapp), Rayna, 12–13, 15

religion: hierarchical system and, 149–50; marriage and religious authorities, 363n82; misplaced scale and, 149; sex negativity and, 148; in South Carolina, 4–5

religious right. *See* right wing conservatives

reproduction, 37–41

"Rethinking Sex" conference, 195, 196, 215

Revolutionary Union, 122

rhetorical tactics, 208, 256, 398n57

Rich, Adrienne, 287–88, 389n80

Rich, B. Ruby, 174, 395n2

Rich, Frank, 29–30

right wing conservatives: on AIDS, 171; antipornography movement and, 183, 274; antiprostitution movement and, 85–86; child protection and, 218; erotophobia and, 109–10; feminist antipornography discourse and, 173; McCarthyism and, 143–44; neoconservativism and, 25–26, 143–44, 280, 290; s/M and, 136

Risch, Gregg, 119

Riversdale, Paule (pseud. for Van Zyulen and Vivien), 104–5

Robinson, Paul, 417n32

Roe, Clifford G., 70–71

romantic friendship standard, 288–89

Rove, Karl, 30

Royère, Jean, 90

Russell, Diana, 123, 207–9

Sacher-Masoch, Leopold von, 306–7

Sade, Marquis de, 306–7

sadomasochism (s/M): Canadian laws and, 191–92; coming out and, 123–24, 129–31, 132; consent and, 129, 134, 176; custody law and, 119–20; Deleuze on masochism, 306–7; Deutsch on masochism, 56; in England, 192; feminist movement and, 124–29, 169–70, 174, 202–6, 207–12; heterosexual, 116, 131–32, 210, 308–9; image vs. production of, 267–68; injuries and, 117–18; "leather" vs., 308; legal vulnerability and police harassment of, 113–16, 134; lesbian social organization and, 132–33; masculinity and, 308–9; misinformation about, 116–21; movement against, 121–22; panic potential of, 169–70; pornography conflated with, 169–70, 207–8; rethinking sexual politics and, 135–36; San Francisco Catacombs and, 232–34; s/M porn, 258; social conflict over sex and, 109–11; social forces against, 125–26

safe-sex practices, 236–37

Sahli, Nancy, 288–89

Sahlins, Marshall, 11, 278

Samoa, 65

Samois, 123–24, 132–33, 174, 203–12, 225, 290

San Francisco: adult theaters in, 258; attrition of gay neighborhoods in, 222; crackdowns in, 140, 141; Great Parties in, 225–26; Hothouse, 402n12; leather bars and s/M in, 116–22, 224–25, 233–34; real-estate politics in, 24, 167–68; Society of Janus, 210, 225, 233; South of Market neighborhood in, 24, 222, 224–25; spatial distribution of gay sites in, 325; Women's Building, 124, 356. *See also* Catacombs of San Francisco

San Francisco Chronicle, 120

San Francisco Lesbian and Gay History Project, 22, 199–200, 248, 302

Sappho, 92

scale and scope: fallacy of misplaced scale, 149; fear of "sex offenders" and, 219–20; trafficking size and scope claims, 77–82

scapegoating: "hardcore" conception and, 211; "homosexual invasion," 167–68;

moral panics and, 169; obscenity laws and, 211; of pornography, 122, 169, 257, 272–73; San Francisco housing politics and, 222; Weeks on, 165

Schlafly, Phyllis, 171

Schneider, David, 299, 339–40, 413n24

school desegregation, 3–4

"second aspect of material life," 39, 41

Sedgwick, Eve, 398n72

segregation, 3–4

separatism, in women's movement, 366n25

Sex and Society (Thomas), 315

sex changes, 350–51. *See also* transgender practices

sex education, 83–84, 188, 220–21, 264

sex/gender system: defined, 34; Engels's theory of society and, 38–41; kinship and the exchange of women, 41–47; Marxist failure to conceptualize sex oppression and, 35–38; "mode of re-production" vs., 39–40; patriarchy vs., 13, 40–41; political economy of sex and marriage systems, 61–65; psychoana-lytic failure and, 58–60; psychoanalytic theory of feminism and Oedipal com-plex, 47–57; reorganization of, 57–58, 60–61; sexual system vs. gender, 178–79

Sex Information and Education Council of the United States (SIECUS), 143

sex negativity, 148

"sex offenders," 139–40, 219–21

sexology: erotic speciation and, 156; igno-rance of, 155; as layer of queer knowl-edge, 351–54; paradigms of, 304; on sexual variety, 293–94; Vivien and Barney and, 92

sex panics. *See* moral panics and sex panics

sex research, 125, 155. *See also* sexology

sex toys and equipment: hierarchy of sexual values and, 151; leather gear, 115, 228, 263; legal crackdowns on, 114–15; Meese Commission on, 263

Sexual Behavior in the Human Male (Kinsey et al.), 313, 329, 418n62, 418n65

Sexual Conduct (Gagnon and Simon), 330

Sexual Deviance (Gagnon and Simon), 322–27

sexual essentialism, 146–48

sexual psychopath laws, 140

Sexual Stigma (Plummer), 329, 330

sexual variation: benign concept of, 154–55; brainwash theory, 177; custody laws and punishment for, 119–20; in feminist literature, 289–90; Foster's "sex vari-ance," 18; limited concept of, 133, 154, 208; sexology and, 293–94; social sci-ences vs. pathology models of, 311

Sex Variant Women in Literature (Foster), 15, 17–18, 88, 348

sex workers. *See* prostitutes and sex workers

Shields, Larry, 296

Shilleto, Violet, 91, 98–100, 102, 105–7

Simon, William, 155, 320–27, 330, 336, 419n78

Slater, Cynthia, 233–34

slaves, 34

S/M. *See* sadomasochism

Smith-Rosenberg, Caroll, 288–89

social construction of sexuality: defined, 197–98; essentialism and, 146–48, 333–34; gender identities and, 403n3; of homosexuality, 295–96; Plummer and McIntosh in development of, 327–30; *Radical History Review* and, 335; social change and, 283; Weeks and develop-ment of, 330–32

Social Evil in Chicago, The (Chicago Vice Commission), 78–79

"Social Integration of Peers and Queers, The" (Reiss), 322, 326–27

social sanctions, 163–65

Society for the Study of Social Problems, 319

Society of Janus, 210, 225, 233

"sodomites," 156, 247

sodomy, 155, 156, 297
sodomy laws, 139, 162, 175, 297
Sonenschein, David, 336–38
Sontag, Susan, 109, 149
South Carolina, 3–8
speciation, erotic, 156–57
Spitzer, Eliot, 75
Spooner, Lysander, 165–66
statutory rape laws, 112
Stead, W. T., 68
Steakley, Jim, 302
Steinem, Gloria, 264
Stephens, Boyd, 117, 120
stereotypes, in antiporn politics, 259
Stern, Jess, 348
stigma: barriers to community entry and,
  119; of boy-lovers, 143; class, overtness,
  and, 341–42; defenselessnes and, 168;
  on drag, 338, 342; Goffman on, 319, 320;
  hierarchy of sexual values and, 149; of
  homosexuality, 155, 294, 320, 323–24,
  342; of masturbation, 149; media and,
  150; numerical exaggeration and, 78;
  "perverts" and, 382n6; on pornography,
  272, 273, 287; redevelopment projects
  and, 222; on sex workers and prostitution, 85, 157, 170, 268–69, 271; s/m and,
  113, 131–33, 211–12; subculture normalization and, 307; on transsexuals,
  386n46, 406n28. See also hierarchy of
  sexual behavior; stratification systems
Stigma (Goffman), 319, 320, 329
Stoddard, Lothrop, 72
Stoller, Robert, 14
Stone, Sandy, 285
"stranger danger," 218–20
stratification systems: articulation of,
  302; female impersonators and, 342–43;
  marriage and, 63–65; moral panics and,
  168; sanctions and, 158–65; Weber on,
  217–18. See also hierarchy of sexual
  behavior
Strauss, Anselm, 416n28
"street fairies," 342

structuralism, 278–79, 283–84, 296, 364n4
Stryker, Susan, 215–16, 363n81
Stuart, Lee, 15, 16–17, 348
Students for a Democratic Society (SDS), 9
study groups, 199
Sturges, Jock, 187
subcultures: "discovery" of homosexual
  world and, 315; Newton on drag queens
  and, 20; normalization and, 307–8;
  Sonenschein on, 338; urban emergence
  of, 331; youth, 26
Suggs, Robert C., 313–14
Sullivan, Louis, 188, 248
Surpassing the Love of Men (Faderman),
  288–89
surveillance: by Alcoholic Beverage Com-
  mission, 199; by FBI, 110–11, 140; prosti-
  tution and sexual surveillance of
  women, 74, 316
Sweet, Michael J., 328
Swinburne, Algernon, 90
Symonds, John Addington, 352–54

Take Back the Night (Lederer), 262, 284
Tarn, Pauline Mary. See Vivien, Renée
Tavarossi, Tony, 226
teenage sexual behavior, 188
Teen Chastity Program, 144
temporal awareness, 326
territorial wars, 166–68
theoretical and descriptive work, 304–7
"theory," 301, 304–7
"Thinking Sex" and politics of sexuality:
  battlegrounds of sexual conflict and,
  165–71; benign sexual variation concept
  and, 154–55; context of, 280, 283–87,
  301–2; domino theory of sexual peril
  and, 151; erotic speciation, sexual ethnogenesis, and, 155–58; fallacy of misplaced scale and, 149; feminism's limits
  and, 171–80; gender vs. sexuality and,
  177–80; hierarchical system of sexual
  value and, 149–51, 152, 153, 164–65; need
  for, 137–38; requirements for radical

theory and, 145; rightward shift in U.S. and, 183; sex negativity and, 148; sexual essentialism and, 146–48; sexual stratification, sanctions, and, 158–65; sex wars and, 138–45

Thomas, W. I., 75, 315–16, 416n28

Thompson, Denise, 214

Thompson, E. P., 51, 295, 334–35

Thorne, Barrie, 10, 416n27

Thorner, Susan, 233

Thorstad, David, 302

Three Strikes and You're Out law (California), 219

Thursday Night Group (Ann Arbor), 10–11

Tilly, Charles, 2, 295

"Time, Work-Discipline, and Industrial Capitalism" (Thompson), 335

Times Square, 128, 222, 388n70

Tonga, 64

Tool Box (San Francisco), 224

Toronto, 114–15, 141, 191

"To the Sunset Goddess" (Vivien), 376n33

tourist clubs, 343

"Traffic in Women" (Goldman), 66, 82–84

"Traffic in Women, The" (Rubin), 12–15; Engels on production and reproduction and, 38–41; gender vs. sexual system and, 178–79; genesis of sexual inequality and, 33–35; Goldman's "Traffic in Women" and, 66, 84; kinship systems and, 41–42; Lévi-Strauss on kinship and, 42–47; Marx's analysis of capitalism and, 35–38; political context of, 276–80; political economy of sex and, 61–65; psychoanalysis and, 47–48, 58–60; psychoanalytic theories of femininity and, 48–57; title of, 66

trafficking: as feminist target, 214–15; Goldman's "Traffic in Women," 66, 82–84; Mann Act, 73–76; organizations against, 76–77; resurgent feminist and conservative movement against, 84–86;

size and scope claims, 77–82; as term, 66–67; white slavery panics, 68–73

transgender practices: DSM and, 215–16; female-to-male transsexuals (FTMS), 243, 248–51, 406n25; "intermediate" bodies, 251; lesbians and, 248–51; male-to-female transsexuals (MTFS), 249; organizations relevant to, 405n22; sex changes and, 350–51; sex system vs. gender system and, 386n46; sexual orientation and, 404n8; transsexual porn, 257–58

transvestism, 216

Trautmann, Thomas, 22, 360n44

Trobriand Islands, 43, 64

Troubridge, Una, 96–97

Turner, George Kibbe, 70

Turner, William, 332–33

Ulrichs, Karl Heinrich, 352

United Nations, 76

United Nations Educational, Scientific and Cultural Organization (UNESCO), 143

University of Chicago, 314–20, 339, 416n28

University of Michigan, 8–15, 278, 285–86, 348–49, 383n16

urban space and migrations: barriers to, 166–67; gentrification and redevelopment projects, 24, 222; industrialization and urbanization, 295–96; military and, 166–67; Park's "moral regions," 317–18; sexually motivated, 130, 157; territorial wars and real-estate politics, 167–68; Weeks on subcultures, 331; white slavery panics and, 72–73. See also ethnography of urban gay communities

utopianism, 279–80

Vance, Carole: Barnard Conference and, 195–97, 200–203, 204–6, 213–14; on gender and erotic flexibility, 283; on rhetorical tactics, 398n57; on sex panics, 26; on social construction theory, 283,

Vance, Carole (*continued*)
333, 335; on study of sexuality, 333; on
trafficking, 66–67, 371n27
Van Zuylen de Nyevelt, Baroness Hélène,
99, 100, 103–5
Vashti, Queen, 93–94
Vaverde, Mariana, 395n2
"Veil of Vashti, The" (Vivien), 93–94
Vietnam War, 9
Viguerie, Richard, 280
Village Voice, 203
violence: hustlers and defense of boundaries with, 327; pornography conflated
with, 256, 257; pornography faulted for,
265–69; 61; sex equated with, 128; s/m
equated with, 117–18; trivialization of,
273
Vivien, Renée: archive of, 373n7; Baroness Van Zuylen and, 100, 103–5; "Brown
like a Hazel-Nut," 95; career of, 88;
childhood and background of, 90–91;
death of, 105–6; "The Eternal Slave,"
94–95; feminism and, 93; gay history
and, 107–8; lesbian self-awareness
and, 92; "Let the Dead Bury Their
Dead," 101; Marks on, 17; Natalie and,
88, 91–92, 97–103; Parisian context of,
88–90; personal life after 1904 of, 103–5;
"The Profane Genesis," 93; Riversdale
collaborations of, 104–5; as romantic,
101; Shilleto and, 91, 98–100, 102, 105–6;
"To the Sunset Goddess," 376n33; "The
Veil of Vashti," 93–94; *A Woman Appeared to Me*, 17, 92, 97–99, 106–8;
"Words to My Friend," 95–96

Walker, Bill, 23
Walkowitz, Judith, 69, 85–86, 139, 146, 335
Weber, Ed, 16, 349
Weber, Max, 215, 217–18, 356
Weeks, Jeffrey: *Coming Out*, 18, 107, 302,
330–31; essentialism and, 146, 196–97;

on moral panics, 26, 165, 168; sexolo-
gists and, 353–54; social construction
and, 295, 330–33
Westley, William A., 322–23, 419n78
Weston, Kath, 345
Whall, Thomas, 4–5
White, Dan, 24, 379n7
White Citizens Councils, 4
white slavery panics, 68–73, 77–78, 82,
85, 139
White Slave Traffic Act (Mann Act, 1910),
73–76, 316
Wilde, Dolly, 97, 376n37
Williams, Linda, 211
Willie, John, 383n16
Willis, Ellen, 174, 196, 203, 206, 264, 395n1,
407n8
Wilson, Robert N., 80–81
Wittig, Monique, 15, 42, 368n54
Wolf, Deborah Goleman, 344
Wolff, Charlotte, 369n58
Woman Appeared to Me, A (Vivien), 17,
92, 97–99, 106–8
woman-identified-woman, 287, 405n13
Women against Pornography (WAP), 174,
185–86, 202, 255
Women against Violence in Pornography
and Media (WAVPM), 206–11, 255
Women's Building, San Francisco, 124, 356
"women's community," 356
women's movement. *See* feminism
"Words to My Friend" (Vivien), 95–96
working-class movement, 60

xenophobia, 249

Yentl (film), 245

Zambaco, Demetrius, 137
Zillman, Dolf, 265
Znanieki, Florian, 315
Zorbaugh, Harvey Warren, 318

Gayle S. Rubin *is an associate professor of anthropology, women's studies, and comparative literature at the University of Michigan.*

Library of Congress Cataloging-in-Publication Data
Rubin, Gayle.
Deviations : a Gayle Rubin reader / Gayle S. Rubin.
p. cm.
"A John Hope Franklin Center Book."
Includes bibliographical references and index.
ISBN 978-0-8223-4971-6 (cloth : alk. paper)
ISBN 978-0-8223-4986-0 (pbk. : alk. paper)
1. Gay and lesbian studies. 2. Queer theory.
3. Feminist theory. 4. Homosexuality—
Political aspects. I. Title.
HQ75.15.R83 2012
306.76′601—dc23   2011027554